Man, Crime, and Society

Man, Crime, and Society

Second Edition

By Herbert A. Bloch and Gilbert Geis

Second Edition revised by Gilbert Geis,
California State College at Los Angeles

Random House   New York

This book is dedicated to the
memory of Herbert A. Bloch
(1904–1965)
and
Adeline Supove Bloch
(1900–1968)

Foreword

I

The years between the publication of the first edition of this book in 1962 and the present edition have been momentous ones for the study of crime. Public clamor for "law and order" probably has concentrated more attention upon criminal behavior than ever before in human history. Political response to public indignation has brought into the limelight many issues that once were confined to intramural debates among specialists. Questions regarding the causes of crime arouse intense debate: Are men fundamentally evil, do they need to be restrained by stern laws that are rigorously enforced, or are they basically well-behaved and likely to engage in criminal depredations only when pressed by the imperatives of their social existence? Do poverty, poor housing, and inadequate medical attention contribute significantly to crime, or is criminal activity rampant in all segments of the society, among the powerful and affluent as well as the deprived and depressed, perhaps indicating a basic moral condition in man?

Public concern with crime has, for the criminologist, produced more opportunities to formulate and refine previous thinking than ever before existed. National commissions are allocating funds for new studies and foundations are providing resources for imaginative experiments, thereby attracting the keen intellects of persons who regard the study of crime as a challenge to their abilities. The result has been a prolific production and refinement of information about crime and greater insight into its genesis.

Not all of the developments of recent years have, however, been so advantageous. Public clamor almost always diverts attention from fundamental issues unrelated to public policy; commissions and foundations most often want answers to "practical" questions and programs for action rather than theoretical formulations whose immediate applicability cannot readily be seen. Researchers tend to respond to such demands often before their material can definitively provide responses to pragmatic questions. In addition, some areas of inquiry tend to be neglected in the attempt to concentrate on other issues of more immediate concern.

It is against such a background of events that the present edition of *Man, Crime, and Society* has been written. It goes without saying that these events dictated a complete revision and updating of the first edition, and it is hoped that the present volume reflects the convolutions that have taken place in the study of crime as well as the quieter, sometimes more penetrating analyses that have proceeded against this background. The attempt has been made, for instance, to incorporate the intellectually exciting insights of the "labelling" theorists, who point out that what comes to be called crime is a function of "moral entrepreneurs," who have the power by which to denigrate and outlaw activities routinely learned and performed by others in more vulnerable positions in the social structure.

Labelling theory is but one aspect of the phenomena of crime, and we have tried to examine carefully different views that offer supplementary or contradictory interpretations of the same behavior. No apology is offered for this kind of approach, since it is a fundamental tenet of this volume that "reality" is a multidimensional condition and that behavior may be seen from diverse vantage points that offer penetrating and valuable insights into it. The organization of data into theoretical frameworks is always preferred, as such scholarship advances an accumulation of unrelated facts into comprehensive and comprehensible schemes, points out gaps, and offers prospects for prediction. But a textbook need not select among competing theories and assemble all data in terms of one. Were it to do so, it would concentrate on a given view rather than unfold relevant materials from which students and scholars could abstract insights and viewpoints that are best suited to their intellectual value systems and their action aims.

This book has also been revised with the belief in mind that academic writing need not be pompous and pretentious in order to be scholarly. Too often in the past, although much less so today, social-science writing has employed obscure language to camouflage obscure thinking. The aim in this volume is to present the material with clarity and simplicity, although, of course, not all thought can be reduced to elementary statements.

On occasion facts are included merely because they appear to be interesting. Bertrand Russell noted that science began because man was curious, and Aldous Huxley pointed out that often in the course of the history of science a little fact was the undoing of a big theory. Someday, hopefully, all the little facts will be integrated into impermeable big theories. Pending that scientific nirvana, however, curiosity, even regarding the ephemera of scientific information, is something less than venial sin, something that it is reasonable to indulge, if such indulgence does not unduly detract or distract from fundamental tenets.

II

There is a particular sadness involved in the present edition of this book. In 1965, the present writer's collaborator, Herbert A. Bloch, died. This volume bears the unmistakable imprint of Professor Bloch's inquisitive and penetrating mind; it also reflects, it is hoped, the pleasure of the common effort that brought the first edition to fruition. In tribute to Professor Bloch, the following section reproduces portions of the Foreword to the first edition, most of which were written by Bloch, and which put forward many of his basic intellectual convictions.

III

In his effort to analyze crime phenomena objectively and scientifically, the criminologist does not tend to regard himself as a social reformer. The concerns of science are *not* those of social reform, no matter how closely they may touch at various points. The scientist, whether his scrutiny be directed to phenomena of the physical world or to the complex patterns of relationships that comprise human behavior, is motivated primarily by an intense desire to *know*—an effort to find answers to his probing questions concerning the world or his fellow man. For this reason, the nature of his questions and the answers he seeks are apt to be circumscribed, frequently to the discomfiture of the layman who, in contrast, raises sweeping questions and expects sweeping answers. Whereas the layman asks, "What causes crime?" the scientist asks himself what particular aspect of a particular kind of crime is capable of explanation in terms of a sharply defined facet of human nature. The order of these two types of question is quite different. The usages of the first type depend upon "common sense," that fallacious and traditional repository of misinformation and bias which, inexorably, answers questions in the same way and with the same prejudices. The second type of question, while not opening doors to Utopia, slowly but ineluctably paves the way for broader understanding.

The dangers of "common sense," ironically, and especially in the human field, continually lurk around us, inviting us to follow the dictates of deeply-laid habits. To this end, the scientist, whether he be a physical scientist or a newer member of the breed—a social or behavioral scientist—must be constantly on his guard to escape the blandishments of the common-sense errors implicit in so much of our knowledge. A sense of history, the correct understanding of tradition, enables us to remain in the full stream of our social development and its great potential. A devotion to the common-sense errors of that tradition, however, may commit us to an undeviating sense of the failures in man's understanding of himself and his destiny. Science, to a considerable degree, enables us to escape this sense of unavoidable dilemma in man's progress by indicating the fallacy of committed belief and the virtually limitless potential of man's understanding.

To free himself from the dangers of untested committed belief, the scientist devotes much of his effort toward the perfection of techniques that will safeguard him against error—especially those errors which indicate bias and make him prey to unconscious habit. Probably the greatest virtue of the scientific method is this implanted procedure of self-correction. In this sense, it is knowledge at its most self-conscious level. For the social scientist, this mode of thought imposes a dual burden. Not only must he be extremely careful in the development of techniques which are self-corrective, but, at the same time, in his pursuit of truth he must escape the dilemma of profound human involvement. The entire nature of his discipline and his subject-matter frequently cry out against this. Indeed, in the matter of the social sciences, a primary issue which continually impinges upon the character of its scientific investigations is whether or not the scientist can escape becoming humanly, and hence, emotionally, involved.

The human disciplines, so called, face a peculiar problem in this respect. Emerging from the great liberalizing and humanitarian traditions of the late eighteenth and nineteenth centuries, only lately have they begun to appreciate the social emphases and implications of the scientific era initiated by Darwin. The early pioneers in criminology, under the inseminating influence of the French rationalists and encyclopedists, were deeply imbued with a humanitarian purpose and even, it may be said, a sense of historic mission. Men such as the eminent Italian jurist, Beccaria, lived during a revolutionary epoch when men believed that the world was ripe for reform. The profound scientific interest of the late nineteenth century, however, as embodied in Beccaria's countryman, Lombroso, has left an intellectual legacy which frequently fluctuates between reformist zeal and scientific enterprise. Lombroso more than any other is the progenitor of the view that crime may not only be studied scientifically but that it is essentially to be viewed as a form of human behavior.

The truth of the matter, perhaps, lies in the view that science itself is a vast reforming instrumentality. Aside from the fact that the true scientist, regardless of whether he plies his craft in the world of physical phenomena or in the field of criminology, abominates the hasty and incautious judgment, there is also a deeply human ethic in science itself. It is probably no accident of history that those periods marked by great compassion and reformist zeal were also periods in which the scientific spirit was also given free rein. Given sufficient

time—and this is probably the most crucial problem of our day—
the scientific spirit in itself may help to bring about the reform which
the humanist so urgently craves.

This book is primarily concerned with scientific efforts to understand crime, and to understand man in relation to crime phenomena.
In pursuing this interest, it is likewise concerned with crime as an
indicator of social change. Although largely neglected as a field of
social research, the changing face of crime is, quite likely, one of the
most crucial indices of the changing social scene. For crime, as conceived in this volume, constitutes a special form of adaptation to the
body politic. When the social structure itself is viewed in its enormous
complexity, in terms of its structural parts and its class stratification,
the various forms of crime constitute adaptive systems of behavior,
spontaneous outgrowths in behavioral form of attitudes, values, and
social perceptions. The changing pattern of crime, therefore, is probably one of the most sensitive social barometers. Nowhere is this better
exemplified, perhaps, than in the changing rates and types of crime,
characteristic of different age and class groups, occurring in this century in the industrialized Western world and the similar pattern of
criminal maladaptations which are now beginning to take form in
the slowly emerging industrial nations of the East.

Crime, as such, represents a special form of social deviance—that
form of deviance defined as such by law. A knowledge of the social
structure and the character of its value-orientations will readily indicate those forms of deviant adaptation that the social structure more
commonly condemns. If societies may be known by the "crimes they
keep," they may also be known by their attitudes toward the convicted and the imprisoned. Long before the modern scientific interest
in criminology, Sir Thomas More indicated that a society may be
gauged by the attitudes it maintains toward its helpless and its imprisoned. If anything, our modern understanding would tend to add
scientific confirmation to this view. With all of the strictures and
criticisms one may heap upon our modern penal system, for example,
the "concentration camp" sheds light upon a type of mentality and
social order different from our own.

The view stressed in this book, that crime constitutes special
forms of adaptation to the social structure, represents a unique and
newly emergent scientific interest in the field of criminology. Unlike
the older views of Lombroso and his immediate followers, which
sought statistical proof in the measurable and, particularly, the physical aspects of crime, this more recent view seeks empirical and measurable data in terms of the character of the adaptation itself. It
welcomes evidence in relation to the specifically formulated conditions determining a particular type of crime. To find such evidence
at this stage for all types and manifestations of crime is impossible.
Also, to see all forms of crime as separable and self-enclosed systems

of behavior is not yet quite possible in the light of the limitations of our knowledge. Nevertheless, the effort has been made in this volume to view crime whenever possible in this light and to formulate the broad categories under which similar forms of criminal behavior should fall.

To attempt to write a comprehensive work in criminology is, in itself, an act of presumption. To bring together into some coherent form the endless materials of the law, legal and social history, sociological theory, the wide range of empirical research into separate phases and types of crime, the attempts toward therapy, modern psychological conceptions and viewpoints, and the vast literature of penology, reform, and social justice, would appear, at first glance, to be more than human scholarly enterprise could attempt to encompass. Nevertheless, such a work may be profitably undertaken if it is recognized that it may contain a sampling of a rich and variegated field and, especially, if we remember that the materials of such a field may be viewed within a logical and coherent frame of reference. This the authors have attempted to do.

IV

This book owes its origin to Charles D. Lieber, now president of Atherton Press, who first conceived of it and of my collaboration with Professor Bloch. His successors as college editors at Random House—Theodore Caris and Arthur Strimling—have been of constant help and good cheer during preparation of the second edition. I also want to thank Leonore C. Hauck and Jane P. Alles for their work on the manuscript of the first edition, Sybil Maimin and Stefanie Gold for their work on the present volume, and Virginia S. Munns for her assistance in tracking down citations. My debt to my wife, Robley, is beyond the possibility of verbal expression; her interest and support permeate the book. I would like to take the advice of my daughter, Jeanie, who cautioned me to make certain that "all the kids" get their names into print. So thanks, too, to Joe and Kay and their children, Emily and Patrick, Ted and Chris, Adrian and Annie and their child Eric, Ellie, and, of course, Jeanie herself.

Los Angeles   G.G.

Contents

Foreword   vii

Part One   Crime and Society

Chapter 1   Crime, Criminals, and Criminology   3

Public Agitation Regarding
  Crime   6
Implications for the Study of
  Criminology   11
Historical Definitions of Crime and
  Delinquency   14
Toward Forming a Scientific
  Definition of Crime   16
The Law as a Social Force   21
Crime and Criminal Law   23
Summary   25

Part Two   Law and Science of Criminology

Chapter 2   The Law, Social Control, and Criminal Behavior   31

Law and Social Science   32
Components of Social Control   36
Criminology and Social
  Control   39
The Definition of Crime as a
  Legal Concept   39
Who is a Criminal?   50
Areas of Criminological
  Interest   52

Chapter 3 History and the Relativity of Crime 54
Early Criminal Law 56
Theft and Social Values 60
Contrast Between Soviet and
  American Criminal Law 69
The Relativity of Crime 73
Crime and Culture: An
  Overview 75
Summary 76

Chapter 4 The Science of Criminology 79
Pioneers in Criminology 84
Sociology of Criminal
  Behavior 91
Typologies: Configurational
  Analysis 101
Individual Offenders 106

Part Three Extent of Crime

Chapter 5 Perspectives on Crime Measurement 111
The Extent of Unreported
  Crime 113
Official Criminal Statistics 117
Crimes Known to the Police 124
Toward the Refinement of
  Crime Measures 126
Population Structure and
  Crime 128
Crime: What of the Future? 130
The Response to Crime 134

Chapter 6 Characteristics of Reported Crime 137
Extent of Reported Crime in the
  United States 141
Monthly and Seasonal Variations
  in Crime 144
Age-Levels and Crime Rates 146
Sex Composition in Arrest
  Statistics 150
Minority Groups and Crime 154
Urban-Rural Crime
  Differentials 159
Summary 162

Part Four   Behavior Systems in Crime

Chapter 7   Professional Crime   167

Professional Crime in History   168
Self-Image of Professional
    Criminals   170
Confidence Games   173
Forgery   178
Shoplifting   182
Hustling as a Criminal Way of
    Life   185
Hierarchy of Crime   187
Summary   187

Chapter 8   Organized Crime   190

Early History of Organized
    Crime   194
Culture Context of Organized
    Crime   197
Infiltration of Legitimate
    Business   205
Mafia and/or La Cosa
    Nostra?   210
Control of Organized Crime   214

Chapter 9   Homicides and Assaults   218

The Violent Male?   220
Background to Homicide   221
The Definition of Homicide   222
The Extent of Homicide   224
Correlates of Homicide   226
Patterns in Criminal
    Homicide   229
Roots of Homicide   233
Homicide and its Motives   235
Homicide and Suicide   237
Assault and Battery   238

Chapter 10   The Sex Offenses   243

Sex and the Individual   244
Sex and American Society   246
Forcible Rape   248
Summary   269

Chapter 11   Property Offenders   272

Social Conditions and Theft   275
Typologies of Property
  Offenders   278
Specific Property Offenders   285
Summary   297

Chapter 12   White-Collar Crime   299

History of White-Collar
  Crime   301
Parallels Between White-Collar
  and Traditional Crime   305
Varieties of White-Collar
  Crime   307
Is White-Collar Crime "Really"
  Crime?   317
Sutherland's Defense of His
  Concept   318
Research Issues in White-Collar
  Crime   319

Chapter 13   Public Order Offenses   324

Public Drunkenness   326
Narcotic Offenses   335
Marijuana   343

Chapter 14   Juvenile Delinquency   350

Roots of Concern with
  Delinquency   350
What is Juvenile
  Delinquency?   354
Behavior Systems in
  Delinquency   361
Conclusion   377

Part Five   Police, Administration of Justice, and Correction

Chapter 15   The Police   383

Police and Minority Groups   385
Police and Social Control   388
Structure of American Law
  Enforcement   391

Police Brutality 397
Police Discretion 399
Foreign Law Enforcement 401
Summary 404

Chapter 16 Administration of Criminal Justice 407

Criminal Justice and
  Misdemeanants 409
Mechanics of Criminal Justice:
  Felonies 413
The Police-Court
  Controversy 426
Summary 432

Chapter 17 Punishment of Criminals 435

The History of Punishment 435
Correction and Its Ideology 437
Capital Punishment 442
Alternatives to Capital
  Punishment 448
Conclusion 457

Chapter 18 Reformation and Responsibility 460

Jails 461
Perspectives on Prisons 465
Criminal Responsibility 476
Civil Commitment 481
Alternatives to Incarceration 483
Summary 493

Bibliography 497
Books and Articles 497
Cases 536

Index 539

About the Authors 553

Figures and Tables

Figure   I   Estimated Rates of Offense Comparison of Police and
Bureau of Social Science Research Survey Data   116

Figure II   Crimes Cleared By Arrest, 1967   123

Figure III   Crimes Against the Person   146

Figure IV   Crimes Against Property, by Month   147

Table   5.1.   Comparison of Survey and UCR Rates   115

Table   5.2.   Reporting System Changes (UCR Index, Figures
Not Comparable With Prior Years)   121

Table   6.1.   Volume of Crime in the United States, 1960-1967   141

Table   6.2.   Crime Rates per 100,000 Population for 1967 as
Compared to 1960 and 1966   143

Table   6.3.   Total Arrests of Persons Under 15, Under 18, Under
21, and Under 25 Years of Age, 1967   148

Table   6.4.   Total Arrests, Distribution by Sex, 1967   152

Table   6.5.   Total Arrests by Race, 1967   156

Table   6.6.   Distribution of Crime in Three Major Statistical
Areas, by Volume and Rate, 1967   160

Table   9.1.   Homicide Rate per 100,000 Population, United
States, 1933-1966   225

Table   9.2.   Homicide Rate per 100,000 Population, Selected
Countries, 1965   226

Table   9.3.   Murder and Nonnegligent Manslaughter Rates per
100,000 Population, by Regions, 1967   226

Table 10.1.   Age of Offender in Sex Offenses   263

Table 14.1.   Twenty-One Incentives for Theft   377

Table 17.1.   Civil Executions in the United States, 1952-1968   444

Table 18.1.   Year-End Population for State and Federal Institutions, 1940-1964   465

Table 18.2.   Present and Ideal View of Purpose of Prison   468

Table 18.3.   Explanations of Views Regarding Rehabilitation or Punishment   469

Part I
Crime and Society

1

Crime, Criminals, and Criminology

The study of crime can be a fascinating enterprise, for criminal activity often arouses intense passions. Fear, enmity, admiration, and envy may all coalesce to whet an impelling sense of curiosity about the roots of a particular criminal offense and about the forces that led the victim and the offender to their fates. In its more sensational form, crime can produce an almost obsessional interest among a nation's population, with greatly heightened feelings of morbid excitement. Edward Gibbon, the renowned chronicler of the story of the Roman Empire, in a paraphrase of Voltaire, called history "little more than the register of the crimes, follies, and misfortunes of mankind."[1] Today, involvement in criminal activity often opens up for public scrutiny intimate areas of the lives of the law violator and his victim, providing vicarious involvement as well as otherwise taboo information about the way in which some people live their lives.

In the United States, stories of brutal violence, clever robbery, and ingenious swindle continually beguile the public imagination. Such stories receive a prominent place in social conversation, conspicuous positions in the newspapers and periodicals, and much attention on radio and television. Mystery and detective fiction provide a consistently high proportion of the American reading diet. "In no other country," it has been noted by Francis Busch, "are crimes and the exploits, successful and unsuccessful, of criminals given greater publicity."[2]

In addition to its extraordinary appeal to the public imagination, crime is also the object of much sober concern, considerable head-shaking, and, often, a large amount of strong distaste, disquiet, and horror. Crime threatens the property and the lives of all citizens. Un-

1 Gibbon, *Decline and Fall of the Roman Empire,* Vol. I, p. 69, paraphrasing Voltaire, *L'Ingénu,* p. 275.
2 Busch, *Prisoners at the Bar,* p. 205.

like a disease such as cancer, which tends to be regarded as an immutable aspect of the roulette of human existence, crime is seen as a phenomenon that somehow might be avoided and controlled in order to allow the potential victim surcease from his uneasiness.

Crime may also represent, as Karl Menninger and Joseph Satten have noted, a "denial of our cultural philosophy," challenging by its existence the consensual roots of the social order.[3] Durkheim has suggested in this regard, however, that crime serves the subtle function of reinforcing collective sentiments of a majority of the members of a society by uniting citizens against the defined offender, who is labelled as an outsider and ostracized.[4] Without crime, there would be less occasion for vivid reaffirmations of the "rightness" of certain forms of law-abiding behavior.

Much crime is, of course, considerably more mundane than the flamboyant offenses that are catapulted into the public limelight. Police detectives are wont to note that an overwhelming amount of their work involves tedious tasks such as filling out and filing forms and talking to inarticulate, often uncooperative and unreliable witnesses about routine, everyday violations, most of which are unlikely ever to be solved. Run-of-the-mill crime and its practitioners, however, tend to flourish in the shadows of the society, areas rarely known to the average citizen but about which he might have considerable curiosity. Note, for instance, the following description by William Manchester of the underworld realm allegedly frequented by Jack Ruby, assassin of Lee Harvey Oswald, the man accused of killing President Kennedy. Few readers will fail to notice Manchester's own emotional intensity as well as his patent appeal to what he conceives to be the prurient interests of his readers. Attention might also be paid to the "loaded" manner in which a way of life other than his own is portrayed by Manchester:

> the maggotty half-world of dockets and flesh-peddlers, of furtive men with mud-colored faces and bottle blondes whose high-arched over-plucked eyebrows give their flat glittering eyes a perpetually startled expression, of sordid walkup hotels with unread Gideon Bibles and tumbled bed-clothes and rank animal odors, of police connivance in petty crime, of a way of life in which lawbreakers, law enforcement officers, and those who totter on the law's edge meet socially and even intermarry. There is no mystery about Jack Ruby's relationship with Dallas cops. His type is depressingly familiar in American police stations. . . . He worships patrolmen and plain-clothes men, and the fact that he is occasionally arrested doesn't dim his ardor. Often he is proud of his record. It is proof of his virility. He is usually overweight, middle-aged, has puffy eyes, wears broad lapels and outrageous neckties, and decorates his stubby fingers with extravagant costume jewelry. . . .[5]

3 Menninger and Satten, "The Development of Criminology," p. 164.
4 Durkheim, *Rules of Sociological Method*, pp. 68–71.
5 Manchester, *Death of a President*, p. 380.

Much of what appears to be an abiding interest in crime and criminals may stem from our need to repress our own impulses toward lawlessness and violence. Certainly, crime is one of the most efficient methods of achieving those things that society values. All of us may have aspects of the offender and the tempter within us, and our concern with crime may represent a vicarious interest in watching others give expression to motives and impulses we also hold. David Abrahamsen suggests that "What the citizen really does is to punish the delinquents for the evil he himself feels and thinks. Filled with his own pent-up resentments and hostilities, which might be transformed into antisocial actions, he instead lets off steam in other directions and often against the offender."[6] Ben Hecht, a popular writer, expressed the same idea in his observation about public response to notorious crimes by political and business leaders. He believes that people are "inclined to grin" at such corruption and ruthlessness and that "These malefactors are their dream selves. The American does not aspire to overthrow the thieves and oppressors half as much as he does to become one of them."[7]

Whatever the explanation offered, no one denies that criminal matters, as an integral part of the American national scene[8] and as a subject of engrossing interest, represent an important realm of human behavior that is deserving of scientific study and philosophical debate. It has been estimated, for instance, that 50 million Americans have criminal records, 10 million of which are felonies, offenses considered serious.[9] Crime is also a major American business enterprise. There is a huge force of persons whose vocational efforts are directed toward dealing with crime, including policemen, judges, probation officers, and prison personnel. Insurance companies derive considerable business from theft policies, and, in an indirect manner, other industries, such as public welfare, derive a considerable amount of their work as a byproduct of the activity of criminals and their removal from society. "If it were somehow possible to eliminate all crime suddenly, the effect on our entire economic structure would be as disastrous as the collapse of any other industry of similar magnitude," E. R. Hawkins and Willard Waller have observed. "The repercussion would be the same in kind, if not in degree, as that which typically follows a great war."[10] The duality of our attitudes toward crime— mingling attraction with repulsion—seems to tell us a great deal about some peculiar ambivalences in human nature and represents a rich source of potential knowledge about human beings and about the societies of which they are a part.

6 Abrahamsen, *Who Are the Guilty?*, p. 287.
7 Hecht, *A Child of the Century*, p. 415.
8 See Bell, "Crime as an American Way of Life."
9 Rubin, *Crime and Juvenile Delinquency*, p. 145.
10 Hawkins and Waller, "Critical Notes on the Cost of Crime," p. 693.

Public Agitation Regarding Crime

It is only in very recent years that crime has become a matter of intense public concern. Periodically throughout American history there have been forays against outlaws, reformist outcries, and similar manifestations of a malaise about criminal behavior. As Allen Churchill notes, however, "until the assassination of President Lincoln, the United States could hardly be called a crime-conscious nation"; American cities and towns possessed their quotas of murder, thievery, mayhem, arson, and rape, "but in the absence of telegraph and telephone communication these had remained localized, so that one community was largely ignorant of sensational events—criminal or otherwise—in places nearby."[11]

It took almost a century, from the assassination of Lincoln in 1865 to the national election in 1964, to bring crime to the point of seething public concern that exists today. Further improvement in communications, particularly the diffusion of television with its ability to depict criminal activity in "living color," and in transportation, bringing with it a burgeoning movement of people to the cities and the growing exposure of persons once safely confined within their respectable neighborhoods, to crime carried on by offenders who could travel rapidly from the slums to outlying suburban areas, contributed to this movement. Rapid social change and a deepening alienation of a considerable segment of youth, which is aggravated by controversial overseas military commitments of the United States and, in particular, the rise of militancy among the blacks, cause upheavals that focus public attention on violence as a major national blight. Concern appears to be based not on a rise in criminal behavior itself, but rather on secondary elements, such as student rebellion and the black power movement, and extends to the political realm in which politicians strive to appease the electorate's concern. "Crime," obviously wrong, truculent, evil, is a much handier scapegoat than the complex matters of social rearrangement, which contain elements that are both right and wrong, admirable and deplorable, and, at the very least, matters open to dispute.

Prior to 1964, most Americans focused their anxiety on the phenomenon of juvenile delinquency. This anxiety was rooted in what Robin Williams, Jr. calls "the strikingly high evaluation of 'youth' as a time of life" that permeates American culture.[12] Delinquency was seen as a threat against adult hegemony and adult standards, an irritating and sometimes infuriating undermining of the unusual emotional investment that Americans tend to make in their children. To fear and threat, Erik Erikson adds a rather poignant third source of American discomfort regarding youthful wayward-

---

11 Churchill, *They Never Came Back*, p. 13.
12 Williams, *American Society*, pp. 77–78.

ness: guilt. "A peculiar guilt can haunt those of the older generation
—the guilt over having caused what they cannot guide to a foreseen
completion. This can make them look at youth as a cast of characters
looking for a scenario not yet written; or worse, a cast populating a
play with a scenario already in production and badly in need of re-
writing."[13]

THE PRESIDENT'S COMMISSION

During the 1964 presidential campaign, Barry Goldwater, the Re-
publican candidate, concentrated much of his fire on the alleged
failure of the incumbent administration to cope with adult crime,
particularly crimes of violence, such as armed robbery, assault, and
rape. Taking heed of public responsiveness to the issue, President
Johnson directed considerable attention to the subject of crime after
his election. In March, 1965, he told Congress that "crime has become
a malignant enemy in America's midst," noting also that crime "will
not yield to quick and easy answers," but that "we must identify and
eliminate the causes of criminal activity whether they lie in the environment around us or deep in the nature of individual men. We
must arrest and reverse the trend toward lawlessness."[14]

Toward this end, the President appointed a Commission on Law
Enforcement and Administration of Justice. The report of that Commission, nine volumes of 2,248 double-columned pages, appeared
in 1967 and, by its very promulgation, served to focus further public
attention on crime. The Crime Commission report, in addition to
offering a sophisticated review of much of what was known or suspected about crime, contributed new information, particularly about
the amount and kinds of unreported crime occurring throughout the
nation. The Commission's theoretical orientation was essentially
eclectic, embracing quite diverse explanations of crime and offering
diverse insights into its problems. "The causes of crime are numerous
and mysterious and intertwined," it was observed.[15] "Each single crime
is a response to a specific situation by a person with an infinitely complicated psychological and emotional makeup who is subjected to
infinitely complicated external pressures."[16] The Commission intensively examined the pattern of crime in the Town Hall district of the
city of Chicago for a seven-day period and attempted in its summary
of events there to place into clearer focus the public's concern with
"crime on the streets":

> What the crimes of that week in Town Hall strongly suggest is that,
> although there is always some danger in the city of being robbed and
> perhaps injured on the street and a considerable chance of being bur-

13 Erikson, *Youth: Change and Challenge*, p. ix.
14 *New York Times*, March 9, 1965.
15 President's Commission, *Crime and Its Impact*, p. 2.
16 *Ibid.*, p. 1.

glarized, what people have to fear most from crime is themselves: their own carelessness or bravado; their attitudes toward their families and friends, toward the people they work for or who work for them; their appetites for drugs and liquor and sex; their own eccentricities; their own passions. Crime in Town Hall that week, like crime anywhere any week, consisted of the brutal, frightening, surreptitious, selfish, thoughtless, compulsive, sad, and funny ways people behave toward each other.[17]

Action programs suggested by the President's Commission, embodied in a series of more than 200 recommendations,[18] met with small favor when they were presented to the Congress. It was not until late 1968 that an Omnibus Crime Control and Safe Streets Act was passed, and the provisions of the new bill were clearly responsive to public fears, usually going against the advice of the President's Commission. The Act undercut restrictions placed by the Supreme Court on the right of the police to interrogate suspects, permitted wiretapping under certain conditions, provided for greatly expanded training for law enforcement officers, placed limited controls on the sale of handguns, and authorized federal grants of $400 million for a two-year period for planning and launching crime control programs by the states. The President, with strong reservations, signed the bill because he believed it contained more good than bad.

FURTHER INVESTIGATORY WORK

The issue of crime developed into public demands for "law and order," a term embracing reactions not only against traditional kinds of crime but also against riots, resistance to the military draft, and outbreaks of rebellion on college campuses. In a Harris public opinion poll in 1968, the public, by a margin of 81 percent to 14 percent, voiced the belief that law and order had broken down in the United States. This issue, termed by the pollsters as "new and emotional" and as one "coming to dominate public attention," showed a hard-line approach from most respondents, who indicated their belief that its roots lay in four major causes: (1) The growth of organized crime, (2) "Negroes who start riots," (3) "Communists," and (4) The opinions of the courts on criminal matters.[19] The preeminent position of crime found by the Harris poll was supported by a 1968 Gallup poll, which indicated that "crime and lawlessness are viewed as the top domestic problem facing the nation for the first time since the beginning of scientific polling in the mid-thirties."[20]

In the midst of the national debate on law and order and in the wake of the report of the President's Commission on Law Enforce-

17 *Ibid.*, p. 13.
18 President's Commission, *Challenge of Crime in a Free Society*, pp. 293–301.
19 *Washington Post*, Sept. 9, 1968.
20 *New York Times*, Feb. 27, 1968.

ment and Administration of Justice, three major groups, influenced
by the aggravated mood of the public, made additional investigations.
Most controversial among them was the report of the National Advisory Commission on Civil Disorders, chaired by Otto Kerner, then
Governor of Illinois. The Commission had been asked to look into
the causes of riots and looting, which, beginning in the Watts area
of Los Angeles in 1965, had swept through Negro neighborhoods in
many metropolitan areas each summer thereafter.[21]

The blunt finding of the Kerner Commission elicited both strong
endorsement and intense opposition: "This is our basic conclusion,"
the Commission report stated, "Our nation is moving toward two
societies, one black, one white—separate but unequal."[22] The Commission was not convinced that one single cause of rioting in the cities,
such as unemployment, lack of education, poverty, or exploitation,
could be found; rather, it pointed out, the cause was all these conditions combined, plus, overridingly, "an insidious and pervasive white
sense of the inferiority of black men."[23] The essence of this allegation
was further expressed: "What white Americans have never fully understood—but what the Negro can never forget—is that white society
is deeply implicated in the ghetto. White institutions created it, white
institutions maintain it, and white society condones it."[24] Summarizing the Kerner report, Wicker notes that people other than those
traditionally regarded as the criminal element in American society
were involved in the rioting:

> As for the rioters—those ominous looters and arsonists whose eruption
> into violence precipitated this massive study—they tended, curiously,
> to be somewhat more educated than the "brothers" who remained un-
> involved. By and large, the rioters were young Negroes, natives of the
> ghetto (not of the South), hostile to the white society surrounding and
> repressing them, and equally hostile to the middle-class Negroes who ac-
> commodated themselves to that white dominance. The rioters were
> mistrustful of white politics, they hated the police, they were proud
> of their race, and acutely conscious of the discrimination they suffered.
> They were and they are a time-bomb ticking in the heart of the richest
> nation in the history of the world.[25]

Improvement of the social and economic conditions of slum
dwellers provided the major focus of the Kerner Commission's recommendations for the reduction and control of rioting. The nation's
welfare systems, it said, required reform and upgrading so that they
would provide basic sustenance for needy persons and so the breakup

21 See, for example, Mattick, "Form and Content of Recent Riots"; Dynes and
   Quarantelli, "What Looting in Civil Disorders Really Means"; Hersey, *Algiers
   Motel Incident;* Sauter and Hines, *Nightmare in Detroit.*
22 National Advisory Commission on Civil Disorders, *Report,* p. 1.
23 *Ibid.,* p. vii.
24 *Ibid.*
25 *Ibid.,* p. x.

of families would be discouraged. The Commission urged the creation of 2,000,000 jobs within the next three years, with remedial training for the unemployed where necessary. It was argued that such a program would reduce crime and delinquency significantly by aiding persons most responsible for such behavior, such as out-of-school, out-of-work young men. Overhaul of the public educational system was also stressed by the Kerner Commission, which advocated a twelve-month school year in disadvantaged city neighborhoods. They believed that such programs would relieve the insecurity of daily life in the slums by taking people off the streets and thereby reducing the amount of predatory crime. The Commission noted, for example, that while low income and high crime rates go together, low-income black areas have significantly higher crime rates than low-income white areas. "This reflects the high degree of social disorganization in the Negro areas," the Commission report observed, "as well as the fact that poor Negroes, as a group, have lower incomes than poor whites, as a group."[26]

The assassination of Senator Robert F. Kennedy in June, 1968, the assassination five years earlier of his older brother, President John F. Kennedy, and the murder of Martin Luther King, Jr., a noted civil rights leader, in April, 1968, were largely responsible for the appointment of the National Commission on the Causes and Prevention of Violence, the second group, which was charged with examining the role of brutality and physical force in American society. Among other things, the Commission was asked to determine whether candidates for public office should be required to minimize their physical contact with the public to protect themselves from "the deranged individual and obsessed fanatic."[27] Ironically, the members of the Commission were sworn in at a White House ceremony while standing under a portrait of Andrew Jackson, probably the most personally violent of the American presidents, who had killed a man in a duel in 1806.

The Violence Commission recommended in its 1969 report that, among other things, more careful attention be paid to providing financial and other necessary resources to victims of criminal violence. It noted that victims remain neglected at the same time that great cost goes into the prosecution, incarceration, and treatment of the offender.[28] In addition, the Violence Commission reported results of the most penetrating study on homicide, aggravated assault, robbery, and forcible rape ever conducted throughout the nation. A 10 percent sample of the records of the police in seventeen metropolitan areas

26 *Ibid.*, p. 267.
27 Johnson, "The President's Remarks to Members of the Commission," p. 936.
28 National Commission on the Causes and Prevention of Violence, *Report*, pp. 106–120. See also Graham and Gurr, *Violence in America;* Walker, *Rights in Conflict;* Massotti and Corsi, *Shoot-Out in Cleveland;* Skolnick, *Politics of Protest.*

were combed to provide information on both offenders and victims, the time and locations of offenses, and the involvement of either drugs or alcohol in offenses.[29]

Finally, the third of the investigatory groups, the Joint Commission on Correctional Manpower and Training, which worked primarily with funds supplied by the federal Vocational Rehabilitation Administration, in 1969 completed a far-ranging examination of the methods employed in the United States to handle criminal offenders. Concentrating particularly on the relationships between social conditions and criminal activity, the Commission stressed that the correctional apparatus is asked to resolve problems produced by deep-seated elements in American life, and that it is often blamed for its inability to resolve those situations, which have defied the powers of many other institutions, such as the family, church, and schools.[30] National surveys of the Joint Commission found that of the 79,000 jobs in juvenile and adult correctional facilities 5 percent were unfilled, and that there is an average annual turnover of 16 percent in such positions, a percentage far in excess of those for other social service occupations.[31] Among its rather gloomy findings on the current state of work with criminal offenders, the Joint Commission noted the following about correctional administrators:

> The administrators studied are clearly isolated and inward-directed as they seek to perform their difficult task. They are effective neither in communicating their felt imperatives to the outside world, nor in drawing from that world much of the potentially available assistance to help them become more effective problem-solvers. This condition is reflected in the pervasive indifference of the universities, of private enterprise, and the public at large. . . .
>
> Some themes seem to predominate: The frustration involved in not knowing what is working and what has not worked in the armament of correctional techniques; the difficulty of obtaining and keeping staff capable of performing the onerous tasks required; the unending problems of implementation—planning, financing, organizing, and, most of all, securing the support and resources necessary for continued operation.[32]

Implications for the Study of Criminology

The work of the various investigatory bodies—the President's Commission on Law Enforcement and Administration of Justice, the National Advisory Commission on Civil Disorders, the National

29 *Ibid.*, pp. 135–170.

30 Joint Commission on Correctional Manpower and Training, *A Time to Act*, pp. 31–34.

31 Joint Commission on Correctional Manpower and Training, *2d Annual Report*, pp. 2–3.

32 *Ibid.*, p. 5.

Commission on the Causes and Prevention of Violence, and the Joint Commission on Correctional Manpower and Training—has contributed more information in recent years about the extent and roots of crime and the methods for dealing with offenders than was gathered during any earlier, equivalent period of time in the history of the study of criminology. Perhaps more important is that today there is a considerably clearer picture of those things that remain to be discovered before scholars and the public can say with assurance that they adequately comprehend matters relevant to the formulation of intelligent, comprehensive policies regarding crime.

It is important to emphasize that governmental inquiries undertaken in response to public and political pressure tend to concentrate on finding means of resolving the issues that initally made the inquiry necessary; there is ordinarily relatively little soul-searching about fundamental philosophical questions. A commission studying the causes of riots, therefore, devotes its efforts to seeking methods to end riots. It might be argued, however, that measures that stop riots today constitute a disservice to rioting groups and perhaps to the society in general, since they tend to foreclose redress of what might be the far-reaching aims of the riots. Higher welfare payments, for instance, while they might bring slum quiescence, fail to achieve more deep-rooted reforms. But, on the other hand, rioting itself is destructive and deplorable and constitutes an undesirable technique in a society dedicated to change by peaceful and democratic methods. Following this argument, it can be said that the achievement of public order is a necessary prerequisite to the creation of an atmosphere in which the elimination of injustice can be given adequate, calm attention, and that riots lead primarily to retaliation and further distress rather than to adequate resolution of real grievances.

These viewpoints are, of course, not demonstrable by recourse to strictly scientific methods of research and experimentation, although historical evidence might be employed to approach an understanding of the dynamics of the situation. The issue of causes, and similar questions, do constitute matters that are of prime significance for the study of criminology, as a field oriented to the understanding of criminal behavior in as thorough and nonjudgmental a manner as possible, and not necessarily as a pursuit dedicated to the reduction of crime. John Stuart Mill wrote that "Improvement consists of bringing our opinions into clearer agreement with facts. We shall not be likely to do this while we look at facts only through glasses colored by those very opinions."[33]

The study of criminology, therefore, in addition to probing why persons often show such intense interest in behavior generally regarded as repellent, also examines the conditions that seem to produce

33 Quoted in Overholser, *The Psychiatrist and the Law*, p. 134.

crime and the views of both law-abiders and criminals toward such conditions and toward the laws that have been violated. Motorists apprehended for speeding or for tail-gating, for example, are rarely satisfied with the writing and the enforcement of traffic laws, but they may become puzzled when the juvenile delinquent shows as little enthusiasm for and compliance with the laws against shoplifting.

Criminal activity *may* be studied to advance personal or social goals—such as those favoring crime control—but criminology need not be tailored to such goals. It can be argued forcefully that the laws against murder are supremely just, because it is immoral for one man to assume the right to take another's life without that person's voluntary consent. In such terms, we may want to determine how murder occurs in the United States, who commits it, who suffers from it, and what the society is wont to do about it. But the same kinds of information may be used to defend the position that in the final analysis murder is a useful part of social life. Some may argue, as Émile Durkheim did, that murder serves to unite the law-abiding more cohesively. Or, some may maintain that murder eases life somewhat by reducing those pressures of over-population that create anguish and suffering. From such a value position—with which few, if any, Americans are likely to be in sympathy—a policy-maker might decide that efforts to reduce the homicide rate in an Indian city like Calcutta should not be encouraged. We know that among Eskimo groups the killing of infants, invalids, and old people is an accepted form of homicide, based on the principle that only those who are able or potentially able to contribute to the subsistence economy of the community may survive.[34] No ethnographic evidence from anthropologists exists regarding the opinions of the condemned about this matter, or if in fact they give it much thought.

The study of criminology can reveal a good deal about the forms of control by which a society attempts to maintain its equilibrium; the types of stress that seem to promote behavior that either characterizes or leads to crime; the variations in the forms crime takes in different cultures; and the different techniques used to deal with criminal behavior. We shall also attempt to discover why one society has comparatively small amounts of theft, whereas another is marked by pervasive dishonesty; the elements within a culture that lead it to designate some types of acts as sexual offenses, while other societies regard similar behavior as acceptable; the ingredients that appear to compel one individual to resolve a dilemma in a law-abiding manner, while another resorts to a criminal offense for apparently similar reasons. In addition, we try to understand why some societies react with almost indifferent leniency to offenses that other societies regard with horror and punish with extraordinary stringency. These are just some

34 Hoebel, "Law-Ways of the Primitive Eskimos," pp. 670–677; East, *Society and the Criminal*, p. 7.

of the areas that absorb the interests and the research energy of criminologists.

The scientific perspectives of the criminologist also make possible an understanding of how various types of social control and legislation arise, why certain patterns of human control are more effective than others, and, indeed, why some appear to be doomed to failure. Above all, criminology and its basic principles should aid us considerably to comprehend more fully the mechanisms and dynamic forces that affect both individuals and the societies themselves. Just as the student of abnormal psychology develops insights into the functioning of the "normal" personality, the student of criminology acquires a vantage point for understanding law-abiding behavior in his probe of the roots of certain forms of illegal behavior. Finally, although the fact is not always sufficiently appreciated, variations in the amount and forms of crime within a society may serve as a highly revealing index of the process of social change.

Historical Definitions of Crime and Delinquency

There is surprisingly little agreement, even among specialists, about the definition of "crime," although it is essential to a scientific approach that a precise conception of the subject under examination be understood, even though its basic assumptions, by their definition, impose limitations and procedural restrictions for its investigation. The fact that the meaning of "crime" is open to so many interpretations has led inevitably to claims and counterclaims by specialists dealing with differing realms within criminology. Much of the confusion arises from the fact that the vantage points from which specialists—sociologists, lawyers, psychiatrists, clinical psychologists, social workers, and penologists—view crime differ, and therefore their fundamental conceptions of what crime is, or should be, also differ.

Even cursory examination reveals that the word "crime" is one of the least precise terms in the English language. In common usage, it covers literally a multitude of sins and includes acts that are proscribed by law, acts that deviate from the imperatives of various ethical systems, and innumerable other forms of human behavior that, at one time or another and in some guise, appear to some persons and by some standards to represent improper behavior. There is not much in the lexicon of human behavior that has not in the past and might not today under certain conditions be regarded as crime. This looseness of definition has long been a major stumbling block in the attempt to outline clearly the province of the study of criminology.

Is it possible, then, to develop a coherent and incisive view of crime when so many people interpret its meaning so differently? An examination of the etymological roots of the word itself is not entirely helpful. The Romans, for example, despite their penchant for law and the fact that they laid the foundation for much of Western jurisprudence, were quite wayward and erratic in formulating a precise definition of the meaning of crime. This may in part reflect the homogeneity of the early Roman social structure and their general consensus on social issues. In homogeneous societies like the Roman society, a common term or designation may encompass a variety of different behaviors, and the term may express a public attitude rather than condemn a specific act or set of acts. Indeed, the general idea of public censure regardless of the act censured, may very well be the genesis of the word "crime."

The term "crimen" first referred to a judicial decision or verdict and only later included a charge, accusation, or reproach. In this early usage the term applied specifically to those accusations that were unfounded. This emphasis in Roman jurisprudence presisted until the reign of Emperor Augustus (27 B.C.–A.D. 14) when the term "crimen" was expanded to include the specific complaints of the accuser, whether or not they were accurate.[35] Ovid, for instance, who was exiled from Rome by Augustus, first refers to the charge that led to his banishment as "crimen" and later refers to it by the Latin word *error,* or mistake.[36] Probably the early use of the term implied formal disapprobation of various kinds of conduct for which public redress might be incurred.

Throughout the course of Western history, the tortuous twists of meaning and public understanding of the term "crime" has resulted in a legacy of widely divergent perspectives. The word "criminology" itself, for instance, represents a euphonious corruption of the term "criminal anthropology," indicating the academic focus of much early work in the study of offenders. Suggested in 1899 by Paul Topinard (1830–1911), a professor at the École d'Anthropologie in Paris,[37] the designation was adopted with enthusiasm by the popular press to describe "the branch of anthropological science which has the best promise of affording results of immediate practical value."[38]

JUVENILE DELINQUENCY

The term "delinquency," another fundamental category in the study of law violation, shows equally ambiguous roots. Derived from the stems *de* (away, from) and *linquere* (to leave), the Latin infinitive *delinquere* translates as "to omit" in its original, earliest sense. It was apparently used in Roman times to refer to the failure of an individual to perform a task or duty.

The first grouping of the idea of "delinquency" with "crime" appears about A.D. 196 in the work of Tertullian, a Christian theologian. When Tertullian uses *delinquentia* in his treatise *De Res-*

---

35 Andrews, *A New Latin Dictionary*, p. 482.
36 Ovid, *Tristia*, Vol. IX, pp. 9, 64.
37 Ellis, *The Criminal*, p. 30; Bonger, *An Introduction to Criminology*, p. 1.
38 "Science," p. 325.

16   Crime and Society

surectione Carnis Liber,[39] he has in mind religious transgressions rather
than delinquencies as these are broadly viewed today. The Latin connotation of delinquency ultimately found its way into English and, in
1484, William Caxton, printer of the first English books, used "delinquent" to describe a person guilty of an offense against the customs.
In his translation from the French of *The Book of the Ordre of
Chivalry*, Caxton renders as "delinquents" the original French term
that signified "evil men" in a passage commenting on obligations of
knights: ". . . in lyke wise is thoffyce of a knyght establysshyd for to
punysshe the trespacers and delynquants."[40]

Shakespeare gave the term a similar emphasis in *Macbeth* (1605),
where one of the characters asks ". . . did he not straight/In pious
rage two delinquents tear/That were slaves of drink and thralls of
sleep?"[41] Shortly thereafter, the designation "delinquents" was used to
refer to persons who fought on the side of Charles I during the Civil
War in England from 1642 to 1660.[42] In 1824, it was found in the
United States in an observation by Washington Irving about "delinquent school-boys."[43] The first official use of the term in its current
sense probably was in 1825 when the Society for the Prevention of
Pauperism in New York City changed its name to the Society for the
Reformation of Juvenile Delinquents.[44]

That language usage may both reflect and condition social policy
can be noted from one of the earliest references to the term "delinquent" in English law. In Cowell's *Institutes*, a compendium of laws
published in 1651, reference is made to the idea that "from . . .
Delinquencies proceed greater crimes."[45] Such a statement provides
a verbal climate for intervention against young offenders for behavior
that for adults would not constitute a criminal offense, justified on
the ground that it can prevent subsequent and more serious violations.

Toward Forming a Scientific Definition of Crime

Certainly, if scientific understanding is to be developed with respect to the study of crime, definitions of an operational, verifiable,
and testable nature, insuring that we are gazing at the same kinds of
phenomena, must be forthcoming. Fundamental to definitional agreement would appear to be the commonplace observation that crime
involves human action that is reproved by legal sanctions. Even this
broad definition, however, is open to question. Certain acts are legally

39 Evans, *Tertullian's Treatise on the Resurrection*, p. 42.
40 Caxton, *The Book of the Ordre of Chivalry*, p. 42.
41 Shakespeare, *Tragedy of Macbeth*, Act III, Sc. 4.
42 Churchill, *History of the English-Speaking Peoples*, Vol. II, pp. 170–186; Clarendon, *History of the Rebellion*, Vol. III, p. 231.
43 Irving, *Tales of a Traveller*, Vol. I, p. 276.
44 Society for the Reformation of Juvenile Delinquents, *1st Annual Report*. See
also Pickett, *House of Refuge*.
45 Cowell, *Institutes*, p. 209.

defined as crimes, for example, although they do not include positive forms of action, but rather constitute a *failure to act* on occasions when the laws insists upon a certain standard of performance. Thus, factory owners who fail to provide required safety equipment for the protection of their employees or eligible persons who fail to register for military service may be guilty of criminal behavior.

In this sense, as a nineteenth-century Italian criminologist Francesco Carrarra once noted, crime constitutes "not action . . . but infraction."[46] Behavior defined as "failure to act" can, of course, be analyzed in essentially the same manner as other forms of action, since failure to behave in a prescribed way includes selection of a course of action other than the required pattern.

It should already be apparent that, although crime is a condition that all men seem to recognize, a definition in which all men might concur is not easy to formulate. Each move toward a resolution of the true meaning of crime raises further dilemmas. Are acts that are ignored by the police and sanctioned by a large segment of the public to be regarded as crimes? There was widespread violation of the prohibition laws while they remained in force and yet neither convicted individuals nor the public-at-large seemed to regard such offenses as crimes, regardless of their legal definition. Similarly, should infringements of the so-called "blue laws," which forbid certain pursuits on the Sabbath, be classified as criminal offenses even though the public might not regard them as such? In other words, does a crime cease to be a crime when laws appear anachronistic and are no longer supported by community opinion or followed by community custom?

Arguments favoring the view that acts should be regarded as noncriminal if a large segment of public opinion does not support the transgressed statute might maintain that it is inconsequential if the laws remain on the books, since it will be only a matter of time until they will be altered. This position is not quite as straightforward as it might appear, however, given the complexities that determine when a law is enacted and when it is repealed. In addition, archaic or rarely used laws are sometimes used to ensnare persons who have been able to avoid prosecution for other, usually more serious, offenses. In the absence of concrete evidence for major crimes, Al Capone was convicted of income tax evasion rather than murder, just as other offenders with long histories of involvement in violent crimes may also be charged with perjury, adultery, or violation of similar laws that under other circumstances would not likely be enforced. This occasional tendency of enforcement officials to use secondary offenses for more far-reaching purposes is not without troublesome implications. For example, in one case, a man gave a woman a lethal overdose of narcotics and then deposited her body in a trunk on the lawn of

46 Quoted in Radzinowicz and Turner, "The Meaning and Scope of Criminal Science," p. 12.

a country estate. Unable to prove that he gave the narcotics to the victim, the authorities tried and sentenced the man for transporting a dead body without a permit from the Health Department.[47] The analytical problems for the study of criminology involved in such a procedure are of fundamental importance.

Further definitional difficulties are raised when questions regarding prosecution and conviction are considered. Is an act a crime if the person accused is freed by a jury that is misled by an effective smokescreen raised by a clever defense attorney? Is his act a crime when the perpetrator, who obviously committed the offense, is set free because of a legal technicality, such as a faultily worded indictment or an incorrect lower-court ruling on the admissibility of a given piece of evidence? How are we to regard acts that are not "really" offenses but that result in convictions because of a miscarriage of judicial procedures? Obviously, we must look very closely at the behavior itself and then evaluate it in terms of the standard employed to determine *criminal* behavior.

As we move into the realm of moral issues, especially when strong institutional and public support exists for the right to take what is believed to be an honorable and sacrificial course of action, the analytical problem may become quite complicated. Has a dying parent, for example, committed a crime by killing a mentally defective child under the belief that this is the only way to safeguard the child against the uncertainties ensuant upon the absence of parental care? Although a violation of the law against homicide, is such an act of mercy-killing a crime if the district attorney refuses, as is his prerogative, to bring the case to trial?

The criminologist is not merely being captious when he demurs at many of the common usages that are applied to the word "crime" and when he expresses concern over the necessity for deriving a precise conception of so kaleidoscopically viewed a thing as crime, in the interest of scientific investigation. We shall first examine various frameworks that have been suggested for the study of criminal behavior before we return and attempt to establish what we conceive to be a reasonable and potentially fruitful approach to the scientific study of criminal behavior.

MORAL ABERRANCE, PARASITISM, AND DEVIANCY

Frustrations over problems of definition have led to occasional demands for the abandonment of the concept of crime and its legal base and a concentration on categories such as moral aberrance, social parasitism, and deviant behavior. Practically all of these ideas are mingled indiscriminately in the definition of crime offered by Maurice Parmelee in the first comprehensive American criminology textbook,

47 Anslinger and Tompkins, *Traffic in Narcotics*, p. 300.

published in 1918. Parmelee categorizes crime as "an act forbidden and punished by law, which is almost always immoral according to prevailing ethical standards, which is usually harmful to society, which it is ordinarily feasible to repress by penal measures, and whose repression is necessary or is supposed to be necessary to the preservation of the existing social order."[48]

The definition proposed by Hermannus Bianchi, a Dutch criminologist, in a similar vein, centers on *moral aberrance*. Bianchi advocates regarding crime as "a sinful, ethically blameworthy, defiant and erroneous act, eventually prohibited by penal law, at any rate deserving to be followed by conscious counteraction on the part of the society."[49] Among other things, the inordinate complexity of attempting to achieve consensus among investigators about acts that are "sinful and ethically blameworthy" hardly advances the concept of crime into reasonable definitional realms. Such views, encompassing the limits of human transgression, usually serve primarily to disclose the special biases of the researcher.

A different approach occurs in the effect to regard crime as a form of *social parasitism*. The parasite is seen as one who receives sustenance from others without giving anything in return. The problem, however, remains one of determining with precision the criteria by which the utility of various acts can be measured and by which scientifically heterogeneous forms of behavior can be studied. As the concept of social parasitism is employed, it usually becomes more a figure of speech and a derogatory label than a scientific instrument.

The value of the concept of parasitism, Wyatt Marrs claims, is that it provides a meaningful measure by asking whether behavior contributes to society or takes something of value from it.[50] The simplistic charm of such a formula, however, breaks down in its application. Using this approach, for example, many American women may be judged parasitic, since they appear to subsist on male effort without making any direct economic contribution to what may be defined as the total product of the society themselves. The difficulty lies in arriving at an accurate specification of the value of diverse acts: How much importance should be attached to child-bearing, housecleaning, and the emotional contribution to a family's well-being? What of the struggling artist or the unfulfilled scholar? Under this scheme, one rater's social parasite might turn out to be another's social paragon.

Social deviance represents behavior that constitutes "deviations from social norms which encounter disapproval and to which theory and concepts derived from sociology and social psychology may be

48 Parmelee, *Criminology*, p. 32.
49 Bianchi, *Position and Subject-Matter of Criminology*, p. 6.
50 Marrs, *The Man on Your Back*, pp. 3-13.

applied."[51] There is little doubt that such a concept can shed valuable light on a variety of situations that are regarded as disorders by different segments or even the entire society; however, the wide-ranging nature of the concept fails to distinguish the highly specific nature of the criminal act. The concept resembles in part the concept of *social dysfunction*, which is oriented to the functional approach to the study of society. The "social deviance" point of view stresses departure from norms of behavior—which are often extremely difficult to establish—while the "social dysfunction" approach tends to stress the consequences that follow from various kinds of acts. The emphasis on deviance avoids the pitfall of having to pass judgment on the utility of a given type behavior. Nonetheless, there is a tendency when looking at deviants to assume that their acts are regrettable and require reformative attention. As Leslie Wilkins points out, "it is usual to find 'deviant' behavior almost automatically connoting 'bad' behavior," although "there is deviant behavior which is 'good' or functional to society. The genius, the reformer, the religious leader, and many others are 'deviant' from the norms of the society as much as is the criminal."[52] It need only be added that "the criminal," legally defined, in some circumstances need not himself be deviant; he may reflect a pervasive pattern of social behavior, even admirable behavior.[53] In addition, of course, judgments of functionality—that is, whether certain acts contribute to the well-being of a social system—can be highly intricate undertakings. Hindsight constantly reminds us that a social pattern that in its time was viewed as superbly valuable to a society, at a much later date might be identified as the very item that sealed the group's doom.

Both the "deviance" and "functionalist" views assume the determination of recognizable forms of behavior as norms to which adjustment is being sought, and which exercise pressures for conformity upon members of society. Both are prepared to recognize a wide range of divergent behavior falling within their province. This *mélange* includes behaviors whose source and focus differ so widely from those forms generally recognized as crimes that we must stretch our imagination to consider them as similar aspects of a common process.

The value of a concept such as social deviation—and it does offer considerable opportunity for fruitful study when carefully stipulated frames of reference are established—is that it indicates some of the characteristic stresses and strains of a society while it acknowledges that criminal behavior constitutes a specialized and distinctive category of deviation.

As soon as we focus on the problem in this way, we recognize a number of further items that the concept of social deviation appears

51 Clinard, *Sociology of Deviant Behavior*, p. vii. See also Cohen, *Deviance and Control*.
52 Wilkins, *Social Deviance*, p. 45.
53 Quinney, "Is Criminal Behaviour Deviant Behaviour?" p. 136.

to neglect. Crime as a distinct category provides a significant index of patterns of social change and a reflection of disruptive stress in the whole social structure. In addition, approaches that broadly equate crime with social deviation often bypass meaningful questions concerning the enforcement of certain statutes and the origins of those statutes. Finally, views like these tend to overlook one of the most critical elements in the study of criminal behavior—the degree to which an awareness of the nature of statutes and the possibility of the invocation of sanctions enter into human behavior.

Thus, the broad categories of antisocial behavior—whether considered as moral digression or waywardness, social parasitism, social deviancy, or social dysfunction—fail to characterize those highly distinctive features that make a unique phenomenon of crime. It is necessary to separate qualities and conditions that distinguish crime out of these conceptual categories. In doing so, we discover that among the elements that place crime in a distinct category, the socially endorsed stipulations of the criminal codes are vital. Shlomo Shoham has put the the matter into an instructive analogy:

> The norms of the criminal law, although very often crude and arbitrary from the psychological, sociological, and moral point of view, may be likened to the political boundaries of a state; these boundaries are largely arbitrary and artificial and quite often transcend the natural and topographical structure of the surrounding areas, but nobody can regard these boundaries as unreal or non-existent. They are there and one has to be provided with a permit, be examined by customs and change currency in order to pass them. We hold that to expand the concept of crime to include non-legal norms is highly precarious and problematic, because then our subject matter will become "social deviation." The difficulties in defining a deviation from a social norm are obvious. . . .[54]

The Law as a Social Force
Criminal law is the crucial element in the specification of criminal behavior. In multifarious ways, individuals learn, though not always in detail, what the law expects of them and what they may and may not do. Recognition of the sanctions contained within the law may affect their behavior and personality in a variety of ways. This does not necessarily indicate, in the classic philosophical view of Thomas Hobbes, that all individuals function because of fear of the law.[55] It does suggest, however, that an awareness of the law provides restraints and incentives to perform in a specified manner, even if, for some reason, the law may be distasteful. How law makes its impact depends

54 Shoham, "The Norm, the Act, and the Object of Crime as Bases for the Classification of Criminal Behaviour," p. 273.
55 Molesworth, *English Works of Thomas Hobbes of Malmesbury*, Vol. II, pp. 68–72.

upon given individuals and their particular qualities, but that the law operates as a significant social force can hardly be questioned. The racial desegregation cases, for example, have shown that, while morality itself may not be legislated, the law may provide a set of conditions under which the practice of morality may be made more feasible.[56] Sol Rubin, stressing the operation of law as an educative instrument, has said that "It is not only a framework for action; it is itself a force. . . . It is a great educational tool, declaring or implying standards of conduct in a highly authoritative way."[57]

A substantial segment of the population, as Marion Barnes points out, "habitually manipulates its own responses and activities to align with prevailing rules,"[58] while Paul Tappan, addressing himself to the same theme, notes that "from introspection and from objective analysis of criminal histories one cannot but accept as axiomatic the thesis that the norms of criminal law and its sanctions do exert some measure of effective control over human behavior."[59] A demonstration of this theme was provided by a study of the influence on behavior of a new ordinance altering the legal parking limit in New Haven, Connecticut. Observations made before and after introduction of the regulation indicated, as might have been expected, significant behavioral changes.[60] It should not be assumed, however, that legal enactments necessarily decrease the proscribed acts; they may, in fact, provide an element of excitement or an ingredient of self-harm previously unattached to the behavior. Baruch Spinoza (1632–1677), the Dutch philosopher, stated the matter well when he advocated the elimination of laws restricting activities that do not harm a second party. Spinoza said, "Nay, so far are they from doing anything to control the desires and passions of men that, on the contrary, they direct and incite men's thoughts the more toward those very objects; for we always strive toward what is forbidden and desire the things we are not allowed to have. . . . He who tries to determine everything by law will foment crime rather than lessen it."[61]

The legal categorization of crime, however, creates a special area of human transgression that may be studied efficiently and effectively. The law itself becomes an important variable in interpreting changes in behavior that relate to it. It must always be kept in mind that legal norms, unlike the more tenuous norms of other social institutions, are explicitly spelled out in written codes. Explanatory concepts that fail to take legal norms into account are inextricably caught up in the inherent difficulty of making scientifically valid determinations of pre-

56 Tumin and Rotberg, "Leaders, the Led, and the Law."
57 Rubin, *Crime and Juvenile Delinquency*, p. 16.
58 Barnes, *Treatise on the Law of Crimes*, p. 7.
59 Tappan, "Who Is the Criminal?" p. 101.
60 Moore and Callahan, "Law and Learning Theory."
61 Spinoza, *Theologico-Political Treatise*, p. 261.

vailing and past social norms. They then face the compounded problem of relating these norms to individual behavior.

Crime and Criminal Law

It seems inescapable that the study of criminology should proceed from
the formulations of criminal law, and should restrict itself to these
formulations. As Jerome Michael and Mortimer J. Adler concluded
after a penetrating examination of the scientific aspirations of criminology, "the most precise and least ambiguous definition of crime is
that which defines it as behavior which is prohibited by the criminal
code"; indeed, they continue, "this is the only possible definition of
crime."[62] This observation has been echoed by other scholars. Karl N.
Llewellyn, generalizing about a common, but hardly universal, pre-
dilection in sociological studies of crime, has written that, "The sociologist says, . . . 'I take the sociological, not the legal, approach to crime,'
though it is surely somewhat obvious that when you take the 'legal'
out, you also take out 'crime.' "[63] Francis A. Allen, Dean of the University of Michigan Law School, has commented in the same vein
that, "It may be doubted that so complete an elimination of the legal
content of the concept of crime has well served the development of
criminological theory."[64] Finally, Jerome Hall has argued that "criminology is synonymous with Sociology of Criminal Law," and that
"criminology must be concerned, first, with the meaning of the rules
of criminal law."[65]

Disagreement with views like these seems to be partly rooted in
the fact that criminologists have at times failed to differentiate adequately between the precise legal conception of a crime and the
criminal behavior for which the individual may be prosecuted. The
performance of an illegal act may involve many forms of illicit behavior, and an offender may be prosecuted for only a phase of his
activity that is not in keeping with its essential character. A person
who commits robbery thus may be charged with being the recipient of
stolen property instead of robbery, if, for example, that charge is an
easier one to prove or if it carries a heavier penalty.

This difficulty arises because of the distinction between the
functional aspects of crime—the performance of a given act in defiance
of legal codes—and the *procedural* aspects of legal machinery devised
to obtain successful prosecutions. The most basic aim in any science is
to formulate categories that are rigidly and mutually exclusive; scientific criminology, therefore, is interested in examining crimes of similar
or identical character. The distinction between the highly flexible and

62 Michael and Adler, *Crime, Law, and Social Science*, p. 2.
63 Llewellyn, "Law and the Social Sciences—Especially Sociology," p. 1287.
64 Allen, "Pioneers in Criminology—Raffaele Garofalo," p. 377.
65 Hall, *General Principles of Criminal Law*, pp. 558-559.

often erratic machinery set up to deal with crime and the painstakingly clear legal definitions of what constitutes crimial behavior may perhaps be understood more readily by an analogy from medicine. Tuberculosis remains a reasonably discernible diagnostic category, whether the victim of the disease is placed in a sanitarium or treated as an outpatient. And, even though the disorder may be incorrectly diagnosed, it obviously continues to be tuberculosis. Tuberculosis is, of course, a condition, whereas crime is an act, but the parallel remains analytically appropriate, even though accurate diagnosis of the precise characteristics of a criminal act is apt to be more difficult than the diagnosis of a physical condition.

This is not an insuperable problem, however. It may be resolved by classifying forms of criminal behavior, regardless of the charge brought against the person, in terms of what the law explicitly states the crime to be. Although an individual who committed robbery may be prosecuted and sentenced for being the recipient of stolen property, the crime is still robbery. Similarly, in certain instances, acts generically similar to automobile theft have been prosecuted as embezzlement, largely because in some jurisdictions it is necessary to prove intent to steal in order to obtain a conviction for automobile theft, whereas embezzlement convictions require only that the person converted a piece of property to his own use that he neither owned nor had permission to take.[66] Another illustration involves the occasional use of statutes prohibiting "attempted suicide," an act that remains a crime in several American states, to prosecute an offender caught driving far in excess of the speed limit. The attempted suicide law may carry a heavier penalty than speeding, and in a particular instance the district attorney might want to make an example of the accused.

In the attempt to overcome such idiosyncrasies in the administration of criminal justice, criminologists have been seeking to redefine certain types of crime more precisely in order to analyze only persons falling within the scope of the restricted definition. Donald Cressey, for instance, redefined embezzlement as "criminal violation of financial trust," after observing that "persons whose behavior was not adequately described by the definition of embezzlement were found to have been imprisoned for that offense, and persons whose behavior was adequately described by the definition were confined for some other offense."[67]

Since the study of criminal behavior involves an awareness of the distinctive characteristics of each type of crime, a category that includes divergent types of offenses would make it impossible to develop general explanatory principles for a specific type of criminal behavior. Useful generalizations obviously cannot be drawn from data where resemblances are only superficial. The intellectual danger

66 Snyder, *Introduction to Criminal Justice*, p. 437.
67 Cressey, *Other People's Money*, p. 19.

of such a procedure, as Robert K. Merton observes, is that it "naturally leads us to assume that it is what these behaviors have in common that is most relevant, and this assumption leads us to look for an all-encompassing set of propositions which will account for the entire range of behaviors"; Merton further notes that it is like trying to find a theory of disease, rather than distinct theories of disease—of tuberculosis and arthritis, of typhoid and syphilis—theories that are diverse rather than single.[68]

To avoid this pitfall, the scientist will attempt to formulate a definition that will guarantee the fundamental similarity of his data without destroying the framework within which he operates. His definition must precisely cover the intentions, motivations, and operations of the individual who performs a certain type of criminal act, without at the same time destroying the fundamental conception inherent in the law. In Cressey's work, to avoid including offenders such as automobile thieves in his analysis of embezzlement, he established two basic conditions: First, he stipulated that the person must have accepted a position of trust in good faith and, second, he must have violated that position by the commission of a crime.

Commenting on the merits of this approach, Cressey notes that it had "the effect of providing a rigorous definition of the behavior under investigation so that a generalization about all instances of the behavior could be attempted, but it did not do violence to the legal definition of 'embezzlement' or of other crimes."[69] The soundness of this position would seem apparent; its general application for sophisticated study in criminology of the panorama of offenses proscribed by law would appear to resolve satisfactorily debates concerning definitions of "crime" and relevant areas for criminological investigation.

Summary

We have seen in this preliminary chapter that crime is a far more dubious and difficult concept than the average person ordinarily realizes. While societies have always indicated a concern about transgressions against the constituted social order, wide variations exist as to the precise meaning of criminal behavior. The public also—especially the present-day public—displays a considerable interest in crime, apparently as a consequence of a fascination for forbidden behavior and because of the need to repress more serious forms of illegal activity in the name of the integrity of the person and property.

Crime, as we have noted, cannot readily be equated with other kinds of antisocial behavior, whether conceptualized as moral way-

68 Merton, in Witmer and Kotinsky, *New Perspectives for Research on Juvenile Delinquency*, p. 27.
69 Cressey, *Other People's Money*, p. 20.

wardness, social parasitism, social deviancy, or social dysfunction. The all-inclusive scope of such categories disregards the precise nature and function of crime itself, which, inescapably, is deeply involved in the legal determinants of acceptable and nonacceptable behavior. The criminal law, in a variety of subtle but unmistakable ways, enters into the functioning personalities of members of society and may be visualized both as a social force and as an educational instrument for the imposition of standards supported by those in a position to make an impress on the laws. As Hermann Mannheim has noted, "In the history of criminal justice it has happened again and again that legislation pretending to be the inescapable result of the trend of public opinion did actually itself create that state of public opinion which had not, or at least not as strongly, existed before."[70]

The study of criminology must concern itself with those forms of proscribed behavior derived from legal stipulations. In the interests of scientific study, it has been recognized that the purport of the law in its definition of criminal behavior may become the basis for sociological definitions of crime; this insures the similarity among forms of behavior under investigation.

Since legal concerns set the state for important criminological considerations and influence the character of the control that a society exercises over its members, we will now turn to a more detailed consideration of legal concerns. Specifically, we will investigate the meaning of social control, its changing nature, and those specialized aspects of the law that underlie the nature of criminal behavior.

For Further Reading

Following is a listing of the major bibliographic sources for material in the fields of criminology and criminal justice.

ABSTRACTS ON CRIMINOLOGY AND PENOLOGY. The Hague: Criminological Foundation.

> Volumes 1 through 8 (1961–1968) were published under the title *Excerpta Criminologica*, with the new title beginning with Volume 9 in 1969. The *Abstracts* are issued bi-monthly, in January, March, May, July, September, and November, and are particularly useful in locating foreign studies. Citations of material are accompanied by 100 to 500-word abstracts of their content.

NATIONAL CLEARINGHOUSE FOR MENTAL HEALTH INFORMATION. *Crime and Delinquency Abstracts*. Washington, D.C.: Department of Health, Education, and Welfare.

> These *Abstracts* are available free of charge to individuals working actively in the field of crime and delinquency control. They contain summaries of current published scientific and professional literature as well as information regarding ongoing research projects. Volumes

70 Mannheim, "Criminal Law and Penology," p. 268.

1 through 3 appeared under the title *International Bibliography on Crime and Delinquency*.

SELLIN, THORSTEN AND LEONARD D. SAVITZ. *A Bibliographical Manual for the Student of Criminology*. New York: National Research and Information Center on Crime and Delinquency, 1963.

This 105-page manual is undoubtedly the most useful first source of literature relevant to criminological issues. It is not a bibliography but rather, in the words of its compilers, "a tool designed to be a time-saving device for students and researchers who are working on criminological problems and need assistance in locating published source data in the form of articles, books, or reports issued in the United States." The entire manual also appears in the *International Bibliography on Crime and Delinquency*, Volume 1, Number 3.

TOMPKINS, DOROTHY CAMPBELL. *The Offender: A Bibliography*. Berkeley: Institute of Governmental Studies, University of California, 1963.

Subdivided by offense types and then divided into sections on the victim and social conditions relating to crime, this bibliography provides easy access to major studies focused on behavior systems. Prior volumes, four of them compiled by Mrs. Tompkins, are: Tompkins, Dorothy Campbell. *Administration of Criminal Justice, 1949–1956*. Sacramento: California Board of Corrections, 1956; Tompkins, Dorothy Campbell. *Sources for the Study of the Administration of Criminal Justice*. Sacramento: California Board of Corrections, 1949; Culver, Dorothy Campbell, *Bibliography of Crime and Criminal Justice, 1932–37*. New York: H. W. Wilson, 1939; Culver, Dorothy Campbell. *Bibliography of Crime and Criminal Justice, 1927–1931*. New York: H. W. Wilson, 1934; Kuhlman, Augustus Frederick. *A Guide to Material on Crime and Criminals*. New York: H. W. Wilson, 1929.

UNITED NATIONS, DEPARTMENT OF SOCIAL AFFAIRS. *International Review of Criminal Policy*. ST/SOA/Ser. M.

Many of the volumes of this periodical contain bibliographies of writings published throughout the world in regard to criminology. Publication began in January 1952.

There are many textbooks in criminology that supply varying approaches to the study of criminal behavior and reflect diverse theoretical emphases. The list includes the following recent titles: Barnes, Harry Elmer, and Negley K. Teeters. *New Horizons in Criminology*. 3rd ed. Englewood Cliffs, N.J.: Prentice-Hall, 1959; Caldwell, Robert G. *Criminology*. 2nd ed. New York: Ronald Press, 1965; Cavan, Ruth Shonle. *Criminology*. 3rd ed. New York: Crowell, 1962; Gibbons, Don C. *Society, Crime, and Criminal Careers*. Englewood Cliffs, N.J.: Prentice-Hall, 1962; Johnson, Elmer Hubert. *Crime, Correction, and Society*. Rev. ed. Homewood, Ill.: Dorsey Press, 1968; Korn, Richard R. and Lloyd W. McCorkle. *Criminology and Penology*. New York: Holt, 1959; Reckless, Walter C. *The Crime Problem*. 4th ed. New York: Appleton-Century-Crofts, 1967; Sutherland, Edwin H., and Donald R. Cressey, *Principles of Criminology*. 7th ed. Philadelphia: Lippincott, 1966; Taft, Donald R., and Ralph W. England, Jr. *Criminology*. 4th ed.

New York: Macmillan, 1964; and Tappan, Paul W. *Crime, Justice, and Correction.* New York: McGraw-Hill, 1960.

Collections of readings in criminology include: Cressey, Donald R., and David A. Ward. *Delinquency, Crime, and Social Process.* New York: Harper & Row, 1968; Clinard, Marshall B., and Richard Quinney. *Criminal Behavior Systems: A Typology.* New York: Holt, Rinehart, and Winston, 1967; Dressler, David. *Readings in Criminology and Penology.* New York: Columbia University Press, 1964; Knudten, Richard D. *Criminological Controversies.* New York: Appleton-Century-Crofts, 1968; and Wolfgang, Marvin E., Leonard Savitz, and Norman Johnston. *The Sociology of Crime and Delinquency,* 2nd ed. New York: Wiley, 1970.

Material of interest to students of criminology may also be found under appropriate headings in the following index services: *Index to Legal Periodicals, Psychological Abstracts, Public Affairs Information Service, Reader's Guide to Periodical Literature, Social Sciences and Humanities Index* (prior to 1965, entitled *International Index*), and *Sociological Abstracts.*

Part II
Law and Science of Criminology

2

The Law, Social Control, and Criminal Behavior

Legal definitions provide an anchor for the investigation by social scientists of criminal behavior. Such investigations should embrace considerations of the forces giving rise to legislative enactments and the segments of the society that support the enactments. They should also be concerned with the study of persons who violate laws and are apprehended for their violations and persons who may violate laws but escape official retaliation as well as persons who do not engage in illegal acts. Law-abiding behavior is apt to be produced by fear of punishment, but it may also be mediated by aspects of social existence beyond the legal system that have been incorporated as part of what is referred to as the "conscience." Failure to violate the law may also spring from the lack of opportunity, or merely an unwillingness, to expend energy. As John Steinbeck has remarked regarding desegregation statutes, "There's an awful lot of inactive kindness which is nothing but laziness, not wanting any trouble, confusion, or effort."[1]

Try to ponder, for instance, your personal reactions to a dilemma such as the following: You are faced with a pressing need for $25,000 because a beloved member of your family must have, but is hopelessly unable to acquire, that amount to pay for immediate medical treatment to reverse a condition that, left untreated, will result in a quick and painful death. Suddenly, you are offered the opportunity to press a button, which, once pressed, will result in the instantaneous death of an anonymous peasant in a remote Near Eastern rice field, a man who is already suffering from a disease certain to take his life within the next year. For this act, you will be paid $25,000 (or perhaps $50,000? (and will be given an absolute guarantee that your act will not become known and that you will suffer no official consequences from it.[2]

1 Steinbeck, *Winter of Our Discontent*, p. 50.
2 Cohen, *Reason and Law*, p. 68.

The question is, how many of us would accept the offer and press the button? Most of us are apt to avoid a response to a hypothetical situation by insisting that it is altogether too fanciful and unlikely to be given serious attention. But if you were to accept the facts as true, the question then involves, among other things, a determination of the balance among motivation, legal and social rules, and the capacity to act in the face of extrapersonal sanctions against so universally condemned an act as cold-blooded murder. It is perhaps indicative of the lack of consensus in American society on so fundamental a matter, that most student groups faced with this question divide about evenly in predicting whether or not they would press the button.

Law and Social Science

Law may thus be seen as one of a considerable number of elements bearing upon human behavior. It is often observed that the study of law may be undertaken with the same tools and techniques used in the attempt to comprehend any other social science. It has been noted by Sidney Simpson and Ruth Field, for instance, that "anthropologically considered, law is merely one aspect of our culture —the aspect which employs the force of organized society to regulate individual and group conduct and to prevent, redress or punish deviations from the prescribed social norms."[3] Nicholas Timasheff adds the observation that the "legal order is a part of the social order, with the social force called law always tending to mold individual behavior in accordance with preestablished patterns imposed by individuals who play the role of 'supporters of patterns.' "[4] A similar view, stressing the necessity for a social science approach to legal scholarship, is expressed by Huntington Cairns:

> Law itself is a social science, and if it is to achieve its full power, if it is to meet with success the incalculable risks and apalling surprises inevitably encountered in any attempt to order human society, it must join with the other social sciences in a united effort to solve the problems common to all.[5]

Finally, in a decision of the United States Supreme Court, Justice Felix Frankfurter made note of the fact that the pigeonholing of knowledge tends to obscure the reality of phenomena that have ingredients that cannot readily be encapsulated within a single academic discipline:

> The problems that are the respective preoccupations of anthropology, economics, law, psychology, sociology, and related areas of scholarship are merely departmentalized dealing, by way of manageable division of analysis, with interpenetrating aspects of holistic perplexities.[6]

3 Simpson and Field, "Law and the Social Sciences," p. 858.
4 Timasheff, *Introduction to the Sociology of Law*, p. 10.
5 Cairns, *Law and Social Sciences*, p. 266.
6 *Sweezy v. New Hampshire*, pp. 261–262.

Despite such observations, there has been a considerable intellectual estrangement between law and the social sciences, reflected in part by the tendency of criminologists to look into extralegal realms for the definition of their subject matter. "The concept of a routine working relationship between law and sociology is still limited to the self-chosen initiates," Alfred Blumrosen recently noted, "and has not become part of the routine kit of working tools of either profession."[7] In part, this estrangement also reflects distinctions between the professional personalities and working methods of lawyers and social scientists. The lawyer, by the nature of his craft, is concerned with the practical necessity of using the law to safeguard the interests of his client. His outlook, consequently, tends to be almost wholly utilitarian and pragmatic, whereas the social scientist's interests are theoretical, dealing with assumptions on the nature of human behavior. Furthermore, the courts tend to accentuate the highly partisan nature of the lawyer's interests,[8] despite the fundamental requirement of law to determine the accuracy of evidence within a given case. As Percy Forman, the attorney who defended James Earl Ray against the charge of assassinating Martin Luther King, Jr., in 1969, put it, "The trial of a criminal case is a tug-of-war between the prosecution and the defense. It's more like an athletic contest, with each side trying to 'win' instead of trying to arrive at the facts of a case to determine justice under the law based on such facts."[9] This partisanship is in direct contrast to the point of view of the social scientist, who, by virtue of his training and commitment, is primarily dedicated to determining the factual evidence within a given situation in the spirit of objective and dispassionate inquiry. Even though total objectivity is often not realized by social scientists, improvements of methodologies in research procedures tend to free social scientists from the more glaring types of prejudice that are sometimes found in the practice of law.

In addition, members of the legal profession are not always familiar with the techniques developed by the contemporary social scientist. The legal specialist frequently confuses the areas of social science, social work, and social reform. Thus, for instance, Chief Justice William Howard Taft of the United States Supreme Court as long ago as 1913 recommended that the education of a judge ought "to include a study of economics and a study of sociology" so that he could meet the "sociological reformer on a common ground."[10] Differences between legal functionaries and social scientists may also be found in the early philosophical viewpoints of the two groups. Auguste Comte, the frequently acknowledged father of sociology, believed law to be nothing more than an emanation of the metaphysical spirit,

7 Blumrosen, "Legal Process and Labor Law," pp. 185–186.
8 Blaustein and Porter, *The American Lawyer*, Chap. 8.
9 *New York Times*, Nov. 12, 1968.
10 Taft, *Popular Government*, pp. 237–238.

something that would disappear as society became more rational.[11] Comte's view is echoed by Lester F. Ward, the first president of the American Sociological Society (1906–1907), who grudgingly conceded that legislatures might have to be maintained, although he believed that "more and more they will become a merely formal way of putting the final sanction of society on decisions that have been worked out in the sociological laboratory."[12] Ward, trained in law, by profession a government geologist and paleobotanist, and by avocation a sociologist, indicated sociological attitudes toward the legal profession in his appraisal of the legal career he had not pursued because his "conscience would not allow it:"[13]

> There is scarcely a doubt that if nine out of every ten members of the legal profession were eliminated from it and turned into some useful occupation, the ends of justice would thereby be immensely the gainer and thousands of laborers would be added to the industrial pursuits. But this is the class whom the masses intrust with the framing of their laws, and as long as they continue to do so, they must pay the penalty for their stupidity.[14]

Yet, despite historical antipathy and some basic differences in outlook, there recently have been encouraging signs of growing rapport between law and the social sciences, particularly as the latter have come to deal more directly with significant social and legal problems. One of the most vigorous justifications of such a rapprochement has been made by William J. Brennan, Jr., Associate Justice of the United States Supreme Court, who placed specific emphasis on the increasing tendency of the courts to rely upon the findings of economics, sociology, and social psychology:

> The mind of the layman unfamiliar with the judicial process supposes it to exist in the air, as a self-justifying and wholly independent process. The opposite is, of course, true—that judicial decision must be nourished by all the insights that scholarship can furnish, and legal scholarship must in turn be nourished by all the disciplines that comprehend the totality of human experience.[15]

It is anticipated that social science findings will eventually lead to more effective administration of criminal justice, producing programs based not only on the vast experience of the judicial system, but also on solid foundations of experimental research. The need in these areas has been outlined by Sheldon Glueck, who has figured prominently in the move to bridge the gap between law and social science:

> First there is need of a deep-probing reexamination of the criminal law—its underlying philosophy, its aims, its basic definitions of types

11 Comte, *Cours de Philosophie Positive,* Vol. VI, p. 651.
12 Ward, *Applied Sociology,* pp. 338–339.
13 Ward, *Pure Sociology,* p. 488.
14 Ward, *Psychic Factors in Civilization,* p. 167.
15 *New York Times,* Nov. 26, 1958.

of wrongdoing, and the instrumentalities for its administration. Such a modern approach to criminal law should perform two absolutely fundamental tasks long overdue: (a) greatly simplify the legal concepts involved in the definition of conduct prohibited by law as socially harmful; (b) transform the simplistic and largely unsound theory and inefficient mechanisms of guilt-punishment into a socio-legal apparatus for reducing crime through understanding its causes and directing social action towards these causes.[16]

This is not to imply that there now exists or that there will soon be a state of felicitous cooperation and mutual understanding between law and the social sciences or between criminology and criminal law. David Riesman, a perceptive theorist trained in both law and the social sciences, has pointed out that lawyers are still "very apt to be scornful of the findings of social science."[17] Riesman attributes much of this attitude to the fact that the social sciences, because of their relative newness and their dynamic character, tend to introduce novel insights and uncertainty into the comparatively rigid legal system, thereby representing a kind of threat to the established system of law and its practitioners. However, conceptions that tend to undermine a structure from which individuals derive their support and professional sustenance are not easily thrust aside. In this respect, lawyers may have to readjust their values and predilections to reconcile with the disclosures of scientific investigation.

The disagreements, though, are not entirely the result of conflict of interest. Well-established systems of thought provide their own intellectual priorities. Lawyers often express the view that social scientists display what appears to be a highhanded disregard for the logical niceties of the law and tend to ignore what lawyers consider the rational product of centuries of trial and error.[18] The legal system, they claim, has been flexible enough to accommodate itself to the needs of society but has nevertheless remained solidly rooted to the bedrock of social reality; it has been slow to change, but equally slow to respond whimsically to each minor ideological breeze. The social sciences, A. Delafield Smith charges, have shown a "grievous absence of understanding of the law's objectives, a resulting failure to apply legal methods, and little awareness of the real contributions of legal philosophy to social objectives."[19] On the other hand, Louis D. Brandeis, one of the most eminent of United States Supreme Court justices, quoted with approval the comment that "a lawyer who has not studied economics and sociology is very apt to become a public enemy."[20]

There can be little doubt that in the intricate processes of social

16 Glueck, *Crime and Corrections*, p. viii.
17 Riesman, "Law and Sociology," p. 651.
18 Fahr, "Why Lawyers are Dissatisfied with the Social Sciences."
19 Smith, *The Right to Life*, p. 5.
20 Brandeis, "The Living Law," p. 325.

control—how society maintains its equilibrium and social order—the system of laws not only provides one of the most effective deterrents to human violence, civil discord, and social disorganization, but it is also closely interwoven with the entire fabric of the society's moral conceptions. It remains for the criminologist, therefore, to recognize the significance of the law as an agency of social control, while acknowledging at the same time the need for determining the limitations of its effectiveness. Talcott Parsons, considered by many the foremost theoretician in the field of sociology, has said, "The sociologist must regard the legal profession as one of the very important mechanisms by which a relative balance of stability is maintained in a dynamic and rather precariously balanced society."[21] In criminology, where the laws deal with what are often regarded as the most severe deviations from socially desirable behavior, the function and importance of criminal law in maintaining balance and stability in society cannot be overemphasized.

Components of Social Control

Social control consists of the various mechanisms that a society has developed to maintain itself as a coherent and functioning unity. It includes customary and institutional patterns of behavior, traditional values, and public morality, as well as an accumulation of habitual patterns and acquired inhibitions. Its nature is extremely complex in even the simplest societies. The law, as a formally devised procedure for the regulation of human behavior, is a relatively late development in the history of the human race.

The components of social control may be classified as *institutional* and *legal*. Individuals conform to the mandates of society because of a vast superstructure of folkways, mores, and institutional and legal patterns that the society has reared.

INSTITUTIONAL COMPONENTS OF SOCIAL CONTROL

The *folkways* and *mores* represent those phases of social control that have arisen out of the peculiarities of historical circumstance and that reflect the innumerable forms of natural adaptation that the society has made to its physical and social environment. The pressure that such traditional forms exert upon the members of the society represents, in part, learned reactions of individuals who recognize those usages as proper and fitting. Social forces like these function in the form of conglomerates, that is, complex institutional structures comprising a multitude of different customary usages that embrace virtually every phase of man's social life—his family, as well as his economic, political, religious, esthetic, and ideological interests.

While the components of these institutional structures may be

21 Parsons, "A Sociologist Looks at the Legal Profession," p. 385.

differentiated as folkways and mores—depending upon the degree of moral pressure that particular norms impose and the degree to which individuals consider them optional or mandatory—the institutional structures themselves differ sharply from the legal statutes that men have devised.

THE LAW AS DISTINCT FROM OTHER NORMS

The function and place of legal rules in a society was broadly described in the following quote by the anthropologist Bronislaw Malinowski, "There must be in all societies a class of rules too practical to be backed by religious sanctions, too burdensome to be left to the mere goodwill, too personally vital to individuals to be enforced by an abstract agency"; he continued that, this constitutes "the domain of legal rules."[22] The law as distinct from customary controls over human behavior tends to be more *specific* about behavior defined as an offense and about the nature of the sanctions or punishments to be meted out. Second, the law is conceived as *universal* in its scope, within the confines of a given society. While the folkways and mores tend to achieve conformity in behavior by virtue of the pressures of public opinion, group distaste or repugnance, ridicule, and anger, they nonetheless usually have an optional character, particularly in modern complex societies, where wide variations in customary behavior exist. The law, however, is meant to be applicable to all segments of the society and to impose the same degree of sanction, regardless of group, class, ethnic, and sectional differences.

The law is also a *formal enactment*. Unlike customary usages, which tend to arise spontaneously out of the necessities of group living, the law is deliberately contrived through some type of formal mechanism in which specially delegated personages and legislative bodies play significant roles. For this reason, the law is frequently a more rational procedure and, in any event, a more explicit and concise formulation than other social norms that not only lack definitional precision but also differ in the character and degree of sanctions that may be used by the community against the deviant individual.

There are, of course, occasions when adherence to a given custom—or the particular reaction of an individual to such a custom—may appear more significant than obedience to the law. Such occasions, however, are relatively rare compared to the overwhelming sense in which the law maintains its priority—despite the classic view of William Graham Sumner that mores were more persuasive than the law in channeling and coercing human behavior,[23] a view echoed by Edward A. Ross, a pioneering sociologist. Ross considered the law, with its "blade playing up and down in its groove with iron precision,"[24] to be "the most specialized and highly finished engine of

22 Malinowski, *Crime and Custom in Savage Society,* pp. 67–68.
23 Sumner, *Folkways,* Chap. 2.
24 Ross, *Social Control,* p. 94.

control employed by society."[25] But, nonetheless, the law was deemed by Ross as "hardly so good a regulative instrument as the flexible lash of public censure."[26] What such men like Sumner and Ross overlooked was that mores ordinarily cover a vast area of human behavior in which the laws do not operate. As Will Durant noted, writing of early Chinese civilization, "the reach of law was narrowed to major or national issues, while the force of custom continued in small matters; and since human affairs are mostly minor matters, custom remained king."[27]

There are instances in which mores prevail over law. At times, youngsters in slum areas will take serious risks to commit theft rather than face the opprobrium of their fellows by "chickening out." Ideological systems may also prove to be more inviolate than legal systems. Conscientious objectors, for example, may defy the government rather than oppose principles that dictate against killing other human beings, regardless of the circumstances. The following report also illustrates how "the flexible lash of public censure" may on occasion be dreaded more than the possible retaliation of the law:

> In Scotland, even more feared than the pillory was the punishment of having to appear in church every Sunday for a given number of weeks, usually twenty-six or fifty-two, to be harangued for half an hour in front of the congregation by the minister—for which, in some churches, offenders were fastened to the wall in iron collars, or jougs. This was the penalty for adulterers and fornicators of both sexes, and was greatly feared. So much so, that it caused a sharp rise in the infanticide rate, for women who had illegitimately become pregnant preferred to risk the capital penalty for infanticide rather than admit the facts and suffer such extreme public humiliation.[28]

Such examples, however, simply show that in moments of crisis individuals will make choices dependent upon the weights of a variety of social, psychological, and cultural factors. The law itself is subtly related to mores in inextricable ways and frequently becomes a basic part of the mores. This interactive process has been nicely described by Benjamin Cardozo in the following manner:

> The constant assumption runs throughout the law that the natural and spontaneous evolutions of habit fix the limits of right and wrong. A slight extension of custom identifies it with customary morality, the prevailing standards of right conduct, the mores of the time. . . . Life casts the moulds of conduct, which will some day become fixed as law. Law preserves the moulds, which have taken form and shape from life.[29]

When we speak of the law as an instrument of social control, we must recognize that the sources of power within a given political state

25 *Ibid.*, p. 106.
26 *Ibid.*, p. 94.
27 Durant, *Our Oriental Heritage*, p. 646.
28 Graham, *Social Life of Scotland in the 18th Century*, pp. 321–324, 489–490; Taylor, *Sex in History*, p. 166.
29 Cardozo, *Nature of the Judicial Process*, pp. 62–64.

may be endlessly diverse. In the ultimate balance of power, a given group or class, because of its strategic position in the mechanism of the state and because of the complexion of values at the time, may be primarily responsible for determining the direction of social events and, more specifically, the form and content that the laws of the period assume.[30] Thus, for example, the major source of control of society at a given period in its history may be the hierarchy of the church, the landed aristocracy, the military, a managerial group, or an industrial elite. This is not to suggest, of course, that such power must be absolute.

Criminology and Social Control
Criminology, in terms of the preceding discussion, is the study of a major segment of the network of social control, which deals with written criminal law. It is unique because it constitutes the end product of a formal process of decision-making that emerges from the deliberation of legislative bodies and courts. Criminology concerns itself with deviations from this system and, more particularly, with the explanation of such deviations. Whereas the criminal lawyer is concerned with the problem of whether or not a given individual has committed a certain crime, the criminologist is concerned with the "why" of his behavior and its relationship to a host of problems concerning class, social status, and the structure of the groups with which the offending individual is identified.

The criminologist also devotes himself to an examination of those types of information that have direct relevance to the violation of criminal statutes—information concerning the formation of criminal codes, their relationship to other values in the society, and their fusion with the inherited and learned patterns of the individual personality. Criminology, like other branches of social science, attempts to extract meaningful patterns from this mass of data and relate those patterns to coherent and integrated theories. On the basis of such theories, efforts are made toward prediction, which not only enables us to indicate the conditions under which crime is more apt to arise but also helps to shed light on a host of factors that contribute either directly or indirectly to crime. Criminology, in this sense, represents the scientific study of the system of criminal law and, more particularly, of individual behavior in relation to that system.

The Definition of Crime as a Legal Concept
We are now in a better position to comprehend the meaning of crime and to arrive at a more precise definition of its exact nature. It is obvious by now that crimes can only arise in violation of criminal

30 Quinney, "Crime in Political Perspective."

statutes and not as a result of infractions of other codes. Clarence Darrow has observed, for instance, that though an act is forbidden by the
law of the land, "it does not necessarily follow that this act is either
good or bad: the punishment follows for the violation of the law and
not necessarily for any moral transgression."[31] Many legal questions
are in fact morally indifferent, such as the issue of whether drivers
should proceed on the right or the left side of the road. In other
instances, actions that most people would regard as immoral are
ignored by the criminal law. For example, a person who could easily
prevent another from drowning and fails to do so, does not violate any
law, even though his failure to act might stem from a desire that the
other person die.[32] The level of crime is therefore no certain measure
of the moral temperature of a nation. A society may have very little
crime, but may be in the throes of complete moral disintegration; on
the other hand, it may have what is defined as a high level of morality
and yet also have a high crime rate, depending upon the character of
the outlawed acts and their relation to the particular system of
morality.

Criminal conduct should also be clearly distinguished from acts in
violation of ethical codes. Many professional bodies and groups in fields
such as business, labor, management, medicine, and engineering have
attempted to bring about compliance with regulatory codes of ethics
or self-governing principles. One of the tenets of the physician's code
of ethics, for example, is the strict rule against advertising professional
services. Hard-pressed physicians will on occasion, however, evade
this regulation by a number of less obvious publicity devices, such as
bringing their names before the public by political activity, conspicuous membership in civic or social organizations, or even having
themselves paged at mass spectator events. Whereas these and similar
devices may be patterned attempts at evasion of the fundamental regulation against advertising, none can be regarded as a crime, regardless
of the distaste with which it may be viewed by the physician's professional associates.

"A crime," in the classic statement of William Blackstone, the
renowned historian and compiler of English common law, "is an act
committed, or omitted, in violation of a public law either forbidding
or commanding it."[33] Contemporary legal analysts, such as Barnes,
have amplified this definition by stressing that the criminal act must
be construed as being against the public interest in contrast to "a mere
private wrong or civil injury to an individual."[34] Ronald A. Anderson,
another criminal law scholar, indicates further that the person who
commits a crime must likewise be distinguished by the fact that he

31 Darrow, *Crime: Its Causes and Treatment*, p. 1.
32 Seavey, "Principles of Torts," p. 77. See also Seavey's "Failure to Rescue: A Com-
    parative Study."
33 Blackstone, *Commentaries*, Vol. IV, p. 5.
34 Barnes, *A Treatise on the Law of Crimes*, p. 92.

had the "capacity" to perform such an act.[35] Paul A. Tappan, whose interests bridged the legal and sociological aspects of criminology, suggests that "crime is an intentional act in violation of the criminal law (statutory and case law), committed without defense or excuse, and penalized by the state as a felony or a misdemeanor."[36] Finally, Helen Silving, a professor of law at the University of Puerto Rico, offers the formulation that "a crime is a conduct occurring under such circumstances and causing such events, combined with such psychological factors of intent or recklessness, as required by the statutory definition of a given crime, provided that the defendant is not exempt from punishment by reason of mental incapacity."[37]

Taking account of these various definitions, we may define a criminal act as an infringement of a criminal statute, either by violation of a specific code of law or by the failure to act in a manner that the law has prescribed, conceived as an act against the public interest, to which specified sanctions as defined by law may be applied. Implicit in this definition is the understanding that the individual is legally responsible for his action. Although definitions in this controversial area are hazardous, such a formulation appears useful, provided that we recognize that in the comparative and critical analysis of various types of crime, we must take into account the specific objectives for which a given criminal statute was framed. This latter qualification enables us to consider, for analytical purposes, the distinction between the result of the judicial process and the nature of the offense that the individual has committed and that may, or may not, have led to his apprehension.

TORTS AND CRIMES

The foregoing definition indicates clearly that not all offenses against the legal order can be regarded as crimes. Offenses in which certain private and individual interests are concerned—such as in business and contractual arrangements—fall under the aegis of the civil codes and are not regarded as crimes. Such offenses are characterized as *torts* and involve a different form of legal process.

Tort law functions to lend assistance to an individual who believes that he has been injured in some way and who requires the assistance of the State to obtain redress. The legal action is considered a private matter in which one individual takes action against another; it begins with a "complaint" filed with the court and terminates with an "order" by the court for the restitution to be made. The primary purposes of criminal law, as Warren Seavey indicates, concern considerations such as revenge, retribution, appeasement, deterrence, and reform. In tort law, such items may also apply, but its primary function is to deter-

35 Anderson, *Wharton's Criminal Law and Procedure*, p. 11.
36 Tappan, "Who Is the Criminal?" p. 100.
37 Silving, *Constituent Elements of Crime*, p. 81.

mine when loss shall be shifted from one individual to another and when it shall be allowed to remain where it has fallen.[38] Criminal litigation, in contrast, is formally initiated not with a complaint, but with an indictment or information in which the person is charged with the crime for which he will be tried. In the event of successful prosecution the case is terminated with a conviction. The criminal case is regarded as *an offense by the individual against the people of a given political community*.

Why certain transgressions have come to be defined as crimes while others have retained their private character is difficult to say, especially since early jurisprudence was largely construed as civil in nature, rather than criminal. It is quite possible that recognition of the public principle was closely allied to the pervasive sense of sin and wrongdoing in moral and religious convictions of certain societies. Thus, acts considered morally reprehensible, such as murder and rape, have traditionally been invested with feelings of emotional revulsion, stemming from deeply embedded religious beliefs.

Despite the fact that civil offenses are differentiated from criminal acts, there is considerable difficulty on occasion in separating the two. It is possible, in fact, for an individual to be tried as either a civil or criminal offender in cases such as those involving the sale of defective or deleterious merchandise or those in which failure to perform an expected contractual obligation resulted in physical or psychological harm to another.

If we are to understand criminal acts objectively and scientifically, the basic distinction between private injury and public wrong should be clearly fixed in mind. Our definition must be broad enough, however, to encompass a given act as criminal if the major consideration in the act was or reasonably could have been regarded as criminal, despite the legal machinery employed in dealing with the case.

FELONIES AND MISDEMEANORS

In addition to the distinction between civil and criminal offenses, there is within the category of criminal offenses a further subdivision of acts into felonies and misdemeanors, though the basis for classification into one or the other group is often tenuous. Misdemeanors, which are relatively minor offenses that include such things as disorderly conduct, vagrancy, and petty theft, are usually distinguished by the fact that they may be punished by confinement in a local jail for a period not in excess of a year and by imposition of a limited fine, or both. Felonies, the more serious charges, are frequently identified as those offenses for which the individual may be incarcerated in either a state or federal penitentiary or prison for a period in excess of a year and subject to a considerable fine, or both.

This distinction does not always apply, however, and it frequently

---

38 Seavey, Keeton, and Keeton, *Cases and Materials on the Law of Torts*, p. 1.

produces misunderstanding. An act that may be regarded as a misdemeanor in one state may be considered a felony in another, and vice versa. There is a tendency to label the guilty person either as a "misdemeanant" or "felon" on the basis of the charge of which he was convicted, suggesting differences in behavior that might not exist. Actually, a study by Stuart Queen concluded that distinguishing characteristics between felonies and misdemeanors were difficult to establish with any clarity and that many aspects of the acts categorized in one way or the other were overlapping.[39] Also, state legislatures sometimes change the statutory classification of offenses from one category to another for a variety of expedient reasons—even due to overcrowding in state penal facilities—so that the distinction between misdemeanors and felonies may represent little more than the product of legislative caprice.

CRIMINAL INTENT

In most criminal offenses, regardless of how they are classified, the law is concerned not only with the illegal act, but also with the intention of the offender. If an individual inadvertently dislodges a flower pot from the window sill of his dwelling and thereby causes the death of a pedestrian passing below, he is absolved of criminal responsibility, unless criminal carelessness on his part can be demonstrated, though the victim is as dead as if he were deliberately killed with a lethal weapon. The reasons for this fundamental tenet of criminal law are of inestimable significance. They are deeply rooted in the tradition of the law and are based upon fundamental principles relating to human discretion and free will.

Traditionally, crime has encompassed two distinct entities: the *act* that is outlawed and the *intent* of the actor. As complicated as the first item may be when applied as a yardstick of behavior, the second is incalculably more complicated. The problem of "criminal intent" has been a major obstacle in the scientific attempt to coordinate law and the social sciences. Intent is closely related to the ancient legal doctrine of *mens rea*, or "guilty mind," a prerequisite for criminal conduct. "In the entire field of criminal law there is no more important doctrine than that of *mens rea*, embedded as are its roots in the principle that no man shall be punished for committing a crime unless a guilty mind can be imputed to him," J. L. J. Edwards notes in a thoroughgoing analysis of the doctrine.[40] The implications involved in the determination of a "guilty mind," in light of modern psychological knowledge and changing conceptions of moral responsibility have created serious doubts as to how and whether the principles should be employed. As Graham Hughes notes, attempts are being made to refurbish the concept of *mens rea*:

39 Queen, *Passing of the County Jail,* pp. 87–94.
40 Edwards *Mens Rea in Statutory Offenses,* p. xiii.

Mens rea, which creaked through the criminal courts for centuries, has recently been dug up, scrubbed, repainted, and paraded for the admiration of criminal lawyers. The old mumblings about "guilty mind" have been replaced by the ice-cutting concepts of intention and recklessness.[41]

Whether denoted *mens rea,* willfulness, maliciousness, or wantonness, the concept of guilty mind has preoccupied legal scholars almost as endlessly and exhaustively as the subtleties of seemingly inconsequential theological argumentation has fascinated medieval pedants. In its simplest form, "intent" signifies that the person who committed the act must have desired at each stage of his performance to bring about the act that is outlawed. Or, put negatively, as an Australian court has done, "the absence of *mens rea* really consists in an honest and reasonable belief entertained by the accused of the existence of facts which, if true, would make the act charged against him innocent."[42] Thus, for instance, a person to whose clothing some piece of merchandise had inadvertently become attached as he left a store could not be held responsible for shoplifting since he did not intend to do so.

Laws differ in the quality of intent that they require before the person charged can be convicted. Burglary, for example, generally requires that a person enter a structure with the intent to commit either larceny or another felony. If a police officer were to enter a private dwelling in order to make a legal arrest and then were to steal some money while on the premises, he could not be charged with burglary, because his original intent did not encompass the entire definition of burglary. On the other hand, the law normally takes the position that a person's intent, all other things being equal, need not be proven since the assumption usually prevails that he "intended to do what he did."[43] Or, in Justice Oliver Wendell Holmes' dictum on intent, "Even a dog distinguishes between being stumbled over and being kicked."[44]

Intent has sometimes been broken down into a number of separate psychological behavioral conditions, such as (1) general or *presumed* intent, in which the intention is assumed from the mere performance of the act; (2) *specific* intent, in which it must be proven that the act was done with the aim of committing a crime; and (3) *constructive* or *transferred* intent, in which the intent of the original act is carried over to apply to consequent acts. Thus, if "A" shoots at "B," intending to kill him, and accidentally hits "C" instead, he is held, by transfer of intent, guilty of murder or manslaughter in regard to the slaying of "C." Recklessness, another aspect of behavior involved with intent, implies that the person performing a particular act used less caution

41 Hughes, "Criminal Omissions," p. 600.
42 Quoted in Barry and Paton, *Introduction to the Criminal Law in Australia,* p. 24.
43 Williams, *Criminal Law Outline,* p. 4.
44 Holmes, *Common Law,* p. 3.

than a hypothetically "reasonable" person would have employed under similar circumstances. A father disciplining a child, for instance, might not necessarily be held responsible for harmful inadvertent consequences of his behavior, since discipline is his legal prerogative. He will be held responsible, however, if he insists that the child remain lightly clothed in the basement overnight in sub-zero weather and the child subsequently contracts a fatal illness, since a reasonable parent would presumably have considered the possible results of such a form of punishment.

One trend in the concept of intent has become particularly evident in recent years. It is a move in the direction of making specified acts criminal regardless of the intent of their perpetrator—a trend viewed with considerable alarm in many legal circles.[45] This movement was, according to John Winchell, "preordained by confusion surrounding the idea of intent and the development of the sociological and pragmatic view of law."[46] It embraces in different jurisdictions such acts as bigamy, sale or possession of narcotics, possession of an automobile with the serial number removed, exceeding the speed limit, carrying concealed weapons, and passing worthless checks.[47]

Changes in the concept of criminal intent are related to a variety of significant social and psychological problems. They suggest the manner in which basic legal principles have become transmuted in the face of significant social pressures and the claimed insights of new knowledge—ideological, scientific, and psychological. Fundamentally, the law functions as a behavioral instrument, in that it is forced to infer the characteristics of human behavior by what people do and say. It is not generally concerned with probing the psychological depths of human behavior. Consequently, the law looks to behavior as providing the most basic clue to why a given breach of law has taken place.

Thus, carrying a dangerous weapon, regardless of knowledge of the person's intent to use it, presupposes the likelihood that the weapon *may* be used, provided the provocation is strong enough; that there is knowledge that it *could* be used, if necessary; and that *may* be used, if conditions warrant it. In what is essentially a common sense approach to human behavior, the law implies that the carrying of a dangerous weapon hardly constitutes a form of personal adornment but represents an implicit threat and a token of intent. The difficulty with this view is that, once it presupposes the presence of intent by the mere commission of a prior act like carrying a weapon, it becomes involved in a variety of devious psychological problems. Thus, psychological studies indicate quite clearly that intent may vary in a chronological sequence from situation to situation. In this light, there are levels and degrees of intent: the mere thought of gain-

45 See, for instance, Hall, "Prolegomena to a Science of Criminal Law."
46 Winchell, *"Intent in Criminal Law,"* p. 35.
47 Sayre, "Public Welfare Offenses," pp. 84–88.

ing possession of a dangerous weapon; purchasing a gun; carrying a gun; and using it. Intent must be distinguished from *motive*, which has no direct relationship to criminal guilt or innocence, though it sometimes carries great weight with juries and may influence the sentence imposed on an offender. Sir Fredrick Pollock, an eminent historian of English criminal law, has noted, for instance, that "a man who steals food for his hungry children is a thief as well as one who steals money to buy liquor and get drunk, but they will hardly be punished alike under a system which leaves any discretion to the judge."[48] Motives may be conceived as the reasons for the development and maintenance of an intent. Intent and motive have been distinguished in the following manner. "The intention is a determination to act in a certain way, whereas the motive is that which incites one to form the intention."[49]

Finally, it should be noted that guilt is not related to the knowledge that the behavior is outlawed. *Ignorantia juris neminen excusat*—ignorance of the law does not excuse—is one of the most deep-lying principles of Anglo-Saxon jurisprudence and has only a few minor exceptions. The possibility of such an exception, however, is illustrated by a case in which the Supreme Court reversed a conviction for the failure of a felon to register with the police on the ground that the appellant was not aware of the regulation. "Where a person did not know of the duty to register and where there was no proof of the probability of such knowledge, he may not be convicted," Justice Douglas ruled for the court's majority, continuing that, "Were it otherwise, the evil would be as great as it is when the law is written in print too fine to read or in a language foreign to the community."[50]

CRIMINAL CAPACITY

Criminal capacity, "the ability to engage in rational conduct and to incur guilt therefrom,"[51] is the last of the essential ingredients of a criminal act and the most controversial. It is inseparably tied to the commitment by criminal law to a philosophy of free will, which insists that individuals, except under rigidly specified circumstances, are responsible for all their actions. It implies further that all individuals are equally responsible, with only minor exceptions—a presumption that led Anatole France to make his famous remark that "the law, in its majestic equality, forbids both the poor man and the rich man to sleep under bridges, to beg in the streets, and to steal bread."[52]

In terms of capacity, Oliver Wendell Holmes once noted that laws

do not merely require that every man should get as near as he can to the best conduct possible for him. They require him at his own

48 Pollock, *First Book of Jurisprudence*, p. 152.
49 Kearny, *A Treatise on the Law of Crimes* p. 80.
50 *Lambert v. California*, pp. 229–230.
51 Mueller, "Criminal Law and Its Administration," p. 84.
52 France, *The Red Lily*, p. 91.

peril to come up to a certain height. They take no account of in-
capacities, unless the weakness is so marked as to fall into the well-
known exceptions, such as infancy and madness.[53]

Few scholars of criminal law would personally subscribe to the
almost limitless doctrine of personal responsibility that underlies the
law, but many defend it as a necessary working principle.[54] Thurman
Arnold, for instance, though he believes that the doctrine of criminal
responsibility is scientifically indefensible, argues for its retention on
the ground that as a piece of "folklore," similar to the fictive beliefs
of many primitive communities, the principle serves as a basis for
integrating social values and maintaining a stable moral order.[55] This
is reminiscent of the famous belief of Blaise Pascal (1623–1662), a
French scientist and religious philosopher, that even if free will did
not exist, it would be necessary to invent it in order to maintain human
balance.[56] Other writers believe that it would be pointless and virtually impossible to hold, for instance, that a middle-class boy, because
he had more opportunities and advantages, was "more" responsible
for a theft than a lower-class boy committing the same act. Nevertheless, the erosion of the principle of moral responsibility could throw
the whole system of criminal law into chaos.

Actually, the dispute about responsibility as it inheres in the
criminal law seems to revolve not so much around the doctrine itself
as around the exceptions that are made to it. Thus, lawyers, social
scientists, and theologians of all inclinations would probably agree
that it is both arbitrary and often absurd to dichotomize human
behavior into gross categories such as sane and insane, and to hold
persons in one group totally responsible for their actions while another
group is held totally incapable of forming a criminal intent. Human
traits such as sanity are never discrete entities, but rather are degrees
along a continuous line describing the amounts of contact with
"reality" that a person is maintaining at any given moment. The
situation was aptly described by a British judge, writing more than a
hundred years ago:

> The difficulty to be grappled with arises from the circumstances that
> the question is almost always one of degree. There is no difficulty
> in the case of a raving madman or a drivelling idiot. . . . But between
> such an extreme case and that of a man of perfectly sound and vig-
> orous understanding there is every shade of intellect, every degree of
> mental capacity. There is no possibility of mistaking midnight for noon;
> but at what precise moment twilight becomes darkness is hard to de-
> termine.[57]

53 Holmes, *The Common Law*, p. 50.
54 Kaplan, "Barriers to the Establishment of a Deterministic Criminal Law."
55 Arnold, *Symbols of Government*, Chap. 1.
56 Fletcher, *Pascal and the Mystical Tradition*, pp. 126–127; Broome, *Pascal*, p. 99.
57 *Boyse v. Rossborough*, p. 45.

Recent debate centering around the relationship of chromosome makeup and criminality indicates the intricate nature of the doctrine of criminal capacity. It has been alleged that a chromosomal formation known as "XYY" predisposes a male to such things as low intelligence and aggressiveness. Normally, individuals have 23 pairs of chromosomes that determine countless inherited traits, such as eye color and sex. Female sex is determined by an XX combination, male by an XY pattern, but in some instances—estimates range from one in 300 to one in 2,000—men are born with an extra "Y" chromosome.

The propensity toward violence associated with having an XYY chromosomal makeup has been supported by work with killifish, the small cyprinodont fishes often used as bait by anglers. Killifish with an XYY makeup are said to act as "supermales," winning female favor around 88 percent of the time over their more normal competitors, and acting, as best as can be told, in a more aggressive and more competitive manner than their fellows.[58] Studies in Australia and Scotland also indicate that persons with XYY chromosomes are apt to constitute disproportionate elements in hospitals for the criminally insane.[59]

On the basis of such evidence, some defense lawyers maintain that persons with XYY chromosomes should not be held legally accountable for their behavior. Instead of prison sentences, it is argued, they should be handled more benignly, perhaps under a regimen of tranquilizers in a relatively open, hospital-like situation. The XYY plea was used successfully in Australia on October 9, 1968, when a jury found a twenty-one year old Melbourne man not guilty of a murder charge because of his chromosome abnormality. A week later, however, a French court refused to accept an allegation of such an irregularity as relevant to the conviction of a thirty-two year old man for strangling a prostitute in a Pigalle hotel. Testifying for the defense, a biologist noted that the phenomenon of a "born criminal" does not exist, but he said that persons with XYY chromosome makeups stand a 30 percent greater chance than others of committing criminal offenses. Whether such statistical odds, even if accurate, should result in reduced criminal liability merely highlights the extraordinarily complex problems of weighing accountability and the pressures toward categoric, operational standards by which judges and juries may readily and with "common sense" guidelines reach some decision on the facts before them.

Perhaps the most attractive suggestion regarding determination of criminal capacity is that offered recently by Helen Silving, who suggests that current psychiatric judgments of criminal capacity are

58 Stock, "XYY and the Criminal."
59 Price and Whatmore, "Behavior Disorders and Pattern of Crime Among XYY Males"; Jacobs, Brunton, and Melville, "Aggressive Behavior, Mental Sub-Normality and the XYY Male"; Weiner, *et al.*, "XYY Males in a Melbourne Prison"; Montagu, "Chromosomes and Crime."

concentrated too much on medical phenomena. She believes that the issue fundamentally should be one of the individual's relationship to his own society, not to an abstract diagnostic system rooted in medical ideas of illness and disease. Silving further suggests that persons should be exempt from punishment if they fall into a class that is clearly psychologically and sociologically "non-average." She expands and defends this measure in the following quote:

> This test defines as exempt persons whose integrative functioning is so impaired that they have considerably greater difficulty conforming to social demands and rules than the majority of community members. The community is the population of the district from which . . . a jury might be drawn and the narrower community to which the accused belongs, whether it be educational, professional or social. The disability is of general scope, affecting the subject's relationship to social demands and rules rather than merely his relationship to the specific conduct with which he is charged.

> This test is expected to eliminate the false assumption implicit in other mental incapacity tests as though we were concerned with a specifically psychiatric issue. Law is a social discipline and is concerned with social and antisocial conduct. The social nature of law ought to be emphasized in every legal rule, including that on mental incapacity . . .[60]

Underlying all formulations are issues concerned with free will and determinism as contrasting explanations of man's behavior. The legal system operates on the assumption that man has free will, except when such will is clearly overwhelmed by specific disabilities. Criminological science is committed to a deterministic position, operating on the assumption that individuals who deviate from the demands of the legal code do so for sufficient and adequate causes that reside both in themselves and in their experience. This does not mean that criminology seeks to exonerate offenders or to justify their wrongdoings. It simply means that criminology makes a distinction between the purely analytical view, which attempts to understand why a certain form of crime has come about, and the judgmental view, which attempts to fix blame and responsibility.

It is one of the anomalies of this position that criminology, which emphasizes a deterministic form of investigation, stands closer to the thinking of the Roman Catholic Church—probably the most articulate proponent of the doctrine of free will—than it does to the system of criminal law, with its adherence to the concept of an almost undiscriminating sense of moral responsibility. In a statement by Pope Pius XII to the Italian Association of Catholic Jurists, in which the position of the Catholic Church was elaborated, great stress was laid upon the need for extensive reforms in carrying out criminal

60 Silving, *Essays on Mental Incapacity and Criminal Conduct*, p. 138.

penalties in the light of a more profound understanding of the individual. The statement emphasized that "the community should see to it that it is disposed to welcome charitably the man who comes forth from prison into liberty"; and, with respect to the determination of guilt and punishment, the leader of the Catholic Church declared that courts should take into account

> not only the external act, but also the influences, both internal and external, which have cooperated in the decision of the criminal, such as innate or acquired dispositions, impulses or obstructions, impressions from education, stimulation from persons or things in the midst of which the person lives, circumstantial factors, and in a peculiar way the habitual or actual intensity of the will-act, the so-called 'criminal urge,' which has contributed to the accomplishment of the criminal act.[61]

Most criminologists make the assumption that the "criminal urge" referred to above, is still another of the influences operating on the individual and traceable to his prior conditioning. By careful study, they seek to uncover the sources for this tendency and other relevant factors that have contributed to the constellation of traits comprising the individual's behavior. But beyond this qualification, both the deterministic and free-will approaches to criminal behavior are in agreement that the individual deviant is largely, if not totally, the product of the forces of his heredity and his environment, and that a consideration of these forces is vital to an understanding of his behavior. To this extent, also, there is agreement that the doctrine of criminal responsibility, apart from its value in holding together a tenable method of law enforcement, falls seriously short of squaring with empirical reality.

Who is a Criminal?

If the establishment of criminal responsibility and the fixing of guilt pose extremely difficult problems, how can we define "the criminal?" The term "criminal," denoting a person who has deviated from the demands of the criminal law, has serious shortcomings, which need to be made manifest in order to clarify the problems and procedures involved in the scientific study of criminology. The word "criminal" lacks rigorous reference and has often been the basis for some of the most untenable generalizations put forward about the nature of persons who violate the law. A primary difficulty lies in the impossibility of applying the term either to homogeneous personalities or to homegeneous behavior unless it is severely restricted. As Robert Rice notes, the dictionary defines a "criminal" as "one who has been found guilty of a crime." He then goes on to point out the shortcomings of this characterization:

61 Quoted in *New York Times*, Feb. 16, 1958.

any definition that in nine words, eight of them monosyllables, is able to effectively blanket such assorted personalities as John Dillinger, Harry K. Thaw, Loeb and Leopold, Waxey Gordon, Robert Whitney, Willie Sutton, Lizzie Borden, and Robin Hood is pretty primitive, and is no more enlightening than the observation that whales, giraffes, two-toed sloths and disc jockeys are all mammals, or that quail, deliquescence, pique, and cumquat are all common nouns containing the letter "q".[62]

In popular usage, "criminal" refers to the more obvious violators—and particularly to those who have been declared guilty and have been subsequently incarcerated. But generalizations based on this group inevitably omit the more adroit violators, those who escape adjudication and prison and those who commit acts that, while outlawed, do not for one reason or another result in judicial proceedings.

In Dostoevsky's famous novel *Crime and Punishment*, the main character illustrates, without unduly stretching the bonds of logic or imagination, how the term "criminal" might readily be applied to individuals normally considered the leaders of society. The student, Raskolnikov, who has committed murder, attempts to link himself to an illustrious brotherhood, reasoning as follows, that

> legislators and leaders of men, such as Lycurgus, Solon, Mahomet, Napoleon, and so on, were all without exception criminals from the very fact that, making a new law, they transgressed the ancient one, handed down from their ancestors and held sacred by the people, and they did not stop short of bloodshed either, if that bloodshed—often of innocent people fighting bravely in defense of ancient law—were of use to their cause.[63]

Individuals who break the law do not do so constantly and, when they do, they are not always apprehended. Even if we try to confine the use of the designation "criminal" to lawbreakers, there are always chronological limitations as to how the term should be employed. Does an individual become a criminal at the moment he violates the law? If so, how long does he remain a criminal? Must he persistently commit crime to retain this label, or are notorious single acts of crime, such as murder, equivalent to a number of pettier acts, such as shoplifting? These are virtually irresolvable questions, just as generalizations about "criminals" are inadequate unless they specify with more precision the group of law violators to which they apply.

A healthy scientific trend in recent criminological studies appears in the attempt to concentrate on particular categories of crime, such as arson, embezzlement, automobile theft, and murder, and on homogeneous systems of criminal behavior. We shall employ this more promising approach in the following chapters, rather than draw

62 Rice, *Business of Crime*, p. xiii.
63 Dostoevsky, *Crime and Punishment*, p. 226.

broad generalizations or present sweeping correlates on the behavior
of so nebulous a group as "criminals."

Areas of Criminological Interest

We have described criminology as the study by social scientific
methods of those conditions and attributes that give rise to different
types of crime and the relation of such crimes to sociolegal trends.
There are, in addition, many related areas that engage the attention
of specialists. In some cases, these areas, such as the study of social
control, may have a direct impact upon our central concern in
criminology. Other areas are more remote and have the same relation
to the main stream of criminology as the specialized study of cellular
tissue has to the broad field of biology.

Generally speaking, the areas of criminology are: (1) *criminology
proper*, the sociological, social psychological, and psychological conditions associated with the causes of crime; (2) *jurisprudence*, concerned
with the development and interpretation of criminal statutes; (3) *law
enforcement*, dealing with techniques of official response to criminal
behavior, including the specialized branch of *criminalistics*, which has
to do with scientific techniques of detection, collection and preservation of legal evidence, and the use of natural science approaches to the
identification of individuals and episodes associated with crime; (4)
administration of justice, covering the operation of the legal system
in its official and informal response to crime; and (5) *corrections* or
penology, an area encompassing the detention, imprisonment, treatment, and possible rehabilitation of offenders, including the operation
of systems of probation and parole.

As we examine the various areas of criminological interest, we
should recognize that crime and the methods of response to it, which
societies have developed, reflect the onrushing course of history.
The observation of Walter Schaefer, a prominent judge, that "the
quality of a nation's civilization can largely be measured by the
methods it uses in the enforcement of the criminal law,"[64] may or may
not be altogether accurate, but it does indicate possibilities for generalizing beyond criminological data to broad areas of scientific and
humanistic concern.

From our discussion of social control and the reciprocal relationship among social values, social institutions, and law, we are compelled to recognize that as social values change, so do conceptions of
what constitutes either a serious or a minor crime as well as the
proper responses to such acts. In fact, as noted earlier, the character
of crime at various periods in history and the nature of response to it
are deeply revealing about the character of social change itself. While

64 Schaefer, "Federalism and State Criminal Procedure," p. 26.

this is implicit in much of what has already been considered, we have thus far concentrated on some of the more static elements of the legal structure. We will now turn to the relativity of crime within different historical contexts and to the significance of changing social values in relation to the meaning of crime.

For Further Reading

DAVIS, F. JAMES, HENRY H. FOSTER, JR., C. RAY JEFFERY, AND E. EUGENE DAVIS. *Society and the Law: New Meanings for an Old Profession.* New York: Free Press of Glencoe, 1962.

Written by two sociologists, a law professor, and a practicing attorney, this book indicates how the behavioral sciences can contribute to an understanding of legal problems and how the law may be utilized to resolve social issues. Also valuable is William M. Evan (ed.). *Law and Sociology.* New York: Free Press of Glencoe, 1962, a collection of nine essays on problems of mutual importance for law and sociology.

EDWARDS, J. L. J. *Mens Rea in Statutory Offenses.* New York: St. Martin's Press, 1955.

An authoritative work on the ancient doctrine of *mens rea,* or "guilty mind," which shows the enormous complexities involved in the application of that principle to specific cases in criminal law.

KAPLAN, SIDNEY J. "Barriers to the Establishment of a Deterministic Criminal Law," *Kentucky Law Journal,* Vol. 46 (Fall, 1957), pp. 103–111.

An analysis of the functional reasons why the theory of free will appears to be important to the system of criminal law. The article considers items such as personal responsibility, deterrence, justice, and the psychological outlets involved in criminal procedure.

MICHAEL, JEROME, AND MORTIMER J. ADLER. *Crime, Law, and Social Science.* New York: Harcourt, Brace, 1933.

A thorough review of the scientific aspirations of criminology and a polemic for a legal approach to its subject matter.

SILVING, HELEN. *Essays on Mental Incapacity and Criminal Conduct.* Springfield, Ill.: Charles C. Thomas, 1967.

Written by the "First Lady of Criminal Law," the essays in this collection, in their author's words, "deal with the problem of designating the mental states which in a rational system of law ought to qualify an offender for exemption from punitive responsibility and for potential treatment by nonpunitivite preventive and protective penal law sanctions."

3
History and the Relativity
of Crime

The content of a criminal code and the enforcement of various criminal laws are, as we have noted, the product of many factors that in large measure reflect a society's ultimate power structure—that is, the ability of certain persons and certain segments of society to translate their desires into public policy.[1] The study of politics, as Harold Lasswell notes, is the study of influence and the influential; the influential, he further observes, "are those who get most of what there is to get."[2]

Since the specifications of criminal law reflect the ethos of a society at a given time, a scholar may, with caution, extrapolate from its criminal code the mainstream of the society that promulgates the code. Insecure societies, for example, will generally concentrate the wrath of their criminal laws, both in terms of acts proscribed and of punishment levied, on those who betray state secrets and who seemingly undermine the security of the country. A religiously-oriented society, on the other hand, will stress disproportionately violations of theological precepts, deeming it unnecessary to seek further than divine will for justification of its rules.

How systems of criminal justice highlight and are responsive to the culture of the societies in which they are rooted are shown in the following examples. In Japan, for instance, the law reflects an intense concern with kinship patterns; it levies a heavier punishment against persons killing their own or their spouse's lineal descendants than against those who commit other kinds of homicide.[3] In France, it is considered inhumane to let a condemned man know the date of his execution; not until the morning when the governor of the prison comes into his cell, does the prisoner know that he will die that day.[4]

1 Rosenblum, *Law as a Political Instrument*, Chap. 1.
2 Lasswell, *Politics: Who Gets What, When, How*, p. 3.
3 Belli and Jones, *Belli Looks at Life and Law in Japan*, p. 129.
4 Bedford, *The Faces of Justice*, p. 297.

Condemned men in France are permitted to drink alcohol prior to their execution, whereas in the United States all efforts are made to keep the condemned man totally sensible, reflecting religious views that insist that the prisoner be given every last opportunity to make his peace with God. In many continental countries, a prisoner need not work if he chooses to remain idle, since it is believed that deprivation of liberty constitutes a harsh enough penalty and that, in any event, work is not necessarily a punishment. In the United States, on the other hand, prison sentences often designate that the prisoner serve "at hard labor." The reflections of Gustave Auguste de Beaumont and Alexis de Tocqueville, who in the 1800s made an inspection tour of American prisons, further indicate how penological practices can mean different things in different cultures. Responding to the then-prevalent American practice of forcing prisoners to exist in total silence, the two Frenchmen observed about the practicality of such a system that "the law of silence would be infinitely more painful to Frenchmen than Americans, whose character is taciturn and reflective."[5]

Testimony to the group cohesiveness and military values of the Cossacks in the sixteenth century might be found in Nikolai Gogol's later report that if "a Cossack were a thief and stole any trifle, it was regarded as a disgrace to the whole body of Cossacks; he was bound to the whipping post as a thief, and beside him was laid an oak cudgel, with which every passer-by was obliged to deal him a blow, until in this way he was beaten to death."[6] The attempt to enhance group solidarity by making a vivid example of the disruptive may also be read from the Cossack punishment for murder in which a pit was dug and the murderer lowered into it alive. Above him was placed the coffin containing the body of his victim, and then both were covered with earth.[7]

The indecisiveness and indulgence of Creek Indian society might be gathered from Angie Debo's report that Creek law provided for increasingly severe penalties for repeated criminal offenses, with death prescribed for the third violation. Being merciful, however, the Creeks almost invariably pardoned the man faced with death; then, not knowing what to do with him on his fourth offense, they merely began the count all over again as if it were his first.[8] The adaptation of criminal procedure to national character is also seen in the Italian method of forcing two witnesses whose evidence is contradictory to confront each other in an open courtroom, in what often ends up to be a violent emotional outburst that brings forth the truth of the matter.[9] Finally, the no-nonsense, pragmatic values of early midwestern society

5 de Beaumont and de Tocqueville, *On the Penitentiary System in the United States,* p. 121.
6 Gogol, *Taras Bulba,* pp. 31–32.
7 *Ibid.,* p. 32.
8 Debo, *Road to Disappearance,* pp. 228–229.
9 Young, *Montesi Scandal,* p. 214.

in the United States can be seen in statutes such as that passed by the lower house of the Indiana legislature in 1899, which set the value of *pi* as 4.0.[10]

Early Criminal Law

Early criminal law was essentially a private matter in which individuals and families exacted retribution against those who had wronged them. As Max Weber notes, regular *ex-officio* prosecution for a delict, or offense, was non-existent.[11] Patriarchs judged the deeds of family members who violated official rules. This concept of personal justice is clearly visible in all early laws, including the Code of Hammurabi, the Roman tablets of laws, the Mosaic Code, laws in early Greek society as revealed in the *Iliad* and the *Odyssey*, and the laws of Tacitus prevalent among the Germanic peoples. The system finally broke down when radical alterations took place in the structure and role of the family, and when injustices became too intolerable, such as when there were no punishments if a family unit was weak or too severe punishments if the family unit possessed great power.

The superimposition of formal political organization on kinship systems of justice dramatically changed the character of early criminal law and procedure. In England, for instance, as Ray Jeffery notes after carefully tracing this development, the first step involved promulgation of rules that no violence or feuding would be tolerated in the presence of lords and bishops.[12] Gradually, this concept was applied to special occasions, special cities, and special days, until finally it was regarded as the "king's peace" or the general law of the land. Soon, itinerant justices were traveling throughout England administering the law of the King's Court to people who earlier had depended upon kinship ties to support and defend them. By the twelfth century, the system of payment of compensation to the family of a wronged individual by the offender had all but disappeared in face of the disintegration of the kinship unit. In addition, the character of land ownership had altered so that comparatively few resources were available to the accused to buy himself free. By intervening, the Crown literally kept the peace but, as defaults on fines occurred, alternative modes of punishment, such as death, mutilation, transportation (that is, banishment to a foreign territory), and outlawry had to be established. Outlawry, for instance, was employed as a means of preventing feuds by removing the wrongdoer from the scene. He could seek sanctuary in a church, and from there he could leave the realm within forty days, after being assured safe passage to a port.

10 Ginger, *Six Days or Forever,* p. 8.
11 Rheinstein, *Max Weber on Law in Economy and Society,* p. 55.
12 Jeffery in Davis, *et al., Society and the Law,* pp. 268–272.

The Code of Hammurabi is the first comprehensive legal document that has come down to us virtually intact, though it appeared several centuries after that of Ur-Nammu, a Sumerian king whose laws are the most ancient discovered to date. The monument on which the Code of Hammurabi is engraved was found in December, 1901, on the acropolis of the city of Susa, capital of the ancient territory of Elam, north of the Persian Gulf, by an expedition sent out by the French Government. The Code was written on a block of black diorite, nearly eight feet high, which had been broken into three pieces that were easily rejoined.[13] It has a neat, conventional structure; the laws, written in prose, are encompassed by a prologue and epilogue in poetry.[14] The importance of the rich agricultural land of ancient Babylonia to the social structure of that country is clearly reflected in the many explicit provisions relating to cultivation and maintenance of the land. The Code also neatly mirrors the rigid social stratification of Babylonia, with different rules applying to each of the three classes: the freemen, the serfs, and the slaves. It also pays heed to the religious tone of the Babylonian society, stipulating, for instance, that a priestess should be burned alive if found entering a tavern. In addition, the constant menace of scarcity in Babylonian society is reflected in detailed regulations concerning the marketing of commodities and the fixing of prices. Finally, a strict retributive rule of *lex talionis*—"an eye for an eye, a tooth for a tooth"—prevailed; a physician was to have his hands severed if he performed a careless operation, and a man's daughter would be killed if the man was responsible for causing the death of another female through miscarriage. The story is told of the judge of ancient times who was faced with a case involving a man who had fallen from a very high tree limb while picking fruit and landed on another man, instantly killing him. The relatives of the deceased demanded vengeance, "an eye for an eye." In a moment of supreme wisdom, the judge ruled that the accusers could have their wish—one of them could climb to the top of a high tree, and while the accused walked beneath it, he could fall upon him.[15] The laws, however, applied only to wrongs against members of the freeman class. Serfs were to be compensated for offenses against them with money rather than through equivalent vengeance. "If a freeman causes a serf to lose his eye," one section of the Code states, "he shall pay one mina of silver," whereas the same offense committed against a freeman would cause the perpetrator to lose his own eye.[16]

Biblical literature strikingly illustrates the close accord between crimes and moral deviancy in certain historical periods. Moshe Silberg, for instance, has observed that "there is no legal system in the world,

13 Harper, *Code of Hammurabi*, p. xi.
14 Gordon, *Hammurapi's Code*, p. 3.
15 Cairns, *Law and Social Science*, p. 37.
16 Seagle, "Hammurabi, King of Babylon," pp. 13–30.

whether modern or ancient, in which the principles of morality and law are so intertwined, so interfused, as in Jewish law." He suggests that in large measure the blending of religion and law in Jewish jurisprudence was due to the need for national law to protect religious identification and, equally important, due to the lack of a politically-based coercive force to execute the law in ancient Hebrew society. While in exile and while subject to the power of other nations, the Jews inevitably had to rely heavily upon group pressure and threats of supernatural sanctions to gain conformity to their edicts.[17] The fundamental premise of Jewish jurisprudence was that the revealed will of God was the sole source of legislation; consequently, every punishable act constituted a violation of God's will. The Hebrew language, in fact, contains no equivalent for the word "crime." "It is a strange fact," Goldin writes, "that we find Hebrew words for sin, iniquity, and other synonymous expressions, but we do not meet with words or phrases corresponding to the expressions *crime* and *criminal law* in their legal senses. Every offense, no matter what its nature, is termed in the Talmud *aberrah*, a transgression."[18] The same assumption of punishable acts as violations of God's will underlay much of early Christian thinking; much later, in fact, every law in the Massachusetts Bay Colony appended a proper Biblical reference to indicate its essential authority.[19]

Mosaic law included thirty-six capital crimes, punishable by one of four methods of death: stoning, burning, decapitation, and strangulation. The types of acts leading to death clearly reflect the nature of the society, and include such items as necromancy, idol-worship, sorcery, cursing one's father and mother, and sexual relations with a betrothed female.[20] Jewish law also included the provision that witnesses who testified falsely would be liable to the same penalty that the accused would have suffered if he were convicted on the basis of their testimony.[21] This provision, certainly more likely to inhibit prosecutions than any current rule of evidence, duplicates similar stipulations in many early legal systems. In the Code of Hammurabi, for instance, it was specified that if a man had accused another of murder but had not substantiated the charge, the accuser would be put to death.[22]

Other early systems of criminal law serve equally well to underline the close relationship between the systems themselves and the societies that nurtured them. In its earliest period, Greece also resorted to the policy of personal retribution, in which offenses against the individual or against family groups were dealt with privately. The Greeks neatly

17 Silberg, "Law and Morals in Jewish Jurisprudence," pp. 321–322.
18 Goldin, *Hebrew Criminal Law and Procedure*, p. 11.
19 Elliott, *Crime in Modern Society*, p. 22.
20 Goldin, *Hebrew Criminal Law and Procedure*, pp. 18–37.
21 Leigh, *Man's Right to Life*, p. 34.
22 Meisel, "The Code of Hammurabi," p. 200.

provided for the legitimacy of divine will by flexibly accommodating their codes to changing conditions; they assumed that the laws had been received from their gods, although imperfectly, that the expression of the will of the gods had been humanly warped, and that changes therefore could be made at any time and justice done.[23] Flagrant attacks on the community, as the poems of Homer vividly portray, were punished by direct and spontaneous action on the part of the populace—actions that were little more than mob uprisings.[24] Later, however, a decisive step was taken in Greece toward criminal law as we know it today, when Solon, an Athenian statesman, at the beginning of the sixth century B.C., gave every Athenian citizen the right to initiate prosecutions for certain offenses, including attacks upon individuals and the state.[25] Solon also put forward laws reflecting his own mercantile background and his interest in industry and industriousness. Persistent idleness was made a crime, and no man who lived a life of debauchery was permitted to speak in public. Solon limited the size of dowries, wishing that marriages be contracted by affection of the mates and for the rearing of children. And, as Will Durant notes, "with childlike trustfulness," Solon forbade women to extend their wardrobes beyond three suits. He condemned pompous ceremonies, expensive sacrifices, and limited the goods that might be buried with the dead. Finally, Solon established that the sons of those who had died in war should be brought up and educated at the expense of the government, a precedent that Durant believes served as "a source of Athenian bravery for generations."[26] Also prominent in Greek jurisprudence was the *dikastery*, in which controversies were submitted to blocks of several hundred citizens in order to reach some understanding of the will of the people. Socrates, for instance, was tried by a jury of 501 persons, and when Alcibiades was tried for treason, it was by a jury of 1,501.[27]

Roman law, finding much of the Greek system unsuitable to its particular needs, revealed a considerably different pattern of growth. Criminal law was slow to develop in Rome and never attained an importance comparable to that of private law.[28] The pragmatic Romans were not concerned with abstract principles of justice, but only with what they considered to be just and effective punishment.[29] Special circumstances were taken into consideration in each case, and wide powers were granted to authoritative judges. Toward the end of Roman hegemony, the influence of Christian theology began to pervade the criminal law, with new stress placed especially on the punishment of

23 Henson, *Landmarks of the Law*, p. xi.
24 Calhoun, *Growth of Criminal Law in Ancient Greece*, p. 6.
25 Linforth, *Solon the Athenian*, Chap. 3.
26 Durant, *Life of Greece*, pp. 116–117.
27 Curtis, *It's Your Law*, p. 102.
28 Wolff, *Roman Law*, p. 53.
29 Schultz, *Principles of Roman Law*, p. 176.

religious and sexual deviancy.[30] This influence carried over to the law of the Middle Ages and to much of American colonial criminal law. Witchcraft, for instance, a form of religious deviance, was believed rampant in the American colonies and alleged witches were commonly burned at the stake. (In 1967, in fact, the state of Massachusetts, in a moment dedicated to conscience-clearing, enacted a legislative resolve wiping from the books the conviction of six women who had been hanged for witchcraft during the seventeenth-century hysteria that swept the town of Salem.[31]) In early Maryland, the law called for penalties against a person who was a "common swearer, blasphemer, or curser," and there are records of a number of prosecutions, including one against Captain Thomas Bradnox, a justice of the peace, who was charged with having uttered at least "one hundred oaths."[32] In June 1969, the 246-year-old Maryland law against blasphemy was finally declared unconstitutional in *West v. Campbell* after an appeal by a man who had been convicted for swearing at a police officer following his arrest. Circuit Court Judge Edward O. Weant, Jr. noted that in England in 1656 the penalty for a first offense of blasphemy might be a hole bored in the tongue. Someone committing a second offense could be stigmatized by burning the letter 'B' on his forehead. The stress of such early law still persists, although to a lessening extent, in contemporary American criminal law. Today, statutes exist against such practices as prostitution, homosexuality, and gambling—landmarks to the Biblical heritage of our society.

Theft and Social Values

Few systematic and detailed studies have been undertaken to relate changes in criminal law to changes in social values, despite (or possibly because of) the vast amount of material available in this area. The classic work in this vein remains the ground-breaking effort by Jerome Hall, a law professor at Indiana University, who examined the law of theft, using social theory as his dominant perspective.[33] The ways in which legal problems concerning theft were met in eighteenth-century England, Professor Hall shows, were closely related to unmistakable cultural changes, and when the substantive law lagged behind social need, both technicalities and legal fictions were resorted to in order to bridge the gap.

Hall reports a typical instance of the use of technical artifice to bring the law into line with public feelings. In 1774, a man was indicted for the capital offense of "stealing a cow." Twelve jurors agreed, however, after carefully weighing the evidence, that because the animal stolen had never had a calf, it was a heifer, not a cow. Since

30 Schultz, *History of Roman Legal Science*, p. 298.
31 See Miller, *The Crucible*.
32 Semmes, *Crime and Punishment in Early Maryland*, p. 162.
33 Hall, *Theft, Law and Society*.

the offense did not square with the indictment, the accused was set free. Also set free was another defendant, who was charged with stealing a live turkey. The turkey found in his possession was dead; the court ruled that possession of a stolen dead turkey was not adequate to support the charge of theft of a live fowl. Quite typical also was the finding of a jury that a defendant had stolen items worth only four shillings, ten pence (the theft of five shillings called for the death penalty), though the defendant had sold the stolen items for one pound, five shillings.[34] Eventually, the laws were altered to fall more accurately in line with the sentiments of the times; thereafter, they were both enforceable and enforced.

Hall found, in his careful evaluation of the cultural winds that served to produce the law of embezzlement, that the following developments existed:

> (1) Expansion of mercantile and banking credit and the use of credit mechanisms; (2) employment of clerks in important positions with reference to dealing with and, in particular, receiving valuables from third persons; . . . (3) a change in the attitude regarding the public importance of what could formerly be dismissed as merely a private breach of trust; and (4) a series of sensational cases of very serious defalcation which set the pattern into motion and produced immediate action.[35]

Hall's fifth point, showing that notorious cases were important in providing the final catalyst for legislation, is shown in recent enactments in the United States, such as the law that makes air piracy (forcibly seizing or trying to seize an airplane in interstate or international commerce) a crime punishable by death, and the law that provides for a five-year penalty for persons claiming that a bomb has been placed aboard an airplane. Plane hijacking, particularly by persons seeking to go to Cuba, and a mass killing of airplane passengers by a bomb placed in the luggage of one passenger provided the impetus for the aircraft laws.

BLUE LAWS

The same interaction between a society's values and its criminal code can be discerned through an examination of chronological changes in "blue laws," restrictions applied against Sabbath activities. These rules trace their origin to the Biblical command that, "You shall keep the Sabbath therefore, for it is holy unto you: every one that defileth it shall surely be put to death." (Exodus 31:14.) In A.D. 321, after his conversion to Christianity, the Emperor Constantine first gave legal teeth to this Biblical edict, requiring by law that all work cease on the Sabbath, that "all judges, city people, and craftsmen shall rest on the venerable day of the Sun," although he exempted

34 *Ibid.*, pp. 121–124.
35 *Ibid.*, p. 66.

farmers from this prescription on the ground that "the right season is of short duration." And, blue laws trace their Anglo-Saxon origin back to Henry VII of England who, in 1237, forbade the frequenting of markets on Sundays. Early blue-law statutes in the American colonies were aimed at frivolous Sunday activity, such as traveling fairs. Later, however, the ban was extended to include most other forms of active or worldly behavior. In 1610, the colony of Virginia decreed that church attendance was compulsory on both Sunday mornings and afternoons. But as American society became secularized and urbanized, various activities, such as fire and police patrol, gained exemptions from Sunday restrictions. Later, exceptions to the rules were widened to include roadside enterprises and, then, as they gained greater economic standing, their business competitors, caught between religious and economic considerations, demanded equal treatment. Today, many cities have food stores that are open seven days a week. Athletic contests take place in virtually all parts of the United States on Sunday, supplying Sabbath recreation for many and Sabbath work for others.[36]

There are a number of theories on how the term "blue laws" came into existence. One belief is that the laws take their name from the color of dye used on cotton stockings by the poorer classes in colonial days. Others believe that the term derives from the blue color adopted by New England Puritans in opposition to the British royal red, while a third school favors the idea that the term dates from the colonial period when volumes of laws applying religious standards to civil conduct were bound in blue. Connecticut, in fact, was once nicknamed the Blue Law State. Whatever the origin of the name, however, blue laws clearly illustrate historic variations in religious orthodoxy in different regions of the United States; they are extensive in the East and gradually decline in number as one moves westward. They also illustrate an erratic and sometimes contradictory approach to what seem to be similar items. In Mississippi, for instance, grocery stores must close on Sunday, but drive-in markets may remain open. The drive-in can sell butter but not oleomargarine; beer but not cat food. On Sunday in Kansas City, Missouri, you can buy a bottle of perfume, but not a baby bottle, charcoal for an outdoor broiler, but not the fluid to light it, a potted evergreen tree, but not an electric fuse. And, to the despair of merchants who try to obey the Missouri blue laws that were enacted in 1825, a person can cross the state line into Kansas and buy anything, except liquor, that is offered for sale.

In Massachusetts, public dancing is forbidden on Sunday, and it is illegal to change the oil or grease in an automobile. In New York, according to Article 2 of the General Business Law, "all labor on Sunday is prohibited, excepting the works of necessity and charity . . . whatever is needful during the day for the good order, health, or com-

36 Chell, "Sunday Blue Laws."

fort of the community." The law continues that, "the first day of the week being by general consent set apart for rest and religious use, the law prohibits the doing on that day of certain acts hereafter specified, which are serious interruptions of the repose and religious liberty of the community." In 1965, however, New York passed a Fair Sabbath Law that allows so-called "mama-and-papa" stores to stay open on Sunday if they are closed another day for religious purposes. Sabbath-breaking in New York is a misdemeanor, punishable by a fine of $5 to $10 and up to five days' imprisonment for the first offense.

All states but Alaska, California, and Iowa have some form of blue laws.[37] Blue laws, now generally defended not on religious grounds but as items of public health and welfare,[38] were attacked in 1961 in the Supreme Court. They were said to constitute the establishment of religion by favoring those Christian sects that observe their holy day on Sunday, thus violating the religious freedom of Jews and Seventh-Day Adventists, who observe their sabbath on Saturday; Moslems, whose holy day is Friday; and Buddhists, whose holy day is determined by phases of the moon and may vary from week to week. The Supreme Court, however, upheld the constitutionality of the blue laws. Chief Justice Warren observed that blue laws had changed from religious enactments to secular rules since colonial days, and that their basic purpose today was to prevent overwork and unfair competition. He stated that, "People of all religions and people with no religion regard Sunday as a time for family activity, for visiting friends and relatives, for late sleeping, for passive and active entertainments, for dining out, and the like."[39] That persons of some religious faiths were penalized by the Sunday laws was granted by the Chief Justice, but this operated not to make the law unconstitutional, but "to make the practice of their religious beliefs more expensive."[40]

At first glance, a historical review of the blue laws may seem to indicate nothing more than the continued existence of tenets that are no longer of functional importance in society, due to a lag in the ability of the law to keep in tune with current social customs. A closer look, however, discloses a considerable range of information about the society, such as its early religious orientation, its tendency to retain a tradition by redefining its application, its reluctance to interfere at a federal level with state enactments, as well as its social values. With respect to the latter, the laws may indicate, for instance, that some emphasis is placed on good health, relaxation, and recreation—values that, if we could amass corroborative evidence of their importance, would appear to tell us a good deal about this society in contrast to others that may stress alternative ideals.

37 "State Sunday Blue Laws," p. 732.
38 Fellman, *Limits of Freedom*, p. 37.
39 *McGowan v. Maryland*, pp. 451–452.
40 *Braunfield v. Brown*, p. 605.

SUICIDE AND ATTEMPTED SUICIDE

Virtually the same course of development found in the blue laws is evident in the evolution of criminal law in regard to the practice of suicide. Early attitudes toward suicide were contradictory. The Athenians prohibited it, showing their disapproval by cutting off the hand of the suicide and refusing to bury it with the body. Yet Socrates was punished by being made to commit suicide. Plato and Aristotle both held suicide to be immoral, yet the Stoics believed it proper to escape an undesirable life by flight into death. The Roman philosopher Seneca sums up what appears to have been the prevalent Stoic attitude of his time with the observation that, "As I choose the ship in which I will sail and the house I will inhabit, so I will choose the death by which I will leave life. In no matter more than death should we act according to our desire."[41] Ironically, because of his involvement in a conspiracy against the government, Seneca was later sentenced to kill himself, an act he committed by severing a vein while lying in a hot bath, a common form of suicide among the Romans.

The Bible itself contains no prohibition of suicide; at a rather late stage—during the Council of Arles in 452—the Church adopted such a position, supporting it with the thesis that "whoever kills himself, thereby killing an innocent person, commits homicide." Roman law, at the same time, was forced to develop rules for punishing suicides who did away with themselves in order to avoid trial, since conviction on a capital charge was accompanied by the confiscation of the accused's property. Eventually the Romans declared that suicide itself was equivalent to criminal behavior and should therefore be punished by denial of a religious burial and by sanctions imposed upon the corpse, such as burial in the highway at a crossroad with a stake driven through the body. The crossroad, possibly having theological significance, was also considered necessary to render the morbid properties of the suicide's body harmless and the stake was expected to keep the tainted soul from leaving the corpse.[42] The English continued interring the bodies of suicides ignominiously under public highways until 1823. As Edmond Cahn notes, with both bemusement and sarcasm, there is no record of "whether this mode of burial did more to reduce the incidence of suicide than to disrupt vehicular traffic."[43] The legal tenet regarding the confiscation of the property of a suicide was not repealed in England until 1870.

Other countries have been equally severe in their criminal laws regarding suicide, indicating a combination of theological anxiety, economic harm, and social disruption associated with it. In France, the Criminal Ordinance of 1670 demanded that the body of a convicted suicide be dragged face down through the streets behind a horse-

41 Quoted in Lecky, *History of European Morals*, pp. 217–220. See also Williams, *Sanctity of Life*, p. 253.
42 Radzinowicz, *History of English Criminal Law*, Vol. I, pp. 196–197.
43 Cahn, *The Moral Decision*, p. 236.

drawn hurdle and then deposited in the town's dumping ground.[44] In Sweden, under the 1608 criminal code of Charles IX, the bodies of suicides were burned on a funeral pyre in the woods. The policy regarding suicide in Scandinavia, in fact, is reported to have led to an epidemic of murders in Norway and Denmark in the seventeenth and eighteenth centuries by depressed persons who wanted to die but who would not commit suicide on religious grounds. Such cases are said to have been so frequent that a special law was passed, which excluded such individuals from the death penalty in order to stop their acts of homicide.[45]

Methods of suicide vary from country to country, indicating by a relatively straightforward measure the manner in which material conditions and values of a society both influence and limit choices. In the United States, for instance, men are apt to kill themselves with firearms and women with pills. Britons prefer gas. In Africa, hanging is the most frequently-used method. In Brazil it is poison.

According to the World Health Organization, Hungary has the highest suicide rate: 34 suicides per 100,000 population. Sweden shows 22 suicides per 100,000 persons; England 15; the United States 11; and Italy, with the lowest suicide rate in the world, 7. Certain occupations also produce high suicide rates. British doctors, for example, kill themselves at rates well above the national average.

In many of the United States, attempted suicide is a crime, either by express statutory provision or by virtue of the general incorporation of the principles of English common law into the state laws. Even where the concept of suicide as crime has been repudiated, as in New York, the legislature has hastened to note that, while not a crime, the act of suicide is a "grave public wrong."

Helen Silving, who has carefully analyzed the legal history of suicide, points out that "world legislation on the subject is more widely split than on any other topic."[46] France and Germany, she notes, have preserved the principle of immunity of accomplices to suicide, while the laws of various jurisdictions in the United States range from granting complete immunity to such accomplices, to trying them for first-degree murder. Silving, who believes that suicide should be a personal rather than a legal matter, notes that "the assumption of a legal duty to live seems particularly objectionable in states which still maintain the institution of capital punishment."[47] In Britain, during debate regarding suicide laws, the position opposing them was put in the following terms:

> The arguments advanced for retaining attempted suicide as a crime
> are its deterrent value and the opportunity given the offender to re-

44 Bien, *The Calas Affair*, pp. 9–10.
45 Wolfgang and Ferracuti, *Subculture of Violence*, p. 207.
46 Silving, "Suicide and the Law."
47 *Ibid.*, p. 91.

ceive treatment. The deterrence argument is nonsensical since the only effect of the law must be to ensure that the person genuinely attempting to end his life will make a good job of it. One can grant that the criminal law is a present means of obtaining treatment, but it is hardly a necessary one.[48]

Such views carried the day, and in 1961, Queen Elizabeth II approved legislation removing the crime of attempted suicide from the statute books. The English, however, continue to regard counseling or aiding suicides a criminal offense, with a maximum penalty of fourteen-years imprisonment for such acts.

USURY

The act of *usury*, also treated in a variety of ways under different social and historical circumstances, is the lending of money at exorbitant or unconscionable rates of interest. Usury strikes us today, as John Noonan, Jr. notes, as a rare and inconsequential vice, a moral fault that is not the problem of any large portion of humanity. Noonan clearly shows in rhetorical terms the evolution of social concern with usury from medieval to present times:

> How . . . can we appreciate the intensity of the intellectual interest in usury in the sixteenth and seventeenth centuries, when its nature and extent were as lively an issue, and as voluminously discussed by reflective observers of commerce, as the nature and cure of business cycles are debated in similar circles today? How much less can we grasp the spirit of a yet earlier age whose most perspicacious moralists described usury as the great vice which corrupted cities and Church alike and held all men of property in bondage? Usury today is a dead issue, and except by plainly equivocal use of the term, or save in the mouths of a few inveterate haters of the present order, it is not likely to stir to life.[49]

The designation of usury as a crime involved a blend of economic, legal, and theological considerations. Concern with usury was an amalgam of Biblical injunctions, decisions reached by early church councils, and the works of early Catholic philosophers. Also particularly significant were the writings of Aristotle, who was the first major figure to oppose usury on theoretical grounds. "The term usury, which means the birth of money from money, is applied to the breeding of money because the offspring resembles the parent," Aristole wrote, continuing that, "Wherefore of all modes of making money this is the most unnatural."[50] During the early Middle Ages, when religious concepts required no buttressing beyond their own enunciation, church strictures against usury were accepted categorically. These sanctions were particularly useful in protecting the small landholders, in what

48 "Crime of Suicide," pp. 871–872.
49 Noonan, Jr. *Scholastic Analysis of Usury*, p. 1.
50 Aristotle, *Politics*, Book I, Chapter 10.

was almost a totally agricultural world, from being swallowed up by the large estate owners. The usury laws also served as protection for persons who, in taking part in the Crusades, usually needed to borrow funds to finance their religious expeditions.

Sanctions against usury were first leveled by the church authorities against the clergy, based upon the Biblical text of Psalms 15:5, which declared that he who, among other things, "takes no interest on a loan" may dwell on God's sacred hill. The ban was extended from the clergy to laymen by Pope Leo the Great, who wrote around 450, inveighing against the *turpe lucrum*, or shameful gain, of usury. Finally, for the first time, the theological principle was translated into secular law when the capitularies of Charlemagne outlawed usury in the Holy Roman Empire in the ninth century, defining it as the financial act in which "more is asked than given."

Between 1050 and 1175, the elements of usury were more carefully stipulated. The term was extended to include credit sales—of the type involved in much of today's merchandising—and usury came to be regarded as a crime in which restitution to the victim was demanded. Dante, the principal poet of the medieval church, relegated usurers to the outer edge of the seventh circle of Hell, calling them "the melancholy folk," their eyes "gushing forth their woe."[51] Later, usury began to be regarded as an offense against the words of Christ: "Lend freely, hoping nothing thereby." (Luke 6:35) Only those profits gained from moneylending, not profits from business transactions, were considered sinful, and professional usurers were excommunicated by the Church and prosecuted in secular courts. Moneylending later became by law the special province of the Jews, who were not concerned with the prohibitions of the Catholic Church, and of migrant groups of Lombards from the hill towns of northern Italy, who historically remained unmoved by ecclesiastical and social censure.

The Renaissance, introducing a period of humanism, commercial activity, and economic nationalism, saw the beginning of the decline in opprobrium directed against usury. Money began to be regarded not in the Aristotelian sense of a static commodity, but as a dynamic force creating additional wealth. Its possession by a borrower was seen in terms of use, creating advantages for him that he could reasonably and morally be expected to share with the lender. The risk of moneylending also came to be viewed as a justification for usury.[52]

John Calvin (1509–1524), the Protestant leader, is regarded as the first theologian to have insisted on the "fertility of money."[53] Calvin believed that moneylending should be judged by the Golden Rule; it would be sinful only if it injured one's neighbor, otherwise it was desirable. Each person's conscience was to be his guide. Loans to poor

51 Dante, *Divine Comedy*, Canto VII.
52 Homer, *History of Interest Rates*, pp. 104–132.
53 Noonan, Jr., *Scholastic Analysis of Usury*, p. 394.

persons would be clearly wicked, whereas loans to rich persons or to businessmen were no different from profit on a sale. "Biting usury," or usury that sucks the substance of another while the usurer runs no risk, and usury above the legal limits were both condemned by Calvin. Calvin's theological conceptions gradually became translated into secular law.

It is striking to note how the legal denotation of what is considered usurious and criminal varies with both the economic conditions and the social conscience of the particular society. In the Middle Ages, for instance, the average annual interest rate was about 43½ percent, a figure not much higher than that prevalent among small commercial businessmen in the United States during the 1930s, when, according to Louis N. Robinson and Rolf Nugent, interest normally ran between 30 and 42 percent annually.[54] Until the depression period, in fact, most writers favored a policy of laissez faire in regard to interest rates. The following statement of Christopher Tiedman is typical of that attitude:

> The rate of interest, like the price of merchandise, is determined ordinarily by the relation of supply and demand. Free trade in money is as much a right as free trade in merchandise. If the owner of the property in general has a natural right to ask whatever price he can get for his goods, the owner of money may exact whatever rate of interest the borrower may be willing to give. For interest is nothing more than the price asked for the use of money. No public interest can be urged for imposing this restriction upon the money lender.[55]

Today, in the United States, there is neither a total ban on the early conception of usury nor is there unrestricted freedom regarding interest rates. Policies, in fact, tend to show a crazy-quilt pattern; as the *Wall Street Journal* notes, "legislators in many states have riddled the usury law with so many 'exceptions' that it resembles a Swiss cheese composed mostly of holes with little cheese in between."[56] On regular long-term loans, eleven states set an interest ceiling of 6 percent, while nine states permit interest charges up to 10 percent, and Rhode Island allows charges up to 30 percent. Three states—Maine, New Hampshire, and Massachusetts—have no interest ceilings.

On the theory that the usury laws are designed to protect small, individual borrowers, loans to corporations are usually exempted from the legal interest limits. Even in lending to individuals, exceptions are often made to permit the time-sale financing of automobiles and appliances, the extension of revolving credit to retail charge-account customers, and the granting of small loans to needy borrowers. Small loan companies in New York are therefore permitted to charge up to 30 percent a year on loans of not more than $100, presumably limiting

54 Robinson and Nugent, *Regulation of the Small Loan Business*, pp. 248–265.
55 Tiedman, *Limitations of Police Power*, p. 239.
56 *Wall Street Journal*, June 4, 1968.

this kind of credit to borrowers whose lack of credit standing keeps them from obtaining a better rate. By contrast, persons better able to pay enjoy the protection of the 7½ percent usury ceiling in the same state.

Contrast Between Soviet and American Criminal Law

ROOTS OF SOVIET CRIMINAL LAW

The nourishment of criminal codes by both the philosophy and the history of a country is perhaps nowhere better illustrated than in the Soviet Union, where attempts have been made to mold the criminal code to the shape of the requirements of the Communist regime. Soviet philosophers maintain that there will be no crime whatsoever when the state manages to convince those recalcitrant individuals who persist in violating the law that they have no reason to do so. As one Soviet writer puts it:

> The material basis for crime prevention lies in the expansion of communist construction in the economic, political, and cultural fields. Because there is nothing in the nature of socialist society that could give rise to crime—for in the USSR the fundamental social causes of crime have already disappeared—every step forward in the development of communism increasingly contributes to the complete eradication of crime in our country.[57]

Crime therefore is defined officially in the Soviet Union as a direct affront to the regime, a selfish and stupid act on the part of an individual who does not appreciate the fact that he has no reason to violate the law. That force is employed against law violators is justified by the alleged transient nature of Soviet society. "Force," Marx said, "is the midwife of every old society pregnant with the new." A major difficulty in the Soviet Union, however, concerns the persistence of criminal behavior in the face of theories that insist it ought to disappear. Soviet publicists maintain that the country's crime rate is decreasing yearly, but the Soviet Union is the only western country that fails to publish official crime statistics. In addition, the alleged decrease in crime is difficult to reconcile with the growing use of capital punishment in the Soviet Union. A key ideological question, recently raised by George Feifer, pertains to what will ultimately be the attitude toward deviants under Communism. Attempting to respond to his own question, Feifer offers the following speculation:

> Will punishments be more severe because living conditions are more perfect? Will there be still less mercy for transgressors because Soviet society, rich and socialist, will more than ever be *presumed* to be rid

---

[57] Gertsenzon, "The Community's Role in the Prevention and Study of Crime," p. 17.

of them? The real test will come in two or three decades, and if it turns out that there *is* human nature, and that wrongdoing is part of it, then it will be clear that sordid wrongs have been done again in Russia in the name of a magnificent illusion. It will be the old story of chopping away at man to make him fit a theory and a grand design, of hurting him temporarily "for his own good" so that he will be *happy*.[58]

The expectation held out by Feifer seems to be that ultimately theory will have to give way to fact, that persistent crime will have to be viewed in terms other than traditional clichés about capitalistic decadence, as the following quote by Feifer suggests:

Maybe there will be crisis and change in Soviet criminology. Maybe the dogma will be allowed to erode and the causes for crime will be treated again in their baffling complexity. There are hints of this now; the spirit of inquiry is gathering momentum in Moscow. Progressive criminologists have recently stopped chanting that Soviet crime is a survival of capitalism and have begun to search for the *real* causes. So far, they say, the causes are not really understood.[59]

Pending the unlikely time, therefore, when there will be no crime in the Soviet Union, criminal justice there, as Morris Zelitch notes, will be caught between combative cross currents, since it consciously rejects the Western ideas of justice, yet finds many of those ideals deeply embedded in the spirit and values of the people.[60] The socialist theory has always maintained that the criminal is nothing more than a victim of the circumstances and environment under which he lives, deserving pity rather than scorn,[61] but the Soviet rules can hardly afford to give rein to this attitude in areas, such as crime, where the government feels particularly vulnerable.

Under the newest Soviet code of criminal law, promulgated in 1958, crime is defined as a "socially dangerous act" and capital punishment, "pending its abolition," is leveled as an "extraordinary penalty" for "terrorist acts."[62] The severest penalties in the Soviet Union are placed against acts that are defined as intending to harm, weaken, or overthrow the government, acts such as treason, espionage, assassination of officials of the state, intentional damaging of machinery of a state enterprise, and "giving aid of any character to the international bourgeoisie seeking to overthrow the communist system."[63] This last category, of course, can be quite elastic as illustrated by the sentencing of a woman in Novosibirsk to five years in a labor colony on the charge of "categorically refusing to work" and thus leading an "anti-socialist parasitic life." The Communist ideology, interested in economic

58 Feifer, *Justice in Moscow*, p. 339.
59 *Ibid.*
60 Zelitch, *Soviet Administration of Criminal Law*, p. 363.
61 *Ibid.*, p. 329.
62 *Soviet Criminal Law and Procedure.*
63 Hazard, *Law and Social Change in the U.S.S.R.*, p. 94.

advance, levels its punitive wrath not so much against what it considers minor derangements in the distribution of goods, such as theft
or robbery, but more against acts that interfere with the extension of
production and the preservation of existing goods. "Thou shalt not
steal," becomes transposed into a different principle in the Soviet
Union: "Thou shalt not waste."[64] The intensity of the diatribe on this
subject is indicated in a recent treatise on Soviet criminal justice,
which calls for efforts "to intensify the struggle against all sorts of
wastefulness, extravagance, and unproductive expenditures, directing
efforts toward cultivating thrift in Soviet people and a concern on the
part of each for preserving and multiplying the social wealth"; in the
same vein, Anashkin castigates not murder, assault, and rape, but
economic dereliction, saying that, "A slipshod, careless, criminally
negligent attitude toward the fulfillment of plan goals, which inflicts
damage on the entire economy is profoundly alien to the party and
government, as is every sort of bragging, deception of the state, and
window dressing."[65] Most Americans would probably find the criminal
restrictions on freedom in the Soviet Union personally abhorrent; presumably, citizens of the Soviet Union regard the relative economic
laissez faire in our country as socially—and therefore, ultimately, personally—undesirable and deserving of alteration by criminal sanctions.

It would be misleading, however, to leave any discussion of
Soviet criminal justice without noting that many responses to its operation seem to reflect, in large measure, standard, perhaps universal,
reactions to criminal behavior that are characteristic of urbanized,
relatively sophisticated, and reasonably law-abiding countries with
large middle-class memberships. The following quotation from the
Soviet newspaper *Izvestia* could easily have appeared in any metropolitan daily in the United States, with the substitution of American
designations for their Russian equivalents:

> Crime is being encouraged by paroles for multiple offenders and living
> conditions in the corrective labor colonies that are better than those
> of the courageous pioneers who opened up the new Siberian agricul-
> tural lands. One man has been sentenced to a colony four times for
> the same offense—grand theft. He has been given long sentences but
> never served them out. Why? Because for every 5-year sentence, he
> gets out in at least 1½ years, either through an amnesty, or probation
> for good behavior. This is the rule, not the exception.
>
> When men convicted of homicide, rape, assault, burglary, and robbery
> return to their home towns long before their sentences have been served,
> they arouse the disbelief and indignation of honest, hard-working
> people. Sentenced to 10 years, they come home in two and commit other
> crimes. They lose all respect for the court and the penalties outlined
> in the criminal code.[66]

64 Berman, *Justice in the U.S.S.R.*, p. 164.
65 Anashkin, "Tasks and Trends in the Development of Socialist Justice," p. 50.
66 *Chicago Tribune*, Dec. 15, 1965.

ROOTS OF AMERICAN CRIMINAL LAW

Dissimilar roots and stresses account for some of the emphases in the laws of the United States that differ from those in the Soviet Union, and we shall attempt to unravel and examine some of these American roots and stresses. The process of disentanglement involves numerous elements, some of them seemingly contradictory, for, as Harold Laski has pointed out, there are a great many cross-currents prevalent in the United States playing upon its criminal law. "The American tradition is one in which veneration for the law is at least equalled by the widespread habit of a violence which disregards laws," Laski believed; he traced this situation back to our early frontier civilization, our mixture of races and philosophies, and, most important to him, to the fact that "it was so easy, if the law was put aside, to make one's way to wealth on so immense a scale." Laski felt that there is a real sense in which American respect for law has of itself begotten lawlessness, and he explained this apparent paradox in the following manner:

> The effort to control every field of human conduct by statute—an obvious deposit of the Puritan heritage—with the result that the sale of tobacco and liquor can be prohibited, means that a group of men would arise to supply those wants to which the law refused satisfaction, The more widespread the want, the greater would be the profit in supplying it, and the more earnest would be the zeal of those responsible for applying the law to see that it was enforced. Out of this there developed quite naturally a sense of satisfaction in outwitting the law makers. And once there is that kind of tension in the social environment, which my generation has witnessed in the conflict between those who regarded prohibition as almost an article of religious faith and those to whom it was a wanton interference with personal freedom, the stage is set for the breeding of violence by the attempt to compel obedience to the law.[67]

The proliferation of and ready recourse to criminal law in the United States is a national quality that has been noted continually by commentators attempting to interpret the American scene. Part of this quality is undoubtedly related to the enormous growth in the complexity of life in the United States, which necessitates additional social controls as the fabric of the society becomes more complicated and the individual becomes more anonymous. At least a segment of this attitude, however, appears to lie in an inveterate folk belief that "there ought to be a law." In a recent book, Max Lerner attempted to express and interpret this situation in terms of American national character, with a thesis that would be difficult to establish scientifically, but that contains elements of considerable hypothetical interest:

> America today, as in the past, presents the picture of a lawless society and an overlegislated one. In some of the earlier societies the reliance was less upon detailed legal norms and penalties than upon custom

67 Laski, *American Democracy*, pp. 31–32.

and the sanctions of community opinion. But America is the type-society of the West in which little is left to loose community action, and the characteristic way of dealing with crime is to set down definite statements of legal transgressions and punishments. Nevertheless, Americans consider crime a problem they cannot master, which will continue to grow because it is an outcropping of some inner disease of their society. Recognizing this, they also recoil from it, thus displacing on the criminal their own guilt and powerlessness—which may help explain why the treatment of crime has lagged. To feel mastery over the environment, over things and money, and yet to feel baffled by so elementary a fact as crime, has become a source of frustration.[68]

The Relativity of Crime

Since many factors determine the nature of criminal law, it is apparent that the final product will vary greatly from one society to another and from one time to another. The relative nature of crime provides one of the most difficult problems for the criminologist attempting to analyze criminal behavior with any consistency and to define it with any discrimination. Harry Elmer Barnes and Negley Teeters, for instance, have pointed out that at least three-fourths of the prisoners in American correctional institutions could not have been incarcerated only fifty years ago, since the acts they committed were not then considered criminal violations.[69] The federal criminal law alone has expanded from the thirty-three sections of the Crimes Act of 1790 to the more than 5,000 sections of Title 18 of the United States Code in 1968, not to mention numerous sections that carry criminal penalties, which are scattered throughout other parts of the Code. To a great extent, this variability accounts for the futility of comparative statements on criminal behavior for different periods or among different countries.

Shifting definitions of crime can be illustrated against a background of three variables—time, place, and circumstance. Technological advance is one of the more obvious conditions reflected in the criminal law. In 1957, for example, the Mansfield Society, organized in New Jersey ninety years before, held its final meeting; the group had been dedicated to apprehending horse thieves, but, as the newspapers noted, "the vigilantes are to disband because one can hardly find a horse thief around here anymore. Or a horse, for that matter." Other illustrations abound. Selling adulterated patent medicines—medicines that often contain addictive opium derivatives—was perfectly legal prior to the passage of the Pure Food and Drug Act at the beginning of the century; after the enactment of the law, sales became serious criminal offenses.

68 Lerner, *America as a Civilization*, p. 661.
69 Barnes and Teeters, *New Horizons in Criminology*, p. 74.

Geographic variations in definitions of crime are often revealing, both in terms of the omission of statutory provisions in certain areas and in terms of the seriousness with which different jurisdictions view the same behavior. Even in as relatively homogeneous a juridical region as the United States, we find sharp discrepancies both in the laws and the penalties concerning certain behavior. About one-third of the more than 3,000 counties in the United States, for instance, including all counties in the state of Mississippi, consider the sale of alcoholic beverages, excluding beer, to be a criminal offense, while numerous counties adjacent to them regard the same activity as a perfectly legitimate and respectable business enterprise. Some states place extremely harsh penalties on various sex offenses, while other states deal with them very leniently or ignore them altogether. California, for instance, has a maximum of fifty years for the crime of incest; for the same offense, Virginia sets the maximum penalty at one year and/or a fine of $500. Oklahoma and West Virginia both view second cousins as within the bounds of incestuous consanguinity, a view taken by none of the other forty-eight states.[70]

Divergencies in criminal sanctions tend to multiply as the geographic distance increases and cultural patterns vary. Ultimately, an investigator is forced to accept the broad generalization put forth by a penetrating student of cultural patterns, William Lecky (1838–1903), who wrote, "There is no line of conduct which has not, at some other time and place, been condemned, and which has not, at some other time and place, been enjoined as a duty."[71]

Examples abound of acts that at one time or another have come under the sanction of the criminal law in various places. The Egyptians punished with death anyone revealing the burial place of the sacred bull, Apis, or anyone causing, even by accident, the death of a vulture, a cat, or an ichneumon (a mongoose who was supposed by the ancient Egyptians to devour crocodile eggs). Early Christians were thrown to wild beasts and crucified by Roman emperors on the basis of their religion. During the time of Henry VIII in England, it was a crime to predict the death of the king. Driving with reins was once a crime in Russia, the immemorial custom having been for the driver to ride on the horse or to run by the horse's side.[72]

The circumstances that surround a given act can also determine whether it represents a desirable piece of behavior, a meretricious act, or a criminal offense. If a local building is used as a gymnasium on Saturday night, a spectator might reasonably cheer with abandon for his favorite team. But if he were to engage in the same behavior in the middle of the sermon the following morning when the same building was being used for church services, his behavior could constitute

70 Harper, *Problems of the Family*, p. 281.
71 Lecky, *History of European Morals*, pp. 101–102.
72 Wines, *Punishment and Reformation*, Chap. 2.

the criminal violation of disturbing the peace. Norwood East, a British criminologist, provides a further example of the same phenomenon, showing how closely behavior must be examined before it can be determined whether it is socially desirable or criminal. He tells of a British soldier who volunteered to donate blood to an officer who suffered from a severe wound, which was seemingly a selfless and commendable act. Slightly before the transfusion, however, it was discovered that the soldier suffered from a venereal disease, and that he desired to infect the officer, against whom he had a grudge.[73]

It is apparent, then, that the realm of criminal law changes to keep pace with social emphases, and that the ingredients of an act— its circumstances—must be examined to place it into its proper perspective. In recent years, for instance, criminal offenses relating to airplanes have grown numerously, and it is certain that as air traffic becomes increasingly congested, flying will become more closely circumscribed by laws carrying criminal sanctions. The same tendency is found in regard to space matters, where legal specialists now debate questions such as: who has jurisdiction above our atmosphere?; can a nation shoot down a satellite taking military pictures?; how should space acts, such as piracy, smuggling, and felonious assault, be defined?[74]

Crime and Culture: An Overview

It has often been maintained that a society gets the criminals it deserves. This broad cliché, allegedly first pronounced by the French criminologist Jean-Alexandre-Eugène Lacasagne,[75] might apply to a people's government, religious institutions, and family organization. As with so many clichés of such imprecise reference, it tells us very little beyond the fact that social organizations generate human behavior which reflects in many respects characteristics peculiar to themselves.

If any meaning is to be garnered from such a broad view of culture and crime, it would indicate that the type, character, and frequency of crime within a given society reflect its historic conditions, its psychological and cultural characteristics, its aspirations, and its objectives. Crimes in different parts of the world and in different types of societies mirror the most basic values of a people and the means that the society has devised for the fulfillment and realization of those values. In acknowledging this, however, we must keep in mind that most societies are endlessly complex mechanisms and that the cultural system in each society is itself extensively involved. To say, therefore, that crimes reflect the culture and social structure is of little significance, unless we recognize the variety of interrelated patterns that may

73 East, *Society and the Criminal,* p. 255.
74 Haley, "Law and Upper Space."
75 Söderman, *Policeman's Lot,* p. 329.

alter the meaning of common values for different groups and different individuals within the society and that may deflect or impede the attainment of certain goals for different members of the society.

It is also necessary to keep in mind the different meanings that social values may have for different persons as well as the functional effectiveness of social values, particularly with respect to contemporary reality. It is one thing to cherish a value because it represents a magnificent ideal to which an individual or an entire people may feel themselves committed; it is quite another to have as values the everyday pursuit of objects and objectives. Although historic and idealistic sets of values may play some role in determining the course of the social order, their function as prominent and controlling forces in the life of the society may be insubstantial.

The discrepancy between social statement and social fact also must be kept in mind when examining the written edicts of our own and other societies, even though the social statement remains an avenue of insight into one aspect of a culture. Although there are values that a given society may have learned to esteem, the pragmatic reference to such values may be almost entirely theoretical, transitory, or ephemeral. These are the values to which people may often pay lip service, but they may, in actuality, have limited effect on the daily routine of living. To take a common example, religious sentiments in a number of societies—admirable as the attainment of such value objectives might appear—may relate only slightly to how people actually order their lives. Or strong, even impassioned, sentiments of a given group about its preeminent belief in the fundamental rights of human equality or liberty, may not actually be attainable in the kinds of living arrangements that the society allows. Later, we shall look more intensively into written edicts regarding what criminal behavior constitutes in the United States, and then we shall compare them to actual situations.

Summary

The historical development and variation in conceptualizations of crime and the structure of criminal laws provide a considerable amount of information about the actual societies as they are discerned through the sanctions of their law. Illustrations of varying acts labelled criminal at different times in different places stand as a warning against undiscriminating statements on the specific nature of criminal behavior. In the long run, since criminal statutes invariably reflect the changing conception of criminal morality, we find continual emendations of and additions to the existing body of criminal law as society itself changes. In modern societies, as we have seen, forms of behavior that are presently regarded as criminal were scarcely known a few generations ago and, indeed, were completely unknown a few centuries ago. The rapidity of social change, especially since the turn of the century, largely induced by the technological developments of the contemporary world, has produced and is continuing to produce situations that constantly require redefinition with respect to the meaning of criminal behavior. Biological, medical, and scientific discoveries create new human situations that compel new forms of regulation; the abridgement of such regulations by certain individuals in turn opens up new areas to which the criminal statutes must be adapted.

While the nature of crime depends upon the changing social and historic context, the organization of society determines, to a considerable degree, which segments of it are most likely to commit the principal crimes during a given period. Two things must be considered in this connection: (1) the nature of the *prescriptive* cultural codes, and (2) the structural organization of the society itself. We have thus far emphasized culture from the standpoint of the kinds of values—the goals and objectives—to which the society aspires and which it tends to hold in high veneration. There are, however, *instrumental* values that must likewise be considered. Culture not only tells us what we should and should not want, but also how we should and should not proceed in achieving such objectives. All societies are organized in such a way, in fact, that it becomes relatively easier for some individuals rather than others to conform to the social prescriptions and proscriptions defined by the instrumental culture. By the same token, certain individuals, by the very positions they occupy in society, are far more vulnerable than others to the pressures that facilitate the commission of crimes. This and similar conceptions form the background for attempts to analyze criminal behavior by the use of intuitive and scientific methods. In the next chapter we will examine some of these approaches, both from a historical perspective and in terms of their assets and shortcomings as potential tools leading toward the contemporary understanding of criminal behavior.

For Further Reading

The four following volumes present historical and crosscultural material on the process of criminal law in four different societies, providing a core of information on the relationships between culture and criminal sanctions.

BERMAN, HAROLD J. *Justice in Russia: An Interpretation of Soviet Law,* 2nd ed. Cambridge, Mass.: Harvard University Press, 1965.

CALHOUN, GEORGE M. *The Growth of Criminal Law in Ancient Greece.* Berkeley: University of California Press, 1927.

GOLDIN, HYMAN E. *Hebrew Criminal Law and Procedure.* New York: Twayne Publishers, 1952.

SEMMES, RAPHAEL. *Crime and Punishment in Early Maryland.* Baltimore: Johns Hopkins Press, 1936.

The following sources review and analyze three forms of human activity, often outlawed for reasons that go far back into history. The third selection also offers considerable insight into the manner in which the judicial process functions.

HOMER, SIDNEY. *A History of Interest Rates*. New Brunswick, N.J.: Rutgers University Press, 1963.

SILVING, HELEN. "Suicide and the Law," in Edwin S. Shneidman and Norman L. Farberow (eds.). *Clues to Suicide*. New York: McGraw-Hill, 1957, pp. 79–95.

"THE BLUE LAW CASES," in *United States Reports*. Vol. 366 (1961), pp. 420–642.

HALL, JEROME. *Theft, Law and Society*, 2nd ed. Indianapolis: Bobbs-Merrill, 1952.

This is the classic study in contemporary criminology of the relationship between social structure and the historic development and application of the criminal law, traced through the life history of the law of theft.

4

The Science of Criminology

Criminology represents a branch of social science, and, as such, it is committed to the achievement of an understanding of the roots and manifestations of different aspects of behavior that violate criminal law. All science seeks understanding, but no science is tied in its approach to a value position, unless the attempt to achieve understanding of behavior as a worthwhile endeavor is considered a value position. In the natural sciences, work that led to the control of atomic energy did not dictate whether an atomic bomb should be dropped on Hiroshima, whether atomic energy should be kept only for peaceful purposes, or whether it should never be utilized under any circumstances. In criminology, the understanding of criminal behavior may be utilized for the control of crime, or it may be merely a pursuit desirable in itself, with understanding representing a worthwhile end, whatever its practical consequences.

The eminent English philosopher Bertrand Russell has indicated in the following statement how the findings of science and the practice of science tend to become "practical" enterprises, with investigators and theoreticians trying to gain understanding in order to control and manipulate:

> Science in its beginnings was due to men who were in love with the world. They perceived the beauty of the stars and the seas, of the winds and the mountains. Because they loved them their thoughts dwelt upon them, and they wished to understand them more intimately than a mere outward contemplation made possible. . . . But step by step, as science developed, the impulse of love which gave it birth has been increasingly thwarted, while the impulse of power (control through knowledge), which was at first a mere camp-follower, has gradually usurped command in virtue of its unforseen success. The lover of nature has been baffled, the tyrant over nature has been rewarded.[1]

1 Russell, *Scientific Outlook*, pp. 262–263.

In criminology, the drive for practical application is perhaps more self-evident than in many other kinds of scientific work. Why should a person want to study about behavior such as crime, it might be asked, unless he cares to reduce the amount of crime and help law-abiding persons to be secure in their person and property? It is some-times insisted, in fact, contrary to Russell's position, that understanding as an end of science is itself a luxury and self-indulgence that contemporary society, beset with practical problems, cannot afford. In the words of August Heckscher, director of the Twentieth Century Fund, "research which disavows any responsibility except that of being objective and nonutilitarian may well qualify as 'pure.' But it is a kind of purity which a society—particularly a society in an age of change—can overvalue"; Heckscher further noted, with respect to foundations that make research awards, "it would be a tragedy if the modern foundation, under the false yoke of methodology or scientific objectivity, were to find itself cut off from the public it must serve."[2]

It seems apparent that the bias in criminological work is clearly in the direction of "applied" rather than "pure" research. For example, typologies of prison inmates almost invariably are constructed in terms of, among other things, the inmates' treatment potential and their risk of recidivism. Criminology textbooks, like medical treatises, almost always devote a large portion of their coverage to treatment; even a theory as general as "differential association," which we will consider later in this chapter, has been said to be particularly valuable be-cause its principles may be utilized for the reduction of crime.[3] It needs to be emphasized, however, that the applications of scientific work do not necessarily and need not flow from the work itself, and that it will always be debatable whether or not control of crime is a desirable social end. It might be true, for instance, that a society with few or no criminals—with no objects for the enhancement of self-righteousness among the conforming—becomes so bland and homo-geneous that it will readily fall prey to its external enemies. In this vein, it is sometimes argued that personal security in a country such as Sweden, brought about by far-reaching government social-service programs, has sapped the vitality of the nation and has created various forms of malaise, which are absent in countries with less "desirable" social conditions.[4] This argument, however, is extremely complex, and adjudication of its merits would require clear definition of terms and much more reliable data than we now possess.

Most scientific work pushes toward the formulation of theoretical statements. A sound theory offers a highly generalized explanation that applies to all of the facts that come within its purview, and

2 Heckscher, "Rightly To Be Great," pp. 9, 14.
3 See Cressey, "Changing Criminals"; Cressey, "Social Psychological Foundations for Using Criminals in the Rehabilitation of Criminals."
4 Fleisher, Sweden: The Welfare State.

accounts for a variety of specific circumstances. Theories create a *frame of reference*—a strictly defined vantage point from which a problem must be examined. The frame of reference indicates the nature of the theoretical explanation, the character or structure of the logical processes that are to be employed, and finally the kinds of evidence that must be gathered to demonstrate the validity of the explanation.

In criminology, theories have tended to far outrun the factual foundations upon which they should rest. Lord Acton once noted that "the worst use of theory is to make man insensible to fact."[5] In addition, criminological theories have tended to concentrate on the offender and on the circumstances that brought him into conflict with the law, to the exclusion of other elements in the criminal process. For example, the behavior of the criminal might be taken as a given, and questions raised only about the circumstances that lead the society to outlaw his behavior. In this approach, stress is placed on the ingredients of the social structure that led to proscriptions against certain kinds of behavior, rather than on the causes for the individual's criminal behavior. Finally, as we shall mention later in greater detail, the attempt to establish all-embracing theories of criminal behavior—themes that in one formulation include explanations of incest, shoplifting, malicious mischief, gambling, burglary, and antitrust violations—has tended to produce statements that are either so general that they are applicable with only slight alterations as explanations of all human behavior, criminal and noncriminal, or so tautological that there are merely extended definitions of the behavior that they seek to explain. It is in this sense that Leon Radzinowicz, Wolfson Professor of Criminology at Cambridge University, insisted that the world's criminologists have been guilty of "hunting for far-fetched hypotheses and clouding their search with pretentiousness"; Radzinowicz suggests that attempts to elucidate the causes of crime should be set aside, and that "the most that can be done is to throw light on the combination of factors or circumstances that can be associated with crime."[6]

Omitting consideration of causal explanation is not, however, compatible with the approach in the present book. This book is based on the view that causes of various forms of crime should be sought, but that at this stage of knowledge the search should take diverse forms. Understanding can be found within different perspectives, depending upon the interests of the investigator and the uses to which his findings are put. Some results obviously will prove superior to others in terms of the value system of science, because they are more generalizable and carry with them insights into cognate forms of human activity. Some may have greater predictive value, while others may be apt to stimulate more comprehensive investigation. By no means,

5 Acton, *History of Freedom*, p. 156.
6 Radzinowicz, *In Search of Criminology*, p. 94.

therefore, can all criminological investigations be embraced with equal intellectual hospitality, nor can a hodgepodge of eclectic viewpoints and a scattering of empirical conclusions be paraded as scientific contributions of surpassing importance. However, it is necessary that, in an overview of research and speculation regarding criminal activity, there be a certain receptivity to a broad range of material and views. This conclusion reflects the state of social science and especially criminological theory today—the knowledge that criminological research may serve diverse ends, and the commitment of many to consider all work that meets the requirements of scientific integrity and sophistication. Percy Bridgman, an eminent physicist, indicates the kind of approach in research needed to lay the groundwork for the most fruitful scientific outcomes—a view supported in this volume:

> I like to say that there is no scientific method as such, but that the most vital feature of the scientist's procedure has been merely to do his utmost with his mind, *no holds barred*. This means in particular that no special privileges are accorded to authority or tradition, that personal prejudices and predilections are carefully guarded against, that one makes continued check to assure oneself that one is not making mistakes, and that any line of inquiry will be followed that appears at all promising.[7]

There are various other dicta that can be used to guide the selection and evaluation of materials relevant to an understanding of criminal behavior. Well-grounded theory should always be preferred to an accumulation of factual material, and poor theory should not take precedence over well-documented facts. Unfortunately, in some segments of social science inquiry the professional prestige associated with theory building and generalized speculation tends to denigrate investigations that bring forth previously unavailable data that cannot for the moment be integrated into any substantial explanatory system.

In the same manner, quantified material tends in some social science circles to be granted more credence than matters that are not expressed, and sometimes cannot be expressed, in mathematical form. The result sometimes is a concern with method that obscures the essential meaning of the material being examined. Henri Poincaire, a renowned scientist, once noted that "while the physical scientists devote their time to solving their problems, the social scientists devote theirs to discussing their methods."[8] Numerous similar warnings have been posted regarding the camouflaging of understanding with the trappings, but not the essence, of science. "The real academic job is to absorb an idea, to put it into perspective with other ideas," Robert Penn Warren, the well-known poet and novelist, has written, "not to dilute it with lingo."[9] Paul Goodman, the writer and social critic,

7 Bridgman, *Reflections of a Physicist*, p. 370.
8 Quoted in Cairns, *Law and the Social Sciences*, p. 6.
9 Ellison and Walter, "Robert Penn Warren," p. 200.

has observed that "the present-day preoccupation with careful methodology is academically praiseworthy, but it does not lead to intensely
interesting propositions. One cannot help feeling that a good part of
the current concern with statistics and polling is a way of being
active in the 'area' without being actively engaged in the subject matter.
There is a good deal of sharpening of tools but not much agriculture."[10] David Riesman, in a biography of Thorstein Veblen, addresses
the same issue with the remark that "Veblen is the opposite extreme
from the stereotype of the sociologist who, with no philosophical training, consumes his time affixing exact degrees of significance to in-
significant correlations and never gets around to discovering anything
new about society."[11] Equally noteworthy, finally, is the comment of
the theologian Reinhold Niebuhr that "scholarship is good if it obeys
the standards of objectivity and honesty, but it may still be nothing
but pedantry if the grace of imagination is not added."[12]

It needs to be noted that the quantification of a concept in no
way insures its scientific fruitfulness. Consider, for instance, the following concept: A "b coefficient" is the number of hairs on anybody's
head divided by the number of years he has lived, raised to the fourth
power. The concept is perfectly precise and quantitative, though it has
no scientific significance, since it does not lend itself to any relation,
functional or otherwise, with any other concept. As Edward Madden
notes, "The scientist needs mathematics, to be sure, but he needs even
more a scientific genius for the formation of useful hypotheses."[13]

In criminology today, there is a need for more detailed empirical
studies of forms of criminal behavior and for thoughtful attempts to
categorize such behavior into groups that make sense for particular
purposes and into other groups that prove useful for other purposes.
If, for instance, the aim of classification is to understand, and perhaps
to control, outbreaks of violence, then crime patterns showing underlying violent characteristics might well be examined as a group. If
the attempt is to determine the impact of recent changes in the law
on consequent criminal behavior, then those offenses showing recent
alterations in legal status can be examined together and then broken
down into groups showing similar outcomes. To reiterate, the study
of criminal behavior does not seem at this time to have reached that
point of intellectual sophistication where it appears warranted to foreclose promising investigative paths because they do not coincide with
preconceived theoretical notions. To say that crime is a "social"
phenomena and thus to omit consideration of genetic traits related to
criminal behavior is to act out the cautionary tale of the elephant and
the blind men, each of whom mistook that segment of the animal
which he grasped for its total being. To insist that crime is a function

10 Goodman, *Growing Up Absurd*, p. 261.
11 Riesman, *Thorstein Veblen*, p. 48.
12 Niebuhr, in *Responsibility in Mass Communication*, p. xxi.
13 Madden, *Structure of Scientific Thought*, p. 10.

of psychiatric aberrations is to foreclose prematurely consideration
of numerous other factors of a nonpsychiatric nature that enter into
the occurrence of a criminal act. To say that causation must be the
exclusive concern of criminology is to neglect meaningful areas of inquiry concerned with such things as the social definitions of deviance
and the social responses to it. To maintain that white-collar crime and
organized crime must be explicable by a single theoretical formulation
is to neglect important dimensions of the two forms of behavior that
differ notably one from the other.

Pioneers in Criminology

The development of philosophical and theoretical points of view—
criminological and noncriminological, scientific and nonscientific—
reflects the culture of the period in which such views emerge in certain
fairly precise ways. In the first place, the culture tends to accept only
those emergent or novel points of view that have some congruence
with their culture. The ground-breaking work of Cesare Bonesana,
Marchese di Beccaria, an obscure twenty-six-year-old amateur in criminal law and penology who in 1764 published his famous essay, *Dei
Delitti e delle Pene,* translated as *Essay on Crimes and Punishments,*
for example, was steeped in the humanitarian rationalism of his
times.[14] Second, each culture tends toward a dominant focus, reflecting
the principal interests and institutions of the period. This focus serves
as the arbiter of the great ethical dichotomies of right or wrong, truth
or falsehood, and as the background for judgments of what constitutes
valid and invalid fact. Finally, the effects of a culture are felt in the
permissiveness it grants to novel behavior and its tolerance for a
given point of view. In the last resort, the acceptance of an idea depends upon the extent to which the culture permits individuals to
respond to issues of critical choice.

In the field of criminology, the relationship between culture and
theories of behavior has created a number of anomalous issues. Much
of contemporary criminological and correctional thought, for example,
emanates from the latter part of the eighteenth and the early nineteenth centuries, before contemporary scientific ideology had taken
root. The result has been that, while our thinking has been profoundly
affected by the deeply humanitarian impulses of some of the theorists
of that time, an attempt to scientifically evaluate their viewpoints
creates critical problems. Indeed, many of the dilemmas of contemporary criminology stem from the fact that the rational humanitarianism
of the early classical thinkers in criminology is based upon assumptions
that the modern criminologist regards with considerable scientific
suspicion, although, at the same time, he may support the high-minded
ethical considerations that led to their formulation.

14 Phillipson, *Three Criminal Law Reformers.*

The men who pioneered the development of modern criminology not only reflected their cultural epochs but also left the ineradicable stamp of their own personalities on the field of criminological thought. Among the seventeen notable figures examined in *Pioneers in Criminology*, edited by Hermann Mannheim, the vast majority were Europeans, and the Italians and the English played the most prominent roles in the development of criminology. Only two, Isaac Ray, a groundbreaking New England psychiatrist, and Charles Doe, a New England jurist, were Americans. The backgrounds of the pioneers were as diverse as their nationalities. Eight of them—Cesare Beccaria, Jeremy Bentham, Enrico Ferri, Raffaele Garofalo, Pedro Montero, Gabriel Tarde, Hans Gross, and Charles Doe—were lawyers. Five—Isaac Ray, Henry Maudsley, Cesare Lombroso, Charles Goring, and Gustav Aschaffenburg—were physicians with primarily psychiatric interests. Durkheim and Bonger were sociologists. Alexander Maconochie was a naval officer, and Haviland an architect. Their span of influence, as Mannheim notes, covered a little more than two hundred years:

> The aggregate life span of our pioneers ranges from the year 1738, when Beccaria was born, to 1944 when Aschaffenburg died. Chronologically, only one of them, Beccaria, is entirely an eighteenth-century figure. Bentham and Haviland belong to both the eighteenth and nineteenth centuries. Ray and Doe entirely to the latter; and all the others had their feet in both the nineteenth and twentieth centuries. Chronologically, too, it is interesting to observe that two of the most momentous events in the history of criminology occurred in the sixties and seventies of the eighteenth and nineteenth centuries: the publication of Beccaria's *Dei Delitti e delle Pene* in 1764 and Lombroso's *L'uomo Delinquente* in 1876.[15]

Mannheim asks if we should expect similar "bombshells" in the next two decades and from what direction.

THE CLASSICAL BEGINNINGS

The cultural setting within which Beccaria completed his famous work in 1764 placed great stress on man's rational facilities and his growing sense of individual rights and prerogatives. At the same time, many theological conceptions concerning the origin and destiny of man survived. Significant in the cultural complex that affected Beccaria's thinking was the widespread belief in the contractual beginnings of human society—a compact in which individuals agreed to surrender their sovereignty to rulers of society in exchange for protection from the hazards of total freedom. Permeating this doctrine was the powerful conception that man could determine his own destiny and political future by the controlled use of reason and the accumulation of knowledge based on rational discourse rather than on fear and super-

15 Mannheim, *Pioneers in Criminology*, p. 3.

stition—a conception nurtured by a line of distinguished philosophers beginning with Thomas Hobbes.[16]

Fundamentally, the classical criminologists believed that man was motivated by *hedonistic* impulses, the desire to escape pain and to derive pleasure from his actions. In a satiric comment on Jeremy Bentham, an English social philosopher who shared Beccaria's views, the poet Helen Bevington has written:

> They say he cherished men,
> Their happiness, and then
> Calmly assumed one could
> Devise cures for their good.
> Believing all men the same
> And happiness their aim.
> He reckoned right and wrong
> By felicity—lifelong
> And by such artless measure
> As the quality of pleasure
> For pain he had a plan
> Absurd old gentleman.[17]

More prosaically, critics of the Beccarian position note that different persons have different views of pleasure and pain and that individuals often may not be rational in their calculations of the consequences of acts. Beccaria, to the contrary, believed that man was endowed with the capacity to make rational and free-will choices as to how he should behave when facing different contingencies—a view reflecting the now discredited psychological principle of separate faculties of human behavior.

The discretionary powers accorded to the courts of their day were particularly offensive to thinkers of the classical period. In paraphrasing Gilbert and Sullivan, judges were unable to "make the punishment fit the crime" under statutory codes that failed to define all punishable human conditions and frailties. The result was that justice became arbitrary—offensive not only because of its cruelty and inequity, but because it defied what was believed to be man's normal sense of logic and reason.

Beccaria, inveighing powerfully against this sort of injustice, sought to establish a system of jurisprudence in which the discretionary powers of the courts would be removed and in which, based upon the hedonistic principle of the day, the proper quantum of punishment would be meted out for each quantum of crime. Such a system involved an enormous reclassification of criminal offenses, and became symbolized by the traditional figure of the blind goddess of justice holding the scales of equity. What is not fully appreciated is the fact that the strong statistical emphasis in subsequent criminological re-

16 See Barker, *Social Contract*; Gough, *The Social Contract*.
17 Bevington, "A Bomb for Jeremy Bentham," p. 33.

search was furthered by Beccaria's conception that all crimes should be precisely classified in accordance with a quantitative spectrum. The result has been a legacy that, to this day, dominates a considerable portion of our codes of justice. The criminal law still adheres in large measure to the psychological and free-will doctrines enunciated more than 200 years ago by Beccaria.

THE POSITIVIST SCHOOL

The sharp distinctions between the classical school of criminology and the positivist school have been succinctly drawn by Ray Jeffery in the following terms:

> The Classical School defined crime in legal terms; the Positive School rejected the legal definition of crime. The Classical School focused attention on crime as a legal entity; the Positive School focused attention on the act as a psychological entity. The Classical School emphasized free will; the Positive School emphasized determinism. The Classical School theorized that punishment had a deterrent effect; the Positive School said that punishment should be replaced by a scientific treatment of criminals calculated to protect society.[18]

The positivists—under the intellectual leadership of Cesare Lombroso, physician and psychiatrist and professor of forensic medicine at the University of Turin for a considerable period of his career—are generally credited with being the first to regard criminal behavior within a modern scientific context. In 1876, when the first edition of Lombroso's celebrated treatise on crime, *L'uomo Delinquente (The Criminal Man)*, was published, the entire force of the nineteenth-century scientific revolution in biology and physics was already under way.

The primary intellectual climate of the period was supplied by the work of Darwin. Theological presuppositions were rudely shaken, and to many it seemed that traditional beliefs concerning man and his nature were shattered for once and all. As Joseph Wood Krutch, a modern commentator, put it, prior to this age man might aspire to be one of the angels—now he became a higher form of ape.[19] The theory of evolution became an instrument not only to examine the modification of the species but also to look into all phases of human phenomena. Implicit in all such explanatory attempts was an enthusiastic acceptance of natural causes and the capacity of physical conditions to elicit man's potentialities for his survival. Such a view implied rigorously deterministic explanations of human behavior in a science of inescapable causal chains and concentrated on the search for physical evidence that would fill in the missing parts of the gigantic jigsaw puzzle of man's historical growth and present condition. Confidence in this shattering new intellectual task was eventually to cul-

18 Jeffery, "Historical Development of Criminology," p. 366.
19 Krutch, *Measure of Man*, p. 147.

minate in Herbert Spencer's proud boast that, given a little more
time, there was little about man that modern science would not be
able to answer.[20]

The contemporary significance of quantitative and empirical
evidence comes to sharp focus in the work of Lombroso. It had been
assumed that concentration on a profusion of measurable facts in
the study of crime would lead to wholly naturalistic explanations. This
inductive emphasis differed considerably from modern scientific research in which carefully defined hypotheses and constructs are set
up to be tested. However, an examination of the work of Lombroso
suggests that his approach prompted theoretical views that appeared
sensible in the light of knowlege of the time.

In keeping with the evolutionary doctrine of his day, Lombroso
thought he was able to identify physical characteristics of offenders in
the form of facial, cephalic, and bodily anomalies (subsequently referred to as the "Lombrosian stigmata"), suggesting that criminals
were an atavistic form of man. Corresponding to these physical characteristics of inadequacy were retarded psychological characteristics,
which he believed rendered such individuals incapable of adapting
to more highly advanced social orders and were crucial in bringing
about criminal behavior. The physically retarded types constituted for
Lombroso the so-called "born criminals," or individuals committed
by their deficient heredity to inevitable entry into criminal activity.
Lombroso acknowledged, however, that not all criminals fell into
this class. He felt that more than half of the criminals of his day were
either insane or, in his introduction of a provocative new concept,
criminaloid, that is, individuals who by physical and psychological
constitution were predisposed toward crime in the face of eliciting
circumstances. The criminality of this group would result only if its
members were confronted with environmental conditions capable of
inciting such behavior. Comparable to the medical concept of diathesis
—a predisposition toward a given disease with no certainty that it will
result—this aspect of Lombroso's thinking raises a number of issues
strikingly similar to certain modern social psychological concepts. Indeed, the contemporary criminologist Hans von Hentig, in his doctrine
of "temptation" as a causal factor of crime, indicates that there is
always a vulnerable group in each society.[21] And the psychiatrist
Lucien Bovet, in a study of delinquency, refers to youths who are
vulnerable but not yet delinquents as "the reserve troops of delinquency."[22]

In numerous subsequent editions of Lombroso's work, his view
of the causes of crime was successively enlarged to take into account a
wide range of contributory environmental conditions. Certainly his

20 Spencer, Sociology, p. 321.
21 Von Hentig, The Criminal and His Victim, p. 450.
22 Bovet, Psychiatric Aspects of Juvenile Delinquency, p. 20.

more comprehensive views, removed from the restricted biological perspective with which he has traditionally been identified, indicate that Lombroso drew closer to modern theories of crime as his career matured. Among other items Lombroso examined were climate and rainfall, marriage customs, banking practices, and religious organizations.

On the other hand, the hard-shelled, early biological views of Lombroso have sometimes been regarded with more intellectual compassion than they seem to merit. That Lombroso scorned the armchair and employed the laboratory for his work is no cause for categoric endorsement, unless it can be maintained that poor science is by definition invariably superior to first-rate philosophy. Lombroso's caricatured case histories (". . . a demi-type . . . her ears stand out, she has big jaws, and cheek bones, and very black hair, besides other anomalies, such as gigantic canine teeth and dwarf incisors . . ."[23]), and his elaborate torturings of logic, such as the attempt to relate the fatness of prostitutes, which "strikes those who look at them en masse" to the obesity of Hottentots and, then, to relate both of these to a theory of atavism (insufficient progression along the evolutionary path),[24] represent dolorous twistings of the scientific method. The best criticism of Lombroso remains that of the French anthropologist Paul Topinard (1830–1911), who gave criminology its name and who, when shown a collection of Lombroso's pictures of asymmetric and stigmatic criminals, remarked wryly that the pictures looked no different than those of his own friends.[25] It took many decades, unfortunately, before the main body of criminological thought accepted the validity of this singularly perceptive criticism of Lombroso's work.

PARTICULARISTIC EMPHASES IN CRIMINOLOGY

Cultish outlooks in criminology have been created by public pressures for simple solutions and academic overemphases on transient, single "explanatory" items. Although it must not be assumed that emphasis on a specialized point of view will in itself invariably produce doctrinaire and partisan viewpoints, the history of criminology has shown a peculiar disposition to particularistic points of view. Particularism, as the term is employed in this context, refers to the tendency to overemphasize one set of factors or conditions at the expense of others, or the tendency to overstress a highly selective theoretical viewpoint.

The birth of divergent particularized views has tended to result from attempts to reject or criticize other particularized schools of thought. Thus, while the early classical thinkers were concerned with crime as a legal entity occasioned by man's free will, the positivists,

23 Lombroso and Ferrero, *Female Offender*, p. 90.
24 *Ibid.*, pp. 113–114.
25 Quoted in Tarde, *Penal Philosophy*, p. 220.

largely under the influence of the resurgent biological science of the day, were interested in criminal behavior itself. The powerful impetus of the positivistic approach, still current in some European and most Latin American criminological work, received its major rebuttal in 1913 from Charles Goring, a British research scientist, who, intent upon disproving the Lombrosian theory of physical types, stressed the significance of psychological characteristics, especially defective intelligence, as the basic condition of crime.[26]

The emphasis on defective intelligence, abetted by the development of new psychometric instruments in the early decades of this century, gave rise to a school of mental testers in the field of criminology. A wide-ranging series of studies resulted, intent on demonstrating the demoralizing and antisocial effects of defective intelligence, which was thought to be transmitted mainly through family lines.[27] Studies of the deficient lineages of families such as the Jukes[28] and the Kallikaks[29] reinforced the worst suspicions concerning the source of criminal behavior. This viewpoint was refuted successfully in the 1920s, although the findings were not widely accepted immediately—so reluctant are even professional investigators to abandon their vested interest in a theory—and the hunt for an all-embracing cause of crime began to shift elsewhere. The view in the mid-twenties began to move toward the rising ground swell of Freudian psychology, and various interpretations of the Oedipus complex, oral compulsivity, the primal scene, and sibling rivalry were offered as presumably adequate explanations of criminal activity.[30]

The Great Depression, ushered in by the collapse of the stock market in the fall of 1929, focused attention on economic and related environmental factors in crime, eventually giving rise to consideration of a wide variety of conditions of a cultural nature. The recital of man's sociological "horribilia," such as poor housing, poverty, deficient schooling, disrupted family life, and bad companionship, constituted the central theme of a distinctive school, sociological in nature, located for some years at the University of Chicago and commonly referred to as the "social disorganization" school of criminology.[31]

Despite the fact that the different approaches tend to stress different aspects of a common situation, there has been an unfortunate tendency in criminology to assume that a particularized explanation is a totally sufficient explanation of criminal behavior. Bitter controversies prevail even now between the proponents of a neo-Lombrosian

26 Goring, *The English Convict.*
27 For a useful bibliography, see Fink, *Causes of Crime, 1800–1915.*
28 Dugdale, *The Jukes*; Estabrook, *The Jukes in 1915.*
29 Goddard, *The Kallikak Family.*
30 See, for example, Abrahamsen, *Who Are the Guilty?*
31 See, for example, Thrasher, *The Gang*; Wirth, *The Ghetto*; Cavan, *Suicide*; Anderson, *The Hobo.*

point of view, stressing the significance of bodily factors in criminality, and those who favor a more sociological or psychological frame of reference. The fact is that such views need not be antagonistic; they can be complementary. The difficulty seems to be that these disparate points of view are not rooted in self-contained and consistent theoretical frameworks. If they were, it would be recognized that a given theoretical explanation proceeds from its own frame of reference and is solely concerned with certain types of facts that fall exclusively within its purview. Theoretical points of view beginning with different assumptions need not contend for dominance, although the prevailing cultural climate may tend to favor one more than the other. Such cultural preference is not, however, a scientific problem; it is, as mentioned previously, a matter of historical fact. *A sound theoretical doctrine, whether based on the constitutional facts of a Lombroso, the psychological data of a Goring, or the newer stress on sociocultural characteristics, claims neither priority nor exclusiveness—it simply accounts for behavior from the vantage point of that given theory.*

Sociology of Criminal Behavior

A number of interesting theoretical approaches in the field of criminology have been developed within the past three decades. Some have been able to grasp and invigorate the imagination of criminological researchers and theorists. To a great extent, these formal theoretical doctrines concerning crime have resulted from the great stress within the social sciences on structural and functional theories and on class and subcultural conditions.

Fundamentally, a theory is a way of looking at data or, as the scientist sometimes puts it, a way of "ordering" data. To a psychiatrist, the facts of crime would be taken almost entirely to be manifestations of a psychiatric disturbance or disorder; thus, every type of criminal behavior is regarded merely as a symptom of a basic personality malfunction. For some sociologists, on the other hand, criminal behavior is seen almost wholly as a form of adjustment to the demands of a particular environment. Although it may be possible to reconcile such theories—and occasionally this is attempted—the facts within the contexts of the separate theories themselves are often of a mutually exclusive order. A "symptom," for example, is *not* a form of social adjustment.

With these ideas in mind, we may proceed to examine some of the more recent theoretical views of crime that have won varying degrees of acceptance. It should be recognized, however, that acceptance of these theories is, at best, only partial and is usually limited to only specific phases of the theory. Also, in the field of criminology it is truly rare to find genuine efforts to validate a theoretical position by means of a systematic piece of research. In most current instances, theories offer suggestions that appear plausible to the investigator but have not been rigorously tested with relevant data.

One of the few comprehensive theories developed by an American criminologist to explain criminal phenomena has been the "differential association" theory of Edwin H. Sutherland (1883–1950). The theory first appeared in systematic formulation in the 1939 edition of Sutherland's *Principles of Criminology*. It is difficult to ascertain whether the theory was originally designed as a pedagogical instrument to provide students with a framework by means of which to examine the highly diversified materials in criminology, or whether Sutherland originally conceived "differential association" as a full-grown theory that might lend itself to testing. There is little doubt that of all the recent sociological explanations of crime, Sutherland's theory has exercised by far the greatest influence.

Sutherland's doctrine of how crime occurs is fundamentally a form of *learning theory*. It is of more than passing interest that the statement of the several steps that, according to Sutherland, are integral to criminal behavior appeared at the time the intellectual climate was stirred by Clark Hull's doctrine of learning. In essence, this type of theory, promulgated by Hull, John Dollard, Neal Miller, and others, stresses that all types of behavior, formal and informal, are essentially the result of a learning process in which the elements of cue, drive, response, and reinforcement are present.[32]

Sutherland's point of view is distinctive because it purports to indicate how noncriminal as well as criminal behavior emerges. Its chief difficulty lies in the fact that it fails to specify in detail those precise aspects and characteristics of the process. Donald R. Cressey, who has carried on Sutherland's theoretical work, has maintained, however, that no doctrine of such range can take in all the interstices of human behavior described by the grand plan. In illustration, he points to the Darwinian theory of evolution and natural selection, which, in laying out a broad framework for scientists to follow, did not attempt to indicate the precise mechanisms whereby the process of natural selection occurs.[33]

In its most common form, Sutherland's theory consists of nine integral phases.[34] The theory begins by asserting that *criminal behavior is learned*. While many criminologists have caviled at Sutherland's broad descriptive formulation, it is possible to stretch the term "learning" to include virtually any phase of behavior—even that which appears spontaneous. Criminologists have not taken strong ex-

32 See Hull, *A Behavior System;* Dollard and Miller, *Social Learning and Imitation;* Dollard and Miller, *Personality and Psychotherapy.*
33 Cressey, "Epidemiology and Individual Conduct," pp. 55–57.
34 Sutherland and Cressey, *Principles of Criminology,* pp. 77–100.

ception to this premise, provided that the criminal behavior described is of the professional or habitual type. The chief objection has been the use of the learning process to account for the wide variety of casual, occasional, or episodic offenders.

As his second point, Sutherland indicates that *criminal behavior is learned in interaction with other persons in a process of communication.* This broad statement suggests that within certain environments, the character of interaction, both by virtue of its mode and its content, would strongly predispose certain individuals to engage in criminal behavior. There is little precise articulation by Sutherland of the actual procedures whereby one set of norms is internalized, as opposed to another. In depressed areas, as Solomon Kobrin has shown, the developing youth is exposed to a variety of conflicting norms—delinquent, nondelinquent, and even antidelinquent (that is, norms stressing the repression of delinquency). It is frequently an adventitious circumstance that seems to create criminal behavior in one case and noncriminal behavior in another. Kobrin, for example, shows that consistency between delinquent episodes is not necessary during adolescent and adult criminality.[35] The interactive process is highly complex, and the mere statement of interaction provides only the crudest of blueprints for its understanding. The crucial problem here is to determine the precise nature of the learning process that predisposes certain individuals toward crime and others toward noncriminal activities.

If individuals acquiring criminal habits or propensities were exposed only to situations, circumstances, and personalities of a criminal nature, it would be relatively easy to comprehend how the process of communication brings about criminal behavior. In view of the variations in standards and personalities to which the individual in our society is exposed, however, it is difficult to discern those critical elements that induce criminality without the intervention of some psychological principle.

Sutherland's third point is that criminal behavior is acquired through participation *within intimate personal groups.* The theory suggests the relatively minor role of the mass media, an area that has often been bruited about as an important cause of crime,[36] but its accuracy cannot readily be determined, since it is virtually impossible to separate out an individual's primary group experiences and his exposure to various forms of mass media stimuli.

Fundamentally, this particular stress by Sutherland suggests that the roots of crime must be sought in the socializing experiences of the individual. Unfortunately, the process of socialization has not been effectively unraveled by social science scholars. In most instances, the terms describing such interpersonal processes have been descriptive

35 Kobrin, "Conflict of Values in Delinquency Areas."
36 See, for instance, Wertham, *Seduction of the Innocent.*

and tautological. Through the invention of such concepts as role-playing, we assume that the individual will develop the characteristics of familial and age-level groups, without indicating how this process takes place. This gap becomes especially cogent when we recognize that the behavior to which the developing individual is exposed is often highly inconsistent.

Sutherland's fourth emphasis indicates that the criminal learning process includes not only techniques of committing crime, but also *the shaping of motives, drives, rationalizations, and attitudes.* With respect to the techniques of committing crimes, the processes themselves can be quite complex, involving high degrees of skill. Frank Tannenbaum as well as Sutherland himself, in a well known monograph on the professional thief[37]—illustrated the high degree of competence required in order to be a successful burglar or pickpocket.[38]

Concerning the cultivation of a supportive rationale and an emotional orientation that is conducive to antisocial and criminal behavior, the long process of intimate participation within the fecund environment of the primary group may lay the basis for rather inflexible adherence to codes of a criminal nature. The case studies amassed since the beginning of the century provide ample evidence of this phase of the learning process, portraying primary group associations that reveal a favorable spectrum of attitudes toward socially disapproved behavior, ranging from sheer indifference to lawbreaking to outright encouragement of it.[39] The general orientation of individuals exposed in the family and other primary groups to a wide variety of antisocial behavior patterns deeply affects the entire personality structure. If techniques are developed by means of which this fundamental learning process may be unraveled, then we may be well on the road to comprehending how certain criminal careers are shaped.

Fifth, Sutherland attempts to narrow his focus by indicating the kinds of pressures that condition the learning process toward an acceptance of illegal pursuits. Careful to keep his theory within the legally-defined forms of criminal behavior, Sutherland stipulates that *"the specific direction of motives and drives is learned from definitions of the legal codes as favorable or unfavorable."* There appears to be considerable ambiguity in this particular tenet; it suggests that at certain phases of the individual's development, he becomes aware that his motives are either contrary or favorable to the legal codes— and hence either criminal or law-abiding—on the basis of how the group around him reinforces his attitudes through its own definition of the legal codes. The extremely broad reference to the "definitions" of legal codes and the "direction of motives and drives" leaves more questions unanswered than it clarifies.

37 Sutherland, *The Professional Thief.*
38 Tannenbaum, *Crime and the Community,* Chap. 7.
39 See, for instance, Shaw, *Brothers in Crime*; Shaw, *The Jack-Roller.*

The development of criminal attitudes is hardly a studied or formal process. Before one can accept the attitude, for example, that "everybody's a sucker, and only suckers work," a variety of subtle and reinforcing attitudes have become absorbed by the developing personality, into which a knowledge of legality and illegality does not figure. In other words, a series of deeply implanted experiences becomes part of the total personality outlook long before the personality is conscious of the illegal nature of different courses of action.

Sixth, Sutherland attempts to answer the dilemma posed by the previous condition in terms of the principle of "differential association," which represents the core of his theoretical position. According to this postulate, *"a person becomes delinquent because of an excess of definitions favorable to violation of the law over definitions unfavorable to violation of the law."* It was this aspect of his theory that suggested to Sutherland that the crux of criminality could be most effectively sought in the character of the associations an individual established in his communal and personal relationships. It was the acceptance of this position that made Sutherland a lifelong opponent of the purely individualistic points of view of the psychoanalyst and the psychiatrist who tend to regard criminal behavior as an outcome, phase, or symptom of personality malfunctioning. It was for this reason, too, that Sutherland, in his suggestions for programs to counter crime, stressed the importance of community programs at the "grassroots" level rather than individual approaches.

In a research sense, however, it is extremely difficult to test this crucial doctrine. This difficulty is acknowledged by Cressey, who seems to suggest that such quantification may be held as an ideal, but one unlikely to be realized,[40] though the theory itself appears to stress that its support must be found in purely quantitative terms.

The fact remains that it is virtually impossible to determine with any degree of accuracy how associations "favorable to violation of the law" are established and to measure them in comparative terms. In the first place, identification with others and with behavior patterns is never a limited or unitary process, but involves a great many supporting, contrasting, and conflicting elements. Second, identification may be intimate with and even sympathetic to lawless elements without necessarily producing criminal behavior. Third, it is doubtful whether any standard of behavior to which an individual is exposed, since it is invariably embodied in the behavior practices of others, may be assessed wholly in terms of attitudes favorable or unfavorable to the law.

As a means of demonstrating with greater clarity the character of the associations that have a subsequent effect on behavior, Sutherland states in his seventh point that *"differential association may vary in frequency, duration, priority, and intensity."* Sutherland implicitly ac-

40 Cressey, "Epidemiology and Individual Conduct."

knowledges the considerable significance of the *character* of the personality in responding to different types of intimate influences. *Priority* suggests a hierarchy of values that the personality senses in its acquired needs, while *intensity* suggests the relative potency of different types of contacts in accordance with the reactive tendencies of the individual. Indeed, both priority and intensity largely determine how important the frequency and duration of the individual's contacts are. Frequent contacts may do little more than promote feelings of boredom, indifference, and rejection of a standard of behavior, unless the contacts accord meaningful reference in terms of the priority of needs that the individual has cultivated. Similarly, regardless of the duration of an individual's association with certain behavior patterns, such continuity may have little importance unless it carries an emotional intensity for the individual.

The variable extent of frequency and duration of associations may be roughly approximated, but, as previously indicated, it becomes difficult to state such phases of associational behavior in terms of precise quantitative indices. There can be little doubt, however, concerning the significance of the effects of *frequency* and *duration* of contacts on the course of human behavior, especially when perceived in relation to the *priority* and *intensity* of the contacts.

Sutherland's eighth point concerns the nature of learning in criminal and anticriminal behavior. Learning, in one sense, may be conceived as basic in determining any form of human behavior, unique or generic. In other words, in all human situations, the experience an individual amasses through learning influences the resultant outcomes of behavior. On this basis, there can be little objection to Sutherland's subsequent proposition that *the processes involved in learning criminal and anticriminal behavior involve "all of the mechanisms that are involved in any other learning."*

Sutherland stressed the idea of the inclusive nature of learning in order to overcome the archaic view, which still remained at the time he promulgated his theory, that learning was essentially imitative in character. Learning is a highly complex affair, involving conscious and unconscious elements, in which imitation plays a limited role. Indeed, viewed as an informal process, learning encompasses virtually every phase of human adaptation.

Sutherland's ninth proposition is a reminder that *while criminal behavior is an expression of general needs and values, "it is not explained by these general needs and values since noncriminal behavior is an expression of the same needs and values."* This injunction, against which no behavioral scientist will cavil, indicates that the oversimplified generalizations that are frequently employed to account for crime—such as the view that an individual steals because he craves "esteem" or kills because he is "unhappy" or robs because he "wants money"—have no scientific validity. Men, criminal and noncriminal, are motivated by much the same acculturated needs and values. They become or do not become criminals on the basis of their unique responses to the same drives for prestige, happiness, success, power, wealth, and a myriad other value-needs. This insistence by Sutherland on the need to discover the precise character of the individual's response to a given situation that leads him to criminal behavior, despite its repeated acceptance in principle, cannot be sufficiently stressed.

The surprising thing about Sutherland's last two propositions is that they should have been incorporated in the theory at all. Actually, they are not germane to "differential association," except as a means of emphasizing what Sutherland believed to be the essential sociological character of his theory as compared with psychological theories. While learning may stem from the same drives for all men, each man learns to express those drives in ways that are compatible to his group, class, and ethnic interests, among other things.

Cressey, in his later reviews of Sutherland's position, has acknowledged many of the criticisms noted above. According to Cressey, however, Sutherland's theory, while fundamentally an attempt to describe the "epidemiology" of crime, that is, the rates and distribution of crime in the social structure, is also effective in indicating the way in which the individual processes of crime occur. Cressey suggests that differential association might be more appropriately referred to as a *principle* rather than a theory.[41]

While Sutherland's view has been inordinately helpful in producing an intellectual focus around which criminologists have attempted to sharpen their concepts and their understanding, its principal weakness, despite Cressey's perceptive appraisal, lies in its inability to lend itself to research testing. After a thoroughgoing review of the Sutherland postulates, Melvin De Fleur and Richard Quinney, for instance, reached the following conclusion:

> The present analysis has shown the theory to be at such a high level of abstraction that it is not possible to test it directly with empirical data. In fact, until fundamental problems of taxonomy concerning criminal behavior and the various factors associated with its etiology are clarified, empirical testing of the theory will remain a very difficult problem at best.[42]

In addition, the theory is unable to account for the processes by which individuals respond differentially to similar situations. While Sutherland attempted to account for such differential *responses* by means of the different perceptions individuals develop with respect to past associations (or differential association), such an explanation, when carefully considered, is tautological, that is, it attempts to offer

41 *Ibid.*, p. 55.
42 De Fleur and Quinney, "A Reformulation of Sutherland's Differential Association Theory," p. 22.

an explanation based upon the very principle it purports to examine. There is no way out of this dilemma, it appears, unless we take into account the differences in human perceptions of the variety of common experiences to which individuals are exposed. This, in turn, involves some social-psychological concept of the reasons for the variations in the human mechanisms of social response.

TAFT: CULTURAL "CRIMOGENISIS"
The "differential association" formulation promulgated by Sutherland has been attended to more assiduously over the years than any other behavioral science statement concerning the etiology of criminal behavior. However, other views also have been put forth that have gathered adherents who believe they offer valuable insights into the roots of illegal activity. Among the more notable of such positions are those of Donald R. Taft, professor emeritus from the University of Illinois, and Walter C. Reckless, recently retired from Ohio State University after a distinguished career in sociology and public administration. In addition, in the past decade there has been a proliferation of theories regarding juvenile delinquency, which we will discuss in Chapter 14, that offer some insight into recruitment patterns to adult crime.

Location of "crimogenic," or crime-producing, forces in the general culture of the United States forms the core of Taft's approach to comprehending criminal patterns. Taft grants that there is a wide diversity of cultural stresses in the United States, but he insists that there may nonetheless be some core emphases that, by their nature, encourage criminal activity. Theoretical focus on such items, he suggests, "is somewhat rare and very unpopular" in the United States because it challenges some of our national and personal commitments. Because of this, popular acceptance is usually accorded to individualistic theories of criminal behavior that focus blame for behavior on the offender and his alleged psychological inadequacies.[43]

For Taft, the following, among others, are said to be characteristic of American culture: its dynamic quality, complexity, materialism, growing impersonality, individualism, insistence upon the importance of status, restricted group loyalties, survivals of frontier traditions, race discrimination, lack of scientific orientation in the social field, tolerance of political corruption, general faith in the law, disrespect for some specific laws, and acceptance of quasi-criminal exploitation.

The method by which the general culture is related to the patterning of criminal behavior is spelled out in more detail by Taft in the following vignette:

> Given a culture dynamic, complex, materialistic, and admiring the successful in a competitive struggle but with many falling short of success, relative failures will collect in its slums and there develop pat-

43 Taft, "Influence of the General Culture on Crime."

terns of behavior hostile to the interests of the general community but in harmony with the community's basic values. Assume such a society nominally approving democracy but in practice often rating its members not on the basis of individual virtues but on their accidental membership in such social groups as races, classes, nationalities, or cliques. Weaken in such a culture primary-group controls which prevent serious departure from approved traditional patterns. Develop in such a culture, through processes of social change, a confusion of tongues in definitions of morality and hypocritical rationalizations as to contrasts between the criminal and the noncriminal. . . . Permit white-collar criminals to receive but mild punishment and no status loss. Permit also gigantic social swindles . . . and injuries to the body politic to go unpunished, while no more serious injuries, classed and treated as crime, result in severe punishment. . . . Assume in this culture a holdover of frontier traditions, involving approval of the use of force and mob action by "respectable" groups against those who oppose their interests or arouse their hostile prejudices. Grant the prevalence in that society of Puritanical traditions preventing the legal or "moral" expression of basic sex and other drives—traditions to which lip service continues to be given long after large minorities, at least, cease to follow them. . . .[44]

These cultural traits, Taft believes, plus numerous other traits similar to them, are what inevitably produce in the United States the extent and kind of crime that we have. Taft notes that in a culture such as ours, we "must expect considerable crime which can be attributed basically to its own inherent qualities. . . . In this sense we get the criminals we deserve. When we 'deserve' less crime, we shall have less of it."[45]

Taft's approach serves, of course, to concentrate attention on fundamental matters of social commitment that establish the background for criminal activity. Sutherland tries to tell us why criminal behavior occurs in any society, while Taft attempts to explain why it occurs more often in one society than another. Together they are complementary approaches, concentrating on different segments of a similar process. Both views, however, fall short in predicting criminal behavior. Taft's, in particular, represents a rather retroactive construct, since he knows the culture and knows its crime rate. It is likely that he would be extremely hard-pressed if asked to assign weights to the crimogenic items that would occur in a society that shares some of the values of the United States, emphasizes other values more strongly than we do, and does not share some with us at all.

RECKLESS: CONTAINMENT THEORY

Containment theory, the name given by Walter C. Reckless to his theoretical position, concentrates on two dimensions of the individual's situation in order to determine his crime-proneness—dimensions that

[44] Taft and England, Jr., *Criminology*, pp. 277–278.
[45] *Ibid.*, p. 279.

are labelled "inner controls" and "outer controls." Inner controls involve self-control, good self-concept, ego strength, well-developed superego, high frustration tolerance, high resistance to diversions, high sense of responsibility, goal orientation, ability to find substitute satisfactions, and tension-reducing rationalizations.[46] Outer controls represent the structural buffers in the person's immediate social world that are able to hold him within bounds. Reckless notes that they consist of such items as a presentation of a consistent moral front to the person, institutional reinforcement of his norms, goals, and expectations, effective supervision and discipline, and opportunity for acceptance, identity, and belonging.

Reckless's theory, it can be seen, accounts for both criminal and noncriminal behavior. When an individual conforms, the theory suggests that he does so because the "containments" (the "inner" and the "outer" controls) propel him toward and reward him for acceptable actions, although there may be some questions about an individual who conforms to behavior of a subculture that is defined as criminal by the majority of society. Reckless notes that the theory does not account for acts said to exist in so-called compulsive crimes, such as phobias and hallucinations, organic impairments, and neurotic mechanisms.

The advantages of containment theory, among other things, are that it provides a framework in terms of which discrete factors can be abstracted, tested, and quantified. It is possible, for instance, to develop measures of such things as ego control and self-concept. In fact, Reckless and other colleagues have published a wide range of papers that attempt to differentiate delinquents and nondelinquents in terms of their self-concepts.[47] It may also be possible, though it appears considerably more difficult, to quantify items such as the "presentation of a consistent moral front." But the major barrier to widespread use of this theory lies in the excruciatingly complex problem of balancing the various items in some manner that will allow a predictive statement to be made on the basis of a particular mixture of controls, especially as such a statement relates to a specific criminal act, such as robbery or burglary. Reckless himself suspects that further research ultimately will distinguish one or two elements in inner and outer containment that serve as basic regulators of behavior, that is, as items that act in an independent fashion to influence the other factors.

Containment theory cuts into the reality of criminal behavior at a different point than the theories promulgated by Taft and Sutherland. Unlike Taft, Reckless has no interest in explaining why one society rather than another generates a certain kind of self-concept in

46 Reckless, *The Crime Problem*, pp. 469–483; Reckless, "A Non-Causal Explanation: Containment Theory"; Reckless, "A New Theory of Delinquency and Crime." See also Voss, "Differential Association and Containment Theory."

47 See, for example, Reckless and Dinitz, "Pioneering with Self-Concept as a Vulnerability Factor in Delinquency."

its citizens, or why persons in different social positions commit different amounts and kinds of crime. Unlike Sutherland, he is not interested in the process by which the forces of containment are learned. Instead, Reckless is concerned with constructing a paradigm that will allow the identification of immediate forces acting within and on the individual at any given moment and that will permit an understanding of the form his behavior is apt to take. It is in such terms that an earlier observation merits repetition: A sound theoretical doctrine claims neither priority nor exclusiveness; a theory simply accounts for behavior from its own vantage point.

Typologies: Configurational Analysis

It might be useful in concluding this review of theoretical approaches to set forth an analytical framework to employ for further study and research into criminal behavior systems, rather than a general framework that tries to interpret the entire realm of criminal activity.

It has already been noted that the legal concept or definition of crime need not, and frequently does not, coincide with the behavioral definition of crime. A commonplace example is the case of statutes defining vagrancy, which are characterized, strictly speaking, by lack of visible means of support and vagabondage, but which have been stretched to include virtually every type of offense from prostitution to unlawful assembly to petty larceny.

Assuming that we can find common definitions for similar behavioral groups of crime, it is possible to conceive of an interrelated behavioral pattern within which crimes of a similar nature will fall. The components that follow do not necessarily function in a specific sequential order or even in the same degree. In some forms of crime, such as organized crime, certain components, such as hierarchical arrangements, may function in well-marked and distinctive patterns. In other forms of crime, such as the "public order" offenses of drunkenness and prostitution, such components may function in crude, nascent, or rudimentary forms. For this reason, such forms of criminal behavior are referred to as forms of "truncated behavior." Following is a list of components to be used in analyzing types of crime.

The Eliciting Sociocultural Matrix. Crimes are invariably reflective of and responsive to a given social order and cultural organization at a given period in historic development. Crimes of a certain type are only possible in terms of a given sociocultural matrix. In this sense, the sociocultural organization plays a basic role in determining the nature and distribution of the offenses that will take place. Those who respond to the basic sociocultural elements may be regarded as being predisposed toward a certain type of criminal behavior on the basis of the social-psychological factors that determine the character of role-performance within a given class structure. Inadequate role-performance, however, is not sufficient to bring about a criminal response. A criminal response may be facilitated by certain adaptive mechanisms in the class and subcultural milieu, such as the "opportunity structures" described by Richard Cloward and Lloyd Ohlin[48] or the learning process suggested by Sutherland.

The resultant criminal behavior, however, is distinctive of the culture and its several parts. An illustration may be seen in the operation of certain confidence games common in the United States. One such confidence game involves seemingly affluent businessmen (usually posing as if in the investment business) who prey upon the large, drifting population of widows in Florida and southern California, where a special group of women is vulnerable to victimization, and where a special set of circumstances renders their exploitation feasible. The peculiar sociocultural elements that enable such an operation to flourish include the greater longevity of women in the United States as compared to men; the overwhelming preponderance of life insurance death benefits that accrue to widows; the large amount of other liquid assets in the hands of women; the enormous increase in per capita income in the United States during the past half-century that has encouraged mobility and the establishment of large semitropical areas of retirement and relaxation; the desirability of the marital status; the freedom from parental responsibility for many married women after the age of forty; and a host of other cultural elements.

Another illustration is the high incidence of car theft in the United States, most of which is committed by youths under twenty-one years of age. The propitious conditions that make this possible are the high rate of car ownership in the United States; the car as a status symbol (in many cases, particularly so for adolescents); the widespread knowledge of driving and elementary mechanics among American youth; the encouragement toward tinkering with motors and mechanical gadgets as a feature of American mores; the concentration of cars within restricted areas; carelessness in safeguarding cars and broad insurance coverage; and many other situational factors that contribute to the car-driving complex in the United States.

The significant fact is that these forms of criminal activity constitute patterned responses to certain arrangements of the institutional patterns within a society.

Similarities in Behavior Patterns of Types of Criminal Behavior. Crime that is a response to segments of the sociocultural organization is characterized by similarities in the form and the scope of the behavior. One of the most fascinating aspects of criminal behavior is the fact that the methods, procedures, and outlooks of certain types of offenders—for example, the shoplifter or the pickpocket—are so

---

48 Cloward and Ohlin, *Delinquency and Opportunity*. The theory is described in detail in Chapter 14.

similar. Part of this is induced by the contingencies of the crime situation itself. In shoplifting, for example, there are certain operational safeguards that must be observed because of the nature of the premises. There are also historical precedents that are directly associated with certain forms of crime. For example, pickpocket mobs in Elizabethan England used a precise, specialized system that is still used today. In addition, direct contact and exchange of information among offenders —"shop talk," if you will—contribute considerably toward the development of uniform procedures and techniques. Much of the offender's "training," however, may begin long before he actually undertakes a form of crime as part of the neighborhood and gang lore in his pre-adolescent and adolescent years. The striking result is to bring about forms of criminal behavior that, in some kinds of crime, are so standardized that they could readily be transcribed into the form of job-specification sheets used by legitimate enterprises.

Similarities in Perceptions, Attitudes, and Values. Criminal procedures and techniques are associated with and directly supportive of outlooks and perceptions characteristic of given criminal pursuits. Robert and Helen Lynd have referred to the "Long Arm of the Job" as illustrative of the mode of life and orientation of a worker conditioned by the peculiar socioeconomic conditions of his employment.[49] In a similar fashion, the offender, in common with others of his specialized bent, enjoys certain perceptions, attitudes, and values that may be intensified by his antipathies toward society and his need for personal security.

Perception refers to the ways in which an individual regards persons and agencies around him, and the ways in which he is characteristically inclined to respond to them, both overtly and covertly. Frank Tannenbaum refers to this phase of the criminal's mentality as his "professional insight,"[50] although it is much more than this. The perceptions engendered by a closely circumscribed way of life tend to produce an outlook that extends far beyond the confines of a particular criminal activity. Jack Black, a former professional criminal, put it very well; he said, "I thought in terms of theft. Houses were built to be robbed, citizens were to be robbed . . . That was the atmosphere I breathed."[51]

As an integral part of his perceptions, the offender develops a variety of attitudes and values that determine his behavior toward his close associates and his reactions to the law-abiding world, including the viewpoint with which he may regard his victim. There is often a peculiar affinity between the victim of a criminal offense and the criminal who perpetrates the offense. Hans von Hentig has shown how crimes may not emerge unless the social system produces individuals

49 Lynd and Lynd, *Middletown*, pp. 53–72.
50 Tannenbaum, *Crime and the Community*, pp. 182–183.
51 Black, *You Can't Win*, p. 151.

vulnerable to certain forms of crime. Citing an ancient Hebrew proverb, Von Hentig states that "the mouse is not the culprit but the hole."[52] The impressive feature about the community of attitudes among criminals toward society and their victims may be observed in the statements made by different types of criminals who voice the same sentiments. The confidence man, for example, frequently utters the conviction that his victim also has "larceny in his heart," suggesting a widespread institutional belief. Additionally, each special form of crime produces its own distinctive configuration of attitudes and sentiments toward the victim, the public, and the police, although there may be some overlapping at certain points with other forms of crime.

Reinforcement of Criminal Behavior by Social Practices

A given set of attitudes, distinctive of a certain way of life, is itself reinforced by a wide supportive framework of related items. The boundaries of the system of criminal behavior are determined by particular socioeconomic agencies and institutions that are directly relevant to the criminal practice. Thus, if bank theft constitutes a separable behavioral complex of crimes, its dimensions must be sought in the physical safeguards and security systems that have been set up to protect the property of banks; the protective devices and operating techniques developed by the bank robber through association, custom, and tradition; and the congenial institutional and behavioral patterns of related primary and subcultural groups. The pickpocket mob, which has been studied extensively in this connection, offers a striking illustration of how urban concentration, modern transit and traffic conditions, the policing of public places, and the adaptation of traditional safeguards and skills combine to produce an interrelated behavioral complex, regardless of where it is practiced.[53]

Distinctiveness Through Language

Significant in the behavioral complexes of crime are the highly developed specialized vocabularies and jargons employed by offenders. In one sense, the degree of demarcation of any special social grouping may be determined by the extent to which it has developed a subvocabulary and jargon of its own. There are distinctive vocabularies of age and sex groupings, as well as of ethnic and occupational categories. The criminal's world, however, is rather clearly marked by a special type of occupational vocabulary that reflects a great many of his outlooks and evaluations, as well as his professional skills. Such specialized language not only facilitates communication among the members of a particularized group, but it also serves as a rallying

52 Von Hentig, *Criminal and His Victim*, p. 312.
53 Maurer, *Whiz Mob*.

point for identification and is a source of recognition for the *cognoscenti,* providing closer and more intimate associations. Those who understand the vocabulary and can use it readily experience a form of exclusiveness and separateness from others, while feeling closer to those who share the same shibboleths and symbols at the same time.

Structural and Hierarchical Arrangements

Identification with a given behavioral complex introduces a sense of values that differentiates the various practitioners of the forms employed. Differences in graded status resulting from such reciprocal obligations and attitudes constantly emerge in any form of institutional behavior. The participants in certain forms of criminal behavior are not exempt from this process of role-grading and status-rating, and they sometimes even tend to be more aware of it than others, possibly due to the fact that they often are restricted in their social activity to a limited world.

Thus, the individual who identifies himself with a criminal group or practice may develop a corresponding pattern of evaluative self-attitudes while tending to regard other criminals in a different light. Many shoplifters, for example, do not regard themselves as "criminals" but view other offenders with opprobrium. In the same ranking process, bank robbers constitute a special form of underworld aristocracy in correctional institutions, while confidence men maintain derogatory attitudes toward others who practice less elaborate types of confidence games than they.

Identification and In-Group Loyalty

Being involved in a deviant way of life and holding out the possibility of apprehension and incarceration induces strong moves toward identification with others engaged in the same type of enterprise. This is motivated in part by the experience of rejection and separateness from regular social relations, so that a sense of kinship with individuals faced by a hostile world may develop. Its principal characteristic is a recognition that one is a participant in a "way of life" and that this way of life involves a network of associations and commitments closed to the outsider.

It does not necessarily follow that this sense of identification inevitably leads to a form of in-group loyalty. Whether or not in-group loyalty results is contingent upon the nature of the criminal practices engaged in. The youthful predatory gang and some of the so-called "syndicated" racketeering gangs, for instance, appear to have developed a high degree of in-group loyalty, manifested in codes of prescriptive regulations according to which "squealing" on one's colleagues is the cardinal sin. Other kinds of offenders notoriously operate under a principle of "every man for himself."

.   .   .

A typology of crime, then, refers to a separable complex of behavior, induced in place and time by a given sociocultural organization,
and producing its own similarities in behavior, perceptions, attitudes,
and values. These behavioral characteristics are manifested in specific
attitudes toward the victim upon whom the criminal activity is
focused and toward the public in general. The specific criminal behavioral practices and outlooks are embedded and reinforced within
a broad cultural matrix, including the agencies against which the
crimes are directed and the criminal's primary and subcultural associations. Characteristic of various behavioral complexes, and aiding
in their integration, are distinctions of language and modes of communication, structural relations, and a sense of identification.

It should be recognized that such typologies of crime may be
instrumental in disclosing the associations of a given form of crime
with the sociocultural organization without necessarily indicating
how a given individual embraces criminal activity. In short, the foregoing relate not to a theory of causation as much as to the recognition of and a procedure for the identification of the adaptive forms
that different types of crime assume. For an individual to identify
himself with a specific criminal way of life involves, first, the consideration of specific elements in the role-development of his career
and, second, the character of the access to criminal activity within his
environment.

Individual Offenders

Consideration of crime by means of separable typologies with which
certain offenders may identify themselves appears to suggest "organizations" of criminals, or, at any rate, criminality of a systematic
or professional nature. A vast amount of crime, however, consists
of acts by individual offenders whose behavior appears isolated and
unrelated to a particular deviant way of life. Whereas criminal
complexes such as bank robbery, confidence games, pickpocketing, and
shoplifting may fit into broad patterns, each with its own attributes
and values, what of offenses such as sexual assaults and prostitution?
Since they are performed in violation of legal codes, they must be
construed as criminal acts. Can we say that such offenses fall within
a typology of criminal behavior? The answer is in the affirmative,
providing two items are kept in mind.

First, the nature of the sociocultural organization, with its own
bans, restrictions, and taboos, tends to engender its own pattern of
responses. Sexual offenses, one of many categories, for example, are
presumably a response to a kind of restrictive prohibition emblematic
of our culture. The nature of the response and the character of self-
image produced in the minds of those who break the law contain a

great many similarities. The nature of furtive operations that prostitutes, for example, are forced to engage in, the acceptance of the usual "pay-off" to some legal intermediary, the attitude toward the "trick," and the acknowledged need for some form of organized protection are widespread conditions of prostitution. Other types of "individuated" offenses also bear a great many similarities, no matter where they are carried on.

Second, the standardization of a given mode of behavior and the systematic organization of codes related to it are invariably matters of degree. A skilled confidence man follows procedures that have been proven by experience over a long period of time. A sexual offender does not identify himself with such a procedural complex in the same manner. However, deviant behavior of an illegal nature, regardless of its nature, tends to introduce a series of incipient roles that lead to a form of truncated behavior, in which implications and extensions of that behavior tend to produce the organized arrangements that comprise some of the more standardized criminal complexes. Recognition of the complex of which his behavoir is a part is likely to exist regardless of the degree with which the offender identifies himself with such a behavior complex. The sexual offender, however, may not recognize that his illicit behavior is part of a way of life. By self-image, rationalization, attitudes, values, sentiment, and practices, however, he will often identify himself with patterns that characterize individuals who engage in the same activity, and he will often differentiate himself from others who do not behave similarly.

Under such conditions, it is not surprising that offenders who seemingly are almost totally isolated from one another, such as incest offenders, will often show similar family attitudes, equivalent socio-economic backgrounds, and many other traits and behavior patterns that mark them as a distinctive group of persons.[54]

For Further Reading

BLOCH, HERBERT A. *The Concept of Changing Loyalties*. New York: Columbia University Press, 1934, Part I.

> The first part of the volume discusses the relationship between data and the method by which it should be approached, viewed against sociological work prior to the early part of the twentieth century. It calls for the tailoring of method to the task being performed and the goals being sought.

COHEN, ALBERT K., ALFRED LINDESMITH, and KARL F. SCHUESSLER (eds.). *The Sutherland Papers*. Bloomington: Indiana University Press, 1956.

> This collection of most of Professor Sutherland's published papers includes several articles tracing the intellectual pathways by which he came to the enunciation of his theory of differential association.

54 Weinberg, *Incest Behavior.*

MANNHEIM, HERMANN (ed.). *Pioneers in Criminology*. Chicago: Quadrangle Books, 1960.

Seventeen notable figures in the early history of criminology are analyzed in terms of their backgrounds and contributions, in this series of articles, which were initially published in the *Journal of Criminal Law, Criminology, and Police Science*. Especially noteworthy are two general articles attempting to integrate the historical development of criminology—one by Professor Mannheim, now retired from a career at the London School of Economics, and the second by Professor Jeffery of Florida State University.

SCHAFER, STEPHEN. *Theories of Criminology*. New York: Random House, 1969.

Professor Schafer, a member of the faculty at Northeastern University in Boston, traces the historical and intellectual development of criminological theory, with particular stress on the contributions of the classical school of Bentham and Beccaria and the positivistic school of Lombroso, Garofalo, and Ferri.

VOLD, GEORGE B. *Theoretical Criminology*. New York: Oxford University Press, 1958.

The broad spectrum of theoretical orientations to the study of criminology comes under review in this volume by a former professor at the University of Minnesota. The questions posed by the author go to the heart of issues facing criminologists, and the historical material sheds a penetrating light on the paths that criminology has taken to arrive at its present state.

Part III
Extent of Crime

5
Perspectives on Crime Measurement

The pitfalls involved in estimating and discussing the numerical proportions of crime with some sophistication should by now be painfully self-evident. New statutes create new offenses that feed into the total amount of crime and make comparisons over time hazardous. Changing demographic characteristics of a population distort the protrait of crime. Police efficiency can increase the known amount of crime without any change in the actual amount. Inflation can raise the number of felonies merely by increasing the value of goods that are stolen; for example states that define grand larceny as the theft of goods worth $50 or more may have twice as much grand larceny in one decade as contrasted to an earlier decade without any change in the number and kinds of items that have been stolen.

In the same manner, statements about the total amount of crime in a jurisdiction produce a certain distortion due to the implicit assumption that all offenses are of equal weight. There can be a dramatic decrease in murder, rape, and assault (i.e., from 100 to 50 cases for each in a given year) and a slight increase in auto theft and drunkenness (i.e., from 3,000 to 3,600 cases). On the basis of these offenses, the crime total for the first year would show 3,300 offenses and for the second year 3,750, enough to cause newspaper headlines proclaiming a "rampant crime wave" and editorials deploring the breakdown of the nation's moral character and calling for a vigorous campaign of "law and order," since the totals do not reflect the overall improvement in the picture of the most serious crime.

These are but a few of the innumerable difficulties that make consideration of crime statistics an enterprise to be undertaken with consummate caution. The figures should be examined with a constant awareness of precisely what they purport to measure, from where they are derived, and whether they are presented as gross amounts or as rates. Crime statistics contain numerous labyrinths to trap the incautious, even when presented with the purest intentions. When an effort is made to compare rates in one place against those in another, the difficulties are compounded, not only by idiosyncratic aspects of the reporting systems, but also by variant traits of the sites themselves. When an effort is made to contrast the amount of crime in one period of history against another, the interpreter enters into an area frequented only by the most fearless angels, whose warier colleagues prefer to tread on firmer statistical ground.

The importance of crime statistics in shaping attitudes and policies should not be underestimated. For one thing, numerical material has a tendency to generate trustfulness; there appears to be something quite substantial in a reported figure and a calculated percentage, especially if carried two decimal places. Public policy is much more apt to be responsive to mathematics than to theory, and it is more attentive to a proclamation such as "Crime has increased by 7.13 percent" than to involved explanations of the deficiencies of so categoric a conclusion. Summarizing both the public and professional importance of crime statistics, Albert Biderman takes note of the following:

1. Crime rates are a much used indicator of basic social problems in the nation.

2. They have been subject to extraordinarily great attention in recent public discussion.

3. They illustrate the special kinds of difficulties that occur where the data are developed by, or from, agencies of social policy and action that are involved with the social phenomenon measured.

4. They constitute an illustration of the possibility of an indicator being poorly adapted to reflect the nature and significance of social changes, with the result that it conveys sometimes one-sided, sometimes reversed, value implications.[1]

Difficulties inherent in the measurement of criminal behavior are not, however, insurmountable. During recent years, in fact, more progress has been made toward obtaining better numerical information regarding crime than since the birth of the nation. The completion of several pioneering studies and national surveys on victimization, undertaken by the President's Commission on Law Enforcement and Administration of Justice, added invaluable data concerning a subject that has persistently teased criminological analysts because of its vital importance and the inadequacy of available information. Today, we have a much better idea of the relationship between reported and unreported crime than ever before. We know, for example, which offenses are most likely to be reported to the police and which kinds of persons are most likely to make known their victimization. Given this kind of material, combined with the increasing accuracy

1 Biderman, "Social Indicators and Goals," p. 112. See also Cipes, *The Crime War.*

of official tabulations, we can come much closer to determining the real level of certain kinds of crime in the country for a given period of time.

In this and the next chapter, we shall attempt to abstract from various reporting sources the most reliable information available on the extent of criminal behavior. It is axiomatic, as Thorsten Sellin has noted, that the nearer we come to the source of crime, from the standpoint of administrative procedures, the more accurate our estimates are likely to be of the prevalence of crime.[2] Field surveys of victims probably represent a more accurate picture of crime (though these surveys also produce many errors, particularly errors of recall in which subjects "forget" their victimization) than tabulations of offenses known to the police. Both of these methods are likely to measure the actual amount of crime in a jurisdiction better than conviction rates or counts of prison populations. We shall proceed, therefore, from victimization studies into official reports on crime known to the police and the consequences of such information—arrest, trial, conviction, and sentencing. We will also attempt to answer questions regarding the alleged increase in crime over time and to compare criminal behavior in the United States with that in foreign jurisdictions.

The Extent of Unreported Crime

The actual number of crimes committed will always be an unknown figure. This point cannot be stressed too strongly. There will always be an enormous—one could almost say an infinite—number of crimes that will not become known to any agency by any inventory method, which is a basic problem from a statistical standpoint.

Crimes such as carrying concealed weapons, individual narcotics transactions, or the vast range of sexual offenses that by their very nature are committed privately and by mutual agreement will remain beyond the range of tabulation. In fact, when such acts do not readily fall into discrete time entities, the problem of counting them becomes extremely complex. Suppose, for example, that we were able to determine how many individuals at a given moment violate laws against carrying concealed weapons. Say that we discover that 190,000 persons in the United States carry such weapons each day. Should we list 190,000 offenses for that day, or can the offenses reasonably be divided into two or three parts for the various portions of the day? Perhaps an offense ought to be counted each time the individual emerges from a dwelling, a store, or place of business with the weapon. When the same person goes out with the same concealed weapon on the follow-old one? Such counting conundrums highlight the necessity of keeping ing day, is this a new offense or should it be counted as part of the kinds of crime in separate categories and exorcizing as thoroughly as

2 Sellin, "Significance of Records of Crime," p. 498.

possible statements referring to the totality of crime as if it were a determinable figure.

UNREPORTED CRIME—THE "DARK FIGURE"

"Given the growth of what is literally a vast citizen-interviewing industry in the United States," Albert Biderman and Albert Reiss, Jr. have noted, "it is perhaps surprising that the sample survey had not hitherto [before 1966] been applied to systematic examination of the crime problem."[3] They point out that, until very recent years, national surveys on crime had been confined to exploration of public views on issues such as capital punishment and juvenile delinquency, and they suggest that it was in large measure a growing interest in "victimology"[4] that provided impetus for inventories of unreported crimes and their consequences.

The selective recall of events by persons interviewed constitutes a major difficulty in determining with some precision the discrepancy between official reports of crime and unreported crime. A study of visits to doctors conducted as part of a national health survey indicated the difficulties faced in reconciling the recollection of facts with the facts themselves. Thirty percent of the *known* visits to doctors during a two-week period prior to the week of interviewing were *not* reported in response to questioning; 23 percent remained unreported after three special probe questions were asked.[5] The difficulty may be considerably greater when as complicated an area as crime victimization comes under scrutiny. Several generalizations may be made about selective reporting by respondents: First, underreporting increases with length of time between the event and the interview; second, the degree of social threat or embarrassment is negatively related to the rate of reporting; third, the greater the involvement in institutional processing, the more likely the event is to be recalled; fourth, respondents report their own experiences better than those of others; fifth, the more events of which one has been the subject, the more likely one is to report a known event.[6] A crucial matter is that underreporting is selective among classes of persons and events.

The first intensive attempts in the United States to employ surveys of samples of the general population for estimating the incidence of crime, which was sponsored by the President's Commission in 1966, led to the conclusion that "the actual amount of crime in the United States today is several times that reported" in national tabulations of crime rates.[7] Two sets of data amplifying this position are presented

3 Biderman and Reiss, Jr., "On Exploring the 'Dark Figure' of Crime," p. 7.
4 See Schafer, *The Victim and His Criminal;* Mendelsohn, "The Origin of the Doctrine of Victimology."
5 Biderman and Reiss, Jr., "On Exploring the 'Dark Figure' of Crime," p. 12.
6 *Ibid.,* p. 12.
7 President's Commission, *Challenge of Crime in a Free Society,* p. 25.

in the Commission report. The first, summarized in Table 5.1, compares reported crime rates with estimates from a National Opinion Research Center (NORC) survey of a national sample comprising 10,000 households. Each person interviewed in each household was asked whether he or anyone living with him had been a victim of a crime during the preceding twelve months. The survey estimated the rate of personal crimes to be twice as high as that of reported figures and more than twice as high for crimes against property. Forcible rapes were more than 3½ times the reported rate, burglaries were

Table 5.1   Comparison of Survey and UCR Rates (per 100,000 Population)

Classification	NORC survey 1965–1966	UCR rate for individuals 1965	UCR rate for individuals and organizations 1965*
Willful homicide	3.0	5.1	5.1
Forcible rape	42.5	11.6	11.6
Robbery	94.0	61.4	61.4
Aggravated assault	218.3	106.6	106.6
Burglary	949.1	299.6	605.3
Larceny ($50 and over)	606.5	267.4	393.3
Motor vehicle theft	206.2	226.0	251.0
Total violence	357.8	184.7	184.7
Total property	1,761.8	793.0	1,249.6

* The UCR national totals do not distinguish crimes committed against individuals or households from those committed against businesses or other organizations. The UCR rate for individuals is the published national rate adjusted to eliminate burglaries, larcenies, and vehicle thefts not committed against individuals or households. No adjustment was made for robbery.

SOURCE: Biderman and Reiss, Jr. "On Exploring the 'Dark Figure' of Crime," p. 15.

3 times, aggravated assualts and larcenies of $50 and over were more than double, and robberies were 50 percent greater. Only vehicle thefts were reported to be lower by a small, though "puzzling" amount; it is believed that perhaps people report their cars "stolen" to the police and then find that they themselves "misplaced" the car or that someone else had merely "borrowed" it. Phillip Ennis suggests that persons "may either forget the incident when interviewed or be too embarrassed to mention it."[8] The one homicide reported during the survey was too small a number to be useful statistically.

A larger deviation than that of the NORC was discovered in a survey by the Bureau of Social Science Research (BSSR) in high and

8 Ennis, "Crime, Victims, and the Police," p. 37.

medium crime-rate precincts in the District of Columbia, the results of which are presented in Figure I. Data were restricted to adults and victimization of businesses and transients was excluded from the reported figures. The survey rates for various offenses are from three to ten times greater than the reported rates.[9]

Figure I
Estimated Rates of Offense*
Comparison of Police† and Bureau of Social Science Research Survey Data

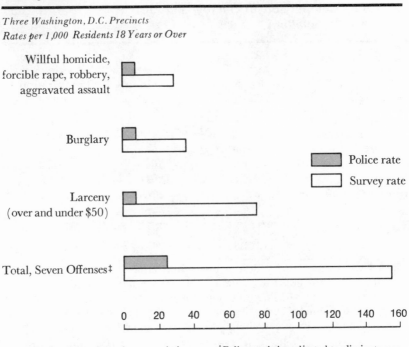

Three Washington, D.C. Precincts
Rates per 1,000 Residents 18 Years or Over

Willful homicide, forcible rape, robbery, aggravated assault

Burglary

Police rate
Survey rate

Larceny (over and under $50)

Total, Seven Offenses‡

0   20   40   60   80   100   120   140   160

* Incidents involving more than one victim adjusted to count as only one offense. A victimization rate would count the incidence for each individual.

† Police statistics adjusted to eliminate non-resident and commercial victims and victims under 18 years of age.

‡ Willful homicide, forcible rape, robbery, aggravated assault, burglary, larceny (over and under $50), and motor vehicle theft.

SOURCE: Albert Biderman, *The Annals*, November, 1967, Page 20.

Victims who had not notified the police of the offenses committed against them were asked during the NORC national survey of households why they had not done so. The reason most frequently given was that the police could do nothing. This reason was offered to survey interviewers by 68 percent of those not reporting malicious mischief and by 60 or more percent of those not reporting burglaries,

9 Biderman, "Surveys of Population Samples for Estimating Crime Incidence," p. 17.

larcenies of $50 and more, and auto thefts. Two brief vignettes of such unreported incidents appear in a news story in *The New York Times*:

> On Saturday, October 26 [1968], Robert Walters went into the vestibule of an apartment building on West 75th Street, leaned over the buzzer board and began searching for the name of a friend. Suddenly, two men appeared, placed a knife at his throat and demanded his money.
>
> Mr. Walters, a visitor from Washington, did not report the armed robbery to the police. "It would have been a waste of my time and police time," Mr. Walters recalled recently. "They only took cash—which couldn't be traced—and the stickup was so fast and professional that I really didn't see their faces."
>
> On the same day that Mr. Walters was held up, Dr. Helen Mitchell, a sociologist and antipoverty official, was away from her apartment in the southern Bronx from 7 P.M. to 9 P.M. During this two-hour period someone broke into her apartment and took her television set and radio.
>
> Dr. Mitchell did not report the burglary to the police. "I didn't bother calling them because there was nothing they could do," she said.[10]

The most frequent reason offered NORC interviewers for failure to report an offense was that it represented a private matter or that the victim did not want to harm the offender. This explanation was given by 50 percent or more of those persons who did not notify the police regarding aggravated and simple assaults, family crimes, and consumer frauds. Fear of reprisal, though least often cited, was strongest in the case of assaults and family crimes. The extent of failure to report to the police was highest for consumer fraud (90 percent) and lowest for auto theft (11 percent). Summarizing the findings prepared for it on unreported crime, the President's Commission offers the following observation:

> The survey technique, as applied to criminal victimization, is still new and beset with a number of methodological problems. However, the Commission has found the information provided by the surveys of considerable value, and believes that the survey technique has a great untapped potential as a method for providing additional information about the nature and extent of our crime problem and the relative effectiveness of different programs to control crime.[11]

Official Criminal Statistics

We are apt in the future to see many more intensive surveys of unreported crime, confined to smaller reporting districts and delimited periods of time. From these, a series of generalizations ought to be

10 *New York Times*, Nov. 29, 1968.
11 President's Commission, *Challenge of Crime in a Free Society*, p. 22.

forthcoming regarding the kinds of crime that go unreported and the persons who do and do not report offenses as well as the conditions favoring reporting and those inhibiting it. We also should soon have results of surveys conducted in the same jurisdictions over time so that we can begin to establish trends in unreported crime and gain deeper insight into the relationship between reported and unreported crime. If, for instance, we discover year after year that armed robberies are reported once for every two times they occur, we can begin to extrapolate with some confidence from reported figures to actual events without the necessity of continuous surveys.

Meanwhile, official crime reports have to be used to estimate the amount of diverse kinds of criminal activity in the United States and variations in crime over given periods of time. The particular shortcomings of compilations should be kept in mind so that corrections can be made for inadequacies and skepticism can be maintained regarding the forthcoming results. The failure of the United States to establish adequate reporting systems for criminal behavior should not be passed by without comment, however. As far back as 1931, the National Commission on Law Observance and Enforcement, popularly known as the Wickersham Commission, commented caustically on the sorry condition of statistics on crime in the United States. The Commission observed that "The eagerness with which the unsystematic, often inaccurate, and more often incomplete statistics available for this country are taken up by text writers, writers in the periodicals, newspaper writers, and public speakers, speaks for itself. . . . Actual data are the beginning of wisdom on such a subject . . . and no data can be had for the country as a whole."[12]

Thirty-six years later, the President's Commission on Law Enforcement and Administration of Justice indicated a concern similar to that of its predecessor, illustrating their concern with specific reference to reported robberies in New York and Chicago, which indicate that crime statistics, like the drunk's lampost, are often used more for support than for light.[13] Though Chicago had less than half the population of New York in 1935, it was reporting eight times as many robberies. Chicago continued to report a higher rate until 1949, when the national crime tabulation discontinued use of the New York figures because nobody had any faith in them any longer. In 1950, when New York installed a central reporting system, robberies rose 400 percent and burglaries 1,300 percent, passing Chicago in both categories. In 1959, Chicago installed its central reporting system and again passed New York. By 1966, with new practices in both jurisdictions, New York was 25 percent ahead of Chicago in robberies.

With some exasperation, the President's Commission noted that

12 National Commission on Law Observance and Enforcement, *Report on Criminal Statistics,* p. 1.
13 Geis, "Crime and Politics."

"it seems unlikely that the level of robbery in New York today is thirteen times what it was in 1940 or triple what it was in 1960, but how does one decide for the purpose of long-term comparisons?"; it was observed that "The real question is not the method of estimation, but whether the yardstick at the present time is too changeable to allow significant trend comparisons to be made at the national level."[14]

UNIFORM CRIME REPORTS

Published annually by the Federal Bureau of Investigation, the *Uniform Crime Reports* remains our major source for official statistical information on the crime problem. The Federal Bureau of Investigation (F.B.I.) was first enpowered in 1930 to collect and distribute statistics pertaining to crime. Since the compilation of such data depends upon the voluntary cooperation of many police agencies in the United States and their willingness to transcribe local data onto the forms prescribed by the F.B.I., complete and accurate coverage has been difficult to attain. The F.B.I. used to indicate in each statistical compilation that it "is not in a position to vouch for the validity of the reports received," though it recently abandoned this caution, despite its obvious truth and importance. In its most recent report, the F.B.I. merely warns readers against "drawing conclusions from direct comparisons of crime figures between individual communities without first considering the factors involved"; then, disregarding its own dictum, the F.B.I. report goes on in its next sentence to suggest that "the national material summarized in this publication should be used, however, as a starting point to determine deviations of individual cities from the national averages."[15]

The inability of the F.B.I. to stand squarely behind the accuracy of the *Uniform Crime Reports,* because of the vagaries of reporting agencies, has been severely criticized in the past. "Even if the word 'Uniform' were omitted from the title and the inaccuracies of the figures pointed out, it is doubtful that the publication of such statistics would not do more harm than good," Sam Bass Warner maintained, adding:

> In spite of anything said in the report, the Federal Government would be giving credence to police statistics by publishing them. Public opinion and legislation would be based upon them. If the Federal Government is to maintain its present reputation for the accuracy of its statistics, it must stand by the slogan: "Better no statistics, than false statistics!"[16]

Experience over the years has underlined the importance of approaching the *Uniform Crime Reports* warily. One of the reasons for major inaccuracies has been indicated by Cressey, who notes that "the

14 President's Commission, *Challenge of Crime in a Free Society,* p. 27.
15 Federal Bureau of Investigation, *Uniform Crime Reports,* 1967, p. vi.
16 Warner, "Crimes Known to the Police," p. 330.

police have an obligation to protect the reputation of their cities, and when this cannot be done efficiently under existing legal and administrative machinery, it is sometimes accomplished statistically."[17] Table 5.2, compiled by the President's Commission, reports instances in which changes in reporting procedures between 1959 and 1965 resulted in increases in reported crime in eleven major cities of between 26 percent and 202 percent. Details on the ingredients of such numerical distortion are supplied by Daniel Bell in a review of statistics supplied by the city of Philadelphia, which in 1953 reported 28,560 major crimes as against 16,773 in 1951, for an increase of more than 70 percent. Bell notes:

> [There] had been no invasion by criminals. Police Comissioner Thomas J. Gibbons, who assumed office in 1952 as part of the reform administration of Mayor Clark, had found that for years crime records, in order to minimize the amount of crime in the city, had been faked. One center-city district, he discovered, had handled 5,000 more complaints than it had recorded. A new central reporting system was installed, and as a result, the number of 'crimes' went up.[18]

More to the credit of the *Uniform Crime Reports* has been the impressive increase in the number of reporting agencies since the time of its inception. Beginning with 400 contributing police authorities in 1930, the *Report* for 1967 includes 8,400 law enforcement agencies representing 98 percent of the United States population living in places defined by the Census Bureau as standard metropolitan statistical areas, 89 percent of the population in other cities, and 75 percent of the rural population. The combined coverage accounts for 92 percent of the national population.

Originally, the Federal Bureau of Investigation published the *Uniform Crime Reports* twice annually, utilizing its own special categories of major and minor crimes, referred to as Part I and Part II offenses. In 1958, on the recommendation of a national committee established to review the publication, methods of compiling and classifying crimes were changed and a series of other improvements were instituted.[19] Chief among these was the restriction of major crimes to seven offenses, which are employed to calculate what the F.B.I. calls "Index Rates" of serious crime. Removal of negligent manslaughter (mostly traffic deaths), larceny under $50, and statutory rape (where force is not used), served to tighten up the category of serious crime to make it more representative of acts generally regarded as particularly socially harmful. As Marvin E. Wolfgang points out, however, offenses such as arson, kidnapping, and assault and battery, which do not appear in the Index, may in fact involve more personal

17 Cressey, "The State of Criminal Statistics," p. 232.
18 Bell, *End of Ideology*, p. 138.
19 Lejins, "Uniform Crime Reports." See also Glaser, "National Goals and Indicators for the Reduction of Crime and Delinquency."

injury than forcible rape, aggravated assault, and other crimes listed in the Index.[20] In addition, since the classifications used in reporting crimes have been modified, data currently compiled cannot be compared with data appearing before 1958.

Table 5.2 Reporting System Changes (UCR Index, Figures Not Comparable with Prior Years)

Name of city	Years of increase	Amount of increase (Index crimes)		Percent increase
		From	To	
Baltimore	1964–65	18,637	26,193	40.5
Buffalo	1961–63	4,779	9,305	94.7
Chicago	1959–60	56,570	97,253	71.9
Cleveland	1963–64	10,584	17,254	63.0
Indianapolis	1961–62	7,416	10,926	47.3
Kansas City, Mo.	1959–61*	4,344	13,121	202.0
Memphis	1963–64	8,781	11,533	31.3
Miami	1963–64	10,750	13,610	26.6
Nashville	1962–63	6,595	9,343	41.7
Shreveport	1962–63	1,898	2,784	46.7
Syracuse	1963–64	3,365	4,527	34.5

* No report was published for Kansas City, Mo., for 1960.
Source: *Uniform Crime Reports*, 1959–1965.

Since 1958, the national crime report has been published only once a year, with quarterly supplements of preliminary figures for the current year for cities of more than 100,000 population. In addition, yearly reports now attempt to adjust figures for population changes during the ten years between the federal censuses to eliminate the more grotesque errors that occurred when figures from the decennial census had been employed through the following nine years as the basis for the calculation of crime rates. The rates for California, for instance, rose astronomically year by year, primarily because crime rates for the state were being calculated without regard to population growth. Every tenth year, however, the California crime rate would drop precipitously when updated census figures were employed in the calculations.

The twenty-seven categories of crime currently used in the annual F.B.I. report are broad in coverage and range from criminal homicide, forcible rape, and robbery to parking violations and a miscellaneous category referred to as "all other offenses." Since the nation's police forces operate under differing classification systems, data must be conscientiously interpreted and redefined. The descriptive categories employed by the F.B.I. are deliberately broad for this purpose. *Rob-*

20 Wolfgang, *"Uniform Crime Reports:* A Critical Appraisal," p. 719.

bery, for example, is defined as "stealing or taking anything of value from the person by force or violence or by putting in fear, such as strong-arm robbery, stickups, robbery armed; assault to rob and attempt to rob." *Aggravated assault* is described as "assault with intent to kill or for the purpose of inflicting severe bodily injury by shooting, cutting, stabbing, maiming, poisoning, scalding, or by use of acids, explosives, or other means. Excludes simple assault, assault and battery, fighting, etc." *Larceny-theft* excludes auto theft, embezzlement, and forgery, and distinguishes between thefts of more or less than fifty dollars in value.

Apart from difficulties involved in accurate accumulation of numerical information and its conversion into index rates, there remain problems with the interpretation of data. In this regard, the performance of the *Uniform Crime Reports* over the years is alleged to be something less than totally satisfactory. Wolfgang, for instance, has entered the following criticisms after a thoroughgoing review of the F.B.I. statistical reports:

> Interesting use of adjectives is made in recent Quarterly Reports. We are told, for instance, that serious crimes "substantially" increased by 7 per cent; pocket-picking decreased by 18 per cent, but with no adjective; while forcible rape had an "alarming" rise of 8 per cent. "Murder" in rural counties was "sharply down" by 16 per cent, but offenses against the person showed a "sharp" increase of 6 per cent. At one time, index offenses increased "alarmingly" by 12 per cent, and aggravated assault had a "sharp" increase of 7 per cent, but at another time when "serious crimes" went up 11 per cent, no adjective was used. This may be a relatively minor objection, but it is certainly difficult to know what is a "sharp," "substantial," or "alarming" change according to these Reports. If these terms are to be used at all, they should at least be applied with discrimination and consistency.[21]

The same author also indicates a further objection to the tendency of the F.B.I. to inject editorial comment into its statistical presentations:

> Keeping in mind what was said earlier about errors in reporting, no one can give very serious attention to the following statement: "Increases were recorded in all crime categories except robbery which was down one per cent. This crime had the most significant rise in 1960 and the reversal of the trend indicates to some extent the success of police efforts to reduce its occurrence." That this change in absolute numbers of one per cent could be a measurement of police efforts is a patently biased comment. Of course no mention is ever made about police efforts to reduce any type of crime when there is a per cent increase, however, "sharp" or "alarming." Moreover, the paradoxical situation may occur that when the police are making greater efforts in their activity, certain types of crime are increasing.[22]

21 *Ibid.,* pp. 736–737.
22 *Ibid.,* p. 737.

Figure II

Crimes Cleared by Arrest
1967

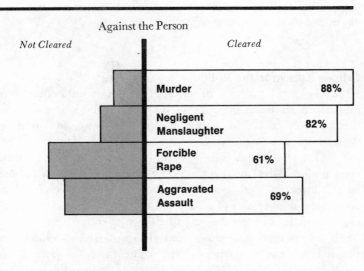

Against the Person

Not Cleared   *Cleared*

Murder   88%

Negligent Manslaughter   82%

Forcible Rape   61%

Aggravated Assault   69%

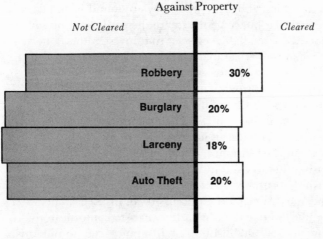

Against Property

Not Cleared   *Cleared*

Robbery   30%

Burglary   20%

Larceny   18%

Auto Theft   20%

SOURCE: *Uniform Crime Reports*, 1967, Page 31

Finally, the allegations of Biderman place in its proper perspective the use of reported crime figures to understand criminal behavior, at least as such behavior becomes known to the authorities. Biderman insists that "most of the sources of error operate to inflate the newer figures relative to the older ones, resulting in a false picture of rapidly increasing lawlessness among the population." He submits the following three items as characteristics of the *Uniform Crime Reports*:

1. The errors and biasing factors affecting the Crime Index largely operate to show spurious increases, rather than decreases in the rate.

2. The Crime Index does not provide a sound basis for determining whether criminal behavior is increasing, or decreasing, in the United States.

3. The Crime Index is highly sensitive to social developments that are almost universally regarded as improvement in the society. Thus, it is altogether possible that year-to-year increases in crime rates may be more indicative of social progress than of social decay.[23]

Crimes Known to the Police

Since the total volume of crime can never be known—and since the information now available on unreported crime is quite fragmentary, replete with methodological flaws—we are often forced to depend upon a category referred to as "crimes known to the police" to provide us with an index of criminal behavior. At the outset, however, it should be noted that "crimes known to the police" are apt to be the most dramatic and the more conventional types of crime. A large volume of crimes of a personal nature and a wide range of minor violations, as well as the so-called "white-collar" offenses involving illicit operations in business and the professions, seldom are incorporated into the category of "crimes known to the police." In regard to white-collar crimes, Harry Shulman has complained that statistics "lie buried in agency files, and sometimes they are found in the annual reports of public agencies, but so scattered are these information sources that they are not easily available to scientific investigators"; he continues that even when numerical material can be located "the statistics are so garbled that specifiic offenses, small in number but qualitatively significant, are concealed through inclusion in broader categories."[24]

In addition to the built-in inaccuracies, reflecting the initial selection of those crimes that will be included in the Reports, there are, as noted earlier, procedural matters that tend to be reflected differentially in them. For instance, the number of reported property offenses is increasing due to insurance against theft. So-called multiple-line comprehensive insurance policies increased twenty-four times between 1955 and 1964. When a theft occurs to an insured homeowner, he is much more likely today than in earlier years to conform to the reporting requirements for establishing an insurance claim. Biderman notes that "The rise in the crime rate attributable to this factor is a useful indicator for measuring the burden of work placed on the police but not for indicating how much lawbreaking is occurring in the United States."[25]

As we move further procedurally from "crimes known to the police," a sizeable shrinkage in the volume of crime as an index takes place. The majority of certain crimes, such as robbery, burglary, auto-

23 Biderman, "Social Indicators and Goals," p. 115.
24 Shulman, "The Measurement of Crime in the United States," pp. 485–486.
25 Biderman, "Social Indicators and Goals," p. 120.

mobile theft, or receiving stolen property do *not* eventuate in arrest. Moving still further along the administrative scale, arrests lead still less to indictments by the grand jury or to the initiation of formal charges upon which the individual will be brought to trial. Trials themselves invariably lead to a smaller percentage of successful convictions, and convictions do not inevitably lead to prison or reformatory sentences. We can see, therefore, that there is a progressive dwindling in the number of criminal occurrences that takes place on each advancing level of the administrative process. Figure II will give some indication of the relatively wide discrepancies that exist between crimes known to the police and those that are cleared by arrest.

It will be noted in Figure II that the number of crimes cleared by arrest is considerably greater for certain types of offenses than for others. In general, crimes against the person result in a much higher number of arrests than crimes against property. Even here, however, except in the case of murder where the percentage of clearances through arrest is relatively high, a substantial number of offenses against the person do not result in arrests. For crimes against property, we are struck by the fact that the vast majority of such offenses are not cleared by arrest, with only a minor fractional part of the larcenies and auto thefts resolved by arrest.

Since the major sources for determining the extent and variations in criminal behavior are law enforcement agencies and the courts, the presence of wide statistical gaps on different administrative levels should be carefully observed. If we take a single category such as robbery, we find that 58 percent of such offenses were not cleared by arrest in 1967 and that of those cleared about 75 percent resulted in charges, of which 49 percent resulted in convictions. Put into numbers, we find that for 100 robberies known to the police (recalling that surveys of unreported crime indicate that for each 100 robberies known to the police, approximately 50 go unreported), only 42 persons are arrested. Some 31 of these persons are apt to be charged, and only 15 convicted of the offense. The biases in studies of robbery or of robbers based on arrested or incarcerated offenders can readily be appreciated from consideration of the number of robbers who escape actionable consequences.

An awareness of the inadequacies of much of our statistical material in crime and our methods for its assessment not only provides us with a more realistic perspective concerning the dimensions of criminal behavior itself, but also gives us a more fundamental understanding of the character of crime in relation to law enforcement and prosecution. Herbert Bloch has shown that statistics concerning crime and delinquency are not necessarily to be construed solely as measurements of the phenomena that they are designed to portray, but, even more, as an index of the state of official and public attitudes.[26] While

26 Bloch, "Juvenile Delinquency: Myth or Threat?"

this has been regarded as particularly true concerning delinquency, it is also true with respect to statistical descriptions of adult crime. Thus, that the police do not always know about the volume of crime in a particular jurisdiction is not only due to the victims' refusal to talk but also to local economic and social policy that may militate against adequate coverage by encouraging non-reporting to protect financial interests (e.g., employment provided by organized crime) or out of sympathy for certain offenders.[27] Thorsten Sellin, for instance, has reported that, in the city of Philadelphia in a given year, three department stores had knowledge of shoplifting offenses in their respective premises that exceeded in number the total thefts of all types known to the police for the entire city.[28] Such episodes and similar conditions could be cited at length for different crimes in different parts of the country.

In review, we note that the development of an adequate statistical index for crime is handicapped by the natural concealments involved in crime; by the character of the police and their efficiency in the apprehension and reporting of crimes; by the relative ease or difficulty with which certain forms of crime come to public attention; and by the categorical and legal differences descriptive of crime in different areas.

Toward the Refinement of Crime Measures

The problems involved in the measurement of crime arise not only from the difficulties of obtaining precise and authentic data, but also from the failure to use an index that is truly representative of the particular phase of crime that is being studied. An index is a measure by means of which we are enabled to gain greater quantitative comprehension of the problem under discussion. Although a large variety of technical problems are involved in how we may arrive at a representative and accurate index, there are three sources of error that are particularly conspicuous—one primarily statistical and the two others pertaining to the nature and composition of the population groups that are employed.

An index may be conceived in certain cases as a simple arithmetic average, a method for providing a type of composite picture of a wide range of data. Thus, in attempting to learn something about the ages of prisoners in selected institutions, their earnings before commitment, or the size of their families, a simple arithmetic average may be computed by adding the sum total of all the items in the series—ages, earnings, or family size—and then dividing by the total number of subjects. If the distribution of the particular series of items is asym-

27 See Van Vechten, "The Toleration Quotient as a Device for Defining Certain Social Concepts"; Wheeler, "Criminal Statistics: A Reformulation of the Problem," p. 319.

28 Sellin, *Research Memorandum on Crime in the Depression*, p. 69.

metrical and uneven, however, such a composite figure may lead to a distorted or misleading conception. In computing average ages of prisoners, for example, a disproportionate number of either youthful or elderly persons in the population group may result in an average index at variance with the true picture. Consequently, other forms of averages might provide a more significant index—for example, the median (the middle age in the sequence) or the mode (the most typical age) or measures that indicate ranges and percentages of distribution. In any event, such averages employed as indexes should be accompanied as a matter of course by measures of distribution such as the *standard deviation,* which indicates the range of distribution of a given group of items around the average. A critically informed attitude is essential in estimating the value of any index.

In addition to problems of a purely statistical nature, there are problems involving the use of samples and their composition as a means of determining the accuracy of a given index. Before we can assume that a certain index is representative of a particular aspect of crime or delinquency, the nature of the sample from which the index was drawn must be carefully assessed. The sample may not be truly representative of cases we would like to examine or portray. For example, prison populations are rarely truly representative of persons who commit given offenses. Prison populations, in some cases, consist of older recidivists, or they may be heavily weighted by members of an ethnic or racial minority. The field of delinquency offers innumerable illustrations of how the selective bias or distorted nature of the sample tends to produce a wholly unwarranted generalization. In samples drawn from urban court-adjudicated delinquents, there is a tendency toward unduly high percentages of youths with alleged major or minor personality disorders, due to the pronounced psychiatric and social-work orientation of many of our juvenile courts. This orientation, reflected in intake policies (that is, policies related to the acceptance of prospective clients) tends to produce selective samples of delinquent youths from which certain indexes cannot be considered truly characteristic. If training-school populations are taken as a basis for deriving indexes about delinquency, the results are apt to be equally distorted because of the high percentage of recidivists and more serious youthful offenders found in such populations.

A third precaution, closely related to some of the considerations just discussed, is concerned with the *composition* of the population from which the sample is drawn. Age, sex, and educational, cultural, and economic differentials must be carefully distinguished in attempting to derive any sort of adequate index about crime or delinquency. A simple illustration will make this clear. If a given population is being examined for its rate of crime, a significant factor affecting such an index is its age composition. An area that is characterized by a disproportionate concentration in the older-age categories would tend to reveal a relatively low index of crime as compared to an area that is weighted more heavily on the youthful side. On the other hand, if the rates for the same two areas are computed only on the basis of those segments of the population most vulnerable to crime— the twenty-one to thirty-five-year age group—the first locality may be found to have an exceptionally high crime rate.

For this reason the index of crime, based upon the rate per 100,000 undifferentiated persons, provides only a crude measure for the country as a whole and for certain large regional and urban areas. It provides a rough index by means of which changes in crime occurrence may be observed. For comparison of rates for related areas and for certain types of crime, however, we would be forced to employ a "refined" rate, that is, a rate based upon those segments of the population most vulnerable to crime, in which age, sex, economic, cultural, and educational levels are taken into account.

Population Structure and Crime

The relationship between the population structure and rates for different types of crime constitutes one of the most fruitful areas for the study of criminal trends and one which has never been fully explored. Such an analysis should properly be concerned not only with the changing size of the population, but also with the changing age-composition of the population, the variable effects of differential birth rates over a period of years, changing patterns of concentration and density of the population, and mobility patterns. Indeed, as Bloch has shown, the pattern of changing crime rates in relation to the totality of the demographic structure may afford us remarkable insight into the fundamental alterations that are occurring in the social structure as a whole and that manifest themselves in crises of differing character affecting different segments of the population.[29]

Class and ethnic differentials may be extremely important in this respect, since the variable nature of crime is commonly associated with different stratified and ethnic components of the population. A study of stratified levels, for example, discloses the type of crime most likely to occur for particular groups. Thus, embezzlement, business frauds, and swindles are largely concentrated among certain groups of the middle class. Further examination of such offenses reveals a good deal about age distribution as well, disclosing that they are rarely found among youthful age categories. Conventional crimes, such as robbery, burglary, aggravated assault, and serious crimes of violence, are primarily concentrated in the lower-socioeconomic strata, with certain offenses, such as aggravated assault, found particularly among certain ethnic groups.

On the assumption that patterns of crime, illustrated in their

29 Bloch, *Research Report on Homicides*, pp. 69–177.

various rates, partially reflect sex, age, class, and ethnic differentials at any given time, the continuance of such rates and their increase or decrease may be predicted, provided we comprehend how the forces of social change are affecting the several parts of the population structure. Certain forecasts may be made with some reasonable assurance, if we stipulate carefully the social conditions on which such rates are contingent. A given forecast, therefore, may vary with differing contingent social conditions. Thus, we may forecast that if police and court activity continue to function as they have in relation to the rising population ratios among our adolescents, rates of adjudicated delinquency and police arrests should continue to increase in a predictable manner among certain depressed socioeconomic and ethnic minorities. In a similar manner, the percentage increase of car thefts among youths under twenty-one years of age during the past fifteen years might have been predicted.

It should be kept in mind, therefore, that membership in certain sex, age, and class groups constitutes *categorical risk* of certain forms of crime, which is proportionately greater for certain individuals and groups than for others. Consequently, a study of the population structure and trends in its growth and decline should, ordinarily, disclose a great deal to us about the shape of crime to come.

Studies that compare the rates of different types of crime with the overall crime total in terms of modifications in the population structure should logically involve specific steps of analysis. Although desirable, however, such a logical progression of analysis is rarely pursued. If done, it might encompass the following steps: (1) As a fundamental priority, a basic investigation should be undertaken to discover where the major geographic concentrations of the particular crime problem are, (2) The broad geographical distribution should then be broken down into distinctive variations within a given area, particularly the differences in specific crime rates between populated areas of different sizes, cities, suburbs, townships, villages, and open-country areas, (3) The distinctive statistical features of such differences should be examined in relation to conspicuous demographic characteristics, such as population growth, marked population differentials, and the movements of population, (4) The distinctive rates for certain types of crime must be compared to other types of crime and to overall rates for the specific areas being studied and for the country as a whole, (5) Considerable attention must be paid to distinctive features of the population in regard to sex, age, class, ethnic, religious, educational, and occupational differences, and (6) An analysis of the growth and decline of types of crime must be undertaken in order to determine whether such manifestations are the result of immediate and transient conditions that exist temporarily in the population structure or whether they represent certain characteristic and deep-seated elements within the society itself.

Crime: What of the Future?

Consideration of items such as the preceding must play a prominent part in the attempt to forecast the direction in which the rates for particular crimes are likely to move during future years. The best evidence that we have available on trends in crime in the United States indicates two distinct tendencies operating in tandem but working against each other. Prognostication is thus extremely difficult. There appears to be good evidence that (contrary to widely-held public beliefs) when measured over broad time spans crime—considered as the sum of conventional kinds of offenses—has been decreasing in the United States. In fact, in regard to some offenses, such as homicide, the decrease is striking. On the other hand, the continuous mass movement of people into urban areas in the United States and the concurrent depopulation of the rural hinterland, where crime has always been relatively low, has tended toward an overall increase in crime. The seeming anomaly of these contradictory trends might be understood through the following hypothetical illustration, which, if thought out carefully, will provide considerable insight into the intricacies of crime statistics:

> Suppose we have a society of 1,000,000 in which 80 per cent of the population lives in villages where the crime rate is 40 per 1,000. The remaining 20 per cent lives in urban areas where the crime rate is 100 per 1,000. The crime rate for such a society would be 52 per 1,000. Now suppose the village crime rate remains at 40 per 1,000, the urban crime rate *drops* to 60 per 1,000, and the per cent of population in urban areas rises to 90 per cent of the total, which is still 1,000,000. The new crime rate for the society has risen to 58 per 1,000 even though the rate has fallen sharply in the cities.[30]

A tabulation by Theodore Ferdinand of the criminal patterns in the city of Boston from 1849 to 1951 provides a major source of information on declining long-term crime rates. The aggregate crime rate in Boston shows an almost uninterrupted decline through the surveyed period, to a level that today is about one-third that of a century ago. Murder, burglary, and assault rates reflect this declining movement, which is interrupted only by upward spurts during wars and depressions. Among the major offenses, only forcible rape shows an upward trend, which is probably influenced by changes in sexual patterns and the advent of the automobile.[31]

The Boston study supports a number of generalizations about the picture of crime in future years. There is reason to believe, for instance, that over a long period—perhaps in 50 to 100 years—crime rates in the United States are likely to drop, possibly very sharply. The Boston study also indicates that cyclical phenomena, such as in-

30 Ferdinand, "The Criminal Patterns of Boston Since 1849," note 22, p. 99.
31 *Ibid.*, pp. 84–99; see Kamisar, "When the Cops Were Not 'Handcuffed.'"

ternational conflict and economic affluence or depression, exert strong influence on crime patterns.

Most important for the immediate future, however, is the indication from the Boston study, combined with corollary data, that the number of persons who commit the kinds of crime presently used in reporting statistics seems almost certain to rise dramatically in the immediate future. Population increases alone, given stable crime rates, will tend to produce higher levels of crime. In addition, the inexorable movement of persons to the cities should more than counteract any intrinsic decline in crime rates for the nation.[32]

A continued decline in the average age of the American population will also result in a higher rate of crime, for the young are notoriously more crime-prone than their elders. In addition, as suburban areas are drawn nearer to core cities by improved transportation, settlements in interstitial areas, and migration patterns, it is likely that crime figures will show an increase in such areas.

The precise nature of the forthcoming increase in crime cannot be stated with precision for a short span of time, largely because of the eddies of extrinsic factors bearing momentarily upon levels of crime. In a Danish study, for example, in order to check the accuracy of their prognostications, researchers attempted to employ crime statistics from the year 1950 to generate conclusions regarding criminal behavior in 1964, *after* the 1964 figures had become available. The result of the attempt to make precise "pretended forecasts," they report, was unsuccessful; it was felt that this was largely due to the general inadequacy of available statistical measures regarding both crime and other forms of social health and malaise.[33] Similar inadequacies seriously handicap attempts to predict the future of crime in the United States.

"If it is true, as Commission surveys tend to indicate, that society has not yet found fully reliable methods for measuring the volume of crime," the President's Commission on Law Enforcement and Administration of Justice noted, "it is even more true that it has failed to find such methods for measuring the trend of crime."[34] Nonetheless, with its numerical reservations on record, the Commission entered a straightforward prediction regarding the likely upward spiral in criminal rates during the next decade as well as its formula for possible remedy of the situation:

> The Commission believes that age, urbanization, and other shifts in population already under way will likely operate over the next five to ten years to increase the volume of offenses faster than population growth. Further dipping into reservoirs of unreported crime will likely combine with this real increase in crime to produce even geater in-

32 Clinard, "Relation of Urbanization and Urbanism to Criminal Behavior."
33 Jepsen and Pal, "Forecasting Crime."
34 President's Commission, *Challenge of Crime in a Free Society*, p. 23.

creases in reported crime rates. Many of the basic social forces that tend to increase the amount of real crime are already taking effect and are for the most part irreversible. If society is to be successful in its desire to reduce the amount of real crime, it must find new ways to create the kinds of conditions and inducements—social, environmental, and psychological—that will bring about a greater commitment to law-abiding conduct on the part of all Americans and a better understanding of the great stake that all men have in being able to trust in the honesty and integrity of their fellow citizens.[35]

The Commission report also supplied evidence on various matters that feed into statements regarding the likely rise in reported crime in the United States during the forthcoming decade. The following ideas, taken from various portions of the Commission's reports, are particularly notable:

1. *There is likely to be a continued proliferation in the number of acts defined as crimes during future years.* There are, the Commission noted, more than 2,800 federal crimes and a much larger number of state and local offenses.[36] While some suasion is now being exerted to remove from the statute books offenses that are regarded as dealing with individual morality, such as abortion and consensual homosexuality between adults, there is a contrary trend to outlaw additional forms of behavior. This is the result of a further effort to protect persons from depredations attached to newer technologies and to extend protection into areas where laissez faire principles previously governed.

2. *There is likely to be a continued increase in the amount of crime reported to the authorities.* In particular, it is believed that changes in expectations among the poor and members of minority groups regarding their rights have led to larger amounts of reporting of criminal offenses than in earlier years. Additionally, improvements in police efficiency and income tax requirements that insist on official reports before deductions are permitted are helping the reporting of criminal offenses. The President's Commission has noted that "even small changes in the way crime is reported by the public to the police, or classified and recorded by the police, could have significant effects on the trend of reported crime. There is strong reason to believe that a number of such changes have taken place within recent years."[37]

3. *There is apt to be a continuing rise in crime rates with the continuation of economic affluence in the United States.* Affluent people do not protect their property well, resulting in the availability of more property that can be stolen. One of the few specific items for which national reports indicate high larceny rates is children's bicycles. Among other things, it is evident that there will be a con-

35 *Ibid.*, p. 31.
36 *Ibid.*, p. 18.
37 *Ibid.*, p. 25.

siderably greater number of bicycles available to be stolen in prosperous times. In 1963, in fact, bicycles constituted 20 percent of all reported larcenies, and between 1960 and 1963 theft of bicycles rose by 40 percent.[38]

Affluence also appears to be crime-inducing in that it tends to introduce a feeling among some less-privileged persons that they are not sharing equivalently in the general well-being of society. More often than in periods of economic depression, such persons are apt to resort to illegal means to secure for themselves a portion of the available material goods. It is one of the time-tested axioms of criminal behavior that it is not poor conditions alone that produce crime, but more often the juxtaposition of poverty and well-being in the same social order, particularly when those less well-off feel deeply that they should have an opportunity to participate more fairly in prosperity.

4. *Further development of "professionalization" of personnel in law enforcement work is apt to produce an increase in reported and recorded crime.* Professionalization tends to increase efficiency as a feeling of occupational pride and an improvement in working standards come into being. In addition, as the President's Commission pointed out, there is a tendency among "professionalized" police forces to arrest more persons and to release fewer of them on the basis of informal settlements (particularly in the case of juveniles) than there is among police forces operating under a less professional working ethos.[39] The Omnibus Crime Control and Safe Streets Act of 1968 (Public Law 90–351) provided substantial financial support to local and state law enforcement efforts; the hoped-for result of upgraded police performance and improved police image should produce an upward surge in reported crime.

5. *There is apt to be a considerable growth in female crime rates as social conditions further blur the distinction between the roles and activities of men and women in the United States.* Among the major "untapped" sources of crime—if the matter can be stated as such—is that of female behavior. Statistics indicate that only one female is involved in the commission of index crimes for every eight males. In some instances, such as rape, the number of female offenders is, of course, negligible. However, females have, on occasion, been convicted of rape in cases involving, for example, the use of force by one woman to make another submit to intercourse. In other instances, such as abortion, where in many states both the abortionist and his client are guilty of a criminal offense, the difficulty of enforcement as well as police and prosecution policies keep down what could be an astronomic influx of females into the criminal justice system. There is also a general reluctance to arrest and convict females for offenses

38 Biderman, "Social Indicators and Goals," p. 119.
39 President's Commission, *Challenge of Crime in a Free Society*, p. 25.

similar to those committed by males, particularly if the women have young children at home.

But the striking absence of female violators in homicide, robbery, and burglary, among other offenses, is an important fact from which considerable comprehension of many of the roots of criminal behavior can be gained, since it tells how different social roles and experiences condition criminal patterns. There is a narrowing of the gap between male and female crime rates as the drive for female equality proceeds.[40] The predicted growing equivalence in crime is seen in offense statistics on juvenile delinquency, although offenses alleged against young girls such as promiscuity and sexual waywardness, do not also result in action against the boys involved with them. In addition, the acts are not a matter of police concern if the girls are beyond the age of juvenile court jurisdiction.

The Response to Crime
Given an increase in reported crime, the social response generated is apt to become more intense, though there is little reason to believe that it will be particularly effective in counteracting the preceding outlined forces. The intricacy of the task of crime control may be illustrated by consideration of proposals that suggest that more stringent enforcement policies and harsher penalties are a necessary first step toward a reduction in criminal offenses. Little empirical evidence can be mustered in support of this view, except in regard to a limited number of offenses that are rationally calculated and a limited number of rationally calculating offenders. On the other hand, the view that sterner measures will reduce crime cannot be rebutted by reference to reliable experimental data. The brutally harsh penalties in earlier centuries hardly led to a disappearance or a notable diminution of crime during these times, but it is impossible to calculate how much crime there otherwise might have been. Certainty of apprehension and punishment rather than severity of treatment has traditionally been viewed as the major deterrent of criminal activity. Total certainty, however, is never likely to be realized—especially in regard to property offenses—and there is no easy method for determining which fraction of probable risk deters and which encourages potential violators.

There are, in addition, views of some persuasiveness that insist that more stringent enforcement of the criminal laws, with higher certainties of apprehension, may in fact contribute to an ultimate increase in the amount of crime. If so, such measures would obviously ill serve the need to provide maximum public protection, both now and in later years. If the police become "overzealous," the President's

40 *Ibid.* p. 41.

Commission observes, taking note of this view, "people better left alone will be drawn into criminal careers."[41]

The relationship between "overzealousness," and subsequent criminal behavior is also difficult to trace with any exactness. But some possible consequences may be spelled out readily enough with hypothetical illustrations. It is known, for instance, that most persons violate many laws even in the course of a single day, and there are studies that indicate that a majority of the population has violated at one time or another laws severe enough to call for imprisonment.[42] Failure to apprehend most of these offenders did not, however, mean failure to keep them from committing a regular string of further serious offenses, in most instances. On the other hand, we may suspect that had they been caught and involved in the web of the criminal process, particularly in terms of exposure to more sophisticated and committed offenders, a number of them would have persisted in regular law-violating behavior. It is in this regard that the failure of the system of law enforcement may, ironically, at times produce those kinds of results claimed for its success.

For Further Reading

BIDERMAN, ALBERT D., and ALBERT J. REISS, JR. "On Exploring the 'Dark Figure' of Crime," in *Annals of the American Academy of Political and Social Science*. Vol. 374 (November 1967), pp. 1–15.

The history of criminal statistics has seen a constant search to illuminate the "dark figure" of crime—that is, occurrences that are not registered in the statistics of public agencies, but that nonetheless meet reasonable definitions of acts constituting criminal offenses. This paper discusses techniques for discovering unreported crime and indicates particular shortcomings of figures on unreported crime as they compare with official sources, which, of course, have numerous shortcomings of their own.

BLOCH, HERBERT A. "Juvenile Delinquency: Myth or Threat?" in *Journal of Criminal Law, Criminology, and Police Science*. Vol. 49 (November–December 1958), pp. 303–309.

A critique of popular statements on the extent of juvenile delinquency, this article shows that much information is based on an inaccurate foundation because of the inadequacy of the statistical sources involved.

ENNIS, PHILLIP H. "Crimes, Victims, and the Police," in *Trans-action*. Vol. 4 (June 1967), pp. 36–44.

Professor Ennis, now on the staff of Wesleyan University in Middletown, Connecticut, served as director of the study of victimization that the National Opinion Research Center carried out for the President's Commission on Law Enforcement and Administration of Justice. His article summarizes some of the more salient points of the NORC investigation and provides answers to questions regarding the kinds of persons who

41 *Ibid.*, p. 104.
42 See, for instance, Wallerstein and Wyle, "Our Law-Abiding Law-Breakers."

summon police aid and the attitudes held by victims and nonvictims toward law enforcement processes.

FERDINAND, THEODORE N. "The Criminal Patterns of Boston Since 1849," in *American Journal of Sociology*. Vol. 73 (July 1967), pp. 84–99.

A member of the sociology faculty at Northeastern University in Boston, Professor Ferdinand examined the annual arrest reports of the Boston police from 1849 to 1951 in regard to seven major crimes. His results show that "when the rates of these crimes are examined collectively, they show a distinct downward tendency." Of the specific offenses, only forcible rape demonstrated a clear tendency toward increase during the last one hundred years.

WOLFGANG, MARVIN E. *"Uniform Crime Reports:* A Critical Appraisal," in *University of Pennsylvania Law Review*. Vol. 3 (April 1963), pp. 708–738.

Professor Wolfgang, of the University of Pennsylvania, has scrutinized the *Uniform Crime Reports* since their inauguration, tracing changes that have been made and indicating shortcomings that continue to exist. Painstakingly comparing some offenses city by city and year by year, he shows clearly that the *U.C.R.*, both in its reporting and in its interpretations, often far exceeds the validity of its raw materials.

6
Characteristics of Reported Crime

The difficulty of obtaining a precise picture of the volume and trend of crime in the United States has been stressed in the preceding chapter. Pending the appearance and validation of more incisive material, information about crime must come from official tabulations, whose shortcomings have been indicated earlier. The strength of official sources lies primarily in the fact that they sometimes report on essentially the same criminal phenomenon over a period of years. That is, if we can determine that no major changes have taken place in a jurisdiction's laws regarding a particular crime, that no notable alterations have occurred in the work or methods of the law enforcement agencies, and that all the numerous other variables bearing upon crime reporting have remained fairly stable, then we might conclude that the figures regarding such an offense accurately reflect changes in the amount of the offense over time.

It should be stressed, however, that such a conclusion supports only observations about *trends,* not about the total amount of the offense in the jurisdiction. We may note that there has been either an increase or a decrease in the reported offense, although we may not know, and probably cannot even estimate, the total number of offenses committed. Thus, the rate of armed robbery may increase from 42 offenses per 100,000 population to 84 offenses per 100,000 population, allowing us to conclude that the reported amount of armed robbery has doubled. But we cannot conclude that armed robbery itself has doubled, although if we cannot locate any other explanation for the reported rise, we may strongly suspect that it does in fact reflect a significant increase in the behavior being examined.

It is in such terms, which involve a good deal of hesitation, qualification, and tentativeness, that material derived from official reports may be studied. In general, conclusions based on changes in criminal behavior over short periods of time may be regarded as more reliable

than those founded upon comparisons between periods far removed
from each other. We have already indicated that the very few studies
of crime patterns in the United States suggest that there has been
a considerable decrease in conventional kinds of crime during the
past century.[1] We know, too, that in all periods of American history
social commentators have deplored what they thought was an inordinate amount of crime. The President's Commission, for instance,
points out that a hundred years ago contemporary accounts of San
Francisco told of extensive areas where "no decent man was in safety
to walk the street after dark; while at all hours, both night and day,
his property was jeopardized by incendiarism and burglary."[2] In the
same period, in one central New York City area near Broadway, the
Commission noted, the police entered "only in pairs, and never unarmed."[3] A noted chronicler of the time declared that "municipal
law is a failure. We must soon fall back on the law of self preservation."[4] "Alarming" increases in robbery and violent crimes were reported throughout the country prior to the Revolution.[5] And in
1910 one author declared that "crime, especially in more violent forms,
and among the young, is increasing steadily and is threatening to
bankrupt the nation."[6]

Crime and violence, the President's Commission notes, has taken
many forms in America's past. During the railway strike of 1877
hundreds were killed across the country, and almost two miles of
railroad cars and buildings were burned in Pittsburgh in clashes
between the strikers and company police and militia.[7] It was only a
half-century later, after pitched battles in the steel industry, that the
long history of labor violence in the United States subsided.[8] The
looting and the takeover of New York City for three days by mobs
in the 1863 draft riots rivaled any contemporary outbreak, while racial
disturbances in Atlanta in 1907, Chicago, Washington, and East St.
Louis in 1919, New York in 1900, 1935, and 1943, and Detroit in 1943
plagued the metropolitan areas.[9] Lynchings took the lives of more than
4,500 persons during the period between 1882 and 1930.[10] And the
violence of Al Capone and Jesse James was so striking that they,
as the Commission observes, have "left their marks permanently on
our understanding of the eras in which they lived."[11]

Overseas, the same conditions may be observed in historical sources

1 Ferdinand, "The Criminal Patterns of Boston Since 1849."
2 President's Commission, *Crime and Its Impact*, p. 19.
3 *Ibid.*
4 *Ibid.*
5 Bridenbaugh, *Cities in Revolt*, p. 110.
6 President's Commission, *Crime and Its Impact*, p. 19.
7 Bruce, *1877: Year of Violence*, p. 13.
8 Rayback, *History of American Labor*, pp. 134–136.
9 See, for instance, Rudwick, *Race Riot at East St. Louis*.
10 U.S. Commission on Civil Rights, *Justice*, pp. 267–268.
11 President's Commission, *Crime and Its Impact*, p. 19.

that comment on crime conditions. The past behavior of gangs in London, for instance, makes contemporary gangs look as if they were made up of gentle and mild-mannered lads out for a playful romp. The following vivid portrayal of gang activity in the eighteenth century by William Lecky, the noted historian of bygone manners and morals, brings into question today's lamentations about the unprecedented nature of juvenile disregard for law:

> The impunity with which outrages were committed in the ill-lit and ill-guarded streets of London during the first half of the eighteenth century can now hardly be realized. In 1712, a club of young men of the higher classes, who assumed the name of Mohocks, were accustomed nightly to sally out drunk into the streets to hunt the passers-by and to subject them in mere wantonness to the most atrocious outrages. One of their favorite amusements, called "tipping the lion," was to squeeze the nose of their victim flat upon his face and to bore out his eyes with their fingers. Among them were the "sweaters" who formed a circle round their prisoner and pricked him with their swords until he sank exhausted to the ground, the "dancing masters" so-called from their skill in making men caper by thrusting swords into their legs, the "tumblers," whose favorite amusement was to set women on their heads and to commit various indecencies and barbarities on the limbs that were exposed. Maid servants, as they opened their masters' doors, were way-laid, beaten and their faces cut. Matrons enclosed in barrels were rolled down the steep and stony incline of Snow Hill. Watchmen were beaten unmercifully and their noses slit. Country gentlemen went to the theater as if in time of war, accompanied by their armed retainers.[12]

Lecky's report of juvenile gang activity in eighteenth-century London brings into focus another possible method of gaining some insight into crime trends: cross-cultural comparisons. There is an adage of statistical inquiry that says that a single small correlation taken by itself provides little support for a thesis, but that if the same relationship appears again and again, it may be taken as fairly strong testament to the fact that something meaningful is being measured. In terms of crime, there has been a reported increase in the kinds of illegal activity measured by official statistics throughout almost the entire world, which lends some credence to the view that the same underlying causes are uniformly producing the same consequences. Such causes may, of course, merely be an improvement in the method of reporting crime both in the United States and in foreign jurisdictions, but the results may also represent an upswing in traditional kinds of criminal behavior traceable to conditions, such as industrialization, affluence, and urbanization, prevalent both in America and abroad.

The figures themselves clearly show a burgeoning rate of re-

12 Lecky, *A History of England in the Eighteenth Century*, Vol. II, pp. 105–113. For similar conditions in fifteenth century Rome, see Gabel, *Memoirs of A Renaissance Pope*, pp. 158–159.

ported crime in nearly every highly industrialized society of western Europe. "Since 1955," the President's Commission on Law Enforcement and Administration of Justice notes, "property crime rates have increased more than 200 per cent in West Germany, the Netherlands, Sweden and Finland, and over 100 per cent in France, England and Wales, Italy and Norway."[13] This increase is not, however, universal. In Japan, property offenses decreased between 1955 and 1964 from 325,893 to 231,323, despite a rapidly increasing population and a considerable increase of larcenies committed by juveniles.[14] The President's Commission also reported an erratic pattern in crimes of violence in the few countries it was able to investigate. Rates declined in Belgium, Denmark, Norway, and Switzerland, but rose more than 150 percent in England and Wales between 1955 and 1964.[15]

The survey of the President's Commission is supplemented by periodic newspaper headlines reporting that "Philippines Crime Rate Sets Record,"[16] "Crime Rate Sets a British Record,"[17] and "Lebanon is Beset by Wave of Crime."[18] More than anything else, such news items underline the exceedingly important research task, yet undone, which will relate conditions in various foreign jurisdictions to their crime rates. Cross-cultural research of such a nature often serves to eliminate some of the grosser ethnocentric generalizations that emerge from investigations that are confined to a single geographic area. It has been argued, for instance, that the elimination of poverty in the United States will reduce the rate of crime against property. British criminologists, however, maintain that the social welfare state, which has cut deeply into economic differentials and provided greater security for all citizens in England, has not reduced the rate of crime against property, but rather that the rate has gone up simultaneously with the introduction of social reforms. The truth of the matter, vital for an understanding of the wellsprings of criminal behavior, would depend upon careful studies that use clear definitions of terms, deriving unimpeachable data of a comparable nature. Hopefully, such studies will emerge as a result of increasingly more cosmopolitan interests of academicians, improved and cheaper transportation, availability of research funds, and more and better-trained manpower.

13 President's Commission, *Crime and Its Impact*, p. 39; "Crime is a Worldwide Problem," p. 9.
14 Japan, *A Summary of White Paper on Crime, 1965*, pp. 3–5.
15 President's Commission, *Crime and Its Impact*, p. 39.
16 *Washington Post*, Dec. 16, 1965.
17 *New York Times*, July 20, 1965.
18 *Reuter's*, Sept. 10, 1961.

Extent of Reported Crime in the United States

Analysis of the reports issued by the F.B.I. between 1960 and 1967 indicates a numerical increase of almost 89 percent in the major felonies grouped as part of the Crime Index and a 71 percent increase when the figures are adjusted in terms of population growth. It will be noted from Table 6.1 that the overwhelming concentration of serious crimes is found in the property offense categories, with burglary leading, followed by larcenies of $50 and more, and then by auto thefts.

Table 6.1 Volume of Crime in the United States, 1960–1967

Classification	Estimated number of offenses		Changes through 1967			
			Since 1960		Since 1966	
	1960	1967	Number	Percent	Number	Percent
Total	2,014,600	3,802,300	+1,787,000	+ 88.7	+538,100	+16.5
Murder	9,000	12,090	+ 3,090	+ 34.4	+ 1,180	+10.8
Forcible rape	16,860	27,100	+ 10,240	+ 60.8	+ 1,770	+ 7.0
Robbery	107,390	202,050	+ 94,660	+ 88.2	+ 44,730	+28.4
Aggravated assault	152,000	253,300	+ 101,300	+ 66.7	+ 21,500	+ 9.3
Burglary	897,400	1,605,700	+ 708,300	+ 78.9	+218,500	+15.7
Larceny ($50 and over)	506,200	1,047,100	+ 540,900	+106.8	+152,500	+17.0
Auto theft	325,700	654,900	+ 329,200	+101.1	+ 97,900	+17.6

SOURCE: *Uniform Crime Reports,* 1967, pp. 5, 61.

It should also be noted that the highest volume of property offenses are of the nonviolent type. Burglaries, for example, occur approximately eight times more frequently than robberies, which are defined as thefts in which force or threat of force is employed. Auto thefts alone, with almost 655,000 in 1967, outnumber all of the crimes of violence taken together, with murder, forcible rape, robbery, and aggravated assault reaching a total of less than 500,000 in 1967. Many auto thefts involve little more than a brief period of joyriding before the vehicle is returned intact to its owner and, while the inconvenience and annoyance may be considerable, the permanent damage suffered is apt to be negligible, particularly in comparison to violent offenses.

Variations in the total amount of robbery are generally regarded as being particularly revealing of underlying trends in crime in the United States. From 1958 to 1959, there was a drop of 5 percent in reported robbery offenses for the nation; from 1959 to 1960, such offenses rose 18 percent. Although it is possible that there was a sharp variation in the actual behavior, it seems more likely that the erratic percentage swings can be traced to the nature of the statistics themselves. More than anything else, however, it was the 28.4 percent rise in robbery between 1966 and 1967 that gave pause to persistent critics of the *Uniform Crime Reports*, since robbery rose more than any other offense by a considerable margin. Lloyd E. Ohlin, professor of criminology at the Harvard Law School, for instance, noted that since robberies tend to involve violence and to be committed on strangers, they are apt to be reported regularly to the police. Under such conditions, Ohlin thought that the considerable rise in robbery in 1967 added credence to figures indicating a general rise in criminal violence during that year in the United States.[19]

It was offenses such as robbery that apparently constituted the core of public concern regarding "crime in the streets," which gave rise to political campaign slogans about "law and order" during the 1968 presidential election campaign. Some persons contend, however, that the explanation of public concern is more racial than numerical and that "crime in the streets" is the white man's response to the black man's surging press toward equality. Another explanation, seriocomic, is that offered by Russell Baker, who observes that

> people simply do not use the streets any longer. It is not fear of crime that deters them. They have lost the street habit. When Americans move today, they move by car. The streets have become places inhabited almost entirely by automobiles, with the inevitable result that any human beings who use them are conspicuously lonely figures, apt to seem easy prey to the thug, suspicious to the policeman or terrifying to the motorist. It can probably be proven statistically that the people who most fear crime in the streets are the people who never set foot in them.

He offers the following explanation for the public mood regarding "crime in the streets":

> At this point we can choose two possible theories. One would be that public fear of crime in the streets is nothing more than man's natural fear of the unknown. The other is that, since so few of us use the streets any longer, we are actually trying to divert the law's attention from what goes on in the places we do use. After all, it's fairly comfortable demanding incessant police vigilance in places you never use. Demanding a federal crackdown on crime in the home or crime in the office is something else. It might be good having a cop there when the burglars come, but most of the time we would prefer to have him otherwise occupied. Stamping out crime in those mysterious streets, for instance.[20]

Examinations of changes in crime based on rates per 100,000 of the population since 1960 until between 1966 and 1967 place the statistical picture in better perspective (see Table 6.2). We note a 71 percent increase between 1960 and 1967, with a 15 percent increase

19 Quoted in *New York Times*, Aug. 26, 1968.
20 Baker, "Crime in the Whats?"

Table 6.2   Crime Rates per 100,000 Population for 1967 as Compared to 1960 and 1966

Crime classification	Crimes per 100,000 inhabitants		
	1967 Rate	*1967 percent change*	
		Since 1960	Since 1966
Murder	6.1	+22.0	+ 8.9
Forcible rape	13.7	+45.7	+ 6.2
Robbery	102.1	+70.5	+27.1
Aggravated assault	128.0	+51.1	+ 8.1
Burglary	811.5	+62.1	+14.6
Larceny			
($50 and over)	529.2	+87.5	+15.8
Auto theft	231.1	+82.3	+16.4
Total	1,921.7	+71.1	+15.3

SOURCE: *Uniform Crime Reports,* 1967, p. 5.

between 1967 and the preceding year. Property crimes clearly pace the rise in crime rates since 1960.

The increase in reported crime in 1967 continues an upward spiral that began soon after the end of World War II, twenty years earlier. During the war, as is usually true in periods of national emergency, the crime rate declined in the United States, partly because of the siphoning off into military service of persons in the most crime-vulnerable age groups and partly, it is often suggested, because of an improvement in national morale emerging from a mission widely accepted among the population. During the immediate postwar period from 1945 to 1950, the crime rate leveled off and for a time appeared to be declining, although the delinquency rate continued a spectacular rate of rise that began in 1943. From 1960 to 1967, the F.B.I. figures indicate a rise in crime seven times greater than that of the population increase in the country.

Despite the F.B.I.'s concern with what it regards as an unprecedented outbreak of lawlessness, it is worth noting again that it remains far too early to tell whether we are in fact experiencing a serious alteration in the total crime picture for the country. This situation is made clear in an examination by Daniel Bell of crime statistics and variations in American culture patterns. The statistics, Bell believes, are about as reliable "as a woman giving her 'correct' age," and changes in the picture of crime represent changes in the social structure more than anything else. Discussing the presumed increase in violence, for instance, Bell offers the following explanation:

> In the last forty years or so, there has been a blurring, culturally and ecologically, of class lines. And in this blurring, in this spilling-over of

classes, there has been not more violence but greater awareness of the dimensions of living that include violence. With the rise of the movies and of other media, the growth of mass audiences, these "windows" into the full range of life, from which the old middle class had been largely excluded, were extended . . . Hence, if violence, once bounded, has flowed over the walls, it is not true that the amount of violence has increased.[21]

After examining historical material on earlier periods in American history, Bell concluded that "a sober look at the problem shows that there is probably less crime today in the United States than existed a hundred, or fifty, or even twenty-five years ago, and that today the United States is a more lawful and safe country than popular opinion imagines."[22] Bell's conclusion, contrasting sharply with public opinion and equally sharply with the verdict of the F.B.I., clearly shows the gaps in definitive information that needs to be filled. One of the few explanations of why the debate on crime statistics has not been more intensive is by Murray Schumach, who suggests the interesting, although far from proven idea that self-serving motives may prompt discrete silence among academicians faced with the claims of the *Uniform Crime Reports:*

> Many of the nation's leading sociologists and criminologists know these weaknesses are built into the national crime statistics. But only a few wish to make a fuss about it. They do not want to antagonize the F.B.I. and they know that as long as there is a sense of panic they will find it easier to get foundation and government grants to look into various aspects of crime that they consider important.[23]

Monthly and Seasonal Variations in Crime

One of the more interesting aspects of the study of variations of crime rates deals with efforts to identify broad cyclical, seasonal, and monthly changes. Theories have been advanced to indicate the reasons for such variations, whenever they could be shown to take place. Though broad rhythmical and cyclical regularities in crime have been difficult to establish, variations in seasonal and monthly frequencies have been observed for some time. Indeed, we would expect, as a matter of logic, that as different seasons and months affect the patterns of employment and human association, crime rates would vary accordingly. This appears to be true universally, and it is a reflection of the ways in which the calendar in each culture regulates life. In Ceylon, for instance, crime rates appear to follow a rhythm determined by the two planting seasons for rice, reflecting the two monsoon seasons and the observation of the major Buddhist festivals.[24]

21 Bell, *End of Ideology*, p. 157.
22 *Ibid.*, p. 137.
23 Schumach, "Crime Statistics: Are They Reliable?"
24 Bloch, *Research Report on Homicides.*

Late nineteenth- and early twentieth-century criminologists attempted to confirm relationships between crime and climate. European data, compiled by scholars such as Enrico Ferri, an Italian, and Alexandre Lacassagne, a Frenchman, seem to support the observation that warmer months and warmer climates are associated with higher rates of crime against the person, whereas cooler climates and months tend to induce higher rates of property offenses. Ferri's study of crime in France and Italy shows that, with the exception of infanticide and patricide, crimes against the person occur with greater frequency during the summer months. He attributes the higher summer rate chiefly to the physiological effect of heat, which leaves a large surplus of energy, to the better nourishment of the population in the summer, and to an enhanced irritability due to oppressive temperatures and humidity.[25] William Bonger, a Dutch criminologist, challenging Ferri, thought the first two of Ferri's reasons "entirely illusory." Crimes of violence, Bonger maintains, are not committed because one is better fed, nor are they refrained from because one is less well fed. Instead, said Bonger, putting on record his own mythology, we should be aware that "the best-fed people commit the smallest number of violent crimes," a generalization that may hold reasonably well within a nation, but hardly seems to stand up in cross-national comparisons; Bonger suggests that a better explanation lies in the fact that in the summer people drink more alcohol and come into contact with each other more often.[26]

The most recent evidence gathered in the United States appears to confirm the existence of marked monthly patterns in the variation of crimes against the person and against property. What is particularly striking about such monthly variations in crime rates is their relative regularity from year to year, as Figures III and IV indicate. December, our most festive month, is the peak crime month of the year, yielding the highest rates of murder, manslaughter by negligence, robbery, burglary, and larceny. Auto theft appears to attain its highest level in October and November, while rape and aggravated assault occur with greatest frequency during the summer months.

It is interesting to note with respect to property crimes that the winter months invariably yield the greatest number of offenses, with December standing out conspicuously as the leading month. A significant item concerning December is that it also figures prominently in crimes in cultures far removed from our own. Even in parts of Southeast Asia, it has been found that December is a leading month for property offenses. Much of this seems due to the increased volume of business and shopping, accompanied by the natural conditions of darkness and weather during December in certain parts of the world. Weather seems basically responsible for the precipitate upward move-

25 Quoted in Bonger, *Introduction to Criminology.* p. 114.
26 Bonger, "An Introduction to Criminology," pp. 114–115.

Figure III

Crimes Against the Person

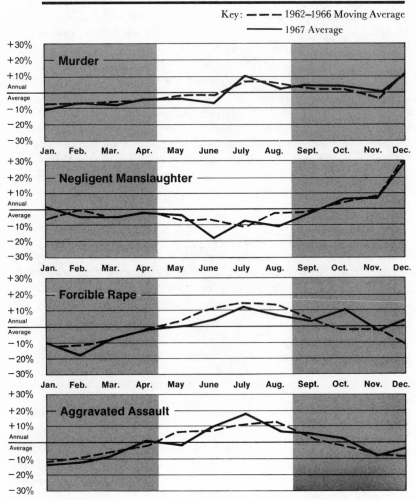

Key: — — — 1962–1966 Moving Average
——— 1967 Average

SOURCE: *Uniform Crime Reports*, 1967, Page 88

ment in negligent manslaughter in December, as seen largely in traffic deaths, which are affected by the more dangerous driving conditions during winter months.

Age-Levels and Crime Rates

A conspicuous characteristic in the development of crime trends during the past three decades has been the increasing proclivity toward crime by youths. Further, this tendency is likely to lead the youthful age groups to commit the more serious and socially harassing crimes.

Figure IV

Crimes Against Property
By Month

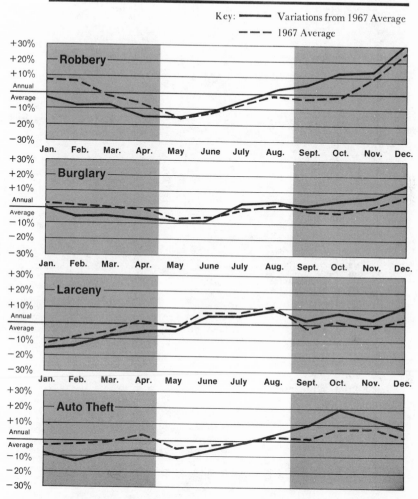

Key: ━━━━ Variations from 1967 Average
     ----- 1967 Average

source: *Uniform Crime Reports,* 1967, Page 19

In 1960, persons under twenty-five years of age made up 32 percent of the total volume of arrests, and one out of seven of all those arrested was under eighteen years old. In 1967, arrests of persons under 25 had risen to 47 percent of the total, and one out of four arrests were of persons under eighteen.

The great bulk of the major felonies are committed by youths under twenty-five years of age, according to arrest statistics (see Table 6.3). Approximately four out of five burglaries for which arrests are made are perpetrated by persons under twenty-five, while more than one-half are committed by those under eighteen years of age.

Table 6.3 Total Arrests of Persons Under 15, Under 18, Under 21, and Under 25 Years of Age, 1967 (4,566 Agencies; 1967 Estimated Population 145,927,000)

Offense charged	Number of persons arrested					Percentage			
	Grand total all ages	Under 15	Under 18	Under 21	Under 25	Under 15	Under 18	Under 21	Under 25
Total	*5,518,420*	*527,141*	*1,339,578*	*2,015,338*	*2,613,887*	*9.6*	*24.3*	*36.5*	*47.4*
Criminal homicide:									
(a) Murder and nonnegligent manslaughter	9,145	137	830	1,948	3,415	1.5	9.1	21.3	37.3
(b) Manslaughter by negligence	3,022	30	246	761	1,295	1.0	8.1	25.2	42.9
Forcible rape	12,659	475	2,515	5,418	8,133	3.8	19.9	42.8	64.2
Robbery	59,789	6,885	18,889	32,305	43,776	11.5	31.6	54.0	73.2
Aggravated assault	107,192	6,559	18,359	31,654	47,520	6.1	17.1	29.5	44.3
Burglary—breaking or entering	239,461	62,510	128,169	169,265	196,538	26.1	53.5	70.7	82.1
Larceny-theft	447,299	134,216	246,057	306,615	344,807	30.0	55.0	68.5	77.1
Auto theft	118,233	19,902	73,080	94,297	104,860	16.8	61.8	79.8	88.7
Subtotal for above offenses	*996,800*	*230,714*	*488,145*	*642,263*	*750,344*	*23.1*	*49.0*	*64.4*	*75.3*
Other assaults	229,928	14,837	37,849	65,822	101,073	6.5	16.5	28.6	44.0
Arson	8,058	3,768	5,236	5,953	6,495	46.8	65.0	73.9	80.6
Forgery and counterfeiting	33,462	806	3,918	9,783	16,572	2.4	11.7	29.2	49.5
Fraud	58,192	643	2,444	8,012	18,534	1.1	4.2	13.8	31.8
Embezzlement	6,073	53	256	810	1,863	.9	4.2	13.3	30.7

Stolen property; buying, receiving, possessing	28,620	3,542	9,901	15,247	19,502	12.4	34.6	53.3	68.1
Vandalism	109,299	54,782	83,571	93,053	98,357	50.1	76.5	85.1	90.0
Weapons; carrying, possessing, etc.	71,684	3,738	12,967	23,984	36,111	5.2	18.1	33.5	50.4
Prostitution and commercialized vice	39,744	97	848	6,729	21,017	.2	2.1	16.9	52.9
Sex offenses (except forcible rape and prostitution)	53,541	4,959	13,075	19,924	27,391	9.3	24.4	37.2	51.2
Narcotic drug laws	101,079	2,812	21,405	49,071	69,565	2.8	21.2	48.5	68.8
Gambling	84,772	343	2,143	5,735	12,865	.4	2.5	6.8	15.2
Offenses against family and children	56,137	264	860	6,435	15,829	.5	1.5	11.5	28.2
Driving under the influence	281,152	57	2,846	17,807	48,975	*	1.0	6.3	17.4
Liquor laws	209,741	4,924	63,587	154,897	169,228	2.3	30.3	73.9	80.7
Drunkenness	1,517,809	3,509	34,621	109,655	225,654	.2	2.3	7.2	14.9
Disorderly conduct	550,469	38,078	110,004	201,169	282,074	6.9	20.0	36.5	51.2
Vagrancy	106,747	1,646	9,777	28,155	41,455	1.5	9.2	26.4	38.8
All other offenses (except traffic)	654,915	76,082	189,921	282,299	364,765	11.6	29.0	43.1	55.7
Suspicion	95,794	5,674	21,800	44,131	61,814	5.9	22.8	46.1	64.5
Curfew and loitering law violations	94,872	23,794	94,872	94,872	94,872	25.1	100.0	100.0	100.0
Runaways	129,532	52,019	129,532	129,532	129,532	40.2	100.0	100.0	100.0

* Less than one-tenth of one percent.

SOURCE: *Uniform Crime Reports*, 1967, p. 128.

Approximately three-fourths of our robberies are committed by persons under twenty-five, while about one out of three robbers are under eighteen. Youthful age groups also figure significantly in many of the other offenses leading to arrest, particularly offenses against property and certain sexual offenses, such as forcible rape, where three out of five are committed by individuals under twenty-five years of age.

The discrepant rise in arrests of youthful offenders can be noted from the fact that between 1960 and 1967 arrests of persons under eighteen rose 69 percent, while the number of persons in this age group, from ten to seventeen years of age, increased 22 percent, and police arrests for all criminal acts, except traffic offenses, rose only 11 percent. It is apparent, therefore, that the involvement of young people, as measured by police arrests, is proceeding at a pace more than three times their percentage increase in the national population, although the F.B.I. takes pains to point out that "a relatively small percentage of the total young age population become involved in criminal acts, about five out of 100."[27]

Sex Composition in Arrest Statistics

Crimes by women, as they appear in official statistics, are, comparatively speaking, small in number. Nevertheless, the figures, examined without regard to particular offenses and particular age periods, may be somewhat deceptive. A disproportionate rise in the annual volume of crime for women as compared to men, modifications of rates for different offenses at different age levels, and the changing character of offenses women are most likely to commit, all reveal a great deal about the crime picture, the social structure, and the status of women in the society.

In 1967, for instance, male arrests outnumbered female arrests in the United States by seven to one, as Table 6.4 indicates. Between 1966 and 1967, however, female arrests rose by seven percent, while male arrests increased four percent. In regard to Index offenses, the involvement of females was primarily in larceny, which accounted for more than one out of six female arrests. Females accounted for 21 percent of the forgery, 23 percent of the fraud, and 19 percent of the embezzlement arrests.

Long-term arrest trends, using the interval between 1960 and 1967, show that arrests for females under 18 years of age rose 71 percent for auto theft and 76 percent for burglary. While arrests of young males greatly outnumbered female arrests during the same period, the male percentage increases in both these categories was not so pronounced, with a 53 percent increase in auto theft and a 40 percent rise in burglary.

27 Federal Bureau of Investigation, *Uniform Crime Reports, 1967*, p. 32.

With the exception of prostitution and commercialized vice, there is no crime category in which women exceed men. But it is notable that the sex ratios in crime vary significantly at different age levels. The ratio of male to female offenses is extremely high for age categories before fourteen, ranging from as much as 8–10 to 1, but tends to become more narrow with advancing age brackets. In the eighteen to twenty-five age bracket, ratios of 4 to 1 are found for many offenses. These figures may indicate a greater leniency on the part of the juvenile courts toward the female offender, who, after eighteen, normally must face the regular adult court.

It is significant to note that in many crime categories the percentage of female crimes is closely analagous to those of males. Thus, in murder both the male and female rates constitute .2 percent of their total crime rate. The same is true in regard to aggravated assaults, with each rate equaling 1.9 percent of the total. Burglary constitutes 4.8 percent of the total female crime rate and only 4.3 percent of the total male rate. Females rates are strikingly higher for larceny, forgery, fraud, and runaway.

Because of the nature of familial and social controls over women and the cultural definitions of permissible role behavior, a large number of cultural activities, beginning with early activities that may have delinquent overtones, are not likely to be found among women. The delinquent subculture, which reinforces illegal modes of behavior, tends to stress masculine values and to recruit primarily boys into its ranks. It should be noted, however, that definitions of appropriate role behavior are largely culturally fixed and not the immutable consequence of sexual characteristics. Ethel Albert, an anthropologist at Northwestern University, has pointed out that "every nice girl of Western culture knows that it is the male who is the sexual aggressor, while the passive female submits with good or bad grace." But, Albert notes, if we ask about sexual aggression among certain Indian or African groups, we are apt to get a different view of the matter: "Obviously, they tell us, women are more driven by sex than men." The Zuni Indians, for instance, have numerous stories about newlyweds, as Americans do, but the Zuni anecdotes feature the groom rather than the bride in a state of anxiety. In Central Africa, anthropological investigation indicates that "everybody knows that men are not suited by nature for hard work, that women are stronger and better workers." Westerners tend to think of women as less stable emotionally than men, but in Iran it is the male who is supposed to cry easily, to prefer poetry to logic, while the woman is deemed to be practical, cool, and calculating. Conclusions from cross-cultural study of sex roles indicate clearly that the disproportionate amount of male criminality in the United States is in large measure a function of defined sex roles and that changes in such roles will inevitably be reflected in crime statistics. "Viewing humanity on a worldwide scale," Albert

Table 6.4 Total Arrests, Distribution by Sex, 1967 (4,566 Agencies; 1967 Estimated Population 145,927,000)

Offense charged	Number of persons arrested			Percent Male	Percent Female	Percent of total*		
	Total	Male	Female			Total	Male	Female
Total	5,518,420	4,829,918	688,502	87.5	12.5	100.0	100.0	100.0
Criminal homicide:								
(a) Murder and nonnegligent manslaughter	9,145	7,650	1,495	83.7	16.3	.2	.2	.2
(b) Manslaughter by negligence	3,022	2,720	302	90.0	10.0	.1	.1	—
Forcible rape	12,659	12,659	—	100.0	—	.2	.3	—
Robbery	59,789	56,689	3,100	94.8	5.2	1.1	1.2	.5
Aggravated assault	107,192	93,343	13,849	87.1	12.9	1.9	1.9	2.0
Burglary—breaking or entering	239,461	229,752	9,709	95.9	4.1	4.3	4.8	1.4
Larceny-theft	447,299	340,355	106,944	76.1	23.9	8.1	7.0	15.5
Auto theft	118,233	113,227	5,006	95.8	4.2	2.1	2.3	.7
Subtotal for above offenses	996,800	856,395	140,405	85.9	14.1	18.1	17.7	20.4
Other assaults	229,928	205,342	24,586	89.3	10.7	4.2	4.3	3.6
Arson	8,058	7,499	559	93.1	6.9	.1	.2	.1
Forgery and counterfeiting	33,462	26,515	6,947	79.2	20.8	.6	.5	1.0
Fraud	58,192	44,678	13,514	76.8	23.2	1.1	.9	2.0

Offense							
Embezzlement	6,073	4,904	1,169	80.8	19.2	.1	.1	.2
Stolen property; buying, receiving, possessing	28,620	26,489	2,131	92.6	7.4	.5	.5	.3
Vandalism	109,299	102,540	6,759	93.8	6.2	2.0	2.1	1.0
Weapons; carrying, possessing, etc.	71,684	66,979	4,705	93.4	6.6	1.3	1.4	.7
Prostitution and commercialized vice	39,744	8,878	30,866	22.3	77.7	.7	.2	4.5
Sex offenses (except forcible rape and prostitution)	53,541	46,569	6,972	87.0	13.0	1.0	1.0	1.0
Narcotic drug laws	101,079	87,097	13,982	86.2	13.8	1.8	1.8	2.0
Gambling	84,772	77,388	7,384	91.3	8.7	1.5	1.6	1.1
Offenses against family and children	56,137	51,140	4,997	91.1	8.9	1.0	1.1	.7
Driving under the influence	281,152	262,925	18,227	93.5	6.5	5.1	5.4	2.6
Liquor laws	209,741	185,149	24,592	88.3	11.7	3.8	3.8	3.6
Drunkenness	1,517,809	1,408,594	109,215	92.8	7.2	27.5	29.2	15.9
Disorderly conduct	550,469	476,022	74,447	86.5	13.5	10.0	9.9	10.8
Vagrancy	106,747	96,354	10,393	90.3	9.7	1.9	2.0	1.5
All other offenses (except traffic)	654,915	564,604	90,311	86.2	13.8	11.9	11.7	13.1
Suspicion	95,794	79,357	16,437	82.8	17.2	1.7	1.6	2.4
Curfew and loitering law violations	94,872	77,457	17,415	81.6	18.4	1.7	1.6	2.5
Runaways	129,532	67,043	62,489	51.8	48.2	2.3	1.4	9.1

* Because of rounding, the percentages may not add to total.

SOURCE: *Uniform Crime Reports*, 1967, p. 124.

concludes, "we find no consensus. Nature makes us male or female, but the beliefs and values of our society make us the kinds of men or women we become."[28]

Minority Groups and Crime

Historically, the most recent immigrant groups entering the United States produced high rates of crime. Beginning with the heavy waves of immigration to America from 1870—first from northern European countries such as Germany, Norway, and Ireland, and later from southern European nations, such as Italy and Poland—each immigrating group made its presence felt by, among other things, a disproportionate contribution to the statistics of crime. This was primarily due to the acts committed by the native-born offspring of foreign-born parents,[29] the so-called "marginal" persons, or individuals caught between two kinds of cultures, comfortable and at ease in neither.[30]

As the processes of assimilation proceeded, however, the high second-generation crime rates came down and groups previously considered intransigent and lawless joined the ranks of the conforming. Middle-class hostility, directed in turn against each migrant group, moved elsewhere to locate scapegoats to bear the burden of our society's failure to fulfill its articulated aim of integration.

Today, Negroes and Spanish-speaking people of Puerto Rico and Mexico are the counterparts of former immigrant groups, performing analogous unskilled services and living in the slums of large, industrial cities. For the blacks, analogy to immigrant ethnic groups is somewhat less than perfect, however. Arriving as slaves, differentiated by color that cannot readily be camouflaged and will not readily be absorbed, tormented by conscious and unconscious color biases that are deeply rooted in the minds of the majority, the blacks face particularly intense pressures that thrust and hold them on the fringes of the society and press them toward resolution of difficulties by violation of criminal codes. In the words of W. I. Thomas, a pioneering sociologist, the black minority is exposed to America's "public culture" but excluded from its "private culture."[31]

Procedural biases also affect the official crime rates of members of minority groups. Sometimes they serve to underplay the total number of crimes, such as when the police fail to take steps against an offender in the ghetto because they believe that public opinion there is less outraged at certain kinds of criminal behavior than it would be in the suburbs. Sometimes procedural decisions serve to inflate the

28 Albert, "The Roles of Women." p. 111.
29 See, for instance, Young, *Pilgrims of Russian-Town.*
30 Stonequist, *The Marginal Man.*
31 Thomas, *Primitive Cultures,* p. 137.

reported rate of crime by members of minority groups, as the following illustration from an article by Geis indicates:

> I was once walking downtown on Main Street in Los Angeles when a patrolman stopped a Mexican boy, nudged him toward the side of the street, and requested that he roll up his sleeves so that it could be determined whether his arms had needle marks. The policeman may have recognized the boy as a possible addict, either through experience or perhaps by the way he walked. (An addict will often swing one arm and hold taut the other into which he has shot the drug because moving it is painful.) Or perhaps the policeman was operating on the assumption that a Mexican boy on this street was much more likely to be a narcotics addict than, say, I was, with my tie and pressed suit. His assumption may have been correct, but it is obvious how readily it becomes self-fulfilling and inflates the "Latin" crime rate. . . . In the same manner, young Negroes—and I have listened to them discuss the matter at length in college classes—driving a relatively new and expensive car in an area not populated with Negroes expect as a matter of course to be stopped by the police as potential auto thieves. For whatever reason, the law enforcement agencies have come to the conclusion that young Negroes are more likely than similarly situated whites to be thieves, or at least that they can more readily and with greater impunity be stopped to determine the ownership of the cars they drive. The procedure obviously serves to increase the number of apprehended and reported Negro car thieves, just as the road blockades during the Christmas season inevitably tend to inflate greatly the total of drunken drivers discovered and arrested.[32]

The results of such conditions, combined with real differences among racial groups in criminal behavior, can clearly be seen in Table 6.5. Though two and a half times as many whites as Negroes are arrested each year, blacks constitute only 11 percent of the population of the United States, and their arrest rate for every offense listed in the *Uniform Crime Reports* is disproportionately higher than that of whites. Among the Crime Index offenses, blacks exceed whites in the number of murders and almost double them in arrests for robbery. In general, the disparity of racial rates for offenses of violence is much greater than comparable differences between the races for offenses against property. The statistics also show that the difference between white and Negro arrest rates is generally greater for those over eighteen years of age than for those under eighteen. The differences between the black and white arrest rates for certain crimes of violence—notably murder, rape, and aggravated assault—have been growing smaller during the past decade. It is worth noting, though, that not only do the races vary in their crime rates, but the victims of crime tend to be drawn in heavy disproportion from different racial groups. Ramsey Clark, former Attorney General of the United States, has observed that the average American has one chance in 400 years

32 Geis, "Statistics Concerning Race and Crime," p. 147.

Table 6.5   Total Arrests by Race, 1967 (4,508 Agencies; 1967 Estimated Population 135,203,000)

Offense charged	Total arrests						All others (includes race unknown)
	Total	White	Negro	Indian	Chinese	Japanese	
				Race			
Total	*5,265,302*	*3,630,787*	*1,462,556*	*121,398*	*1,726*	*3,490*	*45,345*
Criminal homicide:							
(a) Murder and nonnegligent manslaughter	8,218	3,200	4,883	49	2	9	75
(b) Manslaughter by negligence	2,882	2,202	629	15	2	8	26
Forcible rape	11,339	5,737	5,381	81	1	3	136
Robbery	51,672	19,459	31,398	360	6	18	431
Aggravated assault	86,367	42,578	42,367	671	36	26	689
Burglary—breaking or entering	224,699	147,478	73,001	1,609	65	185	2,361
Larceny-theft	425,988	288,406	130,008	2,774	295	481	4,024
Auto theft	109,814	73,389	33,998	996	43	94	1,294
Subtotal for above offenses	*920,979*	*582,449*	*321,665*	*6,555*	*450*	*824*	*9,036*

Offense						
Other assaults	223,595	136,639	83,202	1,630	35	83	2,006
Arson	7,384	5,439	1,849	38	—	5	53
Forgery and counterfeiting	30,169	23,007	6,795	232	19	15	101
Fraud	56,278	45,155	10,564	245	13	23	278
Embezzlement	5,285	4,306	946	18	—	4	11
Stolen property; buying, receiving, possessing	24,045	14,638	9,007	180	7	8	205
Vandalism	102,543	81,791	19,486	431	19	37	779
Weapons; carrying, possessing, etc.	67,776	31,977	34,713	299	14	34	739
Prostitution and commercialized vice	33,456	12,315	20,706	131	8	38	258
Sex offenses (except forcible rape and prostitution)	49,767	36,613	12,221	239	27	79	588
Narcotic drug laws	81,454	57,146	22,848	187	46	137	1,090
Gambling	71,682	18,090	49,007	15	189	689	3,692
Offenses against family and children	55,210	37,354	17,157	449	11	4	235
Driving under the influence	272,664	219,095	48,259	3,783	78	229	1,220
Liquor laws	198,803	165,755	28,746	3,252	90	76	884
Drunkenness	1,489,528	1,071,249	326,152	84,575	152	384	7,016
Disorderly conduct	526,822	333,040	179,775	7,186	131	90	6,600
Vagrancy	100,805	73,665	24,433	1,653	33	80	941
All other offenses (except traffic)	632,082	456,079	161,501	7,772	297	338	6,095
Suspicion	94,451	50,445	43,531	376	14	6	79
Curfew and loitering law violations	93,675	70,951	19,955	901	43	216	1,609
Runaways	126,849	103,589	20,038	1,251	50	91	1,830

Source: *Uniform Crime Reports*, 1967, p. 126.

to be a victim of violent crime, whereas Negroes and Mexican-Americans are apt to be victimized once in eighty years, a member of the white middle class once in 2,000 years, and a white, well-to-do suburbanite, once in 10,000 years.[33]

Interpreting the differences between blacks and whites in arrest and victimization rates, the President's Commission on Law Enforcement and Administration of Justice was inclined to the view that they reflect social conditions. Its report drew the following conclusion:

> Many studies have been made seeking to account for these differences. . . . They have found that the differences become very small when comparisons are made between the rates for whites and Negroes living under similar conditions. However, it has proved difficult to make such comparisons, since Negroes generally encounter more barriers to economic and social advancement than whites do. Even when Negroes and whites live in the same area the Negroes are likely to have poorer housing, lower incomes, and fewer job prospects. The Commission is of the view that if conditions of equal opportunity prevailed, the large differences now found between the Negro and white arrest rates would disappear.[34]

Mention might be made, finally, of arguments that have been advanced suggesting the elimination of racial breakdowns in statistics of criminal behavior. Statistical tabulations of the work of public agencies, it is said, are undertaken to provide a reckoning for examination of the citizen taxpayer and to aid the agencies themselves in performing their job more effectively. It is further maintained that statistics regarding the racial components of arrested persons accomplish neither of these tasks, and that the presence of such statistics reinforces a splintering of the society into compartmentalized groups. In addition, while males and females will not likely find it discriminatory if their crime rates are singled out for attention, minority groups have historically sound reasons to believe, correctly or incorrectly, that something invidious is intended by such distinctions. The argument continues by noting that these fears should not be fed unless there are compelling reasons to do so, asking why we do not indicate the arrest rates of Baptists or Republicans or of migrants from the South, since any of these tabulations might well provide us with data of some value, but presumably not of enough value to make it desirable to differentiate between human beings by singling out particular types for special statistical attention. It is also argued that eliminating racial classifications from public criminal statistics would probably do much good and little harm, and "might allow issues between law enforcement agencies and minority groups to be resolved on grounds more substantial than those provided by rather specious

33 Quoted in *Washington Post*, Dec. 7, 1968.
34 President's Commission, *Challenge of Crime in a Free Society*, pp. 44–45.

statistics."[35] A contrary view suggests, however, that to abandon any source of data for ideological reasons throws social science into the political arena, where it is apt to become the handmaiden of vested interests. Proponents of this view would argue that all useful data— including religion or similar matters now regarded as "private"— should be gathered and fed into social science inquiry. This view appears rather less than persuasive to the present writers, who believe that social science research decisions are to a considerable extent overtly or implicitly ideological decisions, and that the social scientist might better make his own value decisions in areas of fundamental importance than have others make them for him.

Urban-Rural Crime Differentials

Despite the enormous changes in the urban character of the United States since the turn of the century, with the vast concentration of people now living within extensive metropolitan areas, the basic distinctions in urban-rural crime have remained much the same. The large bulk of our crimes and the highest crime rates are concentrated in the larger metropolitan areas, as Table 6.6 indicates. Twenty-six cities of more than 500,000 people, which have less than 18 percent of the total population of the United States, account for more than half of all reported Index crimes against the person and more than 30 percent of all reported Index property crimes. One out of every three robberies and nearly one out of every five rapes occurs in cities of more than one million population. The average rate for every Index crime except burglary is at least twice as great in these cities as in the suburbs of rural areas. With a few exceptions, average rates increase progressively as the size of the city becomes larger.[36]

The F.B.I. employs three major categories in reporting gross variations in crime: the *standard metropolitan statistical areas, other cities,* and *rural areas.* "Standard metropolitan statistical areas" include entire counties or counties containing a city of at least 50,000 population and are characterized by other metropolitan features. The category of "other cities" includes those urban areas falling outside the major classification and comprising approximately 14 percent of the population of the United States in 1960. "Rural areas" consist of the remaining sections of the country that in 1960 held approximately 24 percent of the country's population.

It will also be noted from Table 6.6 that the standard metropolitan areas have a crime rate almost three times higher than the rural areas, with the intermediate cities reporting a rate 1.7 times higher than in the rural districts. There is a rather marked decline in the incidence of crime in every major category from standard metropolitan areas to

35 Geis, "Statistics Concerning Race and Crime," p. 149.
36 President's Commission, *Challenge of Crime in a Free Society,* p. 28.

Table 6.6 Distribution of Crime in Three Major Statistical Areas, by Volume and Rate, 1967

Area	Population	Total Crime Index	Murder and non-negligent man-slaughter	Forcible rape	Robbery	Aggravated assault	Burglary	Larceny $50 and over	Auto theft
United States Total	197,864,000	3,802,273	12,093	27,096	202,053	253,321	1,605,701	1,047,085	654,924
Rate per 100,000 inhabitants		1,921.7	6.1	13.7	102.1	128.0	811.5	529.2	331.0
Standard Metropolitan Statistical Area	134,748,000								
Area actually reporting*	97.5%	3,184,806	8,736	21,921	191,148	196,348	1,320,627	860,193	585,833
Estimated total	100.0%	3,230,337	8,867	22,257	192,367	199,236	1,340,457	874,493	592,660
Rate per 100,000 inhabitants		2,397.3	6.6	16.5	142.8	147.9	994.8	649.0	439.8
Other Cities	24,823,000								
Area actually reporting	89.0%	269,508	832	1,375	4,945	20,404	118,281	88,674	34,990
Estimated total	100.0%	300,372	978	1,545	5,501	23,828	131,759	98,054	38,707
Rate per 100,000 inhabitants		1,210.0	3.9	6.2	22.2	96.0	530.8	395.0	155.5
Rural	38,293,000								
Area actually reporting	75.2%	210,203	1,452	2,387	3,050	19,283	107,077	58,523	18,431
Estimated total	100.0%	271,564	2,248	3,294	4,185	30,257	133,485	74,538	23,557
Rate per 100,000 inhabitants		709.2	5.9	8.6	10.9	79.0	348.6	194.7	61.7

* The percentage representing area actually reporting will not coincide with the ratio between reported and estimated crime totals since these data represent the sum of the calculations for individual states which have varying populations, portions reporting and crime rates. Population by area for each state is 1967 estimate; total population for each state is Bureau of the Census provisional estimate as of July 1, 1967, and subject to change. All rates were calculated on the estimated population before rounding.
Source: *Uniform Crime Reports*, 1967, p. 60.

rural areas, with the exception of murder and nonnegligent man-slaughter, where the rural areas maintain a higher level, which has been characteristic for many decades. In the case of forcible rape, although the rural rate is not as high as the metropolitan rate, it is higher than the rate for the "other cities" category.

The relationship between crime and opportunity, a factor that must inevitably be included in crime statistics that pretend to be complete and sophisticated, is illustrated by the low rate of auto theft in rural areas as contrasted with metropolitan districts. It has been suggested that a much more adequate measure of rural-urban crime differences than we now have would be gotten by dividing the number of offenses by the "number of exposures" that might possibly eventuate in a criminal offense. Under such a procedure, the number of rapes would be divided by a subject's exposure to the possibility of committing a rape offense, that is, at the very least, by the number of women in the area.[37] Of course, such an approach fails to take into account the nature of the exposures to women, the time involved in such relationships, and similar elements presumably related to the likelihood of criminal outcomes.

A particularly exacting investigation into the nature of rural crime in the United States has been conducted by Marshall Clinard[38] and Harold Eastman,[39] one of whom reinvestigated the original findings of the other. The first study, conducted in 1941 by Clinard, used a sample of 200 cases drawn from the Iowa Men's Reformatory, representing sixty farm, fifty-two village, and eighty-eight city boys. The follow-up investigation, done in the same reformatory ten years later by Eastman, employed a sample of 133 cases, similarly sub-divided. The results of the investigations, summarized by Clinard, include the following:

1. Both studies indicated that Iowa rural offenders were more mobile, not as well integrated in their home communities, and more impersonal in their attitudes toward others than non-offenders.

2. In the 1941 study rural offenders more often committed their offenses outside of their home communities in a situation of anonymity. The 1951 study did not find this to be the case.

3. Both studies showed a pronounced difference between offenders from areas of varying degrees of urbanization in the age at which they began criminal activities and in progression in crime.

4. The two studies, considered together, were taken to indicate that the lessening degree of differentiation between rural and urban offenders was a reflection of increased urbanism in Iowa during the ten-year interval between the investigations.[40]

37 See Wilks, "Ecological Correlates of Crime and Delinquency"; Boggs, "Urban Crime Patterns."
38 Clinard, "Process of Urbanization and Criminal Behavior."
39 Eastman, "Process of Urbanization and Criminal Behavior: A Restudy of Cultural Conflict."
40 Clinard, "Relation of Urbanization and Urbanism to Criminal Behavior."

Finally, taking the various correlates of crime rates as a whole, the President's Commission on Law Enforcement and Administration of Justice put on record its discomfort with the task of separating out particular crime-related factors. Available statistics simply were not adequate for the job, the Commission noted. When they could be used, they offered only tantalizing hints to the unravelling of questions concerning the contributions of various factors to particular kinds of crimes. Summarizing its studies on the various correlates of reported crime, the Commission put forward the following observation:

> It would obviously tell us a great deal about the trend of crime if we could analyze all together the changes that have been taking place in urbanization, age composition of the population, number of slum dwellers, and other factors such as sex, race, and level of income. The Commission has spent a considerable amount of time trying to make this kind of analysis. However, it was unable to analyze satisfactorily more than one or two factors in conjunction with each other on the basis of present information. As more factors were brought into the analysis the results differed in some instances substantially from those obtained when only one factor was analyzed. It also seemed clear that as the number of factors was increased, a more accurate picture of the effect of changing conditions on the rate of crime emerged.[41]

Summary
The difficulty of obtaining precise and comparable statistical data remains a basic problem in the study of criminology and the appraisal of national and regional trends in criminality. Despite many improvements in recent years in reporting and recording crime data, statistical information regarding crime remains severely limited. The F.B.I. altered its reporting methods drastically in 1958, adding sophistication to its operation, but making any information derived after the reforms unable to be compared with earlier reports. Within the very severe limitations imposed by the available numerical information, certain restricted conclusions may be set forth regarding the dimensions of crime in the United States.

(1) In terms of broad statements regarding trends in crime rates, the best position appears to be one of skepticism in the face of official proclamations that an unprecedented state of lawlessness exists in the United States and that crime is perennially skyrocketing. Such statements quite often form the foundation for policy pronouncements favoring harsher treatments for offenders as the most efficient means for controlling crime. There exists no truly reliable methods for indicating with much assurance today the direction in which crime has moved in the United States either in recent years or over longer periods

[41] President's Commission, *Challenge of Crime in a Free Society*, pp. 28–29.

of time. For one thing, taking so variegated a behavior as "crime" and looking at it as if it were a homogeneous unit of human activity is a rather vainglorious undertaking. For another, even when particular kinds of criminal acts are examined, too many variables still remain uncontrolled for nationwide comparisons to be accorded much credence. The need remains in criminology for long and short run studies in restricted geographical settings of both unreported and reported criminal activity, examined in terms of specific criminal acts and behavior systems.

(2) Variations in reported crime disclose some significant monthly and seasonal patterns. Moreover, such variations appear to be fairly consistent year after year. Thus, property crimes are more common during the winter months, culminating in the highest rate during December. Murder and nonnegligent manslaughter also reach their peaks in December, although August yields a high incidence of homicides as well.

(3) Reported crimes appear increasingly to have become a propensity of the young. The vast majority of burglaries and robberies are committed by youths under twenty-five years of age. Within the last ten years, rates of arrest for those under eighteen years of age have accelerated seven times as rapidly as rates for those over eighteen years.

(4) While reported crime is still overwhelmingly committed by males, illustrated by the fact that approximately only one out of seven offenders is a woman, the ratio of male to female offenders varies significantly on different age levels. Thus, female delinquency rates are much higher than adult female crime rates. Also, the ratio of male to female convictions narrows appreciably in the eighteen to twenty-four year age bracket.

(5) Serious personal crimes, such as homicides and forcible rapes, constitute only a small fraction of the total volume of serious felonies committed each year. The preponderance of major offenses are burglaries and larcenies of more than $50, which account for approximately seven out of each ten offenses reported each year.

(6) Bearing some similarities to the problem of former immigrant groups in their relation to crime, crime among the Negro and the Spanish-speaking minorities contains some distinctive and unique characteristics as well. The volume of crime among blacks is approximately three times as high as the black proportion of the American population. A by-product of social and economic discrimination, the problem of crime among Negroes contains elements that express the difficulties of black adaptation to today's highly mobile and industrialized society.

(7) Metropolitan districts yield rates of crime roughly three times as high as those in rural areas. Urban areas generally lead in all categories of serious crime with the exception of homicide, where the rural

rates have consistently been higher. Rates of forcible rape are also high in rural areas, and they come very close to approximating the rates found in metropolitan districts.

For Further Reading

BELL, DANIEL. "The Myth of Crime Waves," in *The End of Ideology*. Glencoe, Ill.: Free Press, 1960. Chap. 8, pp. 137–158.
> Historical material provides the background for Professor Bell's claim that statements maintaining that there is more crime today in the United States are part of a "myth" that neither squares with earlier material on our criminal behavior nor is truly supported by contemporary statistics.

Crime in the United States—Uniform Crime Reports. Washington, D.C.: Federal Bureau of Investigation.
> Published annually by the F.B.I., this bulletin of almost 200 pages contains statistical data on numerous aspects of crime as they have been tabulated from material forwarded to the F.B.I.

GEIS, GILBERT. "Statistics Concerning Race and Crime," in *Crime and Delinquency.* Vol. 11 (April 1965), pp. 142–150.
> Two arguments are put forward in this article. The first maintains that the information available regarding crime among minority groups is fundamentally distorted by both the usual statistical errors and special distortions resulting from contemporary race relations. Second, on this ground, as well as in terms of other issues of national policy, it is suggested that it might be desirable to abandon ethnic and racial breakdowns in criminal statistics.

WILKS, JUDITH A. "Ecological Correlates of Crime and Delinquency," in the President's Commission on Law Enforcement and Administration of Justice, *Task Force Report: Crime and Its Impact—An Assessment.* Washington, D.C.: Government Printing Office, 1967. Appendix A, pp. 138–156.
> The major literature relating patterns of criminal behavior to ecological variables is summarized and interpreted by Judith Wilks, of the department of sociology at New York University. Attention is paid to rural-urban differences, intracity and intercity variations, and regional distributions in crime. Summarizing the available material, Professor Wilks wonders whether an attack on crime in the inner city, where its reported rate is highest, will result in a lessening of crime or in a changing spatial distribution of criminal activity.

YOUNG, PAULINE V. *Pilgrims of Russian-Town.* Chicago: University of Chicago Press, 1932.
> This study of the Molokans, a dissident Russian religious group, which migrated from the rural trans-Caucus region into the slums of Los Angeles at the beginning of the present century, is a classic investigation into the eruption of crime and social disorganization among the second generation of a group of conforming and law-abiding migrants. Focusing in particular upon the impact of social work and educational practices in creating alienation, the study contains much of contemporary relevance.

Part IV
Behavior Systems in Crime

7
Professional Crime

Professionalization implies an element of training, a degree of skill, and a clearly-formulated attitude about one's work. Professional criminals exhibit these characteristics and a number of others that are common to their group. The ranks of professional crime include confidence men, professional thieves, forgers, shoplifters, and pickpockets, who generally begin their careers at a relatively early age and persist in criminal behavior with tenacity and purposiveness. The common practice of referring to some offenders as professionals, which is traditional in criminology, does, however, do some injustice to the term's usual usage. Although most parents would likely be pleased if their sons reported that they had decided to enter a profession, few would be apt to remain approving if the choice of a profession was crime.

Most professional criminals develop a routinized pattern of operations and certain individualized techniques, and they become known to the police through their stereotyped exploits—their *modus operandi*, or idiosyncrasies in method of work. It usually takes some time, for example, for a safebreaker to learn how to use an oxyacetylene torch, and once he has become skilled, he will not readily change either to some other method of opening safes or to another form of crime.[1]

Professional criminals are simultaneously proud and squeamish concerning their avoidance of physical force in the accomplishment of their ends. In London, where the police go unarmed, the corps of professional criminals is one of the most diligent groups in eliminating from among themselves persons who employ weapons.[2] The professional criminal, in this instance, is looking out for his own well-being because public concern aroused by a killing or other notoriety-provoking episode may result in more stringent sentences for the

1 Martienssen, *Crime and the Police*, p. 27.
2 Fabian, *Fabian of the Yard*, p. 93; Lefebure, *Evidence for the Crown*, p. 195.

rank-and-file criminal. A rational self-concern, in fact, is one of the major characteristics of the professional criminal. Professional criminals often develop their operations to a point of considerable skill; the adroitness and subtlety with which they "beat" the victim determines their status in the in-group of professional crime. Like other systematic workers in the modern world, professional criminals make strenuous efforts to maximize their returns and to reduce their risks through careful study and analysis of methods, informal group organization, codes of behavior, various forms of insurance that guarantee adequate bail and legal defense, and the perfection of techniques aimed at avoiding arrest, trial, and sentence.

Like the existence of most persons, however, the life of the professional criminal is more often than not a prosaic one. The novelist James Gould Cozzens, making a "tour of that everyday, routine world of professional crime," describes it in the following terms:

> It did not differ as much as the imagination might suggest from the everyday world of those who were not professional criminals. In one, as in the other, the principal problem was how to make a living; and criminals who made good ones were as rare as millionaires. The rank and file could count on little but drudgery and economic insecurity; and for the same reason that most men in lawful pursuits could count on little else. They had no natural abilities, and lacked the wit and intelligence to develop any.[3]

Professional Crime in History

Today's professional crime as a behavior system, despite changes in its verbal trappings, is often virtually indistinguishable from activities of centuries ago. Frank Aydelotte, for instance, writes that there was in England in the 1600s an "elaborately organized profession of roguery with a language of its own and a large number of well-defined methods and traditions. There was a live *esprit de corps* among the thieves, and a pride in clever and dextrous work which made their profession more of an art than a trade."[4] Aydelotte also tells of the routine seventeenth-century ruse of greeting a stranger as a long-lost relative, covering his eyes with a hand and coyly inquiring, "Who am I?" while picking his pocket. More than 300 years later, precisely the same technique is being used daily by professional pickpockets in the United States.

Rather notable is the response of one man, who was robbed by an elderly woman of about 80 who embraced him and cried, "You're the spitting image of my long-lost youngest son!" "I'm not angry," he said, continuing, "I'd like to shake hands with that little old lady. Everybody else waits around for the government to take care of them in

3 Cozzens, *The Just and the Unjust* p. 131.
4 Aydelotte, *Elizabethan Rogues and Vagabonds*, p. 1.

their old age and here she is employing a real, technical skill to take care of herself."

Professional criminals in Elizabethan times, known as "conny-catchers," are immortalized in the works of Shakespeare, with Autolycus in *The Winter's Tale,* referred to us a "snapper-upper of unconsidered trifles," serving as the most notable literary personification of the pickpocket. Today, among other types, we have the "floppers," or persons who routinely fall down on "slippery" places in large department stores, tumble deftly in front of slow-moving automobiles, and collide fortuitously with rocks at the sites of building excavations, and then submit their "damage" claims to the store or insurance company.[5] In early times, there were the "palliards," or beggars, who excited pity by means of artificial sores that were created by placing corrosives against the flesh, and there were the "hookers" or "anglers," thieves who stole clothing and similar items by pulling them through an open window with a hooked stick, a technique still favored by railroad thieves, particularly in the eastern part of Europe.[6]

"Cut-purses," or pickpockets, had an elaborate fraternity, with dues to provide insurance, and they apportioned territories within which each was privileged to operate—a procedure much the same as that used in Philadelphia in the 1920s, when Lincoln Steffens lost his watch to a pickpocket and had it returned by the police, who requested it as a matter of public relations from the thief known to have territorial rights to that particular part of the city.[7] Thomas Wright tells of a school that existed in 1585 in London where pickpockets were trained through the use of dummies with bells attached to them. If the apprentice were too gauche he would brush against the bell, which would signal his ineptness.[8] Punishment at the time for these crimes was unusually severe but apparently did little to deter newcomers from the ranks; pickpockets were often hanged, yet chroniclers tell us that during the hanging, at the moment the culprit was being "turned off," and the spectators' attention was drawn upward, other pickpockets followed their trade among the crowd.

There were widespread forms of professional crime on the frontier in the United States and in places such as the Mississippi riverboats, sites that, like today's conventions and race tracks, were particularly suited for the perpetration of fraud and deception. Two outstanding works of American fiction in the nineteenth century drew upon the confidence game for their motif. The protagonist of James Fenimore Cooper's *Homeward Bound* (1837) is a rogue named Steadfast Dodge, who is said to "partake of the qualities that his two appelations expressed." In the deeply allegorical novel by Herman Melville, *The*

5 Gibney, *The Operators,* p. 111.
6 Elliott, *Crime in Modern Society,* p. 275.
7 Steffens, *Autobiography,* Vol. I, pp. 407–414.
8 Wright, *Queen Elizabeth and Her Times,* Vol. II, pp. 245–251.

Confidence-Man (1857), a series of connivers embark and then myste-
riously debark from the steamboat *Fidèle* as it makes its way down the
Mississippi River. Among other things, they attempt to interest pas-
sengers in such fictitious entities as the Seminole Widow and Orphan
Asylum, the Protean Easy-Chair, the World Charity, the Omni-Balsamic
Reinvigorator, and the Samaritan Pain Dissuader.[9]

Perhaps the best portrait of the confidence games in earlier generations appears in the *Gentle Grafter*, a series of short stories by
O. Henry. The author himself had been imprisoned in Ohio for embezzling, and when released he drew upon the tales of his fellow inmates
for source material. O. Henry writes of Andy, a man with a "hankering
for the oral and polyglot system of buncoing," who had "a vocabulary
of about 10,000 words and synonyms, which arrayed themselves into
contraband sophistries and parables when they came out." Andy
"grafted a dollar whenever he saw one that had a surplus look about
it." Particularly noteworthy is O. Henry's constant drawing of parallels
between white-collar crime and professional crime. Thus, he writes
that Andy "had too much imagination to be honest. He used to devise
schemes of money-getting so fraudulent and high-financial that they
wouldn't have been allowed in the bylaws of a railroad," and he tells
of a woman recruited to assist in a confidence game who "said she was
glad to get a chance to give up her place as a stenographer and secretary to a suburban lot company to go into something respectable."

Self-Image of Professional Criminals

There are a number of identifying characteristics of professional
criminals, perhaps the most impressive of them being their own self-
image. *They regard themselves as professionals*, and they scornfully
separate themelves from déclassé amateurs, or dabblers at crime, who
in their inexperience and inexpertness violate such ironclad rules as
does the professional shoplifter who "grifts on the way out," that is,
takes another item while leaving the store after having stolen the item
he came to steal.[10] The intensity of allegiance to such underworld
mores is no different from that elicited by tea-time rituals and cocktail-
party protocol in the upper-world. "Thieves are as conventional as
Herman Humdrum," one of their number has written; "A man who
allows a woman to be involved in a caper in which she risks her liberty
is automatically sent to the bottom of the class."[11] The thief, in this
quotation, is not expressing a value synonymous with upper-class
chivalry, but rather a rule of criminal expediency. Females, whether
wives or girl friends, are too valuable as go-betweens and as contacts if
things go awry, to be risked as accomplices.

9 See Wright, "The Confidence Man of Melville and Cooper."
10 Sutherland, *The Professional Thief*, p. 13.
11 McKenzie, *Occupation: Thief*, p. 99.

Professional criminals often have long police records that reflect a very minor proportion of their activity. They come to regard fines and incarceration as occupational risks, to be avoided if possible, but, if not possible, to be accepted as part of the inconvenient realities of life—such as income tax audits in the corporation executive's world and the military draft in the young adult male's world.

Among the most significant attributes of the professional criminal is an elaborate system of rationalization, a system that is made up of verbal justifications for a way of life that elicits disapproval from a large segment of society. These rationalizations take a number of different forms, varying with the needs of the individual. In particular, the professional criminal is likely to redefine his own behavior as being equivalent to behavior by a majority of persons in the society, with the (to him, minor) variation that society has chosen, for prudish or perverted reasons, to outlaw his behavior. Professional criminals often catalogue at length the wayward behavior of politicians and the exploitative techniques employed by businessmen, and they are keenly aware of deviations from ethical conduct by law enforcement officers.

Professional criminals, in addition, will often devalue their victims, the "marks" upon whom they prey. Confidence men stress that the individuals they cheat are intent on carrying out schemes that will, in turn, cheat third parties. They scorn the victim as having "larceny in his heart," and believe that he thus deserves no better fate than to be robbed. Many forgers stress that they never steal from "honest" businessmen, which is their equivalent for smaller firms, but instead carry out their work in large department stores that are presumably in a better position to absorb any loss. With this attitude, Erwin O. Smigel indicates that the professional thief reflects a similar belief in the society at large, that it is less blameworthy to steal from a large business organization than from a smaller firm.[12]

Sometimes the professional criminal will romanticize his role to the extent of comparing it to that of a modern-day Robin Hood, taking from the rich and undeserving, and, presumably, by some amorphous process, redistributing ill-begotten wealth among the meritorious but poor. "I did more good than evil," Joseph (Yellow Kid) Weil, the most famous of all confidence men, once airily told a Senate subcommittee, though he failed to explain exactly how his fleecing victims of an estimated $8 million had benefited society; "They wanted something for nothing, I gave them nothing for something," he said of his victims.[13] Perhaps the greatest irony of Weil's career lay in the fact that he lost his entire fortune by poor investments in legitimate business enterprises.[14] The same theme appears in O. Henry's work,

12 Smigel, "Public Attitudes Toward Stealing in Relation to the Size of the Victim Organization," p. 321.
13 U.S. Senate, "Exploitation of Minors in Interstate Confidence Racket," p. 75.
14 Scott, *Concise Encyclopedia of Crime and Criminals*, p. 337.

in which the confidence men return money they swindled to persons they regard as unable to afford the loss. "We never allowed to swindle sick old women and working girls and take nickels off of kids," they say; "In the lines of graft we worked we took money from the people the Lord made to be buncoed—sports and rounders and smart Alecks and street crowds, that always have a few dollars to throw away, and farmers that wouldn't ever be happy if the grafters didn't come around and play with 'em when they sold their crops."[15]

Many of the rationalizations of the professional criminal are gathered together in this statement by one of them during an interview in prison:

> You know how it goes in this dog-eat-dog world. You got to take the other guy before he takes you. You know, the real sharpie outwits the marks. Of course, it all depends on how you get ahead. My way was no different from, say, a lawyer or businessman. You know, a lawyer has a license to steal. The cops should lay off con men. We don't hurt nobody. You can't con an honest man. . . . The cops should do their job and clear the streets of the muggers, heist men, hop heads, and the rest. Why, it's dangerous for a decent man like me to walk down the street at night.[16]

These rationalizations provide psychological support for the professional criminal in periods when he is most aware of the public censure that his role draws. In addition, he may reinforce his ego by reference to the material benefits that his behavior brings to him. He turns back onto the society the standards of judgment that it regularly employs to evaluate "success." Professional criminals may refer to the financial rewards accruing to them—to the leisure, travel, and "individual entrepreneur" advantages of their way of life—which are all general social denotations of adequacy, particularly in our society where wealth and leisure are apt to be respected without regard for their source. In addition, professional criminals are apt to devalue the life of the average citizen and label him a "sucker," a "wage slave," and an unimaginative fellow of plodding mediocrity.

Possibly the greatest protection against social scorn and disconcerting introspection on the part of the professional criminal is his use of isolation, of in-group reinforcement. By restricting his contacts to other persons with similar outlooks in similar occupations, he gains support for his behavior and insulates himself from criticism. Often, the professional criminal only comes into contact with persons holding different values in the course of his work and, in these cases, the contact is either impersonal, as in the instance of shoplifters and pickpockets, or it is with individuals who are themselves intent on dishonest profits, as in the case of victims of confidence men.

A major part of this system of isolation and insulation is a verbal

15 O. Henry, *Complete Works*, p. 336.
16 Roebuck and Johnson, "The 'Short Con' Man," p. 242.

camouflage of slang, such as that found among virtually all specialized groups, particularly if they are functionally peripheral to the mainstream of society, as are jazz musicians and teen-agers, for example. Jargon provides a feeling of both camaraderie and security; it is, as Ned Polsky notes, not only a shorthand manner of referring to technical processes, but also an elaborately inventive, ritualistic, often rather playful way of reinforcing group identity or "we-feeling."[17] A subgroup vocabulary shows that the person has a group to which he belongs and in which he is "somebody." Slang is used in this way to show others and to remind ourselves of our biographical, mental, and psychological background.[18] Professional thieves, for instance, will effectively communicate among themselves when they discuss "burning" (holding out part of the proceeds of a theft for oneself) or talk about a "cannon" (pickpocket), a "moll buzzer" (a pickpocket who victimizes females), or a "wire" (the pickpocket who actually removes the wallet).[19] Some underworld argot terms are international linguistic currency, while others are indigenous. In Italy, for instance, the idea that a pickpocket has stolen a wallet and was placed in a prison cell after a third-degree questioning would be expressed in these terms: "The shoeman was caught lifting a chicken's slipper and ended up in a birdbath at the dark house after a cattle feeding." Much of the language used today in the United States by professional thieves bears a striking similarity to that employed hundreds of years ago by persons in the Elizabethan underworld,[20] while other oddments of jargon appear briefly and are then consigned to linguistic junkheaps. The utility, expressiveness, and the images conveyed by the word presumably determine its life span.

Confidence Games

While the general ethos of professional crime shows striking consistency, regardless of the form of thievery the individual pursues, there are notable differences both in the behavior and in the kinds of individuals who pursue typically diverse avenues of professional crime. A discussion of several major categories of professional crime will indicate their similarities and differences.

The confidence game has been described as "the manipulation of the victim through non-violent methods into a situation of dishonesty in order to take advantage of the victim's dishonesty."[21] The confidence game stands at the top rung in the prestige hierarchy of professional crime. The denotation of the activity comes from the fact

17 Polsky, *Hustlers, Beats, Others,* pp. 106–107.
18 Flexner, "Preface," in *Dictionary of American Slang,* pp. x–xi.
19 Maurer, "The Argot of Forgery"; Goldin, *Dictionary of American Underworld Lingo.*
20 Judges, *The Elizabethan Underworld.*
21 Gasser, "The Confidence Game," p. 47.

that the victim voluntarily delivers up his money or property because
of the confidence he places in the swindler. Confidence men are
smooth, adroit talkers, persons who can "convince you that black is
white."[22] They live by their wits, and a successful confidence man soon
develops "reflexes . . . attuned to the significance of a conversation
overheard, a dropped telephone number, or a letter of introduction
to someone who will introduce you to someone further."[23] "The most
important thing in the rackets is the ability to manipulate people,"
Chic Conwell, a professional thief, has noted. By this criterion confidence men rank supreme. Conwell goes on to summarize the ingredients that make a successful confidence operator:

> Not all persons can be good con men. They generally must have a win-
> ning personality, shrewdness, agility, like the good things of life, and be
> too lazy to work for them, and have great egotism. They must, first of
> all, be good actors. The whole con game is a matter of acting. If they
> cannot put on this veneer of culture, they cannot make it go. A con-
> fidence man must live by his wits.[24]

Confidence games are generally divided into "big con" (or "long
con") and "short con" types, with the major variation being the elabo-
rateness of the build-up and the amount of money taken from the
victim. In a "big con," numerous accomplices and props are employed
to fleece the "mark" after the "steerer" or "roper" (the person who
locates the victim) leads him to the "insideman" (the major actor in
this simulated drama). The victim may be told, for instance, that the
insideman is a disgruntled telegraph company manager who desires
to take his revenge against the company by intercepting race track
results en route to gambling establishments and betting on the victorious horses before the establishment itself has the results. If the
victim cares to participate in this illegal activity, he is put "on the
send" (dispatched home to secure money). Subsequently, various misunderstandings occur and, by the end of these maneuvers, the mark
has been deftly separated from his money. He is then "cooled off."
Sometimes this is accomplished by use of a "cackle bag"—a plastic
bag filled with chicken blood, which is punctured during the course
of a fierce fight between the roper and the insideman, in which the
insideman presumably shoots the roper. The mark, told that he is
now an accessory to murder, is usually more than pleased to be able
to leave the area as rapidly as possible, and he rarely makes further
inquiries about his lost money.[25]

"Cooling off," as Erving Goffman notes in a perceptive analysis,
can be accomplished with more finesse than that employed by use
of a "cackle bag" ruse. When more personal techniques are used, they

22 Whyte, Street-Corner Society, p. 120.
23 McKenzie, Occupation: Thief, p. 87.
24 Sutherland, The Professional Thief, p. 3.
25 Maurer, The Big Con.

rely upon "the art of consolation" and attempt to define the situation to the mark in a way that will make it easy for him to accept the inevitable and yet allow him to retain some image of himself as a relatively able individual rather than forcing him to realize that he was just another "easy mark." Goffman points out that

> For the mark, cooling off represents a process of adjustment to an impossible situation—a situation arising from having defined himself in a way which the social facts come to contradict. The mark must therefore be supplied with a new set of apologies for himself, a new framework in which to see himself and judge himself. . . . Since the mark himself is frequently in too weakened a condition to do this, the cooler must initially do it for him.[26]

In addition to the effectiveness of cooling-off tactics, the embarrassment at having been duped because of his own cupidity often keeps a victim from lodging complaints.

"Short con" ruses take a wide range of forms, with confidence men often improvising new tactics to fit their sense of larceny. Joseph (Yellow Kid) Weil, for instance, tells how he secured money from a man who obviously knew very little about the racing of horses:

> There was one man I strung along for sixteen months. Occasionally, I took him to the track . . .
> "See how dry and dusty the course is today?"
> "Yes."
> "That's what we call a fast track. My horses don't run as well on a fast track, so I usually sprinkle water on it to settle the dust."
> When the water sprinkler came around I pointed it out to him, "It cost me a lot of money, but it's worth it."
> He never questioned that I had to pay the expenses of maintaining the water wagon. He later gave me three hundred dollars to help keep the track watered.[27]

One standard form of short conning is the "smack," a coin-matching procedure in which the mark is led to believe that he can cheat a third party by collaborating with a new-found friend, who is actually a confederate of the third party. Another is the "Spanish prisoner" swindle in which the mark receives a letter, purportedly from a Mexican or Spanish prison, asking for ransom money in return for which he will be allowed to share in a treasure that the prisoner managed to hide before he was jailed. There is also the "green goods" game in which the victim is led to invest money in a machine, complete with colored lights, buzzers, and sponges, which is alleged to convert $1 bills into larger denominations. Still another is the "slum hustle" in which, by clever acting, the confidence man conveys the idea that a practically worthless item that he is surreptitiously selling is actually a piece of stolen property worth considerably more than he

26 Goffman, "On Cooling the Mark Out," p. 456.
27 Brannon, *"Yellow Kid" Weil,* p. 53.

is asking.[28] And, another short con game is the Jamaican switch, a variation of which is described in the following report circulated by a California urban police force:

> 66-year-old male victim was approached by suspect Number 1 at 3:30 p.m., who in broken English inquired as to location of "4019 Peagreen Ave", flashing three large rolls of bills. Suspect was cautioned by victim not to flash the money around and at that time told about paying a woman fifty dollars to get him a bottle of vodka and she had not returned. At this time, Suspect Number 2 approached and also cautioned Number 1 not to flash his money around and advised him to put it in the bank. Number 1 became very excited and said that he had "heard of Communist places where you put your money in and you were beaten and kicked when you tried to draw it out," referring to money always as "grain." Then followed usual procedure of getting victim to draw money out of his bank to show Suspect 1 that it could be done. Number 1 then put the victim's money and his own large amount of bills in a paper sack and rolled it up and then passed victim what appeared to be the same sack and told him to hold it inside his shirt as there were thieves around. Suspects then left, telling victim to wait in the lobby of bank, that they would be right back as they were going to get Number 1 a room so that they would have an address to give the bank when they deposited the money. Sack contained two packs of cigarettes.

Probably the most ubiquitous short con game is the "pigeon drop," a ruse usually practiced by females. In return for the mark's putting up money to show "good will," promise is made that he will be allowed to share in a large sum that one of the confidence actors "happened" to find on the street. Because the pigeon drop is one of the least elaborate confidence games, its operators stand low in the hierarchy of professional crime. The fact that pigeon droppers are often sorely inadequate for the competitive fray has led one investigator to hypothesize that these individuals choose this form of anti-social behavior in an attempt to compensate for feelings of inferiority. In a study of twenty-five inmates in the Eastern State Penitentiary in Philadelphia, all of whom had long records for pigeon dropping, James Barbash found the offenders to have completed only 3.5 grades of school, and to have an average I.Q. of 62.[29]

The pigeon droppers had led seminomadic lives and were known personally or by reputation to fellow artistes throughout the country. They spoke, Barbash found, with "unhidden pride . . . of violence as being beneath their dignity" and considered themselves "professional." Twenty-four of the twenty-five came from low socioeconomic areas. They persisted in a routine that rarely changed and protected themselves with the standard rationalization of confidence men: "I wouldn't of beat him if he hadn't had larceny in his heart." Barbash

28 Anderson, *Beverly Hills is My Beat*, pp. 73–74.
29 Barbash, "Compensation and the Crime of Pigeon Dropping," p. 92.

notes that this statement is "made with such frequency as to assume the proportion of a creed." Pigeon droppers openly expressed enjoyment of the swindle because it involved outsmarting persons who had intended to "beat" them. The mean number of arrests for the group was twenty-one, with the range extending from six in seven years to forty-eight in less than thirty years. Several of the inmates said that only three out of ten attempted routines were successful, with the remainder ending either in arrest or in a prodigious amount of talking to avoid arrest. Barbash notes that his sample may have been somewhat biased, and it is evident that the pigeon droppers he studied in prison represent by definition the least successful of their clan.

The same stricture prevails regarding the study of ten Negro, male, short-con offenders imprisoned in Virginia conducted by Julian Roebuck and Ronald Johnson. For this group the average I.Q. was 100, fifteen points above the norm for the total prison population. In particular, the researchers were impressed by the fact that the con men had assiduously avoided the use of violence throughout their lives. They had not been involved in fighting in their homes, at school, or as members of neighborhood peer groups. They did not destroy property and did not participate in muggings or purse snatching. None of the ten had carried weapons.[30]

In an analysis of confidence rackets as a sociological phenomenon, Edwin Schur calls attention to the fact that they are called "games," while most other criminal offenses receive far less playful appellations; he stresses that such games may have a purposive element, "for even where the game involves a monetary stake . . . to the person who really enjoys it, its attraction lies in the dynamics and hazards of the sociologically significant forms of activity themselves."[31] The point is that confidence games, like the role-playing of the professional actor, represent a symbolic form of activity, drawing into them persons who, for various reasons, derive pleasure from deliberately playing a part. It also seems probable that the power displayed by the confidence man in manipulating his victim is a major attraction. This will-to-power is clearly perceived by Doris Lessing, who writes about a confidence man:

> His strength was—and I could feel just how powerful that strength was —his terrible, compelling anxiety that he should be able to force someone under his will. It was almost as if he were pleading, silently, in the moment when he was tricking a victim: Please let me trick you; please let me cheat you; I've got to; it's essential for me.[32]

This same trait, a trait considered "bizarre and peculiar" by George Thompson, is found many times in professional mendicants and beggars, who seem to derive great satisfaction from having people

30 Roebuck and Johnson, "The 'Short Con' Man," pp. 238–239.
31 Schur, "Sociological Analysis of Confidence Swindling," p. 298.
32 Lessing, *In Pursuit of the English*, p. 53.

believe that they are in need, despite the fact that many of them have amassed considerable sums of money.[33]

Confidence game activity has also been related to some basic values in American society. We reward traits that lead to successful salesmanship and put a premium on "idea men" who have the ability to "sell a bill of goods" and "put across their personality" in addition to being "well-liked" and "good mixers." These socially-sanctioned attributes, as Schur notes, are the very hallmark of the experienced swindler.[34] There is also often a striking similarity between the values of the person swindled and those of the confidence man, which may well allow the victim to identify readily with the confidence behavior and participate in it. At least, as Edwin H. Sutherland once wryly observed, there is no known case of a victim's declining to continue with the confidence scheme after he has learned that its basis was a dishonest plot, allegedly designed to cheat another person.[35]

Forgery

Forgery ranges from elaborate deceptions involving multimillion dollar art treasures to petty alterations on checks. As practiced today, the most common form of forgery involves the cashing of checks—usually to "purchase" merchandise and to obtain change—by persons who refer to themselves as "paperhangers" and refer to their crime as "hanging paper."[36] In English law, forgery did not become an offense until 1562, partly because there was little danger of the behavior, since so few persons could write. When money took on a new significance in the mid-sixteenth century, however, and credit began to be of some importance, the fraudulent manipulation of instruments became dangerous, and the punishment of such offenses became routine.[37]

Forgers further illustrate the finesse, the rational pursuit of illicit gain, and the virtual imperviousness to control that is characteristic of professional criminals. Forgers thrive in a check-oriented atmosphere, which attempts to eliminate the need for carrying large amounts of cash and to lull the inhibitions of buyers by facilitating a form of purchase that seems less "real" than one involving a cash outlay. Today, more than 90 percent of all money transactions in the United States are made with checks. Good commercial public relations demands that purchasers not be questioned too closely or too antagonistically about the validity of their checks lest they be alienated and not return to the store. Forgers are more than willing to take advantage of this sensitive interpersonal relationship between the seller and the check-paying buyer.

33 Thompson, *Psychopathic Delinquent and Criminal,* pp. 58–59.
34 Schur, "Sociological Analysis of Confidence Swindling," pp. 301–302.
35 Sutherland, *The Professional Thief,* p. 70.
36 See Sternitzsky, *Forgery and Fictitious Checks.*
37 Rhodes, *The Craft of Forgery,* pp. 3, 10.

Reliable estimates of the amount of forgery in the United States have never been made. The President's Commission on Law Enforcement and Administration of Justice cited reports placing the forgery loss at a half billion dollars annually, but suggested that this total was the product of limited surveys. The American Bankers Association estimates that forgery of banking instruments comes to about $60 million annually for individuals and business. Banks themselves bear about $4 million of the loss. The Treasury Department indicates that, during the 1965 fiscal year, forged government checks amounted to $4 million.[38] A major difficulty in estimating total forgery losses, however, involves the fact than many stores, after an unsuccessful effort to recoup a loss from a bad check, will merely write the matter off as a regular expense of doing business.

The following newspaper interview with a professional forger shows the mental processes, commitments, and rationalizations of a confirmed paperhanger. (The forger's name and home-town have been altered.)

> "My occupation is check forger—and I'm a good one. I work a 40-hour week with an hour lunch period, and I plan to retire at the age of 55."
>
> That's the way Sally Barnett, 26, Pawhuska, Oklahoma, sums up her life.
>
> The green-eyed brunette was in city jail Saturday—"one of the occupational hazards of my profession."
>
> Detectives described the woman as a "fast check artist" who admitted cashing four forged checks for more than $200 during a 2½-hour spree in downtown department stores.
>
> Getting arrested failed to cloud Miss Barnett's sunny disposition. "It's part of the job," she told a reporter. "However, I've been most fortunate. In my nine years of hanging paper I've only served one year in prison."
>
> She admitted that a return trip to prison appeared rather imminent Saturday. "But if I go to prison it won't reform me. I will start right in forging checks when I get out. I don't want to reform. Check forging is my occupation."
>
> "I have a special talent for it. I can take someone's signature, study it for a few minutes and then forge that signature so that even they wouldn't recognize it as a forgery."
>
> "I've got a record a yard long, but nowhere in my record will you find where I cashed checks at any place but large department stores where the losses are covered by insurance. I don't believe in clipping an individual who must take the loss himself."
>
> "I work my racket the same hours the store employees work—with an hour off for lunch. I'll not tell you how much I make, but in a good town, I will leave after two days with $1,500, about half in cash and half in clothing. I am among the best-dressed women in America."
>
> Miss Barnett says she goes "first class, although I don't spend my money wildly or foolishly. I stay in the best hotels and travel by airliner.

38 President's Commission, *Crime and Its Impact—An Assessment*, p. 51.

You can hit more towns that way. I save money, because I plan to retire when I am 55."

Miss Barnett was strictly an amateur forger nine years ago when she was sent to the women's reformatory at Rockwell, Iowa.

"There I met the queen of forgers, and she taught me all the tricks. I studied under the best. I make mistakes, but I always profit by them."

The ratio of professional criminality to amateur efforts at check forgery has never been accurately determined. In one sample of 1,023 check forgers in Los Angeles, Edwin M. Lemert found that almost 40 percent had prior records for the same offense,[39] but it is impossible to know whether these prior records, in actual fact, were at least partly responsible for the forgery charges being pressed and brought into court. Complainants might well be more lenient toward first offenders who offer to make restitution. On the basis of his data, however, Lemert concluded that the age of the professional paperhanger, with its heyday from the end of the Civil War through the 1920s, is now rapidly coming to an end.[40]

The forgers studied by Lemert were disproportionately concentrated among the male, native white portions of the population. They were also somewhat older than the usual run of apprehended criminals, with many in their late twenties and early thirties, and, in addition, they possessed relatively high degrees of intelligence. Impulsiveness was the trait that Lemert found to be most characteristic of the forger. Several professional check writers, for instance, told him that they shunned confidence games because they required too elaborate a build-up and the denouement was too slow in coming, whereas check forgery provided them with immediate satisfaction.

The "low visibility" of forgery, Lemert hypothesizes, makes it particularly attractive to nonprofessionals, because they can pass worthless checks and yet not place undue strain on their essentially law-abiding image of themselves. The nonprofessionals, whom Lemert labels "naive" check forgers, were found to have become involved in situations that enveloped them so thoroughly that they could not pull back when they came to the point of law violation. A large part of the demands was found to lie in the definition of the role the individual was playing at the time that his funds were not sufficient to sustain his position. A common type of nonprofessional forger was the man on a drinking spree with companions. Rather than pass by his turn to pay for a late round of drinks, despite the fact that he had spent all his money, he would write a worthless check. Prominent also was the man who was enmeshed in pressures to buy gifts for Christmas, but did not have the wherewithal to do so in the manner he felt was required of him.

39 Lemert, "An Isolation and Closure Theory of Naive Check Forgery," p. 297.
40 Lemert, "The Behavior of the Systematic Check Forger," p. 143.

Many of Lemert's findings were supported by an investigation of eighty-one forgers in the Kingston Penitentiary in Canada. These were found to have started their illegal behavior relatively late, beginning at the average age of twenty-five, to have good educations, and to come from "good" families. In general, they had experienced no trouble either in obtaining or holding jobs. Relying on a psychiatric frame of reference, the Canadian investigation maintained that the forgery of these inmates resulted from "inner conflicts which demand relief from tension."[41] The fact that many forgers voluntarily give themselves up provides some support for this hypothesis. Like numerous confidence men, a number of the Canadian forgers told of the pleasure they derived from outwitting victims: "When they accept your cheque," one said, for instance, "you feel proud of yourself. After all, it was so easy to fool somebody who was supposed to know all the angles."[42]

That forgers tend to be more intelligent than other criminals was also documented in a study of 135 forgers imprisoned in the State Prison of Southern Michigan. They were compared to 480 inmates in the general prison population. The mean I.Q. of the general prison population was 89.1 on the Alpha test, which is considered equivalent to the intelligence of an average sample of American adults. The forgers, on the other hand, scored 99.4. The forgers were also found to be eight years older on the average than the general inmate population and to show twice as much recidivism.[43]

Attempts to combat forgery illustrate the constant interplay that occurs between law enforcement and criminal activity.[44] Attempts to fight forgery include the introduction of techniques such as requiring prior registration before cashing a check, insisting on fingerprints on the reverse side of checks, and twin-lens photography of the person and the check he cashes. Commercial firms use check-writing protectograph machines in an attempt to guard funds against forgery. Banks, too, are now beginning to issue personal checks with the photograph of the individual in a top corner. But it seems safe to predict that these methods will, at most, cause professional forgers to concentrate their energies on other, more vulnerable aspects of the marketing system. Most likely, the professional forger will simply develop different devices of his own to counteract advances in methods of control. The ingenuity of the thief who is determined to continue his work has been neatly epitomized by H. Edelston's story of an Arabian pilferer who had his hands amputated as punishment for theft, then continued to steal by using his teeth.[45]

41 Gautier, "Psychology of the Compulsive Forger," p. 63.
42 *Ibid.*, p. 68.
43 Berg, "A Comparative Study of Forgers," p. 233.
44 See Sutherland and Cressey, *Principles of Criminology*, p. 274–276.
45 Edelston, *Earliest Stages of Delinquency*, p. 192.

Shoplifting

The extent of shoplifting in the United States cannot be established with more than vague accuracy, since most stores blend shoplifting losses into their total "inventory shrinkage"—a figure that may include merchandise that is damaged and sold at reduced prices, bookkeeping errors, breakage, and employee thefts, as well as shoplifting losses. Gathering figures from diverse sources, the President's Commission on Law Enforcement estimated that somewhere in the vicinity of $300 to $350 million worth of products are shoplifted each year. The Commission figured that between 75 and 80 percent of all inventory shrinkage is the product of stealing and that such acts amount to a loss of $1.3 million annually. However, a very large percentage of such theft—probably more than 75 percent—is believed to be by store employees, while the remainder is figured as the work of shoplifters.[46]

Accurate information is particularly difficult to obtain, due to the usual store practice of prosecuting only a relatively small percentage of the shoplifters apprehended. This selective process is often based on factors not directly related to the theft itself, such as the attitude of the person arrested or the person's ethnic or racial background and financial standing; Negroes and poor persons are more likely to be prosecuted than middle-class whites. Persons who sign a confession are sometimes released subsequently; those who refuse to sign are more likely to be prosecuted so that the business will not be faced with a false arrest suit.[47] In one study, as noted earlier, Thorsten Sellin found that there were more cases of shoplifting known to three department stores in the city of Philadelphia than there were thefts known to the police force for the entire city.[48] Otto Pollak, surveying the data, concluded that "the relationship between prosecution and incidence of shoplifting is so remote that no reliance whatsoever can be placed on criminal statistics in an effort to gauge the real extent of this . . . type of larceny."[49]

Professional shoplifters can be differentiated from amateurs, who now outnumber them by about twenty-five to one, by the fact that they steal the merchandise in order to resell it to a "fence," an intermediary who will pay the thief about one-third the retail value of the article. There are two major types of shoplifters: the true professional, or "heel," who is rarely involved in other crimes but who shows a long history of shoplifting activity and sometimes concentrates on stealing only particular kinds of goods; and the "boost," an offender who usually steals in order to purchase narcotics or alcohol. The boost will engage in any type of activity that promises financial reward.

46 President's Commission, *Crime and Its Impact—An Assessment*, p. 48.
47 Robin, "Patterns of Department Store Shoplifting," p. 164.
48 Sellin, *Research Memorandum on Crime in the Depression*, p. 69.
49 Pollak, *The Criminality of Women*, p. 51.

Women boosts, for instance, will very often show arrest records for prostitution.

In addition to the professional shoplifters, there is a large corps of amateur pilferers who steal for their own use. Professionals refer to these individuals derogatorily as "snitches." All evidence points to the fact that snitches steal systematically in order to obtain goods that they covet or to avoid the expenditure of money on items that they require. They flourish in supermarkets, where they take too literally the invitation to "self-service."

Mary Owen Cameron, in a comprehensive study of shoplifters apprehended in a downtown Chicago department store, concluded that amateur shoplifters were not compulsive, uncontrolled thieves suffering from severe psychological disturbances, but rather "respectable people who pilfer systematically." She found that they come to the store prepared to steal, and continue to steal until finally apprehended. Once taken into custody, the pilferer rarely repeats his crime. Cameron believes that the damage to the amateur thief's self-concept at the time of his arrest is usually adequate either to push any psychological disturbance into another channel, or, more likely, to inhibit further stealing because of heightened awareness of the consequences. "From the general viewpoint of criminology," Cameron wrote, "this is a very significant fact and an understanding of the why's and how's of it might be important to our total treatment program for first offenders."[50] She continues:

> Pilferers generally do not think of themselves as thieves, and they resist strongly being pushed to conceive of themselves in these terms. . . . It is often quite difficult for the store staff to convince the arrested person that he has actually been arrested, even when the detectives show their licenses and badges. Again and again store police explain to pilferers that they are under arrest as thieves, that they will, in the normal course of events, be taken in a police wagon to jail, held in jail and tried in court before a judge and sentenced. . . . "Yes, I took the dress," one woman sobbed, "but that doesn't mean I'm a thief."[51]

The concentration of shoplifting among women—74 percent of Cameron's Chicago sample[52] and 60 percent of Gerald Robin's Philadelphia sample[53] were women—seems to be traceable to some extent to the fact that advertising pressures are directed specifically toward female shoppers. Women control 80 percent of the purchasing power in the United States, and shopping is an intricate part of the female way of life, exerting stresses, producing ambivalences, inculcating wants. Tremendous effort is made to create lusts for material goods in persons to whom these goods are often financially inaccessible.

50 Cameron, in Edwards, *Shoplifting and Shrinkage Protection for Stores*, p. x.
51 Cameron, *The Booster and the Snitch*, p. 161.
52 *Ibid.*, Chap. 5.
53 Robin, "Patterns of Department Store Shoplifting," p. 167.

Vance Packard has documented the intensive investigation into human fears and anxieties, which is conducted by "motivational research" agencies to provide clues for selling products.[54] Irresistible temptation, in fact, is one of the aims of sophisticated salesmanship, and T. C. N. Gibbens reports that one store in England overhauled its display procedures drastically because it was felt that a low shoplifting rate indicated a lack of attraction in the way merchandise was being displayed.[55]

Some writers have attempted to tie the high rate of females among shoplifters to menstrual tensions, particularly to tensions related to menopause;[56] Cameron, however, by a thorough analysis of the age distribution of shoplifters in Chicago, found this hypothesis untenable.[57] Alex Arieff and Carol Bowie have taken the position that females are attracted to shoplifting because it "may be interpreted as a not-too-aggressive rejection of social restrictions, thus more likely to satisfy women than men, who make attempts at adjustment in more aggressive ways."[58] This idea, however, needs considerably more substantiation before it can be given credence.

Others believe that a condition of kleptomania, or pathological stealing, is behind female shoplifting. Cameron points out, however, that if such a condition does exist, it has little, if any, effect that can be demonstrated in studies of shoplifting.[59] Strictures against the validity of the concept of kleptomania have also recently been advanced by a British criminologist, who doubts if it exists as a clinical entity.[60] Those who support the existence of true kleptomania attempt to tie it to libidinal desires. Milton Barron, for instance, notes that many cases of repeated shoplifting by girls provide an "example of symbolic sex gratification"; the articles that girls steal, he notes, are of a "masculine nature and are associated with sporty and flashy attire, representing an unfulfilled love tryst."[61] This conclusion, however, must be treated with considerable skepticism, particularly in view of Cameron's findings to the contrary, after she tabulated the items stolen from department stores by women shoplifters.[62] It may well be, however, that more detailed research would establish more finite categories among the totality of shoplifting offenders.

Shoplifting, beyond the social and psychological forces mediating it, is also closely tied to the legal definitions of the situation. Merchants are usually wary of interfering with suspected shoplifters, partly out

54 See Packard, *The Hidden Persuaders*.
55 Gibbens and Prince, *Shoplifting*, p. 13.
56 Pollak, *The Criminality of Women*, pp. 125–135.
57 Cameron, *The Booster and the Snitch*, p. 151.
58 Arieff and Bowie, "Some Psychiatric Aspects of Shoplifting," pp. 567–568.
59 Cameron, *The Booster and the Snitch*, p. 119.
60 Neustatter, *Psychological Disorder and Crime*, p. 189.
61 Barron, *The Juvenile in Delinquent Society*, p. 121.
62 Cameron, *The Booster and the Snitch*, pp. 156–157.

of fear of offending a legitimate customer, more out of dread of becoming involved in a suit for false arrest. Some shoplifters have evolved a confidence game routine of deliberately courting arrest by appearing to be stealing when actually not doing so, and then by leveling false arrest charges if detained. To protect merchants from such entrapment procedures, most states have enacted legislation modeled on a pioneering 1955 Florida statute, which allows the storekeeper to make a "reasonable mistake" in detaining a suspected shoplifter if "under the circumstances a reasonable man would make the same mistake."

Hustling as a Criminal Way of Life

The group of professional offenders loosely labelled "hustlers" is marked by a considerable variation in their offense pattern and a lesser commitment to the code of conduct that rules other professional criminal activities. The President's Commission on Law Enforcement described an aspect of "hustling" activities in the following manner:

> For the small-time professional criminal, hustling means moving around the bars and being seen; it means asking "What's up." It means "connecting" in the morning with two others who have a burglary set up for the evening, calling a man you know to see if he wants to buy ten stolen alpaca sweaters at $5 each, and scouting the streets for an easy victim. It means being versatile; passing checks, rolling a drunk, driving for a stickup, boosting a car, burglarizing a store. It is a planless kind of existence, but with a purpose—to make as much money as can be made each day, no holds barred.[63]

The Commission found that run-of-the-mill professional criminals, the hustlers, gather regularly at certain bars and restaurants that function as criminal job placement centers. These sites, it was noted, "do for the professional criminal what want ads, employment offices, and businessmen's luncheons do for legitimate business." Hustling was found to be an unstable vocation. Different crimes require different kinds of personnel and involve different risks, so that the transitory character of operations cuts into routine adherence to a code of conduct. The "no ratting" rule, for instance, implanted in higher-status professional offenders, was found to be archaic among hustlers, who, as one noted, operate on the principle that "The one who gets his story told first gets the lightest sentence." It was felt by the Crime Commission that there has been an absence of adequate research on the work of "fences," who occupy a key place in the market transactions of professional offenders, and the activities of loan sharks, who provide professional criminals with capital and emergency funds.[64]

63 President's Commission, *Crime and Its Impact—An Assessment*, p. 97.
64 *Ibid.*, pp. 99–100.

A biographical statement by Henry Williamson, a man who has spent most of his life hustling, or "doing wrong," as he calls it, provides further insight into this form of career crime. Williamson moved among diverse kinds of offenses, developing a particular expertise in filching safety inspection stickers from automobiles and selling them to persons unwilling or unable to secure their own. "We was so good, that no sooner the guy put it up, we got it!" Williamson notes with pride of craftsmanship; "Gettin' safety stickers in the winter is hard 'cause they freeze to the window. You got to be an expert. I'm not braggin', but I was an expert!"[65]

"Dragging" was another of Williamson's endeavors. "We'd go a certain distance out of the neighborhood, and we'd rob everybody we'd meet. Now we may pass up some people, but we don't pass up many."[66] Such robbery involved a range of skill. Williamson, for instance, never robbed a store without first making a purchase, because he had discovered that cash transactions put salesmen at ease and made them less likely to retaliate. "I liked to get 'em just when they had opened the register to put my money in."[67] He also learned to predict further actions of persons being robbed from their initial responses, just as pickpockets learn that movements in the back of the neck of their victims provide excellent clues to the victim's awareness that he is being jostled and robbed.

Williamson adds personal testimony to the Crime Commission's thesis that ethical codes among hustlers are something other than the traditional credo of professional crime. "Everyone I hustled with I took from," he writes, and he presents a chain of stories of duplicity among crime partners.

There is, in Williamson's story of his life, a strange flatness, a blindness and lack of both comprehension of himself and feeling for his victims that appears often to mark hustling as a way of life. This mood has been caught by John Rechy in a review of Williamson's autobiography:

> Plunging casually into crime, apparently devoid of redemptive qualities, proud only of his brutality, unaware (through incident after incident of savage muggings, kickings, holdups, knifings, shootings) of the horror he creates, he can only narrate the details of a scene that is, inherently, crushingly moving. Not realizing that he intends to rob her, a young Negro girl flirts coyly with him—"puttin' a little switch in her walk . . . givin' a little 'come on' with her eyes." Finally aware, she hands him the money, still smiling even as she sees the gun pointed at her. Williamson is unaffected by the ironic sadness of this. He can *see* it, but he feels nothing.[68]

65 Williamson, *Hustler!,* p. 78.
66 *Ibid.,* p. 82.
67 *Ibid.,* p. 104.
68 Rechy, Book Review of *The Hustler!,* p. 254.

Hierarchy of Crime

The top level in the world of professional crime is made up of big-time confidence operators and professional forgers and shoplifters, who systematically pursue specialized careers. Also very high in the hierarchy are jewel thieves, the "icemen" who concentrate on stealing expensive "flash." Reports indicate that the average professional jewel thief—there are an estimated 4,000 throughout the nation, who account for 20 percent of all stolen jewelry—is a male in his forties, married and the father of two children, living in a $40,000 house in the suburbs; he is said to own two cars, one of which is a Cadillac convertible, and to make between $50,000 and $100,000 a year, a considerable portion of which goes to fix cases when he is caught.[69]

Pickpockets occupy a much lower status on the ladder of professional crime. Their inferior position results from the fact that they are apprehended more often than other professional offenders and because their profits, which are generally meager by the standards of their colleagues, depend upon a considerable amount of activity rather than upon calculating finesse. Pickpockets who operate in groups called "whiz mobs," however, have a fine rank distinction among the members and a systematic division of labor. One member will remove the wallet after a second partner has distracted the victim either by nudging against him or blocking his view or both. The stolen wallet will immediately be passed to a third member of the group so that the "hook," or "dip," as he is called in England, will not have incriminating evidence on his person in the event that suspicion is directed toward him. Pickpockets have been known to plant the wallet on an innocent bystander when circumstances made it necessary, and then subsequently to steal the wallet a second time.[70]

Summary

The precise etiology of professional criminality is difficult to trace. Few studies have attempted to analyze either the personalities or the backgrounds of individuals engaging in these activities or to determine the routes by which they came to professional crime. Mostly, we have only introspective observations by a small number of professionals who chose to write about themselves and their activities, as seen with a selective and perhaps colored memory. Donald McKenzie, a professional thief turned writer, for instance, provides a typical, slim investigatory lead when he notes of his youth:

> At the age of five I was in boarding school and spending alternate vacations with my parents. At an early age I blossomed into an imaginative liar. I breezed into my late teens with expensive tastes and a deep mistrust of anything that appeared dull or humdrum. I didn't like hard

69 Remsberg and Remsberg, "The Aristocrats of Crime."
70 Maurer, *The Whiz Mob.*

work either. As a brat I had the conviction that the world revolved about me and have never been completely able to rid myself of the idea.[71]

Another lead comes from the anonymous thief whose life history has been presented by John Bartlow Martin, and who vividly illustrates many of the points stressed above. In one of the instances when Martin intrudes his own observations upon those of his subject, he attempts to describe an aspect of professional crime:

> They see everything differently than you do. Everything. If you drive down a residential street, you think of property values, perhaps, or of landscaping. They think of burglary. They are America's only proletariat. No other class in America believes lifelong that the rest of the world is their enemy; no other class feels the weight of the rest of us on their backs forever. They have at all times a price on their heads and the price is cheap. They are reviled, hated, and cast down by the rest of us, and they are fair game for anybody with a gun. All this is the criminal viewpoint held by thousands of men. It deserves study.[72]

Martin's last suggestion has, of course, been the aim of the present chapter; an attempt to present in a systematic way the attributes of significant segments of the criminal population. Considerably more study needs to be carried out, study concentrated on homogeneous criminal acts and the correlates pertaining to the individuals who commit these acts, before we will be able to understand the life style of the professional criminal better. Comparison of life histories shows considerable similarity but leaves large gaps in providing more than slim clues to the elements of causation. In addition, many of these elements do not necessarily lie in the individual criminal, but within the society whose values and goals he is reflecting. Sutherland has further pointed to the need to know in detail the process of recognition and tutelage by which a person becomes a professional criminal.[73]

The tenacity of the behavior of professional criminals is clearly illustrated by Martin's subject:

> There never was a day that I ever gave any serious thought to going straight. . . . It looks so foolish to me to work for a living when I look at you. Take like any official, any policeman, anything else, that's doing everything in the book and getting by with it, and here's you that's working your heart and soul out, if you miss three days at work you're three months behind—it looks so foolish.[74]

The quotation suggests an image of himself held by the thief and of his relationship to the society. It represents the end-product of a system of learning, filtered to the individual and, in turn, utilized by him to evaluate both his own position and his immediate and future actions. Partly through experience and its interpretation, and

71 McKenzie, *Occupation: Thief,* p. 53.
72 Martin, *My Life in Crime,* p. 108.
73 Sutherland, *The Professional Thief,* p. 230.
74 Martin, *My Life in Crime,* p. 279.

partly through selective perception of reality, the professional criminal gradually becomes enmeshed and cemented into a way of life. Of all types of crimes, professional crime appears to be among the most "normal" forms of illegal action, in terms of the integration and adjustment to their behavior by the individuals who participate in the activity.[75] This attitude is clearly reflected by the pickpocket who, when queried by his probation officer, "If you had it to do over again, what would you be instead of a pickpocket?" responded immediately, "What's wrong with this racket?"[76]

For Further Reading

CAMERON, MARY OWEN. *The Booster and the Snitch: Department Store Shoplifting.* Glencoe, Ill.: The Free Press, 1964.

> The results of the study of shoplifters apprehended in a Chicago department store throw considerable empirical light on many issues of causation previously arrived at by intuition. Professor Cameron also provides support for the idea that reformulation of the self-image of early offenders may produce changes in their criminal behavior.

MARTIN, JOHN BARTLOW. *My Life in Crime: The Autobiography of a Professional Criminal.* New York: Harper, 1952.

> Martin reports, using many direct quotations, on the life story of a professional criminal, stressing his values and his attitude toward life. The author, who later served as American ambassador to the Dominican Republic, is particularly adept at pinpointing the way in which the offender views the world about him.

MAURER, DAVID W. *The Big Con: The Story of the Confidence Man and the Confidence Game.* Indianapolis: Bobbs-Merrill, 1940.

> This classic, first-hand study of confidence operations was written by a professor of linguistics at the University of Louisville, who started out to study the language patterns of the confidence man and ended by describing his behavior.

SUTHERLAND, EDWIN H. (ed.). *The Professional Thief.* Chicago: University of Chicago Press, 1937.

> A detailed description of the views and exploits of Chic Conwell, a professional thief, growing out of his autobiographical notes and his discussions with Professor Sutherland, who edited and annotated the material.

WILLIAMSON, HENRY. *Hustler!* Garden City, N.Y.: Doubleday, 1962.

> A lifelong career in diversified kinds of criminal activity is summarized by Williamson, a small-time professional criminal, in a series of talks with R. Lincoln Keiser, a social service caseworker in Chicago. A flat tone marks the book, which contains some vivid descriptions of hustling as a way of life. Williamson is presently back in prison on a narcotics charge.

75 Corsini, in Branham and Kutash, *Encyclopedia of Criminology,* p. 113.
76 Dressler, *Parole Chief,* p. 247.

8

Organized Crime

Organized crime extends through a range of activities that include illicit gambling, gangster-controlled prostitution, "shylocking" (the lending of money at exorbitant interest rates), the supply and subsequent sale of narcotics, and a number of extortion practices loosely grouped under the heading of "rackets." Today, it is becoming increasingly difficult to delineate clearly the realms of organized crime, since its practitioners, using the huge profits reaped from illicit activity, are moving into semilegitimate and legitimate enterprises.

Demarcation of the precise boundaries, however, is not essential to the study of organized crime as a behavior system. As Warren Olney points out:

> Organized crime in its modern form is not a special field of activity; rather it is a technique of violence, intimidation and corruption which in default of effective law enforcement can be applied by those sufficiently unscrupulous to any business or industry which produces large profits. The underlying motive, however, never varies. It is always to secure and hold a monopoly on some activity which will produce large profits.[1]

Cressey adds the further definitional note that "an 'organized criminal' is one who has committed a crime while occupying an organizational position for committing that crime,"[2] thus placing the stress on what has been called organized crime's "hierarchical structure involving a system of specifically defined relationships with mutual obligations and privileges."[3]

Criminologists have long been in default in regard to empirical and theoretical investigations into the workings of organized crime. The reasons for this failure shed light on the ramifications of organized

[1] Olney, in Plowscowe, *Organized Crime and Law Enforcement*, Vol. 1, p. 272.
[2] Cressey, in President's Commission, *Organized Crime*, p. 59.
[3] Clinard and Quinney, *Criminal Behavior Systems*, p. 383.

crime itself. Most important, the dearth of scientifically useful material on organized crime springs from the fact that organized criminals rarely come into official contact with law-enforcement and correctional agencies, where they may be studied more closely. In addition, while such criminals as pickpockets and burglars often talk at great length, sometimes almost compulsively, about themselves and their exploits, persons engaged in organized crime usually live by a code of silence.

Membership in this conspiracy of silence is, in fact, one of the more significant identifying characteristics of organized criminals; they depend on an understanding among all collaborators that no one will yield to pressure that will involve others in legal difficulties. "Gangs are organized on a feudal basis; organized upon loyalties, friendships, and dependability," Henry Chamberlin has commented; "Personal loyalty is above the law in these associations."[4] So thoroughgoing is this code of silence that it often overrides what might seem to be elementary doctrines of human behavior. Arnold Rothstein, for instance, who was deeply involved in organized crime in New York, steadfastly refused to name his killer although he lived for two days after being shot by an assailant he undoubtedly recognized.[5] Harry Gross, a bookmaker who pleaded guilty in 1952 to paying more than $1 million per year to members of the New York police force, refused to trade leniency from the district attorney for cooperation in convicting those involved with him. Gross, in fact, led the district attorney to believe that he would supply this information from the witness stand; then, after the trial of his alleged collaborators had begun, Gross refused to testify, thus immunizing all the accused because of the principle forbidding a person to be put in jeopardy twice for the same offense.[6]

Part of this conspiracy of silence, of course, springs from fear; organized criminals rarely hesitate, because it is so vital an aspect of their existence, to underline the need for silence by making object lessons of those who violate the code. The most notorious example undoubtedly is that of Abe Reles, an important cog in a New York syndicate, who decided to supply the police with incriminating details about a number of highly placed gangsters. Despite an around-the-clock guard of policemen, who were stationed on the floor of the hotel where Reles was kept incommunicado, he "fell" to his death from a window.[7] Recent disclosures indicate that by purchasing a funeral home and immuring their victims in the same casket as that of a legitimately deceased person, organized criminals have been able to dispose of numerous troublesome corpses with quiet efficiency.[8]

Another reason for the lack of theoretical material on organized

4 Chamberlin, "Some Observations Concerning Organized Crime," p. 660.
5 Katcher, *The Big Bankroll,* Chap. 1.
6 Arm, *Pay-off;* Reid, *Shame of New York.*
7 Turkus and Feder, *Murder, Inc.*
8 Smith, "The Crime Cartel," p. 18.

crime comes from a certain hesitancy among many academicians to plunge boldly into the vitals of our society. Schur has observed that "ascetic efforts at ethical neutrality" among criminologists "tend to support an approach stressing individual pathology rather than social pathology."[9] This stress on traits of individual deviance seems particularly useless in regard to organized criminals, because it appears likely that successful organized criminals cannot meaningfully be differentiated in terms of individual traits from other persons with similar socioeconomic backgrounds who "succeed" in more legitimate enterprises. Thus, for instance, Frederick Sondern, Jr., writing about Al Capone, notes that "the powerfully-built, enormously energetic little man had administrative capacities which might, if his path and instincts had been different, have made him the head of one of our biggest legitimate corporations."[10]

George Vold of the University of Minnesota has also stressed the dilemmas of personal, as opposed to social, pathology, as they relate to organized crime, by noting that "research of the future must face up to the problem of how to describe and how to interpret the facts of social and economic conflict that seem to be related to the widespread phenomenon of organized crime and corruption."[11] Vold notes that organized criminal groups do not differ radically in structure from small military units, and he further observes that:

> organized crime must be thought of as a . . . developmental adjunct to our general system of private profit economy. Business, industry, and finance are all competitive enterprises within the area of legal operations. But there is also an area of genuine economic demand for things and services not permitted under our legal and social codes. Organized crime is the system of business functioning in this area. It, too, is competitive, and hence must be organized for self-protection and for control of the market.[12]

Bloch has emphasized the same point, noting that cultures reveal themselves in the nature of the lawlessness and nonconforming behavior they condemn, and that civilized societies breed their own types of crime. "Thus, the racket is a peculiar American institution," he notes, "while the *apache* is as distinctive of Paris as is the *nervi* of the Marseilles dock area."[13]

An attempt to trace organized crime to its cultural roots, however, poses a number of analytical problems. There is, for instance, the difficulty of determining the level at which investigation shall be made and the particular angle of approach that shall be utilized. A study

9 Schur, "Theory, Planning and Pathology," p. 227.
10 Sondern, Jr., *Brotherhood of Evil*, p. 71.
11 Vold, *Theoretical Criminology*, p. 280. See also Vold, "Criminology at the Crossroads."
12 Vold, *Theoretical Criminology*, p. 240.
13 Bloch, *Disorganization*, pp. 261–262.

of the operations of a large corporation would produce similar difficulties. The corporation is obviously viewed quite differently by its
executives, its factory workers, its advertising branch, and its stenog-
raphers, as well as by its stockholders and those persons who do not
have a financial interest in the company's success. To each of these
groups the reality that is the corporation is mediated by the particular
segment of that reality which impinges upon and meshes with the
particular qualities of the person and his relationship to the corporation. Parallel considerations arise in connection with organized crime.
Its operation is seen differently when viewed from the top, where
the power is concentrated among a number of extraordinarily wealthy
and powerful individuals, than it is when viewed from the lower
rungs of collectors and runners, who are the small-fry of gambling
operations carried on by professional criminals. In addition, persons
who purchase narcotics, play numbers, or patronize "shylockers" view
organized crime with a different eye than do persons who regard such
activities with abhorrence.

It is important to be aware that organized crime differs from
what might be called "standard" crime in that many of its activities
are concentrated in areas in which the behavior is usually considered
"socially harmful" for other reasons than the coercion of an unwilling
participant, as in murder, rape, assault or property crimes, where a
person is injured or deprived of a possession without his consent. There
are almost always willing participants, rather than involuntary victims,
in activities such as gambling, narcotics, and prostitution. Homosexuality, statutory rape, and abortion are among the comparatively
small number of acts that are outlawed on the same general moral
grounds that lead to penalties against organized criminal activities.

Certain general institutional processes went into the development
of organized crime. Organized crime became a significant phenomenon
on the American scene in 1920, after the advent of Prohibition, an
experiment in appetite control that was supposed to herald an "Era
of Clean Living and Clear Thinking."[14] Prohibition had, at best,
half-hearted support of the society in general, many large segments of
which either approved of the drinking of alcoholic beverages or
regarded it with moral neutrality. "With the unpopular Volstead Act
in the days of Prohibition," Curtis Bok, a one-time Pennsylvania judge
has noted, "juries turned everyone loose, regardless of the evidence,
and went home to their illegal highballs before dinner."[15] It is
significant, in particular, that Prohibition created a crime in an area
of behavior that encompassed activities of persons of high social
status rather than persons who were relatively powerless.

In addition, the story of organized crime provides documentation

14 See Allsop, *The Bootleggers and Their Era;* Asbury, *The Great Illusion;* Lyle,
   The Dry and Lawless Years; Merz, *The Dry Decade.*
15 Bok, *Star Wormwood,* p. 147.

for sociological principles regarding the rise and growth of certain institutions. Churches, labor unions, industrial firms, and governmental agencies, for example, tend to manifest in their early periods an ideological verve coupled with elements of charismatic and often aggressive and individualistic leadership. This early pattern, however, tends to give way to more bureaucratized forms of organization, in which policies are toned down to provide greater amounts of security and certainty for both the leaders and the followers. Written constitutions and tables of organization appear. Fiery, sometimes erratic leaders are succeeded by "safe" bureaucratic administrators, innovators give way to organization men, and the cult of personality, with its elements of uncertainty and insecurity, passes over into planned, blueprinted programs that reduce risks to a calculated minimum.[16]

Early History of Organized Crime

The story of organized crime in Chicago provides a portrait in miniature of the emergence of organized crime throughout the nation.[17] Chicago has often been cited in the past as the most gangster-ridden metropolis in the United States. The Senate Committee to Investigate Organized Crime in Interstate Commerce (the Kefauver Committee), which conducted nationwide hearings from the spring of 1950 to September 1951, noted that "practically every form of rottenness which we found anywhere in the United States was duplicated, in some form or another, in Chicago."[18]

There exist a number of ecological items that help explain organized lawlessness in Chicago. The rapid growth of the city is particularly important. The immigration of people into Chicago within short spaces of time far outpaced concomitant efforts to provide agencies of formal control or to allow time for the growth of fabrics of informal social control. The rapid growth accentuated anonymity of residents in the city; anonymity, in turn, has been related to social disorganization and shown to provide a fertile background for organized criminal activities.[19]

Several statistics will illustrate the rapid growth of Chicago's population. The city was first settled in 1801; thirty years later it had a population of only 4,470 persons, standing fifty-fourth in the nation. Within twenty years, on the eve of the Civil War, Chicago had grown almost 2,000 percent to a population of 109,260 and stood eighth in the nation. Within another forty years, despite the catas-

16 Weber, *Theory of Social and Economic Organization*, pp. 363–373.
17 See Peterson, *Barbarians in Our Midst;* Wendt and Kogan, *Lords of the Levee;* Wendt and Kogan, *Big Bill of Chicago;* Smith, *Syndicate City;* Asbury, *Gem of the Prairie;* Lewis and Smith, *Chicago.*
18 Kefauver, *Crime in America*, Chap. 4.
19 See Thrasher, *The Gang;* Zorbaugh, *Gold Coast and Slum;* Wirth, *The Ghetto;* Cressey, *Taxi-Dance Hall.*

trophic fire of 1871, which virtually leveled the city, Chicago had grown from about 110,000 persons to a population of 1,698,575, and it took fewer than fifty years to double this figure to a total of more than 3½ million.

It is against this background of burgeoning growth that the story of organized crime in Chicago must be examined. Organized crime tends to put its roots into those interstices of society that contain the most hospitable soil, a trait that explains, in part, the contemporary movement of organized crime into semirural and suburban areas where law enforcement tends to be weakest.

Organized crime in Chicago illustrates many of the institutional processes mentioned previously. It began with the execution of Big Jim Colosimo in 1920. Colosimo had controlled prostitution and gambling in a large segment of Chicago, but apparently he was too hesitant about expanding into newly-opened channels for bootleg liquor. Colosimo was succeeded by his chief aide, Johnny Torrio. Torrio, according to underworld legend, did not smoke, drink, or swear, was well-read and an opera devotee. The funeral he arranged for Colosimo illustrates the close connection that existed and continues to exist between crime and politics in many American cities. Honorary pallbearers for Colosimo included three judges, the assistant state's attorney, a member of the United States Congress, several representatives in the Illinois state legislature, and nine city aldermen.

Torrio divided Chicago into a number of jurisdictional areas. Al Capone, an assistant Torrio imported from New York, was put in charge of Cicero, a city of 70,000 persons, completely run by gangsters who nominated and saw to the election of city officials and who appointed and dictated to the police force. The arrangement supervised by Torrio was impressively lucrative. The Bureau of Internal Revenue has estimated that Capone and Torrio together made not less than $100,000 a week during 1925.[20] The six Genna brothers, who were in charge of the west side of Chicago, had an estimated income of $15,000 a month, after deduction of overhead expenses, which included payments to more than 400 Chicago policemen.

With such financial stakes, huge investments to secure friendly political powers were sound business expenditures. Two basic items help to explain the role of organized crime in electoral affairs. First, running for political office is expensive, and a candidate must usually either have personal wealth or secure contributions for his campaign from groups or individuals who have such wealth. Second, groups or individuals who contribute money to political funds usually do so with the understanding, implicit or explicit, that they will later be granted certain benefits, such as being left alone. Money is rarely given for purely altruistic reasons, such as a desire for better government.

20 Sondern, Jr., *Brotherhood of Evil*, p. 69.

Many politicians regard such concessions, particularly if they are in areas that appear to be peripheral to the vital functioning of the body politic, as necessary evils. Others simply balance personal ambition, generalized precepts of morality, and reality, and out of this amalgam they determine what support they will accept and what concessions they will make. In this connection, the observation of the prosecutor of Murder, Inc., an organized crime syndicate, is pertinent: "If the betrothals of gangsters and politicians were broken," Burton Turkus wrote, "organized crime could not last 48 hours."[21] Alfred E. Lindesmith, professor of sociology at Indiana University, stresses the same point, saying that organized crime "requires the active and conscious cooperation of a number of elements of respectable society."[22]

In Chicago, organized crime flourished through campaign contributions to both parties and consequent control of the victorious group. The status quo was disturbed, however, as it often is during the earlier stages of uneasy monopolies, by jurisdictional disputes. One of the Genna brothers refused to pay off a gambling debt to another branch of the syndicate, which led to internecine warfare and the eventual extermination of many syndicate leaders. During the course of the killings, Torrio, the object of an assassination attempt, abdicated from his empire, turned over his interests to Capone, and left the United States for Italy. He returned later and died of a heart attack in relative obscurity in Brooklyn in 1957. The mutual assassinations, meanwhile, reached a peak on St. Valentine's Day in 1929, when five men, three of them wearing police uniforms, lined seven members of the Bugs Moran gang against a garage wall, presumably to search them, and then raked them with submachine guns.[23]

The St. Valentine's Day massacre was the climax of Chicago's criminal warfare. It was as if a gasoline price fight had reduced profits so drastically that all competitors were faced with elimination, or as if two competing labor unions had so decimated each other with recruiting raids that neither was likely to succeed. The only possible solution lay in a compromise, guaranteeing all sides limited but peaceful rights and circumscribed prosperity.

This development in organized crime also took place at Atlantic City, site of numerous conventions of more legitimate organizations. In May 1929, leaders of organized crime gathered on Capone's invitation and agreed to organize their operations so that their existence would be less precarious and more remunerative. It is generally believed that this meeting produced a form of organization that has not

21 Turkus and Feder, *Murder, Inc.*, p. xii.
22 Lindesmith, "Organized Crime," p. 119. For a particularly revealing account of contemporary organized criminal activity in an Eastern American city, see Gardiner, in President's Commission, *Organized Crime*, pp. 61–79.
23 Reeve, *The Golden Arm of Crime*, pp. 52–66.

been radically altered during the past four decades. The new look in organized crime was reflected, for instance, in the subsequent assassination of Dutch Schultz, a New York gangster, who, it is generally believed, intended to murder Thomas Dewey, the special prosecutor in New York. It was felt by the directors of the criminal syndicate that such an act would call too much attention to the machinations of organized crime, that it would, indeed, be poor institutional public relations, or, in modern terms, be bad for the corporate "image."

Culture Context of Organized Crime

It is important to realize how fully enmeshed members of organized criminal syndicates are in a value system that they share with the rest of the society. Their careers, aside from the element of illegality, correspond closely to the myth of Horatio Alger success.[24] "The racketeer is likely to come up from the slums, reaching for quick affluence by breaking the windows of the mansion of American success," Max Lerner writes, "rather than by entering at the door."[25] Organized criminals are among the most socially mobile persons in the United States, advancing with startling single-generation swiftness from the lower rungs of society into positions of power and wealth. Sometimes, in fact, the method of achievement—the criminality—becomes so blurred that it virtually disappears. Al Capone, for instance, received 1,000 fan letters per day, enough to put him in the same class as motion picture stars. Contemporary leaders of organized crime are even more impressive than Capone in demonstrating ability to blend into the upper reaches of the social stream, once they are able to shed the more déclassé traits of their occupation and background.

Particularly significant in this respect is the attempt on the part of many organized criminals to duplicate behavior that corresponds to that of more respected members of the society at equivalent levels of wealth. Such attempts provide supporting evidence concerning the drives that prompt an individual toward competitive success in organized crime. Once he reaches a point that permits a less intensive pursuit of his immediate goal, the organized criminal often cultivates the more esoteric arts, dresses with dignified and expensive taste, takes lessons in elocution, sends his children to select private schools and academies, and makes strenuous efforts to mingle in the more polite elements of society.

Recruitment patterns reflect the potentiality that a career in organized crime offers for movement out of slum ghettoes into gilt-edged elegance, with minimum interference from legal authorities. Coolness in the face of tribulations, reliability, and inventiveness are traits

24 Morris, *Postscript to Yesterday*, pp. 64–68.
25 Lerner, in Tyler, *Organized Crime*, p. 85.

sought among slum youngsters by organized criminals looking for new talent, just as corporate executives look for the same items while canvassing college campuses for management trainees.[26] Irving Spergel indicates that youngsters move into organized criminal careers from neighborhoods that show a tradition of gang rule; in other kinds of slums, they are more apt to become involved in gang-fighting or in thievery.[27] Organized crime, not surprisingly, also reflects the prejudices of the majority society so that, as one Negro put the matter, "a black man's got a better chance of being elected mayor of Selma, Alabama, than of making it into the big money with the syndicate."[28] As elsewhere, Negroes are exploited by organized crime as customers, but barriers are erected against their sharing in the spoils.

These and corollary strains run through the story of organized crime as a behavior system and help to place it into a proper social context. Lindesmith, exploring this context, notes that "organized crime is devoted almost exclusively to economic ends, to the acquisition of wealth" and that "the criminal is in this respect like most of the rest of us." He also points out that organized crime is essentially a big-city phenomenon and traces some of the characteristics of metropolitan life that make the city a hospitable ground for such activity:

> An individualistic predatory philosophy of success, indifference to public affairs, general disregard for law, the profit motive, decentralized government, laissez-faire economics, and political practice which is often as openly predatory as the rackets, have produced in our great cities a fertile breeding place for organized crime.[29]

GAMBLING

Gambling, the core activity of organized crime, represents an invocation of the ethos of luck that pervades our society and serves as an important ingredient in providing continuing motivation for the putative failure. Hard work, touched with vital portions of luck, is regarded as the key to success, and few persons of prominence fail to pay obeisance to luck when they recount the stories of their achievements. If luck plus work represent the mainspring of success, then luck alone represents the major shortcut to success. This is the promise offered by gambling, a promise that also introduces an element of anticipatory hope into what otherwise are often drab existences. As Irving K. Zola points out, in the lower classes, gambling serves as a vehicle by means of which a person is able to "achieve" recognition for his accomplishments by demonstrating ability in the selection of horses or winning numbers.[30]

26 Geis, "Violence and Organized Crime."
27 Spergel, *Racketville, Slumtown, Haulburg.*
28 *Wall Street Journal,* October 6, 1967.
29 Lindesmith, "Organized Crime," p. 120.
30 Zola, "Observations on Gambling in a Lower-Class Setting," p. 360.

It is claimed that psychologically gambling serves as a ritualistic flirtation with an unknown fate.[31] Gambling has been called "a kind of question addressed to destiny," and it has been maintained that the fascination of gambling is that it is "a simulation of life itself." "Speaking pessimistically," Clyde Brion Davis writes, "you might say that life itself is a one-armed bandit slot machine which, in the end, takes all your nickels"; in pointing to the many aspects of everyday living that constitute forms of gambling, he notes that the insurance company "bets you at what might be called pari-mutuel odds that your house will not burn down within the next three years."[32]

Success at gambling is supposed to be transposed by the gambler into a general sign of favor from otherwise inscrutable gods, somewhat in the manner of, for instance, the eminent prize fighter who traced his success to the fact that "Somebody Up There Likes Me," rather than to a fast right hand and an unusual ability to withstand punishment.[33] It was this mental transposition, as Max Weber has shown while tracing the purported origins of capitalism, that led financially successful persons in early Calvinistic societies to credit their wealth to divine approval of their total person and thus to regard it as an indication of a future place in heaven.[34]

Gambling shows an elaborate history through the annals of civilization.[35] Stone-Age people are known to have tossed painted pebbles and to have cast knucklebones, though it is not certain whether their attempt was to win somebody else's stone axe or to invoke magic and to facilitate prophecy.[36] We have records from India from as early as 321 B.C. showing the existence of a governmental department that supervised gambling, with a Superintendent of Public Games who supplied dice for a fee of 5 percent of the receipts.[37] Public lotteries were common in the United States from early colonial times until the 1830s. Many institutions of higher learning, including Columbia, Harvard, and Yale, were financed by public lotteries. Reactions against state-sponsored gambling were due to numerous scandals connected with its operation[38] as well as to a growing sense of moral outrage. This moral feeling, which is related to a person's position in the class structure,[39] is tied to an emphasis on gambling as a form of activity that provides reward without making what is defined as a "productive" contribution to society.

State-operated gambling, however, offers unusual opportunities to

31 See Bergler, *The Psychology of Gambling.*
32 Davis, *Something for Nothing,* p. 12.
33 Graziano, *Somebody Up There Likes Me.*
34 Weber, *The Protestant Ethic and the Spirit of Capitalism.*
35 See Ashton, *A History of Gambling in England;* Asbury, *Sucker's Progress;* Herman, *Gambling;* Allen, *The Nature of Gambling.*
36 Olmstead, *Heads I Win-Tails You Lose.*
37 Durant, *Story of Civilization,* Vol. 1, p. 444.
38 See Ezell, *Fortune's Merry Wheel.*
39 Bloch, "Sociology of Gambling"; Devereux, *Gambling and the Social Structure.*

secure funds through relatively painless methods, though it is often argued that such lotteries tend to be discriminatory, since their brunt is apt to fall most heavily upon lower-income groups. Nonetheless, in 1964, by a 4-1 margin, voters in New Hampshire supported the first legalized lottery in the United States since 1894, and three years later New York followed suit. First prize in the New Hampshire lottery is $100,000, and the proceeds are funneled primarily to school districts, which received $.28 million the first year of the lottery and $1.4 million during each of the following two years—about $50 for each pupil in the state. The nascent revival of state-run lotteries further accentuates philosophical questions regarding the fairness of legalized, state-supported gambling as contrasted to state-proscribed and prosecuted private gambling. As one housewife put the matter to a newspaper interviewer, "Who says it's all right to gamble on bingo at church but wrong to bet on a number at home?"[40]

NUMBERS

The most lucrative form of organized criminal activity is the operation of policy games, or numbers, sometimes called "bolita" or "the bug" in the South. H. L. Mencken, studying the etymology of the word "policy," thought that it might be derived from the Italian "polizza," which means a voucher or receipt. Mencken believes that the word was first applied in the United States to receipts given to players by collectors in the numbers game, which was imported into New York by Italian immigrants between 1885 and 1915.[41] Another writer believes that the term goes further back, at least to the Civil War period.[42]

In New York, officials believe that there are 500,000 daily policy players in the city, who wager about $200 million per year with the "policy banks." Policy banks often have as many as 200 to 300 full-time and part-time employees, in a strictly ordered hierarchy ranging from lay-off persons to pick-up men and finally down to runners, who take bets directly from customers. Odds normally are 600 to 1 against the person selecting the winning, three-digit number, though there are various "cut" numbers—digit combinations such as 111, 222, and 325—which, because of their popularity, are paid off at lower rates. Players may wager a "single action," selecting the first digit of the winning number and receiving 8 to 1 odds if they are successful. Winning numbers are derived from any of several sources. In Chicago, policy wheels, designated by different names or colors, are spun a number of times daily, and winning combinations are drawn from them.[43] Other cities use the last three digits of the total amount of

40 New York Times, June 26, 1964.
41 Mencken, The American Language, p. 222.
42 Matthews, Dictionary of Americanisms, Vol. II, p. 1227.
43 Egen, Plainclothesmen, Chap. 4.

money bet at a designated race track, the final numbers of the last dollar bill printed at the mint, the payoffs on specified horse races, or various other sources.

William F. Whyte, who went to live and conduct research in a semideteriorated Boston neighborhood while a graduate student at Harvard, provides testimony in his book *Street Corner Society* to the importance of numbers in this milieu. At one point, for instance, Whyte's major informant, Doc, tells him, "I'm batted out. I'm so batted out that I don't have a nickel to put on the numbers today. When a Cornerville fellow doesn't have the money to put on a number, then you know he's really batted out."[44]

The integral role of numbers in certain neighborhoods is also underlined in St. Clair Drake and Horace Cayton's study of the Black Belt of Chicago, where the authors found many residents defending the pervasive numbers game as crucial to the economic security of the community because of the jobs it provided.[45] In Cornerville, women would send their children to the grocery store for milk, giving them an extra nickel to put on a number. Publications, so-called "dream books," were sold openly, each one claiming to provide clues to winning numbers.[46] "Policy is not only a business—it's a cult," Drake and Cayton note.[47] But, "It's run like a business," one of Whyte's informants pointed out, "smooth." Competition was eliminated either by mergers or by police action against newcomers, instigated by the organization that controlled the area. The police were paid off regularly, at a "union wage," with a sliding scale for patrolmen, plainclothesmen, and headquarters' officers. Honest law-enforcement officers often found themselves transferred to the cemetery beat. "It's lonely out there in the cemetery," one resident noted wryly; "Nothing ever happens out there." Police duty in Cornerville was particularly desirable because the people "don't complain." "The people that have made good," a resident noted, "most of them have moved out. The people that are left, they just don't care. They let it ride."[48] How "it" rides, that is, how numbers are written in a city such as New York, is indicated in the following vignettes:

Joe stands six mornings a week outside a storefront social club in the "Little Italy" area behind Police Headquarters. He is squat. His long gray sweater blends in color with his thinning hair. Housewives on their way to and from the market, men in work clothes, the unemployed and relief clients stop to exchange greetings with a handshake.

A quarter passes hands, or a half dollar, sometimes a dollar bill—but never a slip with a penciled number. If the police were to frisk Joe they'd find no evidence. He carries the number, given orally, into the

44 Whyte, *Street Corner Society*, p. 115.
45 Drake and Cayton, *Black Metropolis*, Chap. 17; Frazier, *Black Bourgeoisie*, p. 128.
46 McCall, "Symbiosis: The Case of Hoodoo and the Numbers Racket."
47 Drake and Cayton, *Black Metropolis*, p. 474.
48 Whyte, *Street Corner Society*, p. 126.

club inside his head after each encounter. The club interior, where the numbers and amount of play are listed, is forbidden territory to the police without a court-issued search warrant.

A meat market in Harlem gets extremely busy about 2 o'clock. Men and women come and go. They transact business with four countermen, but no meat is wrapped or carried out.

"If you ask for meat around 2 o'clock they'll practically blow your head off," said a neighbor. "But come back around five and they'll sell you meat, and it's good meat, too."

The butcher shop is a "drop," a place where runners bring the numbers and money they have collected for tabulation and transmission to a control office or to the policy bank. The time is important because the third race at Aqueduct goes off at 2:30 P.M. The first digit of the winning number for the day is determined after the prices on that race have been posted.[49]

The relationship between persons controlling gambling and the residents of a socially and economically depressed area provides clues to the stability of the system in the face of periodic crusades to "clean it up." Particularly important is the rapport that exists between the gangster and the slum dweller; the gangster serves as a breakwater between the neighborhood and what often seem to be menacing, anonymous, and immutable outside forces.

The slum dweller often feels a need for some person or organization to transmit and to interpret his needs to the external forces that impinge upon him. Often he finds that he cannot communicate comfortably with the agents of the society, such as the social workers, who may be defined as both condescending and prim. Leaders of the organized crime group, on the other hand, pass no moral judgments and deliver meaningful services. When a slum child gets into trouble with the police, the social worker may map out a long-range plan involving the community center, deliver a lecture on the responsibilities of parenthood, or review the financial position of the family to derive a "more meaningful" plan of living. But often the organized crime boss sees to it that the child receives adequate (i.e., shrewd and somewhat unprincipled) legal defense, so that he perhaps is soon returned home. When a father loses his job, the family is likely to turn to the criminal leader, with his financial resources and connections. From these dealings, a feeling of admiration and respect comes to be attached to the person capable of delivering benevolences.[50] It becomes singularly irrelevant that, by other standards, the society regards these persons as undesirable citizens. Such a judgment carries little weight when it conflicts with the more immediate and real experience of power, opulence, and good will that the criminal can demonstrate.[51]

49 *New York Times,* June 26, 1964.
50 McKay, "The Neighborhood and Child Conduct."
51 See Heard, *The Costs of Democracy.*

BOOKMAKING

Faced with such deep-lying neighborhood roots, where organized crime is highly functional, it is not surprising that the society has had little success in eliminating the numbers game. The same may be said of bookmaking, the taking of bets on horse or dog races, where such activity is statutorily outlawed. Some persons question the democratic propriety of banning off-track betting, while allowing wagers on races, as 25 states do, for those who can afford the time and the money to travel to a race track and deal with the legal pari-mutuel machines.[52] They point to the situation in Britain where bookmaking, or "turf accounting", by telephone has long been legal, and where the state operates a pool on soccer games, which is so popular that an estimated 70 percent of the population participates, and which accounts for 10 percent of the domestic mail during the nine months that it operates.

Proponents of legalized gambling note that British investigatory commissions have consistently supported it. The 1951 Royal Commission, after a two-year study, concluded that, although gambling "may and does cause poverty," it does so no more than smoking, drinking, and other known human "weaknesses," it does not "seriously" interfere with production, it "cannot be regarded as imposing a serious strain on national resources or manpower," and it has not been a significant factor as a cause of crime; the Commission also claimed of gambling that "many of its forms involve some mental activity, and it has a social value as a general topic of conversation."[53]

All legal British gambling was done by telephone, on a credit system, or at the track, until passage of the Betting and Gaming Act in 1960, which permitted bets to be placed in person at neighborhood shops. Major opposition to the Act came from persons who believed that the Act would undermine traditional British concern with good horses and "pure" sportsmanship, or, as one Member of Parliament put the matter, "Racing should not become the appendage of gambling. The tail must not be allowed to wag the horse."[54] But the Act was passed, and now some 15,000 betting shops operate in Britain, and it has been estimated that 2 percent of the national income is wagered on racing alone, although much of the money recirculates among successful bettors. According to Geoffrey Gorer, the new law resulted primarily because of Britain's commitment to welfare state principles, which insisted that gambling rights be extended to the working class and not confined exclusively to credit-worthy individuals who were previously able to make their bets by telephone. Gorer, a well-known anthropologist, believes that part of the abiding British interest in gambling is related to the equation of money with love. British chil-

52 Lawrence, "Bookmaking".
53 Great Britain, *Royal Commission on Betting, Lotteries, and Gaming*, p. 145.
54 Quoted in Kenison, "Off-Track Betting," p. 37.

dren, Gorer points out, rarely receive regular allowances from their parents, but rather are indulged with money erratically, usually on those occasions when they have won their parents' favor.[55]

Many persons insist, however, that conditions in Britain are too different from those in the United States for Britain's experience to be applicable here.[56] The history of sanctioned gambling in Nevada is most often cited to indicate the inability of authorities to keep organized criminals from manipulating gambling enterprises once they are legalized.[57] Nevada first permitted gambling in 1931, in large measure to create revenue for a jurisidiction faced with little prospect of otherwise supporting itself. Today, reported gross earnings of gambling enterprises in Nevada are $240 million yearly, which provide the state with 20 percent of its income. This is well below original expectations, and six states, in fact, realize more money from parimutuel betting. More important, however, are widespread allegations that huge sums of money are regularly drained from patrons of Las Vegas and Reno gambling establishments, hidden from tax investigators (a process known as "skimming"), and funneled into the pockets of organized criminals, who employ the money to invade legitimate businesses. When Las Vegas needed gamblers who knew how to run big casinos, it is alleged that promoters "went to the training halls of Cicero and other underworld fiefs."[58] Another writer notes that "it is common in Las Vegas Strip casinos that among the shareholders will be some with a background in illegal gambling, bootlegging and horsebooks. That is where they sharpened the skills and gathered the capital that permitted them to be successful in the competitive atmosphere of the Strip." When such persons enter into traditional fields of business, they are said "to tend to take with them the same business practices they learned in the backrooms in New York, Chicago, Miami, and Los Angeles—the "fix", the hard shove, the fast fleecing of the unwary." In summary, it is argued that "Las Vegas is the strangest city in America. It is the source of an infectious immorality that rides out of the desert on a golden flood of gambling wealth to spread across the nation."[59]

Further arguments against legalized gambling spring from a belief that the legal legitimization of betting creates an atmosphere conducive to growth of organized crime both in the legal arena and in peripheral areas that remain illegal. In addition, numerous arguments against legalized gambling arise from convictions that it is inherently immoral for the state to support what is viewed as a parasitic method for acquiring wealth. William Parker, former police chief of Los Angeles,

55 Gorer, "British Life—It's a Gamble," pp. 10, 45.
56 Peterson, Gambling—Should It Be Legalized?
57 Reid, Green Felt Jungle.
58 Wessel, "Legalized Gambling," p. 47.
59 Turner, Gambler's Money, Chap. 11.

said, for instance, "Any society that bases its financial structure on the weaknesses of people doesn't deserve to survive,"[60] while Thomas E. Dewey, twice a candidate for the United States Presidency, put his objections to legalized gambling in the following terms:

> It is fundamentally immoral to encourage the belief by the people as a whole in gambling as a source of family income. It would be immoral for government to make available to all of its people a state-wide gambling apparatus with the implied assumption that the gains of chance were a fair substitute for or supplement to the honorable business of producing the goods and services by which the people of the nation live.[61]

Certainly the most ingenious suggestion for ending organized crime's stranglehold on gambling is that of Thomas C. Schelling, professor of economics at Harvard University. Employing standard methods of economic analysis to organized crime as a business enterprise—a task that Schelling chides his colleagues for neglecting in this as well as other areas of illegality—he concludes that the most effective method for dealing with gambling is to place it within organizations that already possess the resources and the tradition to conduct it honestly. He says:

> The greatest gambling enterprise in the U.S. has not been significantly touched by organized crime. That is the stock market. . . . Ordinary gambling ought to be one of the hardest industries to monopolize because almost anybody can compete. . . . If ordinary brokerage firms were encouraged to take horse-racing accounts, and buy and sell bets by telephone for their customers, it is hard to see how racketeers could get any kind of a grip on it. We can still think gambling is a sin, and try to eliminate it; but we should probably not try to use the argument that it would remain in the hands of criminals if we legalized it. Both reason and evidence seem to indicate the contrary.[62]

Infiltration of Legitimate Business

The movement into legitimate and semilegitimate activities represents the denouement of organized criminal careers. "There was a time when you could spot a leading gangster by the hard-eyed bodyguards on either side of him. Not today. Instead the men on either side are apt to be an accountant and a lawyer," one writer notes; "The Mob has shined its boots and placed them in the marketplace."[63] Such a consummation provides greater invulnerability to prosecution and, importantly, surrounds the organized criminal with an aura of respect-

---

60 Quoted in Cook, *A Two-Dollar Bet Means Murder*, p. 203.
61 *Ibid.*, p. 223.
62 Schelling, "Economics and the Public Enterprise," p. 77. See also Schelling, President's Commission, *Organized Crime*, pp. 114–126; Packer, "The Crime Tariff."
63 Smith, "The Mob," p. 91.

ability. This development dovetails with the theoretical explanation that describes a large share of criminality as behavior engaged in by individuals driving toward legitimized social goals by illegal pathways. As was previously mentioned, once the necessity for deviance is no longer present, when enough wealth has been accumulated, the organized criminal often attempts to merge with the mainstream of society, although he may bring attitudes and policies carried over from former operations to his new enterprises. The Research Institute of America, an organization that advises some 75,000 clients on business trends, has indicated the following activities as particularly likely to be carried on by organized criminals in the business world: (1) Gaining control of labor unions to force companies to pay for labor peace, (2) Using loan sharking to force debtors to surrender control of their businesses or to sell stolen goods, (3) Setting up bogus companies that buy heavily on credit and then disappearing with the goods, and (4) Using bribery or threats of violence to secure control or to carve out a monopoly or to win other advantages.

LABOR AND MANAGEMENT RACKETEERING

Organized criminals have notably been without class consciousness in their activities in the labor union movement, selling their skills to whichever side, labor or management, offers the most. The deepest penetration into these activities was achieved by the Senate Select Committee on Improper Activities in the Labor or Management Field under the chairmanship of Senator John L. McClellan of Arkansas.[64] The Committee stressed that it had found undesirable practices in only a small segment of the labor unions, having investigated groups embracing but 2 million of a total of 17 million union members, although its findings were taken as a broader indictment. Many of the unions investigated were called "oligarchies," and were thought to require regulation, and the labor movement was said to be "plagued with a deadly disease beyond its own curative powers" for which "government action was necessary."[65]

The charge of tie-ins between organized crime and unions was documented in particular by the record of a local of the United Auto Workers of America, a one-time American Federation of Labor branch, which was operating as the Allied Industrial Workers of America. Established in 1950, the group soon came under the domination of Johnny Dioguardi, a three-time convicted labor racketeer. The forty men whom Dioguardi brought into the union in positions of responsibility were found to have been arrested some 178 times and convicted 77 times. Their criminal records showed convictions for theft, Harrison Act violations, extortion, conspiracy, bookmaking,

64 See McClellan, *Crime Without Punishment;* Kennedy, *The Enemy Within;* Petro, *Power Unlimited.*
65 Bill, "Corruption and Union Racketeering," p. 345.

felonious assault, possession of an unregistered still, burglary, violation of gun laws, accessory to murder, forgery, possession of stolen
mail, and disorderly conduct. The union exploited its members in
various ways, negotiating contracts for them at about $1 per hour,
which was then the bare national minimum wage, and yet charging
them a $25 initiation fee and $3.50 per month union dues. The union
provided no welfare benefits, no job security assistance, and enforced
its will with ruthless determination.[66]

The activities of James R. Hoffa, then chairman of the International Brotherhood of Teamsters, Chauffeurs, Warehousemen, and
Helpers of America, were said to illustrate further the close connection between organized crime and some union activities. "From
his early years in the labor movement, he formed an alliance with the
kingpins of the Nation's underworld," the committee noted of Hoffa.[67]
Hoffa told the Senators that his friendships with criminals were begun
in order to rehabilitate those individuals, an explanation that the
committee found singularly unconvincing. It would be reasonable,
McClellan and his associates noted, if it were an occasional phenomenon, but "it appears to the committee that a criminal background
was a prerequisite for job placement and advancement within the
teamster firmament."[68]

Finally, the committee documented the thin line existing between the activities of organized criminals and those of presumably
respectable businessmen. It found, for instance, that a large brewery
company had "acted improperly" in granting special favors to a labor
leader because it was "afraid" of him and because it hoped "that it
could secure special favors," which, on occasion, "it sought and secured."[69] A California life insurance company was found to have
advanced a $300,000 loan to Dave Beck, a labor leader, at a lower
than usual interest rate, while at the same time Beck's union was
pouring millions of dollars into the insurance company for policies
for union members.

The McClellan committee's reports furnish contemporary documentation of a condition that has been found to run through the
history of organized crime—that its activities intertwine with allegedly respectable community members, many of whom readily acquiesce
in illegal dealings in order to maximize profits. Al Capone noted with
plaintive logic, in fact, that his activities were no different from those
of persons of presumed merit in the community. He said, "I call myself
a businessman. I make my money by supplying popular demand. If I
break the law, my customers are as guilty as I am. When I sell liquor,

66 U.S. Senate, *Select Committee on Improper Activities in the Labor or Management Field,* First Interim Report, pp. 217–221.
67 *Ibid.,* p. 448.
68 *Ibid.*
69 *Ibid.,* p. 86.

it's bootlegging. When my patrons serve it on a silver tray on Lake Shore Drive, it's hospitality."

THE LOAN SHARK "SHYLOCK"

Shylocking, or "money-moving," has been called the principle vehicle by which the underworld infiltrates otherwise legitimate areas. It is estimated that organized crime's income from moneylending is exceeded only by its income from gambling. Earlier loan-shark activity, with six for five loans (in which when $5 is borrowed, $6 is due the following week) to poor persons, appear to be anachronistic, as does the pattern of vicious beatings to collect unpaid balances.[70] The modern pattern is indicated in the following story constructed from the details of actual cases:

> Businessman Jones was at a difficult point in the history of his company. He had had a bad year because the product he was promoting failed. His whole enterprise was in jeopardy. For these very reasons, credit was hard to come by.

> He needed a small loan to tide him over and had heard about a man who made loans to people on a private basis. . . . The non-secured loan was arranged—and the trap was set. Soon the interest payments—they can run as high as 150 per cent per week—far exceeded the principal he originally borrowed.

> Mr. Jones quickly found that he couldn't meet the payments and, under threat from the loan shark's collectors, he took in a syndicate partner. From this point on, he was on his way out and the syndicate was in.[71]

In shylocking, the prime lender will usually distribute a large sum, perhaps $1 million, among a number of lieutenants, charging them 1 percent per week. These men in turn lend the money to their subordinates at perhaps 1½ to 2 percent weekly, while the third level of shylockers will distribute the money at interest rates not less than 5 percent per week.[72] Loan sharking has been viewed as a "virtually hopeless" problem for law enforcement, despite usury laws that forbid its exorbitant interest rates, because of the surreptitious nature of transactions and the fact that the parties involved are voluntary participants.[73]

PLANNED BANKRUPTCY: THE "SCAM"

Planned bankruptcies, or "scam" operations, represent a rapidly growing organized crime enterprise. The schemes are based on an abuse of credit that is established either legitimately or fraudulently. Planned bankruptcy frauds, as Nathaniel Kossack, an attorney with the U.S.

70 Cook, "Just Call 'The Doctor' for a Loan," p. 55.
71 Will Your Business Be Next?, p. 6.
72 New York Temporary Commission of Investigation, An Investigation of the Loan-Shark Racket, p. 11.
73 New York Times, January 29, 1968.

Department of Justice, indicates, usually consist of five steps: (1) over-purchasing of inventory on credit; (2) sale or other disposition of the merchandise thus obtained; (3) concealment of the proceeds; (4) non-payment of creditors, and (5) the filing of an involuntary bankruptcy petition by creditors.[74]

It is estimated that there are about 200 planned bankruptcies each year, the majority of which are the work of organized criminals. Gains are believed to average about a quarter of a million dollars in each instance. Prime targets are general merchandise fields in which the goods are easily transportable and difficult to trace.

The first step involves the formation of a new corporation, often run by organized criminals or "fronts." A large sum of money is deposited in a bank to establish credit. A warehouse is leased and small initial orders are placed for goods, using the bank account as a credit reference. Early bills are paid promptly. Then the merchants from whom stock has been purchased are used as references so that a later, high credit rating is established. In the concluding step, numerous large orders are placed. Merchandise pours into the warehouse, is removed just as rapidly, and is sold for half or one-quarter its value, which represents pure profit since there is no intention to pay forthcoming bills.

Sometimes the long-term scam operation is shortened considerably by use of an already operative business that has been taken over by organized criminals. Organized criminals who are intent on working a "scam" fraud have also on occasion established firms with names deceptively similar to those of existing businesses, and before the duplication and duplicity was discovered have disappeared from sight.

INTIMIDATION OF COMPETITION

Organized criminals in the business world have concentrated particularly in enterprises where the turnover is rapid and where tax controls tend to be difficult, such as in the restaurant and night club field. An illustration of the tactics of organized criminals is provided by Lawrence Walsh, a former United States deputy attorney general, who tells of a manufacturer who needed an additional sugar quota during the war and, as a consequence, added as a partner a person who he thought had influential government contacts and who had a sugar quota in excess of what he was legitimately entitled to. The new partner soon pushed aside the original man, but then was overshadowed by a third person, who possessed an elaborate criminal record. This third individual did not work, but he drew out of the company a considerable sum of money, and he kept adding persons to the firm's payroll as they left prison. They, too, performed no work. When the original proprietor attempted to protest, his life

74 Kossack, " 'Scam': The Planned Bankruptcy Racket."

was threatened. He could not complain to the authorities because of his own participation in the black-market conspiracy. The new manager, however, felt that the half-million dollar annual company profit was inadequate, and he entered into a tax evasion scheme, which eventually led to his apprehension.[75]

The Kefauver committee pointed out the infiltration of known criminals into the liquor and automobile fields, where they can secure valuable franchises, and into a number of other businesses. Typical was its conclusion concerning organized crime in the laundry and dry cleaning industry:

> The phenomenon of Willie Moretti, one of Costello's associates, in making a success of a large linen-supply company because "he knew a lot of people" and "got plenty of business in a polite way" (which his competitors found not so polite) is one of the darker chapters of American business. In Detroit, Louis Ricardi, an associate of Detroit hoodlums, who was arrested five times for murder, operates a very profitable laundry—the Clean Linen Service Co. Ricardi made $56,000 out of this business in 1949. It is alleged that customers who drop his service may find no other laundry will dare to accept their business.[76]

Mafia and/or La Cosa Nostra?

A majority of writers appear to favor the view that there exists a home-grown, tightly-knit, hierarchically organized society of organized criminals in the United States today. Sometimes the group is labelled the Mafia, indicating historical and current connections between it and a Sicilian criminal organization of much earlier origin; at other times, the name La Cosa Nostra ("Our Thing") is applied to the empire of organized crime, a designation that makes use of the term employed by Joseph Valachi, an underworld hireling who turned informer, who used it in 1963 before a Senate committee. Other writers are apt to describe organized crime merely in terms of local groupings or confederations, without esoteric names, rituals, or similar paraphernalia from the traditional realm of secret societies.

MAFIA

The history of the Mafia in Sicily is a well-documented story.[77] The society was based primarily on a "profound contempt for law"[78] and was one of a number of similar gangs found in Italy, such as the *camorra* of Naples, the *squadracce* in Ravenna and Bologna, the *cocca* in Turino, and the *sicari* in Rome, all of which flourished on the

75 Walsh, "Organized Crime," pp. 3–5.
76 U.S. Senate, *Committee to Investigate Crime in Interstate Commerce,* Third Interim Report, p. 180.
77 Hobsbawm, *Social Bandits and Primitive Rebels,* Chap. 3; Lewis, *The Honored Society;* Alongi, *La Maffia;* Anderson. "From Mafia to Cosa Nostra;" Barzini, *The Italians,* Chap. 14.
78 Crawford, *The Rulers of the South,* Vol. II, p. 366.

foundation of "universal mistrust and uncooperativeness of people of every class toward the government."[79]

In Sicily, the Mafia is considered an immemorial feature of life, though in recent years it is said to be declining in power in rural areas, largely because of the emigration of young men from the countryside. According to Norman Lewis, the Mafia was given a stranglehold on Sicily, an island with a population of some 5 million persons, when its leaders were placed in positions of power by American military and civil authorities in the absence of constituted government following World War II.[80] Intense efforts by the Italian government, using Draconian measures, have, however, decimated the ranks of the Sicilian Mafia leadership in recent years by sending more than 375 Mafiosi into prison or exile. This move is presumably reflected in the homicide rate in Palermo, Sicily's capitol, which dropped from sixty-four in 1960, to forty-six in 1962, to twenty in 1964, and to eleven in 1966.[81]

There is no doubt that many Mafia members migrated to the United States during the 1880s and thereafter, but it seems unlikely that they maintained the organization in its original form. Italian law enforcement officials are said to regard with "incredulity" the American view that the Mafia in Sicily has any relationship with criminal organizations in the United States. It is believed that any links are of a personal rather than an organizational nature, based on "sentimental visits by American racketeers" and on "underworld 'technical assistance' programs for American criminals who have been deported to Sicily."[82]

The Appalachin Meeting

Undoubtedly the most dramatic support for the thesis that organized crime in the United States operates along corporate lines appeared in 1957 when police discovered some fifty-eight persons, all of Italian extraction and many with elaborate police records, gathered at a meeting in the $150,000 home of Joseph Barbara in the village of Appalachin in south-central New York. The "delegates" were all fastidiously dressed, all drove high-priced automobiles, and amongst them were carrying more than $350,000 in cash. Nineteen were from upstate New York, twenty-three from New York City and the adjacent New Jersey area, eight from the Midwest, three from beyond the Rocky Mountains, two from the South, two from Cuba, and one from Italy. A check on their business activities indicated that "ten were primarily interested in the gambling business, nine in narcotics, fifteen in the production of illicit alcohol, and five in union racketeering."[83]

79 Smith, *Italy*, p. 163.
80 Lewis, *The Honored Society*.
81 *New York Times*, April 20, 1967.
82 *New York Times*, March 3, 1965.
83 Sondern, Jr., *Brotherhood of Evil*, pp. 3–17.

As in any highly involved business, the operations were interlocked in a complicated fashion.

In order to acquire information on the meeting, officials offered witnesses immunity from prosecution, hoping to overcome attempts to maintain that their answers might incriminate them. Rather than testify, they all preferred to receive indeterminate jail sentences for contempt and for obstructing justice. Finally, in 1959, twenty of the Appalachin defendants were convicted of conspiring to obstruct justice by lying about the purpose of the meeting. The government hailed the verdict as a new and effective weapon against organized criminals, but, a year later, a unanimous appellate court decision reversed the convictions on the ground that the government's evidence had been insufficient to prove that the alleged conspirators had entered into an agreement to lie to investigative bodies. The major flaw in the government's case against the Appalachin defendants was that, despite the passage of three years, it was still not known what had taken place at the meeting. "In America, we still respect the dignity of the individual, and even an unsavory character is not to be imprisoned except on definite proof of a specific crime," one justice wrote. The government did not, the court said, "have a shred of legal evidence that the Appalachin gathering was illegal or even improper in either purpose or fact."[84]

LA COSA NOSTRA

The testimony in 1963 by Joseph Valachi, before the Senate Permanent Subcommittee on Investigations shed the most penetrating light to date on the structure and activities of organized crime in the United States. Valachi, sixty-years-old at the time, had been sentenced to the federal prison at Atlanta for fifteen years on a narcotics charge. His cellmate was Vito Genovese, reputedly the top leader of the confederation of organized criminals in the United States. According to Valachi, Genovese suspected him of having informed on his fellows and marked him for extermination by kissing him on both cheeks and saying, "One apple gets touched and gets bad, it's got to be taken out." Fearful, Valachi mistakenly thought he noticed a syndicate killer in the prison yard and crushed the man's head in with a lead pipe. His sentence was extended to life imprisonment. Subsequently, saying that he desired revenge on the syndicate, Valachi became a government informer.[85]

The accuracy of Valachi's story is difficult to evaluate. A careful reading of the record indicates particular knowledge of assassinations and internal machinations in organized crime during the 1930s and

84 *U.S. v. Bufalino*, pp. 419–420. See also Dembitz, "The Appalachin 'Conspiracy' "; Fraenkel, "The Appalachin Case."
85 U.S. Senate, Committee on Governmental Operations, *Organized Crime and Narcotics*, Parts 1 and 3.

1940s. At the same time, by his own admission Valachi stood very low in the organized crime hierarchy, despite a thirty-year membership in the syndicate. In addition, as in the case of most informers, Valachi was undoubtedly prompted by hopes of leniency, and he was aware that the better his story, the better his chances for reward. Some experts indicate that Valachi provided confirmation of much of what they already knew; others note that his statements served to overcome widespread public belief that government claims about organized crime were fanciful and self-serving. Nonetheless, some authorities, including law enforcement officers, continued to be skeptical, indicating a belief that much of what Valachi disclosed consisted of "stale rumors and underworld gossip" and that Valachi himself was primarily a "publicity-seeking bum."[86] It was maintained, for instance, that he used the term "La Cosa Nostra" in passing and that his interrogators seized upon it as a grandiose designation of the totality of organized crime in the United States.

Valachi's revelations plus the contents of bulky government dossiers form the background of the report on organized crime by the President's Commission on Law Enforcement and Administration of Justice. Donald Cressey, who prepared part of the Commission's statement on organized crime, insists that he began his work with no preconceptions on the subject, but rather with a lingering doubt regarding the accuracy of government claims about organized crime. "But I am certain," Cressey wrote afterwards, "that no rational man could read 'the evidence' that I read and still come to the conclusion that an organization variously called 'Mafia,' 'La Cosa Nostra,' or 'the syndicate' does not exist."[87]

The Crime Commission indicated that the core of organized crime consists of some 5,000 persons, organized into 24 "families," or *burgatas*. Families may have as few as twenty members or as many as 500, and each is headed by a boss, or *capo*. Most cities with organized crime have only one family; New York City has five, however, while Miami and Las Vegas are regarded as "open cities," without families. Beneath each boss is an underboss, and on the same level as the underboss but operating in a staff capacity is a counselor, or *consigliere*. Often an older member of the family who has retired from an active career in crime, the counselor provides advice and arbitration. Below this level are the lieutenants, or *caporegime*, who maintain communication with persons at the lowest level, the *soldati* or "button men" (Valachi's status), insulating the leaders from direct contact and thereby minimizing their chances of arrest.

The families are confined to persons of Italian descent and are in frequent contact with each other. Their smooth functioning, the

86 *New York Times*, October 3, 1963. See also Hawkins, "God and the Mafia."
87 Cressey, "Methodological Problems in the Study of Organized Crime as a Social Problem," p. 103.

Commission believed, is insured by a national body of overseers, which serves as a combination legislature, supreme court, board of directors, and arbitration board, with its principal activities being judicial.[88]

From a sociological viewpoint, the monopoly on organized crime by Italians, and particularly Sicilians, poses interesting questions regarding cultural diffusion and the transfer of indigenous behavior into new environments. Variations in criminal activity among ethnic groups appear related to a number of phenomena, including the age structure of the group, the amount of similarity and difference between the immigrant culture and that of the receiving country, the urbanness and ruralness of the group, its nationality patterns and heritage, and its wealth and poverty. Such phenomena, among others, help to explain sharp differences between the law-abiding behavior, for instance, of Japanese-Americans, who are members of the Mongoloid race,[89] and American Indians, also Mongoloids, who constitute a severe crime problem in regard to alcoholic offenses.[90] Factors such as these also account for the disproportionate representation of any racial, nationality, religious, or ethnic group in any particular form of criminal behavior.

Control of Organized Crime

It is simplistic to note that organized crime in the United States could be eliminated virtually overnight if society chose to legalize activities that now form the core of gangster control. The same observation is equally true of murder. Were murder to be made legal, we could consider ourselves rid of the troublesome problem of murderers, as indeed we might be rid of the population explosion. It may be true that there exist adequate grounds to legalize acts that are generally labelled human vices, including the fact that doing so might wipe out organized crime syndicates, but this approach does not add measurably to a basic understanding of the etiology of the problem.

Among the more searching programs for dealing with organized crime was that drawn by the American Bar Association's Committee on Organized Crime, a group that came into being as an adjunct to the Kefauver investigations. Its proposals throw a spotlight on the reparable spots in law enforcement as it bears on organized crime.[91]

The Commission recommended that state gambling laws be tightened and modernized. Only five states, it found, had adequate laws dealing specifically with the numbers game. It felt that laws requiring life sentences for habitual criminals should be applied more systematically to organized criminals, who were generally escaping the

---

88 President's Commission, *Organized Crime,* pp. 7–10.
89 Kitano, *Japanese Americans,* pp. 117–122.
90 See Farber, *et al., Indians, Law Enforcement and Local Government.*
91 Ploscowe, *Organized Crime and Law Enforcement.*

full consequence of their behavior through the common practice of "bargaining," a process under which the prosecutor promises a more lenient sentence in return for a guilty plea. The Commission was particularly concerned with the atomization of law enforcement in the United States, which is the result of allowing each police department virtually unchecked local autonomy. It believed that state governments should take a larger part in providing police services. The Commission also recommended that prosecuting attorneys should no longer be elected officials, but rather should be appointed by the Governor and should be responsible to a state department of justice.

The major prong in the federal attack against organized crime took the form of legislation, enacted in 1951, which required a gambler to purchase for $50 yearly an occupation tax stamp, which had to be displayed in a prominent place, and to pay a ten percent excise tax on his profits. Despite the apparent charm of such a program, which would allow the gambler to be prosecuted if he did not secure a stamp, or to be identified and subsequently arrested if he did, it did not prove to be particularly successful.[92] In 1952, when the law first went into effect, 19,855 stamps were sold. The total declined steadily, and in 1967 only 5,917 persons bought stamps. Congress had been told that the bill would provide about $400 million per year in revenue, but the measure brought in only $115 million in its first fifteen years of operation. Finally, in 1968, the law was declared unconstitutional on the ground that it violated the fifth amendment's privilege against self-incrimination by requiring persons to file information that amounted to confessions of guilt.[93]

Besides the tax law, the major attempt to vitiate activities of organized crime has concentrated on controlling betting that makes use of interstate communications facilities.[94] It is through such facilities that syndicates obtain crucial information on horse-race scratches (withdrawals from the race), starting times, changes in pari-mutuel odds, jockeys, track conditions, and final results. These facilities are also vital in the operation of the lay-off system, a program under which gamblers insure against losses by betting against themselves. The lay-off works in the following manner: If a bookmaker has accepted five units of bets on each of A, B, and C, and 20 units of bets on D, the odds presumably being equal on all four, he stands to lose money if D wins. If he himself, however, places a 15-unit bet on D, under no circumstances can he lose money. This system on a much more elaborate, interstate scale lies at the core of organized gambling.

In addition, among the more vulnerable areas of organized crime are those that relate to activities of persons who have at least nominal

92 Mattei, "Use of Taxation to Control Organized Crime". See also "Application of Federal Gambling Stamp Tax Law."
93 *U.S. v. Marchetti.*
94 18 U.S. Code §1084.

obligations to society, such as accountants, lawyers, and politicians. Lawyers are particularly vital in keeping organized criminals out of prison, and the connivance of some lawyers with illegal activities shows clearly the greater seduction of large financial gains when compared with professional ethical standards. One of the most revealing interchanges during the Kefauver hearings took place when the committee questioned a former employee of the Internal Revenue Service who had helped convict a high-level organized criminal of tax evasion. On his release from prison, the criminal approached the accountant, not with a gun, but with a blank check, and hired him away from the government's employ. The Kefauver committee prodded the accountant about this episode:

> Q.: "I'm very anxious to know why you—a former agent of the government, with a background of which I presume you are proud—the man who succeeded in putting this racketeer behind bars—why you are willing to engage in illegal activity?"
>
> The accountant's lawyer objected to the question, but the Committee counsel persisted: "What's the inducement to you? Why do you do such things?"
>
> A. (*vehemently*): "For the almighty dollar. The same as you are doing the job you are doing right now."[95]

Control of organized crime and its practitioners represents a complex problem of deterrence, since its roots are deeply embedded within the framework of our social structure. Paul Tappan observes that perhaps the most effective weapon would be a concentrated campaign of reform focused on the younger age groups, where some possibility of cutting off the supply of recruits for organized crime exists. Tappan doubts that more lenient educative approaches will "reform mature men who have become established in organized criminal activities" and points out that we actually know very little about treatment for such offenders.[96] "The fact is that the law and its administration are not well designed to discover and isolate organized criminals in the vice rackets," he points out; but the severest handicap in controlling and eliminating such activity, he adds, is "the moral hypocrisy in our society that will tolerate and engage inconspicuously in vice that it virtuously prohibits."[97]

For Further Reading

"COMBATING ORGANIZED CRIME," in *The Annals of the American Academy of Political and Social Science.* Vol. 347 (May 1963).
    Twelve articles are included in this symposium on the roots and the

95 Kefauver, *Crime in America*, p. 204.
96 Tappan, in Ploscowe, *Organized Crime and Law Enforcement*, pp. 158–159.
97 *Ibid.*, p. 142.

activities of organized crime, which theoretically stresses contradictions between morality and mores that exist in the United States. Morality, it is noted, is what we preach publicly; mores are what we do privately. As Gus Tyler, the volume editor, notes, "We feed our consciences by writing morality into the law; we feed the underworld by putting our mores into practice."

KEFAUVER, ESTES. *Crime in America.* Garden City, N.Y.: Doubleday, 1951. Highlights of the testimony of the more than 600 witnesses, who were examined by the Senate Special Committee to Investigate Crime in Interstate Commerce in 1950 and 1951, are presented in this documentary account of the Committee's work. Particularly revealing are the occasional verbatim transcripts of emotional outbursts between Committee members and various persons under questioning.

"ORGANIZED CRIME," in *Crime and Delinquency.* Vol. 8 (October 1962), pp. 325–407.
Methods of controlling organized crime are stressed in this nine-article forum in *Crime and Delinquency.* The late Robert Kennedy discusses legislative weapons against organized crime; Herbert Bloch writes about the gambling business and its paradoxical position in American life; Milton G. Rector and Sanford Bates consider the responses of the courts and the correctional system to accused and convicted organized criminals. Particularly helpful is an extensive bibliography on organized crime, compiled by Arminé Dikijian, librarian of the National Council on Crime and Delinquency.

PRESIDENT'S COMMISSION ON LAW ENFORCEMENT AND ADMINISTRATION OF JUSTICE, *Task Force Report: Organized Crime.* Washington, D.C.: Government Printing Office, 1967.
This 126-page, double-columned volume brings together the most recent, substantive material that deals with organized crime, and then it attempts to suggest methods of study and control of the activities of organized crime. Particularly useful are the consultants' papers by Donald R. Cressey, who examines the structure of organized crime from the viewpoint of a sociologist studying institutional structure and process, and the brief contribution of Thomas C. Schelling, which stands as one of the rare attempts to use the analytical tools of economics to bear upon criminal behavior.

TYLER, GUS (ed.). *Organized Crime in America: A Book of Readings.* Ann Arbor: University of Michigan Press, 1962.
Tyler gathers together a comprehensive collection of the major writings on organized crime through the early 1960s. The material also embraces considerations of juvenile gangs and the methods by which youngsters are indoctrinated into the values and attitudes proper for a successful career in the ranks of organized crime. The editor, who is assistant president of the International Ladies' Garment Workers' Union, conducted his study of organized crime with funds from the Center for the Study of Democratic Institutions, which was interested in assessing the impact of organized crime on the democratic process.

9

Homicides and Assaults

On a recent Easter Sunday, thousands of persons in the United States gathered together for diverse kinds of celebrations. In Los Angeles, for instance, an estimated 6,000 hippies, many of them carrying flutes and tambourines, came together for a "love-in," the men often wearing East Indian robes, the girls dressed in miniskirts, their legs painted psychedelic colors. The festivities were marred, however, when one of the celebrants, wandering from the main body, was set upon by a gang of children, aged ten to twelve. The gang boys threw rocks and bottles and flailed the youth with clubs, sending him to the hospital in critical condition with a threatened loss of his right eye. Meanwhile, in a more traditional religious ritual, crowds sat in silence at services in the Hollywood Bowl, at worship, while pickets paraded around the Bowl's circumference bearing signs with messages such as "Would Christ Drop Napalm?"[1]

The counterpointing of events at both the "hippie" and the "square" gatherings provides a fundamental key to the ambiguous role of violence in American society. The duality between peacefulness and passivity, on the one hand, and aggression and violence, on the other, is one that has continuously pervaded American life. Both forms of behavior are at times rewarded, both are encouraged, and both are at different times denounced. It has been said that it is cowardly not to fight, that if you don't throw your weight around people will ignore you, that subtlety is more effective than force, that women should be weak and "nice" but that boys should be strong and aggressive. These, with similar bits of folk wisdom, constitute the variegated indoctrination on violence that is transmitted in the United States. From it emerge diverse amalgams of violent behavior, some of them sanctioned and praised, others deplored and prohibited by the criminal codes.

1 Geis, "Violence in American Society."

Our legal codes select out for attention only certain kinds of violent consequences, even though many things that maim and kill innocent people are tolerated and even approved. If, for instance, a law could be enacted and absolutely enforced that no automobile could travel at a speed greater than 40 or 50 miles per hour, perhaps 10,000 fewer persons would be killed in highway accidents each year and untold numbers of others would be spared injury. Fast driving, within speed limits, is permissible, however, and persons who bring about accidents under these conditions are usually not considered to be "violent." Their victims are written off as sacrifices to an ethos that prefers to move rapidly from one place to another rather than keep alive thousands of driving casualties. It is not, therefore, only the lethal consequences of violence which make it abhorrent.

It would seem that it is only in part the results of violence that contribute to concern about it. It is quick, direct violence that we primarily attend to, probably in large measure because it is so much easier to do so. When we can readily identify the perpetrator and view and pinpoint the immediate wounds brought about by a particular violent act, it is easier to affix blame. It is much more difficult to maintain with certainty that parents have viciously produced a mentally ill, frightened child, or that a remote landlord, charging exploitative rents in a slum district, has contributed to the development of a defeatist, alienated member of a minority group.

A popular assumption is that the uninhibited portrayal of violence by mass media in the United States transmits an image of aggression that is apt to be duplicated by those continuously exposed to its message. Literary violence is not, of course, a new phenomenon. Satirists are fond of dissecting the classic stories of childhood, pointing out that they are indeed a grim and gory collection. There is Captain Hook, his arm waving a spiked hook at Peter Pan, and there are Hansel and Gretel, on the verge of fiery immurement in the ugly witch's oven after a frightening night in a dark and evil forest, having been abandoned to their fate by an indifferent father and a wicked stepmother.

Such portrayals of violence, given their extraordinary longevity and appeal, may be bereft of serious behavioral implications for children. Nobody, at least, has been able to demonstrate conclusively that children raised on such a bedtime diet are destined to reproduce similar grisly events in later life. But, neither has the contrary been proven, nor is it apt to be.

The mass media in the United States often reflect patterns of violence that differ in degree and intensity from those found elsewhere in the world, however. Television viewers, for instance, are apt to be impressed by the ritualistic manner in which violence is portrayed. Reasonably true-to-life stories that are well within the realm of possibility suddenly present fight sequences that defy credence, where individuals inflict punishment on each other that no one could conceivably survive for more than a few seconds. In rapid order, chairs that are bashed over heads will be ignored, punches that would fell elephants will be casually shrugged aside, and kicks ferocious enough to finish off any mortal will be greeted with no more than a momentary grunt from the hero. The pummeling will proceed resolutely for perhaps a minute or more until the villain succumbs.

It is easier to caricature such proceedings, however, than to assay their importance and influence, however tempting such moralizing may be.[2] Research results to date, while far from conclusive, tend to indicate culpability on the part of the media for their inordinate and disproportionate stress on violence.[3]

The Violent Male?

It is important to appreciate that man does not possess an inborn instinct for violence, but rather that expressions of violence are learned in a social context after birth. Konrad Lorenz has pointed out that among carnivores only rats and men have no innate inhibitions against killing members of their own species. It has been noted in this respect that the Latin proverb *homo homini lupus*—man is a wolf to man—represents a libel on the wolf, who is quite a gentle animal with other wolves.[4]

Anthropologists have filled out the biological portrait drawn by Lorenz with ethnographic studies of preliterate tribes that find no pleasure in dominating other persons or in hunting and killing. All such groups want is to be left alone, which they can only do in the midst of their power-seeking neighbors by retreating to inaccessible territories. To Geoffrey Gorer, a prominent anthropologist, the most common distinguishing trait of the peace-loving tribes is an enormous gusto for sensual pleasures—eating, drinking, sex, and laughter. Gorer has also found that these tribes make little distinction between the social characteristics of men and women. In particular, the men have no ideal of brave, aggressive masculinity. No child grows up being told that "All men do X" or that "No proper woman does Y."[5]

For Gorer and others who have studied this, it is here that the key to the riddle of violence lies. They believe that violence that warps and destroys will be controlled only when societies no longer insist that virility and similar masculine status symbols be tied to demonstrations of aggression and violence. Some observers suspect that the "hippies" may in some manner sense this. Sex roles seem

2 See, for instance, Wertham, *A Sign for Cain.*
3 Berkowitz, Corwin, and Heironimus, "Film Violence and Subsequent Aggressive Tendencies."
4 Lorenz, *On Aggression.*
5 Gorer, "Man Has No 'Killer' Instinct."

blurred among them and it is sometimes difficult to distinguish the girls from the boys. The use of drugs also represents withdrawal from combat, a disinvolvement from matters physical and forceful.

The paradox, of course, is that the United States is not an inaccessible territory and its citizens are not likely to be able to survive without some display of traditional masculine-style truculence and aggression. The abhorrence of violence presumably will either have to become universal or violence will prevail. For violence to be expressed only toward "real" enemies but to be inhibited in regard to one's fellows is an achievement that no society has yet been able to realize.

Background to Homicide

Among crimes of violence, homicide is by far the most dramatic. In the United States, stories of homicide occur in a considerable portion of television programs, compete vigorously and quite successfully against foreign news and domestic political affairs for front-page newspaper headlines, and provide a sizable segment of the nation's fictional reading diet. It is also traditional to point out that murder occurs early in the Bible when Cain slays his brother, and that various forms of homicide occupy a prominent position in the classical literature of the world. Stage devotees need only count the corpses in *Hamlet* to appreciate the dramatic potentialities of violence.

In our society, sudden death—and particularly sudden death resulting from homicide—contains a number of items that provide insight into the society itself. Most Americans are carefully shielded from direct contact with death and go through life with well-sublimated feelings about the inevitability of death. Few of us, in contrast to persons in some other societies, evaluate each of our plans in light of the prospect of eventual death and the possibility of sudden death. On the contrary, we generally behave as if we were going to live for a considerable length of time; some persons, in fact, appear to plan as if they were going to live forever.[6]

The act of homicide provides striking evidence of the transiency of human flesh and of the precarious nature of human life. It provides dramatic proof of the fact that, if so inclined, any of us can terminate the mortal existence of anyone else and that our own existence may readily be ended on another's whim. This godlike power is awesome to contemplate and perhaps accounts for the strong interest in stories of persons who have exercised their power to kill in order to resolve real or imagined problems. Psychiatrists would insist further that our interest in homicide, which is similar to the interest of obituary columns readers, is related to the pleasure we derive from learning of other persons' deaths, because their deaths indicate that we have

6 Fulton and Geis, "Death and Social Values."

competed successfully, if only momentarily, in the quest for temporal immortality.

Despite this abiding interest in sudden death in our society, our mass communications media generally do not delve too deeply into the wellsprings of homicide. Marta Wolfenstein and Nathan Leites have documented the sharp variations between the portrayal of murder in American motion pictures and films produced in other countries. Only rarely do American films allow any sense of identification with the victim, so that his demise arouses no emotional feelings. Murders in our motion pictures usually occur early in the film and rarely carry with them a sense of tragic loss. If a "good" person has been murdered, those he leaves behind spend no time grieving, but set out immediately and resolutely to avenge his death. French films, on the contrary, show death as a tragic twist of fate, shattering flimsy human hopes and aspirations, often when it appears likely that they might be realized. French films build up considerable viewer-identity with the potential victim, and those the victim leaves behind are disturbed and frightened rather than vengeful. Wolfenstein and Leites maintain that these motifs reflect real values in the countries producing the different types of films.[7]

The Definition of Homicide

There has developed within the law, as part of our regulatory system, a sharpness of definition with regard to homicide that Albert Morris says "might be used as well as envied by sociologists."[8] From long experience, legal scholars are in reasonable agreement as to the definition of such key words in the law of homicide as "malice," "premeditation," and "provocation." These definitions have been sharpened so that their boundaries are recognized and their essential meanings are commonly understood. The law states, for example, that for an act to constitute criminal homicide, the killing must have occurred after, and not before or during, the birth of the victim. It is not necessary that the criminal act be the sole cause of death, but only that it be a recognizable causal factor. The legal definition of homicide also requires that the death occur within a year and a day from the time the injury was inflicted.[9] These definitional resolutions help alleviate analytical impasses that sometimes occur in the social sciences during attempts by successive workers to define incisively the behavior they are studying.

Traditionally, homicide—the killing of one human being by another—is broken down into four major categories: murder, manslaughter, excusable homicide, and justifiable homicide.

7 Wolfenstein and Leites, *Movies: A Psychological Study.*
8 Morris, *Homicide*, p. 5.
9 Cohen, "Present Status of the Year and a Day Rule."

Murder, in all but ten states, consists of at least two degrees. First-degree murder usually includes the dual attributes of *premeditation* and *malice aforethought,* although in practice many cases that involve both premeditation and malice aforethought are actually prosecuted as second-degree murder. "Premeditation" refers to the prior formation of an intent to kill; even a moment of such intent antecedent to the act is usually considered adequate to fulfill the requirement of premeditation. "Malice aforethought" refers to the manifestation of a deliberate intention to take the life of a fellow creature. Second-degree murder includes malice aforethought—the desire to kill—but not premeditation.

One of the more controversial legal provisions in regard to murder is the *felony-murder* doctrine. Under its provisions, if a death occurs during the commission of a felony, the person committing the felony is chargeable with first-degree murder. A person setting fire to a barn, for instance, who thereby commits the felony of arson, might unintentionally burn to death a tramp who was sleeping in the barn. If so, the arsonist can be charged with murder, though his act lacked both malice aforethought and premeditation. The same situation prevails if a storekeeper dies of a heart attack during the course of a robbery. The felony-murder doctrine has even been applied to cover a charge of first-degree murder against one of a pair of robbers, when a policeman killed the second robber; it was held that the second robber would not have been killed except for the commission of the felony and that, therefore, the partner was legally responsible for the other's death.[10]

The tendency has been to define more precisely those felonies under which the felony-murder doctrine will apply. Many states now enumerate only a limited number, the most common being arson, rape, robbery, and burglary. A large number of states do not include within the felony-murder rule deaths resulting from abortions, on the ground that the victim has consented to the commission of the felony. However, New York considers the felony-murder rule applicable to all felonies, whereas in England the doctrine has increasingly been eliminated from cases in which death was purely accidental or in which death was a consequence that could not reasonably have been foreseen by the offender.[11]

Manslaughter lacks the requirement of malice aforethought. As with murder, it is also generally divided into at least two parts. In first-degree manslaughter, often called "voluntary" manslaughter, death results from conditions under which a fatality might reasonably have been anticipated, as, for instance, in a sudden knife fight between two persons. Second-degree, or "involuntary," manslaughter involves circumstances that are less closely related to the lethal outcome. Second-

10 Crabtree, "Criminal Responsibility for Death of Co-Felon."
11 Great Britain, *Royal Commission on Capital Punishment, 1949–1953,* p. 30.

degree manslaughter might, for instance, be charged against a person who engaged in a fist fight in which his opponent fell and subsequently died from injuries sustained during his fall. Automobile deaths due to the driver's negligence are also usually tried as manslaughter cases, since the driver rarely (though probably more often than is generally suspected) meant to kill anyone.

Excusable homicide includes deaths from accidents or misfortunes, such as those that might occur while a parent is lawfully disciplining his child. In general, excusable homicide is said to apply to deaths growing out of lawful acts, done by lawful means, and in which ordinary caution or restraint is employed.

Justifiable homicide relates to acts resulting in death, which are performed as a result of legal demands. The executioner commits justifiable homicide when he electrocutes a condemned prisoner, as does the policeman who shoots to death a fleeing felon. Self-defense may be either justifiable or excusable homicide, depending upon the particular circumstances. Most states require that the person employing self-defense use no force greater than that needed to protect himself reasonably, and a number of states require that a person does not kill in self-defense unless he has exhausted reasonable opportunities to avoid conflict, such as by running. It is an intriguing illustration of the interrelationship between law and social mores that states that do not require reasonable attempts to retreat before employing lethal methods of self-defense are located in the western portion of the United States, where legislation is tinted with frontier customs.[12]

The Extent of Homicide

All statistical sources indicate that the homicide rate in the United States moved steadily upward from 1900 until the mid-thirties, dropped sharply during the following ten-year period, and then began an upward swing at the close of World War II. It should also be noted that the high postwar homicide rate did not approximate the top levels of homicide reached during the late 1920s and the early 1930s. Table 9.1 presents the figures on homicide since 1933.

Numerically, there are about 10,000 criminal homicides annually in the United States. The figure has been compared to the approximately 50,000 yearly traffic fatalities, toward which our responses, as Morris notes, "appear less vigorous and less emotional," despite the fact that "those who are killed accidentally are just as dead, and just as unwillingly so, as those who are killed by negligence or by malice." Morris believes that there is some basis for arguing that in a high proportion of cases there is as much logic in attaching blame to killings by accident as to killings with legal intent, and he main-

12 Rivkind, "Justifiable Homicide in Texas."

Table 9.1   Homicide Rate per 100,000 Population, United States, 1933–1966

Year	Rate	Year	Rate	Year	Rate
1933	9.7	1945	5.6	1957	4.9
1934	9.5	1946	6.3	1958	4.5
1935	8.3	1947	6.0	1959	4.6
1936	8.0	1948	5.8	1960	4.7
1937	7.6	1949	5.4	1961	4.7
1938	6.8	1950	4.6	1962	4.8
1939	6.4	1951	4.9	1963	4.9
1940	6.2	1952	5.2	1964	5.1
1941	6.0	1953	4.8	1965	5.5
1942	5.8	1954	4.8	1966	5.9
1943	5.0	1955	4.5		
1944	4.9	1956	4.6		

SOURCE: National Center for Health Statistics.

tains that we tend to overestimate the evil intent in the murderer and to underestimate it in the auto driver.[13]

Cross-national comparisons of homicide are somewhat less than satisfactory because of varying definitions of the behavior under scrutiny. On the other hand, homicides, more than other offenses, are readily susceptible to enumeration and relatively immune from vagaries of police practice, political interference, and similar items that distort comparative measurements of criminal behavior. Figures from different nations, presented in Table 9.2, show the relatively high rate of homicide in the United States as compared to other places. The striking discrepancies between South American nations, with Nicaragua reporting a staggeringly high homicide rate and Chile a much lower one, has yet to be adequately explained. It is notable that Spain (and Ireland as well, though it does not appear on the table), both Catholic countries, stand at the lower end of the table, while diverse South American countries, also Catholic, report strikingly higher homicide rates. The table clearly belies insistence that the American homicide rate is a function of our frontier tradition, for both Canada and Australia, which report low homicide rates, have a similar frontier heritage to that of the United States.

The decrease in the homicide rate in the United States over the past decades should, however, serve to put us on guard against ready generalizations based on official statistics. Some persons might claim that the decline in homicide is conclusive evidence that, regardless of what might be said about nuclear weapons and their use, human beings are becoming more "civilized" and less aggressive. This conclusion, however, must be reconciled with the persistent rise in other

13 Morris, *Homicide*, p. 26.

Table 9.2 Homicide Rate per 100,000 Population, Selected Countries, 1965

Country	Rate
Nicaragua	29.3
Guatemala	11.5
Ecuador	6.0
United States	5.5
Panama	4.8
Philippines	2.6
Chile	2.3
Finland	2.0
Australia	1.5
Japan	1.4
Canada	1.3
New Zealand	1.2
France	0.8
Switzerland	0.8
Sweden	0.7
England and Wales	0.7
Norway	0.5
Spain	0.1

SOURCE: *Demographic Yearbook of the United Nations,* 1966, p. 104.

personal crimes of an assaultive nature. Taking everything together, it appears likely that the drop in homicide is a tribute to modern medical and surgical advances as much as to anything else. Many persons who formerly might have died from crimes of violence are now saved on operating tables, and their assailants are charged with assault with intent to kill rather than with murder or manslaughter.

Correlates of Homicide

In general, it can be said that murder and nonnegligent manslaughter increase as one moves away from the New England states. The rate per 100,000 population in various geographical regions in the United States in 1967 is shown in Table 9.3.

Table 9.3 Murder and Nonnegligent Manslaughter Rates per 100,000 Population, by Regions, 1967

Region	Rate
Northeast	4.1
North Central	4.9
Southern	9.4
Western	4.9

SOURCE: *Uniform Crime Reports,* 1967, p. 5.

The high rate of the Southern states points to one of the major items regarding homicide in the United States: the disproportionate presence of homicide among American Negroes. In Alabama, for instance, the state that has the highest homicide rate in the United States, the Negro rate is 41.1 per 100,000 persons, while the Caucasion rate is 11.6. This marked discrepancy in racial homicide does not, however, tell the entire story, for it is important to realize that *both* the Caucasian and Negro murder rates are much higher in Alabama than they are in states such as Maine. The Negro rate in Maine, in fact (3.2 per 100,000), is considerably lower than the Caucasian rate in Alabama (11.6), although it is also quite a bit higher than the Caucasian rate in Maine (1.9). It is obviously not race per se that generates the varying murder rates, but rather a combination of the subculture of the racial group blended with the more general characteristics of the wider environment in which the subculture operates. An attempt to pinpoint those items that contribute most significantly to the Negro homicide rate by use of factor analysis of diverse items has been done by Thomas F. Pettigrew and Rosalind Spier, who suggest that the Negro turns to homicide because, born in the South, he is a product of a region with a violent tradition, and because he is often a migrant to a new and threatening environment that makes it difficult for him to throw off what they consider his cultural thrust toward homicide.[14] Cross-cultural work would seem to indicate clearly the social roots of Negro homicide in the United States.[15]

The present preponderance of Negroes in murder rates requires close examination. The situation shows the necessity for careful scrutiny of all gross correlates of criminal behavior so that sensible explanations can be made about what we know or suspect regarding the operation of the society and its system of criminal justice. Negroes constitute about 11 percent of the American population and account for about 30 percent of all recorded arrests and 60 percent of the arrests for murder and nonnegligent manslaughter. The arrest figures are open to considerable suspicion, however, since they represent the end product of enforcement prejudices and legal discriminations; they do not, for instance, take into account mass white-collar crimes, almost all of which is committed by Caucasians. Murder statistics, even though figures for this particular offense nearly approximate the true extent of the measured behavior, are also less than totally free from bias. Harold Garfinkel, for example, examining 821 homicides in ten North Carolina counties, concluded that proportionately fewer indictments were made when whites killed Negroes; most were made when Negroes killed whites.[16] A similar study in Virgina and North Carolina by Guy B. Johnson found that among 330 homicides there were

14 Pettigrew and Spier, "Ecological Structure of Negro Homicide," p. 629.
15 See, for instance, Bohannan, *African Homicide and Suicide.*
16 Garfinkel, "Research Note on Inter- and Intra-Racial Homicides."

five cases of whites killing Negroes, without a single conviction, and 24 cases of Negroes killing whites, with 22 convictions.[17]

Further explanations for the racial variation in homicide readily suggest themselves.[18] At the heart of the situation probably lies the totality of racial etiquette in the United States, a situation summed up in the poignant phrase of a Negro blues song, "If it wasn't for bad luck I wouldn't have no luck at all." More than forty years ago, Thorsten Sellin, dean of American criminologists, concluded a review of racial variations in criminal behavior with a note that anticipated the 1968 report of the President's Commission on Civil Disorders:

> The American Negro lacks education and earthly goods. He has had very little political experience and industrial training. His contact with city life has been unfortunate, for it has forced him into the most dilapidated and vicious areas of our great cities. Like a shadow over his whole existence lies the oppressive race prejudice of his white neighbor, restricting his activities and thwarting his ambitions. It would be extraordinary, indeed, if this group were to prove more lawabiding than the white, which enjoys more fully the advantages of a civilization the Negro has helped to create.
>
> The responsibility lies where power, authority, and discrimination has its source, the dominant white group. To that group the existence of a high crime rate among Negroes is a challenge which cannot be brushed aside by platitudes about "race inferiority," "inherited depravity," or similar generalizations. . . .[19]

The conditions cited by Sellin combine with a system that relegates Negroes to second-class citizenship, while it at the same time exposes them to the aphorisms, advertisements, mottoes, and ideals of the majority society.[20] The subsequent frustration may well erupt, as the psychologists maintain it often does, into aggressive behavior.

Some substantiation for this view is provided in an analysis by Bertram Karon of Negro personality patterns. Karon notes that the American Negro shares in the diverse personality structures of all individuals in American society, but that "grafted upon these are the special problems involved in adjusting to caste sanctions"; using projective techniques, Karon concluded that "the most serious emotional problems of the Negro concern the handling of aggression," and he attempted to explain the demonstrated difficulties with aggression in the following manner:

> The reason . . . would seem simply to be that the caste sanctions are, in fact, ways in which people are making trouble for the Negro; this

17 Johnson, "The Negro and Crime."
18 See Wolfgang, *Crime and Race;* Korn and McCorkle, *Criminology and Penology,* pp. 224–249.
19 Sellin, "The Negro Criminal, A Statistical Note," p. 64.
20 Jacobs, *Prelude to Riot,* pp. 102–103.

trouble may mean not only inconvenience, discomfort or humiliation, but also real physical danger. Against these problems he may have no defense; any attempt to fight back seems likely to lead to vindictive and inescapable retaliation. He must therefore fight a continuing battle with his own feelings of anger, lest he lose control.[21]

Another characteristic of murder is that it shows an erratic pattern in regard to the size of a city, with higher rates in metropolitan and rural areas than in intermediate-size cities. In an extensive investigation of 489 criminal homicides in Houston between 1945 and 1949, Henry A. Bullock has also shown the "intense variation" in distribution between census tracts within the city. The overall homicide rate in Houston was 22.7 per 100,000 population, but the census tracts showed rates from zero to 76 per 100,000. The highest concentration of homicide appeared near the central business district of the city. Most significant, in addition, was the highly disproportionate amount of homicide on individual streets within specific census tracts in contrast to the total rate for the tracts.[22]

Patterns in Criminal Homicide

The most intensive investigation of patterns in criminal homicide is that conducted by Marvin E. Wolfgang of the University of Pennsylvania, who analyzed 588 criminal homicides occurring in Philadelphia between 1949 and 1952 in order to determine "whether criminal homicide exhibits definite objective order, regularities, patterns, and, if so, what this concatenation of phenomena is."[23] The Philadelphia study cuts into homicide figures in numerous ways, cross-tabulating information on offenders, victims, methods of killing, time of the offenses, and similar items. Of the 588 homicide victims, 550 were killed by a total of 621 known offenders. Thirty-eight of the homicides remained unsolved. The findings, in addition to those of related studies that have examined similar material, indicate the following:

1. The disproportionate presence of Negroes in the total picture of criminal homicide is reemphasized. Eighteen percent of the population of Philadelphia was Negro, yet 73 percent of the homicide victims and 75 percent of the offenders were Negroes. In an examination of felonious homicides in Cleveland from 1947 to 1953, Robert C. Bensing and Oliver Schroeder, Jr., discovered that 76 percent of the persons accused were Negroes, although Negroes made up only 16 percent of the city's population.[24] Equivalent results also have been

21 Karon, *The Negro Personality*, p. 172.
22 Bullock, "Urban Homicide in Theory and Fact."
23 Wolfgang, *Patterns in Criminal Homicide*.
24 Bensing and Schroeder, *Homicide in an Urban Community*, p. 99.
25 Harlan, "Five Hundred Homicides."
26 DePorte and Parkhurst, "Homicide in New York State."

reported in studies in Birmingham, Alabama,[25] upstate New York,[26] and Massachusetts.[27]

2. Men are heavily overrepresented in homicide statistics, accounting for 82 percent of the offenders in Philadelphia and 86 percent in Cleveland. The figures show the following rates in Philadelphia per 100,000 population: Negro males (41.7), Negro females (9.3), white males (3.4), and white females (.4). Wolfgang notes that "the difference in frequency of criminal homicide is significantly greater between the races within each sex than the difference between the sexes within each race."[28] The majority of females kill males, and in homicide statistics for both races females are victims more often than they are offenders. The sex ratio is even more skewed in other jurisdictions. In both Puerto Rico and Ceylon, for instance, men constitute about 96 percent of the homicide offenders.[29] Pollak contends, however, that these figures are misleading, because women are more able to conceal their homicides, which typically involve food poisoning.[30] Such an explanation seems exaggerated, however, as does the rebuttal by Mabel Elliott, who maintains that "it is doubtful . . . if as many women murderers escape detection as men, since their guilt reactions are generally observable"; she further points out however (and with considerable truth), that women murderers usually kill persons close to them, and that, since poisoning has become more easily detected, the number of unknown female homicides has been cut.[31] Durkheim's explanation is particularly persuasive, though. He feels that women are less deeply involved than men in the struggle of life. He maintains about women that "whenever homicide is within her range she commits it as often or more often than men," and he cites abortion and infanticide as examples of female homicide.[32]

3. Only thirty-four (6 percent) of the homicides in Philadelphia crossed racial lines. In fourteen cases Negroes were slain by whites, and in twenty instances whites were murdered by Negroes. In terms of rates per 100,000 population, it is interesting to note that while Negro offenders (1.0) crossed the race line more often than whites did (.2), Negroes were victims (.7) of white offenders approximately three times more frequently than whites were victims (.2) of Negro offenders.

4. Homicides are usually brutal and direct, and the weapons employed are relatively commonplace. Of the 588 Philadelphia victims, 39 percent were stabbed to death, 33 percent were shot, 22 percent died as a result of beatings, and 6 percent constituted miscellane-

27 Stearns, "Homicide in Massachusetts."
28 Wolgang, *Patterns in Criminal Homicide*, p. 32.
29 Wallace and Canals, "Socio-Legal Aspects of a Study of Acts of Violence," p. 187; Wood, *Crime and Aggression in Changing Ceylon*, p. 68.
30 Pollak, *The Criminality of Women*, Chap. 3.
31 Elliott, *Crime in Modern Society*, p. 200.
32 Durkheim, *Suicide*, pp. 341–342.

ous cases, in which death resulted from such things as gas, poison, and arson. It is curious, however, that Wolfgang's sample diverges considerably from the 2,700 murders between 1950 and 1951 in Boston. This group, analyzed by Morris, showed death resulting from shooting more often than all other means combined. Obviously, the manner of death-dealing is a function of cultural forms and weapon availability. In England, for instance, no weapons were employed in 30 percent of the country's murders, while blunt instruments were used in 25 percent and guns were used in but 10 percent.[33] Females in Philadelphia, however, used stabbing four times as often as males to commit homicide. In general, such stabbings resulted from domestic quarrels, and the weapons used were domestic utensils.

5. The high point for Philadelphia homicides was Saturday, just as it was in New York and Cleveland,[34] and 50 percent of the Philadelphia homicides took place between eight o'clock in the evening and two o'clock in the morning.

6. In 36 percent of the Philadelphia cases, there was no evidence of alcohol present in either the victim or the offender. In 44 percent, both had been drinking prior to the commission of the offense. In 9 percent of the cases, only the victim had been drinking, and in 11 percent only the offender had been drinking. In total, 64 percent of the cases showed at least one party to the offense had been drinking before the homicide took place. These findings on alcohol and homicide underline the possible connection between the eruption of violence and the release of inhibitions, with the liquor serving as a superego solvent. In Finland, Veli Verkko has attempted to relate virtually all of the variations in that country's homicide picture to the drinking habits of the people.[35] Wolfgang and Franco Ferracuti, however, make the observation that before alcohol can be labelled a direct cause of homicide, it is necessary to determine on how many occasions other than the one in which he is involved, the homicide offender drinks. "If we knew the incidence of alcohol-related homicide among all alcohol-related social interactions," they ask, "would we be at all impressed by the coefficient?"[36]

7. Persons involved in homicide have had a large number of previous contacts with the police. Of the 621 offenders, 65 percent had an arrest record (almost double the figure, incidentally, found in England[37]). Of the 588 victims, 47 percent had previous records. Of those offenders with previous records, almost half had been arrested for aggravated assault.

8. A majority of the Philadelphia homicides involved persons

33 Gibson and Klein, *Murder*, pp. 20–21.
34 *New York Times*, Feb. 26, 1963; Bensing and Schroeder, *Homicide in an Urban Community*, p. 9.
35 Verkko, *Homicides and Suicides in Finland*.
36 Wolfgang and Ferracuti, *Subculture of Violence*, p. 265.
37 Gibson and Klein, *Murder*, p. 34.

closely related in primary group contacts. In 65 percent of the cases, the victim was a close friend of the killer, a family member, a paramour, or a homosexual partner. Forty-one percent of the female victims were killed by their husbands. Research done elsewhere suggests that this victimization pattern is prevalent in highly industrialized societies.[38] In England, for instance, it is reported that "murder is overwhelmingly a domestic crime in which men kill their wives, mistresses and children, and women kill their children."[39]

9. The varying national rate of murder that is followed by suicide provides interesting food for theoretical speculation. Of the 621 murderers in Philadelphia, only 4 percent subsequently killed themselves,[40] a percentage approximated in studies in Baltimore, Maryland,[41] and New Jersey.[42] In England, however, 50 of the 150 persons who annually commit murder subsequently kill themselves. Not surprisingly, the murder-suicide group in England is more confined to intra-family offenses than the regular murder sample. It includes a large number of young mothers who kill their infant children and then take their own lives, prompted by a combination of feelings of desperation and compassion.[43] The infanticide method used most often was gas, probably because such a method is viewed as more humane.

The foregoing items indicate some of the gross correlates of the kinds of homicide that constitute the daily routine of metropolitan police departments, a routine that is interrupted only infrequently by the flamboyant headline-grabbing murders that are reported detail-by-detail to the American public. The figures do not, of course, provide information on the dynamics of the relationship between offender and victim, both of whom represent carriers of a culture that has not been able to inhibit murderous behavior. It might be important, in this regard, to determine what in the national culture of Iceland, a country with a gory history during the saga era,[44] led to the reported absence of any act definitely known to have been murder during the past few centuries.[45]

A sophisticated attempt to add theoretical flesh to empirical studies of homicide appears in a recent monograph by Wolfgang, written in collaboration with Franco Ferracuti of the University of Puerto Rico. The authors suggest that homicide becomes prevalent when psychological and social forces coalesce into what they label a "subculture of violence." Their theoretical explanation is not concerned with premeditated homicides, but rather concentrates on what they call "passionate" murders, which make up the bulk of homicides.

38 Svalastoga, "Homicide and Social Contact in Denmark," p. 41.
39 Morris and Blom-Cooper, A Calendar of Murder, p. 280.
40 Wolgang, "Suicide by Means of Victim-Precipitated Homicide."
41 Guttmacher, The Mind of the Murderer, p. 9.
42 Gibbens, "Sane and Insane Homicide," p. 114.
43 West, Murder Followed by Suicide, p. 31.
44 Tennant, The Scandinavian Book.
45 Palmer, A Study of Murder, p. 5.

The theory attempts to move interchangeably between sociological and psychological concepts and to embrace research findings from diverse scholarly viewpoints. The notions of a subculture of violence are said to be built upon three foundations: (1) sociological theory on culture, social and personality systems, culture conflict, differential association, and value systems, (2) psychological theory on learning, conditioning, developmental socialization, differential identification, and (3) criminological research on criminal homicide and other assaultive crimes.[46]

The theory contains the seven following points: (1) No subculture can be totally different from or totally in conflict with the society of which it is a part, (2) To establish the existence of a subculture of violence does not require that the actors sharing in these basic value elements express violence in all situations, (3) The potential willingness to resort to violence in a variety of situations emphasizes the penetrating and diffusive character of this culture theme, (4) The subcultural ethos of violence may be shared by all ages in a subsociety, but this ethos is more prominent in a limited age group that ranges from late adolescence to middle age, (5) The counternorm is nonviolence, in the sense that the adult male who does not defend his honor or his female companion will be socially emasculated, (6) The development of favorable attitudes toward, and the use of, violence in a subculture usually involve learned behavior and a process of differential learning, association, or identification, and (7) The use of violence in a subculture is not necessarily viewed as illicit conduct, and the users therefore do not have to deal with feelings of guilt about their aggression.[47]

The authors note that they are not, for the moment, "prepared to assert how a subculture of violence arises," and they indicate that "probably no single theory will ever explain the variety of observable violent behavior"; but they suggest that the subculture-of-violence approach offers "the advantage of bringing together psychological and sociological constructs to aid in the explanation of the concentration of violence in specific socioeconomic groups and ecological areas."[48]

Roots of Homicide

Both popular writers and scientific investigators have focused considerable attention through the years on case-history backgrounds of individual murderers, in the attempt to understand particularly violent or bizarre killings or those in which prominent persons were involved. In addition, psychiatrists, examining defendants for the courts, have accumulated elaborate dossiers on a number of murderers.

46 Wolfgang and Ferracuti, *Subculture of Violence*, pp. 312–314.
47 *Ibid.*, pp. 159–161.
48 *Ibid.*, pp. 161–163. See also Hartung, *Crime, Law and Society*, pp. 136–158.

Several clues pointing toward the direction in which such investigations might head are provided by a pilot study of six murderers serving life sentences in the Minnesota State Prison at Stillwater. Five collaborators from several academic disciplines conducted the research. Their subjects were chosen because they were normally intelligent members of the white race, not associated with gangs or with groups for whom crimes of violence were part of a way of life. The murder each committed was an isolated act, and the murderer himself showed no prior record of violent crime. All six murderers came from middle-class backgrounds, had no history of drug or alcohol use, and showed no traces of organic disease or epilepsy. The research team felt that offenses such as those studied "are sociologically determined and are more or less predictable, and that prevention is largely a broad social problem."[49]

Both parents of each of the six murderers, as well as the murderers themselves, were interviewed. The researchers were impressed with the readiness with which the murderers discussed both the crime and the events leading up to it. They found that the prisoners did not either try to escape responsibility for their crime or to lay the blame on others. Almost without exception, when the stories of the prisoners and their families were at variance, the prisoners were found to be telling the truth.

The study confirmed a finding that has received attention in the field of juvenile delinquency—that the worst offenders do not tend to be those who have been undisciplined, as public opinion often assumes, but those who have been strenuously subjected to constant physical punishment. The Minnesota research team found that for the six murderers "remorseless physical brutality at the hands of the parents had been a constant experience. Brutality far beyond the ordinary excuses of discipline had been perpetrated on them; often, it was so extreme as to compel neighbors to intercede for the boy."[50] The study does not, of course, claim to have unraveled a total etiological pattern, but it is noteworthy in pointing to a common thread in the cases: Conditioned to violence, each of the murderers eventually restored to the techniques that had been indelibly impressed upon him.

A similar finding concerning the importance of brutality by the father in subsequent criminal behavior has been reported by William and Joan McCord, who differentiated a large group of boys on the basis of various parental roles displayed toward them. Interestingly enough, the McCords found that a son appears to identify with a cruel or neglecting father only if the father's behavior is deviant. They interpret this finding in the following manner: ". . . perhaps a child's 'identification with the aggressor' occurs only when the model provides a 'permissible' outlet for the aggressive feelings created by the aggres-

49 Duncan, et al., "Etiological Factors in First-Degree Murder."
50 Ibid.

sion—that is, when the father himself encourages by his behavior the child's aggressive urges."[51]

Physical beatings by parents as part of the developmental history of murderers and manslaughter offenders are also reported by Stuart Palmer in his study of fifty-one New England prison inmates. Palmer found a whole complex of frustrating experiences in the backgrounds of the murderers; his research supported the hypothesis that there is a significant, positive, functional relationship between the amount of frustration experienced by individuals in infancy, childhood, and adolescence, and whether or not they later commit murder.[52]

Homicide and Its Motives

At its root, nonnegligent homicide represents the product of a conception by the offender that the person he kills stands in his way, blocking him from the achievement of some desired goal. Some homicide, of course, may be the inadvertent result of an act directed toward other ends, such as in felony-murder cases. If we exclude these and similar cases, however, we may gain considerable insight into the roots of homicide from an analysis of what the killer sought to accomplish by his act. Wolfgang and Ferracuti, for instance, point out that "motivational analysis remains a tool of paramount importance for the understanding of homicidal behavior and serves as a guideline for an evaluation of the etiology of the violent impulse"; they also suggest that the less clearly motivated a murder is, in the sense that it is impossible to comprehend its motives, the higher is the probability that the homicidal subject is abnormal.[53] It must be realized that the end sought is either inherent in the genetic requirements of the individual or is learned within the culture and thus represents a commentary on the values indoctrinated into the individual and the barricades erected against the realization of these values. It is true that different types of societies produce different amounts and kinds of homicide. Alister Kershaw notes, for instance, that "while many of the Prohibition-era gangsters began their careers in the Unione Siciliano . . . they very soon developed a fashion of assassination which was wholly American"; he cites the case of Jean-Louis Verger, a French priest who killed his superior, which Kershaw believes could only have occurred in France, since he maintains that there is no record "of, say, an Englishman murdering for a purely philosophical motive."[54]

A tentative effort to categorize types of murder has been made by F. Tennyson Jesse, who groups murderers into six categories, ar-

51 McCord and McCord, *Origins of Crime*, pp. 93–94.
52 Palmer, *A Study of Murder*, p. 8.
53 Wolfgang and Ferracuti, *Subculture of Violence*, p. 209.
54 Kershaw, *Murder in France*, p. 11.

ranged according to the motive of the killer. Her types are: (1) murder for gain, (2) murder for revenge, (3) murder for elimination, (4) murder for jealousy, (5) murder for the lust of killing, and (6) murder from conviction. Most murders, Jesse says, are committed for gain, although "the gain for which the murder is committed is very small, often problematical."[55] Murder for the lust of killing embraces such offenders as Nathan Leopold and Richard Loeb who killed a thirteen-year-old boy in Chicago in 1924 for reasons which, as even Leopold admits today, remain incomprehensible.[56] Political murders and assassinations come under the heading of murders from conviction, and include slayings such as those of Abraham Lincoln by John Wilkes Booth, John F. Kennedy by Lee Harvey Oswald, Robert Kennedy by Sirhan Sirhan, and Martin Luther King, Jr. by James Earl Ray.

Eleven categories of murderers have been noted by Mannfred Guttmacher who, before his recent death, headed the psychiatric clinic of the Baltimore courts. Guttmacher's categories overlap considerably, and presumably he would classify individual cases according to the characteristic most outstanding in the total picture. His categories are: (1) "The normal murderer," an individual marked by a reckless disregard for human life, although he is not psychotic, seems to kill because he does not appear to appreciate the deprivation he inflicts on others, (2) "the sociopathic murderer," fitting into Robert Lindner's description of a "rebel without a cause,"[57] who is an individual whose depredations are acts of war he is waging against society, (3) "the alcoholic murderer," (4) "the avenging murderer," who responds to the sudden withdrawal of erotic affection with murderously aggressive acts, (5) "the schizophrenic murderer," who is characterized by the hostility that is one of the dominant psychological traits of schizophrenia, (6) "the temporarily psychotic murderer," who is marked by episodic dyscontrol and typically shows a pattern of extreme parental violence and severe emotional deprivation in his background, (7) "the murderer whose act represents symbolic suicide," who, in psychiatric terms, destroys a part of himself that has been projected onto the victim, (8) "the gynocidal murderer," who kills a woman as a defense against castration fears, (9) "the homosexual murderer," who kills his partner, (10) "the passive-aggressive murderer," including individuals whose "hostile-aggressive reactions are constantly denied expression and are often so deeply buried that they themselves are totally unaware of them . . . [until] . . . there comes a stimulus of sufficient force to break through their defenses and the pent-up aggression explodes with all its volcanic force," (11) "the sadistic murderer."[58]

55 Jesse, *Murder and Its Motives*, pp. 9–62.
56 Leopold, *99 Years Plus Life*.
57 Lindner, *Rebel Without a Cause*.
58 Guttmacher, *The Mind of the Murderer*, pp. 3–108.

These eleven categories, while they may point to the dominant motifs in various murders, only form a somewhat convenient classification system, without telling us what elements in the individual or the society lead to specific forms of murder or what elements determine the form that will predominate. At best, the groups provide classificatory boxes into which we can put murderers before we dig deeper in an attempt to find distinguishing items that separate members of different groups.

A third attempt to delineate murderers is that developed by Max Grünhut, an English criminologist. Grünhut distinguishes between three classes of murderers in which: (1) the offender kills his wife, his mistress, or his wife's lover, (2) murders result from sexual impluses or are produced by a fight, (3) murders are committed in the course of robbery or burglary. Grünhut utilized his classification scheme to show that the rather sharp drop in homicide in England in recent years is not actually a uniform decline, but rather a downward movement marked by a striking decrease in killings that fall within the first group, whereas murders from sexual impulses and acquisitive motives have been increasing both absolutely and proportionately in England.[59]

Homicide and Suicide

The relationship between homicide and suicide has often provided an avenue of intriguing, sometimes almost mystical, research in criminology. Psychiatrists tend to see homicide and suicide as similar aspects of the same aggressive coin. Karl Menninger has theorized that suicide is made up of three components: the urge to kill, to be killed, and a desire to die.[60] Other theorists insist that if an individual is "undersocialized" he will direct his aggression toward others, but if he is "oversocialized" he will likely turn his aggression inward, upon himself. A variety of this theme has recently been expounded by James E. Teele who, on the basis of experimental evidence, concluded that commitment to broad cultural values, in contrast to a more traditional and narrowly based orientation, is likelier to result in suicidal behavior than in assaultive behavior. The most striking finding of Teele's study was that of a clearcut relationship between the social isolation of a person's mother and the individual's subsequent recourse to either homicide or suicide. More specifically, mothers who were highly participant in the culture were much more likely than isolated mothers to have suicidal children, while the reverse was true with respect to assaultiveness.[61]

The most intensive investigation of the hypothesis that homicide

59 Grünhut, "Murder and the Death Penalty in England."
60 Menninger, *Man Against Himself*, p. 71.
61 Teele, "Suicidal Behavior, Assaultiveness, and Socialization Principles," p. 517.

and suicide are inversely proportional to one another—that is, that cultures having high homicide rates should show low suicide rates, whereas those with high suicide rates should show small amounts of homicide—has been conducted by Andrew F. Henry and James F. Short, Jr. They concluded that a more realistic statement than the psychoanalytical position was that "suicide varies negatively and homicide positively with the strength of external restraint over behavior."[62] This finding blends somewhat with the position taken by Murray and Jacqueline Straus after an investigation into the relationship between the social structure in Ceylon and suicide and homicide. Although they found support for the psychoanalytical position of an inverse relationship between homicide and suicide, they felt that the relationship was more inadvertent than revealing. They concluded that "the suicide rate will vary directly, and the homicide rate inversely, with the degree to which a society is closely structured," defining a closely structured society as one in which little variation in individual behavior is sanctioned.[63]

Recent research has tended toward the view that suicide and homicide occur as comparatively independent acts and that their performance is tied to the definitions given to either or both by a particular society. Richard Quinney, for instance, after a study of rates in forty-eight countries, concluded that suicide rates tend to be high and homicide rates tend to be low in countries with high economic development, which is measured in terms of industrialization and urbanization. He was inclined, however, to the position that suicide and homicide are causally separate phenomena.[64] Palmer, studying geographically diverse, preliterate societies, found a high positive relationship between frequencies for *both* murder and suicide, and he suggested that in many societies the impetus toward aggression does not differentiate whether that aggression will be directed in suicidal or homicidal channels.[65]

These diverse studies, as well as the varying reported rates of suicide and homicide, which show some jurisdictions with high rates, others with low rates of both acts, and others with high rates of one type and low rates of the other, indicate that there is an intricate amalgam of items involved in the ultimate production of either suicidal or homicidal behavior.

Assault and Battery

Most of the offenses against the person that do not result in death —apart from several that we shall consider with the sex offenses—represent some form of assault and battery. Assault, contrary to popular

62 Henry and Short, Jr., *Suicide and Homicide.*
63 Straus and Straus, "Suicide, Homicide, and Social Structure in Ceylon."
64 Quinney, "Suicide, Homicide and Economic Development," p. 404.
65 Palmer, "Murder and Suicide in Forty Non-Literate Societies."

definition, in legal terms does not refer to the infliction of an injury, but rather to an incomplete *attempt or threat* to physically harm another person. The attempt must be reasonably related to the probability of harm actually ensuing, a requirement that has led to a morass of exquisitely differentiated court rulings. There is no question, for instance, that a person who brandishes an automobile tire jack against another person is guilty of assault, but the question becomes somewhat more complicated if a threat to injure is voiced on the telephone. It is considered an assault to shoot at a man, frighten him, and miss him. The flexibility of the definition of assault in Britain is, in fact, nicely illustrated by legal provisions that define the withdrawal of a person's blood without his consent as assault, whereas urinalysis conducted without consent is defined as theft.

Battery represents the nonlethal culmination of an assault. It is the carrying out of a threat. It is possible in some jurisdictions to have separate cases of either assault or battery. An assault need not be carried out; similarly, a battery can be committed without any prior threat or intimidation, as, for instance, in the case of an injury inflicted on a sleeping person. Many jurisdictions, in fact, label the more serious batteries as assault with a deadly weapon, aggravated assault, or assault with intent to commit murder. These statutorily defined assaults are invariably considered felony offenses, whereas simple assault and battery is usually a misdemeanor.

Little research has been undertaken regarding assault, partly because it seems so run-of-the-mill. Many of the offenders are often in the courts, and in a sizeable number of cases it is only the sheerest luck that prevents the incident from sliding over into the realm of criminal homicide. It is also true that threats against other persons that are uttered in quick temper are almost never reported to the police, unless the recipient of the threat is motivated by deep malice or considerable fear. Most simple batteries are private affairs between two or more disputants, and, unless the injuries inflicted are quite serious, the participants either shake hands and make up or go home and nurse their wounds and grievances in private. In many, if not most, segments of the society such affrays are considered to be the business only of the individuals involved and not of the police.

The most comprehensive investigation of aggravated assault is that by David J. Pittman and William Handy, which indicates the similarity in many respects between aggravated assault and homicide. The research team examined a 25 percent sample of 965 offenses classified as aggravated assault that were committed in St. Louis during 1961. Most of the acts, it was discovered, took place between ten and eleven o'clock in the evening, and a majority occurred on Saturday. The aggravated assaults that came to the attention of the police primarily were made on the streets rather than in taverns or private residences. A slightly greater number occurred during the summer than during the winter, a conclusion supporting the generalization that, all other things being equal, the more contact individuals have with each other, the more likely it is that such contacts will end in aggravated assault. Warm weather undoubtedly increases contact, and it is also likely that the hot weather of the summer frays tempers. Such fraying, however, would appear to be related as much to the culture as to the inherent nature of tempers, since many societies with very warm temperatures show low rates of aggressive crime.

Knives were the weapons used in 126 of the 241 cases in the St. Louis study, while guns were employed in only 39 cases, perhaps accounting for the fact that the incidents remained aggravated assaults rather than becoming criminal homicides. In thirty-five cases, both the offender and the victim were seriously wounded. The pattern of verbal aggression that spills over into physical force was particularly pronounced. In addition, in almost all cases (193 out of the 241), the identity of the offender was known to his victim, to the police, or to witnesses, and the cases were readily resolved by arrest. Alcohol figured into about one-quarter of the assaults and in equal proportions among offenders and victims. In fact, in 41 of the 241 cases, the offender and victim had been drinking together prior to the commission of the offense. There was a slight and interesting discrepancy in ages of offenders and victims, with the former being older in 106 cases and the latter in 82 cases. Even more pronounced was the variation in marital state, since 86 percent of the victims were married, whereas only 43 percent of the offenders were. As in homicide, very few (10 out of the 241) of the incidents of assault cut across racial lines. Arrest records indicated that many of the offenders had been charged previously with disturbing the peace but that few of them had been arrested for more serious crimes.[66]

An investigation of a group of battery offenders also presents a number of tantalizing clues to the theoretical explanation of this behavior, which should spur additional research. The study, by Kenneth G. Bromage and Harry V. Ball, confined its sample to fifteen cases, all juveniles who had committed battery, residing in San Bernardino, California. It found that 30 percent of the sample recidivated within a very short period of time, compared to only 2 percent of the juveniles charged with offenses other than battery. The battery offenders were discovered to be, in general, short and muscular, and each of the fifteen was reported to have an average or better intelligence. In contrast to most of the other juvenile offenders, the fifteen boys charged with battery were not known gang members. Each of the fifteen was active in boxing, wrestling, or some other form of muscle-building, although none engaged in standard competitive athletics at school.

Most eye-catching was the finding that the fathers of each of the

66 Pittman and Handy, "Patterns in Criminal Aggravated Assault"; see also Schultz, "The Wife Assaulter."

boys "refused to disapprove of his son's fighting to either the legal officials or to the boy." In addition, the fathers were found to be more aggressive than the boys' mothers. The amount of disturbance among the boys' mothers was also striking; seven of the fifteen mothers had been hospitalized in some mental institution, two others had received psychological treatment in a private sanatorium, and two admitted that they suffered from "nervous breakdowns." Bromage and Ball, evaluating the material they had gathered on the fifteen boys, conclude that there are "numerous similar elements in marked forms."[67] Unfortunately, they go no further in trying to draw these various elements into an explanatory pattern that relates to battery offenses, although their material suggests a number of hypotheses. Psychiatrists have constantly pointed to the deleterious effect of weak and passive fathers, who are superseded in child raising and child discipline by aggressive, domineering mothers—a pattern that is alleged to be particularly prevalent in the United States. Is it possible that weak or absent mothers may also be related in some manner to different forms of offenses? Or does a certain type of father influence his male son toward aggression at the same time that he pushes his wife toward nervous disorders? And what elements in the social structure lead certain fathers to put a high value on uncontrolled aggressive behavior, despite the social sanctions raised against uninhibited expressions of such behavior? These are only a few of the questions that need to be answered before we will be within range of a satisfactory understanding of crimes against the person.

For Further Reading

BOHANNAN, PAUL (ed.). *African Homicide and Suicide*. Princeton: Princeton University Press, 1960.
> The records of seven African tribes are examined in order to bring together information concerning the amount and type of homicide and suicide found within them. The book is particularly useful in putting European and American records and hypotheses into better perspective. The editor also supplies two chapters discussing relevant explanatory schemes for homicide and suicide.

PALMER, STUART. *A Study of Murder*. New York: Thomas Y. Crowell, 1960.
> Professor Palmer of the University of New Hampshire interviewed fifty-one murderers, their mothers, and a number of their relatives to acquire material for this study. Concentrating in particular on early home environment, the book also provides several elaborate case histories for interpretation.

WEST, D. J. *Murder Followed by Suicide*. Cambridge: Harvard University Press, 1966.
> The striking prevalence of suicide following murder in England and

67 Bromage and Ball, "A Study of Juvenile 'Battery' Cases."

Wales (about one-third of the murder cases) in contrast to the United States, prompted this inquiry into the dynamics of murder-suicide. The author concludes that the most striking distinguishing features of his murder-suicide sample were the large number of women offenders and child victims, the very small number of offenders with previous convictions, and the total absence of the young offender who kills during theft or robbery.

WOLFGANG, MARVIN E. *Patterns in Criminal Homicide.* Philadelphia: University of Pennsylvania Press, 1958.

The city of Philadelphia provides the locale for this elaborate investigation of homicides committed during a four-year period. As a source of numerical data, providing a base for further theoretical analysis, this volume is extremely valuable.

WOOD, ARTHUR L. *Crime and Aggression in Changing Ceylon,* in *Transactions.* Philadelphia: American Philosophical Society, December 1961.

This volume appraises crimes in Ceylon, especially homicides and suicides, on the basis of variations in reactions by the offenders to strains imposed upon their subjectively defined status. The study has particular value in terms of its cross-cultural insights.

10
The Sex Offenses

Sex offenses point up many of the shortcomings of broad classifications of illegal behavior. The general category of "sex offenses" includes some forms of behavior that are almost universally regarded as serious breaches of the social order, other forms that are but mild deviations from sanctioned behavior, and still other forms that, while outlawed, are engaged in by a large majority of the adult members of our society.

This is but one of the unique aspects of sexual offenses. Sexual behavior in our society represents one of the most emotion-laden areas of life and deep and sensitive feelings about it often serve to shunt aside dispassionate consideration of its dynamics. We are often simultaneously attracted and repelled by different aspects of sexual behavior. The result has been that much misinformation surrounds sexual offenses, which has led to distortions in dealing with sex offenders.

In addition to the emotional biases that handicap scientific consideration of sex offenses, there is the general difficulty of delineating clearly the bounds of these offenses and the specific character of acts that fall within such bounds. Some psychiatrists, for instance, insist that all human behavior can be traced to a sexual base, and by obvious extension, therefore, that all criminal behavior can be tied to sexual or libidinal sources. Thus, one who exceeds the speed limit is said to do so because such behavior provides him with sexual satisfaction, and a murderer is claimed to dispatch his victim because of the offender's unresolved sexual conflicts. The denominator of such a position apparently is that all human action is meaningful in terms of some attempt to achieve emotional satisfaction. If all emotional satisfaction is by definition regarded as sexual in nature, then it can be maintained that all crimes are sexual crimes. But this position hardly sheds much useful light on the distinctive nature of overtly sexual crimes.

An approach to sex crimes that confines itself only to acts that are generally considered to fall into this category must admit that there are additional offenses that, while not usually considered sex crimes, obviously have deep-lying sexual implications. William Heirens, now confined to the Illinois State Penitentiary, never committed an act that might formally be considered a sex crime, yet in the course of his activities Heirens took part in more than 300 burglaries and admitted achieving orgasm merely from entering strange residences. When interrupted during his burglaries, Heirens three times killed the females he encountered and on each occasion spent considerable time afterwards carefully washing the bodies of his victims. It was Heirens, also, who left the strange message, written with lipstick in large letters on a living-room wall, where he had just murdered a woman: "CATCH ME BEFORE I KILL MORE I CANNOT CONTROL MYSELF." No one can dispute the camouflaged sexual meaning in many of Heirens' acts.[1]

Sexual offenses can be broken down into a number of types. Stanton Wheeler, for instance, distinguishes four broad categories of sex offenses. First, are offenses that involve a *degree of consent,* such as in statutory rape. Second, are offenses that grow out of laws that place limits on the *nature of the sexual object.* Most states, for example, restrict legitimate sex objects to humans, of the opposite sex, of roughly the same age, and of a certain social distance in kinship terms. Third, are offenses against legal restrictions that are placed on the *nature of the sexual act,* which is restricted largely to acts of heterosexual intercourse. Fourth, are offenses against laws that attempt to control the *setting in which the sexual act occurs.* Relationships and behavior that otherwise would be ignored may be subject to interference when they occur publicly.[2] Each of the categories admits of many variations in the characteristics of the persons involved, the dynamics of the activities, and the particular forms the behavior takes.

Sex and the Individual

Within the limits of their physical characteristics, human beings are capable of any type of sexual activity. It remains to be shown with greater precision how personal and cultural conditions blend with genetic traits to induce any given individual to participate in certain types of sexual activity and to provide him with adequate incentive to continue in such behavior.

Much philosophical and legal debate concerning sexual offenses centers around definitions of the word "normal," since our society outlaws many sexual activities on the ground that they are abnormal

1 Freeman, *"Before I Kill More."*
2 Wheeler, "Sex Offenses: A Sociological Critique," pp. 79–80.

acts. Acceptance of one or another definition of normality leads to diverse interpretations of the behavior being judged. Some persons maintain that sexual acts that result in reproduction constitute the only type of normal sexual behavior. By this criterion premarital petting and various marital sexual techniques may be defined as abnormal.

Other persons insist that normal and abnormal can best be defined by reference to theological writings and proscriptions. Considerable controversy, however, ensues concerning the extent to which theological doctrines should be translated into criminal codes. It is sometimes maintained that the enactment of theological concepts into law unjustly forces individuals who do not accept such concepts to refrain from activities that they may regard as moral and that have not been shown to injure the general society. Speaking of homosexuality, Bertrand Russell says,

> If it were still believed, as it once was, that the toleration of such behavior would expose the community to the fate of Sodom and Gomorrah, the community would have every right to interfere. But where such factual beliefs do not prevail, private practice among adults, however abhorrent it may be to the majority, is not a proper subject for coercive action for a state whose object is to minimize coercion.[3]

A contrary view maintains that, as a traditionally Christian nation, we have a duty to insist on standards of Christian morality from all members of the society.

Our legal codes take no consistent stand on this problem. Some acts, such as homosexuality and other forms of sodomy, are outlawed primarily because they are offensive to theological precepts; in other cases, behavior that is condemned in the Judeo-Christian religions, such as masturbation, is ignored by our laws.* Adultery, too, a heinous religious sin, is not outlawed by a number of American states, and only a handful of jurisdictions have statutes that punish fornication or sexual relations between unmarried persons, although this form of behavior has always been regarded as a serious breach of religious morality. This morality is, in fact, almost uniquely a characteristic of societies such as ours, for, as Clyde Kluckhohn points out, not more than 5 percent of the world's population condemns fornication and, in this respect, "our sexual code is even more of an ethnological curiosity than is cannibalism or the couvade."[4]

A third position regarding the judgment of normality concentrates on comparisons between behavior in humans and behavior in infrahuman species. The assumption in this approach is that forms of

3 Quoted in Hayek, *Constitution of Liberty*, p. 451.
* Exceptions are Indiana (Stat. Ann. §10-4221, 1956) and Wyoming (Comp. Stat. §6-98, 1957) which consider it a crime to "entice, allure, instigate or aid" a person under 21 to masturbate.
4 Quoted in Murdock, *Social Structure*, p. 47.

sexual conduct that are found, for instance, among chimpanzees are "normal" forms, which have only come to be labelled "perverted" through social interpretations. Seymour L. Halleck observes that "almost any kind of [sexual] behavior humans can think of has some phylogenetic and ontogenetic basis."[5] Somewhat similar to this approach is that which examines behavior from a cross-cultural perspective. Proponents of this view maintain that if societies can be found in which all or most members engage in certain forms of sexual behavior, then logic is stretched unreasonably by defining such behavior as abnormal for the human species.

All of the foregoing points of view compete for acceptance in the determination of the forms of sexual behavior that legally shall be tolerated. As noted, American society has reacted with various compromise approaches that are rather inconsistent in nature. We have traditionally shown a tendency to reflect, although belatedly, variations in sexual mores by alterations in laws and even more by failure to enforce statutory prohibitions against forms of behavior that are no longer offensive to the moral feelings of the community. Robert V. Sherwin's observation about the condition of today's laws regarding sexual behavior that, "The normal forty to sixty year lag which has always existed between the creation of mores and the codification of such mores into statute seems about up, so that one has hope that the dawn of appropriate legal administration of human sexual behavior is closer at hand than would appear on the surface."[6]

Sex and American Society

The importance of sexual components in American culture can hardly be overestimated. Sexual offenses must be tied to these cultural roots, since both the denotation of offenses and their prevalence vary significantly from culture to culture.

In the United States there exists a strong cultural stress on sexuality, which contrasts strikingly to the rather severe limitations placed upon participation in many forms of sexual activity. On the pattern of propellants and restraints in the American ethos regarding sexual conduct, Paul H. Gebhard and his associates in the Kinsey Institute at Indiana University say that:

> It is difficult to find logic in our culture vis-à-vis adult heterosexuality. On the one hand we stress and encourage the development of heterosexual behavior—the literature, the advertisements, the movies, everything relentlessly dins in the order: be sexually attractive, find romance, get a mate! On the other hand we strive to prevent heterosexual coitus, the logical end-product of the social campaign for heterosexuality, in any situation other than legal marriage. We tread on the accelerator

5 Halleck, *Psychiatry and the Dilemmas of Crime*, p. 178.
6 Sherwin, "The Law and Sexual Relationships," p. 109.

and brake simultaneously; this may result in the desired speed, but it is rough on the mechanism.[7]

At least a segment—possibly a very large segment—of sexual offenses appears to represent an attempt by the individual to respond in some manner to almost imperative social demands for sexual behavior. Such responses follow paths that are compatible with the experiences and definitions of permissible conduct that are implanted in the individual as these combine with available types of opportunity. The homosexual need never indulge his sexual appetite, for instance; he could remain sexually inactive, as do some segments of the world's population. It might be postulated that he engages in homosexual behavior, however, because of cultural pressures stressing the desirability of heterosexual behavior as these combine with cultural roadblocks, such as those that limit the number and type of females available for heterosexual activity, that define women (the male's mother, most particularly) as asexual individuals, and that indoctrinate him with deep guilt feelings about the sinfulness of heterosexual conduct prior to marriage. It might be hypothesized, on this basis, that a society that places strong stress on heterosexual behavior in contrast to homosexual behavior and also presents the individual with adequate opportunity to engage in such behavior would produce few, if any, homosexuals. When a society, on the other hand, stresses heterosexual behavior but does not provide adequate opportunities for such behavior, sexual deviation will be one major form of response. Finally, where sexuality is not stressed, and where few opportunities are available, heterosexual activity as well as deviation from it will be at a minimum.

Albert Cohen clearly marks the constellation of behavior that constitutes one aspect of the social equation discussed above. He describes the sexual patterns of girls interested in vertical social mobility—that is, movement up the ladder of social success—who must submit themselves to a strict behavior regimen to achieve their goals. The regimen should be interpreted in terms of the response it might induce in others:

> With respect to sexuality, it is not repression which is required . . . but something perhaps more difficult: the development of skills in the management and husbandry of her sexual resources. She must make shrewd use of her sexuality but must employ it with discretion . . . and must display her carefully cultivated charms as provocatively as "good taste" will allow. She must, like a magnet, exert an attractive force on male objects; unlike a magnet, she must keep those objects rotating in a narrow orbit around her person without actual contact with them. It is a delicate art but there are many adepts.[8]

7 Gebhard, *Sex Offenders*, p. 108.
8 Cohen, *Delinquent Boys*, p. 146.

Complementing Cohen's observations is an illustration of how female stratagems may affect a young man, in this instance a war veteran returning to his home town as portrayed by Ernest Hemingway:

> [The young girls] were too complicated. There was something else. Vaguely he wanted a girl but he did not want to have to work to get her. He would have liked to have a girl, but he did not want to have to spend a long time getting her. He did not want to get into the intrigue and the politics. He did not want to have to do any courting. He did not want to tell any more lies. It wasn't worth it.[9]

Sexual offenses develop in this manner from the stresses and strains within a society. Sex offenders represent individuals in our society who have not learned to abide by those rules of behavior that are reflected in the criminal codes, or do not care to do so, or in one manner or another are incapable of doing so. The erratic nature of the laws as well as the diverse characteristics of the offenders must always be kept in mind. It should also be remembered, as Hulsey Cason notes, that no matter how repulsive or ridiculous some deviations may appear, at some time and at some place almost all have been socially approved and accepted.[10] Albert Ellis and Ralph Brancale, studying sex offenders, make a similar observation concerning our cultural ambivalence toward premarital sexual acts that, they note, "are actually considered to be both nasty and tasty, both frightful and delightful."[11] Illegal responses to such ambivalence is what we shall now consider.

Forcible Rape

Legally, rape is defined as sexual intercourse by a male with a female other than his wife, by force or threat, and without consent. Consent cannot legally be given by women who are insane, mentally incompetent, or insensible at the time of the act because of intoxication, narcotic stupor, or similar indispositions. Some criticism has been leveled against these restrictions because they fail to account for varying culpability, such as when a female willingly produces the state of intoxication through her voluntary behavior.[12] In common law, adopted by the American states from Britain in 1776, a male under the age of fourteen was legally incapable of committing rape, and this provision still applies in Britain,[13] but many American jurisdictions no longer set a specific age limit.

There is much incorrect information surrounding the extent of

9 Hemingway, *In Our Time*, pp. 92–93.
10 Cason, "A Case of Sexual Psychopathy."
11 Ellis and Brancale, *Psychology of Sex Offenders*, p. 124.
12 Ploscowe, *Sex and the Law*, pp. 174–175.
13 Radzinowicz, *Sex Offences*, p. 324.

rape offenses, some of it apparently promulgated in attempts to frighten females into thinking of themselves as potential victims. While forcible rape is often an explosive act containing potentialities for serious harm, the number of such acts is generally widely overestimated. Sutherland, tabulating national reports of female murders in the years 1930, 1935, and 1940, found that there were 324 females killed in those years. Only seventeen deaths were reported to involve rape or suspicion of rape. Nearly 60 percent of the murders of females were committed by relatives or intimate acquaintances, and in one of the three years surveyed, as many women were murdered by policemen as by so-called "sex fiends."[14] Interpreting these findings, some persons have made the facetious observation that the American female is actually safer on a dark street than in her own kitchen.

Most attempts to measure the extent of rape in our society have involved projections from figures reported by police forces throughout the nation to the F.B.I. In 1966, there were reports of about 25,000 cases of forcible rape. It has been claimed that only one out of twenty rape cases becomes known to the police, which would raise the total appreciably.[15] The survey of victimization conducted by the President's Commission on Law Enforcement and Administration of Justice, however, concluded that rape occurs some $3\frac{1}{2}$ times more often than it is reported to the police, although this estimate was considered to be conservative.[16] The F.B.I. is inclined to believe that of serious offenses "forcible rape is probably the most underreported, due primarily to fear and/or embarrassment on the part of many victims."[17]

In actual fact, neither the reported figures on forcible rape nor those arrived at by surveys or extrapolation are altogether reliable. Many rape offenses reported to the police do not represent crimes, but rather are charges leveled to save reputations or for purposes of blackmail. In addition, it is well known that reports to the police of alleged rape offenses tend to increase after widespread publicity concerning any notorious sex crime, although subsequent investigations demonstrate that many of these reports are totally unfounded. Also, it can never be determined accurately how many forcible rape cases involve real resistance to the attack and how many involve merely token resistance in which the criminal charge is an afterthought. In a number of instances, the victim is known to the offender, although the exact percentage of such cases is a matter of some dispute. Gebhard and his associates, for instance, report that 72 percent of the victims were strangers to the offender, 17 percent were "friends" and 9 percent were acquaintances.[18] Menachem Amir, however, investigating 646 cases of rape in Philadelphia, found that in 48 percent of the cases the

14 Sutherland, "Sexual Psychopath Laws."
15 Quoted in Wittels, "What Can We Do About Sex Crimes?", p. 30.
16 President's Commission, *Crime and Its Impact*, p. 17.
17 Federal Bureau of Investigation, *Uniform Crime Reports, 1966*, p. 11.
18 Gebhard, *Sex Offenders*, p. 195.

victim and the offender were known to each other.[19] The discrepancy between the two studies may be a function of their samples. The Gebhard probe was confined to imprisoned white males, while Amir, ranging more widely, used police reports that included both Negro and white cases as well as some 120 cases that had not been solved and that, by definition would have been outside the Gebhard study. It is also possible that prison sentences are less likely to be imposed upon persons charged with rape when the complainant is well known to them, on the assumption that the victim was at least in part responsible for the offense.

Amir also found that rape was essentially an intraracial event and that Negroes constitute a higher proportion of offenders than whites. Both Gebhard and Amir were impressed with the role of alcohol in rape offenses. Gebhard noted that liquor involvement is "omnipresent" in rape as well as in all sex offenses.[20] Amir indicated that in 217 of his cases there was clear evidence of the use of alcohol by one of the participants, and in 63 percent of these cases both the victim and the offender had been drinking. Perhaps most eye-catching is Amir's finding that 19 percent of the *victims* of rape offenses had arrest records, and 56 percent of these had been for "some sort of sexual offense."[21]

Youthful offenders are particularly prevalent among persons convicted of forcible rape. The average age of the rapists in the Gebhard sample at the time they committed their offense was 24½ years.[22] Only 6 percent of the rapists studied by Manfred Guttmacher in his job as psychiatrist for the Baltimore courts were past the age of thirty,[23] and Emil Frankel, using statistics from New Jersey, reported that forcible rape seemed to be committed most frequently by persons under the age of twenty-five.[24] Partly because of their concentration among younger persons, the majority of rapists are unmarried, which relates in some cases to a concomitant lack of available sexual partners. Also entwined in this etiological context are the characteristics of the offender that have kept him from getting married, which may aid in explaining his rape offense. In his study of rapists in the Wisconsin prison population, for instance, John Gillin found that many rapists had physical disabilities, which he believed constituted important factors in their failure to make morally and socially sanctioned sex adjustments.[25]

Analysis of the prior criminal records of offenders discloses that rapists show no significant history of previous, less violent sexual offenses, such as indecent exposure. Among the thirty-six most serious

19 Amir, "Patterns of Forcible Rape," p. 67.
20 Gebhard, Sex Offenders, p. 201.
21 Amir, "Patterns of Forcible Rape," pp. 63–65.
22 Gebhard, Sex Offenders, p. 193.
23 Guttmacher, Sex Offenses, p. 67.
24 Cited in Karpman, Sexual Offender and His Offenses, p. 36.
25 Gillin, Wisconsin Prisoner, p. 129.

sex offenders that he encountered as chief medical officer for the Baltimore courts, Guttmacher found only one who had previously been involved in serious sex difficulty.[26] Such findings lead to one of the most significant conclusions concerning sex offenders in general: *The sex offender rarely progresses from less serious to more serious offenses.* Paul W. Tappan notes that progress occurs only in exceptional cases,[27] and a Michigan study of sex offenders underlines the same point: "There is no evidence that sex offenders in general progress in any significant numbers . . . from sex misdemeanors to sex felonies."[28] The explanation for lack of progression in offense lies in the fact that sex offenses are undertaken to satisfy particular desires—and, to the extent that the offenses do in fact serve their purpose, the actor will usually persist in the same pattern or a pattern closely related to it in terms of its basic dynamics.

In addition to research conclusions that show that rapists have not graduated from less serious offenses to this more serious one, other studies disclose that rapists are more likely to have prior criminal records for nonsexual offenses, in particular, for robbery and burglary, than for sex offenses. Also, among all sex offenders, rapists are the least likely to have *any* prior criminal records. Of 250 sex offenders studied at the Diagnostic Center in New Jersey, forcible rapists constituted 3.2 percent of the offenders, but those with previous records constituted only 1.3 percent of the total number with previous criminal records.[29]

In an effort to account for the variations among rapists and rape offenses, Guttmacher divided rapists into three categories: (1) those in whom the assault is an explosive expression of pent-up sexual impulse, (2) sadistic rapists, who want to injure the victim, and (3) aggressive criminals. Guttmacher does not consider this last group true sex offenders but, rather, criminals who are out to "pillage and rob" and for whom rape is "apparently just another act of plunder."[30] Many of Guttmacher's types show up in the five major varieties of rapists discerned by Gebhard and his associates, who believe that the most common type is the "assaultive variety," which is composed of men whose behavior is marked by "unnecessary violence" and who have a "strong sadistic element" in them. From one-quarter to one-third of the total number of offenders were considered to fit this category. The second most common variety was labelled "amoral delinquents," who pay little heed to social controls and operate on a level of egocentric hedonism. They are not hostile to females, but look upon them solely as sexual objects whose role in life is to provide sexual pleasure. The third group is classified as the "drunken variety" and the fourth

26 Guttmacher, *Sex Offenses*, p. 113.
27 Tappan, "Sexual Psychopath," p. 354.
28 Dunham, *Crucial Issues in Sexual Deviation*, p. 10.
29 Ellis and Brancale, *Psychology of Sex Offenders*, pp. 31–34.
30 Guttmacher, *Sex Offenses*, p. 50.

as the "explosive variety," men whose prior life offers no surface indications of what is to come. The fifth group is called the "double-
standard variety," and is composed of men who divide women into
good females, to be treated with some respect, and bad females, who
are not entitled to consideration if they become obstinate. These
five categories account for two-thirds of the rapists Gebhard studied.
A few of the remainder could be classified as clear cases of mental
defectives and a few others as psychotics, but the rest of the forcible
rape offenders were seen as mixtures of the described varieties.[31]

CULTURAL PERSPECTIVES ON RAPE

Rape represents in our society the most serious of the sexual offenses
and, in fact, judged by the penalties prescribed, the most serious
of all criminals offenses, with the exception of murder. Conviction
on a forcible rape charge carries the death penalty in three states—
Arkansas, Louisiana, and North Carolina—while fifteen other states
punish rape with either death or life imprisonment. All of these
states—except Nevada—are southern or Border States, and capital
punishment is almost always applied only in cases of miscegenous
rape, that is, rape offenses by Negro males against white females.
There were 444 executions for rape in the eighteen states between
1930 and 1962, and 399 of those executed were Negroes. Six of the
states have never executed anyone but a Negro for rape. Since 1908,
for instance, when Virginia got its electric chair, forty-one persons have
been executed for rape, thirteen for attempted rape, one for rape and
robbery, and one for attempted rape and robbery. All were Negroes,
despite the fact that Negroes make up only twenty-five percent of the
state's population and despite the fact that whites have been convicted
of 44 percent of the rapes in that state.[32]

There are some societies in which rape is virtually unknown.
The Arapesh, a mountain-dwelling New Guinea tribe, for instance,
according to Margaret Mead, know nothing of rape "beyond the fact
that it is the unpleasant custom of the Nugum people to the southeast
of them"; she further reports that Arapesh do not have any conception
of a male nature that would make rape understandable to them.[33] On
the other hand, the Gusii, a tribe located in the Kenya highlands,
shows a rape rate that is conservatively estimated to be four to five
times higher than that in the United States. The dynamics of rape
among the Gusii provides extraordinary insight into the manner in
which a culture can elicit aggressive sex offenses. Marriages, for instance, are viewed as intersex contests involving force and pain-in-
flicting behavior, largely because the male has to obtain a bride from
an adjacent tribe, traditionally the enemy of his own, because of

31 Gebhard, *Sex Offenders*, pp. 197–205.
32 Partington, "Incidence of the Death Penalty for Rape in Virginia," p. 43.
33 Mead, *Sex and Temperament in Three Primitive Societies*, pp. 80–81.

exogamous demands. Girls resist sexual encounters with their husbands and berate them ceaselessly in regard to their sexual competence.
There is also a good deal of the same kind of teasing behavior found
in the United States, as Robert LaVine's ethnographic statement
indicates:

> Gusii girls who have no desire for sexual relationships deliberately en-
> courage young men in the preliminaries of courtship because they enjoy
> the gifts and attention they receive. Some of them act provocatively,
> thinking they will be able to obtain the desired articles and then es-
> cape the sexual advances of the young man. . . . An aggressive conclu-
> sion is particularly likely if the girl is actually married. In the early
> stages of marriage brides spend a good deal of time in their home
> communities visiting their parents. Such a girl may . . . pretend to be
> unmarried in order to be bribed and flattered. No matter how emo-
> tionally and financially involved in her a young man becomes, the
> bride is too afraid of supernatural sanctions against adultery to yield
> to him sexually. After she fails to appear at several appointments . . .
> he may rape her in desperation the next time they meet, and she will
> report the deed.[34]

Four items are believed to be present in the Gusii situation,
which will be found in any group with a high frequency of rape: (1)
severe formal restrictions on nonmarital sexual relations of females,
(2) moderately strong sexual inhibitions on the part of females, (3)
economic or other barriers to marriage that prolong the bachelorhood
of some males into their late twenties, and (4) the absence of physical
segregation of the sexes. The fourth condition distinguishes high
rape societies from societies in which women are secluded, where rape
is not feasible and homosexuality may be practiced instead. The
four items, LaVine notes, are necessary conditions for a high frequency
of rape, but not sufficient ones, since these conditions may also be
found in societies with prostitution or other functional alternatives to
rape.[35]

ENCEPHALITIS AND RAPE

Benjamin Karpman has observed that rapists manifest a high number
of cases of postencephalitic brain damage. His implication is that
encephalitis infections, which affect brain cells and, particularly among
younger persons, can sometimes lead to personality disturbances, are
directly related to subsequent rape offenses.[36] This implied relationship between postencephalitis and criminal behavior constitutes one
of the more controversial areas in criminal theory, since it challenges
the theoretical belief that *all* criminal behavior is the outcome of
learning and association processes.

Encephalitis is characterized by its sudden onset, high fever,

34 LaVine, "Gusii Sex Offenses," p. 983.
35 *Ibid.*, p. 987.
36 Karpman, *Sexual Offender and His Offenses*, p. 92.

headaches, and dizziness. Within a day or two drowsiness and stupor overcome the victim, and he becomes mentally confused and has speech difficulties. In severe cases convulsions and coma develop. The viruses of encephalitis damage the spinal cord and brain, disrupt or destroy nerve cells, and frequently damage small blood vessels that supply the brain. While mosquitoes get most of the blame for spreading the disease, it is believed that birds, both wild and domestic, may be the reservoir where the mosquitoes and possibly other insects pick up the virus and then infect humans through their bites.[37]

The case for postencephalitic conditions as a causative factor in crime relies on a considerable number of histories of individuals who prior to the onset of the syndrome were apparently well-adjusted and law-abiding but then subsequent to the attack erupted into a wide range of uninhibited and criminal behaviors.[38] Caryl Chessman, a California criminal, claimed to have suffered as a child from encephalitis.[39] Sol Levy studied 100 delinquents, all postencephalitis cases, whom he describes as overactive, restless, with short attention and concentration spans, unpredictable, acting before thinking, destructive, and usually not showing any remorse and not learning by experience.[40] Nolan Lewis, discussing arson, maintains that "encephalitis assumes the foremost place as a precipitating factor with the juvenile and post-adolescent incendiaries and their largest number are dangerous pyromaniacs,"[41] while David Abrahamsen insists that in a small number of cases, including those of persons who have acquired a disease such as encephalitis, the label "born criminal" is valid.[42]

Sutherland, on the other hand, maintains that while the case for encephalitis as a causal factor appears to be strong, the relationship between the disorder and crime is by no means as direct as it might seem to be. He offers three possible explanations for the association between encephalitis and crime, all of which involve social learning. First, there is the fact that the lesions in the central nervous system produce irritability and reduce efficiency and inhibitions, and consequently the child acts impulsively. These effects may then persist beyond the acute stage of the disease, Sutherland points out, because of habit formation. A second explanation is that the inferiority resulting from the disorder lowers the child's status, and criticisms and ostracism, such as that from parents and teachers, cause the child to do less well than previously, and "drive the child desperate." A third possible explanation offered by Sutherland is that the encephalitic patient who has subsequent behavior problems comes in general from

37 Laurence, "Gain Reported in Fight Against Encephalitis."
38 Bond and Appel, *Treatment of Behavior Disorders Following Encephalitis*, pp. 9, 14, 17; Pfeiffer, *Human Brain*, pp. 116–117.
39 Chessman, *Cell 2455*, pp. 29–30.
40 Levy, "Post-Encephalitic Behavior Disorder"; Levy, "Juvenile Delinquency."
41 Lewis and Yarnell, *Pathological Firesetting*, p. 387.
42 Abrahamsen, *Who Are the Guilty?*, p. 227.

a family with other difficulties, such as extreme poverty and mental illness.[43] These explanations, standing as hypotheses, need considerable further investigation, as does the entire area of scientific problems relating to brain injury and criminal behavior.

STATUTORY RAPE

Sexual intercourse by a male with a consenting female who is under a specified age constitutes the crime of statutory or consensual rape. It is generally irrelevant whether or not the male is actually aware of the girl's true age, and it is equally irrelevant that he might have been misled by her to believe that she was above the age of consent. The first small break in this doctrine appeared, however, in a 1964 case in which a conviction for statutory rape was reversed on the ground that it was necessary to prove criminal intent, and that an offender could not possess the requisite intent to commit the offense if he was unaware that the victim was underage.[44] In general, however, courts take the following viewpoint on deception or culpability on the victim's part; the flowery, victorian prose of the court's opinion can be taken as an indication of a major source of the laws against statutory rape:

> It matters nothing that this girl was forward. . . . The statute was enacted to protect just such girls as this one from their own folly. The legislature has said, in effect, of the adolescent girl under 16 years: "The brook has not yet met the river. She is merely a child—a child perplexed at the disquiet of puberty; confused by emotions she cannot fathom, and unable to comprehend the significance of those emotions to her own being, or their relation to society. She is incapable of consenting to the desecration of her incipient womanhood." The statute makes her sexual profanation a ravishment, even though invited. It has therefore erected a barrier of years around wilful girlhood—a barrier across which the profligate proceeds at his peril.[45]

There have been cases of males who were prosecuted for statutory rape for having engaged in sexual relations with a professional prostitute when the girl was under the age of consent. The age specified by law for consent varies throughout the United States, although it has risen considerably above the ten- and twelve-year-old limits that were formerly part of the English common law. In the United States, the lowest is fourteen in Georgia, and the highest is twenty-one in Tennessee. Most states use the age of eighteen, and it is noteworthy that in many jurisdictions the legal age of consent to sexual relations is well above the legal age a girl may marry. In fact, it is possible in most states for a man to be prosecuted for statutory rape if he engages in a sexual relationship with a consenting married female

43 Sutherland and Cressey, *Principles of Criminology*, pp. 168–169.
44 *People v. Hernandez;* Myers, "Reasonable Mistake of Age."
45 *State v. Adkins*, p. 734.

under the age of eighteen.[46] The maximum penalties for statutory
rape are exceeded only by those for murder and equaled only by
those for forcible rape and kidnapping. Unless the jury recommends
mercy, the death sentence is mandatory in six states, and a death
sentence is possible in an additional ten states.[47]

Many persons do not understand the precise legal components of
statutory rape, and offenders who are convicted of the offense often
find that they are regarded with the same scorn that society turns
upon more serious sex offenders. Part of this problem could be allevi-
ated if the United States used the less inflammatory designation of
"unlawful carnal knowledge," as England does,[48] for it is clear that
in most instances statutory rape is not similar to rape because there
is no element of force or threat.[49] Comparing the general public,
criminology students, and prison inmates on how serious they felt
various crimes to be, G. M. Gilbert discovered wide discrepancies in
their evaluations of statutory rape, which he reported as follows:

> statutory rape is ranked fairly high in severity by the general public,
> sharing a rank order of 5.5 with armed robbery. The criminology stu-
> dents, however, drop it down to about midpoint in the criminality
> scale (10.5), along with larceny, while equating actual rape with armed
> robbery. The wide difference . . . would be attributed by this writer
> to the thoughtless emotionalism of the public toward the rapist symbol,
> contrasted with the better-informed evaluation by the criminology
> students of an offense which constitutes rape in name only. The in-
> termediate ranking by the convict group (7.5) evidently reflects a tem-
> pering of their better-informed state by the deprecatory attitude toward
> sex crimes revealed in their written comments.[50]

Statutory rape dominates the statistics regarding sex offenses.
The Mayor's Committee investigating sex offenses in New York City
in the 1940s found that 59 percent of all such offenses in the court of
general sessions and in the county courts were statutory rape.[51] H.
Warren Dunham's study in Michigan found a somewhat smaller percentage, with statutory rape constituting 30 percent of all sex offenses.[52]
That prosecutions represent but a minute fraction of offenses can
readily be seen by reference to the findings reported in the Kinsey
study of the sexual behavior of American females. Somewhat more than
10 percent of Kinsey's sample reported having engaged in sexual
intercourse at age seventeen or earlier.[53] If this finding has wider
validity than the sample interviewed, it would indicate the commission

46 Ploscowe, *Sex and the Law*, pp. 178–184.
47 Kinsey, *Sexual Behavior in the Human Male*, pp. 287–288. See also Drummond,
   The Sex Paradox, pp. 347–348.
48 Hughes, "Consent in Sexual Offenses," pp. 678–679.
49 Sherwin, *Sex and the Statutory Law*, p. 73.
50 Gilbert, "Crime and Punishment."
51 New York City, Mayor's Committee, *Problem of Sex Offenses*, p. 45.
52 Dunham, *Crucial Issues in Sexual Deviation*, p. 15.
53 Kinsey, *Sexual Behavior in the Human Female*, p. 333.

of statutory rape offenses involving at least 4 or 5 million American women and probably as many males.

Considerable research evidence points up that persons convicted of statutory rape represent the least aberrant of all sex offenders. R. W. Bowling reports no personality deviations whatsoever in cases where there was little age discrepancy between the participants,[54] a finding corroborated in other studies.[55]

The failure of the criminal law to specify more clearly the social harm inherent in the various types of behavior that it labels "statutory rape" and to separate trivial acts from meretricious behavior permeates consideration of this offense. Few persons would deny that the law has a right to protect young girls from exploitation, particularly if they lack the sophistication to be aware of the implications of their behavior. It seems valid to maintain, however, that statutory rape laws as they now stand often do an injustice. Such laws seem to discriminate in particular against segments of the society that have social and sexual mores that are not necessarily harmful but are merely different from those of the progenitors of the laws defining the criminal offense of statutory rape.

VOYEURISM

Voyeurism, or scoptophilia, is the act of window-peeping, generally for the purpose of viewing a female disrobing. Comparatively little research has been conducted concerning sociological correlates of this form of behavior, although we have an elaborate psychiatric framework that attempts to interpret it. The psychiatric approach maintains that window-peeping represents the acting out of thwarted impulses to view female nudity and heterosexual activity, impulses that are strangled in the growing child and disallowed in the adult. Empirical support for this position is derived from studies that characterize voyeurs as products of restricted and inhibited home environments. This element alone, however, cannot account for the behavior, because, as Yushi Honde points out, Japanese children are severely punished for peeping activities, yet Japan's police reports show hardly any adult voyeurist behavior.[56]

Voyeuristic acts have a well-established history in both past and current folklore. Tennyson immortalized the tale of Peeping Tom who was said to be a curious tailor who dared view Lady Godiva riding nude on a palfrey through the market place in Coventry, and was struck blind for his impunity.[57]

> And one low churl
> Boring a little augur hole in fear

54 Bowling, "Sex Offender and the Law."
55 See, for instance, Ellis and Brancale, *Psychology of Sex Offenders*, p. 55.
56 Quoted in Karpman, *Sexual Offender and His Offenses*, p. 558.
57 Hartland, *Science of Fairy Tales*, pp. 71–79.

Peeped—but his eyes before they had their will
Were shrivelled into darkness in his head
And dropt before him.[58]

Contemporary cartoons constantly poke fun at the ogling of pretty girls by middle-aged men, while the burlesque show with its strip-tease represents an institutionalized form of voyeurism.

Elements in our social structure that lead to voyeurism seem rather clear. Both nudity and coital activities are regarded as highly private matters. On the other hand, a certain social attraction is inculcated in virtually all males toward viewing sexually-keyed behavior unobserved; as Gebhard notes, "even a gynecologist will stop or slacken his pace at least momentarily to look at a pretty girl undressing before her window."[59] Kinsey has spelled the matter out in greater detail:

> There are probably very few heterosexual males who would not take advantage of the opportunity to observe a nude female, or to observe heterosexual activity, particularly if it were possible to do so surreptitiously so they would not suffer the social disgrace that the discovery of their behavior might bring. To many males, the observation of a female who is undressing may be erotically more stimulating than observing her when she is fully nude, for the undressing suggests, in fantasy, what they may ultimately be able to observe. Consequently, we have the peeper who gets into difficulty with the law, the peep show which was formerly common in this country . . . and the more surreptitious and unpublicized peeping in which most males engage, at some time in their lives, from hotel windows, and from wherever they find the opportunity to observe.[60]

The element of surreptitiousness that is a characteristic feature of voyeurism cannot be overlooked in interpreting it. The stories of Adam and Eve and of Pandora's box both testify to the lure of the forbidden, which is seemingly underestimated in analyses of criminal behavior. In Samoa, for instance, where there are numerous opportunities to witness sexual behavior, youngsters nonetheless delight in embarrassing lovers who seek privacy near the village,[61] a pastime that has parallels in our society. Part of the explanation of voyeurism may lie in the curiosity of individuals to observe behavior that is not oriented to them, such as through party-line eavesdropping, theater-going, and reading, especially of fiction and biography, since the opportunity to observe others' "private" behavior is rarely afforded in our society.

Kinsey attempts to interpret the absence of voyeuristic activities among American females by references to dissimilarities between the sexes. Human females, Kinsey believes, are not usually aroused by viewing nudity or other items that males consider sexually stimulat-

58 Tennyson, "Godiva."
59 Gebhard, Sex Offenders, p. 374.
60 Kinsey, Sexual Behavior in the Human Female, pp. 663–664.
61 Mead, Coming of Age in Samoa, p. 62.

ing.[62] Guttmacher, on the other hand, maintains that voyeurism has a basic attraction to all persons, although it may take different forms. He equates window-shopping by females, for instance, with voyeurism among males. In both instances, he says, there is a subtle belief that one can have what one sees.[63] There are further interpretations of voyeurism that relate it to mythological ideas regarding seeing, such as those concerned with "the evil eye,"[64] those insisting that the eyes of a dead person be closed, and those among some primitive tribes that maintain that possession of a person's picture provides power over that person.[65]

All authorities agree that voyeurs are passive individuals who desire no further contact with the persons they observe, as opposed to the view that they are "sadistic menaces."[66] Voyeuristic behavior is often more dangerous to the perpetrators than to the objects; voyeurs are on occasion killed by irate householders because it is difficult to distinguish the true voyeur from a potential housebreaker or more serious offender.[67] Peeping is chiefly a young man's avocation, partly because it requires a certain agility to out-race indignant neighborhood residents if discovered. Gebhard reports that the average age at first arrest among his sample of voyeurs was 23.8 years.[68] The same author also noted that peepers are "persevering optimists," and he compares them to ardent fishermen, "undaunted by failure and always hoping that the next time their luck will be better."[69] Studies indicate that voyeurs are generally unmarried and show a continuous pattern of peeping. They are, Guttmacher observes, pathetic instances of individual maladjustment, but "from society's point of view they are seldom harmful."[70] Most jurisdictions regard voyeurism as a misdemeanor, whose criminality springs from the fact that the act is considered a public nuisance as well as an interference with rights of privacy. In Michigan, for instance, it is punishable by a maximum sentence of ninety days.

EXHIBITIONISM

In American society, exhibitionism, or indecent exposure as it is called in law, usually involves public genital exhibition on the part of the male. Few, if any, females are arrested for this offense. It is believed that the motivating force in exhibitionism is an anticipation of sexual interest on the part of the female viewer. Psychiatrists often press this idea somewhat further, maintaining that exhibitionism is essentially

62 Kinsey, *Sexual Behavior in the Human Male,* pp. 651–689.
63 Guttmacher, *Sex Offenses,* p. 41.
64 Seligman, *Der Böse Blick.*
65 Yalom, "Aggression and Forbiddenness in Voyeurism," pp. 308–309.
66 Quoted in Falk, "Public Image of the Sex Offender," p. 605.
67 For a fictional treatment, see Robbe-Grillet, *The Voyeur.*
68 Gebhard, *Sex Offenders,* p. 374.
69 *Ibid.,* p. 359.
70 Guttmacher, *Sex Offenses,* p. 132.

undertaken to reassure the male involved of his own masculinity by way of shocked reactions from female onlookers.[71] We have records of exhibitionists whose behavior was received with nonchalance by females and who report in such instances a total lack of satisfaction.[72]

Many psychiatrists believe that exhibitionism is generated by faulty mother-son relationships and that the exhibitionistic act is a symbolic attempt to rupture what are seen as overwhelming conditions of dominance of the male by his mother. Morris Ploscowe, however, finds this explanation superficial. He notes that precisely the same forms of mother-son relationship that are claimed to lead to exhibitionism exist in large segments of the society where they produce no such result.[73] Psychiatrists report that in addition to the dominating mother, exhibitionists also generally come from families in which the father is passive, relinquishing his duties and privileges as household head to his wife. Nathan Rickles, who conducted the most comprehensive psychiatric study of exhibitionism, found that, in every case, he could trace to acts of exhibitionism a precipitating trauma, such as a broken engagement, death of the mother, or the mother's remarriage after divorce.[74]

Like voyeurs, exhibitionists are generally considered to be rather harmless individuals, although it is usually pointed out that when they perform their acts in the presence of children, the behavior may produce undesirable consequences, such as lifelong sexual fears. Betty Smith, in the novel *A Tree Grows in Brooklyn,* traced in fictional detail the presumed unnerving consequences on a woman of having witnessed an exhibitionist act when a youngster. Exhibitionist behavior increases during the summer months and often takes place from automobiles. Guttmacher notes that more than half of the exhibitionist acts reported in Los Angeles in 1949 involved automobiles, and he believes that these figures indicate a desire for punishment on the part of the exhibitionist, since he knows that he can readily be apprehended by anyone with enough presence of mind to copy down his license number.[75] Exhibitionists are generally between twenty-three and thirty-nine-years old, with a median age of thirty years. The majority are reported to be unusually timid, retiring, often highy conscientious individuals, with only a minority who incorporate exhibitionism into their total personality, which is marked by loud and brash forms of attention-seeking.[76]

Exhibitionism undoubtedly has a social as well as a sexual significance. In Mohammedan societies, for instance, exposure of the

71 Rickles, *Exhibitionism.*
72 Apfelberg, "Psychiatric Study of 250 Sex Offenders," pp. 765–766; Smith, "Exhibitionism," p. 265.
73 Ploscowe, *Sex and the Law,* p. 163.
74 Rickles, *Exhibitionism,* Chap. 6.
75 Guttmacher, *Sex Offenses,* p. 39.
76 Kopp, "Character Structure of Sex Offenders," p. 65.

face by a female may be considered as reprehensible as genital exhibitionism is considered in our society. Quite a few societies exist
in which members of neither sex wear clothing, so that it would be
difficult to imagine that exhibitionism as we know it would have any
significance for them.[77] In addition, American society provides sanctioned forms of exhibitionism, such as on bathing beaches and in
nudist camps.

SODOMY OFFENSES

The crime of sodomy subsumes so many divergent forms of behavior,
involving so many different types of individuals, that it represents an
analytical swampland. Part of this chaos is undoubtedly traceable
to cultural inhibitions regarding public discussion of sodomy. So
chary are we, that even legal indictments are often excused from spelling out the particulars of sodomy offenses, a requirement otherwise
basic to the Anglo-American system of judicial procedure.[78] As one
court put the matter:

> It was never the practice to describe the particular manner of the de-
> tails of the commission of the crime, but the offense was treated in
> the indictment as the abominable crime not fit to be named among
> Christians. The existence of such an offense is a disgrace to human
> nature. The legislature has not seen fit to define it further than by the
> general term, and the records of the courts need not be defiled with the
> details of different acts which may go to constitute it.[79]

In the broadest sense, sodomy is generally defined as a "crime
against nature." The term "sodomy" is derived from the city of Sodom,
a Biblical site that was considered a citadel of wickedness. Originally,
sodomy referred only to male homosexuality, but it has been expanded
to become a catchall for all kinds of sex acts considered "unnatural
and abnormal." Specifically, it refers to types of sexual intercourse
involving patterns other than genital-to-genital intromission. So defined, sodomy covers acts between married partners, men and young
children, persons of the same sex, and humans and nonhumans. Below,
we will attempt to group some of the more prevalent forms of sodomy
and consider them as behavioral units.

Marital and Adult Heterosexual Sodomy

Considerable concern has been expressed regarding laws that
punish some forms of sex behavior that are engaged in by considerable
portions of the adult population. It is felt that such statutes tend
to inhibit what is considered by some persons to be desirable behavior
as a prelude to sexual relations. Kinsey, the most ardent exponent of
this viewpoint, notes that comparatively few persons, including most

77 Ford and Beach, *Patterns of Sexual Behavior,* p. 95.
78 Heller, *Sixth Amendment,* pp. 103–104.
79 *Honselman v. People,* p. 305.

attorneys, are aware that sodomy laws can be extended to married persons and that the penalties for such acts in some jurisdictions are exceeded only by the penalties for murder, kidnapping, and rape. Kinsey points out that one appellate court decision went so far as to uphold the conviction of a man for soliciting his wife to commit sodomy with him. He grants that there are few prosecutions of married persons under these laws, but he believes that "as long as they remain on the books they are subject to capricious enforcement and become tools for blackmailers."

Kinsey is also adamantly opposed to sodomy laws as they relate to voluntary behavior among adult heterosexual couples. He notes that the Judeo-Christian codes specifically condemn activities that bring erotic arousal without having procreation as their ultimate objective. In regard to "petting techniques," which sometimes include acts that violate the laws against sodomy, Kinsey notes that "evidently the religious and public condemnation has had a minimal effect on the behavior of youth of more recent generations"; he also expresses concern that many of those who engage in the behavior do so with a sense of guilt, which when extreme, he believes, "may give rise to a variety of personality problems, sexual maladjustments, difficulties in making sexual adjustments [and] sometimes the substitution of homosexual activities."[80] This view, of course, does not account for possible consequences of unchecked sex behavior that may, depending on the individual and the situation, lead to various other deleterious results.

Wide variations are found in the practice of sodomy acts among the social classes in American society. There is evidence that the behavior is more common among the better-educated portions of the population. However, a large majority of the adult population of the United States has at one time or another violated sodomy statutes and committed acts that carry heavy prison sentences.

Pedophilia

Pedophilia—sexual behavior directed toward a child—often involves some form of sodomy, although pedophilic acts are prosecuted under a wide range of legal rubrics, such as child molesting, indecent assault, contributing to the delinquency of a minor, lewd and lascivious behavior, carnal knowledge, statutory rape, and incest.

Pedophilic criminals run a wide gamut. Gebhard, for instance, distinguishes between offenders whose victims are below twelve years of age and those whose victims are between twelve and fifteen years of age. He further compares pedophiles involved in heterosexual activity to those involved in homosexual activity, and he finally differentiates between offenders who use force to obtain their object and those who employ more peaceable methods.[81] The breakdown, as

80 Kinsey, *Sexual Behavior in the Human Male*, p. 370.
81 Gebhard, *Sex Offenders*, Chaps. 4–8, 13–14.

Table 10.1 indicates, shows that the largest number of imprisoned offenders falls into the group involved heterosexually with very young children without the use of force. It is also notable, as the table illustrates, that such offenders have the highest median age of any sex offender: slightly above 35 years.

Table 10.1 Age of Offenders in Sex Offenses

Offense	Age–%				Median age	Total offenses N
	16–20	21–30	31–40	41+		
Heterosexual offenses vs.						
Children	12.8%	26.0%	30.8%	30.4%	35.1	273
Minors	31.6	34.7	15.8	17.8	24.7	196
Heterosexual aggressions vs.						
Children	3.3	40.0	33.3	23.3	31.7	30
Minors	41.4	44.8	13.8	0.0	23.2	29
Homosexual offenses vs.						
Children	14.6	37.4	26.8	21.1	30.6	123
Minors	8.2	38.3	29.6	24.0	32.6	196
Peeping	33.0	51.6	9.9	5.5	23.8	91
Exhibition	10.1	44.1	30.6	15.3	29.6	288

SOURCE: Gebhard, *et, al., Sex Offenders,* p. 809.

In some three-fifths of the cases, the heterosexual offenders against children were involved with youngsters previously known to them. Kinsey points up the fact that the behavior by elderly males—a group rapidly increasing with expanded life expectancy—who make up a sizeable portion of the heterosexual pedophiles, may be misinterpreted by children. He notes that "such fondling as parents and grandparents bestow" can be misunderstood, particularly if a child has been made crushingly aware of the alleged terrors of child molestation.[82] The interactive relationship between pedophiles of this type and their ultimate victims has been characterized in the following terms:

> As a rule pedophiles like children, frequently consort with them, and in spite of the great disparity in their age differences enter into a peer type of relationship with them. The precocious and aggressive children quickly sense the infantile characteristics of the pedophile and very soon lose the awe of adult authority and treat him as if he were one of them.[83]

[82] Kinsey, *Sexual Behavior in the Human Male,* pp. 237–238.
[83] Revitch and Weiss, "Pedophiliac Offender," p. 75.

A further typology of pedophiles, concentrating upon the seeming motivations of the behavior, is offered by J. H. Fitch, based on a sample of 139 British offenders, of whom 77 had been involved in heterosexual and 62 in homosexual offenses with victims under the age of 16. The types include: (1) those whose offenses appeared due to their inability to identify themselves with an adult sexual role, (2) those whose offenses seemed to be a reaction against sexual or emotional frustration at an adult level, who reverted when made to feel insecure, (3) those whose sexually aberrant acts seemed part and parcel of a generalized inability to achieve social conformity and who had records of instability in many fields of behavior, (4) those whose sexually abnormal behavior seemed due to pathological rather than emotional states—psychosis, mental defect, and organic impairment, and (5) those whose offenses, frequently isolated and compulsive acts, did not appear to relate to any obvious pattern of emotional or sexual difficulty.[84] Following the careers of the 139 men, an average of five years after his original study, Fitch found that thirty-five had been subsequently reconvicted for a sex offense—twenty-five of them members of the homosexual group, and ten of the heterosexual group.[85]

The reactions of children to pedophiliac approaches has been the subject of penetrating research, and the findings tend to oppose what might seem to be the likely conclusions. Augusta Rasmussen studied fifty-four children who had sexual experiences with adult males between their ninth and thirteenth birthdays, and reported that after a lapse of twenty years, forty-six of them were none the worse for their experience.[86] Lauretta Bender and Abram Blau concluded, after examining eleven girls and five boys who had been involved in sex behavior with adults, that they showed remarkably little evidence of "fear, anxiety, guilt or psychic trauma"; in fact, the authors found the children had unusually attractive and charming personalities, and that the children probably played an active or even initiating part in the experience,[87] a conclusion often reached by other researchers. John H. Gagnon, using materials from the Kinsey studies, discovered 333 females who had reported sexual experience with an adult before the age of thirteen. Only 6 percent recalled that there had been a report of the incident to the police. After reviewing their subsequent life histories, Gagnon notes that only 5 percent of the 333 women could be considered to have had adult lives that had been severely damaged for whatever reason, and that of these,

84 Fitch, "Men Convicted of Sexual Offences Against Children," pp. 29–31; Mc-Caghy, "Child Molesters," p. 86.
85 Fitch, *ibid.*, p. 25.
86 Rasmussen, "Bedeutung Sexueller Attentate auf Kinder Unter 14 Jahren für die Entwicklung von Geisteskrankheiten und Charakteranomalien."
87 Bender and Blau, "Reaction of Children to Sexual Relations with Adults"; Mohr, "Pedophilias," p. 258.

only three women related their current condition to their early sexual experience.[88]

Homosexuality

The etiology of homosexuality constitutes one of the more controversial scientific questions of our day. There is strong insistence that all homosexuals are products of faulty parental training, and equally vehement insistence that homosexuality springs from early indoctrination into the behavior. There are schools of thought that believe that endocrine imbalance, hormonal disturbances, and/or physical characteristics of the opposite sex cause homosexual behavior. It has been stated categorically that the origin of homosexuality is "always constitutional or biological, never environmental or acquired."[89] Finally, some Freudian theorists put forward the viewpoint that all human beings are "latent" homosexuals, carrying within themselves a repressed drive toward such behavior.

Eclectic opinion is inclined to equivocate in the debate by maintaining that there are different types of homosexuals, produced by different syndromes, Benjamin Apfelberg, Carl Sugar, and Arnold Pfeffer, for instance, classify homosexuals into three groups: (1) genetic, (2) endocrine dysfunction, and (3) psychological.[90] Such an approach seems more expedient than accurate, and the trend today is clearly toward the view that homosexual behavior is the outcome of social conditioning. After noting that it is more difficult to understand why "each and every individual is not involved in every type of sexual activity" than it is to understand homosexuality, Kinsey offers the following explanation:

> There is no need of hypothesizing peculiar hormonal factors that make certain individuals especially liable to engage in homosexual activity, and we know of no data which prove the existence of such hormonal factors. There is no sufficient data to show that specific hereditary factors are involved. [Our] data indicate that the factors leading to homosexual behavior are (1) the basic physiological capacity of every mammal to respond to sufficient stimuli; (2) the accident which leads an individual into his or her first sexual experience with a person of the same sex; (3) the conditioning effects of such experience; and (4) the indirect but powerful conditioning which the opinions of other persons and the social codes may have on an individual's decision to accept or reject this type of sexual conduct.[91]

Some writers who accept Kinsey's opinion would probably elaborate on his fourth point by stating that certain types of family constellations appear to be more likely than others to lead to the acceptance

88 Gagnon, "Female Child Victims of Sex Offenses," pp. 188–189.
89 Greenspan and Campbell, "Homosexual as a Personality Type."
90 Apfelberg, "Psychiatric Study of 250 Sex Offenders," p. 788.
91 Kinsey, *Sexual Behavior in the Human Female*, pp. 447, 451. See also Hoffman, *Gay World*, pp. 120–123.

of homosexual behavior. Among these, they particularly stress the importance of maternal roles, with mothers who are domineering and assertive as well as those who are too angelic, both conveying the idea to the child that women are asexual objects.

Historical and cross-cultural material strongly supports the social base of homosexual behavior. Many early civilizations, such as that in Greece, apparently regarded homosexual affection as the most noble of all forms of love. Ruth Benedict notes that "Plato's *Republic* . . . is the most convincing statement of the honorable estate of homosexuality" in Greece,[92] a situation traced by Freud to the fact that children were raised by male slaves.[93] In some preliterate groups, such as the Swanis of Africa, all men are expected to engage in homosexual activity, and those who do not, are regarded as "peculiar."[94] On the other hand, undoubtedly because of the need for procreation to insure survival, there is no known society in which homosexual behavior is the predominant form of sexual activity.

Few acts of homosexuality are prosecuted in comparison to the actual extent of the behavior. Kinsey reported in 1948 that 4 percent of the American, adult, white males are "exclusively homosexual throughout their lives after the onset of adolescence," a figure much higher than earlier estimates, and that between 30 and 45 percent of American males have engaged in some homosexual activity.[95] Females, on the other hand, despite popular conceptions, participate in homosexual behavior much less often than males, and they are almost never prosecuted for such behavior, although it, too, is illegal.[96] Negroes are believed to constitute a disproportionately low share of homosexuals, probably because they have fewer heterosexual inhibitions than whites.

Personality traits of homosexuals are as much a matter of dispute as causal explanations. Evelyn Hooker's work indicates that the presumed psychopathological nature of the homosexual's character may be factually inaccurate. She tested a samply of thirty homosexuals drawn from the general community, rather than from institutions or therapy groups, and a matched sample of thirty heterosexuals with a battery of projective techniques and attitude scales, also conducting intensive life history interviews. Two expert judges, knowing nothing about the individual subjects, examined the test results and experienced great difficulty in distinguishing between the homosexual and heterosexual groups. Hooker reports that neither judge was able to do better than guess: "In seven pairs both judges were incorrect; in twelve pairs, correct; and in the remaining eleven they disagreed."[97]

92 Benedict, *Patterns of Culture*, p. 243. See also Licht, *Sexual Life in Ancient Greece*, pp. 365–405.
93 Quoted in Abrahamsen, *Who Are the Guilty?*, p. 187.
94 Ford and Beach, *Patterns of Sexual Behavior*, pp. 131–132.
95 Kinsey, *Sexual Behavior in the Human Male*, p. 651.
96 Kinsey, *Sexual Behavior in the Human Female*, Chap. 11.
97 Hooker, "Adjustment of the Male Overt Homosexual."

Nonetheless, possibly because of the social definition of their behavior, homosexuals appear to be dissatisfied with their lot. Eighty-three percent of a sample of 300 homosexuals, for instance, indicated that they would not want a son to follow their paths, while only 2 percent answered that they would, and the remainder said that they would leave the choice up to the hypothetical son. On the other hand, an overwhelming 97 percent of the respondents said they would not change their own behavior, even if change were easy.[98]

Legal attitudes toward homosexuality have generated much debate and have shown very different responses. At the same time that California was raising penalties against homosexuality, for instance, New York was lowering them. Enforcement procedures vary, although the general rule is that policemen will not bother homosexuals unless their behavior occurs in public and is flagrant. On the other hand, the existence of punitive statutes makes homosexuals targets for blackmail. A former attorney general of England, for instance, indicated that 95 percent of all blackmail cases reported to his office concerned homosexual victims.[99] When discovered, homosexuals are discharged from government employment as security risks, presumably on the ground that they can readily be coerced into divulging national secrets. Such a policy has been criticized as being circuitous inasmuch as homosexuals become blackmail-prone primarily because of the laws against them. Benjamin Karpman, a psychiatrist who vociferously opposes the national policy, calls it "baseless, stupid, political, and productive of nothing except glorious encouragement of blackmail which, in the light of abstract morality, is the worst and most contemptible of possible crimes."[100] Other persons object to the government's policy on the ground that it eliminates from national positions a group of men whose sexual confreres have made outstanding contributions in other fields of endeavor and who might make equivalent contributions to public life.

Punishment of homosexuality as an offense leading to a prison term contains rather quixotic elements inasmuch as the encouragement of homosexual behavior is one of the charges often leveled against prison life. Rather colorful prose has been used to describe the irony of incarcerating homosexuals. "To send a homosexual to prison," John T. Rees and Harley V. Usill note, "is as futile as to hope to rehabilitate a drunkard by occupational therapy in a brewery."[101] In the same vein a judge ruling on the appeal of a conviction for homosexuality was moved to observe that "putting P—— into the North Carolina prison system is a little like throwing Brer Rabbit into the briarpatch."[102]

98 *New York Times*, Dec. 27, 1963.
99 Schur, *Crimes Without Victims*, p. 82.
100 Karpman, *Sexual Offender and His Offenses*, p. 471.
101 Rees and Usill, *They Stand Apart*, p. 6.
102 *Perkins v. North Carolina*, p. 337.

In actual fact, however, few homosexuals are sentenced to prison for their offenses, even when apprehended.[103] In a comprehensive survey of the judicial handling of homosexuals Jon J. Gallo and his colleagues found that fewer than 1 percent of 493 persons charged with felonious homosexuality in Los Angeles County were ultimately dealt with as felons. Virtually all defendants pled guilty to charges that were reduced to misdemeanors, and they were placed on probation or given jail terms. Almost 80 percent of the men taken into custody were Caucasians, and a large majority—274 out of 493—were arrested in public restrooms. The remainder of the arrests took place in vehicles (108), private residences (24), jail (18), public parks (17), and steam baths (11), with twenty-six additional arrests taking place either in other sites or not being listed on the official records. Some 345 of the persons arrested showed no previous criminal record, while 86 had at one time been arrested for sexual crimes and one for a crime of violence. None of the 493 men had ever been arrested for an offense involving children.[104]

Defenders of the laws against homosexuality maintain that such laws serve to reduce the amount of the behavior, an assumption that may contain an element of truth. It is also true, however, that the statutes forbidding homosexuality may encourage the behavior. Oscar Wilde reported, for instance, that enactment in 1885 of an English law that proscribed homosexual "indecencies," even if practiced in private, provided added reason for him to engage in the behavior: "It was like feasting with panthers, the danger was half the excitement."[105] Another common argument for outlawing homosexual activity is that homosexuals often proselyte within the adolescent population. Most persons believe that it is desirable to take reasonable steps to prevent the sexual exploitation of young persons. It appears specious, however, to place all homosexuals outside the pale of the law because some homosexuals may direct their attention to youngsters; it would be similar to outlawing all heterosexual activity because some heterosexual persons exploit youngsters.

The movement toward permitting consensual adult homosexual behavior practiced in private is one of the evident features of statutes concerning sexual behavior. In 1957, Great Britain undertook a thoroughgoing review of national policy in regard to homosexual offenses, primarily as a result of public agitation concerning the severity of penalties as well as concern over the apparent sharp rise in the behavior. Prosecutions for homosexuality in England and Wales had risen from 299 per year in the 1935–1940 period to 1,685 in 1955. The penalty for sodomy was life imprisonment, and for attempts to commit "unnatural offenses" ten years. The British investigation, embodied

103 Bickel, "Supreme Court Fissures."
104 Gallo, "Consenting Adult Homosexual and the Law," pp. 783, 803–830.
105 Wilde, De Profoundis, p. 106.

in the Wolfenden Report, concluded that homosexuality was a matter of morals and not of law when engaged in privately by persons twenty-one years of age or older. The committee said that it had found no evidence supporting the view that homosexuality is "a cause of the demoralization and decay of civilizations."[106] Some of the strongest support for the Wolfenden committee's views came from church leaders, who held that it was useless to try to make sins into crimes without further justification and that such attempts aroused contempt both for law and for morality.[107] Parliament adopted the recommendations of the Wolfenden report regarding adult homosexuality nine years later, in 1966, although it retained the penalty of life imprisonment for homosexual offenses against boys under age 16. In addition, the new law provided that an act of "gross indecency" against a youth between the ages of 16 and 21 could bring five years' imprisonment and that a public act of "indecency" could be punished by two years in prison. In the United States, essentially similar views are incorporated into the Model Penal Code, adopted to date in regard to sex offenses only in Illinois, which now permits all but "deviate sexual behavior" defined as behavior involving force, young and immature persons, or acts that disturb the peace because of their open and notorious character.[108]

Summary

In a society such as ours, in which attitudes toward sexual behavior are in a state of considerable flux, it can perhaps be expected that social policies in regard to sex offenders combine diverse elements of folklore, prejudice, tolerance, and, above all, confusion. The most significant need at the moment appears to be a rationale for determining the degree of social harm inherent in divergent forms of sexual behavior, the methods and potentialities for reducing these forms of behavior, and the proper sanctions to be carried through against offenders. It might be desirable that the laws against some types of behavior either be repealed or enforced more stringently and uniformly so that we can determine their consequences more accurately. Most authorities appear inclined toward the lifting of legal sanctions against behavior that is exclusively a violation of moral codes. Meanwhile, other persons note that investigation of the behavior of sex offenders and the dynamics of their behavior represent one of the more significant frontiers of social science, a frontier still inadequately explored because of lingering taboos. Ellis and Brancale have stressed our research needs in clarion terms:

106 Great Britain, *Report on Homosexual Offences and Prostitution*, pp. 25–26.
107 Buckley, *Morality and the Homosexual;* Bailey, *Homosexuality and the Western Christian Tradition.*
108 "The Crime Against Nature," p. 185; "Deviant Sexual Behavior Under the New Illinois Criminal Code."

What is presently known about sex offenders and the offenses they commit is infinitesimal compared to the lack of knowledge. . . . More research, still more research, and still more research again is vitally needed at the present time; and only after such research is at least partially completed will many of the serious problems involved in sex offenses begin to be seen in their true light, and possible solutions to them begin to become apparent.[109]

For Further Reading

GALLO, JON J., et al. "The Consenting Adult Homosexual and the Law: An Empirical Study of Enforcement and Administration in Los Angeles County," in U.C.L.A. Law Review. Vol. 13 (March 1966), pp. 643–832.

Senior law students at the University of California, Los Angeles, investigated the operation of the superior and municipal court systems in regard to the disposition of homosexual cases. Material gathered includes characteristics of the offenders, place and method of arrest, previous criminal records, and actual time served on the charge.

GEBHARD, PAUL H., JOHN H. GAGNON, WARDELL B. POMEROY, AND CORNELIA V. CHRISTENSON. Sex Offenders. New York: Harper & Row, 1965.

Produced by the Institute for Sex Research at Indiana University, this volume represents the most thorough and painstaking analysis of sex offenders in prisons. Types of offenders are compared to each other and then examined in terms of a control group. The major drawback of the volume is the selective nature of the sample.

GREAT BRITAIN, Report of the Committee on Homosexual Offences and Prostitution. London: Command 247, 1957.

The thorough investigation by a committee headed by Sir John Wolfenden, vice-chancellor of the University of Reading, into homosexuality and prostitution in England as well as into the correct attitude the Government should take toward these activities. Providing stimulating intellectual fare, this report moves with logical precision. The Committee concluded that prostitution should be more tightly controlled, but that consensual adult homosexuality should not be a statutory offense.

KINSEY, ALFRED C., WARDELL B. POMEROY, AND CLYDE E. MARTIN. Sexual Behavior in the Human Male. Philadelphia: W. B. Saunders, 1948.

This first of the well-known studies by Professor Kinsey and his research associates pays considerable attention to the violations of laws regarding sexual behavior, since such laws are primarily directed against males. Despite statistical flaws, this and the subsequent Kinsey volume on females remain standard, basic sources of the most reliable information we have in a difficult research area. Kinsey's polemical views on statutes concerning sexual behavior should be regarded as ideological positions rather than scientific observations.

109 Ellis and Brancale, Psychology of Sex Offenders, p. 92.

"Sex Offenses," in *Law and Contemporary Problems*. Vol. 25 (Spring 1960), pp. 215–375.

The entire issue is devoted to a series of papers on various aspects of sex crimes, examining them from legal, sociological, anthropological, and psychological viewpoints. Criminology students should find particularly interesting the carefully thought out views of Stanton Wheeler, a sociologist who is now on the faculty of the Yale Law School, Albert Reiss of the University of Michigan, and Weston LaBarre, an anthropologist from Duke University.

11
Property Offenders

A desire to acquire that which is defined as belonging to another is not a trait common to all mankind. Jealousy of the property of others, lust for personal goods, and competitive striving for material possessions derive from cultural emphases, which also give rise to theft—the taking of goods from another by stealth or force. Theft is particularly apt to be encouraged when a society places heavy stress on possession of material wealth but limits legitimate opportunities for the acquisition of such wealth.[1]

We know of some people—for example, the Papuans who live in the interior of New Guinea—among whom, although murder is common, theft, cheating, and embezzlement are unknown. The Dakota Indians, to take another cultural example, have an emphatic attitude against placing value on goods or possessions, thus undercutting the motivation for theft. The accumulation of material things is considered suspect by the Dakotas, and prestige attached to property is derived from giving it away.[2] In the same manner, undue wealth is regarded among the Navaho Indians as the result of lack of generosity, perhaps even the product of malicious witchcraft.[3] After analyzing cross-cultural material, Theodore Newcomb concluded, in fact, that the attitude toward property among the Dakotas and Navahos is probably characteristic of more cultures than is the kind of acquisitiveness generally found in industrialized societies.[4]

Historically, Christian civilizations, particularly in their early period, fought a constant battle to inhibit acquisitiveness. In both ancient Jewish and early Germanic law, the surreptitious taking of goods was regarded as more serious than many crimes of violence. It was a

1 Merton, *Social Theory and Social Structure*, pp. 131–194.
2 Mirsky, "The Dakota," pp. 384–385.
3 Lee, *Freedom and Culture*, pp. 10–11.
4 Newcomb, *Social Psychology*, p. 136.

Hebrew idea that the thief who committed his crime in secrecy believed himself not to be watched by God, and that therefore he should be punished all the more.[5] The Germanic tribes regarded stealing, because it was premeditated, as more serious than crimes against the person, and therefore punished theft with death, while allowing fines to be paid to atone for maiming or murder.[6] The Bible, undercutting the motive for theft by inveighing against acquisitiveness, exhorts individuals to strip themselves of worldly possessions in order to prepare more adequately for a heavenly state. It is pointed out that it is more difficult for a rich man to achieve divine indulgence than for a camel to pass through the eye of a needle. Despite these unequivocal dicta, few persons in nominally Christian societies such as ours appear to take religious injunctions against the accumulation of wealth very seriously.

Other moral and legal codes have also attempted through punitive measures to put down acquisitive impulses. The oldest part of the Roman criminal code that has survived contains twelve tables, the eighth of which deals explicitly with thievery: "Whoever by night furtively cuts or causes to be grazed crops raised by ploughing, shall be put to death if an adult, or if he is under the age of puberty shall be flogged at the discretion of the praetor and made to pay double values as damages." Thieves taken in the act were to be beaten with rods and adjudged as slaves of the person they had been in the process of robbing. If the thief was already a slave, he was first to be beaten and then to be thrown to his death from the Tarpeian Rock. Youths were to be beaten at the discretion of magistrates and then condemned to repair any damages they might have inflicted.[7]

Neither religious warning nor legal harshness, however, appear to have had much impact in eliminating acquisitiveness from Western societies, which R. H. Tawney finds "concentrate attention upon the right of those who possess or can acquire power to make the fullest use of it for their own self-advantage."[8] Tawney further describes such societies:

> To the strong they promise unfettered freedom for the exercise of their strength; to the weak the hope that they too one day may be strong. Before the eyes of both they suspend a golden prize, which not all can attain, but for which each may strive, the enchanting vision of infinite expansion. They assure men that there are no ends other than their ends, no law other than their desires, no limit other than that which they think advisable. Thus they make the individual the center of his own universe.[9]

5 May, "Jewish Criminal Law," p. 442.
6 Lieber, in de Beaumont and de Tocqueville, *On the Penitentiary System in the United States,* p. 23.
7 Stephen, *A History of the Criminal Law in England,* Vol. I, pp. 9–10.
8 Tawney, *The Acquisitive Society,* p. 29.
9 *Ibid.,* pp. 30–31.

Under such conditions, Hermann Mannheim notes, it becomes un-thinkable, for instance, to hold an owner liable for the malicious destruction of his own property, even though that property is valuable for the well-being of the society.[10]

Max Weber has hypothesized in a classic statement, that the rise of sanctioned acquisitiveness in Calvinistic society and its subsequent spread through Western civilization represented a blend of religious ideas and secular interests. Capitalism arose in the Calvinist states, according to Weber, because of the psychological devastation of the theological doctrine of predestination. The believer could not tolerate the uncertainty of not knowing the fate divinely decreed for him. Therefore, he came to equate worldly success, particularly material gain, with divine approval.[11] From this belief, it was but a short step to the view that acquisitiveness was a divine command and even a shorter step to the view that gain in and of itself was a worthwhile pursuit. The occasional cries of dismay from persons who scorn materialistic aspects of the society only serve to emphasize their per-vasive presence. Thoreau, for instance, complained bitterly about the stress on material items in nineteenth century America, berating, among other things, the frenetic race to California for gold:

> The rush to California . . . and the attitude, not merely of merchants, but of philosophers and prophets, so called, in relation to it, reflect the great disgrace on mankind. So many are ready to live by luck, and so get the means of commanding the labor of others less lucky, without contributing any value to society. . . . I know of no more startling de-velopment of the immorality of trade, and all the common modes of get-ting a living. The philosophy and poetry and religion of such a mankind are not worth the dust of a puff-ball.[12]

Equally notable are the observations of the noted novelist Franz Kafka, who observed that "For someone an old shirt is riches. Others are poor on ten millions. . . . Wealth implies dependence on things which one possesses and which have to be safeguarded from dwindling away by new possessions and a further dependence. It is merely materialized insecurity."[13]

Thoreau's diatribe regarding the pursuit of gold is a step or more removed from the Biblical injunction against wealth, taking the com-promise position that wealth without work represents sinful behavior. Thoreau and Kafka are, however, but feeble voices, eccentrically sounding against the clarion dictate of the inherent desirability of gain. It was this dictate, combined with the disproportionate lawmaking power of the propertied, that produced the stringent laws protecting material assets against thievery.

10 Mannheim, *Criminal Justice and Social Reconstruction*, p. 192.
11 Weber, *Protestant Ethic and the Spirit of Capitalism.*
12 Thoreau, *Life Without Principle*, p. 29.
13 Janouch, *Conversations with Kafka*, p. 31.

Social Conditions and Theft

Though definitions of private property vary from culture to culture—both early Christian and Roman societies, for example, in the manner of many of today's preliterate societies, regarded adultery as a crime against property, since a man's wife was considered his chattel[14]—there remains a nuclear agreement that there are some things that must remain inviolable. It may be commendable in some societies to live modestly, but in no society is it considered desirable to give away or to allow to be stolen *everything* that one possesses. As Kingsley Davis points out, a state of social chaos would ensue if a man dared not leave his home for fear someone might immediately take possession of it, or if he dared not use his car for fear of having it stopped and appropriated.[15] If a generalization might be ventured, it would be that the more complex the society, the more meaningful property rights become.

Nonetheless, societies in relatively similar stages of industrial development show quite discrepant rates of theft, and within any given society there are likely to be marked differences among groups in terms of honesty. In Tokyo, for instance, where population density is heavy and industrialization is far advanced, there were only 658 robberies in 1966, 177 fewer than the previous year. This reflects a pattern of earlier social conditions, which are marked by Lafcadio Hearn's observation that he had lived in Japanese districts "where no case of theft had occurred for hundreds of years" despite the fact that people left their doors unfastened both night and day.[16] The viability of such cultural traits—even when a group is transplanted—is evident from test results in the United States that indicate that 99 percent of the Japanese children surpass the average Anglo-Saxon child in honesty.[17]

It is from cultural emphases such as these and from individual and group customs that rules regarding acquisition emerge. The behavior that ensues will be mediated by defined needs. The lower-class person who does not possess an automobile will be more inclined to steal one, particularly when he defines possession of the car as important for status and entertainment goals. The individual farther along the social scale will have no pressing need to steal a car if he already owns one, although he may take alternate illegal pathways, such as embezzling or cheating on his income tax, to gain the resources to purchase a better car. He would presumably resort to these alternate methods because they reduce the chances of being apprehended and because possession of the better automobile is not so overwhelming a desire. Too much can be lost by the middle-class person through automobile theft, and, further, it is not temporary ownership of the automobile that is so

---

14 Radcliffe-Brown, *Andaman Islanders,* p. 50; Murray, "Ancient Laws on Adultery," p. 89.
15 Davis, *Human Society,* p. 451.
16 Hearn, *Japan: Attempt at Interpretation,* p. 17.
17 Klineberg, "Mental Testing of Racial and National Groups," p. 289.

important, but rather the act of acquiring the car through normal commerical channels, so that he appears to be able to "afford" it.

It is, of course, an elementary fact that it is considerably easier to be honest if temptation is not present. Millionaires do not steal cars because they can acquire them otherwise, and peasants do not steal pebbles because pebbles have no social meaning to them. In attempting to understand crimes against property in this chapter, we must always keep in mind that the definitions of property and the desires to acquire such property ultimately trace their origin to the value structure of the particular society.

THE LAW OF THEFT

All of the modern law of theft is a product of the eighteenth century, except the Carrier's Case decision in 1473[18] that held a bailee criminally responsible for opening and taking goods entrusted to him for delivery, and two similar rulings in the sixteenth century. The laws regarding theft illustrate clearly the relationship between things men hold dear and their legal recourse to help them protect those things. Early theft laws, for instance, were based primarily upon the importance of cattle, which were vital at the time for food, transportation, communication, and the waging of war, as well as for the tillage of fields. Cattle, in fact, were often used as a medium of exchange. The original laws of theft in England, which were oriented toward cattle, specified that a thing could not be stolen unless it was (1) movable, and (2) under somebody's control. Thus, things affixed to the soil could not be stolen; in fact, a 17th century case dismissed an accusation of taking a tree from a manor because there was no legal provision against such an act.

Exceptions to the law of theft, however, were systematically narrowed by Parliament as it sought to protect the interests of the landowning classes and the rising industrial groups, and as it sought to take account of advances in agriculture, the arts, and finance. Dilemmas continue to exist, however, regarding the precise nature of items that can be stolen. An early case reported by Hall involved a defendant who had used the idle facilities of a factory to comb his own raw wool. Charged with theft, he denied that he had physically taken anything and stated that he certainly had not carried anything away, so that his act lacked the necessary legal element of *asportation*. The court agreed, noting that, "It may be conceivable that if these defendants stole the use of the spinning facilities . . . they carried the 'use' away, or appreciably changed its location, although the work was done on the premises," but it added that "to conceive this [however] requires a certain intellectual flexibility which is probably not possessed by the average person."

If this early illustration seems somewhat academic, attention might

18 Hall, *Theft, Law and Society*, pp. 1–33; Allen, "Offenses Against Property."

be called to dilemmas involving current definitions of theft. Can electricity, for example, be stolen? Certainly all property cannot be subject to theft. The right to produce oil, for example, is property, but it is difficult to see how the right could be "stolen." Other contemporary problems involve such things as "good will," which is often defined as an item of property.

It can be seen that the law of theft is one of the most complex segments of any modern criminal code, embracing offenses such as larceny, which was considered earlier in relation to professional criminals, and such intricate conditions as false pretenses, fraud, and intent to deprive of ownership. Some general definitions, therefore, may help to clarify subsequent material:

Larceny is the broadest form of stealing or theft, and involves the taking of property from a person, without his consent, and with the intent to deprive him permanently of its use. Larceny is usually broken down into *grand larceny* and *petit larceny*, depending on the value of the property stolen. This division has, in fact, been cited to support the view that theft statutes reflect a class bias.[19] It is argued that the theft of $5 from a man who has no more is at least as serious as the theft of several hundred dollars from a man who possesses many times that amount. Regardless, the first act in many jurisdictions is regarded as petty larceny, a misdemeanor, while the second is usually defined as grand larceny, a felony.

Robbery is a form of larceny in which goods or money are taken from a person against his will *through the use of violence or fear*. It would not be robbery to take property suddenly from a person, if there was no resistance and if no force was employed beyond the mere act of grabbing. Also, the fear involved must be of such a nature as to arouse a reasonable apprehension of danger in a reasonable person. Robbery is a more serious crime than larceny, regardless of the amount of money or the value of goods involved. If the robber is armed with a dangerous weapon, he may be sentenced to death in eight states, to life imprisonment in nineteen, and to more than twenty years in twenty other states.

Burglary is generally classified as a crime against the dwelling and represents the most common serious crime in the United States. A burglar is a person who breaks and enters the dwelling house of another in the night with the intent to commit a felony therein. Statutes have greatly extended the original scope of burglary laws to include warehouses, storehouses, offices, and similar buildings and structures as "dwelling houses." "Night" in common-law England, before the time of watches and clocks, was regarded as any time when there was not sufficient light to discern a person's features. Contemporary statutes have taken to define its limits more clearly. England now regards night as from nine in the evening to six in the morning, New York specifies

19 Mannheim, *Criminal Justice and Social Reconstruction*, pp. 90–93.

the hours from sunset to sunrise, and Massachusetts sets the time at an hour after sunset to an hour before sunrise. New York divides burglary into three degrees: burglarly three, which occurs by day and in an unoccupied site, burglary two, in which a human being is present in the dwelling, and burglary one, which is a nighttime offense, or one in which the burglar is armed with a dangerous weapon, or one in which he commits assault while on the premises.

Most burglars prefer to avoid contact with persons, largely because identification and apprehension are less likely if they remain unobserved. An anecdote about a burglar who found a lady present on the premises he had entered illustrates this; when he saw her he became flustered, and warned her, "If you make a noise, Madàm, I'll scream."[20] Like many offenders, burglars tend to develop special patterns. Many routinely "loid" doors, using celluloid strips to snap locks open. Others, finding a door locked from the inside with the key still in position, will place papers under the door, push the key out of its hole onto the papers, and then retrieve it by sliding the papers out.[21] When better locks were developed to protect against burglary, burglars soon learned that door manufacturers were now able to market flimsier products, and they turned their attention to doors. Most burglars steal only jewelry and cash, although occasional sophisticates will take bankbooks and identifying material and withdraw their victims' bank balances, often before the books' absence is realized.

Typologies of Property Offenders

Crimes against property occur along a continuum of criminal behavior, sometimes falling into the realms of professional crime and white-collar crime. Bank robbers, for instance, are often career specialists and share with other professional thieves their way of life and general attitudes. Embezzlers, on the other hand, are almost invariably drawn from the more "respectable" elements of society and resemble persons designated as "white-collar" criminals more than they resemble other thieves. Between these two extremes there is a vast behavioral gulf bridged most basically by the shared fact that property offenders employ illegal methods to expropriate for themselves material wealth belonging to others.

Several attempts have been made to construct typologies of property crime and criminals to reduce the myriad forms to analytical order. As Richard O. Nahrendorf points out, the desire of man to create "types" is probably as old as man himself, and it represents a vital process in the attempt to comprehend and study diverse phenomena.[22] Some property offense typologies are impressionistic and imaginative,

20 Black, "Burglary," p. 64.
21 Shaw, Brothers in Crime, p. 66.
22 Nahrendorf, "Typologies of Crime and Delinquency," p. 15.

while others tend to be tortuously extracted and highly specific types drawn from rather limited universes. The basic object of most typologies has been to supplement legal definitions with analyses that are tied to conduct patterns as well as to differentiate between specific crimes and crime in general. As Jack Gibbs points out, "Crime as legally defined is not a unitary concept, because certain types of behavior are subsumed under it which, when reduced to rates, vary independently of each other; as such, the overall legal category is causally heterogeneous." To support this position, Gibbs cites the finding of a coefficient of correlation of only +.168 between urban assault and larceny rates for the years 1946 to 1952,[23] noting that such a low correlation suggests strongly that the cause of the variability in assault rates could not possibly be the cause of the variability in larceny rates, and that independent explanations must be sought. Gibbs further notes that "it should be abundantly clear that theories which treat crime as though it were a unitary concept are particularly prone to failure, and that the search for something which explains crime in general is the blind spot in criminology."[24]

Requirements for typologies in crime have been summarized as follows:

> First, an adequate criminal typology should include a major part of the offender population. Second, a good typology should describe and discriminate between offender types at any given point in the lives of a cohort of offenders. It should describe the developmental history and provide an etiological description of each type. Third, the characteristics of criminal types must be clearly specified, so that actual offenders may be classified within the typology with clarity, reliability, and precision; otherwise, the typology would not be amenable to validation, nor would it be of particular value in the field of corrections. Finally, an adequate typology should be parsimonious. That is, the number of types should be relatively few.[25]

Using these standards, Don C. Gibbons and Donald L. Garrity differentiate the following types of property offenders: (1) The Professional Thief, (2) The Professional Heavy Criminal, (3) The Quasi-Professional Property Offender, (4) The One-Time Loser, Property Crime, (5) The Embezzler, (6) The Check Writer Who Drinks, (7) The White-Collar Criminal, and (8) The Auto Thief-Joyrider.[26]

As an illustration of the qualities associated with these classes, the "quasi-professional property offender" is described in part as an offender who identifies with a criminal subculture, viewing himself as a criminal and taking some pride in his status. He is from a lower-class urban environment, and his home background is characterized

23 Shannon, "The Spatial Distribution of Criminal Offenses by State."
24 Gibbs, "Needed: Analytical Typologies in Criminology."
25 Gibbons and Garrity, "Some Suggestions for the Definition of Etiological and Treatment Theory in Criminology," p. 53.
26 *Ibid.*, p. 55.

by parental neglect and, in some instances, by family tensions. He usually has been a member of a delinquent gang, and he generally has a long record of juvenile offenses beginning with petty theft and truancy, proceeding to more serious theft. His institutional prognosis is poor in terms of treatment potential. He is not likely to be involved in institutional difficulty, but at the same time he is not easily recruited into treatment programs.

Typologies of property offenders such as that by Gibbons and Garrity possess the virtue of abstracting from the mass of offenders certain patterned regularities that appear in enough instances to make them significant parts of the total picture of criminal activity. Various things may then be said about the types of offenders as a group, and a number of predictions may be ventured regarding the cause of their behavior and the prognosis for their future. The difficulties with these types of typologies, however, are at least as important as the virtues and perhaps outweigh them. For one thing, by merging criminal activity with noncriminal behavior into a single category, such as "The Check Writer Who Drinks," there is a loss of useful information regarding both aspects of the configuration; that is, we really do not learn what we might want to know about forgers in general and the relationship between this particular subgroup and the larger category, and we certainly fail to learn about these persons as drinkers, compared to other drinkers who do not, for example, write insufficient-funds checks.

It appears more rewarding, for reasons such as these, to focus initial attention upon the legally-defined offense category and then, once its dimensions have been drawn, to subsume under it those units of homogeneity that offer further insight into the major behavior. Such an approach has the special values of more readily allowing cross-cultural probes and of avoiding idiosyncratic flights that fail to educe cumulative information. The concentration on offense categories also points more clearly to the necessity not only to establish explanations in general for the particular crime but also to determine those elements of the social system that result in the labelling of certain kinds of behaviors as criminal offenses, the functions that such labelling serves, and the historical record of the particular offense category. It is for reasons such as these that we shall examine categories such as robbery, embezzlement, and arson, following a discussion of property offenders in general.

GENERAL PROPERTY OFFENDERS

Various studies attempt to differentiate between persons engaging in property offenses and those who follow more honest pathways or who commit other kinds of offenses, particularly assaultive crimes. The design of such comparisons indicates in part some of the difficulties regarding generalizations about property offenders, since it is one thing to compare burglars and murderers, but quite another to compare high school students who report engaging in diverse kinds of petty theft as opposed to other persons who deny such behavior.

Such diverse approaches do provide some overall information regarding property offenders, however, when they are viewed side by side. Robert Dentler and Lawrence Monroe, for instance, report several differences between junior-high-school pupils in Kansas who indicated considerable involvement in stealing (a so-called High Theft Score) and those who indicated less involvement. As might be expected, a much greater number of boys than girls had High Theft Scores. Less expected was the finding that youngest siblings are most likely to report stealing practices and oldest siblings are least likely to do so. On the other hand, the authors found no significant relationship between size of family, broken families, residential mobility and reported theft. The High Theft Score respondents were found to confide in their mothers and fathers significantly less often than their peers, to define themselves as very disobedient more often than others, and to perceive their families as essentially unloving.[27] Part of the difficulty of such results concerns the problem of chronology, however; it is always possible that self-definitions and perceptions of relationships follow, rather than precede, the behavior being studied. In this manner, for instance, a child with more to hide from his family may erect communication barriers between himself and them and then subsequently report his family as "unloving."

Such an interpretative impasse is particularly obvious in a recent report that attempted to discover the relationship between adolescent stealing and "temporal orientation," that is, awareness of time spans. In the experiment, a child was summoned to a school office, where he found the experimenter looking flustered, her purse contents scattered, and 65¢ in change lying about the desk. The experimenter then said that she had to go elsewhere for a while and asked the child to gather together some of the papers on the desk. On returning, the experimenter surreptitiously counted the money and found that 49 out of 120 children had stolen an average of 7.3 cents. Various tests were then administered to determine the temporal orientation of the subjects.[28] The difficulty in granting credence to the results lies, of course, in the fact that children who only moments before had stolen money were probably laboring under considerably more strain than their fellows, and their responses were apt to represent the product of such strain and to have little or nothing to do with their possible propensity for theft.

A much tighter experimental design was found in the Cambridge-Somerville study, which is one of the most informative sources of information regarding the characteristics of property offenders. The

27 Dentler and Monroe, "Early Adolescent Theft."
28 Brock and Del Giudice, "Stealing and Temporal Orientation."

Cambridge-Somerville project attempted to determine if a certain form of treatment—in this instance, friendship, example, and under-standing—would deter delinquency and/or produce other changes in the behavior and personalities of a group of boys who in many in-stances seemed headed for difficulty. The study was begun in 1938, with the intention of continuing it for ten years, but World War II forced the research to be concluded at a time when most of the boys had received five years of attention, and no one subject had received more than eight years.

The experimental design of the Cambridge-Somerville study matched 325 boys in a treatment group with 325 boys in a control group. Large amounts of data were collected about each of the boys, and treatment group members were then assigned to one of ten coun-selors. During the period of the study, the counselors attempted by whatever means they felt appropriate to assist the boy toward social adjustment and law-abiding behavior.

The results of the study were extremely discouraging. Evaluations made in 1949 showed that the behavior of the boys in the treatment group did not differ significantly from that of those in the control group. In fact, the treatment boys had a slightly higher rate of delin-quency, although their offenses were somewhat less serious. Various explanations were offered for the failure of the program. Among them, it was suggested that the boys had been too old for real help (their average age was 10½ years) and that the workers had not used standard, professional, social-work techniques. Some hope was held out that perhaps the treatment would manifest subsequent results by giving the boys internal resources,[29] an assumption that was tested in 1955, ten years after the termination of the project, but proved illusory. The treatment boys and the control group again showed no significant differences. The 1955 follow-up also drew upon the previously secured data to examine the subsequent life histories of individuals in the study. As the authors point out, their approach had at least one unique facet: All of the material they used had been gathered prior to the boys' difficulties with the law, and it was therefore not biased by the retroactive factors usually found in studies that look into an in-dividual's life and attitudes after he gets into trouble.

The largest and most amorphous category of Cambridge-Somer-ville offenders was that embracing crimes against property, which included a broadly defined list of crimes whose target was ostensibly either material property itself or a violation of the general rules safe-guarding property. Of the 263 boys whose records were still available, 86 had been convicted at least once for a crime against property. The analysis disclosed the following about these offenders as contrasted to individuals who had committed other forms of violations:

29 Powers and Witmer, *An Experiment in the Prevention of Delinquency.*

A high proportion of [property offenders] had been raised by neglecting mothers and fathers; they had either not been disciplined at all or had been controlled by erratically punitive measures; their homes were characterized by neglect and conflict; and their intelligence usually fell in the normal range. Furthermore, the majority had criminal fathers.[30]

Sixty-five percent of the boys raised by mothers who neglected them committed property crimes as compared to only 31 percent of the sons of all other types of mothers. Fifty-one percent of the criminal fathers had sons who committed property crimes as compared to 35 percent of the alcoholic or sexually unfaithful fathers and 28 percent of the "nondeviant" men. Forty-three percent of the Cambridge-Somerville boys who had experienced lax discipline or who had been subjected to erratic punitiveness committed property crimes as compared to only 24 percent of those disciplined in any other manner. The Intelligence Quotient (I.Q.) results were unexpected by the researchers, who found that 39 percent of the men with I.Q. scores between 81 and 110 committed property crimes as compared to only 25 percent of those with either high or low intelligence. Negatively, the researchers found no significant relationship between property crimes and neighborhood, and they concluded that "property crimes are not simply a result of economic poverty."[31]

The Cambridge-Somerville follow-up study conclusion that poverty itself is not a direct cause of theft finds support in an investigation conducted in England by William Oldham of fifty "common thieves." Study subjects, who were men incarcerated in a local prison, were chosen because of their history of property crime and an absence of crimes of violence. Of the fifty men, forty-two were said to have been motivated by "acquisitiveness" rather than by "dire financial need." Three men were believed to have stolen for revenge, one against a previous employer, and two against family members. Five were drunk at the time of their offense and believed that it would not otherwise have occurred. Finally, one man, who stole clothing, is said to have done so out of need.

Oldham was particularly struck by the absence of guilt among members of his sample. He noted:

Not one of the fifty expressed any shame at his offense, or had any feelings of remorse or guilt. Not one concerned himself with the distress or discomfort which he had caused to his victims. A few of the younger thieves worried about the anxiety which they had caused to their parents. Self-pity was marked and occurred in about half of the cases.[32]

Perhaps this finding adds support to the observations of both Ned Polsky and David Bordua, who point out that one of the lures of thievery is the unfettered existence it holds out, provided the practi-

30 McCord and McCord, *Origins of Crime,* p. 127.
31 *Ibid.,* pp. 127–130, 151.
32 Oldham, "The Common Thief," p. 117–118.

tioner is adept. "Indeed, one of the most genuinely appealing things about crime to career criminals and part-timers alike—though one would hardly gather this from the criminology texts," Polsky observes, "is that for most crimes the working hours are both short and flexible."[33] In the same manner, Bordua underlines the barriers to reform implicit in the "working hours" of criminal activity with the observation that "long-term involvement in the 'free undisciplined' street life with money at hand from petty theft and with the days devoted to play was not exactly ideal preparation for the humdrum life of the job."[34]

Finally, a number of studies attempt to determine the differences between acquisitive and assaultive criminals, although such efforts have generally been more in the nature of exploratory probes than conclusive pieces of research. Working with sixty women inmates in Indiana, Elsie Sjostedt administered a battery of psychological tests that yielded results in thirty-four areas. Half of the women had records showing only crimes against property, while the other half had criminal records concentrated in offenses against persons. The two groups were found to have virtually similar I.Q.s (Assaultive, 92.9; Acquisitive, 92.2) and to exhibit no significant differences in fantasy activity, conventionality of thought, sensitivity to stimuli of an emotional nature, introspection, erotic needs, or concern over bodily functions. The study also failed to uncover support for George Gardner's supposition that the thief is characterized by "oral receptivity" and by an "attitude that things are to be received by him without the concomitant necessity of giving anything of himself in return."[35]

In contrast to the assaultive individuals, who were subject to periods of depression and mood swings vacillating between the explosive, the impulsive, and the depressed, the acquisitive criminals were found to be "relatively restrained, passive individuals" who, in comparison with assaultive women, appeared to be "rather conforming."[36]

In St. Louis, after discovering that official arrest records of offenders often tend to be characterized by stable deviancy patterns (i.e., individuals who commit crimes against persons or crimes against property but not against both), Richard A. Peterson, David J. Pittman, and Patricia O'Neal attempted to differentiate nine violent from ten nonviolent offenders. On the basis of this small sample, they concluded that violent offenders are often characterized by the presence of long-standing psychotic disorders, particularly schizophrenia, while nonviolent offenders are marked by "sociopathic" personality disturbances due to chronic alcoholism and "sexual inversion." Responses

33 Polsky, *Hustlers, Beats, Others,* p. 103.
34 Bordua, "Delinquent Subcultures."
35 Gardner, "The Primary and Secondary Gains in Stealing," pp. 437–438.
36 Sjostedt, *A Study of the Personality Variables Relating to Assaultive and Acquisitive Crimes.*

to partial Rosenzweig Picture-Frustration tests, projective inventories that portray traumatic incidents happening to the subject and then request him to fill in his responses to the episodes, showed the violent offenders to be characterized by self-justification and direct verbal attack, while nonviolent criminals were characterized by passivity, denial, and compliance. Both personal and property offenders were similar in economic and class status. While broken homes, severe rejection, and cultural deprivation were common to both types of offenders, these factors occurred more frequently and grossly in the early lives of the offenders against the person.[37]

The findings of the exploratory studies in Indiana and St. Louis show similarities and provide several clues to distinctions that are characteristic of property offenders; for example, their general social conformity and compliance. Both studies, however, are handicapped by their small samples, and taken together they demonstrate a discrepancy in vocabulary that makes precise comparison difficult—a familiar shortcoming of social science research. In addition, there exist contradictions between them that require deeper investigation.

Specific Property Offenders

PERSONAL ROBBERY

It is noteworthy that the offense of robbery was selected by the President's Commission on Law Enforcement and Administration of Justice to epitomize the varied nature of criminal activity and the futility of recourse to simplistic, uni-dimensional kinds of solutions. On the opening page of the initial volume of the Commission's eleven-volume report, the complexity of robbery is discussed:

> Consider the crime of robbery which, since it involves both stealing and violence or the threat of it, is an especially hurtful and frightening one. In 1965 in America there were 118,916 robberies known to the police: 326 robberies a day; a robbery for every 1,630 Americans. Robbery takes dozens of forms, but suppose it took only four: forcible or violent purse-snatching by boys, muggings by drug addicts, store stickups by people with a sudden desperate need for money, and bank robberies by skillful professional criminals. The technical, organizational, legal, behavioral, economic and social problems that must be addressed if America is to deal with any degree of success with just those four kinds of events and those four kinds of persons are innumerable and refractory.[38]

Following this observation the Commission report proceeds to point out that many of the presumed causative factors influencing robbery are not directly within the ambit of criminal justice systems,

37 Peterson, Pittman, and O'Neal, "Stabilities in Deviance."
38 President's Commission, *Challenge of Crime in a Free Society*, p. 1.

but that they represent more fundamental matters of social arrangements:

> The unruliness of young people, widespread drug addiction, the existence of much poverty in a wealthy society, the pursuit of the dollar by any available means are phenomena the police, the courts, and the correctional apparatus, which must deal with crimes and criminals one by one, cannot confront directly. They are strands that can be disentangled from the fabric of American life only by the concerted action of all of society . . . unless society does take concerted action to change the general conditions and attitudes that are associated with crime, no improvement in law enforcement and administration of justice . . . will be of much avail.[39]

The President's Commission observation highlights problems confronting criminological analysis and understanding, not only in pointing up the diversity of offender types, but particularly in emphasizing the deep-rooted nature of causative factors in crime. At the same time, the Commission's observations, however well taken, also indicate commonplaces that are likely to arise in the absence of sophisticated criminological research upon which to base policy decisions. We know, for instance, that poverty differentially provokes persons to robbery and that the unqualified pursuit of the dollar enrolls only some persons in the race and only a few of these in robbery. However important such items are—and they are very important in setting in place criminogenic factors in our culture—they have differential impacts, both in terms of the number of criminal offenses and in terms of the persons who commit one or another kind of offense.

Historically, robbery was a relatively rare form of crime at the beginning of the century, probably because, to be successful, it necessitated careful disguise, considerable geographical mobility, or withdrawal from regular society. The offense, however, began to increase strikingly during the depression period of the 1930s. At that time, stringent measures were thought necessary to control depredations against property by the large number of unemployed, and many states used the death penalty for robbery, particularly when there was serious injury to the victim. In addition, the growing anonymity of urban existence undoubtedly contributed significantly to the increase in the robbery rate.

Our best information on robbery comes from a recent study conducted in England by the Cambridge Institute of Criminology. As always in studies confined to a single setting, it represents an enterprise of uncertain value in transferring without qualification results uncovered in one setting to a more general canvas; the need for cross-cultural criminological studies is vital. The British study emphasized the urban character of robbery, noting that 50 percent of the country's robberies occurred in London and six provincial cities, which together

39 *Ibid.*

account for only 27 percent of England's population. The British investigation also highlighted variations in criminal rates among different countries. In London, for instance, there is an average of about two robberies reported to the police each day; about one-sixteenth the rate for a city such as New York.

The British investigators desired to arrange robberies in terms of the motive of the perpetrator, but found that available data precluded definite conclusions about each offender's intent. Instead, offenses were broken down into five categories, and their 1957 numerical occurrence was tabulated: (1) Robbery of persons who as part of their employment were in charge of money or goods (174 cases), (2) Robbery in the open following a sudden attack (162 cases), (3) Robbery on private premises (42 cases), (4) Robbery after preliminary association between victim and offender—mainly for heterosexual or homosexual purposes—(71 cases), and (5) Robbery in cases of previous association of some duration between victim and offender, as with friends, lovers, workmates (13 cases).[40]

Investigation of the trends of robbery in London showed a total increase of 61 percent between 1950 and 1957, but it also indicated that the proportion of offenses in each of the five categories had remained fairly constant. Most victims of robbery were men, and weapons were carried by robbers in about one-third of the cases, with the most common being blunt instruments. Firearms were used in one case in 1950 and two cases in 1957, although they were carried in about 10 percent of the robberies. About half of the offenses were not cleared by arrest, a figure higher than that for offenses against the person, but considerably lower than that for other property offenses. If the robber escaped the scene of the crime, his chances for evading later detection were about seven in ten. The British study also illustrated how changes in surrounding circumstances can have a sharp impact on robbery rates. Thus, the Street Offenses Act of 1959, which banned solicitation by prostitutes on public thoroughfares, also eliminated totally a previously common pattern involving robbery of a prostitute by a client or by a person lying in wait for her at the end of her night's work. In addition, there was a noteworthy decrease in the number of robberies of persons decoyed by prostitutes, probably a result of the fact that former streetwalkers were now operating from semipermanent residences.

Figures from the United States indicate much greater recourse to weapons than in England. In contrast to the one-third of the total London robbers, one-half of the robbers in the United States carry weapons. Ironically, the likelihood of a victim being injured during a robbery increases if the offense involves "yoking" or "mugging," that is, unarmed robberies from the rear, than if weapons are used. A survey of 279 robberies conducted by the District of Columbia Crime

40 McClintock and Gibson, *Robbery in London*, p. 16.

Commission found that some injury was inflicted in 25 percent of the cases, a figure that included injuries to victims in 40 percent of the muggings and only 11 percent of the armed robberies.[41]

The best study of robbers in the United States is that undertaken by Julian Roebuck and Mervyn L. Cadwallader, although it confines itself to incarcerated Negro offenders. The thirty-two subjects, who showed numerous arrests for armed robberies, differed significantly in many respects from the remaining Negro prison inmates. Among other things, all armed robbers had police contact prior to the age of eighteen, as compared to 51 percent of the other offenders. More frequently than the remaining prisoners, the armed robbers' mother or mother substitute was the dominant parent, was a migrant from the South, and had worked as a domestic servant. The self-image that the robbers put forward was one of bravery and daring, and they scoffed at criminals who were nonviolent property offenders. According to them, robbers showed the following sterling personality characteristics:

> You got heart, you can get that bread in a hurry! Course you got to figure the angles. These pimps and con men ain't nothing. Those suckers are punks on the street just like they are here. Holler at one and see him keep getting up.[42]

The difficulty with Roebuck's and Cadwallader's study, however suggestive of further investigation it may be, lies primarily in its delimited sample and particularly in the contrast group employed. Thus, the results may not represent distinctions between Negro armed robbers and other Negro offenders, but rather between Negroes who are differently located in the social structure. In addition, the sample to which the armed robbers are compared represents a group filtered through the system of criminal justice, and alterations in that system could dramatically transform the comparative portrait of armed robbers, although the group studied might remain precisely the same.

BANK ROBBERY

Bank robbery, as a specialized form of criminal activity, merits separate consideration. Bank robberies, constituting frontal assaults on accumulated wealth, appear to be the successors in the United States to the train robberies that began in the early 1870s and continued for the following sixty years, reaching a peak at the turn of the century.[43] Since 1934, bank robberies have been prosecuted as federal offenses because of national insurance programs to which banks almost invariably subscribe. This centralized enforcement allows for rather uniform statistical information. The statistics, collected by the F.B.I.,

41 District of Columbia Crime Commission, *Report*, p. 94.
42 Roebuck and Cadwallader, "The Negro Armed Robber as a Criminal Type," p. 24.
43 Block, *Great Train Robberies of the West*, pp. 8–13.

show a dramatic decline in bank robberies, almost to the point of nonexistence, followed by a rapid increase that continues to this day. In 1943, there were only twenty-four bank robberies. By 1950, the figure had risen more than three times, but the total was still only eighty-one robberies. By 1959, however, the figure had increased to 346 robberies, and in 1967 it had risen to 1,730 offenses, up 50 percent from the previous year.

The most comprehensive review of bank robberies appears in a study conducted by the F.B.I. of 238 offenses that took place during the three summer months of 1964. The most likely time for a bank to be robbed proved to be Friday, between 10 A.M. and 2 P.M., and in eighty-six of 100 cases the robbers made away with money, averaging $5,591 per robbery. Most of the offenders operated alone (172 cases), and about half concentrated their attention on branch banks, which are usually less well guarded and architecturally more vulnerable. In all but sixty-seven of the robberies some weapon was employed, primarily hand guns. Of the 238 robberies, 19 involved violence before, during, or immediately following the offense. In two cases there were deaths, both instances involving law enforcement officers. In five cases the robbers took hostages with them to aid in their escape. By a year later—in April 1965—210 of the 332 robbers involved in the 238 cases had been apprehended. In examining the total sample of cases, the F.B.I. investigators were particularly taken with their haphazard nature:

> Many of the violations . . . revealed that the robbers seldom made any well-defined plans as to their methods of operation or getaway. . . . One pair of armed robbers jumped from their car and dashed up to the doors of a bank only to find they were locked. Seven robbers were arrested inside the bank by guards or police officers who were summoned while the teller stalled. Twenty-four who attempted robberies were thwarted by bank employees who either refused to comply with their demands, screamed, or merely ducked behind their cages or calmly walked away. In one of these cases, the bandit fled when the teller fainted, and in another, the teller advised the would-be-bandit that she was going to faint and he told her to go ahead, then calmly walked out.[44]

Somewhat more sophisticated than the F.B.I. count of bank robberies and the tabulation of their correlates is a recent study by George M. Camp, who interviewed 132 bank robbers in five federal prisons and surveyed 300 banks. Camp, pointing out that arrests for bank theft are higher than for any other major property crime, believes that there is little direct relationship between fear of apprehension and willingness to undertake bank robbery. Both bankers and bank robbers, he maintains, believe that they have nothing to lose from the robberies. Banks count heavily on insurance to cover their losses

44 "Profile of a Bank Robber," p. 21.

and take few preventive measures. Robbers therefore regard the
bank as a passive and willing victim, and think that the gamble is
well worth the risks. The bank robber, according to Camp, "views
the consequences of arrest and punishment to be no worse than the
consequences of his present conditions. On the other hand, he can
visualize a significant gain by successfully robbing a bank."[45] That
bank robbery does not arouse guilt feelings in offenders is likely tied
to more general convictions about the morality of banking itself. In
this respect, for instance, there have been reports of bank robbers
who undertake their offenses to secure funds with which to make
overdue installment payments. Not paying one's just debts is what is
bad, not bank robbery—or, as one practitioner put the matter, "I was
determined to protect my credit rating."[46]

Particularly noteworthy has been the infiltration of first-time
offenders into the ranks of bank robbers. Of the persons apprehended
by the F.B.I., about one in four has no prior record for any offense
whatsoever, and almost that number have records for only minor
misdemeanors. The elite of bank robbers, who exhibit many characteristics of professional criminals, except that they often employ the
threat of violence instead of subtler arts, are now vanishing. Their
attitudes are seen in the autobiography of Blackie Audett, who
participated in at least twenty-seven bank robberies. Audett relates
with considerable pride that he never killed a person, although he
admits that, if he had been forced to kill to save himself or his
confederates, he would not have hesitated. Audett's first robbery was
that of a Canadian mail train, when he was only nineteen; the holdup
netted him $1,500,000. He illustrates the professional specialization of
the accomplished bank robber as well as the importance of tutelage by
saying, "I had pretty well cut my teeth on bank heisting in Pueblo
and the Rose City bank job. But it was Al Sutton who really showed
me the business. I picked up a pretty good knack for it from Al and it
was my trade, off and on, for quite a while."

Frequently, Audett and other bank robbers purchased plans from
an individual who did nothing but prepare elaborate outlines for
bank robberies. This man would spend weeks investigating a bank's
routine, the influx and outflow of money, and the habits of employees.
He would then scout all of the highways and sideroads for as much
as seventy-five miles on all sides of the bank, testing speeds, surfaces,
intersections, and traffic flow. Before the robbery, gasoline cans would
be cached along the roads that were to be used and along alternate
routes. Cars would be equipped with medical supplies, and stand-by
cars would be hidden at strategic places in case of emergencies. For
his services, the planner, who never participated in the robbery, would
receive either a flat sum or a percentage of the loot.

45 Camp, *Nothing to Lose.*
46 "The Boom in Bank Robbery," p. 115.

Audett's pride in his status and his abilities is typical of professional thieves. During a trip to Europe to avoid arrest, Audett observes that the Continent was "crawling with all sorts of jewel thieves, con men, and boosters. Cheap crooks. Honest crooks like bank robbers, who don't make no bones about what they are, wasn't bothering Europe none."[47] Noteworthy is Audett's self-righteous designation of bank robbers as "honest crooks."

EMBEZZLEMENT

Standard explanations of embezzlement insist that it is a crime brought about, to quote one source, by indulgence in "bookies, babes, and booze."[48] The word itself derives from the French *bezzle*, which means "drink to excess, gluttonage, revel, waste in riot, and plunder."[49]

Embezzling has commanded more attention than most crimes committed by white-collar persons, probably because it represents an obvious violation of the substantive criminal law and because the offender is an individual rather than a more amorphous corporate entity. Embezzling offenses are, however, often camouflaged, and many victims do not press the prosecution of offenders, even when they are discovered. For one thing, there is a fear of publicity and loss of public confidence in a business that is known to have been bilked. For another, companies are sometimes afraid of what they call a "flareback" effect, brought about by the complexity of the case, an acquittal by a confused jury, and a subsequent civil suit against the firm for harassment and false arrest.[50] It is known that bank embezzlements exceed bank robberies by a substantial margin and that the ranks of bank embezzlers in 1960 included 100 bank presidents, 65 vice presidents, 145 managers, 345 cashiers, and 490 others, principally tellers and clerks. The President's Commission on Law Enforcement and Administration of Justice notes that estimating losses from embezzlement is like "guessing the size of an iceberg"; extrapolating from available data, however, the Commission suggests that each year more than $200 million is embezzled in the United States.[51]

The effect of embezzling on the vitality of businesses should not be underestimated. Two-hundred businesses were reported by the New York State Labor Department to have failed in a single year, solely because of employee embezzling. Embezzlers, the New York agency reports, steal more than five times as much money as all other criminals combined. The average embezzler is described as "socially genteel, enjoying the respect of his fellow workers and community." He is usually about thirty-five years old, married, with one or two children, living in his own mortgaged home, and driving a medium-

47 Audett, *Rap Sheet.*
48 "Embezzlers: The Trusted Thieves."
49 Cort, "The Embezzler."
50 Jaspan and Black, *Thief With the White Collar,* p. 242.
51 President's Commission, *Crime and Its Impact,* p. 47

priced automobile. He has generally obtained a position of financial trust through "ability and diligence." The New York department maintains that neither greed nor the pressures of a materialistic society fully account for embezzlement. Rather, it feels, embezzlement is the result of "the gradual weakening of the national moral fiber."

Somewhat similar conclusions on the social characteristics of embezzlement have been reached by Cressey, who studied a total of 133 embezzlers imprisoned at Joliet, Illinois; Chino, California; and Terre Haute, Indiana. He found embezzlers to be a group apart from other prisoners, with the highest intelligence scores and the least amount of recidivism. Cressey notes three conditions that he considers essential in leading a person to violate a financial trust[52]:

(1) *When the person conceives of himself as having a financial problem that is nonshareable.* By a nonshareable problem, a category containing many subdivisions, Cressey means a dilemma that an individual cannot resolve by seeking the help of another person, on account of his own nature and the defined nature of the situation. A bank teller who conceives his social role as one requiring more money than he is earning, or a person who loses money at gambling but cannot face his new financial condition because his unworthiness would be implied, are both defined as individuals with nonshareable problems. Cressey maintains that he did not discover any embezzler who had taken money because of any stereotypic rationale, such as that implied in definitions of gluttonage and plunder.

(2) *When the person becomes aware that his nonshareable problem can be secretly resolved by violation of his financial trust.* Cashiers, accountants, and persons similarly employed are aware of the techniques necessary for fraud, but before they embezzle they must, Cressey maintains, make a mental connection between this abstract awareness and the immediate realization that they can resolve their financial difficulties by utilizing these techniques.

(3) *When the person is able to apply to his own conduct rationalizations that enable him to adjust his conception of himself as a trusted person to his conception of himself as a user of the entrusted funds or property.* We have previously examined the important role of rationalization in buttressing an individual's self-conception against the harsher perceptions of society as it judges his behavior. For embezzlers, rationalization usually takes the form of an expressed belief that they are only "borrowing" the money and will eventually return it, that "some of our most respectable citizens got their start in life by temporarily using other people's money," and similiar palliatives.

Cressey's approach uses a methodological technique known as analytic induction, and it has been viewed with some reservations. William Robinson notes that this approach, by attempting to posit a

52 Cressey, *Other People's Money*, pp. 16–20.

universal explanation of a phenomenon, must limit and restrict the definition of the phenomenon. Cressey's conclusions, therefore, fit only persons who accept their positions in good faith and not those who accept a trust for the express purpose of violating it. Second, the method of analytic induction does not allow predictive statements to be made about individual possibilities of embezzling behavior. Robinson argues that since Cressey's explanations cannot be used as a basis for prediction they represent only partial explanations.[53] Karl Schuessler summarizes the difficulties involved in Cressey's study in the following manner:

> This book, like all serious studies, is not without its methodological difficulties. The chief one, characteristic of all similar *ex post facto* studies, is based on the fact that the sample was composed of persons who had already engaged in the behavior to be explained. The finding that all cases in the sample had a single set of circumstances in common does not, unhappily, prove that all persons in such circumstances will embezzle. The empirical validation would require an unselected group of persons having in common the hypothesized circumstances who then should all subsequently display the expected behavior. Needless to say, Cressey's proposition is impossible to test.[54]

ARSON

The meaning of fire presents a number of intriguing problems in symbolism. In our society, the color red is considered the warmest, the most stimulating, and the most exciting of the various shades along the spectrum. Lipstick and nail polish are almost invariably red-tinted. Theologically, hell is portrayed as a fiery place, although some people might find a location with a perpetually freezing temperature a more fearsome doom. The American language is replete with fire symbols to express deep emotions. A person who is angry is said to "see red" and to be "burned up"; an enamored individual "carries a torch" and his affective object is "a ball of fire"; a person of deep religious conviction has a "burning zeal." The symbolic idea of fire is shown too by the use of an eternal flame to mark the grave of John F. Kennedy and by the lighting of candles to commemorate the dead. The fascination of fire is readily discovered by watching youngsters when they have the opportunity to play with fire.

The relationship between these characteristics and the crime of arson is difficult to establish, however. It would be of interest to determine the universality of fire symbolism and to ascertain cross-cultural patterns in arson. There is a particular need to discover the meaning that fire comes to have in the ideational life of the person who uses it to commit crime. Information on the early fire contact

---

53 Robinson, "The Logical Structure of Analytic Induction."
54 Schuessler, review of *Other People's Money*.

of a youngster and the emotional significance of such contact might provide keys to arson.

Statistical information relating to arson is flimsy, primarily because of the difficulty of extracting from the total number of fires those that are incendiary in nature. The law of arson presumes that fires are of accidental origin, and it becomes necessary to prove beyond reasonable doubt that a particular fire was maliciously set.[55] This means eliminating from consideration other possible causes, such as carelessness, spontaneous combustion, and faulty wiring. Arson is considered to be the "easiest crime to commit and the most difficult to detect." The fire itself is apt to destroy crucial evidence.

It seems likely that there is less arson in the United States today than there was twenty-five years ago.[56] Most earlier arson offenses took place in rural areas and were directed against farm buildings. The urbanization of the society would therefore account for a drop in such offenses. In addition, growing sophistication among arson investigators and fire insurance companies may have helped deter illegal fire-setting.

Many arsons, like other crimes against property, appear to be related to materialistic ambitions. Fires may be set in commercial concerns with outdated stock, too large an inventory, or seasonal decreases in consumer demand. Over-insurance, representing valuations far in excess of the real worth of the merchandise, may encourage a person to "sell his property to the insurance company."[57] On the periphery of the commercial world there are often professional "torches," individuals who contract to set fires in return for a percentage of the insurance profits. Such persons employ elaborate celluloid devices, candles, or mechanical gadgets to set off fires long after they have left the scene. However, the more elaborate the apparatus, the more likely apprehension will be, for nothing is so hard to trace as a burned match, and few things are so easy as elaborate timing devices, even though partially damaged by heat.[58] There is at least one case on record in which a fire insurance agent burned a house to convince community residents of the desirability of purchasing policies. Automobiles are also often the object of fires aimed at collecting insurance money. Burned cars needing considerable mechanical overhaul, or those in which the owner is far behind on installment payments, are always viewed with suspicion. Vivid evidence of the extensiveness of automobile arson was shown during World War II, when there was a sharp drop in the rate of "accidental" automobile fires, undoubtedly the product of the difficulty of purchasing new cars during this period.

55 Cohn, "Convicting the Arsonist."
56 Battle and Weston, *Arson*, p. 34.
57 A common commercial joke concerns two men who meet at a luncheon counter. "How was that fire in your store last week?" asks the first. "Shh," says the other, finger over lips, "that fire is next week."
58 Kirk, *Crime Investigation*, p. 361.

Apart from commercial motives, arson is often committed by persons who seek revenge. It has also been used to cover up other crimes, particularly murder, and to divert attention from an area in which another crime is going to be committed.[59] Cases of murder followed by arson are sometimes interpreted as symbolic attempts to eliminate all traces of the victim from existence, thereby reinforcing a delusion that the victim never was really alive. Diverting attention by arson is a rather risky business, since arson itself is generally a more serious offense than other property crimes. A considerable number of fires are also set by individuals who seek notoriety, such as volunteer firemen, applicants for night watchman positions, rookie policemen, and would-be-heroes. Finally, there is a group of so-called compulsive fire-setters, loosely gathered under the heading of "pyromaniacs."

Nolan Lewis, in an intensive investigation into pathological fire-setting, notes the particular appeal that arson has for certain personality types. Fire is an excellent means of destruction, provides an indirect outlet for pent-up aggression, and produces spectacular effects. Lewis found that arsonists initiating fires for other than commercial reasons, such as insurance fraud, were both physical cowards and exhibitionists and that pathological fire-setters tended to be persons of low intelligence, with 48 percent of his sample falling into the moron category. In addition, arson appears to be outstandingly a crime of adolescents and young adults.

Lewis believes that the pyromaniac suffers from a physical inferiority that leads to compensatory efforts culminating in the flamboyant exhibition produced by a spectacular fire. Pyromaniacs show classic symptoms of irresistible impulse before they embark on their fire-setting. They report mounting tension, restlessness, an urge for motion, and conversion symptoms such as headaches, ear ringing, and heart palpitations, all culminating in a state in which there appears to be a loss of identity. Most psychiatric writers believe that pyromania has a sexual basis and point to research evidence gained from studies of apprehended pyromaniacs who say that they receive great sexual satisfaction from their behavior. Lewis, however, thinks that such sexual satisfaction is more likely to be symbolic than real. He points to the great number of baby carriages set on fire in urban apartment houses and maintains that such activity represents symbolic hostility against infants, although it appears equally tenable that the carriages are the most flammable objects in the hallways of big-city tenements. After studying a large number of fire-setters, Lewis concludes:

> A desire for exhibitionism is the fact most common to each of the men described, as though they began life with an exaggerated wish to become leading participants in the contemporary drama, and then, when it was realized that fate had relegated them to insignificant roles, they

59 Considine, *Man Against Fire*, pp. 192–193.

secretly staged a drama of their own, in which they were author, stage director, and the leading actors.[60]

Arson and Epilepsy

Several writers report a rather puzzling relationship between the disorder of epilepsy and the crime of arson. The relationship has been summed up by a New York fire marshal, who said, "Epilepsy is found in an important number of persons found to be pyromaniacs. I am sorry to have to bring this point up, and as far as I have been able to determine there is no medical opinion on the reasons for the tendency of epileptic pyromaniacs."[61] The marshal's reluctance to speak of the possible epilepsy-arson relationship undoubtedly is a reaction against a long and vicious tradition in criminology, begun by Cesare Lombroso, which insisted that epilepsy and crime inevitably went hand in hand, that epileptics were, almost by definition, criminals.[62] Later writers tempered these viewpoints, although there were nonetheless a considerable number of treatises using such phrases as "moral epilepsy." It was not until C. L. Anderson's work in Michigan that empirical evidence tested the Lombroso thesis. Studying the extent of epilepsy in the general population and among prison inmates, Anderson found that 210 out of 100,000 persons in the general population and 254 out of 100,000 prisoners were epileptics, a difference of no statistical significance.[63]

The failure to establish any direct tie between epilepsy and crime is not surprising when we delve further into the dynamics of the disorder. There are between 500,000 and 1,500,000 epileptics in the United States—the range of estimates is partly due to variations in definitions of epilepsy—and about 80 percent are able to control their seizures through medication.[64] Lombroso's concentration on epilepsy as a "degenerative" disease reflects little more than a traditional attitude toward a badly misunderstood condition. The Bible related epileptic seizures to visitations by the Devil (Luke 9:37-43) and the early Greeks labelled it the "sacred disease," although Hippocrates, who wrote around 400 B.C., said that it was "folly to ascribe to divine malediction an affection that is wholly human."[65] Such outstanding persons as Buddha, Socrates, Alexander the Great, Julius Caesar, Mohammed, Peter the Great, Feodor Dostoyevski, and Napoleon are all reported to have been epileptics.[66] Epilepsy is now regarded not as a disease, but as a symptom of various kinds of disorders.[67] It does

60 Lewis and Yarnell, *Pathological Firesetting.*
61 *New York Times,* August 4, 1953. See also John Clarke, "Delinquent Personalities," p. 156.
62 Ferrero, *Lombroso's Criminal Man,* p. xvi.
63 Anderson, "Epilepsy in the State of Michigan."
64 Barrow and Fabing, *Epilepsy and the Law,* p. 3.
65 Drake, "Current Drug Theory of Epilepsy."
66 Bryant, *Genius and Epilepsy.*
67 Tower, *Neurochemistry of Epilepsy,* p. 11.

not appear to be inherited, although a predisposition to epilepsy may be genetically transmitted as a recessive trait.

These facts, however, do not explain the relationship that may exist between epilepsy and arson. Otto Mönkemöller felt that epileptics during their confused periods see visions of fire and destruction, and he found twenty-seven cases of epilepsy among the 240 arson cases he investigated.[68] Gustav Aschaffenburg simply observed that "epilepsy, arson, mysticism, cruelty and sexual excitement are all interrelated," taking in rather indiscriminately a large piece of psychic territory.[69] Nolan D. C. Lewis, after examining more than 1,000 arsonists, expressed doubt that arson and epilepsy are associated to the extent commonly believed, concluding that "the type of firesetting seems to depend entirely on the basic personality trends . . . and there is no special pattern for the epileptic as such."[70] Whatever the true state of facts, it is certainly obvious that there is no automatic identity between arson and epilepsy.

Summary
Property offenses are generally the routine, run-of-the-mill events that occupy much of law enforcement and judicial energy. Insurance coverage often allows for replacement, blunting long-lasting concern among victims regarding their losses. The absence of drama in most property offenses seems to be reflected in the paucity of in-depth criminological studies of these offenses and their perpetrators. Such studies, which would make stimulating intellectual work, would have to cut into the roots of economic philosophies, the development of wants, the cultivation of attitudes toward work, and similar items in order to bring about deeper understanding of property crimes.

For Further Reading
CRESSEY, DONALD R. *Other People's Money: A Study in the Social Psychology of Embezzlement*. Glencoe, Ill: The Free Press, 1953.
    From his investigation of 133 embezzlers, Professor Cressey constructs, through the employment of analytic induction, a theoretical explanation for the violation of financial trust. The volume is instructive both for the insight it provides into the act of embezzlement and for the method it employs in approaching its subject matter.

GIBBONS, DON C., AND DONALD L. GARRITY. "Some Suggestions for the Development of Etiological and Treatment Theory in Criminology," in *Social Forces*. Vol. 38 (October 1959), pp. 51–58.
    That criminal typologies provide a valuable framework for the development of explanations of particular kinds of crime and the treatment of

68 Quoted in Lewis and Yarnell, *Pathological Firesetting*, p. 20.
69 *Ibid.*, p. 24.
70 *Ibid.*, p. 386.

different kinds of offenders is the thesis of this paper. The authors support their viewpoint by putting forward a fourteen-category typology, including within it many property offenses. They then indicate the treatment implications of their typological approach.

Lewis, Nolan D. C., and Helen Yarnell. *Pathological Firesetting (Pyromania)*. New York: Nervous and Mental Disease Monographs, 1951.

In a definitive psychiatric examination of both pyromania and arson, the authors delineate distinct behavioral categories, both in terms of the personalities of the perpetrators and the motives for their acts. Short on social explanations, the volume is nonetheless replete with elaborate case histories that provide food for speculative interpretation. The volume also includes a thorough review of the literature regarding arson, much of which is of European origin.

McClintock, F. H., and Evelyn Gibson. *Robbery in London*. London: Macmillan, 1961.

Researchers at the Cambridge Institute of Criminology looked into diverse aspects of each of 462 robbery offenses that had taken place in London in 1957. The offenses were classified into five categories, primarily in terms of the relationship between the victim and the offender and the place where the offense occurred. Following this, the investigation looked at robbery in London in 1950 so that comparisons could be drawn between the two periods, not only in terms of offense patterns, but also in regard to sentencing practices and recidivism rates.

McCord, William, and Joan McCord, with Irving Kenneth Zola. *Origins of Crime: A New Evaluation of the Cambridge-Somerville Youth Study*. New York: Columbia University Press, 1959.

Drawing upon the extensive material gathered in the original Cambridge-Somerville study, and comparing these data to the subsequent careers of the subjects, the authors develop a number of statistically significant differences between types of offenders, although they are limited to the background items originally explored. The book is particularly valuable in discussing the implications of various types of family constellations upon behavior.

12
White-Collar Crime

The designation "white-collar crime" has come to cover a wide array of illegal and illicit enterprises by both individuals and corporate bodies. A white-collar criminal is generally defined as a person of high socioeconomic status who violates the laws designed to regulate his occupational activities.[1] The term is often used to embrace, rather indiscriminately, behavior such as restraint of trade, monopoly practices, pilfering of office supplies, income tax evasion, and fraudulent advertising. Sometimes the label "white-collar-crime" is applied to forms of behavior that represent "sharp" business practices, but against which no statutory laws or administrative fiats lie. Such usage, however, is patently contrary to the requirement that, to be considered a crime, an act must of necessity be violative of a statutorily proscribed standard.

Despite its unfortunately loose definition, the idea of white-collar criminality does carry within it a number of elements of basic importance to the study of criminology. It provides substantive information on a relatively unexplored facet of illegal behavior; more important, it sheds penetrating light on and raises basic issues regarding theoretical explanations of criminal activity.

It was from just such a twin perspective that Edwin H. Sutherland undertook his investigations of upper-class and middle-class illegal behavior, particularly as it appeared in the world of corporate endeavor.[2] Sutherland declared that he was not concerned with muckraking, but rather with adding a crucial dimension to criminal theory. The dimension was represented by a defense and elaboration of the theory of *differential association* (see Chapter 4) and a concomitant denegation of psychiatric explanations of criminal behavior and of explanations based on items pertinent only to particular social classes.

1 Sutherland, in Branham and Kutash, *Encyclopedia of Criminology*, p. 511.
2 Lindesmith, "Edwin H. Sutherland's Contribution to Criminology."

Differential association is essentially a restatement of postulates of basic learning theory. It is built on the deterministic proposition that criminal behavior is learned in interaction with other persons. If criminal behavior is learned, Sutherland maintains, it can be learned at all levels of society, not only at the lower levels represented by the traditional criminals. Sutherland stated his case against psychiatric explanations of criminal behavior after he had documented evidence of widespread illegality on the part of leading American corporations with the following statement:

> We have no reason to think that General Motors has an inferiority complex or that the Aluminum Company of America has a frustration-aggression complex, or that U.S. Steel has an Oedipus complex, or that the Armour Company has a death wish or that the Duponts desire to return to the womb. The assumption that an offender must have some such pathological distortion of the intellect or the emotions seems to me absurd, and if it is absurd regarding the crimes of businessmen, it is equally absurd regarding the crimes of persons in the lower economic class.[3]

White-collar criminality, in addition to the theoretical issues it raises, also cuts to the heart of questions of social health and integrity. The President's Commission on Law Enforcement and Administration of Justice, for instance, suggested that

> White-collar crime affects the whole moral climate of our society. Derelictions by corporations and their managers, who usually occupy leadership positions in their communities, establish an example which tends to erode the moral base of the law and provide opportunity for other kinds of offenders to rationalize their misconduct.[4]

It is sometimes argued, along these lines, that traditional kinds of crime serve to unite community sentiment against the violator and to reinforce adherence to desired standards. On the other hand, white-collar crimes, being more subtle, less visible, and emanating from sectors of the social structure that are supposed to supply leadership, undermine public confidence, create dissent, and ultimately contribute to the decline of those civilizations that are unable to control them. Such a hypothesis, however, requires a considerably more decisive reading of the histories of present and past civilizations before it can be accepted at face value. It may be true, for instance, that social unrest in the presence of white-collar violations tends to create opportunities for moral leaders to emerge—such as Christ did in regard to the moneylenders of his time—and to restructure a society in a manner that would not otherwise have occurred in the absence of flagrant predatory activity.

3 Sutherland, "Crime and Business," p. 96.
4 President's Commission, *Crime and Its Impact*, p. 104.

History of White-Collar Crime

The emergence of the concept of white-collar crime has been labelled as "possibly the most significant recent development in criminology."[5] The concept has also been called "a propagandistic weapon, which under the meretricious guise of science is to be used for the establishment of a new order."[6] Certainly it is true that the present study of white-collar crime is "as controversial as it is provocative."[7]

Critics contend that the term "white-collar crime" blurs distinctions between violators of criminal law who are publicly stigmatized as criminals and those who are not. Persons with training in law sometimes also insist that the concept has been misapplied to actions that are essentially civil wrongs, and that it confuses torts with crimes; they also believe that offenses handled by administrative agencies should not be called crimes.

Proponents of more intensive investigations of white-collar offenses, on the other hand, believe that criminology should study all violations of law that are similar to traditional crimes, no matter how they are named or processed. Sutherland once defended this view by analogy, pointing out that tuberculosis remains a clinical entity whether the bearer is isolated in a sanatorium or treated on an out-patient basis with drugs. So, too, he believes, white-collar transgressions should be considered violations of criminal law, whether they result in "cease and desist" orders, in fines, or in prison sentences. The difficulty of the analogy, however, inheres in the fact that society is not apt to vary the treatment of tuberculosis in terms of the manner in which the disease was contracted, and it is not interested in such ideas as "guilt" or "innocence" in determining how to deal with tuberculosis.

The present criminological interest in white-collar crime finds its roots in biblical tradition, particularly in the writings of prophets such as Micah, who castigated exploitative behavior by persons in positions of trust and power.[8] The tradition reached its heights in the United States in the 1920s, in the work of a group of writers known collectively as the "muckrakers"—persons such as Frank Norris, Ida Tarbell, and Lincoln Steffens.[9] At the same time, a corps of novelists, including writers such as Sinclair Lewis, ripped into the self-satisfieds and selfish shibboleths of the established order.

Muckraking lingers today in the works of social critics such as Vance Packard[10] and Ralph Nader,[11] but its force has largely dissipated by the correction of the more blatant evils it pinpointed and by the

5 Newman, "White-Collar Crime," p. 735.
6 Caldwell, Book Review, p. 282.
7 Sykes, *Crime and Society*, p. 205.
8 See Heschel, *The Prophets*.
9 Chalmers, *Social and Political Ideas of Muckrakers;* Weinberg and Weinberg, *The Muckrakers;* Swados, *Years of Conscience.*
10 See, for instance, Packard, *Hidden Persuaders.*
11 Nader, *Unsafe At Any Speed.*

emergence of subtler tactics that require more elaborate forms of analysis and corrective policies. The fictional component of the social reform movement gave way to a tendency among writers to concentrate on intra-psychic mechanisms rather than on broad social themes. Commercial exploitation today is apt to be treated in novels, if it is dealt with at all, in terms of the drives and motivations underlying the protagonist's behavior, traced to his early life and psychological makeup, rather than as a matter of greed, cruelty, and avarice.

Sociology, coming into the academic picture in the 1890s, clearly saw itself as a reformist enterprise, employing the tools of science to correct social evils.[12] Lester F. Ward, the first president of the American Sociological Association, did not hesitate to note in a treatise entitled *Pure Sociology* that "as you look out a car window, the rocks and trees are placarded all over with lies."[13] As Ward saw it, once sociology became established, legislatures would become outmoded, although they might be used as "a merely formal way of putting the final sanction of society on decisions that have been worked out in the sociological laboratory."[14]

Ward's nephew by marriage Edward A. Ross, another preeminent sociologist of the time, directed his fire against persons he labelled "criminaloids," individuals who would later be defined as white-collar criminals by Sutherland. It was Ross' belief that it was not sycophancy, admiration of success, or the reluctance to take action against persons in high positions that inhibited social retaliation against white-collar crime. Public passivity, Ross believed, was related to perplexity; the newer kinds of offenses lacked "the brimstone smell." Ross suggested that the goals of the criminaloid were acknowledged social goals—money, power, consideration—and that it was in his haste to achieve these goals and in his lack of particularity regarding the methods employed that the criminaloid differed from his law-abiding fellows. Of the discrepancy between the criminaloid's personal and commerical standards, Ross said, "He is unevenly moral; oak in the family and clan virtues, but basswood in commercial and civic ethics." He said that the criminaloid engages in a "mimicry of the good" marked by "flag-worship, old-soldier sentiment, observance of all the national holidays, perfervid patriotism, party regularity and support." The criminaloid knows full well, Ross noted, that "the giving of a fountain or a park, the establishing of a college chair in the Neolithic drama or the elegiac poetry of the Chaldaeans, will more than outweigh the dodging of taxes, the grabbing of streets, and the corrupting of city councils." For Ross it was essential to the control of white-collar crime that there

12 See Geis, "Sociology and Sociological Jurisprudence," pp. 271–279.
13 Ward, *Pure Sociology*, p. 488.
14 Ward, *Applied Sociology*, pp. 338–339.

be a growth of moral indignation regarding the newer offenses,[15] a view that also has contemporary support.[16]

Scathing denunciations of white-collar criminal activity, such as those contained in early sociological writings, became unfashionable as sociology self-consciously groped toward a more scientific, neutral position on social issues. Two recent presidents of the American Sociological Association, looking backward with a certain condescension, indicate the low status now assigned to the ameliorative efforts of their predecessors. Robert K. Merton, for instance, has been critical of what he saw in himself as an early "slum-encouraged provincialism of thinking that the primary subject-matter of sociology was centered in such peripheral problems of social life as divorce and juvenile delinquency,"[17] and Howard P. Becker has caricatured early sociology as an enterprise concerned primarily with "Three S's—sin, sex, and sewage."[18]

The depression period in the United States nonetheless inevitably focused criminological attention on certain ills of the economic system. In his 1935 textbook, Albert Morris, of Boston University, foreshadows current focus on white-collar crime by calling attention to persons he labels "criminals of the upperworld." Difficulties arise in identifying upperworld criminals, Morris points out, because "our general ethical notions are befogged or dulled by the near universality of sharp, if not illegal, business practices." Nonetheless Morris believes that upperworld criminals are genuine, not metaphorical criminals, and that they remain unidentified only because our society falls into the "unjustifiable habit of limiting that appellation to the obstreperous, socially inferior denizens of the underworld; the day laborers in the field of crime." He also adds:

> Unlike the criminals of the underworld, the permissive criminals of the upperworld have never been marked off and dramatized as a distinct group upon which public disapproval could be focussed. They have never been rounded up by the police nor gathered together in a prison where they could be examined, crushed into some semblance of uniformity, and talked about as a special type of human beings. . . . It is doubtful that they look upon themselves as criminals. Failure to be caught and brought to account keeps many of them from being jolted out of their complacency.[19]

Widespread attention was called to this form of illegal behavior when Sutherland pinned the eye-catching name "white-collar crime" on it during his presidential address to the American Sociological

15 Ross, "The Criminaloid."
16 Kadish, "Some Observations on the Use of Criminal Sanctions in the Enforcement of Economic Legislation."
17 Merton, *Social Theory and Social Structure*, p. 17.
18 Becker, "Anthropology and Sociology," p. 145.
19 Morris, *Criminology*, pp. 153–158.

Association in 1939. In this address, Sutherland maintains that causal explanations of criminality that concentrate on such items as poverty, slum environments, and "deteriorated" families are misleading, because they represent conclusions based on studies only of lower-class criminals, rather than of the total aggregate of offenders. Sutherland's often-reiterated emphasis on the theoretical importance of his work, in contrast to its possible implications for social reform, clearly reflect his sensitivity to the dominant sociological ethos of the time, that there was something untoward in activist sentiments.

The so-called "robber barons" of the latter half of the nineteenth century were pictured as the historical forebears of contemporary white-collar criminals.[20] It was in regard to these men that Veblen passed the biting judgment that the ideal captain of industry was like the ideal delinquent "in his unscrupulous conversion of goods and persons to his own ends, and a callous disregard of the feelings and wishes of others, and of the remoter effects of his actions."[21] The robber barons were succeeded by persons such as Ivar Kreuger, the Swedish match king who swindled investors out of an estimated $3 billion,[22] Philip Musica, who, posing under an alias, gained control of a leading drug company and embezzled vast sums through fictitious transactions,[23] Richard Whitney, a former president of the Stock Exchange who was convicted of stealing millions of dollars,[24] and Albert Fall and Harry Sinclair, who were key figures in the Teapot Dome scandal during the presidential term of Warren Harding.[25] These persons were said to represent only the more visible segments of a massive iceberg of white-collar criminality that was expressed in forms such as misrepresentation in the stock exchange, commercial bribery, bribery of public officials to secure favorable contracts and legislation, misrepresentation in advertising and sales, misapplication of funds, short weighting and dishonest grading of commodities, as well as tax frauds and misapplications of funds in receiverships and bankruptcies.

Subsequent research regarding persons listed on Sutherland's roster of white-collar criminals tends to concentrate on their alleged personality congruence with the more traditional kinds of criminals, precisely the kind of endeavor that Sutherland desired to eliminate. A popular account of Kreuger's machinations, for example, calls attention to his "peculiar insensitivity to pain," an item that is said to contain "a key to his whole character," much as the same trait was regarded as fundamental to an understanding of Billy Heirens, the

20 Josephson, *The Robber Barons.*
21 Veblen, *Theory of the Leisure Class*, p. 237.
22 Churchill, *Incredible Ivar Kreuger.*
23 Hynd, "Coster-Musica"; Keats, *Magnificent Masquerade.*
24 Mehling, *Scandalous Scamps*, pp. 1–23; Bromberg, *Crime and the Mind*, pp. 384–389.
25 Werner and Starr, *Teapot Dome;* Noggle, *Teapot Dome.*

young man who committed numerous burglaries and murdered three women before he was apprehended.[26] The further observation that "the more Kreuger was tempted the more contemptuous he became of those who gave," echoes standard research findings regarding confidence men.[27]

Sutherland's theoretical arguments against recourse to personality traits to explain crime can be seen to have compelling validity, not in terms of the more prominent offenders, but rather when white-collar crime is viewed as an almost ubiquitous phenomenon in the business world. If this is true, Sutherland points out, then it is absurd to maintain that *all* businessmen have personality disturbances that explain their behavior. The same observation might be said to apply to traditional crime. It may be true (although it is extraordinarily unlikely) that all or most traditional offenders share background characteristics or personality portraits that are causative of their violations. But if we see society as composed of persons who have at some time or another committed a criminal act, then it becomes analytically absurd and fruitless to put forward the position that crime is caused by personal aberrancy.

Parallels Between White-Collar and Traditional Crime

Financial losses due to white-collar crime, Sutherland points out, are probably many times as great as the financial cost of all acts customarily included in the so-called "crime problem." The President's Commission noted that just one conspiracy involving the collapse of a fraudulent salad-oil empire in 1964 created losses of $125 to $175 million.[28] White-collar crime is not only expensive in monetary terms, but it also may be dangerous to life and safety, to the same or to a greater extent than more traditional forms of crime; "new" cars created by welding together undamaged halves of wrecked cars may fall apart, and bald tires that are regrooved without the addition of new rubber may blow out.[29]

The most thorough attempt to indicate similarities between traditional crime and white-collar crime grew out of Sutherland's study of the records of the seventy leading corporations in the United States. Together their average corporate life was forty-five years, and during this period 980 adverse decisions had been rendered against them, with at least one decision standing against each of the corporations. Of the 980 decisions, 158 were the result of criminal proceedings, 298 were handled by civil courts, and 129 by equity courts, with the remainder representing administrative actions. Virtually all of these

26 Freeman, *"Before I Kill More,"* p. 220.
27 Shaplen, *Kreuger,* pp. 10, 103.
28 Miller, *Great Salad Oil Swindle.*
29 President's Commission, *Crime and Its Impact,* p. 50.

offenses, Sutherland notes, were not "discreet and inadvertent violations of technical regulations." They were, he maintains, "deliberate"
and showed "a relatively consistent unity."

Comparing corporate white-collar crime and professional criminality, Sutherland draws the following parallels:[30]

1. Both groups are persistent in their behavior, with a long record
of recidivism.

2. In both instances, the illegal behavior is more extensive than
prosecutions indicate.

3. The businesman who violates the laws that are designed to
regulate business does not customarily lose status among his business
associates. Neither does the professional criminal lose status among
his underworld peers.

4. Both groups customarily feel and express contempt for law,
for government, and for government personnel.

Sutherland's statements on corporate crime have been criticized as
being highly misleading, however. Thomas I. Emerson, a Yale law
professor, points out, for instance, that the seventy corporations, which
Sutherland treats as if a single individual, are actually gigantic, ram-
bling enterprises, often with tens of thousands of employees, and are
subject to hundreds of statutes and thousands of administrative regulations. Thus adverse decisons in court need not necessarily indicate
culpability on the part of the total corporation. Emerson believes that
Sutherland's inferences are equivalent to saying that the state of Rhode
Island is criminalistic when a resident of Providence violates the
criminal law.[31]

Emerson's critique would appear to be eminently sound. Corporations are, of course, legal entities that can be subjected to criminal
processes, although they cannot, for obvious reasons, be imprisoned.[32]
In 1885, the Supreme Court recognized the corporation as an "artificial
person" entitled to the protection of the fourteenth amendment, a
decision that led contemporary wits to define an "artificial person" as
"something which is neither flesh nor fish but often foul."[33] For the
purpose of criminological analysis, however, corporations cannot be
considered persons, except by recourse to the same type of extrap-
olatory fiction that once brought about the punishment of inanimate
objects, such as railroad cars, for their "criminal acts" in maiming
people.[34] Sutherland's anthropomorphic attitude toward corporations
undoubtedly was a function of the absence of reliable data regarding
individual offenders within the corporate structure, and it was diver-

30 Sutherland, *White Collar Crime*, Chap. 13.
31 Emerson, review of *White Collar Crime*.
32 See Williams, *Criminal Law—The General Part*, Chap. 22; Laski, "Personality
of Associations."
33 Levy, *Corporation Lawyer*, p. 57.
34 See, for instance, Evans, *Criminal Prosecution and Capital Punishment of Animals*.

sionary tactics such as this, in fact, that left Sutherland open to charges that he was a "moralist."[35] Such strictures, however irrelevant, have tended to distract from the essential elements of Sutherland's position and to hinder its reexamination and the absorption of its more viable portions into the main body of criminological theory.[36]

Varieties of White-Collar Crime

One of the major shortcomings of studies of white-collar crime, as noted earlier, has been the failure to delineate clearly homogeneous types of offenses in terms of such things as *modus operandi*, legal categories, characteristics of the perpetrators, impact on particular victims, or the social context in which the offenses arose. As a starting point, it might be desirable to distinguish among offenses committed (1) by individuals as individuals (e.g., lawyers, doctors, and so forth), (2) by employees against the corporation or buisness (e.g., embezzlers), (3) by policy-making officials for the corporation (e.g., in antitrust cases), (4) by agents of the corporation against the general public, (e.g., in advertising fraud), and (5) by merchants against customers (e.g., in consumer frauds). Some of these types follow.

MEDICAL WHITE-COLLAR CRIME

Medical white-collar crime illustrates pointedly that illegal activities need have no relationship to real economic need and deprivation, and that such items as poverty and slum conditions can hardly be considered adequate causes in explaining all kinds of criminal behavior. Material on crime in the medical profession provides support for Aristotle's thesis, expressed in his *Politics*, that "the greatest crimes are not committed in order to acquire the necessary, but the superfluous."[37]

In the medical profession, generally regarded as one of the more law-abiding professions in our society, reports indicate the presence of white-collar crimes such as fee-splitting, ghost surgery, and unnecessary surgery. Fee-splitting, which is illegal in twenty-three states,[38] involves a kickback from a specialist to the general practitioner who sent the patient to the specialist. According to medical sources, fee-splitting is rife among doctors,[39] partly because many medical practitioners refuse to grant legitimacy to the laws that forbid it, and partly because there are easy and well-known tactics that make fee-splitting difficult to detect. For one thing, patients are apt to place inordinate trust in medical honesty and are not likely to demand itemized bills. Investigators can also readily be deceived, especially when billing arrangements

35 Jones, *Crime and the Penal System*, pp. 6–8.
36 Geis, "Toward a Delineation of White-Collar Offenses."
37 Aristotle, *Politics*.
38 See, for instance, *Wisconsin Statutes Annotated*, §147.225, 1957.
39 Whitman, "Why Some Doctors Should be in Jail."

are made whereby the practitioner bills the first patient for the total amount and the specialist bills the next patient. In this way, no money changes hands, although victims are routinely overcharged to make their payments cover the demands of two doctors, only one of whom renders service. Some medical associations have fought strenuously against fee-splitting, but there is no record of a doctor's ever having been convicted for the practice.

In regard to ghost surgery, Dr. Paul R. Hawley, a former director of the American College of Surgeons, reports the case of a surgeon who appeared each morning at the hospital and performed operations at the request of other doctors on patients whom he had never seen before. For this he received a portion of the fee paid to the "real" doctor, and the anesthetized patient never realized the difference. Hawley believes that "inevitably the 'ghost surgeon' performed unjustified surgery in the course of cutting on patients whose cases he had never studied."[40] Writing to his former teacher, a surgeon seeking a location to begin practice provides further documentation of ghost-surgery and fee-splitting in his letter:

> I had a wonderful offer, as far as money goes . . . from a group of five doctors. The head doctor wined and dined my wife and me for the afternoon and into the night before he finally told us the setup. What it amounted to was that each of the doctors scheduled his own surgery and told the patient he would do the case; then I would do the surgery. They would collect the fee and give me one half.[41]

Unnecessary surgery might be said to be the same as traditional kinds of assault and battery, or, perhaps equivalent to armed robbery against an unsuspecting victim. Hysterectomies, appendectomies, and gall bladder operations are the major kinds of surgery said to be most often performed more for the fee than for compelling medical reasons. A partial explanation for unnecessary surgery may lie in the practice of doctor's owning hospitals and their desire to keep their facilities— known as "butcher shops" if they make a practice of engaging in needless operations—filled to capacity. In a study of appendectomies performed in three accredited community institutions and two university hospitals in Maryland, J. Frederic Sparling concluded that fewer than half of the operations were necessary. He believes that 21 percent were patently unnecessary and that the balance were "doubtful." The university institutions did better than the community hospitals, but one of three of their appendectomies, according to Sparling, was unnecessarily performed.[42] Another study, reviewing 6,248 hysterectomies performed in 35 west-coast hospitals, found that 40 percent had aspects that could be criticized. In 12.5 percent of the cases nothing was discovered to support the need for the operation, and in an

40 *Associated Press*, Oct. 9, 1954.
41 Whitman, "Why Some Doctors Should be in Jail," p. 27.
42 Sparling, "Measuring Medical Care Quality."

additional 24 percent of the cases subsequent study concluded that "more conservative" procedures were medically indicated.[43]

Physicians who violate criminal laws, like other white-collar offenders, seem to be the products not of personal pathology but rather of deeply imbedded social processes. C. Wright Mills interprets the situation in the following manner:

> Many of the problems of "white-collar" crime and of relaxed public morality, of high-priced vice and of fading personal integrity, are problems of *structural* immorality. They are not merely the problem of the small character twisted by the bad milieu. And many people are at least vaguely aware that this is so. As news of higher immoralities breaks, they often say, "Well, another one got caught today," thereby implying that the cases disclosed are not odd events involving occasional characters but symptoms of widespread conditions. There is good probative evidence that they are right.[44]

If we accept the thesis that white-collar crime parallels criminal activity in the lower, more vulnerable strata of our society, then Sutherland's demand for a theoretical explanation of this behavior becomes a critical issue in criminology. It will not do to resuscitate time-worn ideas that "every man has his price" or platitudes about "greed" to explain violations by doctors. Perhaps the most telling of Sutherland's postulates regarding criminal behavior is that it is "an expression of the general needs and values," but that it could not "be explained by those general needs and values since non-criminal behavior is an expression of the same needs and values."[45] The good sense of this view is underscored when two equally "greedy" doctors choose alternative methods to satisfy their avarice; one may fee-split, the second may press his wife into working, increase his hours at the office, cut down on home visits, take to writing popular articles, or engage in other perfectly legal activities to satisfy the need that is alleged to be causal in propelling his colleague to illegal behavior. It seems clear, as Sutherland notes, that a need cannot adequately explain criminal behavior if it also satisfactorily accounts for law-abiding, even exemplary, conduct.

CORPORATE CRIME: THE ELECTRICAL CONSPIRACY

The basic criminal nature of a segment of the varied group of behavior patterns that Sutherland brought together under the label "white-collar crime" was clearly demonstrated in 1961 when seven executives of the country's leading heavy electrical equipment manufacturers received jail sentences for violation of the Sherman antitrust law. In all, twenty-nine companies and forty-five of their executives pled guilty or *nolo contendere* to conspiring to fix prices on their

43 Doyle, "Unnecessary Hysterectomies."
44 Mills, *Power Elite*, pp. 343–344.
45 Sutherland and Cressey, *Principles of Criminology*, p. 82.

products and to rig bids on government contracts.[46] Their offense was described by the government as a severe blow to the principle of free competitive business operation. The defendants had held frequent secret meetings—which, interestingly enough, they referred to as "choir practice"—and parceled out Government contracts among themselves, submitting low bids in rotation.

The defendants, described as "middle-class men in Ivy League suits—typical businessmen in appearance who would never be taken for law-breakers"—were pictured by their attorneys when time came for sentencing as "pillars of their community." Several were deacons or vestrymen of their churches, one was president of his local Chamber of Commerce, another was a hospital board member, and another was chief fund-raiser for the Community Chest. Knowledge that they were deliberately violating a criminal statute is apparent from the manner in which the conspirators behaved. As one told a Senate investigating committee:

> It was considered discreet to not be too obvious and to minimize telephone calls, to use plain envelopes if mailing material to each other, not to be seen together in traveling, and so forth . . . not leaving wastepaper, of which there was a lot, strewn around a room when leaving.[47]

It is noteworthy that the officials would often file false travel claims in order to camouflage their meetings, but they never asked for expense money to places further than they had actually gone—on the theory, apparently, that whatever else they were doing, it would not do to cheat the company.[48]

Particularly revealing was a defense attorney's statement in an attempt to secure mitigation of the jail sentence for his client, a forty-five-year-old executive earning $135,000 annually. The attorney called the government lawyers "cold-blooded," saying that they did not understand the consequences to his client's career and personality if he were to be put behind bars with "common criminals who have been convicted of embezzlement and other serious crimes." The defendant was, nonetheless, sentenced to thirty days in jail, where he and his co-conspirators proved to be "model" prisoners, who performed admirably on a project to systematize the prison records. None of the seven men had visitors during their period of imprisonment, all indicating a desire not to be seen by their families or friends; this might be a significant item for the study of self-concept as it relates to the deterrence of white-collar offenses. On release, the forty-five-year-old

46 See Geis, "Heavy Electrical Antitrust Cases of 1961"; Herling *Great Price Conspiracy;* Fuller, *Gentleman Conspirators;* Walton and Cleveland, *Corporations on Trial;* Goodman, *All Honorable Men,* pp. 13–54; Cook, *Corrupted Land,* pp. 32–72; Smith, "Incredible Electric Conspiracy."

47 U.S. Senate, "Administered Prices," Part 28, p. 17396.

48 *Ibid.,* Part 27, p. 16760.

executive resigned from his original job, indignant that his salary had not been paid while he was in jail, and shortly thereafter he was appointed president of another corporation at an estimated annual salary of $65,000.

Attempting to bare the roots of the antitrust offense, Judge J. Cullen Ganey made the following observations:

> I am convinced that in the great number of cases, the defendants were torn between conscience and an approved corporate policy, with the rewarding objectives of promotions, comfortable security and large salaries—in short, the organization or company man, the conformist who goes along with his superiors and finds balm for his conscience in additional comforts and the security of his place in the corporate set-up.

Analysis of the personal motives, rationalizations, and behavior of the sentenced violators might provide criminology with a wealth of valuable material on corporate crime. The complexities of such an investigation cannot be overlooked, however, for as Roy Lewis and Rosemary Stewart indicate, "we know more about the motives, habits, and most intimate arcana of primitive people in New Guinea than we do of the denizens of executive suites."[49] We would particularly like to know what forces in the society led to the antitrust violations. John Kenneth Galbraith suggests that a quest for price certainty and stability underlies much antitrust behavior, something he notes, that should be easy enough for college professors who press for tenure appointments to understand.[50] Other questions concern the views of the participants. How did they explain what they were doing to themselves? How did they become involved in the offenses? What alternative choices were open to them, and why did they not choose such paths? How could the offenses have been avoided?

Some documentary material on these matters emerged from hearings of a Senate investigating committee. The defendants almost invariably testified, for instance, that they came new to a job, found price-fixing an established way of life, and amiably entered into it as they did into other aspects of their work. "My first actual experience was back in the 1930's," one official reported. "I was taken to a meeting by my boss to sit down and price a job."[51] When asked, "Why did you go to the meetings?" another executive replied, "I thought it was part of my duty to do so."[52]

A good example of the rationalizations of the violators was expressed by a sales manager of one of the smaller companies, as he engaged in some soul-searching before the Senate committee:

> One faces a decision, I guess, at such times, about how far to go with company instructions, and since the spirit of the meetings only ap-

49 Lewis and Stewart, *Managers*, pp. 111–112.
50 Galbraith, *Affluent Society*, p. 84.
51 U.S. Senate, "Administered Prices," Part 27, p. 16879.
52 *Ibid.*, Part 28, p. 17550.

peared to be correcting a horrible price level situation, that there was not an attempt to actually damage customers, charge excessive prices, there was no personal gain in it for me, the company did not actually seem to be defrauding. . . . So I guess morally it did not seem quite so bad as might be inferred by the definition of the activity itself.[53]

Perhaps the simplest explanation came from the highest level executive caught in the price-fixing conspiracy, who said, "I think the boys could resist everything but temptation."[54]

The ruthless quest for wealth may appear to contain a key to the antitrust violations, but, as observed earlier, this explanation begs the issue since many persons are motivated by the same desire and yet express their motivation quite differently. In fact, the economist John Maynard Keynes once observed about the drive for wealth, that it sometimes offers a comparatively harmless outlet for human proclivities that might otherwise find dangerous expression "in cruelty, the reckless pursuit of personal power and authority, and other forms of self-aggrandizement. It is better that a man should tyrannize over his bank balance than over his fellow citizens."[55] Whatever the basic ingredients involved, however, it is clear that the government has given warning that deliberate violation of antitrust laws is just like any other crime, and not just an error in judgment. In the words of the former head of the Department of Justice's antitrust division, an antitrust violation is "a serious offense against society which is as criminal as any other act that injures many in order to profit a few. Conspiracy to violate the antitrust laws is economic racketeering. Those who are apprehended in such acts are, and will be treated as criminals."[56] Former Supreme Court Justice Tom C. Clark, in addition, points out that neither the National Association of Manufacturers nor the Chamber of Commerce saw fit to reprimand companies indicted for the electrical industry violations, "Nor was the businessman thought to have done anything wrong." Clark added, however, that if there is no change in behavior, "more businessmen may find themselves in jail."[57]

INCOME TAX EVASION

Failure to file accurate income tax returns sometimes appears to be a national pastime in the United States, although the exact extent of deliberate tax evasion is difficult to determine. It has been said by T. Coleman Andrews, a former Commissioner of the Internal Revenue Service, that "we are becoming a nation of cheats and liars,"[58] a view contradicted by Sheldon S. Cohen, the present Commissioner, who

53 Ibid., p. 17403.
54 Ibid., Part 27, p. 17070.
55 Keynes, General Theory of Employment, p. 374.
56 Loevinger, "Recent Developments in Antitrust Enforcement," p. 102.
57 Associated Press, Aug. 9, 1961.
58 Tulley, Treasury Agent, p. 233.

maintains that most Americans dutifully meet their tax obligations.[59] It is sometimes suspected, however, that the present Commissioner's statement is designed as much to provide incentive for tax honesty as it is to describe facts. It seems likely that the advent of routine computer scrutiny of tax returns under the Automatic Data Processing system encourages honesty, which illustrates the importance of external situations, particularly the fear of apprehension, in inhibiting certain kinds of criminal behavior. Fear, in fact, is a technique assiduously cultivated by the Internal Revenue Service, which typically, in the words of a special agent, keeps a large tax fraud case "on the back burner of the stove and just cooking slowly, then brings it forward to the front burner right around the time that tax returns have to be filed."[60]

A major difficulty in tax collecting relates to widely held beliefs in the United States that persons with sizable incomes are permitted by law, through such things as depletion allowances, stock options, tax-free bonds, "charitable contributions," and individually tailored legislation, to keep an inequitable portion of their incomes. It is estimated, for instance, that $40 billion are lost by the Treasury each year because of tax loopholes favoring wealthy citizens.[61] Figures indicate that persons with incomes of $1 million or more annually pay an average tax of 26 percent[62]—about the same as that paid by many semiskilled workers—despite the theoretical ceiling of 71 percent under our system of graduated taxes. In 1965, in fact, seventeen persons with million-dollar incomes paid no taxes whatsoever.[63]

Tax evasion contains information about the likelihood that Americans will commit surreptitious thievery when faced only with a blank tax-return form, the restraints of their conscience, and a vague awareness that the chances of being apprehended for a criminal violation are comparatively slim. Judge Learned Hand notes that "most Americans do not regard the crime of income tax evasion as a serious moral deviation."[64] It is impossible, of course, to determine how much the failure to report taxable income is the result of deliberate evasions and how much represents carelessness or an unawareness of precise tax obligations. Efforts to defraud the government on taxes, however, sometimes approach the ludicrous, as in the case of a man who deducted the cost of a swimming pool on the ground that it represented a "water purification" experiment, and of a funeral director who substracted vacation expenses on the ground that his was a business trip, since he had spent much time taking photographs

59 Cohen, "Morality and the American Tax System," p. 840.
60 Quoted in Surface, *Inside Internal Revenue*, p. 6.
61 Stern, *Great Treasury Raid*, Chap. 1.
62 Pechman, "Individual Income Tax Provisions of the Revenue Act of 1964," p. 263.
63 Surface, *Inside Internal Revenue*, p. 179.
64 *U.S. ex rel Berlandi v. Reimer.*

of tombstones. Equally curious is the thinking of a man who deducted all of his grocery expenses on the ground that his wife made important business contacts while she was shopping for food.

It is the unique quality of the filing of a tax return that makes it of particular criminological interest. Few persons consciously take seriously the possibility of robbing a bank or burglarizing a house to obtain money, but some 68 million Americans annually wrestle at close quarters with the reporting of income and deductions. In this sense, tax evasion represents an excellent measure of the abstract honesty of a society.

Tax evasions that are considered sufficiently important to merit criminal prosecution appear to be closely related to self-employment. In 1965, almost two-thirds of the criminal prosecutions were against self-employed persons, with the medical, legal, and accounting professions heading the list (20 percent), followed by persons in the real estate, building, and construction trades (6 percent), and then by farmers (4 percent).[65]

Tax evasion cases also provide fundamental data regarding the possibility of deterrence, a major aim of criminal statutes. It is suggested that the predominance of rational considerations in tax fraud makes heavy sentences particularly valuable in warning potential offenders against the likely consequences of their violation.[66] There is little likelihood, for instance, of an offender repeating his violation; of the 1,186 persons convicted of criminal tax fraud in 1963 and 1964, only two were recidivists. On the other hand, the extraordinary variations in sentencing policies by federal judges faced with tax violators would appear to undercut the efficiency of deterrence, if any exists. In the years 1946 through 1963 the ratio between convictions and prison sentences showed a range from zero in South Dakota and 3 percent in the western district of Virginia, to 88 percent in the western district of Washington, and 93 percent in the western district of Tennessee. In all, imprisonment was imposed in 38 percent of the cases.[67]

CONSUMER FRAUD

The line dividing shrewd business practice from illegal exploitation is least clear in regard to practices that deceive consumers, such as in packaging, weights, interest rates, advertising, and sales tactics. At stake are values pressing for freedom of business from governmental regulations that are seen to inhibit initiative, as opposed to values insisting that the anonymous and complicated nature of today's marketplace demands that consumers be provided adequate information with which to make reasonable purchasing judgments. The trend is obviously in the direction of imposing criminal sanctions on vendors

65 President's Commission, *Crime and Its Impact*, p. 113.
66 Bennett, "After Sentence—What?" p. 24.
67 President's Commission, *Crime and Its Impact*, p. 114.

who engage in practices that are defined as exploitative. For criminologists, a basic issue is the determination of the impact of newly declared sanctions on behavior, for it is characteristically true that some persons routinely align their behavior with the demands of the criminal law, while others are indifferent to the definition of the behavior as criminal, and a third group seems encouraged toward certain forms of behavior only after they are proscribed by law.

The widespread nature of fraudulent business practices was vividly underscored in a series of experiments by the *Reader's Digest*. Investigators for the magazine disconnected a coil wire in an automobile, a relatively easily diagnosed problem, and then took the automobile to 347 garages in 48 states. Of these, 129 immediately noted the trouble and either charged nothing or a nominal fee. The remainder—63 percent—overcharged, inserted unnecessary work, charged for work not done or parts not needed, or perpetrated similar frauds or misrepresentations. In addition, almost two-thirds of the radio repair shops visited by magazine representatives deliberately cheated them, as did about half of the watch repair shops in similar experiments.[68]

Two sociological studies provide further documentation of widespread fraud in consumer practices. Clinard notes about his investigation of black market operations during World War II that 1 million cases were dealt with by the government, and that large segments of the American population violated with impunity regulations that the government had established to aid in the prosecution of the war. The violations were primarily concentrated in the area of price-ceiling controls and were particularly flagrant in the meat industry. In regard to gasoline rationing, Clinard said, "At a time when gasoline meant life or death to many of our soldiers, some people almost everywhere were conniving to obtain extra gasoline for nonessential purposes, resulting in one of the most sordid aspects of the entire black market."[69]

In Detroit, Frank E. Hartung analyzed 122 cases involving 195 different offenses in the wholesale meat industry against regulations of the Office of Price Administration (O.P.A.), dividing them into three categories: (1) open overceiling sales or purchases (65 cases), (2) evasive overceiling sales or purchases (58 cases), and (3) violations in reporting or recording (72 cases). These offenses resulted in fines of more than $97,000, damage awards of $132,880, and some prison sentences that ran from three months to one year. Hartung was particularly convinced that O.P.A. violations were a significant, though neglected, aspect of criminal behavior, parallel in relevant respects to traditional crime.[70]

Misrepresentation in advertising, dealt with by the Federal

68 Riis and Patric, *Repairman Will Get You If You Don't Watch Out*, pp. 53–184.
69 Clinard, *Black Market*, p. 155.
70 Hartung, "White-Collar Offenses in the Wholesale Meat Industry."

Trade Commission (F.T.C.), represents one of the more visible kinds of consumer fraud. The F.T.C. was created by Congress in 1914, primarily to combat unfair labor practices, particularly those that restricted free competition. In time, the agency came to define the suppression of fraudulent advertising as part of its function on the ground that such advertising provided one company with an unfair advantage over its competitors.

Yearly reports of the F.T.C. provide indications of the flourishing nature of deceptive advertising. Typical cases involve fraudulent claims that certain vitamin and mineral preparations will overcome nervousness, restlessness, listlessness, worry, irritability, tension, depression, and loss of vigor. The Commission has moved in recent years against a manufacturer of swimming equipment who falsely claimed that his product would render the wearer unsinkable, a manufacturer of a massaging couch who claimed the couch would reduce weight, and a manufacturer of a water filtration device who maintained that it would remove disease-producing, waterborne micro-organisms and viruses.

The need to supplement the work of the F.T.C. by an office dealing more directly with consumer affairs resulted in the establishment in 1964 of a federal Committee on Consumer Interest. The Committee was besieged by more than 30,000 written complaints during its first two years of existence. Analysis indicated that the complaints express intense frustration and anger in dealings in the American marketplace, which the Committee believes underlay in large measure the recent outbursts of racial violence in Los Angeles, Cleveland, Newark, and other cities. The source of minority group displeasure with ghetto merchants has been portrayed in several studies, the most notable of which is by David Caplovitz,[71] and is epitomized in an autobiographical observation of Claude Brown:

> I thought about the way Mama would go down to the meat market sometimes, and the man would sell her some meat that was spoiled, some old neck bones or some pig tails. Things that weren't too good even when they weren't spoiled. And sometimes she would say, "Oh, those things aren't too bad." She was scared to take them back, scared to complain until somebody said, "That tastes bad." Then she'd go down there crying and mad at him, wanting to curse the man out. She had all that Southern upbringing in her, that business of being scared of Mr. Charlie.[72]

The movement toward outlawing deceptive merchandising practices is evident in bills, such as that on "truth-in-packaging," that have been intensely debated in Congress during recent years. The packaging bill, enacted in 1967, for instance, forbids designations such as "full half-quart" and "jumbo pound" on packages, and outlaws containers

71 Caplovitz, *The Poor Pay More.*
72 Brown, *Manchild in the Promised Land,* p. 274.

that have empty spaces that serve no functional purpose. The bill received strong impetus toward enactment from a study that showed that thirty-three young married women were unable in two out of five instances to purchase the most economical package in regard to twenty different products.[73] A second study indicated that four-fifths of the families who do not comparison shop for the best terms when purchasing automobiles on time payments are charged an average interest rate of 22.9 percent, while the remaining families, shopping around, are able to negotiate a 12 percent interest rate.[74] On the basis of such evidence, a "truth-in-lending" bill was enacted by Congress in 1968.

Is White-Collar Crime "Really" Crime?

The most severe critics of the concept of white-collar crime have generally been persons with training in law. Francis A. Allen of the University of Michigan Law School has observed that Sutherland's efforts to explain white-collar crime "are among the least perceptive and satisfactory of his many valuable contributions,"[75] while Paul W. Tappan, who held doctorate degrees both in law and sociology, charged that the category of white-collar crime tends to fall between the bounds of civil and criminal law, to create a veritable analytical no man's land in criminology.

In his writings, Tappan criticizes the fact that Sutherland veers from his initial statement on white-collar crime, which was defined as the behavior of individuals of the upper socioeconomic class who violate the *criminal law*, usually by breach of trust, in the ordinary course of their business activities.[76] Tappan believes that with the passage of time the definition was expanded to include behavior well beyond the boundaries of criminal law, and the realm of white-collar crime soared "into vacuity, wide and handsome"; Tappan said: "One seeks in vain for criteria to determine this white-collar criminality. Is it the conduct of one who wears a white collar and who indulges in behavior to which some particular criminologist takes exception? For purposes of empirical research or objective description, what is it?"[77]

Robert G. Caldwell, another sociologist with legal training, writes in the same vein as Tappan, insisting that, as the concept of white-collar crime now stands, the shrewd businessman, the inefficient workman, the immoral politician, the unethical doctor or lawyer can all be condemned as criminals "by the stroke of the pen" rather than by more stringent legal procedure.[78] Jerome Hall, a leading figure in the study of criminal law, believes that there is a real philosophical difference

73 Friedman, "Consumer Confusion in the Selection of Supermarket Products."
74 *New York Times*, April 16, 1966.
75 Allen, "Criminal Justice, Legal Values, and the Rehabilitative Ideal," p. 228.
76 Sutherland, "Crime and Business," p. 112.
77 Tappan, "Who is the Criminal?" p. 98.
78 Caldwell, *Criminology*, p. 70.

between traditional criminal offenses and white-collar offenses that are directly contrary to the criminal law. Civil law, Hall holds, is concerned with the distribution of economic losses, while criminal law is (or should be) confined to punishment for conduct that is morally culpable. The precepts of criminal law, Hall believes, are more frequently integrated into the mores of the society, whereas the rules of civil law largely represent an adaptation to the prevailing economic system, and as such become integrated into the mores to a much lesser extent than do the criminal laws. Hall believes that criminologists should confine their investigations only to those offenses that are directly violative of the traditional criminal law.[79]

Somewhat similar positions on white-collar crime have been taken by a number of criminologists, although their strictures are usually less directly related to distinctions in the history and body of the law and legal processes. George B. Vold, for instance, calls the term white-collar crime "ambiguous, uncertain, and controversial" and attacks its use on the ground that "there is an obvious and basic incongruity involved in the proposition that a community's leaders and more responsible elements are also its criminals."[80] Ernest W. Burgess adds the further objection that white-collar criminals cannot be considered valid offenders because a "criminal is a person who regards himself as a criminal and is so regarded by society."[81] Such viewpoints, however, appear to initiate more confusion than they resolve, since they put forward both a subjective and objective index and ask that these be used to determine "true criminality." Although it cannot be disputed that white-collar criminals almost always retain the good will of the community, it seems logical that rather than abandon the concept of white-collar crime altogether, the characteristic of community acceptance of business dereliction should be considered one of the attributes of the offender and his offense.

Sutherland's Defense of His Concept

Sutherland felt compelled in 1945 to defend against critics his views regarding white-collar crime. He believed that the basic question to be answered in order to judge the authenticity of his category as a unit of criminological concern was whether the word "crime" could legitimately be applied to corporate and similar offenses. To him, the answer to this question was part of a semantic problem inherent in the definition of "crime." Sutherland felt that there are two necessary ingredients in a crime: first, legal description of an act as socially injurious and, second, legal provision of a penalty for such an act. Both of these criteria, Sutherland felt, are fulfilled in white-collar offenses.

79 Hall, "Criminology," p. 353.
80 Vold, Theoretical Criminology, p. 253.
81 Burgess, Comment on Hartung, p. 34.

Modern laws against white-collar crime are merely adaptations to contemporary settings of early common law principles; for example, false advertising rules are no more than present-day restatements of the early law on fraud. In addition, punishment is present in adverse decisions against corporations, Sutherland maintained, because such decisions "result in some suffering on the part of the corporations against which they are issued and also in that they are designed by legislators and administrators to produce suffering." A considerable part of the suffering also involves "public shame," which is not different from early penalties, such as the sewing of the letter "T" on the outer clothing of a thief in order to bring public humiliation to him.

Three factors were said to explain the differential implementation of the law relating to white-collar crime: (1) the status of businessmen in our society, (2) the trend away from punishment, and (3) the relatively unorganized public resentment against white-collar criminals. But differential treatment of white-collar offenses, Sutherland insisted, has no bearing whatsoever on their etiological history or on their significance as items of criminological concern.[82]

Research Issues in White-Collar Crime

The concept of white-collar crime has been of great importance in expanding the horizon of study of criminal behavior. Nonetheless, at this moment the concept is suffused with controversy, inexact demarcation, and moral connotation, all of which detract from its potential substantive and theoretical value. Following are some of the items that appear to require investigation and clarification in regard to white-collar crime:

Questions of definition. Characterization of offenses by the social or occupational status of their perpetrators is one of the weaker elements of the Sutherland formulation. Clinard and Quinney, for instance, point out that studies of white-collar crime have dealt with milk that was watered-down for public consumption, over-charges on property rentals, and similar violations, committed not by white-collar workers, but by farmers, repairmen, and other similar individuals. For this reason they suggest that the term "occupational crime" is a more apt designation than white-collar crime.[83] At the same time, foreign writers, particularly in the Soviet Union and in East European countries, have regularly employed the term "economic crimes" to designate what we call white-collar crimes in the United States. It appears to be particularly necessary that some agreement be reached on those offenses to be grouped as white-collar crimes, or under an equivalent rubric, and that the special ingredients of these offenses be delineated.

The approach to white-collar crime has also differed greatly from

82 Sutherland, "Is 'White Collar Crime' Crime?"
83 Clinard and Quinney, *Criminal Behavior Systems*, p. 131.

the approach to traditional crime, because studies of white-collar crime have concentrated almost exclusively on the criminal act, rather than on the act and the actor viewed together in an attempt to place both into a broader social context. Field studies of selected corporations or business enterprises, involving interviews with decision-making persons and utilizing analytical tools developed in industrial sociology, could provide criminology with much-needed case material on white-collar crime. In addition, cross-cultural studies might discover quite varying characteristics of white-collar crime in countries other than the United States. In the Soviet Union, for instance, white-collar criminals are not those who try to restrict free competition, but, as Mannheim notes, those who try to compete with the economic activities of the monopolistic state.[84] In addition, there has been some research indication that bribery and corruption, reported as omnipresent in some underdeveloped countries, may serve a useful function in mediating between impersonal, disorganized state forces and the legitimate requirements of an otherwise dispossessed citizenry.[85]

Questions regarding social responses to white-collar crime. It is one thing to remark that there has been official neglect of white-collar crime and considerable attention to the more traditional kinds of lawbreaking, but it is another thing to determine with some precision why this has been true. In one of the few research probes into this area, Donald J. Newman found that citizens did not differ too widely with the statutorily prescribed penalties for food adulteration, although they did favor harsher penalties than those imposed by the courts.[86] The more far-reaching issues concerned with the formation of public opinion, the relationship between such opinion and legislative response, and, ultimately, the relationship between legislative action and enforcement behavior, have rarely been examined.

Accumulation of data regarding official response to white-collar crime requires a careful and sensitive reading of social and historical materials. The task is equivalent to that of determining why the plight of the Negro was largely ignored prior to the Supreme Court decision in 1954, and why poverty, long with us, suddenly became the focus of intensive national action in the 1960s. Cressey, in his foreword to the 1961 reissue of Sutherland's monograph on white-collar crime, indicates some of the dimensions of this research issue:

> The lasting merit of this book is not its demonstration that corporations and corporation executives in white collars break the criminal laws regulating their business activities. It is its demonstration that a pattern of crime can be found to exist outside both the focus of popular preoccupation with crime and the focus of scientific investigations of crime and criminality. Explanation of why such a pattern could re-

84 Mannheim, *Comparative Criminology*, p. 497.
85 Bayley, "Effects of Corruption in a Developing Nation," pp. 726–730.
86 Newman, "Public Attitudes Toward a Form of White Collar Crime."

main for so long outside both popular and scientific purview is a sociological question of first-rate importance. . . . Why does a society report the crime it reports, why does it overlook what it overlooks, and how does it go about deciding that it has, in fact, overlooked something.[87]

Questions concerning the characteristics of white-collar offenders. Little is known about the motivations, rationalizations, biographies, and other traits of white-collar criminals. We have scant information, in fact, concerning even the most fundamental kind of identification material about such offenders, except for a single British study. In it, John C. Spencer investigated a random sample of white-collar violators imprisoned at Leyhill, finding them predominantly middle-aged and elderly, with two-thirds of them being more than forty-five years old. Only twenty-five had no previous convictions, indicating the likelihood that it was repetition itself that led to the imprisonment of many persons in the study sample. Interestingly, Spencer found that the violations of the majority of offenders were not part of a long-standing pattern, but were rather the culmination of a series of dubious business enterprises during the previous three or four years.[88]

Spencer, like most criminologists, is keenly aware of the disadvantages of conducting research on an incarcerated group and attempting, on this basis, to say something about the type of offender in general. If an offense is pervasive in a society, however, it may be worthwhile merely to study those who are inept or unfortunate enough to be apprehended and to try to determine what they are like and what is involved in the social processes that brought about their capture. Studies of white-collar crime, however, have hardly advanced to such a discriminating stage. At the moment, the dearth of useful information regarding apprehended and convicted offenders, much less that concerned with the offender operating beyond the attention of the legal system, remains a basic gap.

There are, in addition, numerous questions concerning such fundamental areas as deterrence and social policy. Little is known regarding what kinds of white-collar offenses are responsive to what kinds of sanctions. It has been guessed that, to a greater extent than most traditional violators, white-collar criminals are apt to align their behavior with the threat of sanctions, partly because they have more to lose from the stigma and shame of public prosecution. There are, of course, strong arguments insisting that the potentiality of deterrence is hardly adequate reason to punish a lesser violator more seriously than another man whose act causes greater harm, when such harm is measured by reasonable standards of personal and social injury.

Until the resolution of definitional matters and the inauguration and completion of empirical and descriptive studies, it appears premature to move too deeply into theoretical statements regarding white-

87 Cressey, "Foreword," *White Collar Crime*, p. xii.
88 Spencer, "White Collar Crime."

collar crime as a criminological entity. Huntington Cairns notes that "the history of social theory is too largely a record of generalizations wrung from insufficient facts," a warning that is notably pertinent in regard to white-collar crime.[89]

For Further Reading

CLINARD, MARSHALL B. *The Black Market: A Study of White Collar Crime.* New York: Holt, Rinehart and Winston, 1952.

> Professor Clinard's study of black market offenses during World War II has meaning both in terms of its implications of national behavior and in terms of the study of criminal activity. "This is not," the author states, "a story of one of the more pleasant aspects of American life." The author, an analyst with the Office of Price Administration from 1942 to 1945, ties his many statistical findings to theoretical explanations about wartime profiteering.

GEIS, GILBERT (ed.). *White-Collar Criminal: The Offender in Business and the Professions.* New York: Atherton Press, 1968.

> Virtually all of the studies undertaken to date regarding white-collar crime are reproduced in this reader, along with the early statements by Ross and Sutherland and contemporary sociolegal debates on the proper delineation of white-collar crime. In addition, there are articles on prescription violations by pharmacists and fraud in home repair, automobile sales and service, and health huckstering.

NEWMAN, DONALD J. "White-Collar Crime," in *Law and Contemporary Problems.* Vol. 23 (Fall 1958), pp. 735–753.

> This thorough paper represents a perceptive defense of Sutherland's position by a scholar acquainted with the intricacies of the system of criminal law. Professor Newman, a member of the faculty of the School of Criminal Justice, State University of New York, Albany, delves into the legal qualities of white-collar crime, and he concludes that its conceptualization possesses great value for the future study of criminal behavior.

SUTHERLAND, EDWIN H. *White Collar Crime.* New York: Holt, Rinehart and Winston, 1961.

> This classic, book-length study of white-collar crime should be read carefully in order to understand Professor Sutherland's strictures against psychological interpretations of criminal behavior as well as his position that white-collar crime is *real* crime. The new edition contains a valuable foreword by Donald R. Cressey, which rebuts many of the criticisms of Sutherland's position while granting the validity of seveeral of them.

TOMPKINS, DOROTHY CAMPBELL. *White Collar Crime—A Bibliography.* Berkeley: Institute of Governmental Studies, University of California, 1967.

> Reading and research in white-collar crime is made inestimably more efficient by Mrs. Tompkins' thorough bibliography of writings on the subject, which was originally prepared for the President's Commission on Law

89 Cairns, *Law and the Social Sciences,* p. 20.

Enforcement and Administration of Justice. As Dwight Waldo notes in his foreword, "It is a probing, exploratory, and original effort . . . Mrs. Tompkins has wrestled with the problems of definition and has covered a wide-ranging literature in specifying and probing relevant categories. For 'white collar crime' has since the coining of the term been more a point of view, an accusation and hypothesis, than a recognizable and accepted area of criminality and criminal law."

13
Public Order Offenses

Most crimes include both a perpetrator and a victim. The victim may be an individual who is harmed, or a social entity, such as a corporation, that is deprived of something properly belonging to it. In some types of white-collar crime, such as misrepresentation in advertising, the victim is more abstract, representing the members of the society regarded as some form of personalized collectivity. In most criminal activities, the harm inflicted on an innocent party is relatively easy to discern. However, a considerable number of criminal offenses exist—including several that lead to the largest number of arrests in the United States—in which the injury done to an innocent person or to the society is not directly apparent and may, in fact, be nonexistent.[1] These crimes include drunkenness, the use of narcotics, vagrancy, and prostitution. In all of them, the injury is primarily done by the person to himself. Abortion is a similar type of offense, in that the abortionist and his subject both engage in the criminal act voluntarily, although the act itself may be defined as socially injurious on the ground that the destruction of the fetus is similar to the killing of an already-born individual.

Several beliefs combine to produce laws against things such as narcotics usage, prostitution, public drunkenness, and abortion. Among them are views insisting that the state has a right to protect an individual from the consequences of his own shortcomings and vices. Such an ethic lies, for instance, behind the Rhode Island statute that makes it a criminal offense for a person to ride a motorcycle without a helmet. The Rhode Island Supreme Court upholds the statute with the argument that the legislature can prohibit persons from engaging in conduct that "could conceivably result in their becoming public charges."[2] A similar law was ruled unconstitutional in Michigan, however, with the court observation that "Under our system of government,

1 See Schur, *Crimes Without Victims.*
2 *State ex rel Colvin v. Lombardi,* p. 627.

the aim is to leave the subject entire master of his conduct, except when the public good requires some direction or restraint"; helmets, it was believed, protect only the individual, not the society.[3]

The same delicate balance of personal and social concerns can be found in the narcotic statutes, which are based on highly speculative estimates of the consequence to the social order of diverse amounts of recourse to opiates and other drugs that are defined as "dangerous." We know that opiates can be taken for lifelong periods without serious physiological harm and that there are many other forms of behavior that can be more deleterious to the human organism than narcotics usage but are not outlawed. Gluttonous overeating, for example, could be said to destroy the willpower of the eater, to detract from the fighting strength of the nation, and to waste an inordinate amount of time and food. Nobody, however, seriously suggests that we create new offenses such as first- and second-degree obesity, or that an S.S. corps (for Supermarket Surveillance) be formed, or that we prohibit the manufacture and import of Swiss chocolate, Israeli halvah, and Italian spaghetti.[4]

Moral and aesthetic considerations are also undoubtedly prominent in leading to the definition of behavior, such as the use of narcotics, as criminal. Prostitution is outlawed because it violates theological tenets against promiscuous sexual behavior—although, again, the taboo is not consistent, since all theologies but few statutes prohibit fornication and adultery and the intense forms of love-making that are often engaged in by unmarried persons in our society. Public drunkenness is forbidden, among other reasons, because it is a nuisance; that is, it tends to offend the aesthetic sensibilities of individuals who are exposed to the sight of the inebriate. But many other acts that may be aesthetically more unappealing than drunkenness do not draw the opprobrium of a statutory ban.

The criminal codes also outlaw some acts, such as vagrancy and narcotics usage, because of the social harm it is alleged will ensue from their operation. Prostitution is forbidden on the assumption that the prostitute will contribute to the rate of venereal infection. Narcotics addicts are legislated against on the ground that to maintain their drug habit they will inevitably resort to antisocial behavior. Vagrancy is outlawed because vagrants are considered to be incipient or practicing felons. Some of these grounds obviously create elements of self-fulfilling prophecy; that is, they create the situations they then employ for their justification. Narcotic addicts, for instance, apparently turn to criminal-activity behavior to obtain narcotics, which are more expensive because they are outlawed, and prostitutes may spread venereal disease because they will not contact medical authorities for fear of incarceration.

3 *People v. Armstrong,* p. 295; *American Motorcycle Assn. v. Davids,* p. 354.
4 See Geis, "Fable of a Fatty."

The moral grounds on which many of the public-order offenses are based are not resolvable by scientific debate, but rather depend upon matters of faith. Abortion is either immoral or it is not, depending upon the definition of "life" that is given to the fetus. Debate, however, can legitimately center around the question of whether theological prescripts should be translated into legal sanctions applicable to large groups of individuals who do not accept the validity of what they regard as partisan religious viewpoints. Debate can also center on determination and judgment of the short-term and long-range impact of certain kinds of behavior on the vitality and well-being of a society. Such matters are, however, rarely susceptible to very precise statement, so that controversy often comes down to matters of preference and guesswork. Patrick Devlin and H. L. A. Hart, for instance, have had an intense debate in recent years that is founded on differing estimates of the social injury implicit in given kinds of regulations. Devlin argues that "society depends upon and is held together by positive morality," and that society "may, to help preserve its existence, enforce that positive morality through the coercive sanctions of law."[5] Hart dissents from the premise that a necessary relationship between positive morality and social coherence exists, and he also differs in his judgments regarding the implications for social integrity of specific kinds of legislative bans.[6] It is empirical questions such as these—questions regarding the relationship between kinds of behavior and social and personal well-being and freedom—that must be answered before we can make surer judgments about public order offenses.

Public Drunkenness

The reasons behind criminal laws proscribing public drunkenness appear in a preamble to the English Intoxication Act of 1606, the predecessor of American and English legislation on the subject. Before 1606, jurisdiction over drunkenness had resided in church courts, but by 1606 the sin of alcoholic overindulgence was considered heinous enough to be incorporated into secular law. The language employed by Parliament is not unlike contemporary diatribes against drunkenness, except for spelling and a little less bluster.

> Whereas the loathsom and odious Sin of Drunkenness is of late grown into common Use within this Realm, being the Root and Foundation of many other enormous Sins, as Bloodshed, Stabbing, Murder, Swearing, Fornication, Adultery, and such like, to the great Dishonour of God, and of our Nation, the Overthrow of many good Arts and manual Trades, the Disabling of Divers Workmen, and the general Impoverishing of many good Subjects, abusively wasting the good Creatures of God.[7]

5 Devlin, *Enforcement of Morals*, pp. 5–21.
6 Hart, *Law, Liberty, and Morality*, pp. 17–24.
7 Quoted in "Alcoholism, Public Intoxication, and the Law," p. 111.

Virtually all American jurisdictions today regard public drunkenness as a criminal offense. Exceptions to the rule are Illinois and New York City, where it is necessary to show disorderly conduct before an inebriated person can be convicted, and Alabama and Georgia, where a breach of the peace is required to make drunkenness a public offense. The procedures employed in New York City have a considerable impact on the nation's crime statistics, since it is estimated that the city would show about 300,000 to 400,000 drunkenness arrests each year, if it observed the same procedures as most other places. For a time, in fact, contrary to law, many derelicts of the Bowery, an area that has been called "the most miserable mile in the United States" and described as a "dingy, tawdry, hopeless stretch dotted with scores of moldering flophouses, some dating back a hundred years,"[8] were arrested and charged with disorderly conduct, although their only offense had been to lie in a comatose state in the streets. Most of the accused pled guilty, but the arrest practice came to an end when Judge John M. Murtagh began insisting that each of the accused persons be provided with an attorney.[9] Murtagh maintained that "putting them in jail doesn't solve a blessed thing," but only "makes certain their further degradation." Use of disorderly conduct statutes against drunks, Murtagh felt, was a verbal travesty. "Who, indeed, is less disorderly than a drunk lying in a doorway or on the sidewalk in the Bowery?" he asks; "He is part of the street scene. He disturbs no one. Visitors go to the Bowery to see him."[10] Diametrical to Murtagh's position is that of Melvin Selzer, a psychiatrist, who maintains that permitting an alcoholic to remain unmolested—whether or not he creates a nuisance or breaks laws—is tantamount to permitting an insidious form of suicide; he also believes that all alcoholics should be placed in custody and attempts made to rehabilitate them.[11]

Intense debate has revolved in recent years about whether there is a need to keep public drunkenness a criminal offense or whether it is necessary to establish civil commitment programs to attempt to rehabilitate alcoholics. There is also a third school that insists that no public action should be taken against alcoholics who are living their lives according to their own idea of the pursuit of pleasure. They believe that all living, since it ends in death, is self-destructive, and that as long as he does not interfere with others, each man should have the right to select his own kind of existential poison.

For a period, it seemed likely that it was the view favoring civil commitment of alcoholics that would prevail. Both the *Driver*[12] and *Easter*[13] decisions in 1966, for instance, in ruling that chronic alcohol-

8 Berger, "Bowery Blinks in the Sunlight," p. 14.
9 Murtagh, "Arrests for Public Intoxication."
10 *New York Times*, Oct. 17, 1959.
11 Selzer, "Alcoholism and the Law."
12 *Driver v. Hinnant.*
13 *Easter v. District of Columbia.*

ism indicates a lack of control over one's behavior, were based on the
common-law principle that acts cannot be declared criminal unless
they are voluntary. This viewpoint was rejected by the Supreme Court,
however, in a 1968 decision involving Leroy Powell, a sixty-six-year-
old Texan, who had asked for medical treatment for an alcoholic condition that had resulted in his arrest at least once a year for each year
since 1949 and in fines that ate up almost 40 percent of his total income. Instead, Powell was fined $20, and his attorney argued on
appeal that this criminal conviction represented "cruel and unusual
punishment" and was thus violative of the eighth amendment of the
federal constitution.

The opinion of the Supreme Court, written by Justice Thurgood
Marshall, merits lengthy quotation for its declaration of the grounds
on which the majority of the Court saw fit to resolve the debate between continued criminalization and civil commitment procedures.
Noteworthy are the emphases on the present absence of adequate treatment facilities and on the possibility of abuses under civil commitment
procedures:

> Facilities for the attempted treatment of indigent alcoholics are woefully
> lacking throughout the country. It would be tragic to return large num-
> bers of helpless, sometimes dangerous and frequently unsanitary in-
> ebriates to the streets of our cities without even the opportunity to
> sober up adequately which a brief jail term provides.

> Presumably no state or city will tolerate such a state of affairs. Yet
> the medical profession cannot, and does not, tell us with any assurance
> that, even if the buildings, equipment and trained personnel were
> made available, it could provide anything more than slightly higher-
> class jails for our indigent habitual inebriates.

> Thus we run the grave risk that nothing will be accomplished beyond
> the hanging of a new sign—reading "hospital"—over one wing of the
> jailhouse.

> One virtue of the criminal process is, at least, that the duration of
> penal incarceration typically has some outside statutory limit; this is
> universally true in the case of petty offenses, such as public drunkenness,
> where jail terms are quite short on the whole.

> "Therapeutic civil commitment" lacks this feature; one is typically
> committed until one is cured. Thus, to do otherwise than affirm [the
> original conviction of Powell] might subject indigent alcoholics to the
> risk that they may be locked up for an indefinite period of time under
> the same conditions as before, with no more hope than before of re-
> ceiving effective treatment. . . .[14]

It is interesting to appreciate that, had the 5 to 4 decision of the
Supreme Court gone the other way, the result would have had a
staggering impact upon criminal statistics. In any given year, about

14 *Powell v. Texas.*

one-third of all arrests in the United States—representing about 1 million cases—are for drunkenness, and this offense category is more than twice as high as any other in the *Uniform Crime Reports.* In addition, disorderly conduct, the second highest offense category, includes, as we have noted, a large number of instances of nothing but public drunkenness.

ROOTS OF ALCOHOLISM

Voluminous amounts of writing have attempted to explain the phenomenon of drinking and the syndrome of chronic intoxication.[15] Little effort has been made, however, to differentiate individuals arrested for drunkenness from other individuals in our society in more than the grossest terms, except for occasional studies of chronic alcoholics whose visits to the police station resemble the action of a "revolving door."[16] We do know that use of alcoholic beverages extends through a considerable portion of our population. Richard H. Blum, for instance, reports that about 68 percent of the adults in our society have at least one alcoholic drink in a given year.[17] There are, according to estimates of the American Medical Association, between 5 and 6.5 million alcoholics in the United States, persons defined as having "a preoccupation with alcohol and loss of control over its consumption."[18] Of these persons, about 1 million are being treated or have been treated for their difficulties with liquor.[19] Only about 8 percent of the alcoholics —and the figure has been declining since the mid-1930s[20]—spend their time on the nation's Skid Rows,[21] or Skids Roads, if Seattle, Washington's original designation for a street used to slide logs into Puget Sound is retained.[22]

Anthropological reports document the presence of alcoholic beverages in virtually all preliterate cultures, except those of the polar peoples, the Australian aborigines, and the primitives of Tierra del Fuego.[23] Equally pervasive as the presence of alcohol are attempts to control its use. As early as 2000 B.C., a Chinese emperor is said to have banished an individual who discovered a method of making wine. In addition, the drinking of intoxicating beverages has been prohibited for centuries by Moslem theology, and in the year 1279 the Mongol Emperor Kubla Khan issued an edict condemning dealers in alcoholic beverages to banishment and slavery. In American colonial times, although the Pilgrim fathers brought with them on the Mayflower a

15 See, for instance, Jellinek, *Disease Concept of Alcoholism;* Pittman, *Alcoholism;* and McCarthy, *Drinking and Intoxication.*
16 Pittman and Gordon, *Revolving Door.*
17 Blum and Braunstein, "Mind-Altering Drugs and Dangerous Behavior," p. 29.
18 *Wall Street Journal,* Feb. 20, 1968.
19 Roueché, *Neutral Spirit,* p. 149.
20 Wallace, *Skid Row as a Way of Life.*
21 Harris, *Skid Row, U.S.A.;* Bogue, *Skid Row in American Cities.*
22 Morgan, *Skid Road;* Peterson and Maxwell, "The Skid Road 'Wino.'"
23 Washburne, *Primitive Drinking.*

generous supply of alcoholic beverages,[24] excessive use of alcohol was almost always defined as criminal. In 1633, for instance, Robert Cole, a citizen of the Massachusetts colony, having been frequently punished for drunkenness, was ordered to wear a red "D" around his neck for a year.[25]

Sociologists have generally looked for group variations in drinking behavior and alcoholism, and they have also attempted to analyze cultural traits of the groups themselves in order to account for these variations.[26] They have found, for instance, that Jews, although only 13 percent abstain totally from drinking, produce a disproportionately low number of alcoholics. Most interpretations of these figures concentrate on the religious proscriptions against alcoholism among the Jews and on the fact that alcohol is traditionally accepted as part of Jewish religious celebrations.[27] Essentially the same pattern is found among the Chinese of New York City, where alcoholic beverages are widely used but the rate of excessive drinking is very low.[28]

Bringing together the material from sociology, psychology, and anthropology, it would seem fair to endorse the conclusion of Fritz Kant that there is no one cause of alcoholism and that there remains as yet unanswered the issue of why, whatever the individual is seeking, he chooses alcohol as the route to his goal.[29] In general, Roueché's observations appear to offer a substantial base line for explanation of the long-standing, cross-cultural appeal of alcoholic beverages:

> The basic needs of the human race, its members have long agreed, are food, clothing, and shelter. To that fundamental trinity most modern authorities would add, as equally compelling, security and love. There are, however, many other needs whose satisfaction, though somewhat less essential, can seldom be comfortably denied. One of these, and perhaps the most insistent, is an occasional release from the intolerable clutch of reality. All men throughout recorded history have known this tyranny of memory and mind, and all have sought, and invariably found, some reliable means of briefly loosening its grip. The most conspicuous result of their search, if not the most effective, is a colorless liquid called ethyl hydroxide, or, more popularly, alcohol. It is also the oldest, the most widely esteemed, and the most abysmally misunderstood.[30]

POLICE-CASE INEBRIATES

Monroe County State Penitentiary, which receives offenders from thirteen western New York counties, was the locale of the most thorough study yet conducted of drunkenness cases that end in sen-

24 Usher, *Pilgrims and Their History*, p. 70.
25 Patrick, *Alcohol, Culture, and Society*, Chap. 2.
26 See Pittman and Snyder, *Society, Culture, and Drinking Patterns*.
27 Snyder, *Alcohol and the Jews*.
28 Barnett, "Alcoholism in the Cantonese of New York City."
29 Kant, *Treatment of the Alcoholic*, p. 32.
30 Roueché, *Neutral Spirit*, p. 9.

tences to correctional facilities. Seventy percent of the 1,919 inmates
who entered Monroe in 1954 were charged with public intoxication,
187 of whom constituted the sample of "chronic police-case inebriates"
studied by David J. Pittman and Wayne Gordon.

Socially, the inebriate was found to be middle-aged or older, probably Irish or Negro, usually an unskilled worker, as likely to be from
a rural as from an urban background, and currently unattached to a
female (although 59 percent had been married). The paucity of education in the group was striking: 70 percent did not advance beyond
grammar school. The police-case inebriate usually had a previous
criminal record for public intoxication or other acts related to the
indiscriminate use of liquor. Occasionally, for those with such a history,
there would be a record of serious criminal behavior, although the
frequency of serious violations tended to diminish after the age of
thirty-five or forty, when they usually settled down to a steady, routine
pattern of arrests for public intoxication. By then, the intoxication
seemed to be an effective control over any tendencies toward aggressive
criminal behavior.[31]

Behaviorally, the Monroe County State Penitentiary inebriate was
clearly distinguishable from the middle-class alcoholic with whom the
Alcoholics Anonymous approach seems to work so effectively. Eighty
percent of the penitentiary group had some experience living in institutions, which may provide support for the psychoanalytical thesis that
alcoholism is a form of dependency need. In contrast to the middle-
class alcoholic who generally drinks alone, the chronic police-case inebriate did his drinking in groups, where he appeared to find emotional
support and reinforcement in the "bottle gang."[32] To such an individual, to employ Skolnick's analysis, "the sober confessional of the
middle-class Alcoholics Anonymous world" seems much like a replica
of Salvation Army ("Sally") evangelism, which, in the eyes of the
police-case inebriate, is no more than "a ritualized exchange of pretended spiritual redemption for institutional bed and board."[33]

The police-case inebriate, according to Pittman and Gordon, cannot be rehabilitated because he was never "habilitated" in the first
place. His behavior is described as "undersocialized," a condition that
is said to stem from a childhood marked by parental death, separation,
divorce, or desertion, and from the failure to acquire social skills with
which to deal with others. The use of the concept "undersocialization,"
however, appears to be of dubious validity, since chronic police-case
inebriates have undoubtedly been socialized, but within a particular
context and in a particular manner. It is this difference in the *character*,
not the amount, of socialization that merits stress and requires interpretation. To assume that the character of this "inadequate socializa-

31 Pittman and Gordon, *Revolving Door.*
32 See Rubington, "Chronic Drunkenness Offender."
33 Skolnick, review of *Revolving Door.*

tion" can be ascertained on the basis of the "structural unity of the family" and from the fact that "the families largely failed to participate in community activities" seems to beg some fundamental issues involved in the concept of socialization.

Data about police-case inebriates represents an indictment of the financial and social waste involved in the "revolving door" process through which these men pass as many as seventy and eighty times during their adult lives. It is reminiscent of the plaintive complaint of a Montana man who had been arrested and sentenced sixty-seven times for drunkenness: "They're giving me life imprisonment on the installment plan." Pittman and Gordon recommended a treatment center for the chronic police-case inebriate where there would be systematic relief of physical ailments, psychological rehabilitation, and social restoration. They further advocated a parole-type release procedure and a "halfway house" or temporary home for alcoholics who have exhibited a pattern of dependence upon institutional living. Similarly, they suggest varying the treatment program according to the particular characteristics of the individual.

The decision in the Powell case, as Justice Marshall clearly indicated, represented in some measure a response to the absence of programs, other than incarceration, which offer hope for the alcoholic. At the moment, several experimental attempts are underway to provide alternatives to criminal prosecution for public drunkenness, so that, at some future date, the Supreme Court might rule favorably to eliminate the offense from the penal codes. The most promising program appears to be that of the Vera Institute of Justice. In 1968, the Institute began a concentrated research effort in New York's Bowery district, which is estimated to contain 6,000 of the City's 30,000 homeless men, a considerable portion of whom are alcoholics. The Institute sends two-man units through the area, each team made up of a plainclothes policeman and a reformed alcoholic. The aim of the team is to offer medical assistance to each person in the Bowery. If the individual indicates disinterest in the proferred help, the matter is taken no further. If he accepts the offer (and three out of four men approached during the early stages of the project have done so), he is then referred for medical help and employment and social service counseling. The aim of the program is to reach some 5,500 persons during its initial year of operation, then to examine success and failure in terms of the expenditure of funds and energy.[34]

DRUNKEN DRIVING

The thin line between the individual convicted of an offense and other individuals who do precisely the same thing but do not come to the attention of the police is clearly shown in the crime of driving while intoxicated. From a theoretical viewpoint, every person who drives an

34 *New York Times*, Oct. 7, 1967.

automobile while he has an illegal concentration of alcohol in his bloodstream is an offender. In practice, very few drivers are apprehended or charged for this, and, in addition, a large number of drunken driving offenses are later reduced in the courts to charges of "reckless driving" or even vaguer misdemeanors.

The number of traffic fatalities related to the use of alcohol is a matter of some dispute, although the National Safety Council estimate, that alcohol is involved in about 50 percent of fatal automobile accidents, is most often cited. In 1967, there were 53,000 fatalities from automobile accidents in the United States, and almost 2 million accidents that resulted in "disabling injuries," that is, injuries serious enough to result in absence from work or suspension of normal activities. Each year, as newspaper headlines proclaim, the total number of automobile deaths increase strikingly, although figures based on more sophisticated measures indicate that automobile accident deaths actually are declining in the United States. Statistics from the World Health Organization show, for instance, that in 1950 there were 23.1 traffic fatalities in the United States for each 100,000 persons in the population, which dropped to 20.6 in 1960. The same organization indicates that the highest fatality rate in terms of 100,000 population is found in Austria, with a figure of 27.5, while the lowest among European and North American countries is in Greece, with 4.7.

Better statistics, however, are those that calculate the amount of mileage traveled as the denominator of traffic fatalities. Mileage traveled can be estimated in terms of domestic use of motor fuel and calculations of miles per gallon achieved by the various kinds of registered vehicles. It is notable that in 1967 the United States registered more than half of the world's 198,996,479 motor vehicles, a figure down from the 73 percent of the world's vehicles found in the United States in 1950. The figures show a significant drop in car fatalities in the United States when estimated in terms of distance traveled, plummeting from 11.3 fatalities per 100 million miles in 1945 to 5.6 fatalities for the same base distance in 1965. The decrease seems attributable to a combination of safer cars, better roads, and more adequately trained drivers. In criminological terms, it is notable that American people seethe with horror and revenge in regard to homicides, and yet tend toward passivity in the face of a traffic fatality rate that is five times higher than the homicide rate, despite the fact that more stringent measures, such as strictly enforced speed-limits, might readily spare the lives of more persons than all those killed in homicides.

The relationship between traffic fatalities and laws defining drunken driving throws considerable light on the general subject of deterrence, an issue that is probably the most important single concern in the administration of criminal justice. In the United States, persons with .05 percent or less alcohol concentration in their blood usually are not considered to be under the influence of alcohol. There is some question about the degree of influence when the concentration falls between .05 percent and .15 percent. A person is definitely considered intoxicated when more than .15 percent concentration is found in his blood. These definitions are embodied in the Uniform Vehicle Code, which has been adopted substantially by thirty-two states and the District of Columbia. Punishment in the United States for driving while under the influence of alcohol covers a wide range, however. In six states the first conviction for drunken driving is considered a felony, whereas seventeen states regard the offense as a misdemeanor until the third conviction. In addition, as noted earlier, there is a considerable tendency to reduce drunken driving charges to less serious violations.

Considerably more stringent policies with regard to drunken driving are found in the Scandinavian countries, where, despite social patterns conducive to heavy drinking, automobile fatalities tend to be low. In Sweden, a driver found with a concentration of .15 alcohol in his blood is routinely sentenced to imprisonment at hard labor, while a concentration of .05 to .15 percent leads to either a fine or imprisonment. License suspension for a period of from one to five years is automatic when the alcoholic concentration exceeds .05 percent. In Norway, an alcoholic content of above .05 percent results in a twenty-one-day jail sentence. Blood tests that establish alcohol concentration need not be undergone, but failure to take the test will automatically result in revocation of driving rights. It is, of course, hazardous to compare fatality rates for different jurisdictions, even when mileage estimates are available. Norway has many tortuously curved driving stretches, particularly in its fjord regions, but it also has considerably fewer automobiles than the United States, so that its fatality rate of 8.6 per 100,000 persons—less than half that of the United States—must be considered no more than a tentative indication of the value of its enforcement procedures.

Somewhat more persuasive has been the early reaction in Great Britain to a new law, enacted in October, 1967, which requires drivers to submit to breath tests if they are stopped by the police. Failure to pass the test results in a $240 fine, a prison sentence, or both. In the first three months after passage of the new law, highway deaths dropped 26 percent below their previous level, patronage of taxis following the closing of pubs at 11 P.M. was estimated to have increased 25 percent, and drinking at home rather than in public places, which was never a British habit, was reported to have risen considerably. The results of the new law were regarded by the Royal Society for the Prevention of Accidents as "spectacular." For criminologists, it would be intriguing to determine precisely what kinds of persons responded in the desired manner to the new law, why they responded in this manner, and how they might respond to a range of other sanctions imposed upon their behavior. It will also be interesting to determine how long the response to the statute will be, that is, whether the downward trend stabilizes, continues, or is dissipated as the statute becomes less familiar and, perhaps, its penalties less threatening.

Narcotic Offenses

Legal responses to the use of certain drugs illustrates vividly an inter-action between social structure and outlawed behaviors. It also illumi-nates clearly the sometimes transient nature of public concern over use and/or abuse of selected kinds of substances. Grouping opiate deriva-tives, such as heroin and morphine with marihuana and LSD, makes about as much taxonomic sense as classifying coffee, alcohol, and chocolate bars together and providing equivalent penalties for inges-tion of any of them. It is worth noting, in fact, that both coffee and alcohol have been legally proscribed in various cultures at different times, although such laws gave way in the face of widespread violation and ensuant dissipation of the statutes' moral persuasiveness.[35]

Drug policies in the United States indicate a profound concern in particular with the use of substances that in some manner contribute to an individual's diminished concern with his environment and with its stress on active participation, energetic self-interest, and competitive-ness. It is the "dropping out" responses of drug-using individuals that apparently most offend the social system, so that widespread recourse to sleeping pills, for instance, is not regarded with disfavor because it only temporarily lulls and ultimately permits the user to return more refreshed to the daily fray. The same explanation provides understand-ing of what otherwise seems to be a notable oddness in our social policies, which, on one hand, encourage mental patients to leave hos-pitals and sustain themselves indefinitely on the outside under drug regimens,[36] and, on the other hand, withdraw persons sustaining them-selves on drug regimens from free society and place them within the confines of prisons or hospitals, sometimes for indefinite periods.

Drugs presently causing the largest concern in the United States— the opiates and marihuana—require separate consideration because they are used by different kinds of persons, for different reasons, and because they are beginning to produce differentiated reactions from the system of criminal law.

THE OPIATE DERIVATIVES

Stripped to its essentials, the business of selling opiates involves a commercial catering to a specialized demand. That monopolistic tendencies permeate the operation of organized crime in the field of narcotics should not be surprising. That the outcome of the practice—

35 De Ropp, *Drugs and the Mind*, p. 428; Chein, *Road to H*, pp. 337–338.
36 Pansamanick, Scarpitti, and Dinitz, *Schizophrenics in the Community*.

the addiction of many individuals—does not lessen the aggressive nature of the operation should not be surprising either. It would only be unusual if we might, on the basis of our cultural patterns, be led to expect that cigarette manufacturers, for instance, would have voluntarily ceased high-pressure selling campaigns in the face of evidence that cigarette smoking is closely related to subsequent death from throat and lung cancer. Given such a relationship, it does not appear unreasonable to maintain that the cigarette industry is partly responsible for the cancer deaths of a number of its customers for the primary reason of financial profit. Such a situation, however, appears in no way to have slowed down the crusade by advertising branches of cigarette companies to raise sales and to obtain new customers, particularly among young persons.

In this respect, although the consequences of a particular behavior system must be considered in an overview of the behavior, the consequences are not adequate bases from which to undertake theoretical criminological investigations. Indeed, even from a moral viewpoint, such an approach often leads to considerable difficulty. If, for instance, it were shown that a specific number of deaths and serious injuries resulted in a given period from narcotic sales, while at the same time it was also demonstrated that triple that amount of negative consequences resulted from the failure of the automobile manufacturers to insist on safety devices in their products, then an assignment of blame might become quite involved. This is so, particularly if it could be shown that both the sale of narcotics and the failure to install safety devices were done for financial profit. In the case of the automobile, it might have seemed likely that the public would resist buying the cars because a large number of safety devices in them would generate mental images of the potentially lethal nature of an automobile, so that the dealer might readily defend his position by saying that he was merely catering to public demand. Similarly, as cigarette manufacturers maintain, nobody forces a person to smoke. And, for that matter, nobody forces another person to use opiates.

These comments are not intended to denigrate the possible social harmfulness of narcotic usage, but rather they are intended to bring into better perspective a problem that has become overladen with a large admixture of emotion. Narcotics represent a commercial product to organized criminals, a product whose mercantile importance has been particularly enhanced by the barriers imposed upon its importation and distribution. Such barriers serve as a tariff, protecting the large profits of the seller by keeping his product in short supply vis-à-vis the demand for it.

The pharmacological and social implications of opiate use indicate in part the justifications that are employed for current statutory prohibitions against addicts. There is, however, almost total medical consensus that persons could use opiates throughout their lives with no serious consequences to their general health that would be directly attributable to the drugs. The user would develop physiological tolerance, however, so that he would require ever-increasing dosages in order to avoid withdrawal distress, and ultimately he would be using amounts sufficient to kill numerous non-addicted persons.

The dangers from opiate use, therefore, lie in various peripheral circumstances. Insensitivity to hygienic considerations produces diseases such as hepatitis, which is transmitted from nonsterile hypodermic needles.[37] Failure to eat and rest properly also leads to a high morbidity rate among opiate users. In addition, there is always the possibility of overdosage, sometimes because of the deliberate failure of the seller to "cut" or dilute the drug to its usual concentration.

CONTROL OF NARCOTICS

It is the commission of crimes to secure funds for opiates that is regarded as the most devastating social consequence of narcotics traffic. Much debate centers around the question of whether addicts are juvenile delinquents or adult criminals who happen to use drugs, or whether it is the establishment of a pattern of drug use that inexorably demands illegal activity for its sustenance from persons who otherwise would have remained law-abiding.[38] In either event, it is clear that opiate users, whether criminals or noncriminals, are unable, in a very large majority of cases, to abandon criminal careers as long as they are unable to cease using drugs.

Because dependence on drugs almost invariably involves criminal activity, such as theft or prostitution, there has been some call for experimental programs under which addicts would have legitimate access to drugs under close medical supervision. It is questioned whether the failure of the forty-four clinics operated during the period between 1919 and 1923—a failure widely publicized by the Federal Bureau of Narcotics[39]—necessarily forebodes the doom of more sophisticated and better-planned proposed contemporary experiments.[40] The major thrust of such programs, in the words of Judge Morris Ploscowe, their leading advocate, would be to "aid in the determination of whether it is possible to rehabilitate addicts, in a noninstitutional setting, so that they can live and function without drugs."[41]

Prior to the passage of the Harrison Act in 1914, the first law to make narcotics use criminal, addiction to opiates was probably more widespread than at present. The inclusion of opiate derivatives in patent medicines created addicts from all levels of the social structure,

37 Appelbaum and Gelfond, "Artificial Transmission of Malaria in Intravenous Diacetylmorphine Addicts"; Batonbacal and Stipman, "Transmission of Viral Hepatitis in Heroin Addicts."
38 See O'Donnell, "Narcotic Addiction and Crime."
39 *Narcotic Clinics in the United States.*
40 Lindesmith, *Addict and the Law*, Chap. 5.
41 Ploscowe, in *Drug Addiction: Crime or Disease?*, p. 103.

although more so for women because of the common use of palliatives containing opiates for "female troubles." Narcotics could be purchased over the counter in drug stores or ordered through the mails. For some of the addicts before 1914, life went on in much the same manner as it always had; for others, the drugs represented stark tragedy. Few persons who have seen the vivid portrayal of the morphine addiction of the mother in Eugene O'Neill's "Long Day's Journey Into Night" will forget the torment that is associated with drug addiction.

After 1914, addicts increasingly were concentrated in the lower socioeconomic classes.[42] In 1935, the federal narcotics hospital at Lexington, Kentucky, was established, and three years later the federal hospital at Fort Worth, Texas, began operation. The opening of the federal facilities marked the end of toleration of addicts by the community, through the existence of special sites to which addicts could be dispatched.[43] There was, in addition, a sharp shift at this time in the public mood regarding drugs, a shift described by O'Donnell in the following terms:

> Public attitudes, which before had regarded addiction as a mildly deviant behavior, harmful to the individual and his family, now regarded it as one of the worst of evils, and as a threat to the community. Achieving abstinence was regarded as requiring only an act of will, so that when addicts relapsed after treatment they were perceived as hopeless weaklings, or as having chosen evil in place of good.[44]

Following World War II, the medical profession completely deserted the field of treatment of drug addiction, partly as a response to implicit threats of criminal prosecution by the Federal Bureau of Narcotics, based upon the Bureau's interpretation of several Supreme Court decisions.[45] In addition, doctors found addicts unrewarding patients, with a high degree of intransigency and a low rate of payment. Law enforcement efforts drove narcotics usage further into encapsulated slum areas, a trend that is evidenced by an examination of the 84,625 admissions to the federal hospitals during the past three decades. The change over time in the characteristics of the hospital populations have been indicated by John Ball:

> The major changes have been that addict patients are younger, a great percentage of those admitted are Negro and Puerto Rican, the use of heroin has increased, and both the number and percentage of addicts admitted from the largest metropolitan areas have markedly increased.[46]

42 Ball, "Two Patterns of Narcotic Drug Addiction in the United States."
43 Isbell, "Historical Development of Attitudes Toward Opiate Addiction in the United States."
44 O'Donnell, "Lexington Program for Narcotic Addicts."
45 Lindesmith, *Addict and the Law;* Eldridge, *Narcotics and the Law;* De Mott, "Great Narcotic Muddle."
46 Ball, "Two Patterns of Narcotic Drug Addiction in the United States"; Winick, "Epidemiology of Drug Use."

At first, ever-harsher criminal penalties, including possible death sentences for selling heroin to minors, were resorted to in an attempt to control traffic in narcotics. But this approach in recent years has given way to an emphasis on civil-commitment procedures.[47] Civil commitment received its greatest impetus when the Supreme Court in the *Robinson* case in 1962 declared that statutes making addiction to narcotics a criminal offense were in violation of the eighth amendment. The court maintained that drug addiction is an illness "comparable to leprosy, insanity, and the common cold" and that criminal punishment could not be inflicted for it. At issue was the question of whether Robinson could be convicted simply on evidence that he was an addict. The prosecution case was based on a series of discolorations and punctures on Robinson's arms, which, it stated, were the result of opiate injections. Robinson testified, although the jury did not believe him, that the marks were due to an allergic condition contracted when he was in the military service.[48] The Robinson case, setting the groundwork for civil-commitment procedures in place of criminal prosecutions, was not without a strong element of irony, for Robinson, free while his appeal was pending, died in a Los Angeles alley nearly a year before the Supreme Court handed down its ruling. According to police reports, the cause of his death was an overdose of narcotics.

CHARACTERISTICS OF ADDICTS

A review of studies on the relationship between pre-treatment variables and later abstinence from drug use shows, almost despairingly, the considerable confusion in present information. Some research probes, for instance, indicate a higher rate of success for males, while others insist that females do better. In general, though, an individual has a better chance for later abstinence from opiate use if Caucasian as contrasted to Negro, female, past thirty years of age, imprisoned for the first time, and from a higher social class. In terms of drug history, a record of first use after the age of twenty-five is more predictive of success than an earlier use-pattern. Short duration of drug usage and addiction on the basis of a legal source, such as in medical cases, both indicate a more hopeful prognosis than their counterparts. Stable employment and absence of a background of a broken home enhance chances of success for addicts. In addition, education correlates positively with abstinence, as does prior military service. A self-concept as a "patient" rather than one as an inmate or prisoner, and lack of involvement in the drug subculture have a high correlation with later abstinence from drug use.

Other items that shed some light on the opiate addict can be reported from a voluminous, though as yet rather uncoordinated

47 See White House Conference on Narcotic and Drug Abuse, *Proceedings*, pp. 173–221.
48 *Robinson v. California.*

literature on the subject.[49] Jack J. Monroe and Robert Astin, for instance, believe that the extent to which an addict identifies with his own stereotype of addicts provides a meaningful differentiation between potential success and failure. Strong stereotypic identification is negatively related to success.[50] Paulus suggests that the higher parole success of women is related to their ability to live stable, quasi-familial existences, while men, without such support, are more often thrown upon the criminal elements in the community. She emphasizes the paramount importance of some tranquility in family relationships as the *sine qua non* of drug abstinence.[51] Charles Winick points out that today's addicts are much more apt than the earlier breed to have milder opiate habits, largely because of the striking dilution of the drug being sold them. Therefore, the trauma of withdrawal for today's opiate addicts is considerably more benign than that of their predecessors. In addition, contemporary narcotic addicts are apt to be polysubstance users more often than addicts of the past generation. In particular, they are likely to move in a so-called "spree" fashion among opiates, including barbiturates, synthetics, and amphetamines, hoping to avoid building up too severe a habit in terms of any one kind of drug, and also, of course, taking advantage of the exigencies of the marketplace.[52] Users of cocaine, a stimulant, however, are notably fewer than in past decades, probably, ironically, because life itself is frenetic enough without the added external stimulation of drugs.

Studies of the marital history of narcotic addicts provide further insight into the possible roots of drug use. O'Donnell and his associates found from a large sample of federal narcotics prisoners that about twice as many of the male subjects as might have been anticipated had never married. There was a striking record of marital instability in the group that had married, and the subjects produced only two-thirds of the number of children that would have been anticipated in terms of their other characteristics. Strong interactive effects were found between the deviance of the subjects and that of their spouses; either they married deviant persons or they led their marriage partners into drug use or other forms of illegal activity.[53]

TREATMENT OF ADDICTS

Treatment approaches for addicts, besides criminal prosecution and fines or incarceration for possession or sale of drugs, and civil commitment, cover a wide range, including community-based programs, treat-

49 Sells, *A Bibliography on Drug Dependence; Bibliography on Drug Dependence and Abuse, 1928–1966.*
50 Monroe and Astin, "Stereotypes and Drug Addicts."
51 Paulus and Halliday, "Rehabilitating the Narcotic Addict."
52 Winick, "Epidemiology of Narcotics Use," p. 16.
53 O'Donnell, "Marital History of Narcotic Addicts."

ments with religious stress, communal-living arrangements, and chemotherapy regimens. Community-based programs operate on the assumption that a man must be acclimated to the milieu that originally led to his addiction. They also attempt to ameliorate evocative conditions in the slums. In addition, agencies and community resources may be mobilized to aid the opiate addict if he is allowed to stay in his own neighborhood instead of being institutionalized.

Perhaps the largest amount of publicity ever accorded any rehabilitative endeavor is that associated with the work of Synanon, a communal-living program run by former addicts to assist other addicts.[54] With vast real-estate holdings, a comprehensive program, and a large contingent of drug-free members and graduates, Synanon has forever dispelled the myth that "once an addict, always an addict." A charge sometimes leveled against Synanon, however, is that it promotes a tendency among its residents to segregate themselves from what may be regarded as productive ways of life.[55] It has been said, for instance, that Synanon is "unlikely to be helpful as a general rehabilitative program because it is a secretive cult. It has returned fewer than 100 persons to the community in seven years."[56] On the other hand, it might be argued that freedom from opiate dependence is itself an inherently desirable goal, and lifelong association with a community-treatment facility is a perfectly reasonable way for a person to spend his time.

Religious programs, such as that run by Teen-Challenge, are common in the treatment of opiate addiction. It is also noteworthy that Karl Marx' most famous statement on theology, that religion is "an opiate of the masses," was based on an analogy to drugs. The efficacy of religious approaches to drug addiction lies in the substitution of deep commitment to religious living for imperative allegiances to heroin.

Chemotherapy programs most generally rely on methadone, a synthetic, pain-killing drug that counteracts heroin by blocking its narcotic action. Patients taking methadone daily build up a tolerance to opiates so that they no longer get "high" from them. By the beginning of 1968, Drs. Vincent Dole and Marie Nyswander, sponsors of the Methadone Maintenance Program in New York, could claim that some 540 former heroin addicts were living useful and successful lives, staying in good health, retaining their alertness, and functioning normally while using methadone.[57] Major objection to methadone maintenance concentrates on the belief that methadone itself is similar to heroin and that no real progress is being made in freeing the addict from

54 See Yablonsky, *The Tunnel Back;* Casriel, *So Fair A House.*
55 Sternberg, "Synanon House." For details of a program using ex-addicts in social-work roles see Bullington, "Purchase of Conformity."
56 Louria, "Cool Talk About Hot Drugs," p. 44.
57 Hentoff, *A Doctor Among the Addicts.*

drug-dependence. It is also said that methadone, being a pain-killer, masks disease symptoms, and that the user may never become aware of suffering from things such as appendicitis. It is claimed also that methadone users constitute public dangers as car drivers and in situations requiring similar control and skill.

The varying treatment approaches reflect in part the continuing primitive state of knowledge regarding opiate addiction. This state was reflected in the cautionary words of Dr. Harris Isbell, who spent a lifetime conducting research on addiction, while addressing the White House Conference on Narcotic and Drug Abuse in 1962. New treatment methods, Isbell warned, are based primarily on intuition. Such innovations, he noted, should be approached experimentally and should be "broadly framed and sufficiently flexible to permit a testing of a variety of approaches, and to permit changes based on ongoing experience." Among key questions posed by Isbell were the following[58]: (1) Is institutional treatment necessary in all cases?, (2) Do small caseloads really contribute over a long period of time to a lower relapse rate?, (3) Are halfway houses needed?,[59] (4) What should be the length of institutional treatment?, (5) What should be the length of post-institutional treatment?, (6) Do Nalline tests, or tests for narcotics in urine, really deter patients from returning to drugs, and which of these two methods is most specific and effective?, and (7) Should relapse to use of narcotics be the sole criterion of success, or should the criterion be adequate social adjustment?

Other informational gaps were also discussed at the White House Conference. The chaplain for Narcotics Anonymous in New York, for instance, said that it might be a myth that addicts need to be treated in special facilities, and suggested that those handled with regular patient populations in hospitals perform better, because otherwise "they talk junk, think junk, and live with it always on their minds."[60] In addition, there was the puzzling information on the careers of physician addicts presented to the Conference. Studies indicate that doctors, pharmacists, and nurses become addicted to narcotics to a disproportionately high degree.[61] Their cure rate, however, is reported to be astronomical. In Los Angeles, for instance, Quinn found that 92 per cent of the physician addicts refrained from drug use for five years after their apprehension, though the sole punishment invoked by the Board of Medical Examiners was withdrawal of prescription-writing privileges.[62] Such a finding would seemingly call into question the effectiveness of treatment procedures that fail to

58 Isbell, in White House Conference on Narcotic and Drug Abuse, *Proceedings*, p. 94.
59 Geis, *East Los Angeles Halfway House;* Miller, "East Los Angeles Halfway House for Felon Addicts."
60 Egan, in *ibid.*, p. 116.
61 Quinn, in *ibid.*, p. 1196. See also Winick, "Physician Narcotic Addicts."
62 Quinn, "Narcotic Addiction;" Bloomquist, "Operation Narcotics."

introduce or reinforce those kinds of items which presumably aid doctors in ridding themselves of the drug habit.

Marijuana

To the criminologist, the marijuana picture today often appears to border on the surrealistic. Much discussion concerns short- and long-term consequences of the use of marijuana. But it would appear to be of secondary importance whether research ultimately proves that marijuana is somewhat more or somewhat less harmful than is currently believed, since there is general agreement that use of the drug is not addictive, and there is little dispute that its consequences are likely to prove less serious than a large range of other indulgences that remain well within the bounds of legality.

The precise parameters of marijuana usage are difficult to locate. The well-publicized 1967 episode of a fifty-eight-year-old elementary school principal in northern California, who told a legislative committee that it had been her habit for the past eighteen years to come home from school to puff on marijuana cigarettes, indicates what is clearly a widespread phenomenon of regular, undetected marijuana usage.

Official policies toward marijuana were established by the Marijuana Tax Act of 1937. Congressional hearings on the act have been said to represent an illustration of the federal legislative process at its poorest[63]; with single-minded dedication, the Congressional committee appeared to move from an untenable set of postulates to a fallacious set of conclusions, making certain to push aside any refractory material along the way. Fundamental to passage of the Act was an apparent unstated linkage between marijuana and the behavior and repute of groups who were then using the drug. This process has been described in the following terms:

> Acts viewed as unattractive, family patterns seen as unappetizing, and similar conditions believed to be unesthetic, items which were indigenous to Negro and Spanish-speaking groups, were implicitly related to the presence of marijuana. It was the same process by which the idiosyncracies of the aberrant in other times and other places have been tied to such things as their style of dress, their heresies, and their ceremonies. Today, in similar manner, campaigns against crime in the streets often represent camouflaged methods for retaliatory tactics against minority group members, who most often commit such crimes, but against whom frontal assaults are no longer fashionable.[64]

This theme is illustrated by a number of wartime studies of

---

63 U.S. House of Representatives, *Hearings on the Taxation of Marihuana;* Oteri and Silverglate, "In the Marketplace of Free Ideas"; Becker, "Marihuana Tax Act."

64 Geis, "Social and Epidemiological Aspects of Marihuana Use."

marijuana use by military personnel. All note a disproportionate number of Negroes among marijuana users who were referred to neuropsychiatric services. In a study of patients at Fort McClellan, Alabama, for instance, fifty-five were Negroes, one white[65]; all but one of thirty-five marijuana cases at March Air Field in California were Negroes,[66] and 95 percent of 150 marijuana cases among servicemen in India were also Negroes.[67] The Fort McClellan study shows the often self-defeating process involved in generalizing from a sample whose characteristics are not measured by adequate sampling or control techniques. The researchers concluded that "the preponderance of Negroes is due, we believe, to the peculiar need marijuana serves for them"; marijuana, they believed, "enables the Negro addict to feel a sense of mastery denied him by his color," a conclusion that has been made somewhat less than prescient by the spread of use today to persons who possess an obvious sense of mastery of both themselves and the world around them. "Fifteen percent of the students at Princeton admit smoking pot—two-thirds of them in the upper academic 20 percent, a third of them members of varsity athletic teams."[68] In addition, the Fort McClellan study went on to detail a panorama of personal and background characteristics found among users, which, three decades later, sound like nothing more than a description of life and its consequences for a large part of the population of the Negro ghetto.

The first significant opposition to the Marijuana Tax Act arose with the publication in 1944 of the report of the Mayor's Committee in New York, under the auspices of Fiorello LaGuardia. Field work for the sociological segment of the report was undertaken by officers of the police department's narcotic squad, who found marijuana usage concentrated most heavily in Harlem among young, unemployed men. Smokers were reported to believe that marijuana made them feel better and that it was not harmful. The report also notes that persons could voluntarily cease using marijuana without signs of discomfort or withdrawal and that it did not appear true that marijuana served as a stepping stone to heroin. The sociological segment of the Report concludes that "the publicity concerning the catastrophic effects of marijuana smoking in New York City is unfounded."[69]

Later research added complementary material to the Mayor's Committee Report. A study by Winick, for instance, indicates that jazz musicians were heavy users of alcohol in the early years of the century, but moved toward marijuana during the 1930s. Following World War II however, heroin began to gain popularity. From inter-

65 Charen and Perelman, "Personality Studies of Marihuana Addicts."
66 Marcovitz and .Myers, "Marihuana Addict in the Army."
67 Gaskill, "Marihuana: An Intoxicant."
68 Gollan, "Great Marijuana Problem," p. 78.
69 Shoenfeld, "Sociological Study"; Arnold, "Meaning of the LaGuardia Report."

views regarding the drug habits of their colleagues conducted during 1954 and 1955 with 357 jazz musicians, Winick estimates that 82 percent used marijuana at least once, 54 percent were occasional users, and 23 percent were regular users. More than half had tried heroin, 24 percent used it occasionally, and 16 percent regularly. Although a majority of musicians believed that marijuana hindered rather than improved their performing ability, a number pointed out that use of the drug seemed necessary for them to face the demands of their job, that without marijuana they would be unable to perform at all. The study also indicates that marijuana may aid in buttressing occupational solidarity and insularity. If true, for instance, the story often told to Winick, that a jazz band had performed such marijuana euphemistic numbers as "Tea for Two" and "Tumbling Tumbleweed" at a police benefit dance, must have been a source of great in-group merriment.[70]

Using similar subjects, interspersed with marijuana users other than musicians, Becker contributes the view that continued recourse to marijuana depends on a sequential series of events, which begin with learning to smoke the drug in a manner that will produce real effects and then proceeding to learn to enjoy the perceived sensations. In short, Becker suggests, "the marijuana user learns to answer 'yes' to the question: 'Is it fun?' " The direction that the drug experience then takes depends on intervening factors, such as moral judgments, availability, fear of arrest or an actual arrest, and social reactions.[71]

It is only very recently that we have acquired longitudinal information with which to examine the continuing careers of persons in the lower-socioeconomic class who have constituted the bulk of marijuana users until the past few years. This information comes from a St. Louis study by Lee Robins and George E. Murphy, which indicates that at the time there was a more widespread use of marijuana than many persons suspected, as well as a striking diminution of use with advancing age. Study subjects were young Negro men who were born in St. Louis between 1930 and 1934, attended local elementary schools, and resided in St. Louis in 1966. Of the 221 persons interviewed, 109 had tried at least one of four drugs during his life: 103 had used marijuana, 28 had used heroin, 37 had used amphetamines, and 32 had used barbiturates. In regard to marijuana, only a very small percentage of either occasional or regular users had come to the attention of the police. It is notable that half of the marijuana users never employed any other drug, that three out of four of the heroin users began with marijuana, and that one out of four of the marijuana users began with the drug prior to his sixteenth birthday. Sixty-nine percent began using it by the time they were twenty years old, and only nine persons from age 24 and afterwards. During the year preceding that in which they were interviewed, twenty-two of the men (about 10

70 Winick, "Use of Drugs by Jazz Musicians."
71 Becker, "Becoming a Marihuana User."

percent) reported that they had used drugs, the majority of whom smoked marijuana.[72] The drug-use rate uncovered by the St. Louis investigation may be slightly inflated by omission of rural and small-town migrants, but it indicates nonetheless a quite pervasive pattern of marijuana use among a minority group in a midwestern city, where drugs are not considered as great a problem as they are in seaport and Mexican border-cities.

The clearest insight into present drug customs in deprived areas is that reported in 1967 by Herbert Blumer and his colleagues. Blumer's work was designed to induce youthful drug users in the flatlands of Oakland, California, an area populated primarily by lower-class blacks and Mexican-Americans, to abstain from further usage, a mission that totally failed. "The real reasons for lack of success," the project workers note, "were the strong collective belief held by the youths that their use of drugs was not harmful and their ability to put up effective arguments, based usually on personal experience and observation, against claims of such harm."[73] Two major types of drug users—the *rowdy* and the *cool*—were identified among the youths. Rowdies, a small minority, used any and all drugs, but preferred alcohol. Cool youths fell into three types: mellow dudes, pot heads (or weed heads), and players. Mellow dudes, by far the most prevalent group, would "try anything once" but did not seek out drugs; their orientation was hedonistic, their pleasures primarily sexual. They used pills and crystal (methamphetamine hydrochloride or methedrine) as well as marijuana. The pot head, who is part of a sizable group, is exclusively a user of marijuana, described as follows:

> He uses no drugs other than marijuana and may even prefer soda pop to drinking alcohol. He is respected by other adolescents, presenting an image of a calm, sensible, solitary figure, soft-spoken, personable, and thoroughly knowledgeable about what is "happening" in the adolescent world. He takes pride in his appearance, always wearing sharp slacks and sweaters, is interested in taking things easy, having a good time, and fostering relations with the opposite sex. He is likely to be involved in conventional life activities, participating in various school functions, athletics, and conventional work.[74]

Initiation into marijuana use is regarded by the Project researchers as something other than a fulfilment of a personality predisposition or a motivational syndrome. Various conditions were found to keep the neophyte from access to drugs, primarily conditions relating to other's estimate of his integrity and his "coolness." Many pot heads were "turned on" by older brothers, intent on preventing them from "sniffing glue, drinking wine, or risking the chances of being ar-

72 Robins and Murphy, "Drug Use in a Normal Population of Young Negro Men";
    see also Bullington, "Concerning Heroin Use and Official Records."
73 Blumer, *World of the Youthful Drug User.*
74 *Ibid.,* p. 79.

rested."[75] Finally, the Oakland study team assails standard personality
theories of drug use, finding them "ridiculous." It is "primarily the
defining response of associates that leads to the formation of whatever
motives may be attached to drug use," they claim; the study evidence
shows "overwhelmingly that the great majority of youngsters become
users not to escape reality but rather as a means of embracing reality"
in a setting in which drug use is extensive and deeply-rooted.[76] It was
the guess of the research team that most pot heads will be assimilated
into conventional life as adults, although their drug experience might
lead a few of them into more serious narcotics involvement.

Given the heavy saturation of segments of lower-class life with
marijuana use in past decades, it is likely that the striking recent
increases in police seizures of marijuana and the skyrocketing arrest
rates for marijuana offenses, represent in considerable measure the
movement of middle- and upper-class citizens into marijuana use.
Much less well studied to date, this group nonetheless presents a major
ideological challenge to marijuana laws and a major rebuff to traditional explanations of marijuana use.

A general overview of available epidemiological material in 1968
by Stanley Yolles indicates that perhaps 20 percent of high school and
college students have had some experience with marijuana. More men
than women students reported involvement, and of those students
reporting use, 65 percent say they smoked marijuana fewer than ten
times, with the most common response being "once or twice." Particularly interesting is that fully 50 percent of the students who tried
marijuana indicated that they experienced no effects from it. Four
explanations were offered for this situation: (1) The agent may not
have been potent, (2) Frequently, effects are seen only after repeated
use, (3) The expectation of the user significantly affects what he experiences, and (4) The social setting in which use takes place has an
effect on the response.[77]

More detailed information may be gained from 1967 surveys of
drug use patterns among high school students on either coast of the
United States. In a study at two senior high schools in Great Neck,
New York, an affluent suburb, some 207 of 2,587 students (8 percent)
self-reported smoking marijuana, while 55 had tried LSD.[78] On the
west coast, in a senior class of a high school in San Mateo county,
California, more than 25 percent of 288 boys and almost 10 percent of
220 girls reported that they had used marijuana at least once, with
more than half of both groups indicating use on three or more occasions.[79]

75 *Ibid.*, p. 49.
76 *Ibid.*, p. 59.
77 *New York Times*, March 22, 1968.
78 *United Press International*, Feb. 16, 1967.
79 San Mateo County, *Narcotics Inquiry Report*, p. 5; see also Goode, "Multiple
  Drug Use Among Marijuana Smokers."

It may be, although we have no trustworthy information on the subject to date, that a disproportionate number of high school marijuana users do not matriculate. Among those most deeply-immersed into drug culture, some may migrate to such drug-use citadels as the Haight-Ashbury district in San Francisco, where research is currently being undertaken to gain a profile of summer transients and permanent residents. Preliminary Haight-Ashbury reports, incidentally, indicate that the largest amount of marijuana use occurs among persons regularly using methedrine. Such persons employ marijuana to put themselves in a more tranquil condition after recurrent methedrine experiences or, in their terms, at the "end of a run."

To summarize, early and continued use by dispossessed elements of American society probably contributed to the present legal position of marijuana, just as shifts in use patterns may contribute to a reexamination of that position. Ultimately, of course, the attitude that society takes regarding marijuana must emerge from a weighing of unquantifiable values. It is worth noting, finally, that that attitude itself will then become, as it has been in the past, one of the most important items shaping use patterns and the consequences of such patterns in regard to marijuana.

For Further Reading

CHEIN, ISIDOR, DONALD L. GERARD, ROBERT S. LEE, AND EVA ROSENFELD. *The Road to H: Narcotics, Delinquency, and Social Policy.* New York: Basic Books, 1964.

> The most intensive study of the subculture of juvenile narcotics use, this volume includes sophisticated statistical analyses, psychiatric speculations, and a thorough humanistic review of the meaning and implications of American drug policies. The monograph also contains a notable discussion of the numerical quicksand involved in estimates of the magnitude of the narcotic problem.

LINDESMITH, ALFRED R. *The Addict and the Law.* Bloomington: Indiana University Press, 1965.

> Professor Lindesmith, a sociologist at Indiana University, has carried on a continuing campaign against what he regards as abuses in the writing and the enforcement of narcotics statutes in the United States. This carefully reasoned volume offers a number of paths for the resolution of narcotics difficulties. Particularly noteworthy is the scalpel-like dissection of arguments that the Narcotics clinics were a dismal failure.

PITTMAN, DAVID J., AND WAYNE GORDON. *Revolving Door: A Study of the Chronic Police-Case Inebriate.* Glencoe, Ill.: The Free Press, 1958.

> Pittman and Gordon present the most comprehensive investigation into the problem of the alcoholic who comes to the attention of the police and is incarcerated. The authors supply a detailed analysis of the background of the police-case inebriate and maintain that he shows

a pattern of faulty socialization. Recommendations are offered for dealing more effectively with the problem.

PRESIDENT'S COMMISSION ON LAW ENFORCEMENT AND ADMINISTRATION OF JUSTICE. *Task Force Report: Drunkenness.* Washington, D.C.: Government Printing Office, 1967.

The recommendation of the Commission that drunkenness alone should not be a criminal offense was rejected in 1968 by the Supreme Court in its decision on the *Powell* case. In part, the Court's decision reflects the paucity of innovative approaches available for handling cases of public drunkenness. The Commission report, although it includes consultant's papers on several of the more imaginative programs in the country, also concludes that there is a striking shortage of adequate facilities to care for alcoholics outside the system of criminal justice.

————. *Task Force Report: Narcotic and Drug Abuse.* Washington, D.C.: Government Printing Office, 1967.

The work of the President's Commission on narcotics and dangerous drugs has been criticized because of what some people regard as its equivocating stand in regard to marijuana laws and its rather amorphous recommendations for dealing with the narcotics situation in the United States. The report is particularly worthwhile for the fair-minded and comprehensive reviews of many aspects of the narcotics issues by Richard H. Blum and his colleagues, which appear as consultants' papers.

14

Juvenile Delinquency

Much can be told about a society from an inventory of those aspects of its life that it believes require particular reformative attention. That juvenile delinquency is regarded in the United States as a separable form of law-violating behavior, although it embraces in large measure acts already proscribed by criminal codes, indicates the concern and unease regarding youth that permeates the social order. This public disquiet need not be related in a realistic manner to the behavior under consideration. There are, by reasonable standards, much worse things than juvenile delinquency that have not been singled out and labelled. It might be just as rewarding, or more rewarding, for instance, to concentrate attention on crimes by persons between the age of thirty and thirty-nine and to define such behavior as "trigintennial criminality."[1] We could indicate that the fourth decade of life is of particular importance for the integrity of society and that it is important to pay particular attention to the malaise, which may eventuate in antisocial conduct, that accompanies incipient middle-age.

Roots of Concern with Delinquency

That juvenile delinquency is a prominent concern among persons in the United States is readily evident. In his comprehensive history of the United States, Samuel Eliot Morison finds delinquency to be a major social theme of the current period, and he moralizes about the phenomenon as "a peculiarly nasty product of the new freedom" involving "teen-age monsters of both sexes who take drugs, rob, riot, and kill 'just for kicks.' "[2] In a more official vein, President Lyndon B. Johnson observed in a message to Congress in 1965 that "Crime has become a malignant enemy in America's midst," and he further noted

1 Margolis, "Juvenile Delinquency"; see also Eisner, *The Delinquency Label.*
2 Morison, *Oxford History of the American People*, p. 909.

that, "It has been said that the fault lies in deep moral decay, particularly among the young; that juvenile delinquency and high crime rates among younger adults have their origins in that decay."[3]

It has been said that public concern with juvenile delinquency reflects the relative newness of the United States compared to other countries. This explanation appears rather spurious, however, since many societies that were formed more recently than America attach much less importance to childhood and adolescence. It may be that the comparatively open-class structure in the United States, the opportunity to have one's children achieve goals beyond the reach of their parents, makes parents particularly concerned with the well-being of the young. It has been suggested, in this vein, that the American emphasis on children is "an expected consequence of a social system founded upon the value of equality and achievement."[4] There are also a number of items operating in the United States, such as the secular attitude toward death,[5] which impart added attraction to youth in contrast to those of more advanced years. The nature of the cosmetics and hairdressing industries, the insistent stress on youth in advertising, and similar items indicate clearly that, given the choice, Americans prefer to prolong as long as possible the illusion of their own youthfulness.

There also appears to be a prevalent belief throughout our society that childhood is a period of freedom and joyfulness. Parents are inclined to stress that life never again will be as attractive as it is when one is young. This belief is, of course, neither true nor false; it represents an emphasis on certain conditions in preference to others. Maturity brings with it a number of different life conditions; the individual superimposes upon such conditions a personal definition. For example, the opportunity to work afforded to an adult may be seen as a chance to be creative and to gain financial rewards with which to purchase desirable items; the same opportunity can also be viewed as a tedious burden that restricts pleasure.

Nonetheless, it is evident that high importance is placed on children in the United States. It is also evident that one of the results of this stress is that delinquency—the falling away of some youngsters from social expectations—is considered a very serious matter. It remains an important task to attempt to pinpoint the reasons for this.

The United States is generally regarded, in the words of Kingsley Davis, as presenting "one of the extremest examples of endemic filial friction in human history."[6] Davis believes that the extraordinary rate of social change in the United States, combined with various role expectations that are severely tried by such change, underlines the

---

3 *New York Times*, March 9, 1965.
4 Lipset, *First New Nation*, pp. 119–124.
5 Blauner, "Death and Social Structure."
6 Davis, "Sociology of Parent-Youth Conflict."

unusual amount of intergenerational conflict. "Not only are the parent and child, at any given moment, in different stages of development," he notes, "but the content which the parent acquired at the stage where the child now is, was a different content from that which the child is now acquiring. Since the parent is supposed to socialize the child he tends to apply the erstwhile but now inappropriate content."[7]

The rapidly changing nature of our society has been particularly influential in prolonging the period of dependency among young persons. The urban, industrial character of the United States has increasingly made the adolescent's labor of little or no value, and his maintenance and education have been a drain on the resources of his family, besides providing him with many experiences that his parents did not have. The impact of this intergenerational conflict, according to Ivan Nye, is related to the socioeconomic level of the family, even when such items as broken homes, size of the family, employment status of the mother, and urban-rural residence are kept constant.[8] Nye offers no explanation for the greater amount of conflict on the lower end of the socioeconomic scale, although interpretations suggest themselves, such as the hypothesis that the working-class family is less able than the middle- and upper-class family to accommodate itself to the perceived needs and demands of the youngster, that it is more rapidly outpaced by the changes in our society, and that it is less able to offer the youngster examples, rewards, and similar incentives for more conforming behavior.

The differentiation of the younger generation—manifest in the definitional distinction of "delinquent" behavior—is reflected in what sociologists label as a "youth culture," although there is some dispute regarding whether such a culture is notably distinctive or whether it represents a precocious replicate of adult forms.[9] The term "youth culture" has been preferred by sociologists to "adolescence," which refers both in its origin and usage specifically to psychological and physiological characteristics dominant from puberty to maturity.[10] The youth culture in the American society, particularly in the middle class, is said to be marked by its efforts to conceal behavior from other age levels. This secrecy serves as an obstacle to the supervision and control of the young by the older age groups. Youths form cliques to bind themselves together into a protective structure, and they employ weapons such as teasing, ridicule, and ostracism to enforce their standards on their fellows.[11]

7 Ibid.
8 Nye, "Adolescent-Parent Adjustment."
9 Berger, "Adolescence and Beyond"; Berger, "On the Youthfulness of Youth Cultures"; Elkin and Westley, "Myth of Adolescent Culture"; Gottlieb and Reeves, Adolescent Behavior in Urban Areas.
10 Tracy, Psychology of Adolescence.
11 Smith, American Youth Culture; see also Eisenstadt, From Generation to Generation; Remmers and Radler, The American Teenager; Coleman, Adolescent Society; Rosenberg, Society and the Adolescent Self-Image.

The major source of adult frustration appears to lie in the fear that adult standards will not be accepted by the younger generation. Erik H. Erikson indicates that ideally the adolescent years should be a period of "psychosocial moratorium" during which the individual remains relatively free from adult pressures and responsibilities, so that he can engage in "identity play" and other forms of experimentation in order to find out who he is.[12] Despite their apparent affection for youth and their general willingness to indulge it, few adults appear able to tolerate so unstructured an exploratory period, possibly because they are so uneasy about its consequences. This uneasiness may spring from their awareness of social change, making their interests anachronistic, as well as from their awareness that many of their articulated criteria for the good life, when scrutinized, will be found wanting. It is "an ultimate contradiction," Smith suggests, that "youth are viewed as disloyal or even punished for trying to carry out the ideal norms of family and religion in adult society."[13]

Delinquency, in the preceding terms, may be seen as a threat against adult hegemony and adult standards. It is a particularly blatant and irritating manifestation because of the unusual emotional investment that Americans make in their children and in younger generations. It strikes so close because it is seen as a challenge to commitments lying at the core of the adult's existence. Adult perception may, of course, be inaccurate; juveniles may in fact be attempting to achieve those very things that adults value—in deed, at least, if not necessarily in word—and may be using tactics that adults, if they would be guaranteed that they would not be injured, would themselves employ. Nonetheless, delinquents are not playing the game according to official rules, and this deviance represents a serious affront to the adult world that defines the rules.

There are also numerous other reasons why delinquency is considered a most serious problem in the United States today, a problem distinct in many ways from crime. Certainly delinquency represents a considerable threat to the physical and material well-being of members of the society who feel that they are entitled to protection and security against such interference. It is also likely that interference with formative behavior patterns will yield better results than if such interference is attempted later, when the patterns have crystallized more completely. William Kvaraceus also observes that there is an emotional release involved in fiery agitation against delinquents:

> The young law violator tends to siphon off much of the adult frustration-aggression that abounds in the complexities of everyday living. The irritating delinquent serves admirably as a handy hate target. He is a perennial and classical institutional scapegoat. In the sanctimonious

---

12 Erikson, "Ego Identity and the Psychosocial Moratorium."
13 Smith, *American Youth Culture*, p. 25.

clucking of many parents can be heard a half-concealed vicarious thrill and delight in the escapades of youth. One can almost sense the adult smacking his lips as he bemoans the "awful" norm-violating conduct of the less-inhibited young. If delinquency is to be prevented and controlled, it will be necessary for many adults to inspect their own problems, and even their own pleasures in the delinquency phenomenon.[14]

What is Juvenile Delinquency?

The laws makes a basic distinction between acts committed by a child and those committed by an adult. Based on a traditional right of "parens patriae" (the state as parent), the juvenile courts may act with juveniles on the basis of the status of being a child rather than on the basis of the offense committed. The individual defined as an adult is accorded the advantages (and disadvantages) of substantive and procedural law. A significant aspect of the legal description of "juvenile delinquency" is that to a considerable extent it has no substantive behavioral reference. The term "juvenile delinquency" is applied variously by the police and the courts to designate diverse forms of youthful activity that are regarded as "misbehavior." In fact, a mere diagnosis that one is "in danger of becoming a delinquent" can be adequate to sustain a finding of delinquency.

The average juvenile delinquent, so adjudicated by the court, therefore is not a "junior criminal," although many delinquent children commit acts that are in violation of the criminal law. The state laws on delinquency, derived from legal concepts of early English chancery courts, typically indicate that being "incorrigible" or "ungovernable" or "habitually truant" are conditions sufficient to constitute juvenile delinquency. If a youth runs away from home, uses "obscene or indecent language," associates with disreputable people, loiters about railroad tracks, solicits money in public places, or is otherwise engaged in a variety of acts of a similar nature he may be taken before the juvenile court, declared a delinquent, and placed under official control. Under such conditions, it is not surprising that the President's Commission on Law Enforcement and Administration of Justice reported that

> Enormous numbers of young people appear to be involved in delinquent acts. Indeed, self-report studies reveal that perhaps 90 per cent of all young people have committed at least one act for which they could have been brought to juvenile court. Many of these offenses are relatively trivial—fighting, truancy, running away from home. Statutes often define juvenile delinquency so broadly as to make virtually all offenders delinquent.[15]

14 Kvaraceus, "Nature of the Problem of Juvenile Delinquency."
15 President's Commission, *Juvenile Delinquency,* pp. 12–14.

It should be noted that no rigid criteria may be employed to characterize forms of behavior that, in the last resort, are fundamentally matters of moral judgment. Thus, what constitutes an "ungovernable" or "incorrigible" child, or "habitual truancy," or the precise occasion that demarks the "running away from home" will depend on how a given juvenile court judge defines such terms, in accordance with his own attitudes and predilections. Because of the very structure of the average juvenile court, staffed by probation personnel or social workers, a selective bias tends to control the kinds of children and youths recommended to the courts for hearing and adjudication.[16]

This difficulty is compounded by the fact that there is little agreement regarding what constitutes an appropriate chronological line of demarcation between delinquency and adult criminal behavior. While there is general consensus as to the lower age at which a child may be dealt with in the courts, there is a wide range of age levels specifying the upper limits at which "childhood" offenses may be handled. The age of seven—regarded in common law as the age when an individual first gives evidence of capacity to reason—is ordinarily utilized by most states as the point at which delinquency adjudications may be initiated. Nine jurisdictions—Connecticut, Georgia, Maryland, New York, North Carolina, Utah, Vermont, Puerto Rico, and the Virgin Islands—consider a person to be an adult when he is sixteen years of age or older. Most jurisdictions, however, have established eighteen years as the upper age limit for legal consideration as a juvenile, while six states hold a person to be a juvenile until he reaches his seventeenth birthday. The federal government, operating under its own statutes, regards eighteen as the appropriate dividing line between juvenile offenses and adult criminality.[17] Particularly disconcerting in regard to these age criteria are regular changes in statutes, displaying no consistency, so that one state in a given year may raise its delinquency age to eighteen from seventeen, while an adjoining state may lower its age specification from eighteen to seventeen.

To add to this confusion, adjudication by states may occur at different age levels for different types of offenses and for differences in sex. Thus, while a state may hold to eighteen as the point of division between juvenile adjudication and adult prosecution, it may use the age of sixteen as the age of separation with respect to certain offenses committed by a girl, particularly if the offenses are of a sexual character. Such differences reflect the social and historic background in the fomulation of age and sex standards within a given area, conditioned by ethnic, religious, and ideological conceptions of social maturity and responsibility. The frontier states, for example, enter-

16 Carr, "Most Courts Have to be Substandard"; Geis and Tenney, "Evaluating a
   Training Institute for Juvenile Court Judges."
17 Sussman and Baum, *Law of Juvenile Delinquency.*

tained conceptions as to when adult status was achieved that were different from those of the more stable mercantile states along the Atlantic seaboard.

The difficulty in establishing by law arbitrary dividing lines between juvenile and adult status has tended (1) to encourage legislation of a discretionary type for handling the cases of youths falling beyond the limiting statute, and (2) to raise serious doubts as to whether an arbitrary system of age categories that permits extremely different legal courses of treatment is wholly justifiable. With respect to the former, it is always relatively easy to argue that special consideration should be given to those who have just recently passed the divide between childhood and legal adult status. But when one proposes the age of sixteen as a dividing line, the question immediately emerges as to why the age of seventeen, or eighteen, or even twenty-one or twenty-five would not do. The impact of the philosophical reasoning behind the juvenile courts, based on primary consideration for the child and *not* for his offense, is making serious incursions on the entire conception of criminal law. Thus, the state of California, having established a Youth Authority for handling cases of juveniles up to the age of twenty-one, subsequently organized an Adult Authority which considers dispositions of offenses by persons beyond that age. Such a change in focus is not to be dismissed lightly. Nor can we necessarily assume that the humanitarian stress of the late nineteenth century, which inspired the development of the early juvenile courts in the United States, is directly applicable to the realm of adult crime. To accept such a position uncritically may constitute a serious hazard to fundamental values, both social and legal.

THE "CHILD-SAVING" MOVEMENT

A historical review of the background of juvenile courts and of the movement to separate out from human activity various forms of behavior undertaken by youngsters places current issues into clearer perspective. The development has been summarized by Anthony Platt in the following terms:

> Contemporary programs of delinquency-control can be traced to the enterprising reforms of the child-savers who, at the end of the nineteenth century, helped to create special judicial and correctional institutions for the labeling, processing, and management of "troublesome" youth. Child-saving was a conservative and romantic movement, designed to impose sanctions on conduct unbecoming youth and to disqualify youth from enjoying adult privileges. The child-savers were prohibitionists, in a general sense, who believed in close supervision of adolescents' recreation and leisure. The movement brought attention to, and thus "invented," new categories of youthful misbehavior which had previously been unappreciated or had been dealt with on an informal

basis. Child-saving was heavily influenced by middle-class women who extended their housewively roles into public service and emphasized the dependence of the social order on the proper socialization of children.[18]

The child-saving movement culmimated in the establishment of the juvenile court. There has been some mild controversy about the exact place of origin of the first juvenile court, but most authorities believe that passage in the spring of 1899 of "An Act to Regulate the Treatment and Control of Dependent, Neglected and Delinquent Children" in Illinois was the first clear-cut step toward an independent institution and is the act upon which most subsequent legislation was based.[19] The Illinois law set up a statewide system of juvenile courts, although only Cook County initially had both the population and facilities to operate a court. The law applied to children under the age of sixteen and specified that one or more judges from the circuit court was to be designated to hear juvenile cases in a special courtroom labelled the "juvenile courtroom." The act eliminated use of warrants for arrests of children, the use of indictments, and many other forms of traditional criminal procedure. It aimed to make the court's "care, custody, and discipline of a child . . . approximate as nearly as may be that which should be given by its parents."

The juvenile court movement initially steered an erratic pioneer course. The first five years of its existence were "largely a period of experimentation, of sentiment, and of missionary work by individuals."[20] By 1904, however, eleven states had enacted juvenile court legislation, and eight years later there were twenty-two states with juvenile court laws. By 1925, all states but two—Maine and Wyoming—had juvenile court acts. Wyoming was the last to join the movement, finally inaugurating a juvenile court system in 1951.[21]

The ease with which the juvenile courts gained constitutional acceptance sheds considerable light on the attitudes that gave rise to and lie behind current concern with juvenile delinquency. Examination of the court decisions in the earliest cases show the emergence of two principles: first, that the court proceedings in no sense could be considered criminal; and, second, as a justification for the first proposition, that the proceedings were designed to serve the best interests of the child. It was not until 1967—two-thirds of a century after passage of the Illinois juvenile court act—that the Supreme Court peered behind the euphemistic rationale of the juvenile court and

18 Platt, "Rise of the Child-Saving Movement," p. 21.
19 Reproduced in Elliott, *Conflicting Penal Theories in Statutory Criminal Law*, pp. 241–249.
20 Lou, *Juvenile Courts in the United States*, p. 22.
21 See, for example, Wunniche, "The 1951 Juvenile Court Law of Wyoming"; Kahn, *A Court for Children*; Popper, *Individualized Justice*; Waybright, "Florida's New Juvenile Court Act."

ordered, in the *Gault* case, that elements of procedural regularity be introduced.[22]

The first appellate decision relating to the juvenile court was *Ex parte Loving,* in which the constitutionality of the Missouri Juvenile Court Act of 1903 was attacked after an eight-year-old boy was sentenced under it to the State Reform School. The boy appealed on various grounds, calling the subject of the law vague, labelling it a local law and class legislation, and maintaining that the law called for an illegal levy of taxes and failed to differentiate between neglected and delinquent children. The act was sustained. It is interesting to note the judge's introductory comment in the decision:

> We confess, at the outset, that the wise and beneficent purposes sought to be accomplished by this act—the prevention of crime, and the up-building of good and useful citizenship—tend . . . to the creation of a desire to uphold it.[23]

The first major case concerning the constitutionality of the juvenile court procedure, *Commonwealth v. Fisher,* was a test of the Pennsylvania juvenile court act of 1903. In its decision, the appellate court enunciated the major rationale for by-passing constitutional guarantees. "There was," the decision noted, "no trial for any crime here," and the *Fisher* case also provided a philosophical bulwark for the juvenile court movement:

> To save a child from becoming a criminal, or from continuing in a career of crime, to end in maturer years in public punishment and disgrace, the Legislature may surely provide for the salvation of such a child, if its parents or guardian be unwilling or unable to do so, by bringing it into the courts of the state without any process at all, for the purpose of subjecting it to the state's guardianship and protection.[24]

By the time of *Pugh v. Bowden,* the court was even more rhapsodical about the benefits being conferred upon a delinquent sentenced under the new juvenile court law:

> The State Reform School is not simply a place for correction, but a school where the young offender, separated from vicious associates, may receive careful physical, intellectual, and moral training, be reformed and restored to the community with purposes and character fitting for a good citizen, an honorable and honest man, with a trade or skilled occupation fitting such person for self-maintenance.[25]

By the time of *In re Sharp* in 1907, the matter had been settled beyond dispute. The Idaho court noted that "These questions have

22 *Gault v. Arizona.* See also Ketcham, "Guidelines from *Gault*"; Dorsen and Rezneck, "Gault and the Future of Juvenile Law"; Neigher, "The Gault Decision."
23 *Ex parte Loving,* p. 508.
24 *Commonwealth v. Fisher,* p. 200.
25 *Pugh v. Bowden,* p. 501.

all been so extensively, exhaustively, and lucidly considered and discussed by so many courts within recent years that we shall content ourselves with a citation of some of the authorities"; it went on to point out that the juvenile court law "is not a penal or criminal statute in nature, but is rather paternal, benevolent and charitable in its purposes and operation, and is intended to confer and grant favors, privileges, and opportunities rather than to impose penalties, burdens, or exactions."[26] To fourteen-year-old Hazel Sharp, sentenced to a term in the Idaho Industrial Training School, if to no one else, this must, indeed, have sounded like a dubious proposition. In fact, the extraordinary malleability of the juvenile court laws was illustrated by an Ohio case in which a boy was committed to the state penitentiary by a juvenile court. A writ of habeas corpus was denied on the ground that, while the penitentiary was assuredly a penitentiary in the case of adults, the same institution was for children "only a school or place of reformation."[27]

STATISTICS ON DELINQUENCY

The earlier review of statistics on adult criminal activity notes that the data is partial and selective, and that in many ways it is more indicative of public attitudes than of criminal behavior. This situation, somewhat characteristic of adult crime, is also pervasive in regard to juvenile delinquency statistics. It is in such terms that the reported numerical tabulations of juvenile delinquency in the United States must be regarded.[28]

The *Uniform Crime Reports,* which provide most of the statistical information concerning adult crime, are much less trustworthy concerning their enumeration of delinquency. The voluntary reporting by local jurisdictions to the F.B.I., which is the basis of the *Uniform Crime Reports,* tends to undercut severely the accuracy of figures on delinquency. For one thing, many police departments will not include in their calculations youth offenses that are referred to juvenile court, especially when the allegation against the youth is stated as "juvenile delinquency" rather than as a specific offense. In addition, in jurisdictions where fingerprinting and photographing juveniles are forbidden by law, arrest statistics on youths forwarded to the F.B.I. are apt to be incomplete. The soundest generalization about the *Uniform Crime Reports* figures is that they tend to report the same phenomenon, with the same limitations, year after year, and that an increase probably (although by no means necessarily) represents a real rise in the phenomenon reported, however unknown its precise dimensions may be.

Most authorities rely, however warily, upon the Children's Bureau

26 *In re Sharp,* p. 564.
27 *Leonard v. Licker,* p. 445.
28 See Robison, *Can Delinquency Be Measured?*

series *Juvenile Court Statistics* for numerical data concerning delinquency. It is noteworthy that both the Children's Bureau's and the
F.B.I.'s data show "a remarkable similarity" in their trends over a
long period of time, despite their differences in definitions, units of
count, and extent of coverage. To interpret the *Juvenile Court Statistics* it must be appreciated that only about one out of three youths
arrested ever appears before the juvenile court, and that the rules, procedures, and enumerations may be very different in different jurisdictions.[29] Also, as *Juvenile Court Statistics* notes, ages of children and
types of cases over which juvenile courts have jurisdiction vary in different states and even within the same state. In addition, the presence
or absence of other social agencies in the community may seriously influence whether or not a particular child is referred to the juvenile
court or sent elsewhere.[30]

It is very evident, after taking these considerations into account,
that a major factor in the overall reported crime rise in the United
States is the burgeoning amount of reported juvenile lawbreaking.
In 1966, some 745,000 juvenile delinquency cases (excluding traffic
offenses) were handled by juvenile courts in the United States. The
estimated number of children involved in these cases—642,000—was
somewhat lower, since in some instances the same child was referred
more than once during the year. The 1966 delinquency population
represents 2.1 percent of all children age ten through seventeen in
the country. The increase in delinquency for 1966 was 7 percent,
while the child population aged ten through seventeen increased by
only 2 percent.

The upward trend in delinquency in 1966 repeats a movement
begun in 1949, which has been uninterrupted since, except in 1961
when a slight decline was reported. The growth in reported delinquency between 1957 and 1966 was 69 percent, compared to a child
population increase of 35 percent. It is predicted now that an American boy aged ten in 1969 stands a 50-50 chance of being arrested
sometime in his life for other than a traffic offense. If the boy lives in
the city, his chance of arrest rises to 60 percent; if he is a Negro living
in the city, his chance of arrest increases to 90 percent.

Contributing to the heavy increase of delinquency in 1966 were
demographic factors, which can play havoc with year-by-year comparisons when the age-base on which the delinquency rate is calculated
varies. Ten-year olds, for example, do not contribute heavily to delinquency, while youths seventeen years of age have very high juvenile delinquency rates. Disproportions in the number of youths
found in the different age categories will readily be reflected, therefore,
in the year's delinquency statistics. In 1965, the large number of ju-

29 Goldman, *Differential Selection of Juvenile Offenders for Court Appearance.*
30 Schwartz, "Statistics of Juvenile Delinquency in the United States."

veniles born in 1947, when birth rates were high in the United States, moved out of the sixteen- and seventeen-year-old bracket into age groups subject to criminal rather than juvenile jurisdiction. Their departure was undoubtedly responsible in large measure for the relatively small reported increase of 2 percent in delinquency between 1964 and 1965. Better balancing in age categories tended to push the increment in delinquency up to its 1966 level of 7 percent.

Other notable aspects of the 1966 figures on juvenile delinquency include the following:

1. Semiurban and rural juvenile courts both experienced increases of 13 percent, almost twice the amount of increase for the country as a whole. Delinquency remains an urban phenomenon nonetheless, with a rate three times higher in the cities than beyond their boundaries. Cities account for two-thirds of the total amount of delinquency in the United States.

2. The increase in delinquency during 1966 showed no differentiation between boys and girls, with the figure for both groups rising by 7 percent. Boys continue, however, to come before juvenile courts more than four times as often as girls, a figure still strikingly different from the 8 to 1 male-female sex ratio in serious adult offenses.

3. The increase in delinquency court cases was found by the Children's Bureau, through its examination of F.B.I. records, not to be a consequence of a disproportionate increase in minor offenses, but rather a result of a higher rate of serious law violations.

Behavior Systems in Delinquency

It was suggested earlier that crime may be conceived of as falling into separable behavioral systems, each with its special set of adaptational mechanisms and its own set of rationales and orientations. For this reason, a history of criminal law may be visualized in terms of separate types of legislative enactments devised to meet unique problems of lawbreaking encountered by a society in its historical development. This is fundamentally different than conceiving of crime in a highly generic sense as consisting of all types of lawbreaking in general. The separable systems of crime that we have attempted to describe and analyze thus far constitute, in a sense, a typology of crime.

In the case of delinquency, such a typology is far more difficult to devise, since delinquency, as presently conceived in the American system of law, is not construed as criminal, even though certain forms of "criminality" are included in its legal definition.[31] Because of the enormously wide and amorphous kinds of youthful behaviors regarded as delinquent, it becomes very difficult to separate out those special types that constitute specific forms of delinquent adaptation. Be-

31 See also Ferdinand, *Typologies of Delinquency.*

havioral systems in delinquency, because of the wide-ranging forms
they encompass, may be regarded as reflecting *social* forms of adaptation within a given environment, or they may be regarded as reflecting
the behavioral systems of groups of *uniquely structured personalities.*
Thus, a typology may be constructed on either of these bases. In the
first instance, for example, children of a given class and ethnic background within a specific slum environment may be impelled, by the
very conditions of their sociocultural surroundings, to make a given
form of adjustment, involving its own attitudes, value-commitments,
and outlooks. Their form of adaptation is directly conceived of as a
social adaptation in which the youth's peer-age associates reinforce
his behavioral tendencies so that a distinctive subculture results. In
the second instance, a given environment may tend to engender specific
forms of personality structure among the children, which in turn may
lead to behavioral adaptations that are regarded as delinquent. Their
behavioral outlooks and practices relate to a specific personality pattern, which elicit similar responses on the part of others who may
tend to reinforce such forms of behavior.

In the following sections, we will consider two distinctive forms
of delinquent adaptation—one, the case of Lee Harvey Oswald, representing a lone individual in conflict with delinquency statutes; the
other, involving juvenile gangs, stands for the more common form of
conglomerate, group delinquency.

SOCIALLY NONADAPTIVE DELINQUENCY: THE CASE OF LEE HARVEY OSWALD
Lee Harvey Oswald was the man whom the Warren Commission,
which investigated the death of President John F. Kennedy, believed
beyond any reasonable doubt[32] to have been the assassin of the President. The commission concluded that he was "profoundly alienated
from the world in which he lived"; it continued to state that Oswald's
life "was characterized by isolation, frustration, and failure. He had
few, if any, close relationships with other people and he appeared
to have great difficulty in finding a meaningful place in the world.
He was never satisfied with anything."[33]

Oswald was born in New Orleans on October 18, 1939. His father,
an insurance premium collector, died two months before his birth.
Two older children were sent to an orphans' home at the time of
Lee's birth, and he joined them there from age three until a little
past his fourth birthday. In August, 1952, the Oswalds moved from
Texas to New York City. An older brother was at a Coast Guard
station nearby, and the second brother had enlisted in the Marines.
Lee was enrolled in a junior high school in the Bronx, where the
other children teased him because of his western clothes and Texas
accent. He began to be truant, staying home and reading magazines

32 But see Epstein, *Inquest;* Lane, *Rush to Judgment.*
33 President's Commission on the Assassination, *Report,* p. 376.

and watching television by himself while his mother worked. Because of his school absences, delinquency charges were brought against him alleging that he was "beyond the control of his mother insofar as school attendance is concerned." He was sent to Youth House, a detention facility (where he stayed for about three weeks), to which children are brought for psychiatric observation, for detention pending court appearance, or for commitment to a child-care or custodial institution.

Lee's mother visited the boy at Youth House and recalled that her pocketbook was searched "because the children were such criminals, dope fiends, and had been in criminal offenses, that anybody entering this home had to be searched in case the parents were bringing cigarettes or narcotics or anything." She remembers that Lee cried and said, "Mother, I want to get out of here. There are children in here who have killed people and smoke. I want to get out." Lee told his probation officer, however, that he did not miss his mother, and he told the social worker who interviewed him, as she remembers it, "The worse thing about Youth House was the fact that he had to be with other boys all the time and was disturbed about taking showers with them . . ."[34]

The psychiatric examination did not indicate that Lee Oswald was potentially dangerous.[35] The psychiatrist reported him to be a tense, withdrawn, and evasive boy who intensely disliked talking about himself and his feelings. He was also described as having a "vivid fantasy life turning around the topics of omnipotence and power, through which he tried to compensate for his present shortcomings and frustrations." The psychiatric summary regarding Oswald read:

> This 13 year old well built boy has superior mental resources and functions only slightly below capacity level in spite of chronic truancy from school which brought him into Youth House. No finding of neurological impairment or psychotic mental changes could be made. Lee has to be diagnosed as "personality pattern disturbance with schizoid features and passive-aggressive tendencies." Lee has to be seen as an emotionally quite disturbed youngster who suffers under the impact of really existing emotional isolation and deprivation, lack of affection, absence of family life and rejection by a self involved and conflicted mother.[36]

The psychiatrist recommended that Lee be placed on probation on the condition that he seek help through a child guidance clinic. He suggested that the boy be treated by a male psychiatrist who could substitute for his lack of a father. He also recommended that Mrs.

34 Stafford, *A Mother in History*. See also Ford and Stiles, *Portrait of the Assassin;* Oswald, *Lee;* Abrahamsen, "Study of Lee Harvey Oswald"; Ansbacher, "Lee Harvey Oswald."
35 Hartogs and Freeman, *The Two Assassins.*
36 President's Commission on the Assassination, *Report*, p. 380.

Oswald seek psychotherapeutic guidance from a family agency. The possibility of committing Lee was to be considered only if the probation plan was not successful.

The social worker handling the case noted that there was "a rather pleasant, appealing quality about this emotionally starved, affectionless youngster which grows as one speaks to him." She thought that he had detached himself from the world around him because "no one in it has ever met any of his need for love." She observed that since Lee's mother worked all day, he prepared his own meals and spent his time alone because he didn't make friends readily with the boys in the neighborhood. The social worker concluded that Lee "just felt that his mother never gave a damn for him. He always felt like a burden that she simply just had to tolerate." Lee confirmed some of these observations by saying that he felt almost as if there were a veil between him and other people through which they could not reach him, but that he preferred the veil to remain intact.

After her interview with Lee's mother, the social worker described her as a "smartly dressed, gray haired woman, very self-possessed and alert and superficially affable" but essentially "a defensive, rigid, self-involved person who had real difficulty in relating to people" and who had "little understanding" of her son's behavior and of the "protective shell he has drawn around himself." Lee's half-brother reported that Lee had slept with his mother until he was about ten or eleven years old.

Lee had an intelligence quotient of 118 on the Wechsler Intelligence Scale for Children. The psychologist who administered this and other tests to him indicated that "although Lee was presumably disinterested in school subjects he operated on a much higher than average level." The probation officer assigned to the case reported that Lee was disruptive in class after he returned to school on a regular basis in the fall of 1953. He refused to salute the flag and was doing very little, if any, work. But looking back some ten years to the time when he had supervised Oswald, the probation officer could only tell the Warren Commission that, "There was nothing that would lead me to believe when I saw him at the age of 12 that there would be seeds of destruction for somebody. I couldn't in all honesty sincerely say such a thing."[37]

The Warren Commission summarized the events following Oswald's first and only contact with agencies concerned with juvenile delinquency in the following terms:

> Lee Oswald never received . . . help. Few social agencies even in New York were equipped to provide the kind of intensive treatment that he needed, and when one of the city's clinics did find room to handle him, for some reason the record does not show, advantage was never taken

37 Ibid., p. 382.

of the chance afforded to Oswald. When Lee became a disciplinary problem upon his return to school . . . and when his mother failed to cooperate in any way with school authorities, authorities were finally forced to consider placement in a home for boys. Such placement was postponed, however, perhaps in part at least because Lee's behavior suddenly improved. Before the court took any action, the Oswalds left New York in January of 1954, and returned to New Orleans where Lee finished the ninth grade before he left school to work for a year. Then in October of 1956, he joined the Marines.[38]

Searching diligently for clues to explain the assassination, the Warren Commission directed its attention to the period of Oswald's return to New Orleans and then to his military career, during which he was in some difficulty, but always difficulty of a rather petty nature. He evinced a growing interest in communism and in Marxist literature, and he began to study Russian. In late 1959, at the age of nineteen, he migrated to the Soviet Union. When the Russians told him that he could not remain there, Oswald made an unsuccessful attempt to kill himself by slashing his wrist, first soaking it in cold water to numb the pain. Three years later, married to a Russian girl, he returned to the United States. The marriage was rocky, marked by several separations. Oswald also experienced difficulty in obtaining and keeping jobs. He went to New Orleans briefly from Texas, passing out leaflets there for the Fair Play for Cuba Committee. In April, 1963, according to the Warren Commission, he attempted unsuccessfully to assassinate Major General Edwin A. Walker, a retired Army officer identified prominently with right-wing activities. Seven months later, according to the evidence accumulated by the Commission, Oswald, acting alone, made his successful attempt on the life of President Kennedy.

The analysis of the character and motivation of Lee Harvey Oswald that the Warren Commission puts forward after examining a voluminous amount of material appears somewhat superficial. Its inadequacy may represent more of a reflection on the state of such interpretations—the inability to penetrate very deeply into the recesses of the human mind and into the pathways of human behavior—than a commentary on the Commission's shortcomings. The Commission report notes:

> Many factors were undoubtedly involved in Oswald's motivation for the assassination, and the Commission does not believe that it can ascribe to him any one motive or groups of motives. It is apparent, however, that Oswald was moved by an overriding hostility to his environment. He does not appear to have been able to establish meaningful relationships with other people. He was perpetually discontented with the world around him. Long before the assassination he expressed his hatred for American society and acted in protest against it. Oswald's search for

38 *Ibid.,* pp. 382–383.

what he conceived to be the perfect society was doomed from the start. He sought for himself a place in history—a role as the "great man" who would be recognized as having been in advance of his times. His commitment to Marxism and communism appears to have been another important factor in his motivation. He also had demonstrated a capacity to act decisively and without regard to the consequences when such action would further his aims of the moment. Out of these and the many other factors which may have molded the character of Lee Harvey Oswald there emerged a man capable of assassinating President Kennedy.[39]

Oswald and Juvenile Delinquency

The Oswald case provides a focus for many basic issues concerning the phenomenon of juvenile delinquency. There are initial questions regarding the intervention by the authorities of the government against a truanting youngster: What rights should the individual be afforded, and what powers should the state be granted? Should truancy be an act of delinquency, or should it be handled by agencies who do not possess the stigma associated with delinquency? If the state should be permitted to move against a boy who fails to attend school, what sanctions are reasonable in such an instance? Should Oswald's mother have been imprisoned or made to quit work and tend more carefully to her wayward son? If so, what would have been the likely consequences? Might interstate compacts and transfers of records involving New York and Louisiana have called the authorities' attention in Louisiana to the behavior and character of the boy as recorded in New York?

What of the treatment itself? Are the diagnoses made by the psychiatrist, psychologist, and social worker shown to have been strikingly inadequate and incorrect in the light of Oswald's subsequent behavior? Are these diagnoses useful, or do they represent little more than an accumulation of professional platitudes? It is always tempting, looking back from a shocking adult crime to manifestations of earlier delinquency, to say that more forceful measures should have been undertaken against the juvenile. But how serious was Lee's delinquent behavior? And how serious a disturbance did the clinical evaluations appear to indicate? How many boys who show similar characteristics and behave in similar or apparently more seriously inadequate ways ultimately adjust quite well, even admirably, to society's demands in later life? One could, in fact, legitimately ask whether the period that Lee spent in Youth House and the time during which he submitted to diagnoses was more harmful than it might have been had no official action whatsoever been taken against him; it is sometimes true that individuals, once defined as bad or aberrant, accept that definition of themselves and behave in the defined manner thereafter, when they might not otherwise have done so.

39 *Ibid.,* pp. 423–424.

Some sociologists point out that the case of Lee Harvey Oswald, as unraveled by the Warren Commission, pays scant attention to the emphases and insights that have marked their work in the field of delinquency. Oswald certainly was not a delinquent member of a boys' gang, so that the sociological relationship between him and his environment is somewhat more difficult to pinpoint in terms of current theoretical emphasis in sociology. But little or no attention was paid to the nature of the neighborhoods in which Oswald lived and to the implications of their social atmosphere on him. What was it like at the Bronx junior high school? What were some of the values of the teachers, and how did these compare with those held by the young boy? While the Warren Commission stresses at several points that Oswald's mother was working a good part of the time, no mention is made of whether or not most mothers in this neighborhood were also employed outside the home. If so, this isolated item would hardly lead us to understand this young boy as distinct from other boys growing up under similar circumstances.

There are, then, a large number of unanswered, even untouched, etiological items in the case of Lee Harvey Oswald as it has been restructured. There are also a considerable number of political and philosophical issues inherent in the details of Oswald's brief career as a juvenile delinquent—issues that relate to the just and efficient use of the state's power over the individual. The Oswald case should serve to illustrate the difficulty of preconceived and simple answers to what are quite complex matters of social science and social policy.

GROUP DELINQUENCY: JUVENILE GANGS

The word "gang" has a long history in our language, and some of that history sheds light on contemporary use of the term and on present social attitudes toward designated groups of adolescents in our cities. In early English usage, "gang" was often employed as a synonym for "a going, a walking, or a journey"; in this sense it traces its origin to the Scandinavian languages. There was also an Anglo-Saxon derivation, which appears in print as early as 1340 and which is equivalent to "a number of things used together or forming a complete set." The linguistic ideas of "a journey" and "a set of things" were shortly combined so that "gang" came to stand for a crew of a ship or companies of mariners.

This verbal representation of a group of maritime persons who were functionally interrelated expanded into the broader designation of gangs as individuals joined together as recognizable entities. The word "gang" also acquired a derogatory connotation, possibly because of a third early meaning attached to it, one which has long since become archaic but which made "gang" synonymous with "privy." Chaucer, for instance, writing about 1390 with characteristic scatalogical zest, likens "fool wommen" to a "common gonge." When Sam uel Johnson put together his dictionary in the late 1700s, he indicated that the word "gang" was "seldom used but in contempt or abhorrence," a view borne out in Shakespeare's *Merry Wives of Windsor,* where a character cries out against "panderly rascals" and notes that "there's a knot, a gang, a pack, a conspiracy against me."[40]

The etymology of the word "gang" provides a starting point from which to examine contemporary social views about juvenile gangs. These social views are constructed from an amalgam of fact, myth, and stereotype, and like all such views, they tend to elicit and perpetuate the process that they seek to describe. It is one of the noteworthy insights of social-science theory that the isolation and labelling of forms of behavior tend to solidify and sometimes increase such behavior. Labelling provides a definitional framework in its recognition of a phenomenon, adding a further dimension to its previous characteristics. It is one thing to drink intoxicating beverages, but it is often quite another thing to violate the law by such behavior. It is one thing to hang around with a group of boys, but it is another thing to be a gang member, and the particular self and social definition imparted to the behavior may sometimes greatly affect the behavior itself.

Cross-Cultural Perspectives

Albert K. Cohen, a sociologist at the University of Connecticut, points out that "the sad truth is that the comparative study of juvenile delinquency does not exist."[41] Cohen quotes two Italian researchers who indicate that gangs, as we know them, are rare in their country, and, where they do exist, they seldom attack other adolescents but direct their activities against adults. "If this is so," Cohen suggests, "the tendency for delinquents to coalesce into gangs and for gangs to war on other gangs, so common in our country, is not necessarily implicit in the idea of delinquency."[42]

An examination of the experience with gangs in the Soviet Union provides additional perspective on the situation in the United States. Following the Soviet Revolution of 1917, large groups of youths, finding themselves adrift in a society that was groping for political order and also finding themselves without adult supervision because of the death or dislocation of parents and relatives, formed marauding bands and lived in cellars and makeshift shelters in and near the large, urban centers.[43] Attempts to incorporate these youths into the majority society after the regime became more stabilized were unsuccessful at first; the explanation offered is "that children who had lived for more than a year on the streets found it difficult to adapt themselves to the

40 From Geis, *Juvenile Gangs.*
41 Cohen, "Sociological Research in Juvenile Delinquency," p. 783. See also Cavan and Cavan, *Delinquency and Crime;* Gottlieb, *Emergence of Youth Societies.*
42 Cohen, "Sociological Research in Juvenile Delinquency," p. 783.
43 UNESCO, *Vagrant Children.*

new life" because they had been "influenced by the picaresque life of the vagabond."[44] This suggests the importance of appreciating the attractions of gang existence—the camaraderie, the self-indulgence, the luxury, and the excitement—and is relevant to gangs in the United States.

The major stress in Soviet efforts to reform the *bezprizornye* (literally, "the neglected"), who numbered more than 524,000 by 1921, was placed on training them for factory employment. Special use was made of the honor code, a code somewhat similar to that found among members of American juvenile gangs:

> In the beginning we made many mistakes, but now we know that, above all, we must teach these children by appealing to their sense of honor. Strange to say, a sense of honor is much more strongly developed amongst the *bezprizornye* than it is in normal children. Locks are of no use at all, for they can easily pick them, so we give them keys. They are really astonished that they are treated like ordinary children.[45]

The Soviets inaugurated a rule that no questions be asked of a boy concerning his past life or record, unless he initiated the subject. They also attempted to put group pressures on individual boys who would not abide by the rules and to instill a sense of shame through ritualized examples of disapproval:

> The children have meetings every evening, and those who have not worked well, or who have done something wrong, are called to account. The unfortunate delinquent has to stand in the middle of a circle and submit to a fire of questions. The worst punishment is temporary forfeiture of the badge of the community.[46]

Tactics designed to control the *bezprizornye*, given time (and the aging process of the juveniles, which is often the most efficacious "reformative" force[47]), blended its members into the society.

Today, however, the Soviet Union continues to have widespread difficulty with deviating youngsters. Understanding of the dynamics of this situation sheds much light on American conditions. It should be appreciated that the Soviet Union can, as efficiently as any large country is able to today, propagandize its younger generation regarding virtues it expects them to manifest; unsatisfactory examples can fairly readily be repressed and contradictory ideas submerged. Nonetheless, a newspaper reporter, who had previously studied juvenile gangs in New York City,[48] notes that many Russian adolescents insist on calling Moscow's Gorky Street *Brudvay*, and he further indicates

44 Halle, *Woman in Soviet Russia*, p. 59.
45 Mehnert, *Youth In Soviet Russia*, p. 116.
46 *Ibid.*, p. 119.
47 Glueck and Glueck, *Juvenile Delinquents Grown Up*; Miller, "The Corner Boys Get Married."
48 Salisbury, *Shook-Up Generation*.

that they engage in the same kind of "nihilistic revolt as that of their coevals in the west":

> Party agitators exhort them. Komsomol bully squads rout them out of the restaurants and cafes and send them home. Photographs of them are plastered on billboards under headings: "Parasites, Get Out." They are shipped to virgin lands or the reconstruction sites in Siberia.

> But nothing that the party has been able to devise wins back the loyalty or the enthusiasm of the bored, nihilistic and disoriented generation.

> "This is our greatest defeat," a middle-aged party man conceded. "The young people have deserted the cause. I do not know how we are going to get them back."

> The number of internal rebels are great. They can be seen everywhere. They dance to Western music. They wear Western-style clothes. They act as much like Westerners as they are able.

> In a play by Ivan Kupriyanov, a rude young man, a complete delinquent, is asked what he wants in life:
> "My golden desire? Well, nobody wants a heart attack. What do I want? Drink . . . restaurants . . . jazz . . . money . . . women . . . a Volga (a Soviet car) . . . a country cottage . . . you know, the complete gentleman's selection."

> In provincial towns and Moscow's sprawling industrial suburb the picture of the "young generation" is hardly attractive. The boys organize in tough gangs that often terrorize people on the streets. The newspapers constantly report that bands of hooligans in various cities have taken control of the streets and ordinary citizens hardly dare venture out at night. The gangs amuse themselves by attacking police posts and beating up militia police officers.

> This kind of behavior baffles the older generation. As a party chief accurately declares in one Moscow theater play:
> "I cannot understand our young people. They have some kind of kink. They are growing up without ideals. They have lost their ideals."

> But the reply is:
> "What kind of ideals were they—that they were so easy to lose?"[49]

A recent study emphasizes that many young persons in the Soviet Union, called derogatorily the *bezdelnichestvo* ("idlers"), reject the production ethic, refuse to work in remote, countryside areas, or refuse to labor at monotonous jobs for minimal reward. The Soviet regime has attempted to link the social misbehavior of the idlers and that of delinquents (*stalyagi*) with political disloyalty by charging it to the impact of Western culture and considering it a form of espionage. Attempts to deal with the disaffiliation of youths are concen-

49 Salisbury, "Lost Generation Baffles Soviet."

trating on the reduction of the salary gap between manual workers and persons holding white-collar jobs or performing more glamorous tasks. There is also a long-range plan to establish boarding schools for virtually the entire school-age population of the Soviet Union in order to reinvigorate the indoctrination of the youth.[50]

The relative intransigency of the problem to date in the Soviet Union, however, sheds considerable light on parallel concerns in the United States. In fact, one of the most intriguing theses concerning gang behavior suggests that, by the very rigor of its demands on youth for rigid conformity, the Soviet Union may be creating a hard-core group of intractable rebels, since it requires a particularly strong will to resist the pressing demands of the government. On the contrary, some hypothesize that the more laissez-faire and permissive attitudes in the United States may, in terms of its very flexibility, be pushing young people toward commitments to one or another of the diverse groups in the society so that they can feel more secure. These commitments may then in turn become strong levers for the further inculcation of conforming behavior. Whether or not this tentative speculation is valid, the general conclusion regarding the present situation in the Soviet Union applies to some degree to juvenile gangs in the United States:

> In spite of all the resources at its command, in spite of its monopolistic advantages, in spite of the unprecedentedly vigorous efforts to indoctrinate entire generations, the youth program does not work well when it is undermined by the actual conditions of the larger society. The program's central imagery—the valor and glory of service to the state through self-sacrificing labor—thorough and persistent though it may be, cannot compete with the more compelling influence of hard reality.[51]

GANG STUDIES IN THE UNITED STATES

All intellectual paths involving studies of gang structure and activity in the United States lead back to the pioneering investigation conducted almost a half century ago by Frederic M. Thrasher in Chicago. Thrasher stressed particularly the ecological aspects of gang emergence, pointing out that gangs tended to thrive in interstitial areas, such as zones of the city lying between commercial and residential neighborhoods. He was also particularly penetrating in his emphasis on feudal, political arrangements as they contributed to the genesis of gangs.[52]

It was not until the beginning of World War II that another gang study—Whyte's *Street-Corner Society*—came up to the standard set

50 Kassof, *Soviet Youth Program*. See also, Hollander, "A Converging Social Problem."
51 Kassof, *Soviet Youth Program*, p. 116.
52 Thrasher, *The Gang*.

by Thrasher. While a graduate student at Harvard University, Whyte took up residence in a Boston working-class neighborhood in order to conduct his study. The result is particularly noteworthy for its penetrating analysis of the relationship between an individual's status in a group and his performance in various group activities. Whyte found, for instance, that low-status group members scored much better in bowling matches when they competed with persons below them in the gang hierarchy than when they bowled against group leaders. The study also describes the interrelationship between organized crime and gang activities, and in the 1955 edition of the book, Whyte adds notes on his views of research work with gangs. He stresses, first of all, his belief that the researcher's own "personality needs must be met in some degree if he is going to function successfully." He must feel that what he is doing has real meaning for him, and must dig into his own background and motives to determine as well as possible why he is performing a particular job. Whyte emphasizes that the researcher's personal life is inextricably mixed with his performance, and artificial attempts to segregate the two areas may prove self-defeating. Whyte notes that his strenuous efforts to learn Italian, the language of the neighborhood, helped immeasurably in gaining acceptance. "My effort to learn the language probably did more to establish the sincerity of my interest in the people," he notes, "than anything I could have told them of myself and my work."[53]

The Hypothesis of the Delinquent Subculture

Further theoretical speculation regarding gangs remained moribund until the appearance in 1955 of Albert K. Cohen's germinal book entitled *Delinquent Boys*. Identifying various attributes of delinquent gang behavior, such as its concentration in depressed areas, its masculine character, and its frequent nonutilitarian function, Cohen encompasses these into the idea of a distinctive delinquent "subculture." Behavior of delinquent boys, Cohen suggests, is created by their identification with the delinquent subculture because of its ability to confer status on them within a context in which middle-class values are largely incapable of fulfillment and are hence rendered meaningless. Cohen's theory revolves around the supposition that, since middle-class values are unobtainable, delinquent boys initiate a reversal process, whereby the delinquent subculture, by means of this process, becomes an inversion, so to speak, of middle-class values. The gang boy, according to Cohen, is in the "market for a solution" to his cultural dilemma, and his behavior is typified by its negative, malicious, and destructive character. Aggression is highly prized, and to achieve a reputation—a "rep" in the parlance of the gang boy—for such behavior is a mark of high distinction.

53 Whyte, *Street-Corner Society*.

Cohen's basic theme is that, "The same value system, impinging upon children differently equipped to meet it, is instrumental in generating both delinquency and respectability"; and according to him, gang delinquency "constitutes a solution to problems of adjustment to which the established culture provides no satisfying solutions." Delinquency is a gang member's response to problems with *status* and *self-respect*. The gang provides "moral reassurance" against "gnawing doubts" and gives "repeated, emphatic and articulate support to the delinquent."[54]

Cohen's comment on the relationship of his theoretical observations to social policy are well-reasoned. Although there are no immediate guidelines for the resolution of problems that are believed to be caused by delinquent gangs, his ideas are worth including:

> Of these various circumstances and features of our social system which are involved in the production of the delinquent subculture, which are subject to deliberate control? How, for example, can we enable the working-class male to compete more effectively for status in a largely middle-class world or, if we want to cut into the web of causation at another point, how can we change the norms of the middle-class world so that his working-class characteristics do not relegate him to an inferior status? *If* these things are possible, we must then ask: What price are we willing to pay for this or that change? Since any social system is a complex network of interdependencies, any change designed to effect a reduction of delinquency may have all sorts of ramifying consequences. What consequences may we anticipate and are we willing to accept them? Many teachers, for example, are intuitively aware of the dilemma: to reward the "meritorious" and implicitly humiliate the handicapped, or to abandon this system of competition and invidious discrimination and abandon therewith a most powerful spur to the development of the kind of character most of us so highly prize. Or need we not contend with such agonizing dilemmas? Is this dilemma, perhaps, a spurious one, or can we enter the web at some other point, where we may obtain as effective results at a lesser cost to traditional values and interests? In any case, the formulation of policy is a matter of choosing among alternatives and our choices must involve not only technical considerations but the balancing of social values.

Cohen's work follows in the earlier tradition of Robert Lynd and W. Lloyd Warner, both of whom attempted through studies of American communities to pinpoint the value system of our society. In his study of Middletown, U.S.A. (actually Muncie, Indiana), Lynd notes, among many other things, the extraordinary emphasis on success and the derogatory labels placed on those who had not been able to achieve such success.[55] Warner, conducting his research in Yankee City (actually Newburyport, Massachusetts), demonstrated the intricate class structure of the community, pinpointing factors that lead to

54 Cohen, *Delinquent Boys.*
55 Lynd, *Middletown, U.S.A.*

membership in one or another social group.[56] Results of such studies have been gathered together by Robin Williams, Jr., who attempts to demonstrate that American values are in many instances quite distinct from those found in other societies. A "value" can be determined in a rough shorthand way by discovering which choice an individual makes when confronted with alternatives.[57] For example, would he pass up an opportunity to swim on a hot summer day rather than patronize a racially-integrated pool? Or, after discovering a $10 bill, how would he spend it?

Delinquent Adaptation Through Differential Opportunity

The idea of a delinquent subculture—a distinctive mode of life among gang boys—put forward in Cohen's work, has formed the basis for most succeeding theoretical statements about gangs. The major differences between Cohen's report and the work of those who have followed lie in the latter stress on different types of delinquent adjustments and the occasional quarrel with Cohen over whether in fact gang boys are primarily reacting to middle-class values.

Richard A. Cloward and Lloyd E. Ohlin in *Delinquency and Opportunity* (1960) attempt to answer why delinquent "norms" or rules of conduct develop and what the conditions of various systems of delinquent norms are. Adaptations by gangs are divided into three major types by Cloward and Ohlin. First, there is the "criminal subculture," which is a type of gang devoted to theft, extortion, and similar illegal means of securing income. This subculture places stress upon a "big score," or making one's "pile" through illegitimate means, knowing the "right guy," and having "connections." Second, there is the "conflict subculture," which is a type of gang in which the manipulation of violence predominates as a means of winning status. The conflict pattern stresses assaultive and predatory gang behavior, aimed in part at gaining respect and instilling fear among peers and adults in the vicinity, in which "heart," or the ability to stand up to physical threats without flinching, is emphasized. Third, there is the "retreatist subculture," which is a type of gang that stresses the consumption of drugs. This subculture advocates sensual pleasures and the maintenance of isolation from conventional persons and values. Incorporated within this way of life are "kicks," in which pleasure is sought through drugs, alcohol, and unusual sex experiences; the "hustle," as a means of getting by without regular employment; the art of being "cool," in which the "cat," through his clothes, manners, and vocabulary, seeks to create an impression of self-assurance and unruffled demeanor.[58]

Of importance in the theory of Cloward and Ohlin is their description of the conditions that evoke one adaptation or the other. The

56 Warner, *Social Life in a Modern Community*.
57 Williams, Jr., *American Society*.
58 Cloward and Ohlin, *Delinquency and Opportunity*.

criminalistic pattern is produced when the organization of the neighborhood affords ready access to both criminal and conventional values for individuals, and individuals are recruited and trained in the one or other pattern that best fits their background, talents, desires, and particular experiences. The conflict pattern most readily emerges when conventional and criminal controls are both absent in the neighborhood. Retreatist adapations are said to occur under neighborhood and family conditions where middle-class aspirations are stressed, though not accessible, and where the individual has developed sufficient inner sanctions against the use of illegitimate means or is restrained in their use by the external conditions of his environment. As today's urban society changes, Cloward and Ohlin see the future producing a greater number of conflict gangs and fewer criminalistic adaptations.[59]

The major critical response to Cloward and Ohlin concentrates on the lack of empirical detail offered to support their theoretical speculations. James Short, Jr., observes that "recent enthusiasm for abstract conceptualization, particularly of varieties of delinquent subcultures, has outstripped the data at hand, and we are badly in need of new empirical studies,"[60] and David J. Bordua notes facetiously that "Cloward and Ohlin's delinquents seem suddenly to appear on the scene, sometime in adolescence, to look at the world, and to discover, 'Man, there's no opportunity in my structure.' "[61]

The seminal nature of the work of Cloward and Ohlin, however, is evident both in the empirical work and the action programs that it has inspired. The Mobilization for Youth project in New York, for instance, was built on *Delinquency and Opportunity*. It de-emphasized traditional forms of intervention that locate pathology in the individual and stressed services speaking to the failure of the social order.[62] Research studies note high aspiration levels, both in occupational and educational goals, among delinquent youths.[63] Irving Spergel, using the Cloward and Ohlin model for a field study of New York gangs, suggests that theft, fighting, and racket activity are dominant gang motifs. He also believes that the racket subculture arises primarily in Italian neighborhoods, where strong adult controls are evident and where there is an established pattern of involvement by "successful" adults in gambling and similar enterprises. He found the conflict gang subculture to flourish in Puerto Rican neighborhoods, where there was little opportunity to succeed either in a criminal or in a noncriminal fashion,[64] and he found the theft subculture in the more

59 *Ibid.*, pp. 193–211.
60 Short in Thrasher, *The Gang*, p. xxi.
61 Bordua, "Delinquent Subcultures." See also Landis, Dinitz, and Reckless, "Implementing Two Theories of Delinquency"; Empey, "Delinquency Theory and Recent Research."
62 Bibb, "Gang-Related Services of Mobilization for Youth."
63 Rivera and Short, "Occupational Goals."
64 For a treatment of such gangs in theatrical form, see Laurents, *West Side Story*.

heterogeneous sections of the city, marked by diverse patterns of law-abiding and criminal behavior.[65]

Delinquency as Adaptation to Lower-Class Culture

The most comprehensive field investigation of gang behavior during recent times is that undertaken by Walter B. Miller in the Special Youth Project in Roxbury, Massachusetts. Conclusions reached by Miller may be derived from a quotation from his as yet unpublished manuscript, *City Gangs,* which reports on the Project:

> Criminal behavior as engaged in by Midcity gang members was in no sense an extraordinary phenomenon. It was not a sport, an idiosyncracy, a temporary quirk of momentarily distraught persons. It was not the product of any conspicuously unusual or obviously transient set of social conditions. Crime was engaged in repeatedly, systematically, regularly, by rationally understandable people as a routine and expected part of their ordinary conduct of life.

Miller presents a rather different viewpoint of the nature of gang behavior from the theorists we have considered thus far. His thesis is summarized in the following paragraph:

> In the case of "gang" delinquency, the cultural system which exerts the most direct influences on behavior is that of the lower-class community itself—a long-established, distinctively patterned tradition with an integrity of its own—rather than a so-called "delinquent subculture," which has arisen through conflict with middle class culture and is oriented to the deliberate violation of middle class norms.[66]

The distinctive lower-class culture that Miller describes is marked by female-based households and a pattern of "serial monogamy," in which many marriages follow, one after the other. In the adolescent adaptation to lower-class cultural traits, boys expect to get into trouble; they assert their toughness, display "smartness," emphasize the ability to outwit or con others, and seek excitement. They accept the dictates of what they see as "fate," and they are constantly concerned with the maintenance of their own autonomy. Gangs, according to Miller, are built around individuals who fall into four distinct subcultures of the society—they are males, adolescents, urban residents, and low-skilled manual workers. When each of these four items appears in "subcultural conjunction" within our society, with its distinct social structure and legal system, they produce, Miller believes, "a propensity to engage in violative behavior."[67]

Miller notes that theft is the overwhelming form of criminal activity among gangs. To account for its prevalence in terms that are meaningful to the boys committing the offenses, Miller outlines four

65 Spergel, *Racketville, Slumtown, Haulburg.*
66 Miller, *City Gangs.* See also Miller, *Violent Crimes in City Gangs.*
67 Miller, "Lower Class Culture as a Generating Milieu of Gang Delinquency."

major incentive categories and delineates broader motives for larceny under some twenty-one headings, which are reproduced in Figure V. Miller proposes a solution that springs directly from his motivational scheme: "Provide law-abiding substitutes for these goals, and the incentive for theft will be vitiated." He suggests that this solution is more practical than sweeping plans to revise the country's entire economic structure in order to eliminate gangs.

Table 14.1   Twenty-One Incentives for Theft

Major incentive category	Incentive
I Acquisitional	1. Immediate Necessity
	2. Extended Necessity
	3. Immediate Facilitative Utility
	4. Extended Facilitative Utility
	5. General Utility
	6. Representational Utility
II Demonstrational	1. Smartness, Craft, Ingenuity
	2. Courage, Daring, Risk Facing Capacity
	3. Positional Commitment
	4. Affiliance, Allegiance
	5. Mild Anger, Annoyance, Pique
	6. Severe Anger, Malice, Spite
	7. Individual Task-execution Competence
	8. Collective Task-execution Competence
	9. Mating Interest
	10. Combat Interest
III Experimental	1. Excitement, Thrill
	2. Amusement, Diversion
IV Justificational	1. Value-inequality Rectification
	2. Injustice Redress
	3. Status-right

SOURCE: Walter B. Miller, *City Gangs*, manuscript.

Conclusion

A nationwide survey suggests that gang fighting is on the decline throughout the United States. From a seven-month study of nine cities, Bernstein concludes that gangs are less obvious than they were formerly, that their names are no longer splashed on walls, and that they less frequently flaunt dark-colored jackets that advertise who they are. In place of rumbles, Saul Bernstein reports greater indulgence in things such as "snagging" or "japping," in which a lookout is stationed to observe the daily movements of individuals from rival gangs, and in which the rival gang is methodically waylaid and beaten up. Bernstein, like many other writers, calls attention to what he regards as a growing emphasis on "coolness" among gang members.[68] One boy, a former member of a fighting gang, attempted to portray the change as follows: "The difference now is that everybody is down on JD's. It is almost square to go down [to fight]. It don't have the kicks it used to. Some of the shrimps take to it, but it ain't what it used to be. It's cliche, man."[69] A member of the one-time Assassins, now named the Socializers, explained the shift this way: "We're cool because everyone wants to go out without worrying about it. The kids want to be, like, grown up. When I was jailed for carrying a zip gun, that was time wasted, man. You can't bring back that lost time. You can waste yourself, man."[70]

Preventive work, particularly that involving the use of street or detached workers with gangs, is given partial credit for the amelioration of gang activity.[71] More importantly, the civil rights movement is said to have caught the imaginations and taken the energies of youngsters who formerly might have joined delinquent gangs. These developments and others of similar nature serve to underscore the observations put forward by Cloward and Ohlin on the basis of their theoretical formulation:

> We hope that we have at least made it clear that services extending to delinquent individuals or groups cannot prevent the rise of delinquency among others. For delinquency is not, in the final analysis, a property of individuals or even of subcultures; it is a property of the social systems in which these individuals and groups are enmeshed. The pressures that produce delinquency originate in these structures, as do the forces that shape the content of specialized subcultural adaptations. The target for preventive action, then, should be defined, not as the individual or group that exhibits the delinquent pattern, but as the social setting which gives rise to delinquency.[72]

For Further Reading

CAVAN, RUTH S. *Juvenile Delinquency.* 2nd ed. Philadelphia: Lippincott, 1969.

A textbook presenting material on the significant phases of delinquency causation and control. The reader should also consult other texts in the field: Barron, Milton L. *The Juvenile in Delinquent Society.* New York: Alfred A. Knopf, 1952; Neumeyer, Martin H. *Juvenile Delinquency in Modern Society.* 3rd ed. Princeton, N.J.: Van Nostrand, 1961; Robison, Sophia M. *Juvenile Delinquency: Its Nature and Control.* New York:

68 Bernstein, *Alternatives to Violence.*
69 *New York Times,* Aug. 7, 1967.
70 *New York Times,* May 5, 1966. See also Gannon, "Harlem's Immortal Five Per Cent."
71 See, for instance, Yablonsky, *The Violent Gang;* Riccio and Slocum, *All the Way Down;* Kolman and Black, *Royal Vultures.*
72 Cloward and Ohlin, *Delinquency and Opportunity,* p. 211.

Holt, Rinehart & Winston, 1960; Shulman, Henry M. *Juvenile Delinquency in American Society*. New York: Harper & Row, 1961.

GIALLOMBARDO, ROSE (ed.). *Juvenile Delinquency: A Book of Readings*. New York: John Wiley, 1966.

The writings of Cohen, Miller, Cloward and Ohlin, and other theorists of delinquency appear in this collection. See also: Cavan, Ruth S. (ed.). *Readings in Juvenile Delinquency*. Philadelphia: Lippincott, 1964; Glueck, Sheldon (ed.). *The Problem of Delinquency*. Boston: Houghton Mifflin, 1959; Quay, Herbert C. (ed.). *Juvenile Deliquency: Research and Theory*. Princeton, N.J.: Van Nostrand, 1965; Roucek, Joseph S. (ed.). *Juvenile Delinquency*. New York: Philosophical Library, 1958; and Vedder, Clyde B. (ed.). *The Juvenile Offender: Perspective and Readings*. New York: Doubleday, 1954.

MacIVER, ROBERT M. *The Prevention and Control of Delinquency*. New York: Atherton Press, 1966.

Following his retirement from teaching, the author, one of the more eminent political scientists of our times, turned his attention to a review of delinquency programs. He notes that, "This book is intended to state a problem and its setting so as to derive from this analysis directions for effective action in the various areas and various stages and types of delinquent behavior." Reviews of experiments being conducted on control of delinquency are also included.

POWERS, EDWIN, and HELEN WITMER. *An Experiment in the Prevention of Delinquency*. New York: Columbia University Press, 1951.

This study reports on an elaborate program of counseling designed for youths in the Cambridge-Somerville area of Massachusetts, revealing a great deal about the extraordinary difficulty of field research and providing many hypotheses about the dynamics of delinquency. For a later review of the outcome of the youths in the program, see McCord, William and Joan. *Origins of Crime: A New Evaluation of the Cambridge-Somerville Youth Study*. New York: Columbia University Press, 1959. For another examination of the general field, see Hirschi, Travis, and Hanan C. Selvin. *Delinquency Research: An Appraisal of Analytic Methods*. New York: Free Press, 1967.

PRESIDENT'S COMMISSION ON LAW ENFORCEMENT AND ADMINISTRATION OF JUSTICE. *Task Force Report: Juvenile Delinquency*. Washington, D.C.: Government Printing Office, 1967.

"America's best hope for reducing crime is to reduce juvenile delinquency and youth crime," the Task Force report notes. The report presents the latest statistical material on delinquency, recommends strongly that many behaviors now handled by the juvenile courts be channeled elsewhere, and suggests tightening the legal procedures by which the juvenile court now operates.

Part V
Police, Adminstration of Justice, and Correction

15

The Police

The role of the police in American society and the behavior of law enforcement officers may be examined in much the same manner that criminal behavior is analyzed. People presumably become policemen, as they become criminals, engineers, or maintenance men, in consequence of the satisfactions they perceive from the role as measured against other alternatives that are open to them. Their abilities, training, experience, and backgrounds, among numerous other things, help determine their career choices. Chance also plays into occupational choice, as, for example, when one finds the position he seeks available. Once on the job, some practitioners also behave differently from others. To discern traits that identify the role performance and its practitioners in a general manner is the task of analysis. There is also a need to identify elements of the social structure that play upon occupational behavior and to differentiate one form of job performance from another.

In recent times, the American police have come to epitomize in a dramatic fashion the authority of the state as it is exerted against persons who are intent on changing some of its rules. During the convention of the Democratic party in Chicago in the summer of 1968, the local police forces were charged with controlling persons who started a number of demonstrations in protest of the operation of the nomination process and the choice of a presidential candidate. Various "confrontations" between the police and groups of demonstrators left some 300 persons injured, including many spectators, and resulted in more than 250 arrests. Television cameras conveyed to a national audience vivid instances of police brutality directed against the demonstrators as they moved toward convention headquarters. Night sticks were wielded, and demonstrators were hit and kicked gratuitously as they were hustled into paddy wagons. More than a score of incidents in which the police allegedly employed undue force against mass media reporters and photographers provoked particularly angry responses from television announcers covering the convention.

Following events in Chicago, it became evident that a large percentage of the nation's population endorsed the action of the police during the Democratic convention. A Gallup poll in September showed that 56 percent of a nationwide sample supported the police action, with 31 percent disapproving. Older persons more often than younger ones and whites more often than blacks were apt to express approval of the police behavior. Such endorsement was in part a response to information indicating that insults and threats, often couched in obscene and inflammatory terms, had been hurled against the police by demonstrators. Improvised weapons, including rocks and potatoes containing razor blades, had also been used by some of the protesters in a phase of the "battle" that went unfilmed. But in larger measure, the public response to the Chicago events pinpointed a structural aspect of the police role—that the public expects from the police categoric control of persons who are seen as disruptive of social tranquility and as challenges to the status quo. The police, caught between these demands and those of the law that restrict the methods by which they may exert control and suasion, tend to identify with the larger public and its pressures.[1] They do so in part because of their background and in part because of their experience,[2] which informs them that those persons defiant of their authority represent serious threats to the well-being of the society and must be dealt with forcefully. That this experience may be distorted and one-sided is as possible as it is for the elementary school teacher to address her adult friends with short words, spoken with painful slowness, and enunciated with meticulous clarity.

The particular form of police experience and its conditioning effects have been reviewed sympathetically by Patrick Devlin, a former justice of the British high court. "The police come into much closer contact with criminals than the lawyer does, and no doubt they find some of them quite despicable and are revolted by the prospect that they may be left at large to hurt others," Devlin writes, maintaining further that the tendency of an officer under such conditions "to press interrogation too hard . . . is a very understandable fault."[3] He adds:

> It is easy for lawyers to say that it is better for ninety-nine guilty men to be acquitted than for one innocent to be convicted; but to those in daily contact with the ninety-nine who see at close quarters the harm that they do the maxim has less appeal. It is not corruption or the desire to pervert justice, nor is it always the natural ardor of the chase (though this no doubt plays its part) that makes the police less fair and dis-

1 Kooken, *Ethics in Police Service*, p. 31

2 Toch, "Readiness to Perceive Violence as a Result of Police Training."

3 Devlin, *Criminal Prosecution in England*, p. 54.

passionate than they should be. It is often just honest indignation. . . . It is easy to talk of the advantages to be derived from requiring the police to be quasijudicial. It means that the police have to conform to a very high standard. In order to discharge the burden that is put upon them, they must be both prosecutor and judge, both player and umpire.[4]

Other pressures that push law enforcement officers beyond the limits of their legal authority can also be identified. Skolnick notes that policemen have a stake in maintaining their position of authority and that there are pressures on individual policemen to produce results—to be efficient rather than legal when the two norms are in conflict. In addition, Skolnick notes, there is ample opportunity for the policeman to behave in a manner inconsistent with the rule of law because of the low visibility of much of his conduct. The result is a conflict between the conception of the policeman as a *craftsman* rather than as a *legal actor,* a skilled worker rather than as a civil servant obliged to subscribe to the rule of law.[5]

An investigative committee of the National Commission on the Causes and Prevention of Violence, the Walker committee, probed into the episodes during the Democratic national convention in Chicago. It concluded that the episodes could best be described as "police riots," which accentuates the discrepancy that can exist between public views and the position of official agencies, such as commissions and courts, regarding the proper performance of the police role. The Walker Report calls the behavior of the Chicago police gratuitous, ferocious, malicious, and mindless. The nature of the police response to provocation was said to be "unrestrained and indiscriminate" and "made all the more shocking by the fact that it was often inflicted upon persons who had broken no law, disobeyed no order, made no threat." The report notes that the police who committed violence were a minority, but it warns that "the effect can only be to discourage the majority of policemen who acted responsibly, and further weaken the bond between police and community." Perhaps most revealing is the disclosure that a large number of the police officers who engaged in illegal violence in Chicago against demonstrators and bystanders first took care to remove their badges with their identifying numbers on them, indicating their awareness that their behavior conflicted with regulations. That they felt free, when anonymous, to act as they did appears to be testimony to the belief that support for their actions existed in the outside society.[6]

Police and Minority Groups

The Chicago episodes served to accentuate the increasingly contro-

4 *Ibid.,* p. 55.
5 Skolnick, *Justice Without Trial,* p. 231.
6 Walker, *Rights in Conflict.*

versial role of the police in today's society. The theme of "law and
order," dominating presidential election politics in 1968, focused
further attention on the performance of the police. Many Americans
view the police as their best hope for avoiding injury and loss of
property attendant upon what they regard as a rampant crime wave,
civil disorder, student rebellion, and minority group unrest. Other
persons define the police as the major oppressors of the civil rights
movement, as uncouth violators of civil liberties, and as the embodiment
of the insensitivity of governmental authorities to the demands for
necessary social change.

The riots sweeping through many American metropolitan areas
have consistently been triggered by incidents of antagonism between
persons in minority group neighborhoods and members of the "Establishment." Most often, as with the riots in Harlem, Watts, Newark,
and Detroit, the outburst is ignited by a routine arrest of blacks for
minor offenses by white policemen. Probably the most vivid portrayal
of antagonism between the police and the Negro community appears
in the *Algiers Motel Incident,* a depiction of events during the Detroit riots, which was written by John Hersey, a Pulitzer-Prize winning
novelist. The National Advisory Commission on Civil Disorders, reporting in 1968, summarizes police involvement in minority group
distress as follows:

> Physical abuse is only one source of aggravation in the ghetto. In nearly
> every city surveyed, the Commission heard complaints of harassment of
> interracial couples, dispersal of street gatherings, and the stopping of
> Negroes on foot or in cars without obvious basis. These, together with
> contemptuous and degrading verbal abuse, have great impact in the
> ghetto. As one Commission witness said, these strip the Negro of the one
> thing he may have left—his dignity, "The question of being a man."[7]

The National Advisory Committee recommended, among other things,
that police departments assign officers with "superior ability, sensitivity, and common sense" to duty in minority group neighborhoods
and that they reward such officers with bonuses or promotion credits.

Two noted Negro writers provide insights into the background
and experience of law enforcement officers as they seem to bear upon
racial unrest and police performance. James Baldwin indicates that
the class origin and the social status of policemen make them cater
to persons better established in the social scheme than themselves:

> Policemen were neither friends nor enemies; they were part of the
> landscape, present for the purpose of upholding law and order; and if
> a policeman . . . seemed to forget his place, it was easy enough to make
> him remember it. Easy enough if one's own place was more secure than
> his, and if one represented, or could bring to bear, a power greater than

7 National Advisory Committee on Civil Disorders, *Report,* p. 303. See also Kephart,
  Racial Factors and Urban Law Enforcement; Edwards, *Police on the Urban
  Frontier.*

his own. For all policemen were bright enough to know who they were working for, and they were not working, anywhere in the world, for the powerless.[8]

Essentially the same view, emphasizing among other things the social class background of the police, is registered by Richard Wright:

> I've long been interested in the psychology of policemen. Of all the functionaries in a country they share the outlook, the fears, the aims, and the attitudes of the group holding power. Enforcers of the law generally partake of the impulses both of the lawmakers and the law breakers and they are mostly men devoid of illusions.[9]

Many policemen come from the upper-lower and lower-middle classes, and they represent socially mobile individuals, although their mobility is slight rather than dramatic. Perhaps class congruence partially explains the fact that a survey of approximately 3,000 persons found that there is "a definite trend among the respondents with the least schooling to look most favorably upon the police, and for the college graduates to look upon them with the least approval."[10] On the other hand, when respondents are divided by race, there is a clear tendency for nonwhites to be more critical of police than whites. A study in Hartford, Connecticut, for instance, found that slightly over two-thirds of the whites were satisfied with the manner in which the police were performing their jobs, compared to about half the Negro sample.[11]

Because of their class backgrounds, policemen sometimes find it difficult to regard some offenders, such as neighborhood gamblers and small-time prostitutes, as seriously as the law would seem to demand. The camaraderie that seems to exist between policemen and professional criminals has often been noted: Each regards the other group as merely doing its job, and each tends to give the other as little unnecessary trouble as possible.[12] The police, however, respond with great indignation to persons such as sex offenders, particularly when children are involved, and to homosexuals.[13] On the other hand, like many citizens, policemen seem to show a grudging admiration for the successful upper-class, white-collar offender.

The position in the social structure from which the police are drawn probably also accounts in some measure for attitudes toward members of minority groups, particularly Negroes. Skolnick points out on the basis of his study of a large, west-coast police force that "the attitudes of policemen toward Negroes are not significantly different from those of most comparable whites such as skilled workingmen

8 Baldwin, *Another Country*, p. 290.
9 Wright, *Black Boy*, p. 208.
10 Gourley, *Public Relations and the Police*, p. 79.
11 McCaghy, "Public Attitudes Toward City Police in Hartford."
12 Cameron, *Booster and the Snitch*, pp. 45–46.
13 Niederhoffer, *Behind the Shield*, pp. 129–130.

and white-collar workers."[14] The police, he notes, operate in many respects much as combat troops in wartime, and they are as little given as soldiers to the more polite vocabularly that sometimes camouflages prejudice. And, because the police world tends to be a masculine one, the language used to address both friends and persons in the out-group is blunt. Finally, the police job insists on stereotyping, or making hunch judgments based on loose correlations. All of these factors tend to bring into open view hostility toward members of minority groups that may be more latent and better repressed in other segments of society.

The ambivalences involved in the performance of the law enforcement role in American society, particularly as manifested in periods of considerable social unrest, are reflected in a survey of police attitudes in New York City, which found that patrolmen have a high level of dissatisfaction with their job and feel that they are misunderstood by the public. Interviews conducted by the Vera Foundation with 1,369 patrolmen led to the conclusion that "patrolmen perceive a general trend toward permissiveness throughout society, particularly with respect to leniency in the administration of justice, and they believe this undermines their relationship with the public and hampers the performance of their duties." The report also notes that "from the patrolmen's standpoint, the chief problem stems from their inability to take more aggressive action against those who create disturbances or commit crimes and do a better job of preventing serious crime from occurring." Finally, the survey documents the significance of recent events in creating growing dissatisfaction among the police with their position, with a total of 63 percent of the police sample indicating their belief that there was more criticism of police action in connection with civil disorders and demonstrations than in any other activity.[15]

Police and Social Control

Policemen who ride in marked cars often wryly remark on how well motorists behave once they sight the long radio aerial and the insignia on the squad car; speeders suddenly find reason to apply their brakes, and drivers intending to pass abruptly change their minds and swerve back into the position from which they were emerging. In this way, the observed presence of police and their presumed efficiency clearly operate to control and prevent illegal behavior. In some states squad cars are marked with large letters in order to deter those who view them, while in other places, police cars go unmarked and occasionally have out-of-state licenses and white-wall tires (since government-owned vehicles tend to have economy features)

14 Skolnick, *Justice Without Trial*, p. 83.
15 *New York Times*, Dec. 19, 1968. See also Clark, "Isolation of the Police."

in order to catch unwary offenders.[16] The choice between camouflaged and marked cars in fact represents at its heart a choice between different philosophies of both crime causation and human behavior.

Police-car episodes also illustrate one of a number of explanations of why individuals do not at any given moment engage in particular criminal acts. On the simplest level, an act may be physically impossible; mental defectives, for example, cannot get caught up in elaborate antitrust violations, and armless individuals might have difficulty shoplifting. In addition, some forms of criminal behavior may never occur to a person, just as few of us would turn to other cultural orientations to find solutions to our problems; for example, few Americans think of exploring Papuan rites or Bushman theology in order to seek salvation, although their adherents claim that their way represents the only true path to eternal life.

Restraint on criminal activity is also engendered by a person's "conscience," which might be described as his imaginative awareness of the consequences of various forms of behavior, as these consequences would affect his self-image. The consequences might be either personal or social. Anticipation of headaches, anxiety, and guilt can be just as effective a deterrent to unsanctioned behavior as anticipation of court appearances, jury verdicts, and imprisonment. Social ostracism, as Sumner clearly documented more than a half century ago, can be more (or less) effective than social sanctions.[17] But, apart from the actual consequences of action, there is the vital element of the individual's anticipation of these consequences. Guilt and anxiety cannot be effective deterrents to the person who does not anticipate these consequences from his activities any more than imprisonment can represent a threat to a person who regards it as highly unlikely that he will be apprehended or incarcerated. And, finally, none of these consequences can be significant as inhibitors of action if the actor desires the consequences, such as persons who apparently welcome imprisonment and those who seem more comfortable with feelings of guilt than without them.

Police both fashion and control crime by the methods of operation they use. Crime may be induced as a response to police oppression and a lack of respect for law enforcement standards. It may be reduced by fear of police action and by police efficiency. The law enforcement officer, acting on information and intuition regarding sources of potential criminal activity makes his actions correspond to some extent with criminal reality. Since police work is essentially combative, with relatively clear lines drawn between the "good guys" and the "bad guys," to introduce definitions and specific guidelines might prove confusing and might render police operations ineffective.

A particularly clear-cut illustration of this theme appears in

16 Holcomb, *Police Patrol.*
17 Sumner, *Folkways.*

Les Misérables, Victor Hugo's memorable novel concerning Jean Valjean, an escaped French convict. Valjean is trailed relentlessly by Inspector Javert, an officer with a single-minded dedication to his job and an inflexible belief that all convicts are beyond trust and honor. After Valjean saves the Inspector's life, Javert feels obligated to grant his request for a period of temporary freedom, although he is certain that Valjean will not return. When Valjean does in fact keep his promise, Javert's *raison d'être,* the commitment upon which he founded his life, collapses. As Hugo notes, "His supreme anguish was the loss of all certainty. He felt that he was uprooted. The code was now but a stump in his hand. He had to do with scruples of an unknown species."[18] Mystifying questions now stupify Javert:

> What? An honest servant of the law could find himself suddenly caught between two crimes, the crime of letting a man escape, and the crime of arresting him! All was not certain in the order given by the state to the official! There might be blind alleys in duty. Was it true that an old bandit, weighed down by condemnations, could rise up and be right at last? Was this credible? Were there cases then when the law ought, before a transfigured crime, to retire, stammering excuses?[19]

For Hugo, the conclusion was inevitable. Javert walks, as if in a daze, to the water's edge, then

> a tall and black form, which from a distance some belated passer might have taken for a phantom, appeared standing on the parapet, bent towards the Seine, then sprang up, and fell straight into the darkness; there was a dull splash; and the shadow alone was in the secret of the convulsions of that obscure form which had disappeared under the water.[20]

Hugo's portrait of the rigid attitudes of Inspector Javert and the consequences of his inflexibility when contrary facts became too overwhelming indicates one of the fundamental difficulties of police work, in which officers are often obligated to enforce laws that they do not personally support. Inevitably, there is a tendency to achieve closure between personal views and professional duty; in many instances, therefore, law enforcement officers transmute and introject the demands of their position, so that it is not only the written law that they enforce; they are also responding to a personal affront against themselves and their beliefs. Nowhere perhaps does this become clearer than when angered persons do not show what is considered the proper respect for police authority, so that "contempt of cop" often becomes a more serious offense than real or alleged violations of the law.

There is, as a result, a move toward categoric positions in the face

18 Hugo, *Les Misérables,* p. 1108.
19 *Ibid.,* p. 1111.
20 *Ibid.,* p. 1114.

of demands for interpretative action. "Society must be protected," one police official notes, "and the policeman is not paid to be a theoretical psychologist or a social reformer."[21] In the same vein, another official remarks, "People expect a policeman to be a demigod on the salary of an upstairs maid."[22] The consequences of these role stresses as they bear upon issues such as police brutality will be explored subsequently; first, we shall examine the structure of law enforcement as it provides the framework within which the police role is played.

Structure of American Law Enforcement

A number of characteristics of American police are unique and provide clues to the level and type of crime in the United States. These characteristics stand out in bold analytical relief when the structure of the police in the United States is compared with its counterpart in countries such as Great Britain and France.

Most significantly, the American police operate under an almost unchecked policy of local autonomy. The tremendous proliferation and segmentation of police work in the United States has had considerable impact upon the quality of service rendered. At the same time, it has devitalized the police as a potentially dangerous force in the give-and-take of internal political affairs, since the absence of coordination among the different departments makes any mass political action by them unlikely. In other countries, leaders often vie for police support for political and revolutionary ends.

Los Angeles County serves as an extreme object-lesson in diffuse police organization, although its example can be duplicated on a lesser scale throughout the nation. The county has within its boundaries forty-six local police units, which are responsible to forty-six different governmental units. The largest police force, that of the county sheriff on occasion has to traverse wide breadths of territory policed by other units to get from one segment of its jurisdiction to another. Cooperation among agencies is a matter of voluntary agreement. Sometimes it is excellent, while other times it is poor, as vested local interests, personal antagonisms, and, on occasion, corruption, interfere with police work. The county is also policed by the State Highway Patrol, which in general concentrates on traffic offenses, by various federal agencies, and by untold numbers of private police who are responsible for railroad property, housing developments, college campuses, and similar sites.

The extraordinary amount of unchecked local political control involved in American policing is duplicated in no other large nation in the world, and undoubtedly this has been largely responsible for

21 Søderman, *Policeman's Lot*, p. 331.
22 Duffy in Bloch, *Crime in America*, p. 156.

the considerable amount of corruption that has occurred throughout the history of American police work.The President's Commission on Law Enforcement and Administration of Justice notes that "metropolitan police forces—most of which developed during the late 1800's when government corruption was most prevalent—have often been deeply involved in corruption." They cite as notorious examples of corruption in recent years both the indictment in 1963 of city officials and police in Newport, Kentucky for permitting organized vice and gambling activities to flourish, and the case in 1961 of ten Boston policemen who were exposed through a nationwide television documentary entering and leaving a bookmaking establishment. The Commission cites as another form of political corruption, the practice of

> police appointments . . . considered a reward for political favors and police officials . . . consequently responsive primarily to the local political machine [which] is still fairly open and tacitly accepted practice in many small cities and counties. It recurs too, from time to time, in larger cities, though generally in less conspicuous form.[23]

The public often accepts this style of city government as simply the "way things are," according to the Commission report, and the policeman who tries to buck such a system is likely to be ostracized by his companions and to forfeit any chance he may have had to advance in his career.

Geographical units are the most significant items in determining the caliber of police forces in the United States, although generalizations can be misleading; some county sheriff's departments, such as that in Los Angeles with 5,515 men, are as large and sophisticated as any metropolitan police department, while others, such as the force in Putnam County, Georgia with one man, are rather primitive. In general, it can be said that federal police units are specialized and efficient, while metropolitan police forces more often tend to become involved in scandals. County police organizations, mostly rural, are primarily vulnerable in terms of their adequacy to deal with any but the simplest forms of crime, although simple forms of crime are generally the only types they encounter. Together the 40,000 separate law enforcement agencies in the United States employ about 420,000 persons and are divided into 50 federal law enforcement agencies, 3,050 county agencies, 200 state police forces, 3,700 city forces, and 33,000 police units in boroughs, towns, and villages.[24]

FEDERAL POLICE

National police forces in the United States have comparatively limited enforcement powers. There is, however, a movement to grant larger

23 President's Commission, *Police*, pp. 208–209. See also Ingersoll, "Police Scandal Syndrome"; Smith, *Tarnished Badge*.
24 President's Commission, *Police*, pp. 7–8.

amounts of jurisdiction to such forces, partly because they are usually better financed, having the national treasury to draw upon, and partly because of the general trend toward expanded federal control over the affairs of the nation.[25] There has always been some reluctance, on the other hand, to place too much authority in a central police force.

Among the better-known federal police units, four operate in the Treasury Department. One unit is the Intelligence Unit of the Bureau of Internal Revenue, which was responsible to a large degree for putting together tax cases against persons such as Al Capone, Johnny Torrio, Waxey Gordon, and other organized criminals who could not be prosecuted for their more flagrant violations of the criminal law.[26] The Treasury Department also houses the Alcohol and Tobacco Tax Division, which enforces revenue laws against manufacturers of liquor and cigarettes, the Secret Service,[27] which combines the jobs of protecting the President and other dignitaries and of detecting counterfeit currency,[28] and the Bureau of Customs.

Other federal police agencies include the Chief Inspector of the Post Office, which is charged with resolving crimes concerned with the use of the mail, and various enforcement groups located within the Department of Justice, including the Immigration and Naturalization Service, the Bureau of Narcotics and Dangerous Drugs (transferred in 1968 from the Treasury Department to Justice), and the Federal Bureau of Investigation.

Federal Bureau of Investigation

The Federal Bureau of Investigation is undoubtedly the best known and most highly regarded police agency in the United States. It is also one of the most controversial forces, primarily because of its work in sensitive areas involving civil rights as they relate to race relations and in espionage and treason cases. The agency also is occasionally the center of controversy because of its director, J. Edgar Hoover, who epitomizes in many respects the forceful combination of honest, tough, and punitive law enforcement. The F.B.I. was organized in 1908 to halt the land-grabbing tactics of big business and in particular to enforce the Sherman Anti-Trust Act, although the agency has since tended to concentrate its attention less on these forms of white-collar crime and more on the apprehension of individuals whom Hoover labels "scum from the boiling pot of the underworld" and "vermin in human form . . . spewed out of prison cells to continue their slaughter."[29]

25 Ottenberg, *Federal Investigators.*
26 Irey and Slocum, *Tax Dodgers.*
27 Tully, *Treasury Agent.*
28 Bowen and Neal, *United States Secret Service;* Baughman and Robinson, *Secret Service Chief.*
29 Editorial, *Journal of Criminal Law,* p. 627.

Hoover took over the leadership of the F.B.I. in 1924, after it had been severely undermined by a series of inept performances and scandals. The professionalization of the F.B.I. and its striking public image are among the contributions that have been credited to him. A particular area of F.B.I. specialization includes identification of offenders, as the F.B.I. serves as a central depository for fingerprints. It also performs laboratory work on items such as fraudulent checks, toolmarks, firearms, hairs and fibers, shoe prints, and tire treads, and it sets up training facilities to keep local agents up-to-date on developments in law enforcement. The list of the nation's Ten Most Wanted Criminals is an F.B.I. innovation that has concentrated public attention on malefactors, and the F.B.I. also publishes *Uniform Crime Reports*, as we have seen, which is the most comprehensive national record of criminal behavior that we have.[30] In addition, in 1967 the F.B.I. inaugurated the National Crime Information Center, a computer program that stores information on things such as missing property and fugitives, and is linked electronically to police forces throughout the nation.

Criticisms of the F.B.I. epitomize in many ways general objections to certain law-enforcement procedures in addition to specific objections to the agency itself. Some complaints have been made that the F.B.I., like local police forces, tends to intrude its own feelings of right and wrong into selective forms of enforcement. Typical criticisms center around the Mann Act, for instance, which was passed by Congress in 1910 to halt commercialized white slavery but was used to prosecute cases of interstate cohabitation by consenting adults[31] until 1961, when the federal courts declared such interpretation to be a breach of Congressional intent.[32]

The F.B.I. is also charged with enforcing the National Motor Vehicle Theft Act, or Dyer Act, passed in 1919, which makes the transportation across state lines of stolen vehicles a federal offense.[33] Kidnaping also comes under federal jurisdiction, on the dubious assumption that the kidnaper will take his victim across a state line. James Bennett, former director of the federal Bureau of Prisons, stated an objection to what he considered the overly literal enforcement of kidnaping laws:

> I had two boys come to me here a little while ago who had gotten drunk, had taken a taxicab, put a soft drink bottle in the back of the neck of the taxi driver, and had him drive them across the State line. Then they all got drunk together and they stayed there all night. The next morning the taxi driver got very belligerent about it, and turned them

30 Whitehead, *FBI Story.*
31 For a dramatized version of this theme, see Sackler, *Great White Hope.*
32 *United States v. McClung.*
33 See Dosick, "Statement."

over to the police. They were held for kidnaping, and got thirty years apiece.[34]

Major complaints against the F.B.I. include the following: (1) That the agency, by insisting on staying outside of Civil Service regulations, violates a basic personnel doctrine of a democratic society. Hoover objects to Civil Service on the following ground: "I do not want the Bureau bogged down with misfits and incompetents or persons possessing communistic beliefs." When he was required by Congress to hire fingerprint clerks under Civil Service, Hoover maintained that he received persons who were "physically disabled, psychotic, criminals, persons with radical tendencies, sufferers from hypertension and cardiac enlargements." In 1969, F.B.I. agents received starting salaries of $11,626 annually, while members of other federal police forces began at a yearly salary of $6,981, although all groups require essentially the same talents. F.B.I. agents may, however, be fired at the will of the director; as a national magazine recently indicated, "any evidence of personal disloyalty to Hoover is traditionally rewarded with instant dismissal."[35] (2) That the Bureau is unnecessarily showy. The late Chief Justice Stone appointed Hoover to head the F.B.I. when he was Attorney General. Always regarding the appointment as eminently sound, he nonetheless noted, ". . . personally, I have been sorry to see the Bureau get the great publicity that it has received. One of the great secrets of Scotland Yard has been that its movements are never advertised. It moves and strikes in the dark and in consequence is more efficient both in its internal organization and its relation to criminals . . ."[36] Former Associate Justice Frankfurter obliquely refers to the same thing, remarking that "the Secret Service . . . is most efficient, non-advertising, non-Hooverian, competent and self-effacing."[37] (3) That the Bureau occasionally violates civil rights and, despite its distinguished record, is not as efficient as it might be. Critics cite the Judith Coplon case in which Miss Coplon, an alleged spy, was searched without a search warrant—an elementary error. In addition, during the Coplon case, F.B.I. agents denied wiretapping Miss Coplon's telephone although it eventually came to light that they had been doing just that, which led a New York newspaper to comment that it had become clear that the Bureau was "deliberately and notoriously violating the law."[38] (4) That the Bureau operates on a principle of vengeance, which is out of line with more modern and accepted principles of criminal reform. Here Hoover is an articulate opponent of advocates of current trends in corrections,

34 Quoted in Lowenthal, *Federal Bureau of Investigation*, p. 409. See also Cook, *FBI Nobody Knows*; Overstreet and Overstreet, *The FBI In Our Open Society*.
35 "J. Edgar Hoover and the FBI," p. 22.
36 Mason, *Harlan Fiske Stone*, pp. 152–153.
37 Phillips, *Felix Frankfurter Reminisces*, p. 42.
38 Quoted in Lowenthal, *Federal Bureau of Investigation*, p. 436.

whom he has called "sentimental yammerheads" and "moronic adults" who show "asinine behavior" and "maudlin sentiment" and "inherent criminal worship." Hoover would prefer to ignore the "moo-cow sentimentalities" of "hoity-toity professors."[39]

RURAL AND URBAN POLICE

Most of the major attention to police work focuses on the performance of forces in the largest cities, where crime tends to be more complex and more concentrated than in the hinterlands. By far the majority of America's police forces, however, are located in counties and small towns. These forces, often shopworn, underpaid, inadequately trained, and unskilled, will someday give way to state law enforcement agencies, although the movement in this direction has been painfully slow.

The county sheriff, found in every American county but Petroleum County, Montana, is characterized by the following: (1) He is elected, which means that he is often involved in partisan politics and therefore often does not have previous qualifications. (2) He is rotated, which means that he cannot usually hold the job for more than two to four years, and must therefore either look around for another position or retain the one he had before becoming sheriff. It also means that the benefit of any training acquired on the job is dissipated. This lack of training becomes particularly acute as crime operations move into the areas surrounding cities to avoid more stringent law enforcement. (3) He is often paid on a fee system that is based upon his maintenance of prisoners in the county jail, which he supervises. Bruce Smith calls attention to what might happen under such conditions:

> In one county a reliable investigation indicates that the cost of feeding a prisoner was eight cents a day while the sheriff received forty-five. In many counties, the sheriff is permitted, either directly or through concessionaires, to sell special articles of food, tobacco, or other so-called luxuries, to prisoners. He is thus permitted to starve them to the point where they or their friends purchase food to supplement the daily ration. He thus enjoys the extraordinary privilege of reaping a profit not only from starvation but from the relief of starvation.[40]

The same kind of graft, involving bribes and payoffs, is also found to a considerable extent in urban police forces, usually in the areas of vice control, such as of gambling and prostitution. The police, of course, are in the public limelight so that lawbreaking in their ranks, when uncovered, is apt to receive widespread publicity. The irony of lawbreaking by law enforcers also calls particular attention to police crimes. In addition, the police operate under conditions of considerable temptation; they are quite familiar with lawbreaking attitudes and techniques, and they undoubtedly become somewhat

39 Editorial, *Journal of Criminal Law*, p. 627.
40 Smith, *Police Systems in the United States.*

callous about crime. In addition, they are readily able to help themselves surreptitiously to additional goods lying around the premises of burglarized stores. Subject to political pressures, sometimes poorly paid, and caught between the demands of a society that officially abhors illegal pleasures and unofficially indulges in them, the police stand in a notably vulnerable position.

These vocational components appear to provide much better insight into police illegality than strained attempts to label the police with personal traits that condition their activities. John H. McNamara notes, for instance, that a large percentage of recruits into the New York City Police Department had also taken the examination for the Fire Department, and that a considerable number of policemen later resigned to work for the Fire Department, although virtually no firemen quit to take up police work. He suggests that it is not the opportunity to tyrannize over one's fellow man that primarily sends men into police work but rather the attraction of a civil service job, with reasonable salary, and early retirement opportunities. Using a punitiveness scale developed by Gwynne Nettler,[41] McNamara found that police recruits tended to be less punitive than community leaders.[42]

Police Brutality

There appears to be a consensus among persons who have observed police work over the years that the use of brutality by law enforcement officers in dealing with suspects and other persons with whom they have contact has been on the decline. Notorious instances of "third degree" tactics, common in the 1920s, appear to be much more unusual today, although by no means nonexistent.[43] Instances of police brutality may be divided into various categories, including (1) brutality directed against sex criminals and "cop fighters," (2) brutality inflicted on people by police officers who enjoy hurting people, and (3) brutality that ensues when policemen are afraid or are under great physical or mental stress.

The most comprehensive survey of police brutality yet undertaken is that conducted in 1966 by Albert J. Reiss, Jr., of the University of Michigan, for the President's Commission on Law Enforcement and Administration of Justice. Observers, usually graduate students, accompanied 450 policemen on a total of 850 eight-hour tours of duty in Negro and white slums in Washington, Boston, and Chicago. One out of ten of the policemen, according to the observers, used "improper" or "unnecessary" force. Incidents placed in this category included situations in which policemen beat a handcuffed man,

41 Nettler, "Cruelty, Dignity, and Determinism," p. 380.
42 McNamara, "Uncertainties in Police Work," p. 195.
43 Burnham, "Police Violence." See also Cray, *Big Blue Line;* Whittemore, *Cop!*.

in which several policemen held a man while a patrolman beat him, and in which two policemen beat a confused mental patient whom they pushed into a telephone booth. Among the cases observed was the following:

> One evening an observer was present in the lockup when two white policemen came in with a white man. The suspect had been handcuffed and brought to the station because he had proved obstreperous after being arrested for a traffic violation. Apparently he had been drinking. While waiting in the lockup, the man began to urinate on the floor. In response, the policemen began to beat the man. They jumped him, knocked him down, and beat his head against the concrete floor. He required emergency treatment at a nearby hospital.[44]

It is the "officer culture"—a code or attitude that is prevalent in police departments—rather than prejudices, that prompts the beatings, Reiss believes. His tabulations indicate that policemen do not tend to select their victims according to race. "The most likely victim of excessive force," Reiss notes, "is a lower-class man of either race."[45]

Other commentators remark on the sensitivity of law enforcement officers to attacks on police personnel. A detective notes, for instance, that

> an attack on a cop is viewed by the police as the most serious thing in the world. The rightful worry about their own safety leads to a belief that any kind of physical response—or sometimes even an angry word —is a cause for a crack across the head. I've seen an old drunk being creamed for having taken a harmless swing.[46]

In the same vein, William Brown, a former inspector of the New York Police Department, now professor of criminal justice at the State University of New York, Albany, notes that the police take the attitude that "anyone who wants to fight me is my potential killer."

Brown also stresses the class discrepancy between the police and various types of offenders, which leads to outbreaks of brutality:

> I think the student contempt of patriotism and materialism is, in some ways, much more difficult for the police to understand than the problems confronting a poor Negro in Harlem. Many cops have just bought houses [in the suburbs], many are in the process of escaping from boyhoods in white slums and this tends to make them super middle class. They really become outraged and confused when they hear some kid question the guts of those fighting in Vietnam or hear some Barnard girl shouting dirty words.[47]

Another student of police work has made essentially the same observation:

44 Reiss, Jr., "Police Brutality," pp. 15–16.
45 *Ibid.*, p. 17.
46 Burnham, "Police Violence."
47 *Ibid.*

Most cops I know will walk into the mouth of a cannon. But they're terrified of words. Don't forget most cops don't have any education, they're inarticulate. In a way, the police feel much more challenged by the words of the Columbia students than by any threat they may actually be. The police feel superior to the Negro, but they don't feel superior to the students. This means they show a tolerance to the Negro that doesn't come so easily to the students.[48]

Presumably, if the diagnoses are correct, law enforcement officers with better educational backgrounds will feel less threatened by student demonstrators than those less well-educated and less secure personally. In addition, brutality directed against lower-class persons would presumably decrease as law enforcement officers developed more understanding attitudes toward sex offenders and drunks, among others, who appear to offend them more aesthetically than in actual fact. How to control retaliation against persons who present potential threats to the police appears much more complicated. For one thing, of course, persons might learn to deal with the police with more respect and less aggression; presumably, this would elicit better police behavior in return. For another thing, the police undoubtedly would have to learn to exercise more care and control of their own behavior if they expect others to treat them more respectfully.

Police Discretion

The police have a great amount of discretion in regard to which laws they will enforce and which laws they will not enforce and against whom they will enforce the different laws of their jurisdiction. This discretion is probably the most important aspect of police operations, although it usually receives less attention than issues of police corruption and such mechanical matters as whether patrol cars should be manned by one or two men. Even granting the significance of corruption, most police forces are not seriously handicapped by it in their enforcement of the laws against routine criminal activity. The way in which discretion is employed, on the other hand, colors the entire picture of any police department's enforcement efforts.

Some persons maintain that the police should enforce all laws exactly and impartially, exercising no discretion whatsoever, in robot-like fashion. Others maintain that the exercise of sound and intelligent discretion, whatever the possibilities of abuse of such discretion may be, is necessary for reasonable and intelligent police performance. The legislature, for example, may write a law against all forms of gambling, even though the presumption is that it did not really intend to include private card games within the ambit of the law. Private games cannot specifically be exempted, however, because professional gamblers would then hide behind the façade of privacy. Therefore,

48 *Ibid.*

the legislature enacts the inclusive piece of legislation and presumes that the police will exercise discretion in carrying out the law.

The most strenuous argument for full enforcement, regardless of its consequences, has been advanced by Joseph Goldstein, a law professor at Yale University. Goldstein points out that police discretion is of extremely low visibility—that is, that the public is barely, if at all, aware of the routine exercise of police decisions not to enforce various laws and/or to enforce them differentially. In a typical metropolitan city surveyed by the American Bar Foundation, there was routine failure to enforce various laws, either through default or based on affirmative departmental policies, Goldstein notes. He points out that this use of discretion represented well-intentioned, honest judgments, and did not involve bribery or concern obsolete laws. In this city, the police chose not to enforce the narcotics laws against certain violators who informed against other "more serious" offenders, not to enforce the felonious assault laws against an assailant whose victim did not sign a complaint, and not to enforce the gambling laws against persons involved in the numbers racket. Rather, they chose to harass these individuals.

Narcotics cases might be examined more closely to see how police discretion operates. In the same city studied, about 80 percent of the narcotics arrests were not prosecuted, generally because a precinct officer decided that the search was illegal or that the evidence obtained was inadequate. There did not seem to be much interest in being more meticulous in searches or obtaining better evidence due to a departmental view that harassing narcotics addicts was equally as effective as bringing them to court. A narcotics suspect was generally given an opportunity to serve as a police informer, to "do himself some good." The hope of a lesser sentence or no sentence at all, plus the desire to avoid withdrawal pains, pushed many addicts toward cooperation with the police. The addicts were usually charged, but final disposition of their cases was postponed until the information they supplied could be tested; if it proved valuable, the offender might be placed on probation or the original case against him dismissed. On occasion he would even be allowed by some police departments to keep a portion of the narcotics he arranged to buy under their surveillance.

Goldstein argues that the decision not to have full enforcement of all laws should not be made by the police department itself, but rather should be subject to review by an impartial body. Such review would make the decisions more visible to public scrutiny and would lead to study of the different effects of varying policies. In regard to narcotics, for instance, Goldstein makes the following observation:

> Full enforcement will place the legislature in a position to evaluate narcotics laws by providing a basis for answering such questions as:

Will such inflation increase the frequency of crimes committed to finance narcotics purchases? Or will full enforcement reduce the number
of users and the frequency of connected crimes? Will too great or too
costly an administrative burden be placed on the prosecutor's office
and the courts by full enforcement? Will correctional institutions be
filled beyond "effective" capacity? The answers to these questions are
now buried or obscured by decisions not to invoke the criminal process.[49]

There are others who insist that the police, like administrative
agencies such as school boards and federal regulatory commissions,
possess a certain expertise—specialized knowledge and information—
and must be allowed flexibility in determining for themselves how to
operate most effectively.[50] It is pointed out that the use of discretion
may on occasion be beneficial. The policy of dealing with minor narcotics offenders seems to most police officials to be the only reasonable
method to cope with the traffic in addictive drugs. Other kinds of
offenders may benefit from police discretion; for example, drunks are
often turned loose after they sober up, instead of being taken to court
and perhaps humiliated for their first offense. Many offenders are
not taken into custody because individual police officers are convinced
that there are mitigating circumstances that may not be adequate as
legal defenses but that vitiate the social harm of the crime. Squad-car
officers, for example, will on occasion condone a statutory rape violation by the simple tactic of "forgetting" to ask the participants, if they
are of nearly equivalent age, to produce evidence of their birth years.
Laws that conflict with the mores of certain groups are sometimes
not enforced as stringently as they are among other groups who take
these enactments more seriously. A bigamy offense may not be pressed
in a downtown slum area, whereas the same offense will be prosecuted
with vigor when the police become aware of it in a suburban section,
particularly if the residents in one area do not feel injured, while
those in the other demand that "justice" be done. Such selectivity
may contain an element of subtle discrimination, but, at least from
the viewpoint of the individual who gains from it, it may seem more
humane than the literal enforcement of the criminal code.

Foreign Law Enforcement
Most European countries maintain the police as a national agency,
although this arrangement has its own hazards, as we have noted, particularly in periods of unrest when the police may exert quasi-military
power. In France, the Paris police (*agents de police* or, in the vernacu-
lar, *flics*) are mainly under the jurisdiction of the local prefecture,
but the rural police (*gendarmerie,* from *gens d'armes,* or "men at arms")

49 Goldstein, "Police Discretion Not to Invoke the Criminal Process." See also
Wilson, *Varieties of Police Behavior,* pp. 83–129.
50 LaFave, *Arrest;* Goldstein, "Police Discretion."

combine both military and civil functions and are under the control of the Ministry of the Interior and the Ministry of War. The *gendarmerie* are stationed throughout France in squads of five and ten men, and they live in barracks with their families.[51] Finally, there is the *Sûreté Nationale*, comprising about 53,000 officers and men, which polices all cities with populations of more than 10,000 except Paris and its environs. Recruits for the lower ranks are gotten from the armed forces, and the *Sûreté Nationale* is in every sense a national police force organized along military lines.[52]

The British police attempt to combine the merits of local control with the advantages of centralized authority by placing reviewing authority in the Home Office, which approves the appointment of police chiefs and sets nationwide standards for law enforcement.[53] In addition, by contributing half the expenses of local police organizations, the Home Office inevitably is able to exert control over their operations.[54] In part too, the rule stipulating that no officer may be a local resident serves to overcome allegiances and obligations that many men tend to take with them when they join law-enforcement organizations.[55]

The 168 English police forces represent, of course, a much smaller and more controllable group than the estimated 40,000 police units in the United States. The British police, however, provide an example of a force established with trepidation that it might result in governmental tyranny that evolved into an organization commanding widespread public support. The early history of policing in Britian offered little prospect that law enforcement would be able to command public respect. The Bow Street Runners, predecessors of the current police organization in London, for instance, were described by Charles Dickens in the following manner:

> I remember them very well. . . . They kept company with thieves and such-like, much more than the [present] detective police do. I don't know what their pay was, but I have no doubt their principal complements were got under the rose. It was a very slack institution, and its headquarters were the Brown Bear, in Bow Street, a public house of more than doubtful reputation, opposite the police-office.[56]

In 1829, Sir Robert Peel established the metropolitan police in London, members of which are still known as "Bobbies" in his honor.[57] Today, in contrast to early forebodings, the British police enjoy wide-

51 Søderman, *Policeman's Lot*, p. 105.
52 Cramer, *World's Police*, pp. 296–298.
53 *Ibid.*, p. 452. See also Martienssen, *Crime and the Police*; Hart, *British Police*; Solmes, *English Policeman, 871–1935*; Chappel and Wilson, *The Police and the Public in Australia and New Zealand*.
54 Whitehead, *Journey Into Crime*, p. 9.
55 Puttkammer, *Administration of Criminal Law*, p. 35.
56 Dexter, *Letters of Charles Dickens*, Vol. III, p. 293.
57 Lyman, "Metropolitan Police Act of 1829."

spread affectionate respect. A survey, for instance, indicates that, despite considerable encouragement to register complaints about the police, 75 percent of a nationwide sample in England could offer no criticisms, while 5 percent were "really hostile," and 13 percent noted minor complaints.[58]

In an intriguing analysis, Geoffrey Gorer, a well-known British anthropoligist, uses the British police to suggest that "the national character of a society may be modified or transformed over a given period through the selection of personnel for institutions that are in constant contact with the mass of the population and in a somewhat superordinate position, a position of some authority." If the character of an institution is generally felt to be benevolent, protective, or succoring, Gorer suggests, then the character exemplified by the personnel of the institution will to a certain degree become part of the ego ideal of the mass of the population. The process proceeds, according to Gorer, along the following lines:

> The mass of the population will then tend to mold their own behavior in conformity with this ideal, and will reward and punish their children in conformity to this adopted pattern. As generations pass, the attempt to approximate this ideal will become less and less conscious, and increasingly part of the unconscious mechanisms that determine the content of the superego; with the ultimate consequence that a type of character that may have been relatively very uncommon when the institution was first manned will subsequently become relatively common, even perhaps typical of the society as a whole, or of those portions of it with which the members of the institution are in most continuous contact.[59]

Gorer suggests that by careful recruitment, constant stress on esprit de corps, unremitting training in polite and fair dealing with the public, and in similar attitudes, the British police came to operate at a level far above the standards of public behavior. Ultimately, Gorer believes, the police came to mold British behavior in their own image. In the United States, he believes, much the same function was served by public school teachers in regard to immigrant children.

Two events, fifty years apart in time, indicate changing ingredients of public behavior toward the police in Britain:

> In June 1780 rioting broke out in London and for nearly a week the city was in the hands of a savage, drunken mob. . . . A mob destroyed chapels and houses, set fire to Newgate Jail and released prisoners. The Constables, Peace Officers and Justices of the Peace were helpless to interfere and the crowds were incensed, rather than intimidated, by the military being called in. One Member of Parliament stood up and shocked the House by observing that perhaps the constables in London could take a leaf out of the books of the French Police and be more

58 Gorer, "Modification of National Character."
59 *Ibid.,* p. 29.

efficient in their duties. (To the Englishman of those days the word "Police" was regarded with much the same loathing as the word "Gestapo" in later years.) By the time the fighting had subsided, many citizens had been killed and wounded and thousands of pounds' worth of damage committed. Later, twenty-five rioters were executed for their part in the affair.[60]

Note, however, a quite different public reaction a half century later, only a year after the new police had come into being:

> With the passage of time, however, the public noticed how patient and restrained these unarmed policemen were, despite all manner of provocation. On one occasion in 1830 a policeman was fatally stabbed whilst endeavoring to apprehend a suspect in the daytime in Gray's Inn Road. A collection of petty criminals who had observed the struggle with laughter and jeers suddenly realized that the dying constable had no cutlass or pistol with which rumor had armed the police. The spectators fell silent at the tragedy then, and with cold anger, turned on the murderer and seized him. He was handed over to justice.[61]

Conditions in Britain, however, appear to be changing again, moving in the direction of those in the United States in regard to the position of the police. Several recent scandals brought disrepute upon the record of the English law-enforcement system. Poor salaries (a sergeant on the London force earns approximately $3,000 a year) have severely hampered recruitment. The lament of a British bobby today, in fact, sounds very much like the plaint of his American equivalent. "You won't get any help in Soho in a punch-up," a bobby recently told a newspaper reporter, "Not even if six of them are having a go at you. Some decent chap might put your helmet back on your head, while you're lying there on the ground."[62]

Summary

The foregoing pages have attempted to survey some of the more important impacts of law enforcement on criminal behavior. Some criminal acts, as we have seen, are beyond the ken of the police because of their very nature. Attempted suicides, for example, are not known unless they are reported, and by definition, virtually all concealed-weapon offenses remain undetected. In addition, the resources available to the police limit severely the amount and the form of criminal activity that will be dealt with officially.

It may be presumed that the failure of the police to operate in some areas of activity that are defined as illegal, will, if nothing else, fail to deter such activity. Whether some forms of crime are or are not promoted by law-enforcement problems is probably related to

60 Cramer, *World's Police*, pp. 16–17.
61 *Ibid.*, p. 19.
62 *New York Times*, Aug. 15, 1964.

the type of act involved; for example, social factors are undoubtedly more important in determining the amount of incest that exists than any police activities are. Police discretion, then—the selection of what offenses to act against and which persons to deal with—undoubtedly influences our official portrait of criminal behavior as well as the actual amount of such behavior.

We have also noted that legal rules inevitably inhibit the full enforcement of criminal sanctions in areas in which the police may be anxious and eager to operate. The presence and fluctuation of such procedural rules is likely to influence criminal activity, since at least a segment of the population that contemplates illegal activity is inclined to engage in acts in which the chance of apprehension is least likely; for example, income tax evasion would undoubtedly decrease if enforcement efforts were tripled or multiplied many times, and gamblers would probably either seek other means of operation or abandon their activities altogether if various search and seizure techniques were not disallowed. In this realm, the delicate balancing of the society's interest in combating crime and its interest in keeping inviolate certain standards of state performance inevitably come into abrasive contact.

Inadequate and conflicting definitions of the roles that the police are expected to play in our society account in large measure for many of the abuses that are charged against policemen. Members of the society want to be secure against criminally caused annoyance and depredation, and they expect the police to provide such security. At the same time, the police are expected to operate within the confines of restrictive laws. These laws are seen as guaranteeing the citizen protection from arbitrary police tyranny, yet, admittedly, they also serve to protect many criminals from apprehension. Thus the police are charged with doing a job, but are handicapped to some extent from doing it well. There would be no conflict, of course, if the police took the position that they would do the very best they could within the rules that society declares to be essential for its freedom. In practice, however, either because of public intolerance or professional impatience and pride, the police often stress disproportionately their duty to apprehend criminals. They thereby underplay and denigrate their obligations to do so only within the rigid confines of controlling laws, which they view as ill-conceived and unfortunate, supported by persons who do not appreciate the realities of criminal activity and the problems of law enforcement.

For Further Reading

BORDUA, DAVID J. (ed.). *The Police: Six Sociological Essays.* New York: John Wiley & Sons, 1967.

　　Nine authors—Bordua, John H. McNamara, Irving Piliavin, Albert

Reiss, Allan Silver, Jerome H. Skolnick, Carl Wertham, James Q. Wilson, and J. Richard Woodworth—contribute six statements on the role of the police in contemporary society. The essays examine the demand for order in civil society, the environment and organization of the police, the relationship of police with gang members, the problems of a morals detail, police morale, and the relevance of a policeman's background and training to his task.

LOWENTHAL, MAX. *The Federal Bureau of Investigation*. New York: Sloane, 1950.

This critical account of the F.B.I. draws heavily upon Congressional investigations and other semiofficial documents. The author feels in particular that the Bureau does not receive the public scrutiny that it should have and that there is some danger in an uncritical hero-worship of any police organization.

PRESIDENT'S COMMISSION ON LAW ENFORCEMENT AND ADMINISTRATION OF JUSTICE. *Task Force Report: The Police*. Washington, D.C.: Government Printing Office, 1967.

Among the many recommendations flowing from this comprehensive review of police operations is the proposal that every metropolitan police department should have community-relations machinery to promote more effective liaisons with minority groups. The Commission also suggested that police departments abandon single entry procedures and establish three levels at which candidates may begin their police careers.

SKOLNICK, JEROME H. *Justice Without Trial: Law Enforcement in Democratic Society*. New York: John Wiley & Sons, 1966.

Basing his book on actual participant observations plus comparative community and case material, Skolnick discusses key issues, such as the organization of the police in America, the effects of police bureaucracy on criminal justice, narcotics and vice investigations, and the informer's payoff and its consequences. His findings are analyzed in light of organizational and legal controls over the police.

WILSON, JAMES Q. *Varieties of Police Behavior: The Management of Law and Order in Eight Communities*. Cambridge: Harvard University Press, 1968.

The study considers how the uniformed officer in eight communities deals with such offenses as assault, theft, drunkenness, vice, traffic, and disorderly conduct.

16
Administration of
Criminal Justice

Criminal behavior might be examined without regard to the activities of the courts of criminal jurisdiction. A murderer remains a criminal whether or not he is apprehended or processed through the courts, just as, to repeat an earlier analogy, a tubercular person remains tubercular whether or not his condition is detected and diagnosed correctly. Yet the operation of the courts, like the operation of the police, produces many subtle fluctuations in the amount and type of criminal activity. It is obvious, for instance, that a considerable number of criminals would not have violated the law had they been certain of being convicted. In this respect, both the failure of the police to apprehend criminals and the failure of the courts to convict them fall short of maximum possible deterrence to those individuals who would take such consequences into account.

There are a number of reasons why the courts fail to convict guilty persons, including the following: (1) The evidence at hand is not adequate to sustain the charge, either because adequate evidence is unobtainable or because it is not obtained, and (2) The process of adjudication serves to liberate the guilty offender.

The second item can be broken down into several constituent elements. Guilty offenders often are not convicted because the various safeguards set up to protect the innocent against conviction serve to free numerous guilty offenders. Edwin M. Borchard estimates that one innocent person is convicted for every nine guilty individuals set free.[1] Most commentators would probably say that this is a generous under-estimate of the unconvicted guilty. Guilty offenders also secure their freedom in some instances because of the effective tactics of their lawyers or through an inaccurate appraisal of the evidence by the judge

---

1 Borchard, *Convicting the Innocent*, p. 407.

or the jury. In other instances, juries may deliberately divert the course of literal justice by ruling in favor of the accused for reasons that appear to them to override the demands of the criminal code. Mercy killers and wives who retaliate homicidally against wayward husbands notoriously benefit from such jury indulgence.

Certainty of conviction is also related to fairness and to perceptions of procedural integrity; they help determine the effect of the process of criminal justice on the offender. As Lord Hewart, at one time the Lord Chief Justice of England, expressed it, "Not only must justice be done, but it must also *appear* to have been done."[2] The same remark appears in the writings of Lord Herschell, another English jurist, who said, "Important as it was that people should get justice, it was even more important that they should be made to feel and see that they were getting it."[3] McCleery, studying the most recalcitrant offenders in two different prisons, discovered that the system of criminal justice produced intense hostility among the inmates. He found that the prisoners' resentment of lawyers was significantly stronger than their resentment of guards and prison officials.[4] Some of this hostility was obviously the product of rationalization, in an attempt to displace blame; for example, it was not the offender who was responsible for his predicament, but rather the prosecutor who conducted the case against him and the defense attorney who was not agile enough to get him off. But other elements in the resentment stem from the inmate's accurate appraisal of American criminal justice; he knows that other persons, equally guilty, manage to "beat the rap," are sometimes allowed to plead guilty to lesser offenses, are granted immunity in return for information, or are allowed to turn state's evidence in return for mild sentences. Such outcomes may undermine respect for the integrity of the court and for its concern with principles of justice. It is a moot question whether such respect would compel more law-abiding behavior in the future. Lloyd McCorkle and Richard Korn argue, for instance, that inmates usually find something or somebody upon whom to project the responsibility for difficulties largely of their own creation and that one scapegoat may be much the same as another.[5] Nevertheless, from an ethical standpoint, the criminal courts often fail to meet desirable standards of justice.

The erratic nature of criminal court proceedings probably creates the greatest emotional malaise in the accused. He feels that if he can unravel the key to the system he can benefit. His lawyer may encourage him in the belief that the operation of the system is a mystical ritual that only the lawyer's expertise can comprehend and manipu-

2 Quoted in O'Donnell, *Cavalcade of Justice*, p. 65.
3 Atlay, *Victorian Chancellors*, Vol. II, p. 460.
4 McCleery, in Cressey, *The Prison*, pp. 294–295. See also Mylonas and Reckless, "Prisoner Attitudes Toward Law and Legal Institutions."
5 McCorkle and Korn, "Resocialization Within Walls."

late.[6] It probably does not matter in terms of the offender's reactions whether or not a court or its officials are corrupt, so long as the accused thinks that its brand of justice can be purchased. To some extent, of course, even the court of total and unimpeachable integrity has a price tag on certain facets of its operations, just as innumerable other aspects of life relating to an individual's liberty and to his very existence depend in some measure on his command of economic resources. The fact that harsh laws of economic survival operate in other parts of society, however, does nothing to obviate the offender's sense of persecution. In some cases, offenders seem to react to court experiences by vowing to obtain financial resources, either by legal or illegal means, which will enable them, if they ever again appear before a criminal court, to purchase the top grade of "justice" on the market.

It is in such ways that the operation of the criminal justice system plays upon the nature of criminal behavior in a society. Within this system, we shall first examine the operation of the so-called "inferior" courts, whose designation reflects only their position in the hierarchy of judicial bodies, although in fact they very often are "inferior" tribunals when measured in terms of reasonable standards of fairness and decency. We shall then look more closely at trial courts that hear felony cases, after which we will examine the role and performance of practitioners associated with such courts. Finally, we will scrutinize several controversial areas of criminal justice—search and seizure, wiretapping, confession rules, and exclusionary rules—in the attempt to exhibit stresses and strains within the criminal justice system as they mirror general social attitudes toward crime and criminals.

Criminal Justice and Misdemeanants

The greatest amount of public attention in the United States is focused on those sensational trials in which the accused is charged with a notorious murder or an offense having sexual overtones. The day-to-day course of the administration of justice is much more mundane, however, than that segment singled out for newspaper headlines.

Misdemeanors, the petty, run-of-the-mill business of the lower courts in America, usually involve offenses carrying sentences of less than one year in the county jail or comparatively small fines. Misdemeanor justice in its usual form is meted out by magistrates or justices of the peace, who as often as not appear to have secured their positions because of their political leanings and activity rather than because of their legal acumen, human compassion, or social insight. As William Beaney notes, "Poorly qualified and inadequately paid, overworked and conscious of their low status in the judicial system,

6 Blumberg, "Practice of Law as Confidence Game."

many inferior court judges use their offices to dispense political favors, occasionally with outright corrupt motives, but, more typically, in an effort to promote their own long-range interests in one of the party organizations of their community."[7]

Misdemeanor justice usually takes place in rather sordid surroundings and involves in many instances defendants who, through considerable exposure to its operation, have become as familiar as the bailiff with its routine. Guilty pleas are the rule. A national survey of municipal courts conducted by senior students in the Harvard Law School presents some first-hand impressions of lower courts. The survey notes that these courts constitute the only contact most Americans ever have with the judiciary and that they therefore are the courts where "more than anywhere the quality of American justice earns the respect or contempt of the public"; it further observes that:

> The physical characteristics of the court may not be an indication of the quality of justice dispensed, but the appearance of the courtroom and the behavior of the court officers are of considerable effect in determining the tone of the proceedings and their impact on the defendants. In one Southern city it was not unusual for the judge to smoke and drink soft drinks in the courtroom; in Philadelphia magistrates often joke with the prosecuting attorney at the expense of the defendant. In some cities the judge may interrupt the trial to give a brief lecture to those in the courtroom on the evils of the offense with which the defendant is charged.[8]

The ingredients of municipal court justice found by the Harvard researchers are supported in a story filed by a metropolitan news reporter after witnessing a day's proceedings in New York's municipal court:

> A Criminal Court Judge balefully surveys a tardy defendant scurrying to present himself before the bench. "Is this the idiot that's supposed to be in this case?" the magistrate inquires. There is nervous laughter in the courtroom.

> Another judge dismisses a prostitute with an admonition: "Stay away from Broadway—all of it." A moment later he discovers that another woman arrested at the same time has inadvertently left the courtroom. "OK—the same thing goes for her," the judge calls out.[9]

The situation described in New York appears neither worse nor better than the quality of justice dispensed in the nation's other municipal courts. The President's Commission on Law Enforcement and Administration of Justice labelled such courts as sites of "inequity, indignity, and ineffectiveness" and offered numerous illustrations to support its charge. In the Recorder's Court in Detroit, the Commission

7 Beaney, "United States Courts and Criminal Justice."
8 "Metropolitan Criminal Courts of First Instance."
9 *Wall Street Journal*, Dec. 7, 1967.

notes, "most of the defendants pleaded guilty and were sentenced immediately, without any opportunity for allocution. When they tried to say something in their own behalf, they were silenced by the judge and led off by the bailiff."[10] Details of such a procedure were illustrated by the following exchange in a Philadelphia courtroom:

> Magistrate: "Where do you live?"
> Defendant: "Norfolk."
> Magistrate: "What are you doing in Philadelphia?"
> Defendant: "Well, I didn't have any work down there, so I came up here to see if I could find . . ."
> Magistrate (who had been shaking his head): "That story's not good enough for me. I'm going to have you investigated. You're a vagrant. Three months in the House of Corrections."[11]

It would be interesting, given the many accounts of the negative conditions of America's municipal courts, to understand more definitively the impact that these conditions have upon defendants. It is easy to caricature the municipal courts—and they certainly earn the derision they receive in Commission reports and other surveys—but the jump from descriptive material to behavioral implications is a long one, particularly when hard data is notably absent. It can be said that unaesthetic judicial proceedings are unacceptable per se, but it should not be concluded without further investigation that such proceedings necessarily have an effect on criminal behavior. It is always possible that the conditions of municipal courts so offend many persons and that their erraticism so appalls others, that offenders make strenuous efforts to avoid further trouble. That such a consequence might appear to be unlikely does not render it untrue until research information is accumulated. It would be of value, for example, to compare the long-range outcome of cases heard in a dignified manner in a well-kept courtroom with those heard under the conditions now prevailing in most municipal courts.

GUILTY PLEAS

Many misdemeanor offenses begin as felonies in which the original charge is reduced by the prosecuting attorney for various reasons. Sexual offenses may be reduced to "disorderly conduct," drunken driving to "reckless driving," and statutory rape to "contributing to the delinquency of a minor." Seasoned offenders are usually well aware of the limits and the techniques of bargaining, called "copping a plea," and they will offer to plead guilty to lesser offenses in return for other considerations.

Prosecutors generally defend the procedure of bargaining, ubiquitous in the administration of criminal justice in the United States,[12]

10 President's Commission, *Courts*, p. 30.
11 *Ibid.*, p. 31.
12 Newman, *Conviction;* Cressey, "Negotiated Pleas."

on several grounds. First, it saves the state a great deal of money by by-passing time-consuming and costly trials. Second, it expedites justice by avoiding clogged court calendars. Third, it allows the conviction and sentencing of many offenders who might otherwise win their freedom if their cases were tried on more serious charges with somewhat shaky evidence. In addition, in some instances prosecutors accept guilty pleas to lesser offenses as a form of rough-and-ready justice, taking into account favorable aspects of the accused's background or personality that might militate against the literal character of the original transgression. Finally, although they would hardly admit it, prosecutors are elected officials who are often politically mobile, seeking legislative posts, judicial appointments, and voter support, and they want to cite a superior record to their constituents.[13] Many prosecutors, for example, are apt to note that they have won, say, 93 percent of their cases, when they have in fact accepted guilty pleas to lesser offenses in virtually all of them and would have lost a considerable percentage had they gone to trial.

Guilty pleas, then, are a mainstay of the administration of criminal justice in the United States. In a detailed analysis of their use, Donald J. Newman found that approximately 94 out of 100 inmates sentenced to prison from a medium-sized Wisconsin county had pled guilty, and if those who had been placed on probation had been included in his figures, the percentage of guilty pleas would probably have been higher. Although few figures are available and practices vary widely in different jurisdictions, it is probably reasonably accurate to state that about 5 percent of all felony charges are tried by juries, whereas some 25 percent are tried by a judge alone. Of the remainder, perhaps 30 percent are dismissed after indictments have been returned and 40 percent are resolved by guilty pleas. Eliminating dismissals, the figures would show approximately 60 percent of the felony cases resolved by guilty pleas. A convict explains how the system works, as follows:

> The D.A. needed my help. His evidence was all circumstances (sic). He knew I done it but he couldn't ever prove it. But I couldn't go to court and take a chance with my record. When I saw he was going to stick me with something, I was willing to make the best deal.[14]

In terms of the large number of guilty pleas, much of the writing concerning fair trials that appears in academic journals actually deals with a relatively minor problem, judged at least in terms of the numbers of persons involved. Higher court decisions rarely concern guilty pleas, since they usually involve few issues susceptible to judicial review. But it is likely that there are more miscarriages of justice involved in guilty pleas than there are in improper remarks to the

13 Tappan, *Crime, Justice, and Correction,* p. 343.
14 Newman, "Pleading Guilty for Considerations," p. 784.

jury, inadequate indictments, lie detectors, and similar matters that monopolize the attention of the higher courts. Many offenders plead guilty to charges out of fear of conviction for greater offenses, when in fact no charges could be sustained. Others assume that a lesser sentence, which might be probation, is more acceptable than the risk of a prison term ensuing from a prolonged jury trial. Some judges have a policy of refusing to give suspended sentences to convicted defendants who insisted upon a jury trial rather than pleading guilty.[15] Some defendants may plead guilty from a misunderstanding of the nature of the proceedings, and still others to avoid the publicity and expense of a more elaborate trial.

Mechanics of Criminal Justice: Felonies

Those felonies that are not settled by dismissal or a guilty plea at an early stage of the proceedings travel through a process evolved from centuries of experience and continual reevaluation.[16] This process is still the subject of considerable controversy, and its major elements follow in skeletal form.

ARRAIGNMENT

The accused, after arrest, is arraigned before a lower-court justice. Prior to arraignment, the defendant's lawyer may force the hand of the prosecuting agency by use of a writ of habeas corpus, demanding that it substantiate the reasons for which it is depriving the accused of his liberty. Habeas corpus, an integral tool in criminal justice, has been declared to be "the most basic distinction between a free people and a tyranny."[17] At the arraignment, the accused is supposed to be informed of the charges against him and of his constitutional rights, although in practice, according to the Harvard survey, "the charge is read only on demand in most jurisdictions, a fact of which the unrepresented defendant is seldom aware."[18] Bail is also set during the arraignment.

The amount of time allowed to elapse between arrest and arraignment is a hotly debated issue today. Here, as in many spheres, federal courts tend to be more sensitive than state courts to the violation of what they conceive to be inalienable individual rights. In the *Mallory* case, for instance, three men were arrested on suspicion of rape; they were questioned and given lie detector tests. One of them confessed, and then, 7½ hours after he had been arrested, he was arraigned before a federal commissioner. The United States Supreme Court reversed Mallory's subsequent conviction on the ground that he

15 *Townley v. State.*
16 See Orfield, *Criminal Procedure from Arrest to Appeal;* Puttkammer, *Administration of Criminal Law.*
17 Frank, *Marble Palace,* p. 215.
18 "Metropolitan Criminal Courts of First Instance," p. 325.

should have been arraigned "without unnecessary delay," as provided for by the Federal Rules of Criminal Procedure, and that the confession was therefore obtained illegally.[19] The police responded by pointing out that an early arraignment would have meant that all suspects, including the two innocent ones, would have had to be burdened with a criminal proceeding and an arrest record. They cited an earlier federal court ruling that notes that:

> if the police are compelled to arraign all potential suspects before questioning . . . we shall have used the artificial niceties and superficial technicalities concerning our liberties to reduce genuine and important rites to absurdity. . . . Every citizen has a right to insist that the police make some pertinent and definitive inquiry *before* he may be arraigned in a criminal charge, which even if it is later abandoned inflicts on him a serious stigma.[20]

The police further noted that if he had been arraigned at once Mallory would have been discharged because of the inadequacy of evidence available at the time. At an arraignment, he would have been told that he need not talk and that he was entitled to legal counsel. Had he secured counsel—and the courts now insist that a defendant be provided with legal assistance at early stages in criminal proceedings[21]—he would immediately have been cautioned to tell the police nothing whatsoever. Under such circumstances, the case would likely have collapsed and a rapist would have been turned loose. Mallory, in fact, after he was freed by the Supreme Court, subsequently committed two offenses against females for which he was convicted in Pennsylvania.[22] The *Mallory* ruling has been adopted by only one state—Michigan—since its enunciation. Although most states have "prompt arraignment" laws, state judges widely tolerate incommunicado police interrogation lasting as long as three days.

The police maintain that they cannot function without some time for interrogation, both to capture guilty suspects and to clear innocent ones. O. W. Wilson, former police chief in Chicago, insisted that the police ought to be allowed to detain anyone for brief periods on "reasonable suspicion." Any "inconvenience" suffered by innocent persons, Wilson contended, "seems to be a small price to pay for the privilege of living securely and peacefully."[23] On the other hand, Justice Douglas of the Supreme Court believes that the police should not interrogate at large and should not attempt to make their cases through information supplied by the defendant.[24] Most policemen would regard this as a naive view; they insist that they could not

19 *Mallory v. United States.*
20 *Metoyer v. United States.*
21 *Escobedo v. Illinois; Miranda v. Arizona.*
22 Inbau, "Police Interrogation," p. 20.
23 *New York Times,* Feb. 19, 1960.
24 Douglas, *Right of the People,* p. 155.

operate with any efficiency if so handcuffed and that society would be inundated by criminal activity. However, Anglo-Saxon countries are almost unique among democracies in allowing interrogation of suspected persons by the police.[25] Critics of Anglo-Saxon jurisprudence maintain that it has persistently overrelied on confessions. The drafters of the 1872 India Evidence Act, for instance, put the problem succinctly: "It is far pleasanter to sit comfortably in the shade rubbing pepper into a poor devil's eyes than to go about in the sun hunting up evidence."[26] Under the Evidence Act, all Indian confessions are inadmissible unless made "in the immediate presence of a magistrate" who has first warned the accused that he need not speak and that anything he does say may be held against him.[27]

BAIL

The seventh amendment to the Constitution specifies that "excessive bail shall not be required," but "excessive" is, of course, a relative term, measured against the wealth and available resources of the accused. Virtually all offenders are admitted to bail, although they may not be able to raise the amount, with the general exception of persons accused of capital crimes where the proof is evident or the presumption of guilt is great.

Bail originated in the period of medieval dungeons when incarceration prior to trial could be tantamount to a death sentence because of epidemics of "gaol fever," a form of typhus, in the prisons. If the accused did not appear for trial, the person who had guaranteed his presence was often required to stand trial in his stead.[28] Today, the problem involving bail centers about the extra period of incarceration for the person of limited means. As James V. Bennett, former director of the Federal Bureau of Prisons, put it:

> When a poor man is arrested, he goes willy-nilly to the same institution, eats the same food, and suffers the same hardships as he who has been convicted. The well-to-do, the rich, and the influential, on the other hand, find it requires only money to stay out of jail, at least until the accused has had his day in court.[29]

If the accused is declared innocent, then the money he had to pay a bail bondsman for the loan of bail funds or the time he had to spend in jail represent punishment unrelated to his prior conduct. The burden of bail may be even more pronounced in the case of material witnesses, individuals who have evidence concerning an important element of a particular case, who may be held in jail if they cannot raise bond to assure their appearance in court. It is not rare

25 Coatman, *Police*, p. 127.
26 Stephen, *History of the Criminal Law of England.*
27 Basu, *India Evidence Act, 1872.*
28 Freed and Wald, *Bail in the United States.*
29 Quoted in *ibid.*, p. 43.

for a witness to spend weeks in jail while the accused is free on bail.

A study of bail in New York City, conducted by a research team from the University of Pennsylvania, provides evidence for the thesis that bail often causes unnecessary detention of accused persons. Almost 50 percent of the accused individuals could not obtain funds for bail, and in many instances the amount set seemed disproportionately high in terms of the relatively minor offenses involved. In such instances, the accused could not gain freedom to find witnesses and to prepare his case. High bail was often demanded by the courts to give the offender "a taste of jail" or to "protect society," a point of view condemned by the study team on the following grounds:

> It is fundamental that the state has no right to punish a person until his guilt has been established beyond a reasonable doubt. And there is no support in the law for the proposition that a person may be imprisoned because of the speculative possibility that he may commit a crime.[30]

The Universtiy of Pennsylvannia report recommends that courts devote more time to studying the financial and moral backgrounds of accused persons, thereby enabling them to fix bail at more equitable levels. It found that about 43 percent of the individuals unable to post bail were detained up to forty-nine days and 38 percent were held from fifty to ninty-nine days prior to trial.

It is only in the past few years that major reforms have been made in the traditional methods of assessing bail. That such changes have been established is largely a testament to the power of a pioneering action program that used sophisticated research. Beginning in 1961, the Vera Institute of Justice inaugurated a program under which brief interviews were held with accused persons soon after they were received in jail.[31] The interviews focused on the person's residential stability, employment history, family contacts in New York City, and his prior criminal record. After the information provided was verified by telephone calls, the defendant was given a score, based on the four factors. If he had accumulated sufficent points, it was recommended to the court that he be released on his "personal recognizance," that is, without the necessity of posting bail.

Between 1961 and 1964, Vera Institute workers interviewed more than 10,000 accused persons. Four thousand were recommended for immediate parole, and 2,195 of them were released on their personal recognizance. Of them, only fifteen failed to show up later in court, a default rate of less than seven-tenths of 1 percent. Over the years, the Institute's recommendation policy became increasingly liberal. At first, release was urged for only 28 percent of the defendants interviewed, but that figure gradually increased to 65 percent, with no marked change in the default rate.

30 Foote, "Compelling Appearance in Court." See also "A Study of the Administration of Bail in New York City."
31 Ares, Rankin, and Sturz, "Manhattan Bail Project."

To study the impact of their recommendations, the Institute research team set up an experimental-control research design, under which only half of the defendants believed by the project to be qualified for release were actually recommended for such disposition. No recommendation was made for persons falling into the control group. In the project's initial year, 59 percent of its recommendations were accepted by the court, while only 16 percent of the control group was released without bail. Subsequent analysis of the case histories of the defendants in both groups showed that 60 percent of the recommended parolees were either acquitted or had their cases dismissed, compared to only 23 percent of the control group. Moreover, of the 40 percent found guilty out of the parole group, only one out of six was sentenced to prison. In contrast, 96 percent of those convicted in the control group were sentenced to serve a jail term, which is testimony not only to the fundamental initial inequity of bail decision but to its strong tendency to affect the decision and disposition of a defendant's case.

The ground-breaking work of the Vera Institute quickly led at least 100 communities and more than half of the states to accept the Institute's model for reforms in bail procedures. Nonetheless, despite this progress, the President's Commission on Law Enforcement and Administration of Justice reports that much needs to be done to modernize bail systems:

> In many jurisdictions there has been no bail reform, and heavy reliance on money bail continues to be the rule. Even in those jurisdictions that have reformed their bail practices, including the Federal system [which enacted the Bail Reform Act of 1966], an excessive rate of pretrial detention frequently prevails. Thus in many places defendants who were formerly released on bail now are released on recognizance, while those formerly detained for want of bail continue to be detained. Improved fact-finding procedures have been instituted in some jurisdictions, but old habits persist, and high money bail continues to be set primarily on the basis of the offense charged.[32]

PRELIMINARY HEARINGS

Felony cases in most jurisdictions proceed from arraignment through the preliminary hearing. At this hearing, which takes place before a lower-court magistrate, the state is obliged to demonstrate that there is "probable cause" to hold the defendant for trial. The state usually reveals the least amount of its case consistent with establishing that enough suspicion exists to support further prosecution. The defendant may cross-examine state witnesses and can gain valuable insights or factual concessions if he is represented by able counsel. However, as the President's Commission on Law Enforcement points out, in many places testimony at the hearing is not recorded or otherwise

32 President's Commission, *Courts*, p. 39.

perpetuated, in some jurisdictions the defense does not have the right to subpoena witnesses, and quite often counsel is not appointed for the accused until after the preliminary hearing.[33]

The preliminary hearing also serves purposes other than those officially expressed. As Jerome H. Skolnick notes:

> Prosecutors and defense attorneys . . . all felt that in *most* cases the real purpose of having a preliminary hearing . . . was *not* to convince a judge there was sufficient evidence against the accused to warrant that he stand trial. That question has usually been settled to the satisfaction of both parties by the time the preliminary hearing is conducted. The prosecutor tends to find the preliminary hearing useful as an opportunity to observe how well the State's witnesses hold up under cross-examination. On the other side, the defense attorney frequently uses the preliminary hearing as a "fishing expedition." . . . in part the preliminary hearing allows him to seek actual flaws in the testimony of the State's witnesses. It also enables him to search for any statement by the witness under oath, in hope that it will later be contradicted by the same witness during the trial, thereby impeaching the validity of the witness's trial testimony.[34]

The routine finding of "probable cause" has been seen as one of the objections to preliminary hearings, since few prosecutors initiate proceedings unless they possess strong elements of a case. Unrepresented defendants often make highly damaging statements at preliminary hearings that they might otherwise avoid, and the time and expense involved in what is often nothing more than a preview of the state's case has been said to make the preliminary hearing an obsolete affair.

Considerable objection has also been raised against newspaper coverage of preliminary hearings, since almost invariably only one side of the issue is presented, and the public, reading the story the following day, seems inclined to regard a "probable cause" action equal to a finding of guilt. In the United States, six states—California, Idaho, Montana, Nevada, North Dakota, and Utah—allow the defendant to bar newspaper reporters from preliminary hearings.[35] The question of newspaper coverage of preliminary hearings is but one aspect of the vexing problem of "trial by newspaper," a meretricious process that pervades the entire system of criminal justice in the United States.[36] Recent reversals of criminal convictions by the United States Supreme Court because of inflammatory newspaper[37] and television[38] coverage may herald more aggressive action against mass-

33 *Ibid.*, p. 43.
34 Skolnick, *Justice Without Trial*, p. 29.
35 Geis, "Preliminary Hearings and the Press."
36 Sullivan, *Trial by Newspaper;* U.S. Senate, Subcommittee on Constitutional Rights, "Free Press and Fair Trial"; Friendly and Goldfarb, *Crime and Publicity.*
37 *Irvin v. Dowd.*
38 *Estes v. Texas.*

media statements that are likely to undermine the right to a fair trial. In the past, American courts have been extremely reluctant to use contempt powers, which are employed with striking severity in England,[39] against institutions as powerful and, on occasion, as ruthless as the press.

GRAND JURY

The Fifth Amendment demands that "no person shall be held to answer for a capital or otherwise infamous charge unless on a present-ment or indictment of a grand jury," but in most jurisdictions there has been a tendency during recent times to by-pass the grand jury in criminal proceedings. In California, for instance, only about 10 percent of the murder cases and 3 percent of other felony cases pro-ceed through the grand jury.[40]

Grand juries were intended to allow the defendant to avoid a public accusation and the trouble and expense of a public trial before establishing the likelihood of his having committed the crime. They were also intended to prevent hasty, oppressive, and malicious pros-ecutions. Grand juries are selected in most jurisdictions by the judges, and they often have more than the twelve members who traditionally make up a "petit" or trial jury. The grand jury may initiate prosecu-tions on its own behalf by the filing of presentments, or it may return indictments in cases called to its attention by the prosecuting attorney. In such instances it returns either a "true bill," indicating probable cause to proceed to trial, or a "no bill" finding, indicating the absence of such cause. In virtually all instances, however, the grand jury merely rubber-stamps the desires of the prosecutor. A grand jury hearing, conducted in secret and outside the presence of the accused, may follow a preliminary hearing or may be conducted without a prelim-inary hearing having taken place.

Grand juries are particularly useful in uncovering criminal actions by public officials, such as police officers or prosecuting attorneys, which might not otherwise have been discerned or acted upon. Some-times, however, grand juries have used their office to harass individuals. It was such harassment that led the British to abolish the grand jury during World War I when indictments were returned indiscriminately against alleged German sympathizers. Restored after the war, the grand jury was again abolished in Britain in 1933. It has also been eliminated in twenty-eight American states.

CRIMINAL TRIALS

Parodied, exaggerated, misrepresented, and glamorized by the mass media, criminal trials represent in the public mind the intense

39 See *Baltimore Radio Show, Inc. v. State*, pp. 921–936.
40 "Some Aspects of the California Grand Jury System," p. 644; Miller and Dawson, "Non-Use of Preliminary Examination."

jousting of a clever defense attorney who is attempting to overcome, in the vein of Perry Mason, the sincere but misguided efforts of the state. Elements of this undoubtedly exist in some criminal trials, blended with a number of other items that taken together may lead to the conclusion that "the administration of justice is no more designed to elicit truth than the scientific approach is designed to extract justice from the atom."[41]

Critics claim that a criminal trial is a "sublimated brawl."[42] They attack the element of surprise in criminal trials and the use of snares and traps to ambush either the accused or the prosecution. Adversary attorneys are said to alter what is presumed to be a search for truth into a form of combat. Trials are sometimes said to be settled only "according to the preponderance of perjury."[43] On the other hand, criminal trials have been defended in pragmatic terms, that is, on the ground that they do get at the truth, however intricate and wayward their path toward it may be. Such trials are also defended on the ground that they represent the best balancing of the myriad and contradictory demands of procedural precision and fairness yet devised; what may seem awkward and peripheral may actually represent a compromise that emerged as the result of historical examples of how certain procedures might, under certain conditions, be exploited to harm both the innocent citizen and the society-at-large.

Although trials supply the public lode of eye-catching material on criminal matters, they constitute, as we have seen, a relatively unimportant aspect of the total picture of criminal procedure. In the following pages, we shall examine trials in terms of some of the participants and some of the major issues.

PROSECUTING ATTORNEYS

Prosecutors are the most powerful figures in the total picture of the administration of criminal justice, primarily because of the wide range of virtually unchecked discretion that inheres in their office. They have broad powers concerning the charge to be placed against the accused, the method in which the case is to be handled, and, most important, whether or not they will proceed with the allegation.[44]

The quality of prosecutors varies remarkably throughout the country. Justice Douglas of the Supreme Court has charged that in recent decades "the quality of prosecutors has markedly declined" and that they "sometimes treat the courtroom not as a place of dignity, detached from the community, but as a place to unleash the fury of public passion."[45] Rural prosecutors often tend to be recent law-school graduates, trying to eke out a meager living until they embark

41 Curtis, *It's Your Law,* p. 21.
42 Frank, *Courts on Trial,* p. 7.
43 Dressler, "Trial by Combat in American Courts."
44 Blumberg, *Criminal Justice,* p. 58.
45 Douglas, "A Challenge to the Bar."

on a private practice, or they are superannuated attorneys who are no longer able to carry on full-time legal practices.[46] On the other hand, prosecutors in large cities and counties are often specialists who are skillful in all aspects of criminal practice.

Possibly one of the most vitriolic comments on the office of prosecutor is that by John Mason Brown which stresses the tendency to develop highly partisan attitudes and procedures designed not to separate the guilty from the innocent but to gain a mounting total of convictions at all costs:

> The prosecutor's by obligation is a special mind, mongoose quick, bullying, devious, unrelenting, forever baited to ensnare. It is almost duty bound to mislead, and by instinct dotes on confusing and flourishes on weakness. Its search is for blemishes it can present as scars, its obligation to raise doubts or sour with suspicion. It asks questions not to learn but to convict, and can read guilt into the most innocent answers. Its hope, its aim, its triumph is to addle a witness into confession by tricking, exhausting, or irritating him into a verbal indiscretion which sounds like a damaging admission. To natural lapses of memory it gives the appearance either of stratagems for hiding misdeeds or, worse still, of lies, dark and deliberate. Feigned and wheedling politeness, sarcasm that scalds, intimidation, surprise and besmirchment by innuendo, association, or suggestion, at the same time that any intention to besmirch is denied —all these as methods and devices are such staples in the prosecutor's repertoire that his mind turns to them by rote.[47]

Some substantiation for Brown's description can be gathered from a book for attorneys called *How to Win Lawsuits Before Juries* Note, for instance, this advice under the general heading of "How to Humiliate and Subdue a Recalcitrant Witness":

> When you have forced the witness into giving you a direct answer to your question you really have him under control; he is off-balance, and usually rather scared. This advantage should be followed up with a few simple questions such as, "You did not want to answer that question, did you?" If the witness says that he wanted to answer it, ask him in a resounding voice, "Well, why did you not answer it when I first asked you?" Whatever his answer is you then ask him, "Did you think that you were smart enough to evade answering the question?" Again, whatever the answer is you ask him, "Well, I would like for the jurors to know what you have behind all this dodging and ducking you have done!" . . . This battering and legal-style "kicking the witness around" not only humiliates but subdues him.[48]

It is undoubtedly the harsh, partisan nature of the prosecuting attorney's actions that strikes most offenders as antithetical to their interests, be they guilty or innocent. Perhaps if more defendants could

46 Geis and Costner, "Oklahoma's County Attorneys."
47 Brown, *Through These Men*, p. 259.
48 Lake, *How to Win Lawsuits Before Juries*, pp. 164–165.

be convinced that a prosecutor is selflessly seeking the truth without blindly pursuing a path toward conviction, rehabilitation of offenders would be aided, although this remains a moot question. In England, there has been particular success in a process under which the same attorneys are called upon both to prosecute and to defend criminals. Former Lord Justice Devlin maintains that "a barrister who appears as often for the defense as for the prosecution acquires no special sympathy for either."[49]

DEFENSE ATTORNEYS

It is axiomatic among individuals accused of crimes that the better the lawyer they manage to acquire, the more likely their chance of gaining freedom. To the extent that the quality of a defense attorney overrides questions of guilt or innocence, then the system of criminal justice becomes that much more quixotic and, presumably, less likely to operate in a rational manner in deterring criminal behavior. Criminal law has always been something of a stepchild of legal practice, and lawyers who specialize in the defense of criminals seem more often than their colleagues in corporation and similar branches of law to engage in chicanery and unethical practices. Those lawyers who defend organized criminals for large sums and who sometimes are paid retainers by criminal gangs are hired because of their ability to avoid the penalties demanded by the law for acts their clients routinely commit. As one writer, a lawyer, expresses the matter, "The success of criminal lawyers . . . is not based upon a deep knowledge of the law, but rests upon an ability to size up quickly what might be called the human nature of witnesses and prospective jurors with an uncanny skill of throwing 'monkey wrenches' into the judicial machinery."[50] The agility of an adept defense attorney is illustrated by an anecdote from the career of one of the most renowned attorneys, Edward Carson. With his thick Irish brogue, he asked a hostile witness: "Are you a drinking man?" "That's my business," the witness haughtily replied. "And have you any other?" Carson roared. According to reports, the jury laughed uproariously, the witness was demolished, and the defendant was acquitted.[51]

Indigent offenders must be supplied with attorneys for serious crimes,[52] based on the Sixth Amendment guarantee that "in all criminal cases the accused shall enjoy the right to the assistance of counsel for his defense." There are three types of counsel generally provided to persons unable to afford a defense attorney of their choice: (1) Public defenders, who are usually appointed or elected, and who work on fixed salaries, (2) Court-appointed attorneys, who are most

49 Devlin, *Criminal Prosecution in England,* p. 26.
50 Mullen, *Let Justice Be Done,* p. 37.
51 Stryker, *Art of Advocacy,* p. 93.
52 *Gideon v. Wainwright;* Lewis, *Gideon's Trumpet.*

often selected from among the newest members of the Bar, and (3) Legal Aid Society attorneys, who are usually volunteer lawyers who donate a portion of their time and services to this Society, which is supported by voluntary contributions.

The public-defender system began in Los Angeles County in 1913 and has been gradually spreading throughout the country, although, despite bills introduced in Congress, it has not yet reached the federal courts.[53] The fact that public defenders are specialists operating with adequate budgetary resources is seen as their particular strength. Several public defenders have testified that they can get a lighter sentence for a client more often than a private attorney might:

> The public defender is able to accomplish more because of the cordial relationship that has been built up over a considerable period of time [with the prosecutor], and his familiarity with criminal proceedings . . . sometimes I think a judge gets sorry for the poor P.D.—stuck with a lot of bum cases and so begins giving some of them lenient treatment.[54]

Criticism of the office of public defender has been leveled on a number of grounds. Judge Edward J. Dimock of New York has maintained that "defense of those charged with crime is the last field we should permit the state to enter" and that "once the state has acquired power over the defense of those it has accused the power of the state would be absolute indeed." Dimock itemizes the following objections to public defenders: (1) They tend to encourage too many defendants to plead guilty rather than submit their cases to a jury, (2) Being on the public payroll, public defenders are not always "intensely partisan," (3) If the public defender gets a better break for his clients, the system is unfair to those who hire private counsel, and (4) The process of electing or appointing a public defender is unlikely to produce or to continue in office any official who works sincerely for acquittals.[55]

The practice of appointing attorneys, however, has disadvantages of its own. Some lawyers tend to be overloaded and cannot give adequate attention to those cases assigned to them. In addition, as Wiley Rutledge, a former Supreme Court judge, points out, "Serious criminal cases are not proper subject matter for legal apprentices, however capable or hardworking."[56] The difficulty with Legal Aid Societies is that, more often than not, they suffer from chronic financial malnutrition that detracts from their work.

Regardless of the method used to provide adequate defense for a person accused of a crime, the importance of the process needs to

53 Havighurst, "Representation of Indigent Criminal Defendants in the Federal District Courts."

54 Quoted in Meyer, *Public Defenders*, p. 17.

55 Dimock, "Public Defender: Step Toward a Police State?"

56 Quoted in Rogers, "Plea for the Public Defender," p. 26.

be stressed. A former Attorney General, in supporting extended use of public defenders, indicates the significance of the problem in terms of rehabilitation of criminals:

> [T]he correctional process for a prisoner cannot begin to operate until the bitterness engendered in him by the legal process has been overcome. The poor and helpless person who rightly believes he was not adequately defended leaves the courtroom with a heart full of hate.[57]

JURIES

The operation of juries in criminal proceedings, like other aspects of the system discussed previously, has been subjected to intense ridicule and defended with equal vehemence by those partial to their alleged assets. Juries succeeded the early processes of Trial by Battle and Trial by Ordeal. The former combined, in the words of one scholar, "the attractions of a prize fight with those of a religious ceremony." In a pitched conflict between the accused and his accuser, it was presumed that the innocent person would win out through divine favor. Trial by Ordeal has been described in the following wry terms:

> It was popular among prosecutors because it eliminated the unpleasant chances of battle. The accused person, being bound hand and foot, was thrown into a pond. If he "swam," as it was expressed, he was taken out and dealt with as guilty. If he sank and drowned, his innocence was manifest and he was buried with all decency and respect. . . . A not unreasonable dissatisfaction was felt among the criminal classes which at that time constituted the bulk of the population.[58]

Opponents of jury trials stress that the average citizen cannot intelligently follow details of a complicated criminal action and that he will judge more often in terms of emotion than of intellect and the intrinsic merits of the case. Lawyers, knowing the importance of the predilections of jurors, will joust endlessly to secure panels presumed to be favorable to their client. In an Illinois case, for instance, it took 22½ weeks and a total of 8,866 prospective jurors before opposing attorneys could agree on twelve individuals. Critics have branded the jury system with such violent labels as "the great obstructing incubus of the administration of criminal law," calling it "as preposterous and out of date as the sun dial of James I or the coach of Charles II" and a "paralyzing yoke."[59]

Defenders of juries generally rely on the good sense and sound judgment of representative groups of citizens as the basis for their support. It is believed that such citizens often render more representative justice than that demanded by the rigid criminal codes or the

---

57 *Ibid.*, p. 58.
58 Quoted in Heller, *Sixth Amendment*, p. 4.
59 Barnes, "Let's Reform Our Jury System"; Newman, "Trial by Jury: An Outmoded Relic?"

partisan representations of either defense or prosecuting attorneys. These and other items are found in Carolyn Simon's panegyric for the jury system:

> Long training in the law, long experience before the bench and administrative tribunals, long dealings with experts, convince many lawyers that juries—"twelve good men and true"—are the best and fairest safeguard we have to insure justice for all concerned. It seems an undue burden to trust one man, be he judge or other specialist. Most of us would rather place our fates in the hands of ordinary people like ourselves. There is an extra-legal benefit too . . . the involvement of the citizen in the judicial process is a vital part of our democratic system.[60]

Comparatively little experimental evidence is available to show how juries actually operate. Part of this informational gap springs from the element of secrecy and sacredness traditionally surrounding jury deliberations. An attempt by a research team from the University of Chicago to "bug" a jury room in Wichita, which was undertaken with permission of the opposing attorneys and the trial judge, led to federal legislation outlawing any future endeavors of such a nature. The Chicago group then proceeded to record a mock trial and to determine how jurors reacted to it. Findings indicated "the extraordinary complexity of the individual jury trial and the countless number of variables that might have influenced the result in one case." In virtually all cases of a jury split on the first ballot, the decision ultimately swung toward the majority view. Blue-ribbon juries—specially selected for intelligence and ability—were shown, as lawyers suspected they might, to be convicting juries. In addition, juries awarded more money to a plaintiff when they were told that the defendant had insurance, but were warned to ignore such information, than when they were not told about the insurance, or were told about it but were not asked specifically to ignore the matter.[61] This last finding bore out long-standing beliefs held by jurists. Jerome Frank compares asking a jury to disregard a remark in court to the story of the young boy who is told to stand in the corner and "not to think of a white elephant."[62]

Many suggestions have been put forward regarding possible reforms in the jury system. Perhaps the most prominent concern reduction of the number of jurors from the traditional dozen and change in the requirement that the jury speak with "one voice," that is, that its verdict be unanimous. In 1967, England began to accept 10 to 2 verdicts in criminal trials, partly, it was said, in the attempt to curb jury bribery and intimidation. English juries are required to spend at least two hours in an effort to achieve unanimity, and they are required to spend even more time in cases judged to be highly com-

60 Simon, "Case for Trial by Jury."
61 Kalven, "Report on the Jury Project."
62 Frank and Frank, *Not Guilty*, p. 113.

plex. There is no announcement of the line-up of votes if the
defendant is found not guilty, because doing so would represent a
"second-class acquittal." In convictions, however, the precise jury
count is made part of the public record.

Several American states have long had requirements in misdemeanor cases similar to those recently inaugurated in England for
all criminal trials. Idaho requires only a five-sixths majority for a
binding verdict in misdemeanant trials, Montana, a two-thirds verdict,
and Oklahoma a three-fourths verdict.[63] Many foreign countries have
gone further and have abandoned the jury system altogether. Israel,
which adopted much of its legal framework from Britain, does not
include the requirement of trial by jury. In Germany, the English-style
jury system was abolished by the Weimar Republic because of a
belief that it resulted in too many convictions; it was believed that
the people left on their own, "proved to be more severe, illiberal, and
prejudiced than the jurists." Weimar juries are now selected at random
from lists of persons of standing in the community. They number not
twelve members, but vary between two, three, or six, depending upon
the offense. Jurors sit on the bench with judges and reach their verdict
after discussions with the judges. A majority decision suffices and
the judge-jury panel must indicate the specific reasons for its verdict.[64]

The Police-Court Controversy

During recent years, the operation of the criminal courts has been
fiercely attacked by persons who insist that appellate court decisions
have made enforcement of the criminal law an excruciatingly difficult
task for the police and prosecutors. The contrary argument is that the
courts have moved to align more carefully the requirements of the
Constitution, which are fundamental underpinnings of our democracy,
with the actual methods by which criminals may be apprehended and
convicted. Debate has focused on two areas—the exclusionary rule
and wiretapping—which we shall examine more closely.

THE EXCLUSIONARY RULE

Exclusionary rules provide that evidence obtained through searches
and seizures in violation of the Fourth Amendment[65] shall not be
admitted in court against the accused. The federal government
adopted the exclusionary rule in 1914 in the *Weeks* case, noting that

63 Kalven, Jr., *American Jury.*
64 Bedford, *Faces of Justice*, pp. 141–144.
65 "The right of the people to be secure in their persons, houses, papers and effects
against unreasonable searches and seizures shall not be violated, and no warrants shall issue but upon probable cause, supported by oath or affirmation and
particularly describing the place to be searched and the persons or things to be
seized."

the police and the courts should not be aided "by the sacrifice of those great principles established by years of endeavor and suffering which have resulted in their embodiment in the fundamental law of the land."[66] This use of the exclusionary rule applied only to federal cases. The Supreme Court, however, on occasion reversed convictions by state courts if it decided that they had been obtained under conditions that violated the "sense of justice" of the people and the higher tribunal. There were reversals in cases involving protracted questioning of dull suspects, flagrant brutality, and holding suspects incommunicado. Typical of such reversals was that in the *Rochin* case, where the police unlawfully entered the defendant's home and, after he had allegedly swallowed evidence, took him to the hospital and pumped his stomach. Justice Frankfurter put the court's view of the matter in the following words:

> [w]e are compelled to conclude that the proceedings by which this conviction was obtained do more than offend some fastidious squeamishness or private sentimentalism about combatting crime too energetically. This is conduct that shocks the conscience. Illegally breaking into the privacy of the petitioner, the struggle to open his mouth and remove what was there, the forcible extraction of the stomach's contents—this course of proceeding by agents of the government . . . constitutes methods too close to the rack and screw to permit of constitutional differentiation.[67]

The states were specifically exempted from the exclusionary rule, however, by the *Wolf* decision, handed down by the Supreme Court in 1949. The Court noted at that time that fewer than one-third of the states had exclusionary rules and it felt that it could not lightly "brush aside [the] experience" of the remainder which had decided to do without such rules.[68] During the intervening years, however, a considerable number of states adopted exclusionary rules, either by judicial fiat or by legislative enactments. Most notably, California's Supreme Court imposed an exclusionary rule on its trial courts after concluding that "other remedies have completely failed to secure compliance [by the police] with the constitutional provisions." Operating without an exclusionary rule, the California courts "had been required to participate in and, in effect, condone the lawless activities of law enforcement officials."[69]

The issue returned to the Supreme Court in 1961 when the residence of an Ohio woman, Dolly Mapp, was forcibly entered. Asked to produce a search warrant, an officer held up a piece of paper, which the woman grabbed. During an ensuing struggle, the officer retrieved the "warrant," manhandling the accused in the process by "grabbing her" and "twisting her hand." Searching the house, the officers dis-

66 *Weeks v. United States,* p. 393.
67 *Rochin v. California,* p. 132; Westin, "Bookies and 'Bugs' in California."
68 *Wolf v. Colorado.*
69 *People v. Cahan.*

covered obscene material, although they said they had been looking for gambling slips and a person suspected of a bombing offense. The "warrant" was never produced at the trial. Because Ohio did not have an exclusionary rule, the defendant was convicted of possessing obscene material. In reversing the conviction, the United States Supreme Court also reversed *Wolf*, now declaring that "all evidence obtained by searches and seizures in violation of the Constitution is, by that same authority, inadmissible in a state court."[70]

Ethical justification of the exclusionary rule is not a matter of empirical research. It is scientifically relevant, however, to determine whether the exclusionary rule does, as the courts appear to believe it does, compel respect for constitutional guarantees by removing the incentive to disregard them. Tentative information points up that court decisions may at times obscure as much information as they highlight, because they deal only with those matters formally brought to the judges' attention. Field surveys of police operations indicate, for instance, that exclusionary rules may, rather than developing police sensitivity to constitutional rights, merely channel police activity into other forms of enforcement.[71] Gamblers may be harassed (the police term is "rousted") and their equipment destroyed. Prostitutes may routinely be brought into the police station and then turned loose after a night in jail. Such activities do not come to the attention of the courts because there is no prosecution and because the victims are in no position to protest. Stuart Nagel indicates that following *Mapp* both those states that previously had exclusionary rules and those now obligated to adopt them tightened up their procedures on search and seizure. His examination of crime rates indicates that both sets of states had essentially similar crime increases, indicating tentatively—because the available material is extremely difficult to analyze with precision—that the rule may not have had any particular impact on crime.[72] Another writer suggests that the exclusionary rule, by increasing police respect for the law of search and seizure, may increase public respect for law in general and thereby decrease criminality.[73] Such a view, however, requires substantiation before it can be directly relevant for the formation of intelligent public policy.

The *Mapp* decision was followed by a number of Court decisions that insisted on closer conformity with what the judiciary saw as the basic requirements of the Constitution. In 1964, in the *Escobedo* case, the Court reversed the conviction of a defendant on the ground that he had not been permitted to see his attorney, although he had so requested and the attorney was at the police station at the time.[74] Inherent in the Court's decision was the belief that the American sys-

70 *Mapp v. Ohio.*
71 Barrett, "Personal Rights, Property Rights and the Fourth Amendment."
72 Nagel, "Testing the Effects of Excluding Illegally Seized Evidence."
73 Kamisar, "On the Tactics of Police-Prosecution Oriented Critics of the Courts."
74 *Escobedo v. Illinois.*

tem of justice should proceed on the principle of accusation and not on that of inquisition, and that guilt should be proved by evidence independent of that derived from the defendant's own words.

Two years later, the *Miranda* decision ruled that a suspect must be informed before interrogation of his rights to remain silent and to have the services of an attorney.[75] The *Miranda* decision led to pained reactions from law-enforcement officials, who maintained that it would make the control of crime very much more difficult. Studies following *Miranda* have attempted to determine if this belief is true. To date, it is suggested, among other things, that earlier ideas about the importance of confessions in police work were exaggerations. Judge Irving Kaufman reports that only 86 out of 1,000 cases in New York City in 1966 were resolved by confessions, with the remainder going forward on independent evidence of the accused's involvement.[76] There were also unexpected reports that the warning itself might not exert inhibiting influence on certain kinds of offenders; a report from Detroit noted that in the first nine months following adoption of the *Miranda* rules, confessions were obtained in 56 percent of all homicide cases, compared with 53 percent four years earlier.[77]

Other studies suggest that the *Miranda* regulations are paid only minimum heed by police officers. Researchers from the Institute of Criminal Law and Procedure at Georgetown University found from interviews with 260 defendants that 29 percent alleged that they had not been warned at all and that 62 percent said that they had not been fully warned of their rights. Interrogations following enunciation of the *Miranda* rules were said to have dropped only slightly—from 55 percent of the cases to 48 percent.[78] In a similar study, Reiss and Black, after observation of 831 cases, reported that only a small fraction of the suspects were warned of their constitutional rights and also that 14 percent of the suspects admitted their guilt to policemen before any formal interrogation was begun.[79]

WIRETAPPING

Wiretapping is an expedient, valuable method of dealing with forms of crime that are by their nature secretive, such as espionage and gambling. Wiretapping also contains potentialities for the invasion of the privacy of citizens and for the surveillance of unpopular rather than criminal individuals. Cross-cultural surveys show that wiretapping is practiced with considerable impunity in most foreign countries.[80] In England in 1957, newspapers learned of wiretapping by the

75 *Miranda v. Arizona.*
76 Kaufman, "Miranda and the Police," p. 47.
77 *Ibid.*, p. 50.
78 Medalie, "Custodial Police Interrogation in Our Nation's Capitol."
79 Reiss, Jr. and Black, "Interrogation and the Criminal Process."
80 U.S. Senate, *Wiretapping, Eavesdropping, and the Bill of Rights*, pp. 137–187; Dobry, "Wire-tapping and Eavesdropping."

British government when disbarment proceedings were brought against a lawyer who had been overheard giving illegal advice to a client. Press reports noted that "most Englishmen have regarded wiretapping as a foreign device associated mainly with the Federal Bureau of Investigation and Congressional investigation committees in the United States and with the Soviet secret police."[81] A Parliamentary review committee granted that the action taken against the lawyer represented a "mistaken decision," but insisted that the government had both a right and an obligation to wiretap, saying that, "Wiretapping is a legitimate function of Government authority provided certain safeguards exist and provided the information obtained by wiretapping is not disclosed to non-official sources."[82]

The history of wiretapping in the United States illustrates the delicate problems involved in balancing the rights of the individual against efficient criminal prosecution.[83] Congress outlawed wiretapping during World War I, not to protect citizens, but to keep spies from intruding on government communications. In the 1920s federal police employed wiretapping extensively to combat bootleggers. The first wiretapping case to be adjudicated by the Supreme Court—*Olmstead v. U. S.* in 1928—was decided by a 5 to 4 vote. The Court took the position that wiretapping was not in conflict with the search and seizure provisions of the Fourth Amendment, since it did not deal with "tangible material facts" and did not involve "actual physical invasion." In a famous dissenting opinion, Justice Oliver Wendell Holmes tagged wiretapping with a label that it has never been able to shake; it is, Justice Holmes said, "a dirty business."[84]

A section buried obscurely in the Federal Communications Act of 1934 put a temporary end to the use of wiretapping in federal courts. Section 605 of the Act was interpreted by the courts to mean that, while wiretapping was legal, any information gained directly or indirectly from it would not be permitted in federal courts.[85] In June, 1968, however, as part of the Omnibus Crime Control Act, Congress authorized the use by federal and state police of wiretaps, if previous permission had been obtained from a judge. A forty-eight hour exception to the need for court permission was authorized for "emergency" cases concerned with national security or organized crime. The law required that persons who were subjected to wiretaps had to be notified within ninety days after the tap was terminated, although such notification could be delayed for "good cause." President Johnson signed the measure with strong reservations. "If we are not very careful," he maintained, "these legislative provisions could result in producing a nation of snoopers bending to the keyholes of the homes

81 *New York Times*, June 8, 1957.
82 Great Britain, *Interception of Communications.*
83 Tompkins, *Wire Tapping.*
84 *Olmstead v. United States*, p. 470.
85 *Nardone v. United States.*

and offices in America, spying on our neighbors."[86] The law was used only sparingly until 1969, when Attorney General Mitchell put it into much wider play as part of the Nixon administration's campaign to bring "law and order" to the country. The stepped-up procedures ran into almost immediate difficulty, however, when the Supreme Court ruled that persons tried on the basis of wiretap evidence must be given full access to transcripts of all the taps in which they had been involved. The Attorney General, fighting the ruling, noted that it provided an offender with an easy immunity; all he had to do was call several espionage agents or notorious organized criminals and identify himself clearly. Later, the Government could be very well obligated to drop the case against him rather than turn over indiscriminately the full wiretap files on cases still in the process of development or too delicate for public disclosure.

The debate regarding wiretapping highlights dilemmas of criminal prosecution. A former police chief of Los Angeles maintains, for instance, that "adequate intelligence of underworld activities is the police administrator's most potent weapon against organized crime." Decisions that would be banned from courtroom use, he felt, would give the illegal criminal a greater benefit than the illegal police officer, a situation that he conceived to be socially self-defeating. He said further that law enforcement is "not a game of 'cops and robbers'" and the public "should not tie police hands." He also believed that the police are not likely to become an instrument of tyranny since they are under stringent public control, nor do they have any reason to intrude on the privacy of innocent, law-abiding citizens. He defended wiretapping with the following arguments:

> When wiretapping cannot be carried on, the most effective method of suppressing crime and ferreting out criminal activities is to keep the men known to be engaged in these activities under close surveillance. This is not only more costly than any police department can afford, but in the vast majority of cases it is impossible. The most effective substitutes for constant and close surveillance are to have an undercover agent inside the organizations, which is extremely difficult to achieve and very hazardous, or to have some means of overhearing what is said, whether by listening at transoms, outside windows, down a ventilator shaft or by dictograph.[87]

The heart of the chief's polemic for wiretapping appears in the following statement: "If society chooses, for reasons of its own, to handicap itself so severely that it cannot or will not deal effectively with the criminal army, it is doubtful that free society as we now enjoy it will continue."[88]

One counterargument on wiretapping has been presented by

86 *New York Times*, June 20, 1968.
87 Parker, "Surveillance by Wiretap or Dictograph," p. 734.
88 *Ibid.*, p. 728.

Richard Donnelly, a Yale Law School professor, who believes that wiretapping either should be completely outlawed or should be tolerated under only the most rigidly controlled conditions that impose effective sanctions against persons who violate the laws against restricted wiretapping. Donnelly believes that all taps that invade the privacy of the individual and that are exploratory dragnets rather than specific attempts to obtain evidence concerning known offenses should be prohibited. He flays wiretapping as a form of expedient morality and asks why, if wiretapping is to be permitted, we do not open up for surveillance the religious confessional and the public mails. He asks if we desire doctors to be forced to disclose patients' confidences if they pertain to criminal offenses, and whether we want to sanction third-degree methods if it is believed that they will clear up a particular case. Contrary to the view that a society that will not protect itself by certain methods may cease to be free, Donnelly submits the observation that a society "which countenances [such] practices ceases to be free."[89]

Summary

It must be noted initially that neither the police nor the courts will ever remotely approach success in apprehending and convicting all law violators. The question then arises as to how much leeway and discretion should be granted to both law-enforcement and adjudicative agencies and how much leakage—or loss of guilty suspects—the system can tolerate in its aim to protect the innocent person and the society. We have seen how intensely controversial this question can be. Although it is true that the accused receives the benefit of numerous doubts in criminal procedures, this situation should not be overstressed. As Jerome Frank notes, unlike the governments of all other civilized nations, we do not advise the accused before trial of the evidence that the state intends to use against him.[90] Also, American criminal prosecutions, unlike those of all Continental countries except England, do not allow the accused's attorney to have the last word to the jury.[91] In addition, the very fact that he is in court tends to raise an initial presumption of guilt against the defendant, and the state usually possesses far greater resources and manpower with which to press its suit than those available to the defendant.

There are persuasive considerations for stress on procedural guarantees despite the loss of convictions. The 462 words in the American Bill of Rights have often been said to be the major difference between a democracy and a totalitarian regime. Henry Commager notes that "it is becoming increasingly clear that it is respect for the dignity of

89 Donnelly, "Comments and Caveats in the Wire Tapping Controversy," p. 806.
90 Frank and Frank, Not Guilty.
91 Kunkel and Geis, "Order of Final Argument in Minnesota Criminal Trials."

the individual that most sharply differentiates democratic from totalitarian systems" and that "any conduct of the state that impairs the dignity of man is dangerous."[92] Benjamin Cardozo writes:

> The great ideals of liberty and equality are preserved against the assaults of opportunism, the expediency of the passing hour, the erosion of small encroachments, the scorn and derision of those who have no patience with general principles, by enshrining them in constitutions, and consecrating to the task of their protection a body of defenders. By conscious or subconscious influence, the presence of this restraining power, aloof in the background, but none the less always in reserve, tends . . . to hold the standard aloft and visible for those who must run the race and keep the faith.[93]

Perhaps the most carefully modulated statement on this subject was that made almost ninety years ago by Sir James Fitzjames Stephen in his classic history of the English criminal law:

> If it be asked why an accused person is presumed to be innocent, I think the true answer is, not that the presumption is probably true, but that society in the present day is so much stronger than the individual, and is capable of inflicting so very much more harm on the individual than the individual as a rule can inflict upon society, that it can afford to be generous. It is, however, a question of degree, varying according to the time and place, how far this generosity can or ought to be carried.[94]

For Further Reading

BLUMBERG, ABRAHAM S. *Criminal Justice*. Chicago: Quadrangle Books, 1967.
Professor Blumberg, a member of the faculty at John Jay College of the City University of New York, argues that the needs of bureaucratic management have led to the inauguration of a system of "justice by negotiation." Blumberg suggests that recent appellate court decisions, rather than enhancing the position of the defendant, may serve to weaken it. He depicts lawyers as "agent-mediators" rather than as antagonistic adversaries, and probation officers as practitioners of an art of disparagement in regard to their clients.

"Metropolitan Criminal Courts of First Instance," in *Harvard Law Review*, Vol. 70, December 1956, pp. 320–349.
Third-year students at the Harvard Law School conducted personal research into the operations of the inferior courts (i.e., the lowest courts on the judicial hierarchy), through interviews with private attorneys, prosecutors, judges, probation officers, newspapermen, and similar individuals. Observations were made of courts in Cambridge, Boston,

---

92 Commager, *Freedom, Loyalty, Dissent*, p. 5.
93 Cardozo, *Nature of the Judicial Process*, p. 92.
94 Stephen, *History of the Criminal Law of England*, Vol. I, p. 354. See also Goldstein, "The State and the Accused."

New York City, Rochester, N.Y., Camden, N.J., Philadelphia, Chicago, Los Angeles, Pensacola, Birmingham, Mobile, and New Orleans.

NEWMAN, DONALD J. *Conviction: The Determination of Guilt or Innocence Without Trial.* Boston: Little, Brown and Co., 1966.

A sociologist who pioneered in the study of guilty pleas, Professor Newman brings to bear large amounts of information accumulated by field surveys that were conducted under the auspices of the American Bar Foundation's Survey of the Administration of Criminal Justice in the United States. The volume is one of a series; others in print are: La Fave, Wayne R. *Arrest: The Decision to Take a Suspect into Custody*, 1965; and Tiffany, Lawrence P., Donald M. McIntyre, Jr., and Daniel L. Rotenberg. *Detection of Crime: Stopping and Questioning, Search and Seizure, Encouragement, and Entrapment*, 1967.

ORFIELD, LESTER. *Criminal Procedure from Arrest to Appeal.* New York: New York University Press, 1947.

Reciting their historical background and contemporary state in different jurisdictions, Professor Orfield presents an elaborate investigation of the various stages of criminal procedure. Unfortunately, some of the material is now out of date, but the volume nonetheless remains a basic starting point for surveys of the process of criminal adjudication.

PRESIDENT'S COMMISSION ON LAW ENFORCEMENT AND ADMINISTRATION OF JUSTICE. *Task Force Report; The Courts.* Washington, D.C.: Government Printing Office, 1967.

The courts, the Task Force notes, "are the pivot on which criminal justice turns." It goes on to suggest that "maintaining a proper balance between effectiveness and fairness has always been a challenge to the courts," and that "in a time of increasing social unrest, and increasing public sensitivity to both, it is a particularly difficult challenge." Perhaps the Task Force Report's most valuable contribution is its concentration on two important nontrial aspects of the process of criminal justice: the prosecutor's decision regarding whether and what to charge and the negotiated guilty plea.

17

Punishment of Criminals

The History of Punishment

It is difficult to reconstruct, after the fact, the motivations that led past cultures to inaugurate various policies toward those persons who deviated from their norms. But it is important to realize that many of those policies have tended to survive long after the reason they were formulated is proven erroneous or unacceptable. Sociologists are fond of pointing to handshaking, toasting, and similar practices, instituted for diverse out-of-date reasons, which persist today, often because social lethargy and inertia keep them alive.

Punishment appears to have its roots in early attempts to placate deities who were thought to be offended by acts contrary to their divine ideas of proper human behavior, and who were believed likely to take revenge. To assuage these gods, the transgressor was sacrificed to them. Combined with this notion, and eventually outliving it, was the idea that the person whose conduct appeared to be the cause of social harm should be held responsible for the harm. Today we might view with some amusement the medieval practice of literally holding all "causal" items responsible for their "behavior." Drawing upon the Biblical injunction that "if an ox gore a man or a woman, that they die, then the ox shall be surely stoned, and his flesh shall not be eaten,"[1] medieval courts sentenced not only animals but also inanimate objects to be punished. These objects, called "deodands," included trees that fell upon persons and rocks against which an individual might have injured himself.[2] Soon such deodands came to be claimed by the monarch for his own. The practice of punishing deodands was not abolished in England until 1846, a development hastened by the coming of the railroads, which did not

[1] *Exodus* 21:28.
[2] Evans, *Criminal Prosecution and Capital Punishment of Animals.*

take kindly to the idea of having their property expropriated when it was involved in an accident.[3]

Expiation of guilt by money payments was prominent among the early forms of Anglo-Saxon punishment in the pre-Norman period. All homicides were adjusted by the payment of a pecuniary fine, called a "wer," to the family of the slain man. For injuries, a payment called a "bót," which was carefully measured in accord with the form and intensity of the injury as well as the status of the person hurt, was transmitted to the injured party. The gravest offenses, such as treason, always remained outside the pale of this rough-and-ready system of justice, and by Norman times money payments had become obsolete, being replaced by *outlawry,* or banishment, and by afflictive punishments leveled at the discretion of the king. The afflictive punishments included death, various forms of torture and mutilation, and/or fines payable to the sovereign. George R. Scott, in two penetrating studies of corporal punishment, traces its manifestation to psychological roots deep in the human animal, which are expressed in sadistic forms if unchecked by the social custom. Whether this view is correct or not, Scott provides vivid testimony to man's incessant cruelty to man. Roman emperors staged spectacles in which captured prisoners and criminals were thrown to animals, to be torn to shreds before bemused spectators. In Deuteronomy there is Biblical sanction of whipping, although the permissible limit set is "forty stripes," a rather arbitrary standard if one takes into account the variability in persons who might perform the whipping.[4] In England, Henry VIII's reign saw the enactment of a Whipping Act in 1530 in which vagrants were tied naked to the end of a cart and beaten while being dragged through the town "till the body shall be bloody by reason of such whipping."[5]

In the United States, Delaware continues to permit whipping of criminals at the option of the judge for 24 offenses including grand larceny, wife beating, horse stealing, and burning a courthouse. The notorious "Red Hannah" whipping post in Delaware, first installed in 1656 under Dutch colonial rule, has been the center of controversy about the value of physical punishment, with the best statistics available indicating that whipping has no effect in preventing crime.[6] On the other hand, British juvenile institutions employed flogging until 1948, and there is a considerable body of opinion in England that believes that the abolition of flogging is responsible for the rise in juvenile delinquency there.

Various forms of mutilation have also been employed throughout

3 Turner, *Kenny's Outline of Criminal Law,* pp. 7–14; Henson, *Landmarks of Law,* p. 232.

4 *Deuteronomy* 25:1–3.

5 Scott, *History of Corporal Punishment;* Scott, *History of Torture Throughout the Ages.*

6 Caldwell, *Red Hannah.*

history in an effort to prevent repetition of particular acts. Thieves have been punished by having their hands chopped off. Branding was also a common form of punishment, used in some cases to allow the authorities to recognize a previous offender or to facilitate social ostracism and to bring about social humiliation. In Victor Hugo's famous *Les Misérables,* for example, Jean Valjean was branded with a "V" (for *voleur)* for the theft of a loaf of bread, and in Nathaniel Hawthorne's *The Scarlet Letter,* Hester Prynne is forced to wear an embroidered "A" on her clothing to mark her adultery.

Gradually, however, the penalty of death replaced mutilation almost altogether. Death, in its turn, was largely replaced by imprisonment. The development of imprisonment has traveled through several stages, but its basic philosophical underpinnings have altered little during the centuries since it was first undertaken.

Correction and its Ideology

Crime may be prevented or reduced by any one of a number of methods. Some of these techniques are unavailable in a given society because they are offensive to principles more basic than that of the reduction of crime. As we have noted, for instance, the police are forbidden to employ a considerable range of effective and expedient methods for the apprehension of malefactors, on the ground that such methods undermine democratic institutions. Correctional programs are also limited by the tolerance of the society. In fact, changes in penal policies during the past 100 years probably represent more of a growth of compassion toward offenders than a fruition of scientific insight and programming.

Policies toward offenders need not necessarily be supported by empirical evidence of their effectiveness. The reduction of crime is but one of a number of possible aims of a society, and other aims may take precedence over it. Few Americans, for instance, presumably would be willing to live under a totalitarian regime even if this regime could demonstrate outstanding effectiveness in combatting crime through the elimination of civil liberties. Nor is it likely that many Americans would support the indiscriminate employment of capital punishment for offenses such as petty larceny, even if it could be demonstrated that such a program would strikingly reduce the amount of petty larceny.

Correctional policies, therefore, must be viewed in terms of some value system as well as in terms of their effect on criminal activity. It is also important to note that "effectiveness" itself involves some criterion of measurement and that the selection of the criterion to be employed will be influential in determining the judgment of a particular program. If a cancer victim is given a certain treatment that prolongs his life for five years, while the average cancer patient in similar circumstances without such treatment lives only three years, has the treatment been successful? If a criminal who was exposed to some institutional program does not repeat his offense for a period of seven years but then recidivates, while others similar to him without exposure to such a program recidivate within four years, can the program be considered a successful one?

At the heart of questions such as these is the fact that various techniques employed to discourage criminal behavior produce different results with different individuals. In addition, criminology is deficient in studies that shed light on the varying utility of such programs. Findings from such studies, however, were they to be done, would probably not support a policy decision to treat harshly offenders who respond to harshness and to treat other offenders, especially for the same crime, leniently. Democratic feelings may insist that it is blatantly discriminatory to deal in highly discrepant manners with two offenders who are subject to restraint because of similar behavior.

Also important in evaluating correctional programs is an understanding of the *total* result produced.[7] It may be demonstrated, for instance, that the most effective technique for reducing criminal behavior is to instill within the individual a sense of guilt and fear, a deeply rooted censoring conscience, which would act in the future as a check on his illegal conduct. It might also be shown, however, that such a procedure could readily lead to mental maladjustment, even to a psychotic breakdown; would that program then be worthwhile and desirable?

That the foregoing considerations are not altogether academic can be seen in disputes that arise over some of the most "progressive" correctional techniques that have evolved in the past century. The use of group therapy, for instance, is a treatment procedure used by virtually all institutions that consider themselves forward looking; in California, for example, such therapy includes in its scope approximately 70 percent of the state's prison inmates.[8] Writing about such programs, Gresham Sykes implies that the programs may have a tendency to employ both the techniques and justifications of "brainwashing."[9] An account in a textbook of a group therapy session strikes Sykes as "more than a little disturbing," and he notes that "if we ever really give up punishing criminals and instead try to cure them, we may find ourselves inflicting psychological barbarities on our prisoners which are far worse than any physical maltreatment."[10]

AIMS OF CORRECTIONAL PROGRAMS

Attempts to deal with criminal behavior involve, in the broadest

7 Morris, "Impediments to Penal Reform," p. 665.
8 Fenton, *Prisoner's Family*, p. 56.
9 Lifton, *Thought Reform and the Psychology of Totalism;* Rickett and Rickett, *Prisoners of Liberation.*
10 Sykes, review of *Criminology and Penology,* p. 304.

sense, five policies, which might be identified as seeking to achieve: (1) *ritual equilibrium*, seeing that punishment and penalties testify to adherence to the rules of the game, that the bad are being disciplined, and that the good, by indirection, are being rewarded, (2) *general deterrence*, that is, deterrence of persons who, without the example of what happens to others, might themselves violate, (3) *specific deterrence*, the effort to keep the particular offender from subsequently committing criminal offenses, (4) *sequestration*, the process of restraining the individual and thereby eliminating for the time being any opportunity for him to violate the laws in the free community, and (5) *reformation*, the attempt to make fundamental changes in the offender through systems of punishment and reward and by training in things such as vocational skills, academic subjects, and work habits.[11]

In general, punishment is basically a desire for revenge against a person who has offended us either directly or in more remote aesthetic or psychological ways. However, it is the idea of general deterrence that underlies the pronouncement of an eighteenth-century judge, who said, "You are to be hanged not because you have stolen a sheep but in order that others might not steal sheep."[12] Recourse to such a principle has led to deep philosophical debate concerning the moral validity of punishing one person in order to deter another. Hoyles notes, for instance, that "there certainly does seem to be something wrong about the infliction of pain on an individual against his will for the sake of making him an example to others. It is nothing more or less than a form of human sacrifice."[13] We know that the deterrent effect of penalties is not necessarily related to their harshness for, as Lord Coke noted sadly many centuries ago, "And true it is, that we have found by woeful experience, that it is not frequent and often punishment that doth prevent like offences, for the frequency of the punishment makes it so familiar as it is not feared."[14] Perhaps the most sophisticated adjudication of the philosophical issue involved in punishment is that offered by C. S. Lewis, who considers the relationship between punishment and principles of justice:

> the concept of Desert is the only connecting link between punishment and justice. It is only as deserved or undeserved that a sentence can be just or unjust. I do not here contend that the question "Is it deserved?" is the only one we can reasonably ask about a punishment. We may very properly ask whether it is likely to deter others and to reform the criminal. But neither of these last two questions is a question about justice. There is no sense in talking about a "just deterrent" or a "just cure." We demand of a deterrent not whether it is just but whether it will deter. . . . Thus when we cease to consider what the criminal

11 Goffman, "On the Characteristics of Total Institutions."
12 Fox, *English Prison and Borstal System,* p. 11.
13 Hoyles, *Treatment of the Young Delinquent,* p. 117.
14 Quoted in Bowen, *Lion on the Throne,* p. 64.

deserves and consider only what will cure him or deter others, we have tacitly removed him from the sphere of justice altogether; instead of a person, a subject of rights, we now have a mere object, a patient, a "case."[15]

Most programs that deal with criminal offenders mix somewhat indiscriminately considerable portions of the various correctional aims outlined above, operating on the unlikely assumption that if one is effective, like an antibiotic in medicine, then the others will at best be neutral. The different approaches may in fact tend to counterbalance each other and to antagonize or defeat whatever virtues any of them might possess independently. In this and the following chapter we will devote attention to each of these approaches in an attempt to place them into a criminological context and to evaluate their assets and liabilities. But it must be kept in mind that no one approach, even if it were to operate unhampered by other considerations, can be guaranteed to work effectively with all offenders, nor is it likely that it would fit the requirements of any contemporary society.

REFORMATION OR PUNISHMENT?

The attempt to control crime by use of punishment is the earliest and most pervasive technique that society has employed to coerce conforming behavior. In its broadest sense, punishment may be defined as any interference with the liberty of the individual. Under such a definition, all societies utilize innumerable forms of "punishment." Punishment for crime represents just one interference to an individual's freedom to do as he pleases, when he pleases; for example, the scarlet-fever victim is forced to remain in quarantine, the adolescent to attend school, the pedestrian to cross with the light. But punishment for crime is characterized particularly by the fact that it is inflicted on the basis of some prior act and on the ground that the offender is not likely of his own will to accept or to prolong the treatment he receives. The quicksand of this definitional resolve should not be overlooked, however. Some individuals regard as punishment various forms of civil interference, such as withdrawal of income through taxes, which most citizens accept, however unenthusiastically, as legitimate functions of the state. And some criminals apparently prefer incarceration to freedom, punishment to the absence of punishment. A considerable number of narcotic addicts, for instance, knowing that they will be detected and institutionalized, nonetheless show up for nalline testing by parole officers after having used heroin and appear to be relieved when they are sent to prison.

The distinction between "reformation" and "punishment" is a very difficult one to draw. Some school pupils undoubtedly regard compulsory education as a punitive imposition, whereas others accept

15 Lewis, "Humanitarian Theory of Punishment," p. 225.

it for what it is meant to be: and educative approach designed to aid the individual. Perhaps we must accept the intent of the administrative organization in designating the essential nature of any program, but here, too, the definitional impasse is impressive. Those persons in charge of the Inquisition during the Middle Ages were apparently honestly convinced that their program was a form of treatment, since those who refused to respond to the torture inflicted upon them were allegedly doomed to eternal perdition. To salvage such almost-lost souls was considered a work both of mercy and compassion by the administrators.

The determination of whether a program is "punishment" or "reformation," therefore, probably must derive from a subjective evaluation of the intent of the program as well as a review of its operating characteristics. But we must not fall into the semantic trap of regarding any program designed for the subject's betterment as reformative and therefore praiseworthy. To the extent that an individual does not prefer to be part of such a program, then the program contains an element of punishment and of deprivation of liberty, and it must be justified on solid and acceptable grounds of democratic procedure, which take into account the elaborate safeguards of the individual against the force of the state[16] as well as the right of the state to protect itself against real dangers to its well-being.

Philosophically, punishment is tied to the doctrine of free will. Criminals are seen as errant individuals who, out of perversity and antisocial self-interest, choose to violate the criminal code. By inflicting injury upon the offender, it is expected that he will be taught in a vivid manner the harmful consequences of subsequent repetition of his criminal activity. That punishment does in fact sometimes accomplish this purpose cannot be doubted; neither can it be doubted that punishment may turn an offender irretrievably into an implacable enemy of authority, deeply set in his intention of "getting even" with those he now regards as oppressors.

An analogy from child training might shed some light on definitional problems in this area. Children must often be impressed with the need to avoid certain forms of behavior. A child must learn, particularly if he is an urban child, to avoid the street and to be careful of automobiles. The lesson may be imparted in various ways. He may be reasoned with, but there is considerable danger that reasoning will not prove effective. Or, he may be carefully protected from any contact with streets and automobiles until he is old enough to deal with them safely, but he may escape surveillance and then enter a street carelessly, unprotected by a deep-rooted fear of cars. Probably the most common technique for dealing with the problem involves a combination of restraining the child near traffic and punishing him at the first sign of his running into the street. The deterrent effect of the punishment is

16 See Cohen, "Sentencing, Probation, and the Rehabilitative Ideal."

usually obvious; the child may resent it. But, the parental assumption
is that the punishment is essential for the protection of the child, whose
hostility will be dissipated by counterbalancing affection and eventually by a mature understanding of the necessity for it.

The analogy does not necessarily tell us how to deal with criminals
and with prison inmates. For one thing, the issue is not to protect the
criminal, but rather to protect persons and property from him. But
the analogy does tell us that all actions must be evaluated *situationally,*
and in a context in which there is a fair balancing of diverse elements
and aims. It is from such a perspective that we will examine various
ways of dealing with criminal offenders.

Capital Punishment

In regard to the numbers involved, the issue of capital punishment
is today a minor one. Yet capital punishment has the ability to arouse
extraordinarily passionate polemics, indicating perhaps that the issue
comes close to some basic emotions in our people.

Today, capital punishment has been abolished over much of
Western civilization. In Western Europe, the death penalty survives
only in the Irish Republic, with hanging; in France, with the guillotine;
and in Spain, with garroting. (Garroting is a practice introduced by the
Moors and Arabs, in which a brass collar containing a screw is fastened
around the victim's neck; the executioner turns the screw until its point
enters the spinal marrow where it unites with the brain, causing in-
stantaneous death.) By the standards of 150 years ago, the number
of executions in these countries is extremely low. In 1957, after
vehement Parliamentary debate, Great Britain excluded all but
a few varieties of homicide from the penalty of death, and in 1965
it declared a five-year moratorium on the use of capital punishment. Austria, Belgium, Denmark, Finland, Iceland, Luxembourg,
the Netherlands, Norway, Portugal, Rumania, Sweden, Switzerland,
and West Germany do not use capital punishment except in cases
of treason. In eastern Europe, in Russia, the policy toward capital
punishment also has fluctuated; the death penalty was abolished between 1947 and 1950 but was restored and gradually expanded to embrace high treason, espionage, sabotage, terroristic acts, banditry, and
certain forms of aggravated premeditated murder. In 1961, it was expanded further to include large-scale embezzling of state property and
counterfeiting.[17]

CAPITAL PUNISHMENT IN THE UNITED STATES
Although capital punishment was widely employed for a broad range
of offenses in England in the 1700s and 1800s, William Penn managed

17 Laurence, *History of Capital Punishment.*

to bring about its abolition for all offenses except murder from 1682 to 1718 in the colony of Pennsylvania. After Penn's death, however, the colony was forced to return to the much harsher English codes. Following American independence, Pennsylvania again pioneered in mitigating the penalty of death by dividing murder into two degrees, a precedent that was followed by most American states during the next half century. During this period, the tendency toward more lenient treatment of offenders in the United States in contrast to England was striking. Jurisdictions such as Kentucky and Pennsylvania, for instance, abolished the death sentence for all crimes except murder at the same time that Sir Samuel Romilly, a prison reformer, was desperately trying to persuade the English Parliament that the British way of life would not be hopelessly endangered if Parliament repealed capital punishment for the shoplifting of goods valued at more than five shillings.

For a generation before the Civil War, there was great agitation in the United States for the abolition of capital punishment. Questions concerning human responsibility, the fallibility of the courts, the progress and decline of society, the metaphysical origins of good and evil, and the authority of the Bible were debated vigorously. On March 1, 1847, Michigan became the first English-speaking jurisdiction to abolish the death penalty. It was soon joined by Rhode Island in 1852 and by Wisconsin in 1853; other states gave up capital punishment but then restored it, usually in the face of notorious crimes that aroused public cries for revenge and social protection. After the Civil War, David B. Davis notes, "men's finer sensibilities, which had once been revolted by the execution of a fellow being, seemed hardened and blunted," and the abolition movement "failed to recapture the widespread enthusiasm and evangelic fervor of the 1830's and 1840's," although Maine in 1887, Minnesota in 1911, and North Dakota in 1915 finally became abolition states.[18]

No other state joined the permanent roster of abolition jurisdictions for thirty-eight years. Hawaii and Alaska had both abandoned capital punishment before their admission to the Union. In 1958, Delaware, which had not had an execution in almost a quarter of a century, officially eliminated capital punishment, but three years later, in response to a brutal murder, the legislature reestablished the death penalty.[19] Shortly thereafter, however, the floodtide of public opinion began to move additional states into the ranks of those without capital punishment. In 1964, after its fourth statewide referendum in fifty years, Oregon abolished capital punishment. In 1965, Iowa, West Virginia, New York, and Vermont joined the ranks of abolitionist states, raising their number to thirteen; New Mexico was added to the list in March 1969. In some instances, the death penalty was retained for

18 Davis, "Movement to Abolish Capital Punishment."
19 Samuelson, "Why Was Capital Punishment Restored in Delaware?"

specified offenses, as in New York where it may be applied in cases in which a policeman is killed during the commission of a felony or in which a guard or inmate is killed by a prisoner serving a life sentence.

More important than the formal declarations of different jurisdictions concerning the elimination of capital punishment have been statistics showing the striking diminution in its use. In the two decades between 1930 and 1950, there were approximately 150 executions each year, but in recent years the number had dropped precipitously, as shown in Table 17.1.

Table 17.1   Civil Executions in the United States, 1952–1968

Year	Number	Year	Number
1952	88	1961	42
1953	62	1962	47
1954	82	1963	21
1955	76	1964	15
1956	65	1965	7
1957	65	1966	1
1958	48	1967	2
1959	49	1968	0
1960	57	1969	0

DETERRENCE AND CAPITAL PUNISHMENT

The major dispute concerning capital punishment centers around its effectiveness as a deterrent of crime. Persons rely on what they consider to be common sense to support their view that the fear of death keeps individuals from resorting to murder to resolve difficulties or to discharge aggressive feelings. It is presumed that life imprisonment presents a less forbidding prospect, particularly when the individual can contemplate the possibility of release within as little as seven years in some states.

The absence of *certainty* as to whether life imprisonment or death will be employed undoubtedly helps to distort any contemplative image that potential offenders might conceive. It does seem likely, however, that there would be more murder if the penalty were reduced to, say, three years. But it remains doubtful whether the choice between life imprisonment, even with the hope of parole, or the death penalty makes much difference to possible offenders, particularly when they doubt that they will be apprehended or convicted.

A major difficulty in the deterrence dispute has been the inability to differentiate among different types of offenders. To many capital offenders their act appears to be so imperative and correct, and their preoccupation with it is so thorough that the penalty involved is probably of little, if any, consequence. It seems very doubtful if capital punishment would affect the number of *crime passionel* murders or those violent homicides that are perpetrated by individuals who appear highly disturbed but who nonetheless fall within the legal bounds of sanity. Thus, for example, capital punishment would seem to be extraneous to offenders such as the eighteen-year-old in Arizona who in 1964 massacred four women and a child and explained, "I wanted to kill about 40 people so I could make a name for myself. I wanted people to know who I was," continuing that he wanted to "see the headlines and stories with my name in them before I die."

The inability of the knowledge of capital consequences to deter crime is seen in instances of pickpockets who worked assiduously among the gaping crowds at early English public executions while other pickpockets were being hanged. In addition, several British hangmen, who should have been well aware of the attributes of the rope, were themselves later executed.[20] Furthermore, there is evidence that executions are sometimes followed by outbreaks of the same type of crime for which the offender was killed. There are also cases in which offenders apparently commit capital offenses in order to be executed, as when a Nevada radio announcer shot to death a total stranger and then told the police that, "I wanted to kill myself but I didn't have the courage, so I decided to kill somebody else and let the state execute me."[21]

Some statistical material has been brought to bear on the subject of the deterrent effect of capital punishment and, to the extent that one can safely generalize, it offers strong evidence of the failure of capital punishment to affect homicide rates. Polemicists are wont to mention that Alabama, which uses capital punishment, had a murder rate in 1967 of 11.7 per 100,000, whereas Maine, which does not employ capital punishment, had a rate of .4 per 100,000; however, the cultures and population composition of the two areas are so diverse that such an intrastate comparison is not valid. More telling have been comparisons of contiguous states in which one is without capital punishment while the other retains it. All data on deterrence have been negative. North and South Dakota, for instance, have almost exactly similar homicide rates, as do Wisconsin and Illinois, Minnesota and Michigan, and Maine and New Hampshire.[22] So, too, states that have abolished capital punishment have not shown any undue increase in the amount of homicide that occurs within their borders subsequent to abolition.

Work has also been done to determine if the use of capital punishment provides an element of safety to police officers. In Great Britain, particular pains were taken to see that any killing of a police officer

20 Duff, *A New Handbook on Hanging*, p. 72; Gribble, *True Book About The Old Bailey*, p. 19.
21 Klare, "Hanging the Sick."
22 Schuessler, "Deterrent Influence of the Death Penalty"; Sellin, *Death Penalty*. See, in contrast, Van Den Haag, "On Deterrence and the Death Penalty."

brought death to the perpetrator. This was said to be one of the major reasons why the British police were able to go unarmed. A detailed investigation in the United States of this hypothesis, however, fails to substantiate it. Thorsten Sellin, studying murders of policemen, finds no significant relationship between capital punishment and the rate of such killings,[23] while Father Campion, investigating the same phenomenon in regard to state police, concludes that the data available "do not lend empirical support to the claim that the existence of the death penalty in the statutes of a state provides a greater protection to the police than exists in states where that penalty has been abolished."[24]

The deterrent effect of capital punishment for crimes that appear to be more rational and deliberate than murder and rape—the two crimes for which capital punishment is most often employed—remains a more complex problem. In particular, there is the question of felony-murder in which death results from an armed robbery. It is sometimes postulated that capital laws enforced vigorously against felony-murderers would lead to the carrying of fewer loaded weapons by robbers and the tendency of fewer of those with loaded weapons to fire them. Here the evidence is vague, although it certainly has not been demonstrated that armed robbers could not be equally deterred by life-imprisonment sentences. Indeterminate sentence policies also serve to complicate the issue. In some states a second conviction for armed robbery may lead to a sentence with a maximum of life imprisonment. If capital punishment were not present, the armed robber could foresee no sentence greater than life imprisonment, and it is said that there would therefore be no reason for him not to attempt to shoot his way out of any difficulty; this remains doubtful, however, for the experienced armed robber usually realizes that he is in a much stronger parole position without a killing on his record.

In summary, it seems reasonable to maintain that, at the present stage of our knowledge, the burden to support their position lies heavily on those who want to demonstrate that capital punishment, as it is presently employed, does in fact deter crime.

OTHER ASPECTS OF THE CAPITAL PUNISHMENT DEBATE

Certain basic questions of value that suround the whole question of capital punishment cannot be demonstrated or rebutted in terms of scientific premises. Biblical sources are often cited both in favor and against capital punishment. The Bible is said to favor retribution, as seen in the divine admonition to Noah: "Whoever shed the blood of man, by man shall his blood be shed" (Genesis 9:6). The doctrine of *lex talionis,* the law of retaliation and vengeance, is sometimes said to be divine law: "An eye for an eye, a tooth for a tooth." Counterargu-

23 Sellin, "Death Penalty and Police Safety."
24 Campion, "State Police and the Death Penalty," p. 735.

ments maintain that the admonition to Noah was merely intended to point out that bloodletting is an inevitable consequence of prior violence, and that "an eye for an eye" refers to nothing more sinister than equivalent monetary payments to the heirs of a dead person. Those in opposition to capital punishment generally rely on Romans 7:19: "Beloved, never revenge yourselves, but leave it to the wrath of God for it is written: Vengeance is mine, I will repay, says the Lord"; and Matthew 5:38–39: "Ye have heard that it hath been said, An eye for an eye, and a tooth for a tooth: But I say unto you, That ye resist not evil: but whosoever shall smite thee on thy right cheek, turn to him the other also."

Proponents of capital punishment also maintain that by employing it a society gives moral expression to its legitimate outrage at a heinous crime and is further integrated and entrenched in its collective desire to avoid such behavior. The truth of this is almost impossible to determine, but few persons would carry it to the point of the English writer who declared that an innocent person about to be hanged should not protest, because by doing so he would only undermine the citizenry's faith in their judicial system.[25]

Capital punishment is also defended on the ground that, were it not used, murderers and similar dangerous criminals would be released on parole and would repeat their original offenses. That some murderers spared the death penalty have been released and have killed again is true,[26] and it can be argued that one such instance is enough ground for valid opposition to the abolition of capital punishment, unless a system of life imprisonment without hope of parole is established in its place. On the other hand, it is pointed out, murderers make extraordinarily good prison adjustments and their recidivism rate for any offense is strikingly low. It is also sometimes argued that capital punishment is a more humane form of treatment than life imprisonment without hope of parole and that, if nothing else, the offender ought to be allowed to choose his own form of punishment among the two alternatives.[27]

The fact that capital punishment allegedly saves the state money is also raised in favor of its employment, but this argument seems specious. The expense of electric chairs and gas chambers, prolonged court appeals in capital cases, and other such costs should not be overlooked. Nor can it be ignored that prisoners can be made virtually self-sufficient. Furthermore, the cost to maintain those persons executed is very negligible compared to the overall price of social policies dealing with persons unable to conform to various standards.

Other opposition to capital punishment is based on the belief that it is a sadistic form of action that by its very nature brutalizes those

25 Paley, *Works,* Vol. II, p. 388.
26 Rice, *Los Angeles Murders,* Chap. 7.
27 Barzun, "In Favor of Capital Punishment."

who take part in it and allow it to occur, and that it cheapens the value of all human life. "It has always seemed to me," the French writer Albert Camus notes regarding capital punishment, "that in fact there were no executioners—only victims."[28] Others maintain that it violates democratic tenets, since those selected out for capital punishment are, disproportionately, men, the poorer persons in the society, and blacks.

A telling argument against capital punishment concerns its irreparability. As leaders of the Protestant Episcopal Church note in opposing capital punishment, the execution of even one innocent man may be "a colossal, irremediable, and final offense which must haunt the Christian conscience." It seems likely that more innocent persons were executed in bygone times than they are today,[29] although the lesson of the Salem witches, who were burned as a result of their own confessions of guilt, has some contemporary relevance.[30] Even today, though, there are cases in which miscarriages of justice seem to have occurred,[31] such as the 1950 English case in which Timothy Evans, a London bus driver, was hanged for allegedly killing his fourteen-month-old daughter, largely on the testimony of a boarder in the house John Christie. Three years later, Christie himself was hanged for the murder of seven women, including Evans' wife, and few persons doubted that Evans was innocent of the offense for which he had been executed.[32] In fact, in 1966—sixteen years after he had been hanged— Evans was given a full pardon by Queen Elizabeth in a gesture of consummate irony designed to quiet the continuing controversy about the case.

Alternatives to Capital Punishment

BANISHMENT

Banishment and/or imprisonment, which arose to mitigate capital punishment, were designed to remove the offender from society so that society could be secure from him. Death, of course, was the most effective method of guaranteeing such safety, but indiscriminate application of capital punishment gradually proved too severe for toleration by humanitarian consciences. Besides, life imprisonment or banishment could provide almost as much of a guarantee to the society against the exorcized individual.

In early English history, criminals were banished from the realms of the king to fend for themselves as best they could. Soon this practice

28 Camus, *Reflections on the Guillotine*, p. 41.
29 Borchard, *Convicting the Innocent*.
30 See Upham, *Salem Witchcraft*.
31 Frank and Frank, *Not Guilty*; Huie, *Mud on the Stars*, pp. 164–177.
32 Jesse, *Trials of Evans and Christie*; Eddowes, *Man on Your Conscience*; Kennedy, *Ten Rillington Place*.

coalesced with a form of self-banishment in which the criminal fled from the major society to join with others like himself in settlements, usually geographically inaccessible, from which he preyed upon more peaceable citizens. The folklore of virtually all European countries contains tales of social bandits, probably real characters transmuted somewhat in the telling, who allegedly benefited the poor and harassed the rich—bandits such as Robin Hood in England. Janŏsik in Poland and Slovakia, and Diego Corrientes in Andalusia.[33] Such outlaw communities are still found in sections of Italy, where they protect themselves by their numbers, their familiarity with the territory in which they operate, and the sufferance or friendship of law-abiding persons in the neighborhood.[34]

Banishment is still utilized in certain forms today to eliminate offenders from a society. The United States has often employed deportation proceedings against aliens, particularly when involved in organized crime. Another form of banishment, used by many municipal court judges, is the threat of incarceration, leveled against vagrants if they are found in a particular community after passage of a specified period of time.[35]

TRANSPORTATION

The most systematic form of banishment occurred from the beginning of the sixteenth century until 1855, as England mitigated its capital-punishment procedures by allowing certain criminals to come under a program of transportation to far-removed territories. Transportation had at least two aims: (1) to eliminate convicts from England, and (2) to colonize inhospitable territories. America and the West Indies became dumping grounds for hordes of English convicts whose offenses were not considered severe enough for hanging. It is estimated that somewhere between 15,000 and 100,000 convicts were transported to America before the Revolution put an end to the practice.[36] Subsequently, England sent convicts to Australia, in a chapter in penal history that contains some of the ugliest illustrations of human callousness and brutality that exist,[37] although it also witnessed the first widespread experiment in inmate self-government.[38] There is no worthwhile information on how effective transportation might have been in preventing crime, but there is no gainsaying that it was effective in eliminating from England a considerable segment of its least desirable elements. Despite the appalling horror of many aspects of transportation, however, an outstanding English jurist of that time believed that

33 Hobshawm, *Social Bandits and Primitive Rebels*, p. 13.
34 Maxwell, *God Protect Me From My Friends*.
35 Foote, "Vagrancy-Type Law and Its Administration," p. 617.
36 Barnes and Teeters, *New Horizons in Criminology*, p. 296.
37 O'Brien, *Foundation of Australia*; Bateson, *Convict Ships, 1787–1868*; Barry, "Founding Felons of Australia"; Shaw, *Convicts and the Colonies*; Robson, *Convict Settlers of Australia*.
38 Barry, *Alexander Maconochie of Norfolk Island*.

transportation should not have been substituted for the gallows because it was nothing more than "a summer's excursion, in an easy migration, to a happier and better climate."[39] The judge's remark illustrates a persistent feeling in most societies at most times that regardless of what is being done to criminals they are being treated altogether too indulgently.

Transportation also played a large and macabre role in the penal history of other European countries. France transported some of her worst convicts to French Guinea—a punishment wryly referred to as the "dry guillotine"—where they resided in the dolorous confines of a small, unhealthy, and degenerate penal colony.[40] Prior to this, France sent most of the convicts it spared from the guillotine to the galleys, which was possibly the earliest form of extensive imprisonment, in an attempt to maintain its naval power and prestige in competition with the Spanish on the Mediterranean littoral. Both captured slaves and *forçats,* or nationals condemned to penal servitude either for a term of years or for life, were delivered to the galleys. To replenish the galleys, the king finally ordered all army deserters, 8,000 of whom were often executed in a single year, to be placed in galley service after first having their noses and ears cut off and then being marked with a fleur-de-lis on each cheek. By the early 1690s, the French galley fleet reached its zenith, with more than 12,000 oarsmen, most of whom were convicts, manning the ships. When steamships became common in the eighteenth century, the galleys disappeared, and convicts who were not to be executed were transferred to penal settlements, the first having been established at Toulon in 1748.[41]

Transportation got underway soon after slavery was abolished in 1848 in French Guinea. Freed Negroes left the cities for the interior, and Indo-Chinese, who had been imported to do agricultural work, refused to remain in such employment after their original term of service expired. Napoleon III then decided to colonize Guinea with convicts. Beginning in 1852 until 1938 when the prison ship *La Martinique* made its last transatlantic voyage with a cargo of convicts lashed to its deck, every French criminal with a sentence of five years' imprisonment or more was sent to Guinea. The convicts fell into three classes: *relégués,* or incorrigible thieves, *déportés,* or political criminals, and *transportés,* or individuals found guilty of murder, robbery with violence, rape, or similar crimes.[42] France was not the only continental country to employ transportation; both the czarist and the communist governments of Russia have used Siberia to store individuals whose actions or thoughts put them in social or political disfavor.[43]

39 Quoted in Radzinowicz, *History of English Criminal Law,* Vol. I, p. 31.
40 Belbenoit, *Dry Guillotine.*
41 Bamford, "Procurement of Oarsmen for French Galleys," p. 40.
42 Seaton, *Isle of the Damned,* pp. xiv–xv.
43 Kennan, *Siberia and the Exile System;* Dostoevsky, *House of the Dead.*

IMPRISONMENT

As early as 525 B.C., Plato, writing in *The Laws,* recommended imprisonment for theft, assault and battery, and as part of the punishment for the crime of "impiety." We also have early historical records of offenders being placed under house arrest. But imprisonment was used only sporadically to deal with criminals until comparatively recent times. "It was not common to keep men in prison," Frederick Pollock and Frederic W. Maitland write of the medieval period, explaining that "this apparent leniency was not due to any love of abstract liberty. Imprisonment was costly and troublesome."[44]

The development of prisons is marked by several background threads. Of considerable pioneering significance was the contribution of Cesare Beccaria, an Italian nobleman who in 1764 published a small but highly influential volume entitled *Essay on Crimes and Punishment.* The sole philosophical justification for punishment, according to Beccaria, was the protection of society by the prevention of crime. Beccaria stressed that uniform maximum severity, particularly widespread capital punishment, was not only morally wrong, but practically ineffectual, and he maintained that milder punishment, proportioned to the offense but inflicted with promptness and certainty, would be more effective than erratic severity in controlling crime. Beccaria also stressed the desirability of programs for the prevention of crime and believed that good legislation was one of the major methods for achieving this end. Laws, he believed, should be clear and simple and should apply equally to all men. Virtue would have to be rewarded in order that it would become the desired goal of men. It was Beccaria's observations, in fact, that provided the intellectual underpinning and impetus for the development of prisons in the place of capital punishment.[45]

Beccaria's philosophical ideas were pushed toward the realm of practical work by the fertile pen of Jeremy Bentham, a philosopher who concerned himself with, among numerous other things, the details of a penal program for England. Bentham considered punishment an evil but one that was, however, necessary to prevent greater evils from being inflicted on the society and thus diminishing the common sum of happiness. Bentham's works have a contemporary relevance as he berates punishment of the following types: (1) Where it is groundless, since there is no offense because consent has been given, or where the evil is more than compensated for by an attendant good, such as in justifiable homicide, (2) Where the punishment is inefficacious because it has no power to affect the will, such as in the case of underage persons, or in circumstances where the acts seem to be absolutely in-

44 Pollock and Maitland, *History of English Law,* p. 585.
45 Beccaria, *Essay on Crimes and Punishments;* Monachesi, "Cesare Beccaria."

voluntary, (3) Where the punishment is unprofitable because the evil of the punishment exceeds that of the offense. In this connection, Bentham notes that it would be wise to pardon an offender who is protected by a foreign state whose goodwill it is essential to obtain, (4) Where the punishment is needless because the end may be obtained as effectively at a cheaper price "by instruction . . . by informing the understanding."[46]

Pushed along by Bentham's philosophical prodding, England began to inaugurate institutions for the incarceration of offenders. The model for this movement arose not in the British Isles themselves, however, but was imported from across the ocean where the first penal institution had been organized in the American colonies.

The American development was spurred by the efforts of the Quakers who, under the guidance of William Penn, established an institution for convicted misdemeanants in Philadelphia in 1682. Although it did not survive Penn's death in 1718, this institution was the direct antecedent of the Walnut Street Penitentiary—the world's first real prison—which was opened in 1776 in Philadelphia. Walnut Street operated, in theory at least, on the principle of solitary confinement with a system of absolute silence. It was presumed that "calm contemplation" would inevitably lead to repentance.[47] In 1819, a congregate prison, in which inmates came together for work, though in silence, during the day and spent the nights in solitary cells, was established at Auburn, New York, and both the Philadelphia and the New York systems then competed for the attention and support of European visitors.[48] But then, as now, there was no pervasive feeling that a method had been discovered that would effectively control criminal behavior. The dilemma of the times was clearly expressed in a letter that Sir Robert Peel wrote in 1826 while he was evaluating problems related to criminal activity:

> I admit the inefficiency of transportation to Botany Bay, but the whole subject of what is called secondary punishment is full of difficulty. . . . We have the convict ships. . . . There is a limit to this, for without regular employment found for the convicts, it is worse even than transportation. . . . Solitary imprisonment sounds well in theory, but it has in a peculiar degree the evil that is common to all punishment, it varies in its severity according to the disposition of the culprit. To some intellects its consequences are indifferent, to others they are fatal. . . . Public exposure by labour on the highway, with badges of disgrace, and chains, and all the necessary precautions against escape, would revolt, and very naturally, I think, public opinion in this country. . . . As for long terms of imprisonment with hard labour, we have them at present, for we have the Penitentiary with room for 800 penitents. When they

46 Bentham, *Rationale of Punishment*, pp. 23–26.
47 Teeters, *Cradle of the Penitentiary*; McKelvey, *American Prisons*.
48 de Beaumont and de Tocqueville, *On the Penitentiary System*; Dickens, *American Notes*.

lived well, their lot in the winter season was thought by people outside to be a rather enviable one. . . . We reduced their food [and] there
arose a malignant and contagious disorder which at the time emptied
the prison, either through the death or the removal of its inmates. The
present inmates are therefore again living too comfortably, I fear, for
penance. I despair of any remedy but that which I wish I could hope
for—a great reduction in the amount of crime.[49]

The years since Peel's disheartened remarks have not produced any
significant resolution of this problem. Prisons have become more
lenient in many overt respects. Striped garments, locksteps, unreasonable rules of silence, and other repressive features have disappeared
from the prison regimen. Radios, television sets, athletic equipment
and facilities, and many other items of creature comfort have found
their way inside the prison walls. But the essential, basic conundrum
remains as pressing and unanswered as it has throughout the life
span of prisons. Is the prison effective in reducing crime? Can it be
effective? And, most important, is it the *most* effective method available
for producing the desired results? Two studies, spaced two decades
apart, shed light on inherent difficulties involved in imprisonment.

The Prison Community
In 1940, Donald Clemmer published a study of a 2,300-inmate
prison, which he describes as "just another place where men do time."
He attempted to gather information on the "culture" of the prison, for
it is this culture, Clemmer believes, that provides the key to the influence of the prison program and that is much more significant than
the superimposed standards of the prison administrators.

Sixty percent of the prison inmates, Clemmer found, were members of informal groups in the institution. These groups had as their
dominant ethos a set of attitudes that was in contrast to the aims of
the institution. Unaffiliated inmates were somewhat older, slightly
less intelligent, more frequently married, and, in general, less criminalistic. A large portion of the unaffiliated inmates remained so because of their strong relationships with their families or friends in the
nonprison community; these relationships controlled their prison behavior and, more than any contribution of the prison itself, determined
their post-release adjustment.

In identifying inmate types and prison roles, Clemmer singled
out for further analysis the informers, whose behavior is considered the
most flagrant violation of the inmate code. He found the following
individuals to make up the informer group:

First is the man who has never before been in prison but whose dealings
in the free world have been shady and unscrupulous, who is weak of
character, desirous of personal comforts, socially immature, not closely

49 Quoted in Fox, *English Prison and Borstal System,* pp. 35–36.

affiliated with any adult groups, and generally dishonest. Such a type is frequently a forger or confidence man. Second, is the man of previous good standing in his own community, who is in prison for the first time, and who feels as one with officials, and identifies himself with them. Such a man is frequently a banker or business man who has come to prison for embezzlement or larceny. Third, is the man who has been criminalistic in an inadequate, non-professional way for years, who has served many terms in various prisons, who has reached the age when the glamor of life is gone, and who wants security and peace. Such a man may be any type of thief, but is usually a burglar. Fourth, is the very young man who is not conditioned to criminality, but who finds himself in prison, and is overwhelmed by the whole thing; he yearns for home and mother. Such a man may be any type of thief, and is more frequently than not the boy who stole an automobile for a joy ride. Fifth, we have the man who considers that thieves and predatory criminals are the scum of the earth. He is the emotionally controlled, and not very intelligent person who is not sure of his status in any group and knows only that he is better than the "real criminals." Such a man is the sex offender, or the man who has murdered during rage.[50]

The informer or "rat" arouses the inmate group to aggression and retaliation, which, in turn, serves to integrate further the grouped inmates, to dramatize their loyalty to a code of opposition, and to dissuade potential transgressors from allying themselves with the prison administrators.[51]

A key bit of insight into prison culture occurs during athletic contests, when the inmates in Clemmer's institution almost invariably rooted for the visiting "free" team. Such behavior sprang from their dislike of their own athletes who were regarded as prison politicians and stool pigeons. There was also the feeling that the guards and other prison officials wanted the inmate team to win; therefore, the prisoners felt compelled to oppose the team on what they considered the consistent ground that they should be against anything favored by the officials. Clemmer remarked that:

> Basic to these reasons, the convicts have a deeply rooted dissatisfaction with their own status, and a rebellious attitude toward any factor or symbol which has caused or maintains it. If a member of a visiting team becomes officious and arrogant, the sympathies of the men revert to the home players, because the visitor is "acting like a guard."[52]

Clemmer's caustic summary remarks are worth repetition.

> The apparent rehabilitating effect which prison life has on some men occurs in spite of the harmful influences of the prison culture. Among the writer's wide acquaintanceship with hundreds of inmates those who were improved or rehabilitated were men who, in the first place, should

50 Clemmer, *Prison Community*, pp. 160–161. By permission.
51 Johnson, "Sociology of Confinement"; Wilmer, "The Role of the 'Rat' in Prison."
52 Clemmer, *Prison Community*, p. 212.

never have been committed to prison at all, and who, in the second place, were engulfed by the culture, or prisonized in only the slightest degree. While sometimes the so-called real criminals are rehabilitated, the occasions are so rare that the total effect is negligible. Such "rehabilitation" as occurs with the actual criminals refers to the type of "treatment" which keeps them in prison until they reach such an age that they no longer have sufficient physical nor mental vigor to commit further crimes. In a cold, objective sense this means of "rehabilitation" has some societal utility, but, at the same time, if other methods had been used the waste of human resources might have been avoided and the dignity of human personalities maintained.[53]

SOCIETY OF CAPTIVES

Clemmer's observations are extended in a study by Gresham Sykes of the New Jersey Maximum Security Prison at Trenton, a more than thirteen-acre institution surrounded by a twenty-foot high wall, which houses the state's older, more recalcitrant male offenders, who have poor records and long sentences. Inmates in the New Jersey prison show the following offense distribution: felonious homicide, 24 percent; larceny, 12 percent; burglary, 24 percent, with the remaining distribution scattered among a variety of crimes. Thirty-five years is the median inmate age. Thirty-eight percent of the offenders are Negro and 63 percent have had fewer than nine years of schooling. The immediacy of the task of returning a "reformed" individual to the society is shown by the fact that at the time of the study in 1958, 55 percent of the prisoners were to be released within two years and 85 percent within four years.

Sykes suggests that the entire idea of "attempting to reform criminals by placing them in a prison is based on a fallacy." He notes that custody demands within the institution take priority over treatment considerations. Escapes create a public uproar and may result in pressures to remove a warden; therefore the major emphasis is to keep the prison as escape-proof as possible. Internal order must also be maintained, and labor must be performed, although the usual incentives for productive work are conspicuously absent. As Sykes points out, "with too many men for too few jobs, hamstrung by worn-out and outmoded machinery, lacking an adequate budget, under pressure from economic interests in the free community, and hampered by their own commitment to competing objectives, the [prison] officials . . . are in an unenviable position."[54]

The basic dilemma of the prison is clearly summarized in the following analysis:

The administrator of the maximum security prison . . . finds himself confronted with a set of social expectations which pose numerous di-

53 *Ibid.*, p. 313.
54 Sykes, *Society of Captives*, pp. 17–18.

lemmas when an attempt is made to translate them into a concrete, rational policy. Somehow he must resolve the claims that the prison should exact vengeance, erect a specter to terrify the actual or potential deviant, isolate the known offender from the free community, and effect a change in the personality of his captives so that they gladly follow the dictates of the law—and in addition maintain order within his society of prisoners and see that they are employed at useful labor. If the policy of the prison sometimes seems to exhibit a certain inconsistency, we might do well to look at the inconsistency of the philosophical setting in which the prison exists.[55]

In the informal structure of the prison, most officials are relatively indifferent when it comes to punishing their wards for past sins and are equally indifferent when it comes to saving them from the sins of the future. Allegiance to the goal of rehabilitation tends to remain at the verbal level, as an expression of hope for public consumption. Imprisonment is likely to be defined as successful only if it does not make the offender worse, while an attempt is made to avoid corrosive abnormalities and to make the prisoner learn compliance.

Prison life itself throws into dramatic relief basic human conditions: the trivial becomes tragic, the absurd becomes profound, and unreasoned faith gives life its only logic. Prisons, Sykes maintains, are organized around a grant of power that is without equal in American society. Most important to Sykes is the need of the prison inmate to maintain a semblance of psychological self-respect, an extraordinarily difficult task in an institutional setting. It does not matter to the prisoner that his rejection by the society has ensued because of his own acts; he feels the need to establish convincing evidence of his own importance as a human being.[56] "Legitimately or illegitimately, rationally or irrationally," Sykes notes, "the inmate population defines its present impoverishment as a painful loss."[57] A man has been, in the words of the Russian novelist Solzhenitsyn, "stripped of his outer bark" and is "ready to be planed."[58] Added to this is the deprivation of heterosexual relationships that compounds the psychological problem, since heterosexual success and security are among the more important methods by which most men evaluate their worth. The prisoner must operate in a milieu similar to that of the child in our society, where certain forms of behavior are expected to occur without explanation of why they should occur. Their loss of autonomy is also a serious threat. The inmate, "rejected, impoverished and figuratively castrated,"[59] fights to create a prison culture that will provide him with evidence of his own worth, in terms of the same set of values that others in the culture from which he springs measure their worth.

55 *Ibid.*, pp. 44–45.
56 For a fictional treatment of this theme see Braly, *On the Yard.*
57 Sykes, *Society of Captives*, p. 68.
58 Solzhenitsyn, *Cancer Ward*, p. 6.
59 Sykes and Messinger, "Inmate Social System," p. 14.

As part of their social system, the inmates subtly compromise the lower range of custodial personnel who are as dependent upon the prisoners for their own well-being as the prisoners are upon them. By being recalcitrant, by teasing, or by failing to perform their work, the inmates can make the custodial official miserable and can jeopardize his chances for retention and promotion. Status accrues to inmates who do their own time, refusing to allow the deprivations of institutional life to eat into their apparent self-sufficiency. These adjustment roles in the institution, however, do not signify any willingness to abandon a criminalistic way of life, but rather represent efforts to come to grips with the system. A prisoner who goes out of his way to antagonize an official is denigrated by other inmates. "He gets all inmates in a jam," they will say; "And besides he's an idiot. He's the sort of person who'll come up and ask you for a stamp when you're washing your hands."[60]

Sykes describes the inmate role that is most admired by the prison population:

> There is no single, fixed term for the inmate who endures the rigors of imprisonment with dignity, but the label of *real man* is applied . . . as frequently as any other. The *real man* is the prisoner who "pulls his own time" in the phrasing of the inmate population and he confronts his captors with neither subservience or aggression. Somewhat aloof, seldom complaining, he embodies the inmates' version of decorum. And if the real man's efforts to maintain his integrity in the face of privation have an important psychological utility—for the real man regains his autonomy, in a sense, by denying the custodians' power to strip him of his ability to control himself—it is also true that his role is of vital functional significance for the social system of imprisoned criminals. In the emphasis on endurance with dignity, the inmates have robbed the rebel of their support; it is the man who can stop himself from striking back at the custodians that wins their admiration and thus their image of the hero functions wittingly or unwittingly to maintain the *status quo*.[61]

Conclusion

No revolutionary breakthrough in the prison impasse is anticipated by Sykes. He believes that social inertia, combined with the economic inertia caused by large investments in existing physical plants, will tend to make prison reform a slow and tedious process. The social demand for vengeance is not apt to diminish very rapidly. Gradual changes in prisons, and recognition of the fact that some escapes, caused by looser regulations and more demanding programs, are the price that must be paid if a majority of the offenders are to be helped, would ameliorate conditions somewhat. Sykes also points out that it

60 Sykes, *Society of Captives*, p. 100.
61 *Ibid.*

is excessively optimistic to expect 100 percent rehabilitation and that public education in the realistic function and price to be paid for correctional ends is an imperative need. In addition, new programs, stressing community participation by convicted offenders, if proven valuable, may ultimately undercut the present rationale for imprisonment. Such programs, as well as the issue of criminal responsibility that lies at the base of corrections, will be considered in the following chapter.

For Further Reading

BEDAU, HUGO ADAM (ed.). *The Death Penalty in America.* 2nd ed. Garden City, N.Y.: Doubleday, 1968.

The most comprehensive collection of materials relating to all aspects of capital punishment, complete with a near-definitive bibliography. Professor Bedau contributes several articles of his own to fill the gaps in the literature on the death penalty. The volume contains a series of articles favoring capital punishment and a number opposing it as well as studies regarding possible deterrent effects of the death penalty.

CRESSEY, DONALD R. (ed.). *The Prison: Studies in Institutional Organization and Change.* New York: Holt, Rinehart, & Winston, 1961.

A number of writers contribute articles on different phases of prison existence. Particularly engrossing are two introductory pieces by Erving Goffman, which dissect what he labels "total institutions" or places such as prisons, army camps, and monasteries, in an attempt to find common patterns. Also noteworthy are essays by Clarence Schrag and a number of his former students at the University of Washington, which attempt to delineate characteristics of inmate types in prison society.

GROSSER, GEORGE (ed.). *Theoretical Studies in the Social Organization of the Prison.* New York Social Science Research Council, 1960.

Six papers, the outcome of the work of the Conference Group on Correctional Organization, under the chairmanship of Frank E. Hartung, are presented in this volume. Each concentrates on a different aspect of the prison, which is viewed as a social system with a complicated network of formal and informal interrelationships.

SELLIN, THORSTEN (ed.). *Capital Punishment.* New York: Harper & Row, 1967.

Several excellent pieces are included in this review of the major literature on capital punishment. A section of the work of Cesare Beccaria forms one chapter, while another chapter reviews an ancient Roman debate between Caesar and Cato on capital punishment. Also included is an article by Walter E. Oberer, which was the major impetus toward judical consideration of the fairness of juries selected on the basis of their stated willingness to impose death sentences.

SYKES, GRESHAM M. *The Society of Captives.* Princeton: Princeton University Press, 1958.

Professor Sykes' study of the New Jersey maximum-security institution in Trenton pays major attention to attempts by immates to retain and restore their image of themselves as worthwhile individuals. Well-written and perceptive, the book contains challenging observations on the basic errors in the use of imprisonment to deal with offenders.

18

Reformation and Responsibility

It is important to appreciate that the various correctional enterprises, such as the prison system, the system of juvenile justice, the systems of probation and parole, and the process of handling misdemeanants, were developed independently of each other and not as segments of a coordinated enterprise. With few exceptions, these programs continue today to function as separate entities. Each enterprise usually has its own standards and goals, and the personnel within each generally identify their careers with that special system rather than with the field of corrections as a whole. Until recently, in fact, the term "corrections" referred only to work with adults; juvenile probation and aftercare workers were more apt to identify with the field of child welfare than with corrections—although in some jurisdictions strenuous attempts were made to differentiate juvenile court workers from welfare personnel on the ground that the latter "give away money" while the former "protect society," deal with "dangerous people," and are, therefore, entitled to better pay and greater esteem. As a result, correctional units have tended to become "institutionalized" and to lack a broad, coherent, and interrelated program to deal with mutual problems.

The necessity for coordination of the services needed by correctional clients is apparent in any overview of the diverse agencies. Shortcomings of any correctional endeavor almost invariably place added strain on another, and the absence of one basic service can hinder the performance of another. Examples of likely chains of events resulting from correctional shortcomings can readily be cited. Failure to provide adequate screening and prehearing studies at the juvenile-court level may result in an untoward number of training-school commitments. Such procedures place an undue burden on training-school resources and may undermine the integrity of the training-school program. Absence of a juvenile aftercare program may result in increased recidivism by training-school graduates, which in turn may add to the caseload of misdemeanant and felony-probation services or to the overcrowding of adult institutions. Inadequate or nonexistent services for misdemeanants may add to the number of disrupted homes, lost jobs, and similar situations, which could produce increased rates of delinquency and crime. Poor probation services in a community usually leave a judge with little choice but to commit an offender to a correctional facility. Overcrowding of such facilities may clog court and parole dockets, forcing some persons to be kept under supervision beyond an optimum point.

The parade of interrelated consequences of inadequate correctional facilities may be looked at almost as long as the spectator cares to watch it pass in review, its ranks swelled by an unwillingness on the part of those on the sidelines to call a halt to practices indisputably detrimental to their own and others' well-being and to insist on a hard, clean look at the entire field of corrections as an interdependent operation. In this chapter, we shall concentrate on several of the key units of the correctional spectrum, beginning with jails and misdemeanant treatment. Following this, we shall examine programs aimed at ameliorating criticisms of the prison system indicated in the previous chapter, including conjugal visiting, work release, and group therapy. Alternatives to incarceration, which are gaining increasing attention, will then be scrutinized, and the question of civil commitment will be examined along with the general issue of individual responsibility that underlies it. Finally, we shall examine probation and parole as they bear on criminal behavior and the social response to such behavior.

Jails

Jails—in early English, *gaols*—were the institutional forerunners of the contemporary prison. In the beginning their exclusive function was to hold malefactors until they could be tried by the courts, following which the convicted person would either be hanged or transported. As one wag put it, the jails were the "ante-room to the New World—or the next."[1]

The early jails and a large number of their successors were indescribably wretched. Often they would bring together felons and misdemeanants as well as males and females. There were no sleeping facilities except straw tossed on the dirt floors, and sanitary conditions were frightfully primitive. Sheriffs in charge of the jails made their living by charging fees for the maintenance of the prisoners as well as for shackling them with irons and chains, since the average early jail was far from escapeproof.

1 Fox, *English Prison and Borstal System,* p. 24.

Today there are, according to Bureau of Census reports, 2,969 local jails and workhouses in the United States. Most are small, with few inmates. Thirteen hundred jails and workhouses at the time of the census had fewer than ten inmates in them; another 800 had between ten and twenty-four. It is estimated that about 1 million persons pass through jails and workhouses each year, with the daily population probably somewhere between 120,000 and 150,000 persons. How many of these individuals serve more than one jail sentence in the course of any given period is unknown; such information is simply not collected by jail administrators.

That all types and classes of offenders are mixed together and that jails are chronically overcrowded can be gathered from a description of the Cook County Jail by Hans Mattick, who was its assistant superintendent. The jail had been designed to hold 1,032 inmates. At the time Mattick was writing, it had a daily population between 1,600 and 2,400 persons:

> In the single building that constitutes the Cook County Jail is housed the most heterogeneous inmate population ever congregated under one roof. The inmates can be classified in any number of ways. The jail houses both male and female adults and juveniles of both sexes. Jurisdictionally speaking, it houses municipal, county, state and federal prisoners. In terms of legal status, it houses both sentenced and non-sentenced inmates. In terms of offense categories, the jail houses persons charged with everything from committing a public nuisance to murder. Sentences range from a few hours in custody to death in the electric chair. In terms of time served, the range is from one day to five years. . . . Ages range from 15 to 85. Sentenced prisoners comprise two-thirds of the population. Ten men are awaiting death by execution.[2]

Census figures permit comparisons between jail populations and populations of prisons and reformatories. The figures show that almost twice as many women are incarcerated in jails as in prisons and reformatories, although the percentage of women is not very high in either—less than 4 percent in prisons and reformatories and slightly more than 7 percent in jails. Age distributions show a disproportionate number of younger persons in prisons than in jails.

Minority groups are severely overrepresented in jails, with more than 30 percent of the 1960 jail population being nonwhite, a figure more than double the nonwhite population in the nation. Most telling is the near 50 percent proportion of nonwhite females in jails—for example, in 1960, there were 3,819 nonwhite females in a total jail female count of 7,805.

Statistics on the numbers and kinds of persons in jails fail by far to convey the waste, despair, and hopelessness of much of the jail routine throughout the country. Federal jail inspectors, who visit

2 Korn and McCorkle, *Criminology and Penology,* p. 460.

local instititutions to determine if they are suitable to house federal prisoners, would often be just in comparing them to "Augean stables." To ferret out accurate information regarding these institutions often seems to be a more formidable task than that which confronted Hercules. Undoubtedly the best information we have is that gathered during 1966, when the National Council on Crime and Delinquency (NCCD) conducted a nationwide survey of correctional facilities on behalf of the President's Commission on Law Enforcement and Administration of Justice. Comments on jails supplied in unpublished memoranda by the NCCD surveyors included the following:

> *Oregon:* Most counties and cities persist in operating their own jails, nearly all of which are nothing more than steel cages in which people stay for periods up to a year. Most jails are custody oriented and supervised by ill-trained, underpaid personnel. In some cases (e.g., the city jail in Dallas—Wasco County) the jail is not manned except as a police officer on duty can look in once during his eight-hour shift.

> *New Jersey:* Staff for local adult institutions are under county merit system, but about 50 per cent of the staff is classed as temporary employees because they cannot meet the qualifications of the merit system.

> *Texas:* One jail had a total staff of two jailers for a three-story jail building. Each man puts in a 12-hour day and the man on the night shift is expected to sleep through the night on a cot in a first floor office with no responsibility to make periodic investigations of the upper floors.

The jail situation in the United States today can probably best be understood by examination of an individual city's program. In Detroit, for instance, many misdemeanants are held in the Wayne County Jail, a facility administered by the Sheriff's Department. The jail is a block-square building, seven stories high, in the heart of the city, and has a 1,000-person capacity. Part of it is old and grimy, whereas a new addition is sparkling clean. The inside of the jail was described by an NCCD field visitor in the following terms:

> One or two man cells and 8–10 man dormitories are mixed on each floor. An exercise aisle, perhaps four feet wide in the old section and somewhat wider in the new, runs outside the cells which are left open throughout the day. Somewhat more space is available in the dormitories. Tables are provided for cards and writing. Most inmates appear to spend their time sleeping, lying on bunks, or talking in pairs or small groups. No organized activity of any kind was visible. An inmate's day apparently consists of killing time as best one can.

Relatives may visit once a week, but visitors and the inmates, although they stand face-to-face and can see one another through a window, must talk by way of a telephone connection. All mail is censored. Cell lights are left on at all times, and meals are served in the cell blocks. The only planned activities are religious services, which are available only to individuals who do not have a bond in excess of $2,500 and against whom no additional charges are pending, and a recently instituted educational program under the auspices of the adult education division of the Detroit schools. The guide taking a field investigator through the jail thought that the school program was "just an excuse to get out of the cell." The schoolroom itself was an unattractive jail-house green cubicle, about twelve by twenty feet, with three tables constituting the only visible equipment.

The jail in Detroit is by no means the worst in the country. Field visits often report more undesirable conditions. In Denver, for instance, the investigator made the typical observation that "while humane, secure, and physically satisfactory, the institution offers not even a modicum of treatment to the inmates who pass through its doors— some 2,200 persons each year." The Women's Detention Center in Baltimore, built in the mid-1800s, was reported to have individual cells that are locked at night, each with an old bucket under the bed to be used for toilet purposes. "It is only infrequently," the widely-traveled field observer reported, "that I have seen a physical plant as bad as this one."

Among the recommended reforms for today's conditions is the return to earlier principles when jails were used only for pretrial detention. In the United Kingdom and Australia persons are never sentenced to jail, but rather are placed in state penitentiaries to serve sentences. A similar program was also adopted in West Germany in May, 1969, in the first major revision of penal statutes since 1871, when the Bonn Republic eliminated almost all jail sentences of less than six months, replacing them with a system of fines based on the ability to pay as well as the gravity of the violation. Under the new system, a theft might result in a $100 fine for a poor man and a $90,000 fine for a millionaire. The new law also abolished the distinction between jails and prisons. Hans Mattick suggests that in the United States a judge should decide which of the following three choices regarding misdemeanants is most applicable: (1) This person merits a sentence of at least six months in a state prison, (2) This person requires some service or treatment in the community and must be supervised to help him to get it, or (3) This person should be released without further supervision.[3] Among other things, Mattick further advocates procedures enabling jail inmates to vote; there is no law forbidding the vote to accused persons, he notes, and no law denying the vote to convicted misdemeanants. "What is required," Mattick maintains, "is a method that will relate the fortunes of the jail and its inmates to the self-interest of the political decision-makers."[4]

[3] Mattick and Aikman, "The Cloacal Region of American Corrections," p. 115.
[4] Ibid., p. 117. See also Geis, "The Right to Vote for Prisoners."

Perspectives on Prisons

The greatest difficulty involved in the reform of offenders concerns alteration of the pattern that led to the original violation. It seems likely that prison experiences of the kind described in the previous chapter tend to reinforce rather than alleviate original criminalistic attitudes and that prisons rather routinely return the inmate to the same milieu from which he emerged, with essentially the same values and beliefs. He may be more concerned about subsequent apprehension, but this may only mean that he will be more careful and circumspect, not that he will be more law-abiding.

The United States relies on prisons more than any other nation in the world. We have approximately 112 adult prisoners for every 100,000 persons in the general population. If we add to this the number of persons held in jails, we get a figure of 178 persons behind bars for every 100,000 of the population. In contrast, England and Wales have only 65 persons under lock and key for every 100,000 citizens, and Japan has only 85.[5] It may be that persons in these other countries are more law-abiding, but it also may be that the United States resorts to imprisonment to a greater extent than is necessary for the well-being of both the offender and society. Henry Weihofen insists that "it is time we Americans realized that we have probably the most ferocious penal policy in the whole world."[6]

That such views have had virtually no effect on public action may be seen from Table 18.1, which presents for even-numbered years

Table 18.1   Year-End Population for State and Federal Institutions, 1940–1964

Year	Number	Rate per 100,000
1940	173,706	131.7
1942	150,384	116.8
1944	132,456	104.1
1946	140,079	99.4
1948	155,977	106.6
1950	166,123	110.3
1952	168,200	108.6
1954	182,848	113.8
1956	189,421	113.4
1958	205,493	118.7
1960	212,953	118.6
1962	218,830	118.1
1964	214,356	112.5

SOURCE: *National Prison Statistics Bulletin*, No. 38, November, 1965, p. 12.

5 Bennett, "Correctional Problems the Courts Can Help Solve," p. 2.
6 Weihofen, *Urge to Punish*, p. 148.

from 1940 through 1964 the number of persons in state and federal prisons, and which also indicates the ratio between prison population and the general population. The most recent drop in prison populations may be traced almost exclusively to federal policies. The number of federal prisoners decreased by 3.4 percent in 1963 and by 6.4 in 1964, while state-prisoner populations fell only .4 percent in the former year and .8 in the latter.

The rate of imprisonment for felons varies strikingly in each state, despite the fact that comparative studies indicate no consistent relationships between the amount of crime in a given jurisdiction and its use of imprisonment, between the rate of growth of a state and the relative size of its prison population, or between the "dangerousness" of convicted felons in a jurisidiction and the inmate count of its prisons. There is a need for more detailed research into such relationships to determine the probable consequences of different degrees to which imprisonment is employed. Figures show ratios of 174:1 between the nonprison and prison populations of Pennsylvania and 149:2 in California, whereas New Jersey, a heavily-urbanized industrial state like California and Pennsylvania, has a ratio of only 69:6. And Massachusetts with a ratio of 37:4, Rhode Island with 33:7, and New Hampshire with 30:6, the lowest ratio in the nation, all have imprisonment rates less than one-fifth that of Pennsylvania. The variations are not merely explainable because of the small size of the three New England states, since Delaware has a ratio of 58:3, Idaho 69:4, Wyoming 100:3, and Vermont 71:1.

Characteristics of persons in state prisons can be derived from the 1960 tabulation, the latest now available, issued by the federal Bureau of Prisons. In 1960, there were 177,703 prisoners confined in state institutions for adult felony offenders, of whom 96.9 percent were men and only 3.1 percent were women. About 85 percent of the prisoners had been confined throughout the year. The median age of the total prisoner group was 30.8 years. Less than 1 percent of the felon population was reported to be foreign-born. Thirty-two percent of the inmates said they were married and 18.6 percent reported themselves divorced; 46.6 indicated single status, which is high considering the median age of the group, and which indicates that there is a problem for correctional programs in dealing with social reintegration of offenders.

Offenses involving violence or the threat of violence (excluding sex offenses) constitute about one-third of the crimes committed by prison inmates. Homicide (11.8 percent) and robbery (16.6 percent) are the two major crimes of violence, while assault (4.9 percent) constitutes the third largest category. About 2 percent of the felon population is convicted of what are regarded as "sex offenses," although the erotic component of such offenses varies greatly, ranging from sometimes consensual acts such as sodomy to forcible rape, so that no easy designation of sex offenses as violent or nonviolent is possible without case-by-case examination.

The time served by felony prisoners varies considerably from jurisdiction to jurisdiction. The median time served throughout the country in 1960 by felons was approximately twenty-one months. About 9 percent of the inmates had been in confinement for five years or more. Among the regions of the nation, the Northeast has the highest median time for its prison inmates—25.1 months. The implications for the crime and recidivist rate in the Northeast, with its pattern of longer periods of imprisonment (but generally fewer prison commitments), is unclear. The least amount of time served in prison is in the Southern states—18.7 months. Within geographical regions, however, there is considerable variation. In the Northeast, for example, Vermont shows the lowest figure in the country—9.1 months—while Rhode Island is among those states with the longest periods of incarceration, which are twice as long as in Vermont. The figures indicate the complexity involved in drawing inferences about the interrelationships among crime rates, conviction and commitment rates, length of prison sentences, recidivism, and a host of other items that distinguish one state from another. The systematic unraveling of such threads is a task that should have high research priority.

Felons are held in some 500 different institutions throughout the United States. The Federal Bureau of Prisons operates thirty-four such institutions, while the Army, Navy, and Air Force have one each. Five institutions are operated by the District of Columbia alone. The Vermont State Prison and House of Correction for Men, which opened in 1809, holds the distinction of being the oldest state prison in the country; its decrepit buildings house a conglomerate collection of misdemeanants and felons from the age of sixteen upward. Next oldest is the Maryland Penitentiary, which opened in 1811. New York's Auburn Prison received its first inmate in 1817. Confinement of prisoners in the first cellblock at Sing Sing, built in New York in 1829, was ended in 1940, exactly a century after it was first condemned as unfit for human habitation.

Prisons are usually termed maximum, medium, and minimum security institutions, in terms of the amount of control they exercise over their inmates. A maximum-security institution usually has a high wall and guard towers, solidly constructed and heavily barred buildings and windows, and cellblocks of the "inside type", having four to six tiers of cells, back to back, with their barred fronts ten to fifteen feet from the cellhouse windows. Maximum-security prisons usually stress custodial control by surveillance, routine and surprise searches for anything contraband, frequent counts of prisoners, and strict enforcement of disciplinary rules and regulations. Relaxation of such conditions and more open accommodations characterize institutions with lesser security classifications.

Most programs in the various institutions are built around security considerations, as these are more or less tailored to fit reformative ends. John Conrad, who surveyed correctional institutions both in the United States and abroad, found custodial concerns ubiquitously involved in all attempts to perform other functions:

> The standard practice of corrections, wherever we went, centered on the containment of the correctional client. Whatever else was done for him, the client was held . . . within arbitrary limits. Much more was done for many clients: They were educated, put to remunerative work, given remedial surgery, and provided with various kinds of psychotherapy. Even more was attempted: A frequently encountered phenomenon was the good idea put into play with inadequate resources. However, control was the guiding consideration of the correctional apparatus. All other operations were shaped to meet the patterns dictated by custody and surveillance.[7]

Nonetheless, in recent years increasing efforts have been made to establish prison programs that make sense in reformative terms. Part of this response has come from what appears to be a public redefinition of correctional goals. In 1967, for instance, the Harris Poll put the following questions to a nationwide sample: (1) Do you feel that most prisons today mainly try to be corrective—that is, try to make criminals into useful citizens—or mainly to be punitive—that is, punish criminals for having broken the law?, and (2) Do you feel prisons should be mainly corrective, trying to rehabilitate criminals, or mainly punitive, punishing them for their crime? Table 18.2 shows the results of the inquiry, and Table 18.3 indicates further explanations of the responses. The results indicate an overwhelming stress—by a margin of 7 to 1—among the respondents regarding the necessity for prisons to become more corrective, although within such verbal answers one person's corrective stress may be like another's punitive emphasis; furthermore, it is easier to be benevolent in abstract verbal sentiments than in practice.

Table 18.2   Present and Ideal View of Purpose of Prison

Response	Prisons are	Prisons should be
Mainly corrective	57%	77%
Mainly punitive	19%	11%
Not sure	24%	12%
Total	100%	100%

SOURCE: Harris Poll, *Los Angeles Times*, August 14, 1967.

7 Conrad, *Crime and Its Correction*, p. 172.

Table 18.3 Explanations of Views Regarding Rehabilitation or Punishment

Why mainly corrective		*77%*
Make better citizens	20	
Should be rehabilitated	10	
Better to correct than to punish	10	
Give them a chance	10	
Criminals should be educated	10	
More correction means less crime	9	
Make safe to protect Society	3	
Costs money to keep in prison	3	
Criminals need mental treatment	2	
Why mainly punitive		*11%*
Teach them a lesson	6	
They're no good	3	
No punishment enough	2	
Not sure		*12%*
Total	100%	100%

SOURCE: Harris Poll, *Los Angeles Times*, August 14, 1967.

Clarence Schrag's appraisal seems to be an accurate summary of today's prisons and their problems. He writes:

> The prison of yesterday, based on a model of constraint, is dead. Neither the goal of penitence nor the strategy of solitary confinement is regarded as viable today. But prisons, like other social institutions, are rarely buried. Thus, today's prison, based on a model of rehabilitation, has to build on its legacy of outmoded physical facilities, inadequate personnel, and erroneous beliefs and theories. And it must build at a time of growing public concern for problems of deviance and justice.[8]

Among the major areas in which changes are taking place or being considered are work programs, conjugal visits, and group therapy.

WORK PROGRAMS

Elaborate work programs have become part of the fare at many institutions on the assumption that offenders who are able to earn good livings through legitimate work will be less likely to turn to illegal channels. Much of prison work, however, involves the creation of artificial tasks, the overassignment of more men than are necessary to jobs that have no meaning in the outside world (i.e., erasing scribbling in textbooks or working a machine that turns out license plates), or doing housekeeping tasks within the institution. However, more men remain idle in most institutions than are involved in any kind of work

8 Schrag, "The Correctional System: Problems and Prospects."

program. In addition, American prisons persistently have difficulty with both private business and labor unions in developing comprehensive programs of prison labor and training. Today, some progress is being made through state-use laws, which demand that prison-made goods be used wherever possible in other state-operated facilities. The outstanding record of American prisoners in producing war goods during World War II is strong documentation of the ability of inmates to perform extraordinary services if sufficient motivation is present.[9]

Part of the work difficulty in prisons lies, of course, in the lack of motivation and incentive among the men. Payment for a full day's work runs less than 50 cents in most American prisons. John Conrad's description of labor in some prisons in the Soviet Union, a country not known for the indulgence of its violators, should give pause to correctional reformers in the United States:

> It would be pleasant to report that an impressive solution to the problem [of the demoralizing nature of prison labor] had been found in the United States or in a western country. It was in the Soviet Union, however, that we saw prison labor most impressively used. We saw well-equipped factories turning out such consumer goods as kitchen utensils, fire helmets, automobile engine parts, and metal tools. The pace looked fast and it was explained to us that the production norms were the same as for civilian industry. We noted that great attention was given to each man's performance. . . . What punitive sanctions spurred on the slacker and inspired the incompetent may not have been clear. Group ridicule of sloth, and eulogy of outstanding production, was everywhere evident . . . but a positive incentive in the form of full pay at regular rates would be enough to account for a considerable difference from the stagnant pace of prison industries in most western countries.[10]

Undoubtedly the most encouraging development in prison labor in this century in the United States has been the establishment of programs of "work release" or "work furlough," as they are sometimes called.[11] Under such programs, inmates are allowed to leave the institution during the day to work at jobs in the outside community. The name of the pioneering statute, which was restricted to misdemeanants and formulated in Wisconsin, is the Huber Law; it was enacted in 1913,[12] but the movement failed to catch on or to be extended to felons until North Carolina adopted work release in 1957. Under the North Carolina program, a man may hold a job for up to sixty hours a week; his eligibility for work-release status is determined either by the sentencing judge or by a review board. In its first eight years of operation, the North Carolina work-release program involved 1,046 prisoners and reported no crimes of violence among the

9 England, *Prison.Labour.*
10 Conrad, *Crime and Its Correction,* pp. 48–49.
11 Grupp, "Work Release"; McMillan, "Work Furlough for the Jailed Prisoner."
12 Schmidt, "Wisconsin Jails and the Huber Law."

men, although 16 percent had to be removed from the program, primarily because of either drinking or visiting wives or girl friends while away from the institution.[13] The North Carolina example led more than thirty states to adopt similar programs in the 1960s, and the federal government to pass the Federal Prisoner Rehabilitation Act, a work-release statute, in 1965.[14]

Major advantages of work-release include its ability to decrease the pace of institutionalization by allowing a man to remain in contact with the outside world on a day-to-day basis. In addition, the program tends to reduce prison and welfare costs, to provide a test by means of which the parole board can better gauge a man's readiness for full release, and to ease the transition for the inmate between prison and the community.

CONJUGAL VISITING

Conjugal visiting, a pattern under which wives are permitted to visit with their incarcerated husbands, has never been sanctioned in the United States, with the notable exception of the state prison at Parchman, Mississippi—although, according to Austin MacCormick, a leading authority on American prisons, there is some surreptitious conjugal visiting in several other institutions.[15] Ruth S. Cavan and Eugene Zemans note that "conjugal visits are not compatible with the mores of the United States since they seem to emphasize only the physical satisfactions of sex," but they point out that home leaves and family residence in prison colonies, both of which emphasize the whole complex of married life and family relationships, might contain rehabilitative potentialities. From a world-wide survey, Cavan and Zemans conclude that other countries, much more than the United States, are expanding family-prisoner contacts, and they ask, "Is it not possible that in the United States a more reflective and experimental attitude toward marital contact is needed?"[16]

Among the more unusual institutions included in the Cavan and Zemans survey is the Tres Marias island penal colony of Mexico, located sixty miles off the coast of Mazatlan. Tres Marias is a neat community, with lofty palms, a plaza, and a bandstand, which looks much like a typical Mexican pueblo. Between 500 and 1,500 inmates live at Tres Marias, representing in general persons in Mexico with the longest sentences and severest offenses. After six months of good behavior, the prisoner may bring his family to live with him at the colony. He has complete freedom of the island's 34,000 acres, and he may pursue an occupation of his choice. Reports indicate that the

13 *New York Times,* Aug. 18, 1965.
14 Carpenter, "Federal Work Release Program."
15 *New York Times,* Aug, 25, 1955.
16 Zemans and Cavan, "Marital Relationships of Prisoners"; Cavan and Zemans, "Marital Relationships of Prisoners in 28 Countries."

morale at Tres Marias is high, with the greatest tensions growing out
of conflict among men who want to marry female prisoners.[17]

Since the Cavan and Zemans study, Sweden, usually acknowledged
to have the most progressive penal policy in the world, has expanded
its system of conjugal visiting by constructing a special penal facility
where wives, fiancés, and children are permitted to visit inmates and
remain for extended periods, providing they pay their own room and
board. Another new Swedish prison has apartments where a prisoner
and his family may live if the inmate is regarded as being in danger
of drifting into hard-core criminality through association with regular
offenders, or if his family is believed to be suffering greatly because of
the absence of a husband and father. By a 1946 law, the Swedish
Riksdag insisted that a prisoner be treated "with respect for his dignity as a human being," although the same law also stated that he
should be treated "firmly."[18] The object of the law was reformative
rather than support for the "vengeful sentiments of the least enlight-
ened members of the society." Most Swedish prisoners receive three
days of leave four times a year after they have been incarcerated for
six months. About 2 percent get into some trouble while they are on
leave, but, since Sweden is a small country, the police have little difficulty apprehending the offenders. The Swedish prisons are highly
decentralized and specialized, with 83 institutions accommodating different types of offenders.[19]

In the United States, the conjugal visiting program at Parchman
is an outgrowth of conditions in the 1900s, when inmates ran the
prison, and wives, girl friends, and prostitutes were regularly brought
inside the institution walls. The conjugal visiting program was enacted into law in 1956. It involves some 500 married women and a
number of common-law wives who are permitted to visit their husbands in separate apartments on the prison grounds from 1 P.M. to
3 P.M. each Sunday and from 1 P.M. to 5 P.M. every third Sunday.
Estimates of the importance and consequences of the conjugal-visiting
program vary. Some maintain that since the program involves less
than one-third of the institution's 1,630 inmates, it only intensifies the
monastic feelings of a majority of the population. Others suggest that
publicity given to the conjugal-visiting program diverts attention from
the basic deprivations of the institution. The prison is run almost
exclusively by armed trustees, prisoners themselves, and is said to be
marked by homosexuality, bribery, and brutality, despite encouraging recent improvements in admistration and facilities.[20] Other evaluations of the conjugal visiting program at Parchman maintain that
interviews with inmates show their enthusiastic support of the program

17 Jewell, "Mexico's Tres Marias Penal Colony."
18 Eriksson, "Postwar Prison Reform in Sweden." See also *Penal Code of Sweden.*
19 Fleisher, *Sweden:The Welfare State,* pp. 205–226; Bixby, "Penology in Sweden and
    Denmark."
20 *New York Times,* Feb. 10, 1968.

and their belief that it represents one of the most progressive and encouraging movements in American penology.[21]

GROUP THERAPY

Group therapy, also called group counseling, among other things, is an institutional regimen that has become of considerable importance in American prisons.[22] First begun with military personnel, then adapted to the New Jersey prisons under the name of "guided group interaction," such therapy aims to develop within prisoners an understanding of the facts that led them to prison. It also provides an opportunity for the inmate to catharsize, that is, to express openly the various angry feelings that the prison might have aroused within him.[23] It is presumed that such activities aid in providing the necessary degree of insight to keep the inmate out of further difficulty.

There are fundamental difficulties involved with group-therapy programs, however, most of which still await resolution. For one thing, they have a tendency to redefine the offender as "sick" rather than as "bad," and it is arguable whether this change in self-image, when accepted, is enabling or detrimental. For another, sessions tend to avoid straightforward discussion of the complexities of personal and social interaction in the genesis of criminal behavior, and they tend to concentrate on the alleged personal inadequacies of the offender. Finally, group therapy is seen by some inmates as the most brutal of all punishments developed by correctional institutions, since it insists on penetrating the mind and promotes self-revelation, which, if he accedes to its demands, lays the offender naked before his captors and his fellow prisoners. If he does not accede to the imperatives of group therapy, he is apt to be retained within the institution for longer periods than his colleagues on the ground that he is resistant and intractable, that he refuses to look at himself intensely and to come to grips with his alleged problems. On the other hand, if he simulates therapeutic involvement, as many articulate and sophisticated inmates do, then he is apt to develop contempt for the group leaders who might respond approvingly to his presumed soul-baring.

The tendency of correctional group therapy to substitute superficial diagnosis for direct discourse is illustrated by a California session, which proceeded in the following manner:

> The discussion centered about a loud complaint by an inmate that he had checked his going-home clothes only to find that his expensive sports jacket had been stolen. What kind of a prison was this, he wanted to know, where the custodial people could not adequately protect a man's property?

---

21 Hopper, *Sex in Prison.*
22 Bixby and McCorkle, "Guided Group Interaction in Correctional Work."
23 McCorkle and Korn, "Resocialization Within Walls."

The group leader, of course, wanted to know what the group thought. They thought it was pretty disgusting and, thus reinforced, the inmate resumed a vitriolic attack on the supposed guardians of his belongings. Again the leader interposed, asking him what he thought of the situation.

The inmate, who had made it quite clear what he thought, reiterated his opinion. Perhaps you can guess the leader's response:

"Why do you think that?" he wanted to know. "What do clothes *really* mean to you?"

Very angry now, the inmate stepped up his attack. But the remainder of the group now began to send out cues.

"Forget about it," they warned. "Don't lose your temper. It's just one of their tricks. They put the stuff someplace else to see how'll you'll take it, and then they'll decide whether you can go home. It ain't worth it."

Duly warned by this unfounded interpretation of the situation, the inmate became quite conciliatory and dropped the subject as soon as the leader would allow him to.[24]

There are empirical as well as moral problems regarding the growing use of group therapy in correctional institutions. The most penetrating study to date, conducted in California by David Ward and Gene Kassebaum, strongly suggests that group therapy has no impact on the subsequent criminal behavior of the inmate exposed to it. The program may, of course, allow for smoother operation of the institution itself, by opening channels of communication between staff and inmate, but Ward and Kassebaum question its value in terms of its goal of reducing recidivism. Their experiment took four groups of prisoners, each with 600 men, and offered three of the groups different kinds of intensive group counseling; the fourth group received the same prison treatment as the other three, except that its members had no involvement in group counseling. A follow-up investigation five years after completion of the experimental program indicated no significant difference in the criminal behavior among persons in any of the four groups.[25]

OTHER PRISON REFORMS

Reevaluation of group therapy programs is but one of the pressing needs in prison work. The President's Commission on Law Enforcement and Administration of Justice also suggests that strong efforts be made to establish "collaborative" institutions. It notes that:

The collaborative institution is structured around the partnership of

24 Geis, "Correctional Work: 'Think Ye That Ye May Be Wrong.'"
25 Kassebaum, Jr., Ward, and Wilner, *Prison Treatment and Parole Survival.*

all inmates and staff members in the process of rehabilitation. It tries to oppose the tendency for an institution to become isolated from the community physically and in terms of values, and instead seeks to assimilate inmates in normal noncriminal ways of life, partly through close identification with staff and partly through increased communication with the outside community.[26]

Setting up such an instituiton would require a thoroughgoing revision of traditional prison rules and procedures. In traditional prisons, for instance, the serving of meals proceeds in a highly regimented fashion, in which inmates march to meals in lines that are closely watched by guards, sit in silence on one side of long, narrow tables, and, in some prisons, are given only large spoons with which to eat, because knives and forks can be stolen and fashioned into weapons. A collaborative institution would install four-man, restaurant-style tables and permit men to go informally to the dining halls during the serving period. Similarly, schedules would become more flexible, with greater discretion left to inmates regarding when they arise, eat, work, and go to bed. Most importantly, there would be an increased degree of decision-making by members of the inmate population.[27]

Suggestions beyond those advanced by the President's Commission have also been made regarding reform of prisons. Among the more intriguing proposals is that of Sykes, who advocates that noncriminals be introduced into prisons, to mix with the regular population. Sykes concedes that finding volunteers to undergo the deprivations of prison life would not be simple, but he believes that students, VISTA workers, and members of various religious groups, among other persons, might contribute to the effort. He suggests three possible outcomes of this. First, there is the primary, planned consequence of creating a countervailing subculture that will influence the attitudes and the behavior of the confined offenders. Second, there is the strong possibility that the regime of the custodians could be reexamined in a new and more rational light when the custodial and administrative staff finds that it faces middle-class noncriminals as well as lower-class offenders. And third, the group of voluntary inmates could unquestioningly learn more about the structure and functioning of penal institutions than would be possible by almost any other means.[28] On the other hand, Sykes admits that the prisoners might corrupt the volunteers.

While the need for internal reforms in prisons is pressing, students of the situation agree that the most fundamental requirement is to siphon out of the prisons all but the most recalcitrant offenders and to establish programs more closely related to community life for those individuals who can benefit from such programs. Actions of this type stand to benefit not only the offender but, by reducing his alienation

26 President's Commission, *Corrections*, p. 47.
27 *Ibid.*
28 Sykes, "Criminals and Non-Criminals Together."

from the mainstream of the society, would likely benefit the society as well.[29]

Criminal Responsibility

Fundamental to procedures for dealing with offenders are questions of criminal responsibility. Responsible persons may be punished, the ethos goes, but persons not responsible for their behavior deserve to be helped. The attempt is to treat the incompetent person for his condition rather than to respond to his crime, while the competent person undergoes procedures designed, presumably, to impress upon his rational faculties the undesirability of criminal activity. This distinction between treatment and punishment, however, and that between responsibility and its absence, stand at the moment in a state of considerable confusion.

One example will suffice to indicate some elements of the dilemma. Individual A commits arson. He is adjudged not to be responsible for his act because he was performing under the direction of a compulsive, pathological drive. He is therefore sent to a mental hospital where, under conditions that are not likely to be much more attractive than those of the ordinary prison,[30] he will be given treatment for his mental condition. When "cured," he may be returned to the community. If not cured, presumably he will be retained within the institution for the remainder of his life. Individual B also commits arson, but a panel of forensic psychiatrists declares that he is not suffering from any mental aberration of a nature to have interfered drastically with his exercise of free will and his option to determine whether or not he had chosen to set the fire. Individual B is sentenced to a correctional institution where he will receive, along with the punishment of imprisonment, some mild forms of treatment. After the lapse of a certain period of time, B will be returned to the community.

Difficulties lie in determining answers to some of the following questions: (1) Is the treatment of A, undertaken for his own good and presumably because he is less responsible, a better or worse fate than that of B? (2) Will the respective dispositions of both cases produce the results desired in either instance or in both instances? (3) If the treatment in the hospital is good for A, why would it not be useful for B? (4) Are either A or B really responsible for their acts, or is the differentiation between them merely an arbitrary and meaningless distinction?

At the heart of such issues lies the question of criminal responsibility. No single issue in criminal law, with the possible exception of capital punishment, has aroused more controversy. The intensity of the conflict may in some measure be traceable to the closely equiv-

29 See Empey, *Alternatives to Incarceration.*
30 See Deutsch, *Shame of the States;* Goffman, *Asylums.*

alent social statuses of the two major groups involved: lawyers and psychiatrists. Each group feels that it has a particular professional stake in its viewpoint, and each feels that the other lacks the knowledge essential to appreciate the necessity for particular definitions and their historical and scientific rationales. The determination of criminal responsibility centers in debates around the M'Naghten Rule.

THE M'NAGHTEN RULE

Adopted in England in 1843, the M'Naghten Rule was formulated by the House of Lords and stated that a person was excused from criminal responsibility if at the time of the commission of his act "he was laboring under such a defect of reason as not to know the nature or quality of the act he was doing; or, if he did know it, that he did not know he was doing what was wrong."[31] The rule subsequently was transplanted intact to most jurisdictions in the United States. It arose when a Scotsman, Daniel M'Naghten, was acquitted on the ground of insanity for an attempt on the life of the British Prime Minister that resulted in the death of the Prime Minister's secretary.

In substance, the M'Naghten Rule remains the law of most jurisdictions in the United States. Fifteen states, beginning with Ohio in 1834, have added to it the concept of "irresistible impulse," by which a defendant who is found to have acted under such an impulse is not held criminally responsible.[32] The concept of "irresistible impulse," however, has been found deficient by some writers in at least five respects: (1) An impulse to do harm by one who can distinguish right from wrong cannot be irresistible but only unresisted, (2) It is difficult to prove the existence of an "irresistible impulse" in a given case, (3) The test is too impractical in its application, (4) Its use is dangerous to society because it dilutes the deterrent effect of the law, (5) It is not needed, since post-conviction clemency can be granted to persons "irresistibly" driven to commit crimes.[33]

Critics of the M'Naghten Rule stress that it is outdated and archaic. They call attention to cases in which the defendant appears to know right from wrong, but nonetheless seems incapable of obeying the criminal law. Such a condition, it is believed, is particularly true of offenders tagged as "psychopaths" or "sociopaths." Calling for revision of the M'Naghten Rule, one judge notes that "the development of psychiatry appears to have transferred the main professional attention from disorganization of the intellect to emotional disturbances" while "the legal definition remains focused upon intellectual disorientation."[34] Others maintain that competent psychiatrists cannot

---

31 *Daniel M'Naghten's Case.* See also Glueck, "Mental Illness and Criminal Responsibility."

32 For a fictional treatment of the criminal see Traver, *Anatomy of a Murder.*

33 Guttmacher and Weihofen, *Psychiatry and the Law,* p. 409; Keedy, "Irresistible Impulse as a Defense in Criminal Law," pp. 987–988.

34 *People v. Horton,* p. 19.

accurately describe a defendant's mental condition in court, using modern terminology, without raising objections from attorneys that such description has nothing to do with the *M'Naghten* criteria. As one writer notes, "If on an issue whether someone had typhoid, the pathologist was told that he must not consider the laboratory tests, but only one symptom, temperature, which is solemnly declared legally conclusive, who would have confidence in such testimony or such procedure?"[35] In addition, it is not as clear in *M'Naghten* whether the concepts of "right" and "wrong" refer to moral or to legal standards; there are advocates of both views—the United States tends to interpret them as moral standards, whereas England tends toward legal criteria.

Defenders of the M'Naghten Rule stress that it has succeeded in practice and in a reasonable way has managed to separate the more seriously disturbed offenders from the less seriously disturbed ones. Most importantly, the rule offers a working definition of responsibility against which evaluators can measure each offender with some precision. Lady Wootton, an astute British writer in the field of criminology, observes that "Once we allow any movement away from a rigid intellectual test of responsibility on *M'Naghten* lines, our feet are set upon a slippery slope which offers no real resting place short of the total abandonment of the whole concept of responsibility."[36] It is said that abandonment of the M'Naghten Rule would throw determination of responsibility open to the anarchistic judgments of psychiatrists who have to date notably failed to come to any agreement among themselves, either in terminology or diagnoses.[37] Lawyers cite numerous cases in which psychiatrists took opposing sides and disputed vehemently the accuracy of interpretations of an accused's mental condition, although the importance of this is challenged by Hermann Mannheim, a British criminologist, who observes that it is naive to expect any complex discipline to show unanimity of opinion, and that psychiatry is at least as sophisticated and shows as much consensus as either law or sociology.[38]

THE DURHAM AND CURRENS RULES

The first breakthrough in the United States against the M'Naghten Rule occurred in 1954 in the *Durham* case, when the Court of Appeals for the District of Columbia declared that it would recognize a new definition of criminal responsibility. Under the Durham Rule, "an accused is not criminally responsible if his unlawful act was the product of mental disease or mental defect."[39] The Durham Rule followed the

35 Sobeloff, "Insanity and the Criminal Law," p. 795.
36 Wootton, *Social Science and Social Pathology*, p. 249.
37 See Hakeem, "A Critique of the Psychiatric Approach to Crime and Correction."
38 Mannheim, "The Criminal Law and Mentally Abnormal Offenders."
39 *Durham v. United States.* See also Wathen, "Criminal Responsibility: Durham Rule in Maine."

position taken as early as 1869 in New Hampshire, which rejected *M'Naghten* on the ground that it installed "old exploded medical theories in place of facts established in the progress of scientific knowledge."[40] As in *Durham*, in New Hampshire there was no attempt to establish with precision the meaning of the terms "mental disease" or "mental defect," but rather they were allowed to remain flexible so that they could be kept aligned with current ideas in the sciences.[41]

Early enthusiasm for *Durham* dissipated, however, as court after court found its rationale unacceptable. Primarily, they felt that the Durham Rule offered no guideline by which judges or juries could determine how much of any action or diagnosis constituted "enough" to conclude that the accused was suffering from a defect or disease sufficient to excuse him. At what point, it was asked, do idiosyncracies shade over into defect and disease?[42]

To obviate such problems and to gain greater acceptance from other courts in the nation, Chief Judge John Biggs, Jr., of the Third Circuit Court of Appeals, in 1961 handed down a new definition of insanity in the *Currens* case.[43] Donald Currens had been convicted of violating the Dyer Act by transporting a stolen vehicle from Mansfield, Ohio to Pennsylvania. In declaring that Currens' mental condition was to be judged under a new concept, Judge Biggs criticized both the M'Naghten and Durham Rules. Judge Biggs claimed that *M'Naghten* actually had roots going back into the sixteenth century and that it mirrored a period in which "belief in witchcraft and demonology, even among well-educated men, was widespread." Furthermore, he believed that *M'Naghten* was "unworkable, an intellectual sham," and an "antique and creaking doctrine"; it was also too vague, and it failed, by ignoring the amount of control the individual might have over his mental state, to provide a workable rule.

To relieve the defendant of criminal responsibility under the Currens Rule "the jury must be satisfied that at the time of committing the prohibited act the defendant, as a result of mental disease or defect, lacked substantial capacity to conform his conduct to the requirements of the law which he is alleged to have violated." *Currens* attempts to tie the mental state of the defendant to the crime that he committed and, of course, to substitute "substantial capacity to conform" for the criterion under *Durham* that the act was a "product" of mental disease or defect.

The position in *Currens* was derived in large part from the formulation put forward by the American Law Institute (A.L.I.) as part of its Model Penal Code. The Institute's provision, which has

40 *State v. Pike*, p. 408.
41 Reid, "Understanding the New Hampshire Doctrine of Criminal Responsibility";
  Reid, "Companion of the New Hampshire Doctrine of Criminal Responsibility."
42 *Anderson v. United States*, p. 127.
43 *United States v. Currens*.

been adopted in Vermont, Illinois, and by the second-circuit Court of Appeals,[44] differs from *Currens* in that it adds the phrase "he lacks substantial capacity . . . to appreciate the criminality of his conduct" as an additional test of responsibility. Judge Biggs in *Currens* believed that those words in the A.L.I. formulation "overemphasize the cognitive element in criminal responsibility and thus distract the jury from the crucial issues,[45] and he therefore omitted them, although he retained the other elements.

Lying at the heart of the matter of criminal responsibility is a philosophical impasse that proponents of any rule cannot resolve scientifically and often prefer to ignore. It is the dilemma inherent in the question of whether human behavior is determined or whether it is the consequence of the exercise of free will. If all human acts, both criminal and noncriminal, are totally determined by prior events, then no individual can be said to be "responsible" for his behavior; offenders should therefore presumably be dealt with in terms of what they have done (putting aside any notion of responsibility[46]) and what their subsequent behavior is likely to be—as well as that can be predicted.

There is also the question of sociological as opposed to psychiatric responsibility. If an offender is to be excused because of his mental condition, why should he not also be excused because of compelling circumstances of his social situation? C. Ray Jeffery explains this issue and offers his interpretation of why it has not as yet been resolved:

> It is assumed by the psychiatrist that the crux of the problem is the M'Naghten Rule. The real problem is, however, the fact that we do not know the causes of criminal behavior. A causal link is assumed to exist between mental illness and crime, and therefore we feel we should not punish the mentally ill. We do not hesitate to punish those who are social criminals, those whose criminal activities are a result of the environment in which they grew up. This is a moral reaction, not a scientific reaction, since social determinants are causal determinants, and social determinism is as real as psychic determinism. Why do we not have sociologists testifying at criminal trials as to the social determinants of behavior? The reason we do not has nothing to do with the scientific explanations of behavior but is related to the fact that the physician has come to occupy an important position in the power structure of the community, whereas the sociologist does not.[47]

Perhaps the best explanation offered for the existence and emphasis in criminal law on the question of "responsibility" is that offered by one-time Supreme Court Justice Robert Jackson, who defends existing concepts on the grounds of pragmatic utility:

44 *United States v. Freeman.*
45 *United States v. Currens*, note 32, p. 754.
46 Goldstein and Katz, "Abolish the 'Insanity Defense'—Why Not?"
47 Jeffery in Davis, *Society and the Law.*

How far one by an excercise of free will may determine his general destiny or his course in a particular matter and how far he is the toy of circumstances has been debated through the ages by theologians, philosophers, and scientists. Whatever doubts they have entertained as to the matter, the practical business of government and administration of law is obliged to proceed on more or less rough and ready judgments based on the assumption that mature and rational persons are in control of their own conduct.[48]

Civil Commitment

The extensive use of civil-commitment procedures, relegating certain types of offenders to situations that are strikingly similar to those of imprisonment but otherwise named, has gained momentum within recent years and requires examination. The thesis of civil commitment is that the offender is excused from the usual consequences of his criminal behavior, or the criminal behavior itself is redefined, because of psychic aberrations or inadequacies associated with the behavior. These deficiencies are labelled "illnesses," and the offender is considered "sick." To assist him, he is placed in a custodial situation where the emphasis is said to be on "treatment."

Excusing an individual from criminal responsibility for his behavior or condition does not necessarily free him from state control, however. It has been pointed out, for instance, that Daniel M'Naghten, although acquitted on the charge of homicide, nonetheless spent the remainder of his life under lock and key in a mental institution. Enlargement of such procedures—the removal of criminal liability but the expansion of civil commitment—has been proceeding apace in recent years. During the four years before the enunciation of the Durham Rule, for instance, only thirteen persons were acquitted in the District of Columbia for insanity; six years after *Durham*, the figure rose to 104; each, under the law, was placed in the District's mental hospital until such time as hospital authorities found, and the court agreed, that the offender had improved sufficiently to be released.[49]

Civil-commitment procedures have, as was noted earlier, also been applied to offenders such as narcotic addicts, who may no longer be punished under criminal law for their condition,[50] but who may be committed on a civil level to treatment centers. Examination of the operation of a few such centers provides material regarding possible consequences of substitution of civil for criminal procedures for certain behaviors.

In New York, for example, reviews of the addict civil-commitment program are summarized in a caustic lead sentence of a newspaper

48 *Gregg Cartage and Storage Co. v. United States*, pp. 79–80.
49 Overholser, "Some Psychiatric Aspects of Criminal Responsibility."
50 *Robinson v. California*.

story: "The State Narcotic Addiction Control Commission, set up two years ago, is in need of rehabilitation itself, a growing number of critics say."[51] At the time—April, 1969—four Commission employees were awaiting trial on charges of beating up addicts with "booted feet, a blackjack, and handcuffs." Most of the addicts committed to the program maintained that it was no different than those run by state correctional authorities and that the results obtained showed no improvement over the criminal approach.

Confirmation of the failure of civil commitment of narcotic addicts to achieve success rates different from those of prison programs is supplied by a comprehensive study of the work of the California civil commitment program for addicts, which has been operating since 1961. By statutory provision, the purpose of the program is to treat, rehabilitate, and control, not to punish. Commitment to the program is based not only on determination that an individual is an addict, but also on the ground that he may be in danger of becoming an addict. The median length of stay in the program has been about fourteen months. Subsequently, the detoxified addict is placed on "outpatient" status for a statutory limit of seven years. Outpatients report regularly to supervising agents, must be tested for drug use, and may be required to attend group counseling sessions. It is said that the restrictions on outpatients "are slightly more encompassing than parole restrictions on nonaddict felons and are usually administered more strictly."[52]

Statistics show that only 35 percent of the 1,209 outpatients released from the program between June, 1962 and June, 1964 remained in good standing for one year and only 16 percent for three years. Most of the failure to remain in good standing came as a consequence of a return to drug use. The rate of failure for the civil-commitment program was found to be essentially similar to that of other regimens for addicts operated under correctional auspices.[53] Under such conditions, arguments for civil commitment become attenuated, since there are no compensating gains to accommodate losses in due-process protections. John Kramer summarized these legal objections by noting that they maintain "that commitment for a treatment which is not proven effective is cruel and unusual punishment and that it is a subterfuge around the stringent protection afforded to a person accused of a crime but not to one "accused" of an illness."[54]

Similar kinds of reservations have been voiced regarding tests of criminal responsibility and programs of civil commitment. Wormuth, for instance, maintains that such programs run contrary to fundamental tenets of democracy. "It is doubtful that democracy could

51 Severo, "Addicts and the State."
52 Kramer, Bass, and Berecochia, "Civil Commitment for Addicts," p. 817.
53 Miller, Himelson, and Geis, "East Los Angeles Halfway House for Felon Addicts."
54 Kramer, et al., "Civil Commitment for Addicts," p. 816.

survive in a society organized on the principle of therapy rather than judgment, error rather than sin. If men are free and equal, they must be judged rather than hospitalized."[55] In more strident tones, Thomas S. Szasz, a psychiatrist, maintains that "most of the legal and social applications of psychiatry, undertaken in the name of psychiatric liberalism, are actually instances of despotism" and that there is a danger abroad in the society of "tyranny by therapy."[56] Szasz, referring to civil-commitment programs, insists that:

> the psychiatric disposition of offenders seems to me a colossal subterfuge. It provides the "offender-patient" neither absolution from criminal guilt *nor* treatment. It is nothing more than an expedient method for "disposing" of persons displaying certain kinds of antisocial conduct. Every form of social oppression . . . has, at some time during its history, been justified on the ground of helpfulness toward the oppressed.[57]

Even more fundamental, perhaps, have been the scathing attacks on psychiatric formulations, which lie at the head of the civil commitment philosophy. Many of these emerge from internal sources. Thus, for instance, two psychiatrists, Corbett H. Thigpen and Hervey M. Cleckley, mount the following verbal assault in calling for more intellectual rigor and vigor in psychiatric work:

> For all its polysyllabic jargon the reigning scheme of popular dynamics narrows down in the end to an amazingly rigid and stereotyped process by which the same stilted and tiresome answers are always ground out. However rich, complex, marvelous, or profound the material of human experience may be, it is at last mechanically reduced by this rule of thumb to unvarying banal and implausible little equations. Anyone so inclined could, by manipulation of trite and essentially simple syllogisms of the prevailing method, construct whatever paradigm his creed demands out of the assumed contents of preverbal memory, the septet of baby fears, various pre-oedipal countercatheses, gelatinations of the libido, interrelations of orality and psychic masochism, embryonic intrauterine emotional traumata, and anally incorporated parental images, as well as out of assumed unconscious fantasies of incest and castration (umbilical as well as penile).[58]

Alternatives to Incarceration

COMMUNITY-TREATMENT PROGRAMS

Various arrangements have been developed over the years in an attempt to keep offenders from the deleterious consequences of imprisonment unless it appears necessary beyond doubt that the person

55 Wormuth, *Origins of Modern Constitutionalism*, p. 212.
56 Szasz, *Law, Liberty, and Psychiatry*, pp. vii–viii.
57 *Ibid.*, pp. 114, 185.
58 Thigpen and Cleckley, *Three Faces of Eve*, p. 222.

needs to be locked up to protect others from potentially serious harm.[59] Probation and parole were early alternatives to incarceration; more recently, a host of community-based programs have emerged and are now in the process of being evaluated and refined. The President's Commission on Law Enforcement and Administration of Justice, strongly endorsing the idea of community-based corrections, called for the establishment of facilities such as group homes for delinquents, halfway houses for adult offenders, and intensive community-supervision programs for persons who, without such supervision, would likely be incarcerated.[60]

The President's Commission was particularly impressed with the work of the Community Treatment Program sponsored by the California Youth Authority, which since 1962 has operated under a tight experimental design directed toward measuring the success and failure of the program.[61] The blueprint of the Community Treatment program calls for the

> differential diagnosis of offenders into sub-types, the selection and training of agents to work with these sub-types, the definition of a treatment plan for each of the sub-types, the development of a host of program resources to be used singly or in combination for the different sub-types, and . . . the development of specialized homes in which certain wards would be housed.[62]

All subjects come from a common pool of eligibles who have been assigned by the courts to the Youth Authority for what ordinarily would be an institutional program. The experimental design allows the random assignment of experimental subjects to the Community Treatment Project; control subjects go to a traditional institutional program. Results indicate that 28 percent of the persons placed in the experimental group have been failures within fifteen months on parole as compared to 52 percent of the control group whose paroles were revoked and who were reinstitutionalized in the same time period.[63] The saving to the community in the costs of institutionalization, in misery and loss due to recidivism, and in the lives of the youths involved, would argue for expanded use and continued intensive evaluation of the Community Treatment Program concept.

PROBATION

Probably the best definition of probation is that supplied by the National Council on Crime and Delinquency in its Standard Proba-

59 For a thorough review of new approaches, see Empey, *Alternatives to Incarceration*.
60 McCorkle, Elias, and Bixby, *The Highfields Story;* Empey and Rabow, "Provo Experiment in Delinquency Rehabilitation"; Geis, *East Los Angeles Halfway House for Narcotic Addicts*.
61 President's Commission, *Corrections*, pp. 41–42.
62 Empey, *Alternatives to Incarceration*, p. 41.
63 Warren, "Case for Differential Treatment of Delinquents"; Warren, "Recent Findings in the Community Treatment Project."

tion Act: "Probation is a procedure under which a defendant, found guilty of a crime upon verdict or plea, is released by the court, subject to conditions imposed by the court and subject to the supervision of the probation service." Historically, probation has some tenuous connections with such practices as "benefit of clergy," and it resembles the early arrangement of releasing an offender in exchange for a surety, or bond, that guaranteed his subsequent good behavior. Some historians find a striking resemblance between modern-day probation and a ruling of King Athelstand of England in A.D. 940, which decreed that a fifteen-year-old boy who was liable to the death penalty should not be executed, but rather should be placed under the supervision of the bishop, and that only if he continued to break the law should he be liable to punishment.[64]

Benefit of clergy, a predecessor of probation, began in the time of William the Conquerer when churches were authorized to try those of the ordained clergy who violated the law. Lay citizens soon found it desirable to become honorary church functionaries, since ecclesiastic justice was notably more lenient than that of the king's courts. Benefit of clergy was later extended to all persons who could read certain Biblical passages, thereby spurring literacy; not long afterward, it applied to those who could recite by memory Psalm 51, which became known as "the neck verse." Those granted benefit of clergy were excused from their violations, but they were usually branded on a thumb so that they could not claim the privilege more than once. Finally, with the passage of time, benefit of clergy was granted routinely to all citizens, and the practice then began to deteriorate as various crimes were declared "non-clergyable." The practice of benefit of clergy persisted until about 1827 when the state established its clear-cut jurisdictional preeminence over the church.[65]

Use of probation in the United States traces its origin to an 1878 Massachusetts law that provided for the appointment of a supervisory officer to look after offenders in Suffolk County, Boston, who were released into the supervisor's care immediately after conviction.[66] The law grew out of the work of John Augustus, "the father of probation," a Boston bootmaker and inveterate court-attender, who in 1841 asked the court to allow him to tend a drunken offender about to be jailed. Augustus returned to the court three weeks later with the misdemeanant, whose apparent regeneration so impressed the judge that he fined him only one cent and set him free. For the following eighteen years, until his death in 1859, Augustus continued his unofficial work as probation officer, supervising more than 2,000 cases.[67] The appointment of probation officers by the court was made mandatory for the

64 United Nations, *Probation and Related Matters*, p. 370.
65 Dalzell, *Benefit of Clergy in America.*
66 Grinnell, "Common Law Origins of Probation in Massachusetts."
67 *John Augustus: First Probation Officer;* Moreland, "John Augustus and His Successors."

entire state of Massachusetts in 1891, and the practice gradually diffused throughout the United States so that all states today have some form of probation for both adult and juvenile offenders. The idea of probation also took root abroad, beginning in New Zealand in 1886, and it thereafter became virtually universal in Western countries.[68]

Typically, probation status may be authorized at the discretion of the courts. The law in Minnesota, for instance, specifies that probation may be granted "whenever the court is of the opinion that by reason of the character of the person or the facts and circumstances of his case, the welfare of society does not require that he should suffer the penalty of law," and it specifies that the offender may continue on probation "so long as he is thereafter of good behavior." Some states, however, exempt from consideration persons who commit certain offenses, which usually include those involving aggravated violence or a deadly weapon, and sometimes include sex offenders, second or subsequent offenders, and offenders whose acts carry more than a specified prison term. The exclusion of such offenders has been criticized on the ground that it places too much emphasis on the offender's act rather than on his prospects for law-abiding behavior. For instance, sex offenders have a much lower recidivism rate than offenders against property, and they often make excellent probation risks, especially if they receive some form of treatment while under supervision in the community—treatment which ordinarily would not be available in prison.

Conditions of Probation

The supervision that a probationer is expected to receive while he lives in the community takes its most formal tone from the regulations that are imposed on him as conditions for his continued freedom.[69] The probationer is expected to permit unhampered visiting of his domicile by supervising officers,[70] and he is required to report to the officer either in person or by correspondence at stipulated intervals. All jurisdictions specify that the commission of another offense provides grounds for the revocation of probation, but it is often a matter of considerable discretion on the part of the probation officer whether he will proceed against the probationer on the basis of minor infractions. Most probation officers probably evaluate the importance of the violation against their assessment of the potentialities of the individual and make their judgments accordingly. On the other hand, officers, who for one reason or another, whether adequate or invidious, no longer desire a probationer to remain at large, will normally have little trouble in uncovering some technical violation to pursue.

Conditions of probation are usually either directly concerned with preventing a repetition of the individual's offense or with incapacitat-

68 See United Nations, *Probation and Related Matters.*
69 Best and Birzon, "Conditions of Probation."
70 Holtzoff, "Power of Probation and Parole Officers to Search and Seize."

ing him from participation in what are seen as disorganizing situations. Probationers are often forbidden to associate with exconvicts, although in some instances such persons are virtually their only source of companionship. Offenders whose crimes seem to be the result of alcoholic overindulgence are often forbidden to use intoxicants or to enter a place where such beverages are served. Sometimes a probationer may not be allowed to ride in an automobile except in connection with his work, and in other instances he may be forbidden to change residences or jobs or to marry without the express permission of the court or the probation officer.

The most usual probation procedure involves the leveling of pecuniary assessments against the offender. Many probationers must pay court and probation service costs as part of the price of their freedom, while others must post bond to insure that they will not disappear. Restitution for damages or injuries perpetrated on a victim is also often part of the condition of probation,[71] although in recent years some states have taken over the task of reimbursing victims for injuries suffered as a result of crimes of violence.[72] Often the probationer must support his dependents, especially when the offense itself has been desertion or failure to support them. Problems arise, however, when the probationer does not make the specified payments, since revocation of his probation hardly ameliorates the initial situation.

Conditions of probation are usually imposed by the court and must be specifically communicated to the offender. The only reins imposed on probation conditions are that they may not require behavior that is illegal, immoral, or impossible. Interpretation of these requirements has tended to become increasingly tighter in recent years. In 1965, for instance, a federal court declared that it was unreasonable to impose a "no drinking" condition on a chronic alcoholic.[73] Probation conditions also may not violate the Eighth Amendment provision against cruel and unusual punishment. In this respect,[74] if probation conditions are violated, probation can be revoked by the court; presumably, although the 1967 Supreme Court decision on the matter will require further elaboration to detail the full extent of the right at every stage of the proceedings, the offender must be represented by counsel at a revocation hearing, where he may rebut the allegations raised against him.[75]

Probation: Theory and Practice

The relationship between the probation officer and his client holds the key to the process of probation. Probation may be defended as

71 See Schafer, *Restitution to Victims of Crime.*
72 Geis, "State Compensation to Victims of Violent Crime."
73 *Sweeney v. United States*, p. 11.
74 *Weigand v. Kentucky.*
75 *Mempa v. Rhay.* See also Cohen, "Sentencing, Probation, and the Rehabilitative Ideal."

neither more nor less than a humane indulgence granted to the offender as a sporting opportunity to reform or as a "second chance," and in many instances it is no more than that. In theory, however, the officer is expected to provide some form of supervision and guidance that will, by presenting and making realistic alternative goals, deter the offender from further crime. The constant threat of imprisonment is not generally stressed as part of the probation program, although it, too, can presumably be effective in convincing the offender to alter his behavior.

The most prevalent creed in probation today is that the offender is to be treated on a casework basis with techniques developed in the field of social work by means of psychiatry.[76] According to Robert Taber, "Casework may be defined as a process of attempting to understand the needs, impulses and actions of an individual and of helping him to recognize these in a way satisfying to himself and yet in accord with the demands of social living"; such insight is expected to ensue from the "constructive efforts of an interpersonal relationship between the officer and the probationer, the course of which is pursued mainly through interviews."[77] Another writer states the probation officer's role in the following terms:

> Probation officers . . . are called upon to make personality diagnoses and plan comprehensively to improve the probationers' environment and economic life, to adjust delicate family problems, find employment, provide for necessary medical treatment and health assistance, determine recreational needs and social needs, stimulate spiritual and moral improvement.[78]

Unfortunately, we have virtually no information on either the actual application or the applicability of casework techniques in probation. What little we do have indicates that most large probation staffs handle their cases in a routine manner, carrying out bureaucratic, form-filling chores in a rather perfunctory fashion. Lewis Diana, a former probation officer with the Juvenile Court of Pittsburgh, claims that most probation work involves little more than administrative functioning. His analysis of 540 probation records in one court shows that the total number of personal contacts between the officer and the offender averaged out to fewer than five in 16½ months, that is, the probationer got to see his officer about once every three months. Nearly 84 percent of the probationers received but one home visit in almost a year and a half.[79]

Like many areas in which the aim is to help people, probation tends to neglect well-designed research evaluations of its assumptions and techniques, presuming often that good intentions produce desir-

76 See, for instance, Meeker, "Probation is Case Work."
77 Taber, "The Value of Case Work to the Probationer," p. 176.
78 Murphy, "Training for and on the Job," p. 98.
79 Diana, "What is Probation?", pp. 198–199.

able consequences. Some ethical difficulty is involved in the problem of withholding from randomly selected individuals procedures that are believed to be worthwhile, but it seems apparent that some such experimental design is needed to determine whether the procedures are accomplishing what they claim to and to determine whether alternative methods might be more effective. For example, it might be desirable to allow randomly chosen offenders to go unsupervised while other violators are placed on probation and then to compare the behavior of the two groups. Different forms of treatment might be provided for matched samples of probationers, and their effectiveness might be determined in regard to various criteria. Although it is routinely claimed that high case loads militate against rehabilitation, we have no firm evidence that reduced case loads would produce any better results. There is also a striking lack of knowledge concerning the type of probation officer who might be most effective with various types of offenders, despite observations such as that by Jay Rumney and Joseph P. Murphy of instances in which an offender is a failure with one officer and an exemplary success with another.[80] In the absence of such knowledge, the "common sense" assignment of women probation officers to youngsters and female violators may be less desirable than is usually supposed.[81] In some jurisdictions, the statutory requirement that probation officers of similar religious backgrounds be assigned to probationers of the same persuasion may not only be of no positive merit but, as one scholar persuasively argues, may be undesirable on therapeutic, ethical, and constitutional grounds.[82] These are but a few of the many problems that await investigation. One former probation officer provides testimony to how important research evidence might have been to his work:

> I cannot think who is so handicapped as is the probation officer by having no opportunity to study the effects of his labors. To evaluate the work on the day the case is closed is not enough, no matter how brightly successful it seems to be. The real test is in the long pull after that. . . . Yet we have usually no way of knowing what is now happening in the lives we touched ten, twenty, or more years ago. They may have done well after a slow start, and now are successful beyond any hope we had for them when last seen. Just as possible—the man who showed the most promising success while on probation may since have proved unable to hold the gains and, unknown to us, have later failed more miserably than before.[83]

PAROLE

The use of parole is tied to the basic fact that about 95 percent of all prison inmates will be released from the institution at one time or

80 Rumney and Murphy, *Probation and Social Adjustment*, p. 42.
81 Geis and Woodson, "Matching Probation Officer and Delinquent."
82 Hager, "Race, Nationality, and Religion"; Hager, "Religion, Delinquency, and Society."
83 Keve, *Prison, Probation, or Parole?*, p. 257.

another. Parole attempts to see to it that they are released under supervision rather than turned loose in a random, haphazard manner. The vituperation that often descends upon parole might be traced to scandals in which some inmates have been released because of political pressure and bribery. There are also common misunderstandings that cause problems. For instance, the mass media often reports an offense by a former convict as a depredation by a "parolee," and it inquires why this particular offender was not still in the institution, failing to appreciate that, by the nature of his sentence, he would have had to be released sooner or later. Former Chief Justice Warren pinpoints a major parole difficulty with the observation that "unfortunately for parole, it is one of those terminal procedures which must absorb most of the criticism for the failures of the intermediate agencies leading up to it."[84]

Parole is defined as a method for selectively releasing offenders from institutions prior to the completion of their maximum sentence, subject to conditions specified by the paroling authority.[85] It is seen as a technique by which society can be protected and the offender can be provided with treatment and supervision in the community. Parole allows the state to retain jurisdiction over the offender and to return him to the institution if it appears that he will not be able to remain out of difficulty in the community. In this manner about 15 to 20 percent of the persons released on parole are sent back to correctional facilities for "technical violations," and it may be presumed that in this manner a number of potential offenses are headed off by a procedure that could not be employed if the offender were made to serve his full sentence and then was released without supervision. There is likely some truth in the assertion that it is not the offender who has a right to parole, but the society that has a right to see that he receives it.

Parole originated in Europe from economic pressures to put into the labor market as many able-bodied men as possible. The term itself is of French origin and means "word," as in "word of honor." It was first employed in 1846 by Samuel Howe, a Boston penal reformer.[86] The system it denotes, however, was used earlier, during the period of transportation of felons, and was embedded in the practice of granting a "ticket-of-leave" to prisoners; this practice began in Australia around 1800, when the colonial governor excused an inmate from further prison work and permitted him to live independently within a circumscribed area.[87] The practice of parole was brought to

84 Quoted in Bell, Parole in Principle and Practice, p. 10.
85 Ibid., p. 65.
86 Giardini, The Parole Process, p. 9.
87 Dressler, Practice and Theory of Probation and Parole, pp. 44–61.

the United States, where all states have parole systems today and where all belong to the Interstate Compact on Parole, which allows them to assist each other in cases that cut across state lines.[88]

In theory, an inmate should be paroled at the precise moment that he seems most likely never to commit another offense. At least two basic questions are involved in this proposition: First, how adequately can this propitious moment be gauged? Second, how much freedom should the parole board be given to release all offenders and, as a corollary, to retain all offenders indefinitely?[89] The complex matter of sentencing is closely tied to these issues.

Sentencing

The erratic nature of sentencing procedures in the United States has long been a subject of criticism. It has been shown that different jurisdictions impose highly discrepant penalties for similar crimes and that within the same jurisdiction statutory sentences may vary greatly for virtually the same behavior. A law enacted by one legislature may impose a severe penalty on a particular form of theft, either because of the mood of that legislature or possibly because of the recent memory of a nefarious act of that type. A subsequent legislature, on other grounds, may enact a law concerning a similar type of theft but place a much milder penalty upon it. Two prisoners, therefore, sentenced under the different laws, may find it difficult to reconcile their fates with their behavior, thus undercutting, in theory at least, subsequent law-abiding behavior by creating additional hostility.

The sentencing idiosyncracies of judges also introduce a quixotic note into the procedure. Various writers have studied comparative sentencing practices of different judges who hear essentially the same types of cases and have found striking variations among them.[90] At a federal judicial conference this theme was clearly demonstrated when twenty-eight judges were given an elaborate presentence report concerning an offender who had robbed a bank, but whose personal characteristics indicated some potentiality for future good conduct. The probation officer recommended probation with restitution by the offender to the bank of the more than $2,000 he had stolen and spent. The judges were then asked what sentence they would impose. One judge demurred, noting that he would not sentence anyone without seeing him. Of the remainder, seventeen said they would imprison the offender, while ten reported that they would place him on probation. Those voting for imprisonment set sentences ranging from six months to fifteen years. The discrepancy between sentences illustrates the

88 Crihfield, "Interstate Parole and Probation Compact"; see also Wendell, "Interstate Compact on Juveniles."
89 See Cohen, *The Legal Challenge to Corrections.*
90 Kahn, *A Court for Children,* Chap. 5.

vagaries of fortune that may determine how a given offender will be treated. Seven of the judges who voted for probation believed that the offender was a "good risk for rehabilitation," while nine of those who would have sent him to prison believed he needed the discipline and training a prison was presumed to be able to supply.[91]

Many persons who have looked into sentencing believe there is a considerable need for systematization of procedures. The American Law Institute recommends that all felonies, excluding those committed by habitual offenders, should be grouped into three classes in which maximum sentences for each class would be: first degree—life, second degree—ten years, third degree—five years. The minimum sentence would be set by the judge for each class, although it could not exceed a specified limit. Thus for third-degree felonies, the minimum could range up to two years, for second degree, up to three years, and for first degree, up to ten years. No minimum sentence could be less than one year, and parole could be granted upon expiration of the minimum sentence less time off for good behavior within the institution.[92]

Major criticism of the Institute's proposals have been raised by Sol Rubin, who believes that judges should be allowed to set only maximum sentences within predetermined limits and that there should be no specified minimum. By imposing a high minimum, Rubin insists, the judge frustrates the paroling authority from releasing an inmate when he is ready to return to the community.[93] Both Rubin and the Institute agree, however, that maximum sentences should bear some relationship to the offender's criminal act and that institutions should not have the power to keep persons for unreasonably long periods of time on the highly speculative ground that they represent poor parole risks.

Parole: Practice and Theory

Only twenty-three states maintain full-time parole boards and about one-third of all offenders are released without parole supervision.[94] The determination of parole eligibility by a board may range from a formal statistical evaluation of the offender's likelihood of future violation to grossly intuitive responses to his behavior at a parole interview. Statistical prediction of the outcome of parole employs procedures much like those used by the life-insurance actuary in determining the mortality experience of a given population and in estimating from it the risk of death at different age levels. The parole statistician calculates the frequency of failure within selected cate-

91 "Test Presentence Report and Summary of Ballot."
92 Wechsler, "Sentencing, Correction, and the Model Penal Code."
93 Rubin, "Sentencing and Correctional Treatment Under the Law Institute's Model Penal Code"; Rubin, "Allocation of Authority in the Sentencing-Correction Decision."
94 President's Commission, *Corrections*, p. 66.

gories and projects these rates into the future. Sociologists have attempted to refine various predictive devices since 1923.[95] Reviewing their efforts, Karl Schuessler reaches the following summary evaluation:

> It must be acknowledged . . . that the application of actuarial methods to parole experience has thus far not provided data that greatly reduce the uncertainty attached to forecasting individual behavior on parole. The reasons for this seem to lie, not in the actuarial method itself, which is indifferent to the nature of the data, but rather in the unavailability of items that sharply differentiate outcome groups, and in the apparent sensitivity of parole adjustment to abrupt social changes which militate either for or against a good parole adjustment.[96]

The Model Penal Code of the American Law Institute leans toward the idea that offenders should be paroled when they first become eligible for release unless there is at least some vaguely substantial reason to the contrary. The Institute obviously has difficulty spelling out the precise reasons for retention but attempts to do so by suggesting that an offender not be paroled if (1) there is undue risk that he will not conform to the conditions of parole, (2) his release at that time would unduly depreciate the seriousness of his crime or promote disrespect for the law, (3) his release would have a substantially adverse effect on prison discipline, or (4) his continued correctional treatment, vocational or other training in the institution, or medical treatment will substantially enhance his capacity to lead a law-abiding life when released at a later date. This implies that the failure of the parole board to demonstrate the existence of any of these items should lead to a decision in favor of parole.

Summary

In examining the changing conceptions of criminal responsibility in an attempt to line them up with current thought in the social science disciplines, there remains the difficult problem of bringing into alignment both a legal system based on the assumption of free will and various fields of scientific investigation committed to a deterministic doctrine. Professor Francis A. Allen, Dean of the University of Michigan Law School, aptly states the problems that exist in this area:

> The values of individual liberty may be imperiled by claims to knowledge and therapeutic technique that we, in fact, do not possess and by failure candidly to concede what we do not know. At times practitioners of the behavioral sciences have been guilty of these faults. At other times, such errors have supplied the assumptions on which legislators, lawyers and lay people generally have proceeded. Ignorance, in itself, is not disgraceful so long as it is unavoidable. But when we rush to meas-

95 See Ohlin, *Selection for Parole;* Allen, "A Review of Parole Prediction Literature"; Kirby, "Parole Prediction Using Multiple Correlation."
96 Schuessler, "Parole Prediction," p. 425.

ures affecting human liberty and human dignity on the assumption that we know what we do not know or can do what we cannot do, then the problem of ignorance takes on a more sinister hue. . . . It is no paradox to assert that the real utility of scientific technique in [corrections] depends on an accurate realization of the limits of scientific knowledge.[97]

During the discussion of criminal responsibility, jails, prisons, probation, sentencing, and parole, the observation has often been made that definitive judgment must await empirical work that will provide basic data. Meanwhile, pending the appearance of crucial data, the importance of initial value commitments should not be overlooked. In this respect, it may be relevant to conclude with a statement by Winston Churchill, delivered to the House of Commons almost sixty years ago:

> The mood and temper of the public with regard to the treatment of crime and criminals is one of the most unfailing tests of the civilization of any country. A calm, dispassionate recognition of the rights of the accused, and even of the convicted criminal against the State—a constant heart searching by all charged with the duty of punishment—a desire and eagerness to rehabilitate in the world of industry those who have paid their due in the hard coinage of punishment; tireless efforts towards the discovery of curative and regenerative processes; unfailing faith that there is a treasure if you can find it, in the heart of every man. These are the symbols which, in the treatment of crime and criminal, mark and measure the stored up strength of a nation and are sign and proof of the living virtue in it.[98]

For Further Reading

COHEN, FRED. *The Legal Challenge to Corrections: Implications for Manpower and Training.* Washington, D.C.: Joint Commission on Correctional Manpower and Training, 1969.
> The thrust of Professor Cohen's monograph is clearly stated in the foreword by James V. Bennett, former director of the Federal Bureau of Prisons, who says: "It will come as a shock to many if not most probation officers, prison keepers, and parole officials that they are not endowed by law and the accouterments of their office with unfettered power to make decisions concerning their charges. It was to make this fact of life abundantly clear and stake out the boundaries of legal prerogatives of their clientele that the Commission requested Professor Cohen . . . to prepare . . . *The Legal Challenge to Corrections.*"

GLASER, DANIEL. *The Effectiveness of a Prison and Parole System.* Indianapolis: Bobbs-Merrill, 1964.
> Financed by the Ford Foundation, this 5½-year inquiry into the federal prisons, directed by Professor Glaser of the University of Southern Cali-

97 Allen, "Criminal Justice, Legal Values, and the Rehabilitative Ideal," pp. 230–231.
98 Quoted in Size, *Prisons I Have Known,* pp. 62–63.

fornia, provides a wealth of material concerning the rehabilitative effectiveness of prisons and their value in areas such as vocational preparation and education.

HART, H. L. A. *Punishment and Responsibility: Essays in the Philosophy of Law.* New York: Oxford University Press, 1968.

A review by Justice Douglas of the Supreme Court aptly summarizes this volume's contents: "This is a scholarly work by a learned Oxford don which combs through legal decisions, treatises, and essays looking for strands of thought that can be used to weave together the Anglo-American philosophy on criminal responsibility and punishment." This volume should whet the reader's appetite for a deeper plunge into the intricacies of the issue of responsibility for criminal acts.

NEWMAN, CHARLES L. *Sourcebook on Probation, Parole, and Pardons.* 3rd ed. Springfield, Ill.: Charles C. Thomas, 1968.

A large amount of relevant material on the subjects can be found in this reader, as well as references to additional source data. Two articles on parole prediction—one by Schuessler and the other by Glaser and O'Leary—are of particular significance, in addition to an article by Chester Bartoo entitled "Hidden Factors in Probation Recommendations." A companion volume is that by David Dressler entitled *Practice and Theory of Probation and Parole.* New York: Columbia University Press, 1959.

PRESIDENT'S COMMISSION ON LAW ENFORCEMENT AND ADMINISTRATION OF JUSTICE. *Task Force Report: Corrections.* Washington, D.C.: Government Printing Office, 1967.

This comprehensive review of the history of American corrections and survey of the more promising approaches in use today pays particular attention to community-based programs that allow offenders to remain under supervision within the area in which they live and must adjust. There is also a delineation of emerging legal standards in corrections, under the title "Concern for Fairness." The report was prepared under the direction of Kim Nelson of the School of Public Administration of the University of Southern California.

Bibliography

Books and Articles

Abrahamsen, David. *Who Are the Guilty? A Study of Education and Crime.* New York: Holt, Rinehart and Winston, 1952.

————. "Study of Lee Harvey Oswald: Psychological Capability of Murder," *New York Academy of Medicine Bulletin,* 43 (October 1967), 861–888.

Albert, Ethel M. "The Roles of Women: A Question of Values," in Seymour M. Farber and Roger H. L. Wilson (eds.), *Man and Civilization: The Potential of Women.* New York: McGraw-Hill, 1963, pp. 105–115.

"Alcoholism, Public Intoxication, and the Law," *Columbia Journal of Law and Social Problems,* 2 (June 1966), 109–132.

Allen, David. *The Nature of Gambling.* New York: Coward-McCann, 1953.

Allen, Francis A. "Criminal Justice, Legal Values, and the Rehabilitative Ideal," *Journal of Criminal Law,* 50 (September–October 1959), 226–232.

————. "Offenses Against Property," *The Annals,* 339 (January 1962), 57–76.

————. "Pioneers in Criminology: Raffaele Garofolo," *Journal of Criminal Law,* 45 (November–December 1954), 373–390.

Allen, Robert M. "A Review of Parole Prediction Literature," *Journal of Criminal Law,* 32 (January–February 1942), 548–554.

Allsop, Kenneth. *The Bootleggers and Their Era.* New York: Doubleday, 1961.

Alongi, Guiseppe. *La Maffia.* Turin, Italy: Biblioteca Antropologico Giurdica, 1886.

Amir, Menachem. "Patterns of Forcible Rape," in Marshall B. Clinard and Richard Quinney (eds.), *Criminal Behavior Systems: A Typology.* New York: Holt, Rinehart and Winston, 1967, pp. 60–75.

Anashkin, G. Z. "Tasks and Trends in the Development of Socialist Justice," *Soviet Review,* 8 (Summer 1967), 46–56.

Anderson, C. L. "Epilepsy in the State of Michigan," *Mental Hygiene,* 20 (July 1936), 441–462.

Anderson, Clinton. *Beverly Hills is My Beat.* Englewood Cliffs, New Jersey: Prentice-Hall, 1960.

Anderson, Nels. *The Hobo: The Sociology of the Homeless Man.* Chicago: University of Chicago Press, 1923.

Anderson, Robert T. "From Mafia to Cosa Nostra," *American Journal of Sociology,* 53 (November 1965), 302–310.

Anderson, Ronald A. *Wharton's Criminal Law and Procedure.* Rochester, New York: Lawyers Cooperative, 1957.

Andrews, E. A. *A New Latin Dictionary.* New York: American Book, 1878.

Ansbacher, Heinz L., Rowena R. Ansbacher, David Shiverick, and Kathleen Shiverick. "Lee Harvey Oswald: An Adlerian Interpretation," *Psychoanalytical Review,* 58 (Fall 1966), 55–68.

Anslinger, H. J., and William F. Tompkins. *The Traffic in Narcotics.* New York: Funk & Wagnalls, 1953.

Apfelberg, Benjamin, Carl Sugar, and Arnold Z. Pfeffer. "A Psychiatric Study of 250 Sex Offenders," *American Journal of Psychiatry,* 100 (May 1944), 762–770.

Appelbaum, Emanuel, and Mennasch Kalkstein. "Artificial Transmission of Viral Hepatitis Among Intravenous Diacetylmorphine Addicts," *American Medical Association Journal,* 147 (September 15, 1951), 222–224.

"Application of Federal Gambling Tax Law," *DePaul Law Review,* 8 (Summer 1959), 362–368.

Ares, Charles E., Anne Rankin, and Herbert Sturz. "The Manhattan Bail Project: An Interim Report on the Use of Pre-Trial Parole," *New York University Law Review,* 38 (January 1963), 67–95.

Arieff, Alex J., and Carol G. Bowie. "Some Psychiatric Aspects of Shoplifting," *Journal of Clinical Psychopathology,* 8 (January 1947), 565–576.

Arm, Walter. *Pay-Off.* New York: Appleton-Century-Crofts, 1951.

Arnold, David O. "The Meaning of the LaGuardia Report: The Effects of Marihuana," in J. L. Simmons (ed.), *Marihuana: Myths and Realities.* North Hollywood, California: Brandon House, 1967, pp. 111–135.

Arnold, Thurman W. *Symbols of Government.* New Haven, Connecticut: Yale University Press, 1935.

Asbury, Herbert. *Gem of the Prairie: An Informal History of the Chicago Underworld.* New York: Knopf, 1940.

———. *The Great Illusion: An Informal History of Prohibition.* New York: Doubleday, 1950.

———. *Sucker's Progress.* New York: Dodd, Mead, 1938.

Ashton, John. *A History of Gambling in England.* London: Duckworth, 1898.

Atley, James B. *The Victorian Chancellors.* London: Smith, Elder, 1906–1908.

Audett, Blackie. *Rap Sheet.* New York: Sloane, 1954.

Aydelotte, Frank. *Elizabethan Rogues and Vagabonds.* Oxford, England: Clarendon Press, 1913.

Bailey, Derrick S. *Homosexuality and the Western Christian Tradition.* London: Longmans, 1955.

Baker, Russell. "Crime in the Whats?" *The New York Times,* January 26, 1968.

Baldwin, James. *Another Country.* New York: Dial Press, 1962.

Ball, John C. "Two Patterns of Narcotic Drug Addiction in the United States," *Journal of Criminal Law,* 56 (June 1965), 203–211.

Bamford, Paul W. "The Procurement of Oarsmen for French Galleys, 1660–1748," *American Historical Review,* 65 (October 1959), 31–48.

Barbash, James T. "Compensation and the Crime of Pigeon Dropping," *Journal of Clinical Psychology,* 8 (October 1951), 92–94.

Barker, Ernest (ed.). *Social Contract: Essays By Locke, Hume, and Rousseau.* London: Oxford University Press, 1958.

Barnes, Harry E. "Let's Reform Our Jury System or Abolish It," *Coronet,* 41 (April 1957), 72–76.

————, and Negley K. Teeters. *New Horizons in Criminology.* 3rd ed. Englewood Cliffs, New Jersey: Prentice-Hall, 1959.

Barnes, Marian (ed.). *A Treatise on the Law of Crimes (Clark & Marshall).* 7th ed. Mundelein, Illinois: Callaghan, 1967.

Barnett, Milton. "Alcoholism in the Cantonese of New York City," in Oskar Diethelm (ed.), *Etiology of Chronic Alcoholism.* Ithaca, New York: Cornell University Press, 1955, pp. 179–227.

Barrett, Edward L., Jr. "Personal Rights, Property Rights and the Fourth Amendment," in Philip B. Kurland (ed.), *Supreme Court Review.* Chicago: Chicago University Press, 1960, pp. 46–74.

Barron, Milton L. *The Juvenile in Delinquent Society.* New York: Knopf, 1956.

Barrow, Roscoe L., and Howard D. Fabing. *Epilepsy and the Law.* New York: Hoeber Medical Books, 1956.

Barry, John V. *Alexander Maconochie of Norfolk Island.* Melbourne, Australia: Oxford University Press, 1958.

————. "Founding Felons of Australia," *Hartwick Review,* 2 (Fall 1966), 29–35.

————, and G. W. Paton. *An Introduction to the Criminal Law in Australia.* London: Macmillan, 1948.

Barzini, Luigi. *The Italians.* New York: Atheneum, 1964.

Barzun, Jacques. "In Favor of Capital Punishment," *American Scholar,* 31 (Spring 1962), 181–191.

Basu, Amar K. (ed.). *The Indian Evidence Act, 1872.* 3rd ed. Calcutta, India: Eastern Law House, 1953.

Bateson, Charles. *The Convict Ships, 1787–1868.* Glasgow, Scotland: Brown, 1959.

Batonbacal, V. I., and A. Stipman. "Transmission of Serum Hepatitis in Heroin Addicts," *New York State Journal of Medicine,* 59 (January 1959), 320–323.

Battle, Brendan, and Paul B. Weston. *Arson.* New York: Greenberg, 1954.

Baughman, U. E., and Leonard W. Robinson. *Secret Service Chief.* New York: Harper & Row, 1962.

Bayley, David H. "The Effects of Corruption in a Developing Nation," *Western Political Quarterly,* 19 (December 1966), 719–732.

Beaney, William M. "United States Courts and Criminal Justice," *Current History,* 53 (August 1967), 65–69.

Beccaria, Cesare. *Essay on Crimes and Punishments [Dei Delitti delle Pene, 1764].* Edward D. Ingraham (tr.). Stanford, California: Academic Reprints, 1953.

Becker, Howard P. "Anthropology and Sociology," in John Gillin (ed.), *For a Science of Social Man.* New York: Macmillan, 1954, pp. 102–159.

Becker, Howard S. "Becoming a Marihuana User," *American Journal of Sociology,* 59 (November 1953), 235–242.

————. "The Marihuana Tax Act," in Becker (ed.), *The Outsiders: Studies in the Sociology of Deviance.* New York: Free Press, 1963, pp. 135–146.

Bedford, Sybille. *The Faces of Justice: A Traveller's Report.* New York: Simon and Schuster, 1961.

Belbenoit, René. *Dry Guillotine.* New York: Dutton, 1938.

Bell, Daniel. "Crime as an American Way of Life," in Bell (ed.), *The End of Ideology.* New York: Free Press, 1960, pp. 115–136.

Bell, Marjorie (ed.). *Parole in Principle and Practice.* New York: National Probation and Parole Association, 1957.

Belli, Melvin M., and Danny R. Jones. *Belli Looks at Life and Law in Japan.* Indianapolis, Indiana: Bobbs-Merrill, 1960.

Bender, Lauretta, and Abram Blau. "The Reaction of Children to Sexual Relations with Adults," *American Journal of Orthopsychiatry*, 7 (October 1937), 500–518.

Benedict, Ruth. *Patterns of Culture*. Boston: Houghton Mifflin, 1934.

Bennett, James V. "After Sentence—What?" *Journal of Criminal Law*, 45 (January–February 1955), 537–540.

———. "Correctional Problems the Courts Can Help Solve," *Crime and Delinquency*, 7 (January 1961), 1–8.

Bensing, Robert C., and Oliver Schroeder, Jr. *Homicide in an Urban Community*. Springfield, Illinois: Thomas, 1960.

Bentham, Jeremy. *The Rationale of Punishment*. London: Heward, 1830.

Berg Irwin A. "A Comparative Study of Forgers," *Journal of Applied Psychology*, 28 (June 1944), 232–238.

Berger, Bennett M. "Adolescence and Beyond," *Social Problems*, 10 (Spring 1963), 394–408.

———. "On the Youthfulness of Youth Cultures," *Social Research*, 15 (Winter 1963), 319–342.

Berger, Meyer. "The Bowery Blinks in the Sunlight," *The New York Times Magazine*, May 20, 1956, pp. 14–15 ff.

Bergler, Edmund. *The Psychology of Gambling*. New York: Hill & Wang, 1957.

Berkowitz, Leonard, Ronald Corwin, and Mark Heironimus. "Film Violence and Subsequent Aggressive Tendencies," *Public Opinion Quarterly*, 27 (Summer 1963), 217–229.

Berman, Harold J. *Justice in the U. S. S. R.: An Interpretation of Soviet Law*. Rev. ed. New York: Vintage, 1963.

Bernstein, Saul. *Alternatives to Violence*. New York: Association Press, 1967.

Best, Judah, and Paul Birzon. "Conditions of Probation," *Georgetown Law Journal*, 51 (Summer 1963), 809–836.

Bevington, Helen. "A Bomb for Jeremy Bentham," in Bevington, *Nineteen Million Elephants and Other Poems*. Boston: Houghton Mifflin, 1950.

Bianchi, Hermanus. *Position and Subject-Matter of Criminology*. Amsterdam: North Holland Publishing, 1956.

Bibb, Marilyn. "Gang-Related Services of Mobilization for Youth," in Malcolm W. Klein and Barbara G. Meyerhoff (eds.), *Juvenile Gangs in Context*. Englewood Cliffs, New Jersey: Prentice-Hall, 1967, pp. 175–182.

Bickel, Alexander M. "Supreme Court Fissures," *New Republic*, 151 (July 11, 1964), 15–16.

Biderman, Albert. "Social Indicators and Goals," in Raymond A. Bauer (ed.), *Social Indicators*. Cambridge, Massachussets: M.I.T. Press, 1966. pp. 68–153.

———. "Surveys of Population Samples for Estimating Crime Incidence," *The Annals*, 374 (November 1967), 16–33.

———. and Albert J. Reiss, Jr. "On Exploring the 'Dark Figure' of Crime," *The Annals*, 374 (November 1967), 1–15.

Bien, David. *The Calas Affair: Persecution, Toleration, and Heresy in Eighteenth-Century Toulouse*. Princeton, New Jersey: Princeton University Press, 1960.

Bill, J. F. "Corruption and Union Racketeering," *Current History*, 36 (June 1959), 343–346.

Bixby, F. Lovell. "Penology in Sweden and Denmark," *American Journal of Correction*, 24 (May–June 1962), 18–25.

———, and Lloyd W. McCorkle. "Guided Group Interaction in Correctional Work," *American Sociological Review*, 16 (August 1951), 455–459.

Black, Jack. *You Can't Win*. New York: Macmillan, 1926.

Black, Susan. "Burglary," *New Yorker,* 39 (December 7, 1963), 63–64 ff., and 39 (December 14, 1963), 89 ff.

Blackstone, William. *Commentaries on the Laws of England.* 14th ed. London: Strahan, 1803.

Blauner, Robert. "Death and Social Structure," *Psychiatry,* 29 (November 1966), 378–394.

Blaustein, Albert, and Charles O. Porter. *The American Lawyer.* Chicago: University of Chicago Press, 1954.

Bloch, Herbert A. *Disorganization: Personal and Social.* New York: Knopf, 1952.

———. *Research Report on Homicides, Attempted Homicides, and Crimes of Violence.* Washington, D.C.: International Cooperation Administration, U.S. Operations Mission to Ceylon, 1960.

——— (ed.). *Crime in America.* New York: Philosophical Library, 1961.

———. "Juvenile Delinquency: Myth or Threat?", *Journal of Criminal Law,* 49 (November–December 1958), 303–309.

———. "The Sociology of Gambling," *American Journal of Sociology,* 57 (November 1951), 215–221.

Block, Eugene B. *Great Train Robberies of the West.* New York: Coward-McCann, 1954.

Bloomquist, Edward. "Operations Narcotics," *Medical Times,* 85 (March 1957), 349–353.

Blum, Richard, and Lauraine Braunstein. "Mind-Altering Drugs and Dangerous Behavior," in *Task Force Report: Drunkenness.* Washington, D.C.: President's Commission on Law Enforcement and Administration of Justice, 1967, 29–49.

Blumberg, Abraham S. *Criminal Justice.* Chicago: Quadrangle Books, 1967.

———. "The Practice of Law as Confidence Game: Organized Cooperation of a Profession," *Law & Society Review,* 1 (June 1967), 15–39.

Blumer, Herbert, Alan Sutter, Samir Ahmed, and Roger Smith. *The World of Youthful Drug Use.* Berkeley: School of Criminology, University of California, 1967.

Blumrosen, Alfred W. "Legal Process and Labor Law: Some Observations on the Relationship Between Law and Sociology," in William M. Evan, *Law and Sociology: Exploratory Essays.* New York: Free Press, 1962, 185–225.

Boggs, Sarah L. "Urban Crime Patterns," *American Sociological Review,* 30 (December 1965), 899–908.

Bogue, Donald J. *Skid Row in American Cities.* Chicago: Community & Family Study Center University of Chicago, 1963.

Bohannan, Paul (ed.). *African Homicide and Suicide.* Princeton, New Jersey: Princeton University Press, 1960.

Bok, Curtis. *Star Wormwood.* New York: Knopf, 1949.

Bond, Earl E., and Kenneth E. Appel. *The Treatment of Behavior Disorders Following Encephalitis.* New York: Commonwealth Fund, 1931.

Bonger, W. A. *An Introduction to Criminology.* Emil Van Loo (tr.). London: Methuen, 1936.

"The Boom in Bank Robbery," *Fortune,* 61 (January 1960), 115–117 ff.

Borchard, Edwin M. *Convicting the Innocent.* New Haven, Connecticut: Yale University Press, 1932.

Bordua, David J. "Delinquent Subcultures: Sociological Interpretations of Gang Delinquency," *The Annals,* 338 (November 1961), 119–136.

Bovet, Lucien. *Psychiatric Aspects of Juvenile Delinquency.* Geneva: World Health Organization, 1951.

Bowen, Catherine D. *The Lion on the Throne.* Boston: Little, Brown, 1956.

Bowen, Walter S., and Harry E. Neal. *The United States Secret Service.* Philadelphia: Chilton, 1960.

Bowling, R. W. "The Sex Offender and the Law," *Federal Probation,* 14 (September 1950), 11–16.

Braly, Malcolm. *On the Yard.* Boston: Little, Brown, 1967.

Brandeis, Louis D. "The Living Law," in Osmond K. Fraenkel (ed.), *The Curse of Bigness.* New York: Viking, 1935, pp. 318–325.

Branham, Vernon C., and Samuel B. Kutash (eds.), *Encyclopedia of Criminology.* New York: Philosophical Library, 1949.

Brannon, W. T. *"Yellow Kid" Weil—Con Man.* New York: Ziff-Davis, 1948.

Bridenbaugh, Carl. *Cities in Revolt: Urban Life in America, 1743–1776.* New York: Knopf, 1955.

Bridgman, Percy W. *Reflections of a Physicist.* New York: Philosophical Library, 1950.

Brock, Timothy C., and Carolyn Del Guidice. "Stealing and Temporal Orientation," *Journal of Abnormal & Social Psychology,* 66 (January 1963), 91–94.

Bromage, Kenneth G., and Harry V. Ball. "A Study of Juvenile 'Battery' Cases," *Alpha Kappa Deltan,* 28 (Spring 1958), 18–24.

Bromberg, Walter. *Crime and the Mind.* Philadelphia: Lippincott, 1965.

Broome, J. H. *Pascal.* New York: Barnes & Noble, 1965.

Brown, Claude. *Manchild in the Promised Land.* New York: Macmillan, 1965.

Brown, John Mason. *Through These Men.* New York: Harper, 1956.

Bruce, Robert V. *1877: Year of Violence.* Indianapolis, Indiana: Bobbs-Merrill, 1959.

Bryant, John. *Genius and Epilepsy.* Concord, Massachusetts: Old Depot Press, 1953.

Buckley, Michael J. *Morality and the Homosexual.* Westminster, Maryland: Newman Press, 1960.

Bullington, Bruce, John G. Munns, and Gilbert Geis. "Purchase of Conformity: Ex-Narcotic Addicts Among the Bourgeoisie," *Social Problems,* 16 (Spring 1969), 456–463.

———, and James Ranea. "Concerning Heroin Use and Official Records," *American Journal of Public Health,* 59 (October 1969), 1887–1893.

Bullock, Henry A. "Urban Homicide in Theory and Fact," *Journal of Criminal Law,* 45 (January–February 1955), 565–573.

Burgess, Ernest W. Comment, *American Journal of Sociology,* 56 (July 1950), 32–34.

Burnham, David. "Police Violence: A Changing Pattern," *New York Times,* July 7, 1968.

Busch, Francis X. *Prisoners at the Bar.* Indianapolis, Indiana: Bobbs-Merrill, 1952.

Cahn, Edmond. *The Moral Decision.* Bloomington: Indiana University Press, 1959.

Cairns, Huntington. *Law and the Social Sciences.* New York: Harcourt, Brace, 1935.

Caldwell, Robert G. *Criminology.* 2nd ed. New York: Ronald Press, 1965.

———. *Red Hannah.* Philadelphia: University of Pennsylvania Press, 1947.

———. Book Review. *Journal of Criminal Law,* 50 (September–October 1959), 281–283.

Calhoun, George M. *The Growth of Criminal Law in Ancient Greece.* Berkeley: University of California Press, 1927.

Cameron, Mary O. *The Booster and the Snitch: Department Store Shoplifting.* New York: Free Press, 1964.

Camp, George N. "Nothing to Lose: A Study of Bank Robbery in America." Unpublished Ph.D. dissertation, Yale University, 1967.

Campion, Donald. "The State Police and the Death Penalty," in Canadian Joint Committee on Capital & Corporal Punishment, *Report*. Ottawa, Canada, 1955, pp. 729–741.

Camus, Albert. *Reflections on the Guillotine*. Michigan City, Indiana: Fidjof-Karla, 1959.

Capolovitz, David. *The Poor Pay More*. New York: Free Press, 1963.

Cardozo, Benjamin. *The Nature of the Judicial Process*. New Haven, Connecticut: Yale University Press, 1928.

Carpenter, Lawrence A. "Federal Work Release Program," *Nebraska Law Review*, 45 (July 1966), 690–701.

Carr, Lowell J. "Most Courts Have to be Substandard," *Federal Probation*, 13 (September 1949), 29–33.

Cason, Hulsey. "A Case of Sexual Psychopathy," *Journal of Clinical Psychopathology*, 8 (July–October 1947), 785–800.

Casriel, Daniel H. *So Fair a House*. Englewood Cliffs, New Jersey: Prentice-Hall, 1963.

Cavan, Ruth S. *Suicide*. Chicago: University of Chicago Press, 1928.

———, and Jordan T. *Delinquency and Crime: Cross–Cultural Perspectives*. Philadelphia: Lippincott, 1968.

———, and Eugene Zemans. "Marital Relationships of Prisoners in Twenty-Eight Countries," *Journal of Criminal Law*, 49 (July–August 1958), 133–139.

Caxton, William. *The Book of the Ordre of Chivalry*, Alfred T. P. Byles (ed.). London: Oxford University Press, 1926.

Chalmers, David M. *The Social and Political Ideas of Muckrakers*. New York: Citadel, 1964.

Chamberlin, Henry B. "Some Observations Concerning Organized Crime," *Journal of Criminal Law*, 22 (January 1932), 652–670.

Chappell, Duncan, and P. R. Wilson. *The Police and the Public in Australia and New Zealand*. St. Lucia: University of Queensland Press, 1969.

Charen, Sol, and Luis Perelman. "Personality Studies of Marihuana Addicts," *American Journal of Psychiatry*, 102 (March 1946), 674–682.

Chein, Isidor, Donald L. Gerard, Robert S. Lee, and Eva Rosenfeld. *The Road to H: Narcotics, Delinquency, and Social Policy*. New York: Basic Books, 1964.

Chell, Eugene P. "Sunday Blue Laws: An Analysis of Their Position in Our Society," *Rutgers Law Review*, 12 (Spring 1958), 505–521.

Chessman, Caryl. *Cell 2455–Death Row*. Englewood Cliffs, New Jersey: Prentice-Hall, 1954.

Churchill, Allen. *The Incredible Ivar Krueger*. New York: Holt, Rinehart and Winston, 1957.

———. *They Never Came Back*. New York: Doubleday, 1960.

Churchill, Winston. *A History of the English-Speaking Peoples*. London: Cassell, 1956.

Cipes, Robert M. *The Crime War: The Manufactured Crusade*. New York: New American Library, 1968.

Clarendon, Edward. *The History of the Rebellion and Civil Wars in England Begun in the Year 1641*. W. Dunn Macray (ed.). Oxford, England: Clarendon Press, 1888.

Clark, John P. "Isolation and the Police: A Comparison of the British and American Situation," *Journal of Criminal Law*, 56 (September 1965), 307–319.

Clarke, John. "Delinquent Personalities," *British Journal of Criminology*, 3 (October 1962), 147–161.

Clearinghouse for Mental Health Information, Public Health Service, *Bibliography on Drug Dependence and Abuse, 1928–1966*. Washington, D.C.: Department of Health, Education and Welfare, 1967.

Clemmer, Donald. *The Prison Community*. New York: Rinehart, 1958.

Clinard, Marshall B. *The Black Market*. New York: Rinehart, 1952.

————. *Sociology of Deviant Behavior*. 3rd ed. New York: Holt, Rinehart and Winston, 1966.

————. The Process of Urbanization and Criminal Behavior," *American Journal of Sociology*, 48 (September 1942), 202–213.

————. 'The Relation of Urbanization and Urbanism to Criminal Behavior," in Ernest W. Burgess and Donald J. Bogue (eds.), *Research Contributions to Urban Sociology*. Chicago: University of Chicago Press, 1962.

————, and Richard Quinney. *Criminal Behavior Systems: A Typology*. New York: Holt, Rinehart, and Winston, 1967.

Cloward, Richard A., and Lloyd E. Ohlin. *Delinquency and Opportunity: A Theory of Delinquent Gangs*. New York: Free Press, 1960.

Coatman, John. *Police*. London: Oxford University Press, 1959.

Cohen, Albert K. *Delinquent Boys: The Culture of the Gang*. New York: Free Press, 1955.

————. *Deviance and Control*. Englewood Cliffs, New Jersey: Prentice-Hall, 1966.

————. "Sociological Research in Juvenile Delinquency," *American Journal of Orthopsychiatry*, 27 (October 1957), 781–788.

Cohen, Fred. *The Legal Challenge to Corrections: Implications for Manpower and Training*. Washington, D.C.: Joint Commission on Correctional Manpower and Training, 1969.

————. "Sentencing, Probation, and the Rehabilitative Ideal: The View from *Mempa v. Rhay*," *Texas Law Review*, 47 (December 1968), 1–59.

Cohen, Isabel R. "Present Status of the Year and A Day Rule," *Intramural Law Review*, 19 (January 1964), 133–155.

Cohen, Morris R. *Reason and Law*. New York: Collier, 1961.

Cohen, Sheldon S. "Morality and the American Tax System," *George Washington Law Review*, 34 (June 1966), 839–845.

Cohn, Herman H. "Convicting the Arsonist," *Journal of Criminal Law*, 38 (September–October 1947), 286–303.

Coleman, James S. *The Adolescent Society: The Social Life of the Teenager and Its Impact on Education*. New York: Free Press, 1955.

Commager, Henry Steele. *Freedom, Loyalty, Dissent*. New York: Oxford University Press, 1954.

Comte, Auguste. *Cours de philosophie positive*. Paris: Bachelier, 1830–1842.

Conrad, John. *Crime and Its Correction: An International Survey of Attitudes and Practices*. Berkeley: University of California Press, 1965.

Consodine, Robert B. *Man Against Fire: Fire Insurance Protection from Disaster*. New York: Doubleday, 1955.

Cook, Fred J. *The Corrupted Land*. New York: Macmillan, 1966.

————. *The FBI Nobody Knows*. New York: Macmillan, 1964.

————. *A Two-Dollar Bet Means Murder*. New York: Dial Press, 1961.

————. "Just Call 'The Doctor' For a Loan," *The New York Times Magazine*, January 28, 1968, pp. 19ff.

Cort, David. "The Embezzler," *The Nation*, 188 (April 18, 1959), 339–342.

Cowell, John. *The Institutes of the Laws of England*. London: Roycraft, 1651.

Cozzens, James G. *The Just and the Unjust*. New York: Harcourt, Brace, 1942.

Crabtree, Robert W. "Criminal Responsibility for Death of Co-Felon," *Hastings Law Journal,* 16 (May 1965), 620–629.

Cramer, James. *The World's Police.* London: Cassell, 1964.

Crawford, Francis M. *The Rulers of the South.* New York: Macmillan, 1900.

Cray, Ed. *The Big Blue Line: Police Power vs. Human Rights.* New York: Coward-McCann, 1967.

Cressey, Donald R. *Other People's Money: A Study in the Social Psychology of Embezzlement.* New York: Free Press, 1953.

———. *Theft of a Nation: The Structure and Operations of Organized Crime in America.* New York: Harper & Row, 1969.

——— (ed.). *The Prison: Studies in Institutional Organization and Change.* New York: Holt, Rinehart and Winston, 1961.

———. "Changing Criminals: The Application of the Theory of Differential Association," *American Journal of Sociology,* 61 (September 1955), 116–120.

———. "Epidemiology and Individual Conduct: A Case from Criminology," *Pacific Sociological Review,* 3 (Fall 1960), 47–58.

———. "Methodological Problems in the Study of Organized Crime as a Social Problem," *The Annals,* 374 (November 1967), 101–112.

———. "Negotiated Pleas," *Criminologica,* 5 (February 1968), 5–16.

———. "Social Psychological Foundations for Using Criminals in the Rehabilitation of Criminals," *Journal of Research in Crime and Delinquency,* 71 (July 1965), 49–59.

———. "The State of Criminal Statistics," *National Probation and Parole Journal,* 3 (July 1957), 230–241.

Cressey, Paul G. *The Taxi-Dance Hall.* Chicago: University of Chicago Press, 1932.

Crihfield, B. E. "The Interstate Parole and Probation Compact," *Federal Probation,* 17 (June 1953), 3–7.

"The Crime Against Nature," *Journal of Public Law,* 16 (1967), 159–192.

"Crime is a Worldwide Problem," *FBI Law Enforcement Bulletin,* 35 (December 1966), 7–10.

"Crime of Suicide," *Economist,* 196 (September 3, 1960), 871–872.

Curtis, Charles P. *It's Your Law.* Cambridge, Massachusetts: Harvard University Press, 1954.

Dann, Robert H. "Capital Punishment in Oregon," *The Annals,* 284 (November 1952), 110–114.

Darrow, Clarence. *Crime: Its Causes and Conditions.* New York: Crowell, 1926.

Davis, David B. "The Movement to Abolish Capital Punishment, 1787–1861," *American Historical Review,* 63 (October 1957), 23–46.

Davis, F. James, Henry H. Foster, Jr., C. Ray Jeffery, and E. Eugene Davis. *Society and the Law: New Meanings for an Old Profession.* New York: Free Press, 1962.

Davis, Kingsley. *Human Society.* New York: Macmillan, 1949.

———. "Sociology of Parent-Youth Conflict," *American Sociological Review,* 5 (August 1940), 523–535.

deBeaumont, Gustave, and Alexis deTocqueville. *On the Penitentiary System in the United States and Its Application in France* [1833]. Francis Lieber (tr.). Carbondale: Southern Illinois University Press, 1964.

Debo, Angie. *The Road to Disappearance.* Norman: University of Oklahoma Press, 1941.

DeFleur, Melvin, and Richard Quinney. "A Reformulation of Sutherland's Differential Association Theory and a Strategy for Empirical Verification," *Journal of Research in Crime and Delinquency,* 3 (January 1966), 1–22.

DeMott, Benjamin. "The Great Narcotic Muddle," *Harper's*, 224 (March 1962), 46–54.

Dentler, Robert A., and Lawrence J. Monroe. "Social Correlates of Early Adolescent Theft," *American Sociological Review*, 26 (October 1961), 733–743.

DePorte, J. V., and Elizabeth Parkhurst. "Homicide in New York State, 1921–1930," *Human Biology*, 7 (February 1935), 45–73.

DeRopp, Robert S. *Drugs and the Mind*. New York: St. Martin's Press, 1957.

Deutsch, Albert. *Shame of the States*. New York: Harcourt, Brace, 1948.

Devereux, Edward C. *Gambling and Social Structure: A Sociological Study of Lotteries and Horse Racing in Contemporary America*. Ph.D. dissertation, Harvard University, 1949.

"Deviate Sexual Behavior Under the New Illinois Criminal Code," *Washington University Law Quarterly*, (April 1965), 220–235.

Devlin, Patrick. *The Criminal Prosecution in England*. New Haven, Connecticut: Yale University Press, 1958.

———. *The Enforcement of Morals*. London: Oxford University Press, 1959.

Dexter, Walter (ed.). *Letters of Charles Dickens*. Bloomsbury, England: Nonesuch Press, 1938.

Diana, Lewis. "What is Probation?" *Journal of Criminal Law*, 51 (July–August 1960), 189–208.

Dickens, Charles. *American Notes and Pictures from Italy*. London: Oxford University Press, 1842.

Dimock, Edward J. "The Public Defender—Step Toward a Police State?", *American Bar Association Journal*, 42 (March 1956), 219–221.

Dobry, George. "Wire-Tapping and Eavesdropping: A Comparative Survey," *International Commission of Jurists Bulletin*, 1 (Spring–Summer 1958), 319–335.

Dollard, John, and Neal Miller. *Personality and Psychotherapy: An Analysis in Terms of Learning, Thinking and Culture*. New York: McGraw-Hill, 1950.

———, and ———. *Social Learning and Imitation*. New Haven, Connecticut: Yale University Press, 1941.

Donnelly, Richard C. "Comments and Caveats on the Wire-Tapping Controversy," *Yale Law Journal*, 63 (April 1954), 798–810.

Dorsen, Norman, and Daniel Rezneck. "Gault and the Future of Juvenile Law," *Family Law Quarterly*, 1 (December 1967), 1–46.

Dosick, Martin L. "Statement," in U. S. Senate, Committee on the Judiciary, Subcommittee to Investigate Juvenile Delinquency, *Part 18 (Auto Theft and Juvenile Delinquency)*, 90th Congress, 1st Session, 1968, 4014–4026.

Dostoevsky, Fyodor. *Crime and Punishment*. [1866] Constance Garnett (tr.). Cleveland: World Publishing, 1947.

———. *Memoirs from the House of the Dead*. [1862] Jessie Coulson (tr.). London: Oxford University Press, 1956.

Douglas, William O. *The Right of the People*. New York: Doubleday, 1958.

———. "A Challenge to the Bar," *Notre Dame Lawyer*, 28 (Summer 1953), 497–508.

Doyle, James C. "Unnecessary Hysterectomies," *American Medical Association Journal*, 151 (January 31, 1953), 360–365.

Drake, Frank R. "The Current Drug Therapy of Epilepsy: A Review," *Journal of Medical Sciences*, 230 (July–December 1955), 98–107.

Drake, St. Clair, and Horace R. Cayton. *Black Metropolis*. New York: Harcourt, Brace, 1945.

Dressler, David. *Parole Chief*. New York: Viking, 1951.

———. *Practice and Theory of Probation and Parole.* New York: Columbia University Press, 1959.

———. "Trial by Combat in American Courts," *Harper's,* 222 (April 1961), 31–36.

Drug Addiction: Crime or Disease? Bloomington: Indiana University Press, 1961.

Drummond, Isabel. *The Sex Paradox.* New York: Putnam, 1952.

Duff, Charles. *A New Handbook on Hanging.* Chicago: Regnery, 1955.

Dugdale, Richard L. *The Jukes: A Study in Crime, Pauperism, Disease and Heredity.* New York: Putnam, 1877.

Duncan, Glen M., Shervert H. Frazier, *et al.* "Etiological Factors in First-Degree Murder," *American Medical Association Journal,* 168 (November 22, 1959), 1755–1758.

Dunham, H. Warren. *Crucial Issues in the Treatment and Control of Sexual Deviation in the Community.* Lansing: Michigan Department of Mental Health, 1951.

Durant, Will. *The Life of Greece.* New York: Simon and Schuster, 1939.

———. *Our Oriental Heritage.* New York: Simon and Schuster, 1954.

Durkheim, Emile. *The Rules of Sociological Method.* [1895] Sarah A. Solovay and John H. Mueller (trs.). New York: Free Press, 1938.

———. *Suicide.* [1897] John A. Spaulding and George Simpson (trs.). New York: Free Press, 1951.

East, Norwood. *Society and the Criminal.* Springfield, Illinois: Thomas, 1949.

Eastman, Harold D. *The Process of Urbanization and Criminal Behavior: A Restudy of Culture Conflict.* Ph.D. dissertation, University of Iowa, 1954.

Eddowes, Michael. *The Man on Your Conscience.* London: Cassell, 1955.

Edelston, H. *The Earliest Stages of Delinquency.* Edinburgh: Livingstone, 1952.

Editorial, *Journal of Criminal Law,* 28 (January–February 1938), 627.

Edwards, George. *Police on the Urban Frontier.* New York: Institute of Human Relations Press, American Jewish Committee, 1968.

Edwards, J. L. *Mens Rea in Statutory Offenses.* New York: St. Martin's, 1955.

Edwards, Loren E. *Shoplifting and Shrinkage Protection for Stores.* Springfield, Illinois: Thomas, 1958.

Egen, Frederick W. *Plainclothesmen.* New York: Greenberg, 1952.

Eisenstadt, S. N. *From Generation to Generation: Age Groups and Social Structure.* New York: Free Press, 1956.

Eisenstadter, Werner J. "The Social Organization of Armed Robbery," *Social Problems,* 17 (Summer 1969), 64–83.

Eisner, Victor. *The Delinquency Label: The Epidemiology of Juvenile Delinquency.* New York: Random House, 1968.

Eldridge, William B. *Narcotics and the Law.* 2nd ed. Chicago: University of Chicago Press, 1967.

Elkin, Frederick, and William A. Westley. "The Myth of Adolescent Culture," *American Sociological Review,* 20 (December 1955), 680–684.

Elliott, Mabel A. *Conflicting Penal Theories in Statutory Criminal Law.* Chicago: University of Chicago Press, 1931.

———. *Crime in Modern Society.* New York: Harper, 1952.

Ellis, Albert, and Ralph Brancale. *The Psychology of Sex Offenders.* Springfield, Illinois: Thomas, 1956.

Ellis, Havelock. *The Criminal.* New York: Scribner, 1892.

Ellison, Ralph, and Eugene Walter. "Robert Penn Warren," in Malcolm

Cowley (ed.), *Writers at Work: The Paris Review Interviews*. New York: Viking, 1959, pp. 185–207.

"Embezzlers: The Trusted Thieves," *Fortune*, 56 (November 1957), 142–144ff.

Emerson, Thomas I. Review of *White Collar Crime*, Yale Law Journal, 59 (February 1950), 581–585.

Empey, LaMar T. *Alternatives to Incarceration*. Washington, D.C.: Office of Juvenile Delinquency and Youth Development, 1967.

———. "Delinquency Theory and Recent Research," *Journal of Research in Crime and Delinquency*, 4 (January 1967), 28–42.

———, and Jerome Rabow. "The Provo Experiment in Delinquency Rehabilitation," *American Sociological Review*, 26 (October 1961), 679–695.

England, Ralph W. *Prison Labour*. New York: U.N. Department of Economic and Social Affairs, 1955.

Ennis, Phillip H. "Crime, Victims, and the Police," *Trans-action—Social Science & Modern Society*, 4 (June 1967), 36–44.

Epstein, Edward J. *Inquest: The Warren Commission and the Establishment of Truth*. New York: Viking, 1966.

Erikson, Erik H. *Youth: Change and Challenge*. New York: Basic Books, 1963.

———. "Ego-Identity and Psychosocial Moratorium," in Helen L. Witmer and Ruth Kotinsky, *New Perspectives for Research in Juvenile Delinquency*, Children's Bureau 356. Washington, D.C.: Government Printing Office, 1956.

Eriksson, Torsten. "Postwar Prison Reform in Sweden," *The Annals*, 293 (May 1954), 152–162.

Estabrook, Arthur H. *The Jukes in 1915*. Washington, D.C.: Carnegie Institution, 1916.

Evans, E. P. *The Criminal Prosecution and Capital Punishment of Animals*. London: Heinemann, 1906.

Evans, Ernest (ed.). *Tertullian's Treatise on the Resurrection*. London: SPCK, 1960.

Ezell, John. *Fortune's Merry Wheel: The Lottery in America*. Cambridge, Massachusetts: Harvard University Press, 1960.

Fabian, Robert. *Fabian of the Yard*. New York: British Book Centre, 1953.

Fahr, Samuel M. "Why Lawyers are Dissatisfied with the Social Sciences," *Washburn Law Review*, 1 (Spring 1961), 161–175.

"Failure to Rescue: A Comparative Study," *Columbia Law Review*, 52 (May 1952), 631–647.

Falk, Gerhard J. "The Public Image of the Sex Offender," *Mental Hygiene*, 48 (October 1964), 612–620.

Feifer, George. *Justice in Moscow*. New York: Simon and Schuster, 1964.

Fellman, David. *The Limits of Freedom*. New Brunswick, New Jersey: Rutgers University Press, 1959.

Fenton, Norman. *The Prisoner's Family*. Palo Alto, California: Pacific Books, 1959.

Ferdinand, Theodore N. *Typologies of Delinquency: A Critical Analysis*. New York: Random House, 1966.

———. "The Criminal Patterns of Boston Since 1849," *American Journal of Sociology*, 73 (July 1967), 84–99.

Ferrero, Gina Lombroso. *Lombroso's Criminal Man*. New York: Putnam, 1911.

Fink, Arthur E. *Causes of Crime: Biological Theories in the United States, 1800–1915*. Philadelphia: University of Pennsylvania Press, 1938.

Fitch, J. H. "Men Convicted of Sexual Offences Against Children: A Descriptive Follow-up Study," *British Journal of Criminology*, 3 (July 1962), 18–37.

Fleisher, Wilfrid. *Sweden: The Welfare State.* New York: John Day, 1956.

Fletcher, Frank T. H. *Pascal and the Mystical Tradition.* Oxford, England: Blackwell, 1954.

Foote, Caleb. "Vagrancy-Type Law and Its Administration," *University of Pennsylvania Law Review,* 104 (March 1956), 603–650.

————, James P. Markle, and Edward A. Wooley. "Compelling Appearance in Court: Administration of Bail in Philadelphia," *University of Pennsylvania Law Review,* 102 (June 1954), 1031–1079.

Ford, Clellan S., and Frank A. Beach. *Patterns of Sexual Behavior.* New York: Harper & Row, 1951.

Ford, Gerald R., and John R. Stiles. *Portrait of the Assassin.* New York: Simon and Schuster, 1965.

Fox, Lionel W. *The English Prison and Borstal Systems.* London: Routledge and Kegan Paul, 1952.

France, Anatole. *The Red Lily.* [*Le Lys Rouge,* 1894] Winifred Stephens (tr.). New York: Dodd, Mead, 1927.

Frank, Jerome. *Courts on Trial: Myth and Reality in American Justice.* Princeton, New Jersey: Princeton University Press, 1950.

————, and Barbara Frank. *Not Guilty.* New York: Doubleday, 1957.

Frank, John P. *Marble Palace: The Supreme Court in American Life.* New York: Knopf, 1958.

Frazier, E. Franklin. *Black Bourgeosie.* New York: Free Press, 1957.

Freed, Daniel J., and Patricia M. Wald. *Bail in the United States.* Washington, D.C.: National Conference on Bail and Criminal Justice, 1964.

Freeman, Lucy. *"Before I Kill More."* New York: Crown, 1955.

Friedman, Monroe P. "Consumer Confusion in the Selection of Supermarket Products," *Journal of Applied Psychology,* 50 (December 1966), 529–534.

Friendly, Alfred, and Ronald L. Goldfarb. *Crime and Publicity: The Impact of News on the Administration of Justice.* New York: Twentieth Century Fund, 1967.

Fuller, John G. *The Gentleman Conspirators.* New York: Grove, 1962.

Fulton, Robert, and Gilbert Geis. "Death and Social Values," in Fulton (ed.), *Death and Identity.* New York: Wiley, 1965, pp. 67–75.

Gabel, Leona C. (ed.). *Memoirs of a Renaissance Pope: The Commentaries of Pius II.* Florence A. Gragg (tr.). New York: Putnam, 1959.

Gagnon, John H. "Female Child Victims of Sex Offenses," *Social Problems,* 13 (Fall 1965), 176–192.

Galbraith, John K. *The Affluent Society.* Boston: Houghton Mifflin, 1958.

Gallo, Jon J. *et al.* "The Consenting Homosexual and the Law: An Empirical Study of Enforcement and Administration in Los Angeles County," *U.C.L.A. Law Review,* 13 (March 1966), 643–832.

Gannon, Thomas M. "Harlem's Immortal Five Per Cent," *America,* 115 (August 27, 1966), 208–209.

Gardner, George E. "The Primary and Secondary Gains in Stealing," *Nervous Child,* 6 (October 1947), 436–446.

Garfinkel, Harold. "Research Note on Inter- and Intra-Racial Homicide," *Social Forces,* 27 (May 1949), 369–381.

Gaskill, Herbert S. "Marihuana, An Intoxicant," *America Journal of Psychiatry,* 102 (September 1945), 202–204.

Gasser, Robert L. "The Confidence Game," *Federal Probation,* 27 (December 1963), 47–54.

Gautier, Maurice. "The Psychology of the Compulsive Forger," *Canadian Journal of Corrections,* 1 (July 1959), 62–69.

Gebhard, Paul H., John H. Gagnon, Wardell B. Pomeroy, and Cornelia V. Christenson. *Sex Offenders*. New York: Harper & Row, 1965.

Geis, Gilbert. *The East Los Angeles Halfway House for Narcotic Addicts:* Sacramento, California: Institute for the Study of Crime and Delinquency, 1966.

————. *Juvenile Gangs*. Washington, D.C.: President's Committee on Juvenile Delinquency and Youth Crime, 1965.

———— (ed.). *White-Collar Criminal: The Offender in Business and the Professions*. New York: Atherton, 1968.

————. "Correctional Work: 'Think Ye That Ye May Be Wrong'," *Criminologica*, 2 (May 1964), 3–5.

————. "Crime and Politics," *The Nation*, 205 (August 14, 1967), 115–116.

————. "The Fable of a Fatty," *Issues in Criminology*, 3 (Spring 1968), 211–214.

————. "The Heavy Electrical Equipment Antitrust Cases of 1961," in Marshall B. Clinard and Richard Quinney (eds.), *Criminal Behavior Systems: A Typology*. New York: Holt, Rinehart and Winston, 1967, pp. 139–151.

————. "Preliminary Hearings and the Press," *U.C.L.A. Law Review*, 8 (March 1961), 397–414.

————. "The Right to Vote for Prisoners," *Presidio*, 35 (July–August 1968), 9–10ff.

————. "Social and Epidemiological Aspects of Marihuana Use," *Journal of Psychedelic Drugs*, 2 (Fall 1968), 67–77.

————. "Sociology and Sociological Jurisprudence: Admixture of Lore and Law," *Kentucky Law Journal*, 52 (Winter 1964), 267–293.

————. "State Compensation to Victims of Violent Crime," in *Task Force Report: Crime and Its Impact—An Assessment*. Washington, D.C.: President's Commission on Law Enforcement and Administration of Justice, 1967, pp. 157–177.

————. "Statistics Concerning Race and Crime," *Crime and Delinquency*, 11 (April 1965), 142–150.

————. "Toward a Delineation of White-Collar Offenses," *Sociological Inquiry*, 32 (Spring 1962), 159–171.

————. "Violence in American Society," *Current History*, 52 (June 1967), 354–358.

————. "Violence and Organized Crime," *The Annals*, 364 (March 1966), 86–95.

————, and Herbert Costner. "Oklahoma's County Attorneys," *Oklahoma Bar Association Journal*, 24 (April 1953), 687–694.

————, and Charles W. Tenney, Jr. "Evaluating a Training Institute for Juvenile Court Judges," *Community Mental Health Journal*, 4 (December 1968), 461–468.

————, and Fred W. Woodson. "Matching Probation Office and Delinquent," *National Probation and Parole Association Journal*, 2 (January 1956), 58–62.

Gertsenzon, A. A. "The Community's Role in the Prevention and Study of Crime," *Soviet Review*, 2 (January 1961), 14–27.

Giardini, G. I. *The Parole Process*. Springfield, Illinois: Thomas, 1959.

Gibbens, T. C. N. "Sane and Insane Homicide," *Journal of Criminal Law*, 49 (July–August 1958), 110–115.

————, and Joyce Prince. *Shoplifting*. London: Institute for the Study and Treatment of Delinquency, 1962.

Gibbon, Edward. *Decline and Fall of the Roman Empire*. [1776] New York: Modern Library, n.d.

Gibbons, Don C., and Donald L. Garrity. "Some Suggestions for the Definition of Etiological and Treatment Theory in Criminology," *Social Forces,* 38 (October 1959), 51–57.

Gibbs, Jack P. "Needed: Analytical Typologies in Criminology," *Southwestern Social Science Quarterly,* 40 (March 1960), 321–329.

Gibney, Frank. *The Operators.* New York: Harper, 1960.

Gibson, Evelyn, and S. Klein. *Murder.* London: Her Majesty's Stationery Office, 1961.

Gilbert, G. M. "Crime and Punishment: An Exploratory Comparison of Public, Criminal, and Penological Attitudes," *Mental Hygiene,* 42 (October 1958), 550–557.

Gillin, John L. *The Wisconsin Prisoner.* Madison: University of Wisconsin Press, 1946.

Ginger, Ray. *Six Days or Forever?: Tennessee v. John Thomas Scopes.* Boston: Beacon Press, 1958.

Glaser, Daniel. "National Goals and Indicators for the Reduction of Crime and Delinquency," *The Annals,* 371 (May 1967), 104–126.

Glueck, Sheldon. *Crime and Correction: Selected Papers.* Cambridge, Massachusetts: Addison-Wesley, 1952.

———. "Mental Illness and Criminal Responsibility," *Journal of Social Therapy,* 2 (3rd Quarter 1956), 134–157.

———, and Eleanor Glueck. *Juvenile Delinquents Grown Up.* New York: Commonwealth Fund, 1940.

Goddard, Henry H. *The Kallikak Family: A Study in the Heredity of Feeblemindedness.* New York: Macmillan, 1912.

Goode, Erich. "Multiple Drug Use Among Marijuana Smokers," *Social Problems,* 17 (Summer 1969), 48–64.

Goffman, Erving. *Asylums: Essays on the Social Situation of Mental Patients and Other Inmates.* New York: Doubleday, 1961.

———. "On Cooling the Mark Out: Some Aspects of Adaptation to Failure," *Psychiatry,* 15 (November 1952), 451–463.

———. "On the Characteristics of Total Institutions," in Donald R. Cressey (ed.), *The Prison: Studies in Institutional Organization and Change.* New York: Holt, Rinehart and Winston, 1961, pp. 15–106.

Gogol, Nikolai. *Taras Bulba.* [1835] Constance Garnett (tr.). New York: Washington Square Press, 1962.

Goldberg, Arthur. "Juvenatrics: A Study of Prolonged Adolescence," *Clearing House,* 38 (April 1964), 488–492.

Goldin, Hyman E. *Hebrew Criminal Law and Procedure.* New York: Twayne, 1952.

———. *Dictionary of American Underworld Lingo.* New York: Twayne, 1950.

Goldman, Nathan. *The Differential Selection of Juvenile Offenders for Court Appearance.* New York: Research and Information Center, National Council on Crime and Delinquency, 1963.

Goldstein, Abraham S. "The State and the Accused: Balance of Advantage in Criminal Procedure," *Yale Law Journal,* 69 (June 1960), 1,149–1,199.

Goldstein, Herman. "Police Discretion: The Ideal Versus the Real," *Public Administration Review,* 23 (September 1963), 140–148.

Goldstein, Joseph. "Police Discretion Not to Invoke the Criminal Process: Low-Visibility Decisions in the Administration of Criminal Justice," *Yale Law Journal,* 69 (March 1960), 543–594.

———, and Jay Katz. "Abolish the 'Insanity Plea'—Why Not?," *Yale Law Journal,* 72 (April 1963), 853–876.

Gollan, Antoni. "The Great Marijuana Problem," *National Review,* 20 (January 30, 1968), 74–80.

Goodman, Paul. *Growing Up Absurd.* New York: Random House, 1960.

Goodman, Walter. *All Honorable Men.* Boston: Little, Brown, 1963.

Gordon, Cyrus H. *Hammurabi's Code: Quaint or Forward-Looking?* New York: Holt, Rinehart and Winston, 1960.

Gorer, Geoffrey, "British Life—It's a Gamble," *The New York Times Magazine,* September 1, 1963, pp. 10ff.

————. "Man Has No 'Killer' Instinct," *The New York Times Magazine,* November 4, 1966, pp. 47ff.

————. "Modification of National Character: The Role of the Police in England," *Journal of Social Issues,* 11 (1955), 24–32.

Goring, Charles. *The English Convict: A Statistical Study.* London: His Majesty's Stationery Office, 1913.

Gottlieb, David, and Jon Reeves. *Adolescent Behavior in Urban Areas: A Bibliographic Review and Discussion of the Literature.* New York: Free Press, 1963.

————, ————, and Warren D. TenHouten. *The Emergence of Youth Societies: A Cross-Cultural Approach.* New York: Free Press, 1966.

Gough, John W. *The Social Contract: A Critical Study of Its Development,* 2nd ed. Oxford, England: Clarendon Press, 1957.

Gourley, G. Douglas. *Public Relations and the Police.* Springfield, Illinois: Thomas, 1953.

Graham, Henry G. *Social Life of Scotland in the Eighteenth Century.* [1899] London: Black, 1950.

Graham, Hugh D. and Ted Robert Gurr (eds.). *Violence in America: Historical and Comparative Perspectives.* Washington, D.C.: National Commission on Causes and Prevention of Violence, 1969.

Graziano, Rocky. *Somebody Up There Likes Me.* New York: Simon and Schuster, 1955.

Great Britain, Committee Appointed to Inquire Into the Interception of Communications. *Report.* (Command 283, 1957).

————, Committee on Homosexual Offences and Prostitution. *Report.* (Command 247, 1957).

————, Departmental Committee on Proceedings Before Examining Justices. *Report.* (Command 479, 1958).

————, Royal Commission on Betting, Lotteries, and Gaming, 1949–1951. *Report.* (Command 8190, 1951).

————, Royal Commission on Capital Punishment, 1949–1953. *Report.* (Command 8932, 1953).

Greenspan, Herbert, and John D. Campbell. "The Homosexual as a Personality Type," *America Journal of Psychiatry,* 101 (March 1945), 682–689.

Gribble, Leonard. *The True Book About the Old Bailey.* London: Muller, 1959.

Grinnell, Frank W. "The Common Law Origins of Probation in Massachusetts," *Massachusetts Law Quarterly,* 45 (October 1960), 70–91.

Grünhut, Max. "Murder and the Death Penalty in England," *The Annals,* 284 (November 1952), 158–166.

Grupp, Stanley. "Work Release: Statutory Patterns, Implementation, and Problems," *Prison Journal,* 44 (Spring 1964), 4–25.

Guttmacher, Manfred S. *The Mind of the Murderer.* New York: Farrar, Straus, 1960.

————. *Sex Offenses: The Problem, Causes, and Prevention.* New York: Norton, 1951.

————, and Henry Weihofen. *Psychiatry and the Law.* New York: Norton, 1952.

Hager, Don J. "Race, Nationality, and Religion: Their Relationship to Appointment Policies and Casework," *National Probation and Parole Association Journal,* 3 (April 1957), 129–141.

———. "Religion, Delinquency, and Society," *Social Work,* 14 (July 1957), 16–21.

Hakeem, Michael. "A Critique of the Psychiatric Approach to Crime and Correction," *Law and Contemporary Problems,* 33 (Autumn 1958), 650–682.

Haley, Andrew G., *et al.* "Law and Upper Space: A Symposium," *Saint Louis University Law Journal,* 5 (Spring 1958), 1–133.

Hall, Jerome. *General Principles of Criminal Law.* Indianapolis, Indiana: Bobbs-Merrill, 1947.

———. *Theft, Law and Society.* 2nd ed. Indianapolis, Indiana: Bobbs-Merrill, 1952.

———. "Criminology," in Georges Gurvitch and Wilbert E. Moore (eds.), *Twentieth Century Sociology.* New York: Philosophical Library, 1945.

———. "Prolegomena to a Science of Criminal Law," *University of Pennsylvania Law Review,* 89 (March 1941), 549–580.

Halleck, Seymour L. *Psychiatry and the Dilemmas of Crime.* New York: Harper & Row, 1967.

Harlan, Howard. "Five Hundred Homicides," *Journal of Criminal Law,* 40 (March–April 1950), 736–752.

Harper, F. R. *Code of Hammurabi.* Chicago: University of Chicago Press, 1904.

Harper, Fowler V. *Problems of the Family.* Indianapolis, Indiana: Bobbs-Merrill, 1952.

Harris, Sara. *Skid Row, U.S.A.* New York: Doubleday, 1956.

Hart, H. L. A. *Law, Liberty, and Morality.* Stanford, California: Stanford University Press, 1963.

Hart, J. M. *The British Police.* London: Macmillan, 1951.

Hartland, Edwin S. *The Science of Fairy Tales.* New York: Stokes, 1890.

Hartogs, Renastus, and Lucy Freeman. *The Two Assassins.* New York: Crowell, 1965.

Hartung, Frank E. *Crime, Law, and Society.* Detroit: Wayne State University Press, 1965.

———. "White-Collar Offenses in the Wholesale Meat Industry in Detroit," *American Journal of Sociology,* 56 (July 1950), 25–32.

Havighurst, Bruce, Peter MacDougall, and Richard P. Schulze, Jr. "The Representation of Indigent Criminal Defendants in the Federal District Courts," *Harvard Law Review,* 76 (January 1963), 579–618.

Hawkins, E. R., and Willard Waller. "Critical Notes on the Cost of Crime," *Journal of Criminal Law,* 26 (January–February 1936), 679–694.

Hayek, F. A. *The Constitution of Liberty.* Chicago: University of Chicago Press, 1960.

Hayner, Norman S. "Delinquency Areas in the Puget Sound Area," *American Journal of Sociology,* 39 (November 1936), 314–328.

Hazard, John N. *Law and Social Change in the U. S. S. R.* London: Stevens, 1953.

Heard, Alexander. *The Costs of Democracy.* Chapel Hill: University of North Carolina Press, 1960.

Hearn, Lafcadio. *Japan: Attempt at Interpretation.* New York: Macmillan, 1920.

Hecht, Ben. *A Child of the Century.* New York: Signet, 1955.

Heckscher, August. "Rightly to Be Great . . . ," in *Annual Report of the Twentieth Century Fund,* New York: Twentieth Century Fund, 1959, pp. 9–14.

Heller, Francis H. *The Sixth Amendment to the Constitution of the United States.* Lawrence: University of Kansas Press, 1951.

Hemingway, Ernest. *In Our Time.* New York: Scribner, 1925.

Henry, Andrew F., and James F. Short, Jr. *Suicide and Homicide.* New York: Free Press, 1954.

Henson, Roy D. (ed.). *Landmarks of the Law.* New York: Harper & Row, 1960.

Hentig, Hans von. *The Criminal and His Victim.* New Haven, Connecticut: Yale University Press, 1948.

————. "Delinquency of the American Indian," *Journal of Criminal Law,* 36 (July–August 1945), 75–84.

Hentoff, Nat. *A Doctor Among the Addicts.* New York: Random House, 1968.

Herling, John. *The Great Price Conspiracy.* Washington, D.C.: Luce, 1962.

Herman, Robert D. (ed.). *Gambling.* New York: Harper & Row, 1967.

Hersey, John. *The Algiers Motel Incident.* New York: Knopf, 1968.

Heschel, Abraham J. *The Prophets.* New York: Harper & Row, 1962.

Hobsbawm, E. J. *Social Bandits and Primitive Rebels.* New York: Free Press, 1959.

Hoebel, E. Adamson. "Law Ways of the Primitive Eskimos," *Journal of Criminal Law,* 31 (March–April, 1941), 663–683.

Hoffman, Martin. *The Gay World: Male Homosexuality and the Social Creation of Evil.* New York: Bantam, 1969.

Holcomb, Richard L. *Police Patrol.* Springfield, Illinois: Thomas, 1952.

Hollander, Paul. "A Converging Social Problem: Juvenile Delinquency in the Soviet Union and the United States," *British Journal of Criminology,* 9 (April 1969), 148–166.

Holmes, Oliver W. Jr. *The Common Law.* Boston: Little, Brown, 1881.

Holtzoff, Alexander. "The Power of Probation and Parole Officers to Search and Seize," *Federal Probation,* 31 (December 1967), 3–7.

Homer, Sidney. *A History of Interest Rates.* New Brunswick, New Jersey: Rutgers University Press, 1963.

Hooker, Evelyn. "The Adjustment of the Male Overt Homosexual," in Hendrik M. Ruitenbeek (ed.). *The Problem of Homosexuality in Modern Society.* New York: Dutton, 1963, pp. 141–161.

Hopper, Columbus B. *Sex in Prison: The Mississippi Experiment with Conjugal Visiting.* Baton Rouge: Louisiana State University Press, 1969.

Hoyles, J. Arthur. *Treatment of the Young Delinquent.* London: Epworth Press, 1952.

Hughes, Graham. "Consent in Sexual Offenses," *Modern Law Review,* 25 (November 1962), 672–686.

————. "Criminal Omissions," *Yale Law Journal,* 67 (Fall 1958), 590–637.

Hugo, Victor. *Les Misérables.* [1862] Charles E. Wilbour (tr.). New York: Modern Library, n.d.

Huie, William B. *Mud on the Stars.* New York: Fischer, 1942.

————. "The Hero of Iwo Jima," in Huie (ed.), *Wolf Whistle.* New York: Signet, 1959, pp. 73–141.

Hull, Clark. *A Behavior System: An Introduction to Behavior Theory Concerning the Individual Organism.* New Haven, Connecticut: Yale University Press, 1952.

Hynd, Alan. "Coster-Musica: The Man Who Dopes the Drug Houses," in Hynd (ed.), *Murder, Mayhem, and Mystery.* New York: Barnes & Noble, 1958, pp. 463–489.

Inbau, Fred E. "Police Interrogation—A Practical Necessity," *Journal of Criminal Law,* 52 (May–June 1961), 16–20.

Ingersoll, John E. "The Police Scandal Syndrome," *Crime and Delinquency,* 10 (July 1964), 269–275.

Irey, Elmer L., and William J. Slocum. *The Tax-Dodgers.* New York: Greenberg, 1948.

Irving, Washington. *Tales of a Traveller.* New York: Putnam, 1850.

Isbell, Harris. "Historical Development of Attitudes Toward Opiate Addiction in the United States," in Seymour M. Farber and Roger Wilson (eds.), *Conflict and Creativity.* New York: McGraw-Hill, 1963, pp. 154–170.

Jacobs, Patricia A., Muriel Brunton, and Marie M. Melville. "Aggressive Behavior, Mental Subnormality and the XYY Male," *Nature,* 208 (December 25, 1965), 1,351–1,352.

Jacobs, Paul. *Prelude to Riot: A View of Urban America from the Bottom.* New York: Random House, 1966.

Janouch, Gustav. *Conversations with Kafka.* New York: Praeger, 1953.

Japan, *A Summary of White Paper on Crime, 1965.* Tokyo: Training & Research Institute, Ministry of Justice, 1966.

Jaspan, Norman, and Hillel Black. *The Thief in the White Collar.* Philadelphia: Lippincott, 1960.

"J. Edgar Hoover and the FBI," *Newsweek,* December 6, 1964, pp. 21–26.

Jeffery, Clarence Ray. "The Historical Development of Criminology," in Hermann Mannheim (ed.), *Pioneers in Criminology.* London: Stevens, 1960, pp. 364–394.

Jellinek, E. *Disease Concept of Alcoholism.* New Haven, Connecticut: Hillhouse, 1960.

Jepsen, Jorgen, and Lone Pal. "Forecasting Crime," *Forward in Europe,* (April–May 1967), 20–23.

Jesse, F. Tennyson. *Murder and Its Motives.* Rev. ed. London: Harrap. 1952.

———. *Trials of Timothy John Evans and John Reginald Halliday Christie.* London: Hodges, 1957.

Jewell, Donald P. "Mexico's Tres Marias Penal Colony," *Journal of Criminal Law,* 48 (November–December 1957), 410–413.

John Augustus—First Probation Officer. New York: National Probation and Parole Association, 1939.

Johnson, Elmer H. "Sociology of Confinement: Assimilation and the Prison 'Rat'," *Journal of Criminal Law,* 51 (January–February 1961), 528–533.

Johnson, Guy B. "The Negro and Crime," *The Annals,* 277 (September 1941), 93–104.

Johnson, Lyndon B. "The President's Remarks to Members of the Commission Upon Signing Executive Order Establishing the Commission," *Weekly Compilation of Presidential Documents,* 4 (June 10, 1968), 936.

Joint Commission on Correctional Manpower and Training. *2nd Annual Report.* Washington, D.C.: The Commission, 1968.

———. *A Time to Act: Final Report.* Washington, D.C.: The Commission, 1969.

Jones, Howard. *Crime and the Penal System.* 3rd ed. London: University Tutorial Press, 1965.

Josephson, Matthew. *The Robber Barons.* New York: Harcourt, Brace, 1934.

Judges, A. V. (ed.). *The Elizabethan Underworld.* London: Routledge and Kegan Paul, 1930.

Kadish, Sanford H. "Some Observations on the Use of Criminal Sanctions in the Enforcement of Economic Legislation," *University of Chicago Law Review,* 30 (Spring 1963), 423–449.

Kahn, Alfred J. *A Court for Children: A Study of the New York City Children's Court.* New York: Columbia University Press, 1953.

———. *Police and Children.* New York: Citizens Committee on Children of New York City, 1951.

Kalven, Harry, Jr. "Report on the Jury Project at the University of Chicago Law School," Address, Conference on Legal Research, Ann Arbor, Michigan, November 5, 1955.

———, Hans Zeisel, Thomas Callahan, and Phillip Ennis. *The American Jury.* Boston: Little, Brown, 1966.

Kamisar, Yale. "On the Tactics of Police-Prosecution Oriented Critics of the Courts," *Cornell Law Quarterly,* 49 (Spring 1964), 436–467.

———. "When the Cops Were Not Handcuffed," *The New York Times Magazine,* November 7, 1965, pp. 34–35ff.

Kant, Fritz. *The Treatment of the Alcoholic.* Springfield, Illinois: Thomas, 1954.

Kaplan, Sidney J. "Barriers to the Establishment of a Deterministic Criminal Law," *Kentucky Law Journal,* 46 (Fall 1957), 103–111.

Karon, Bertram P. *The Negro Personality.* New York: Springer, 1958.

Karpman, Benjamin. *The Sexual Offender and His Offenses.* New York: Julian, 1954.

Kassebaum, Gene G., David Ward, and Daniel Wilner. *Prison Treatment and Parole Survival.* New York: Wiley, 1970.

Kassof, Allen. *The Soviet Youth Program: Regimentation and Rebellion.* Cambridge, Massachusetts: Harvard University Press, 1965.

Katcher, Leo. *The Big Bankroll.* New York: Harper & Row, 1959.

Kaufman, Irving R. "Miranda and the Police: The Confession Debate Continues," *The New York Times Magazine,* October 2, 1966, pp. 36–37ff.

Kearney, James J. (ed.). *A Treatise on the Law of Crimes (Clark & Marshall).* 5th ed. Chicago: Callaghan, 1952.

Keats, Charles. *Magnificent Masquerade.* New York: Funk & Wagnalls, 1964.

Keedy, Edwin R. "Irresistible Impulse as a Defense in Criminal Law," *University of Pennsylvania Law Review,* 100 (May 1952), 956–993.

Kefauver, Estes. *Crime in America.* New York: Doubleday, 1951.

Kenison, Robert S. "Off-Track Betting: A Legal Inquiry Into Quasi-Socialized Gambling," *New Hampshire Bar Journal,* 6 (October 1963), 5–41.

Kennan, George. *Siberia and the Exile System.* Abridged ed. Chicago: University of Chicago Press, 1958.

Kennedy, Ludovic. *Ten Rillington Place.* New York: Simon and Schuster, 1961.

Kennedy, Robert F. *The Enemy Within.* New York: Harper & Row, 1960.

Kephart, William M. *Racial Factors and Urban Law Enforcement.* Philadelphia: University of Pennsylvania Press, 1957.

Kershaw, Alister. *Murder in France.* London: Constable, 1955.

Ketcham, Orman W. "Guidelines from Gault: Revolutionary Requirements and Reappraisal," *Virginia Law Review,* 53 (December 1967), 1,700–1,718.

Keve, Paul W. *Prison, Probation, or Parole?* Minneapolis: University of Minnesota Press, 1954.

Keynes, John M. *The General Theory of Employment, Interest and Money.* New York: Harcourt, Brace, 1936.

Kinsey, Alfred C., Wardell Pomeroy, and Clyde E. Martin. *Sexual Behavior in the Human Male.* Philadelphia: Saunders, 1948.

———, and Paul H. Gebhard. *Sexual Behavior in the Human Female.* Philadelphia: Saunders, 1953.

Kirby, Bernard C. "Parole Prediction Using Multiple Correlation," *American Journal of Sociology,* 59 (May 1954), 539–551.

Kirk, Paul L. *Crime Investigation.* New York: Interscience, 1953.

Kitano, Harry H. L. *Japanese Americans: The Evolution of a Subculture.* Englewood Cliffs, New Jersey: Prentice-Hall, 1969.

Klineberg, Otto. "Mental Testing of Racial and National Groups," in *Scientific Aspects of the Race Problem.* New York: Longmans, 1941, pp. 253–291.

Kobrin, Solomon. "The Conflict of Values in Delinquency Areas," *American Sociological Review,* 16 (October 1951), 653–661.

Kolman, Sam, and Hillel Black. *The Royal Vultures.* New York: Perma Books, 1958.

Kooken, Don L. *Ethics in Police Service.* Springfield, Illinois: Thomas, 1957.

Kopp, Sheldon B. "The Character Structure of Sex Offenders," *American Journal of Psychotherapy,* 16 (January 1960), 64–70.

Korn, Richard R., and Lloyd W. McCorkle. *Criminology and Penology.* New York: Holt, Rinehart and Winston, 1959.

Kossack, Nathaniel. " 'Scam': The Planned Bankruptcy Racket," *New York Certified Public Accountant,* 35 (June 1965), 417–423.

Kramer, John C., Richard A. Bass, and John Berecochea. "Civil Commitment for Addicts: The California Program," *American Journal of Psychiatry,* 125 (December 1968), 816–824.

Kunkel, Marilyn V., and Gilbert Geis. "Order of Final Argument in Minnesota Criminal Trials," *Minnesota Law Review,* 42 (March 1958), 549–558.

Kvaraceus, William. "The Nature and Problem of Juvenile Delinquency in the United States," *Journal of Negro Education,* 26 (Summer 1959), 191–199.

LaFave, Wayne R. *Arrest: The Decision To Take a Suspect Into Custody.* Boston: Little, Brown, 1965.

Lake, Lewis W. *How to Win Lawsuits Before Juries.* Englewood Cliffs, N.J.: Prentice-Hall, 1954.

Landis, Judson R., Simon Dinitz, and Walter C. Reckless. "Implementing Two Theories of Delinquency: Value Orientation and Awareness of Limited Opportunity," *Sociology and Social Research,* 47 (July 1963), 408–416.

Lane, Mark. *Rush to Judgment.* New York: Holt, Rinehart and Winston, 1966.

Laski, Harold J. *The American Democracy: A Commentary and Interpretation.* New York: Viking, 1948.

———. "The Personality of Associations," *Harvard Law Review,* 28 (February 1916), 404–426.

Lasswell, Harold D. *Politics: Who Gets What, When, How.* New York: Whittlesey, 1936.

Laurence, John. *A History of Capital Punishment.* New York: Citadel, 1960.

Laurence, William L. "Gain Reported in Fight Against Encephalitis," *The New York Times,* October 1, 1962.

Laurents, Arthur. *West Side Story.* New York: Random House, 1958.

LaVine, Robert A. "Gusii Sex Offenses: A Study in Social Control," *American Anthropologist,* 61 (December 1959), 965–990.

Lawrence, Louis. "Bookmaking," *The Annals,* 269 (May 1950), 46–54.

Lecky, William E. H. *A History of England in the Eighteenth Century.* London: Longmans, 1920.

———. *History of European Morals from Augustus to Charlemagne.* 3rd ed. New York: Appleton, 1904.

Lee, Dorothy. *Freedom and Culture.* Englewood Cliffs, New Jersey: Prentice-Hall, 1959.

Lefebure, Molly. *Evidence for the Crown.* Philadelphia: Lippincott, 1955.

Leigh, Ruth. *Man's Right to Life.* New York: Union of American Hebrew Congregations, 1959.

Lejins, Peter. "Uniform Crime Reports," *Michigan Law Review*, 64 (April 1966), 1,011–1,030.

Lemert, Edwin M. "The Behavior of the Systematic Check Forger," *Social Problems*, 6 (Fall 1958), 141–149.

———. "An Isolation and Closure Theory of Naive Check Forgery," *Journal of Criminal Law*, 44 (September–October 1953), 296–307.

Leopold, Nathan F. *Life Plus 99 Years*. New York: Doubleday, 1958.

Lerner, Max. *America as a Civilization*. New York: Simon and Schuster, 1957.

Lessing, Doris. *In Pursuit of the English*. New York: Simon and Schuster, 1961.

Levy, Beryl H. *Corporation Lawyer: Saint or Sinner?* Philadelphia: Chilton, 1961.

Levy, Sol. "Juvenile Delinquency: Are We Ignoring Important Causative Factors in Our Present-Day Etiological Approach?", *Lex et Scientia*, 4 (April–June 1967), 69–100.

———. "Post-Encephalitic Behavior Disorder—A Forgotten Entity: A Report of 100 Cases," *American Journal of Psychiatry*, 115 (June 1959), 1,062–1,067.

Lewis, Anthony. *Gideon's Trumpet*. New York: Random House, 1964.

Lewis, C. S. "The Humanitarian Theory of Punishment," *Res Judicatae*, 6 (June 1953).

Lewis, Lloyd, and Henry J. Smith. *Chicago: The History of Its Reputation*. New York: Harcourt, Brace, 1929.

Lewis, Nolan D. C., and Helen Yarnell. *Pathological Firesetting (Pyromania)*. New York: Nervous & Mental Disease Monographs, 1951.

Lewis, Norman. *The Honored Society: A Searching Look at the Mafia*. New York: Putnam, 1964.

Lewis, Roy, and Rosemary Stewart. *The Managers*. New York: New American Library, 1961.

Licht, Hans. *Sexual Life in Ancient Greece*. J. H. Freese (tr.). London: Routledge and Kegan Paul, 1932.

Lifton, Robert J. *Thought Reform and the Psychology of Totalism*. New York: Norton, 1961.

Lindesmith, Alfred R. *The Addict and the Law*. Bloomington: Indiana University Press, 1965.

———. "Edwin H. Sutherland's Contributions to Criminology," *Sociology and Social Research*, 35 (March–April 1951), 243–249.

———. "Organized Crime," *The Annals*, 217 (September 1941), 76–83.

Lindner, Robert. *Rebel Without a Cause*. New York: Grune & Stratton, 1944.

Linforth, Ivan M. *Solon the Athenian*. Berkeley: University of California Press, 1919.

Lipset, Seymour M. *The First New Nation: The United States in Historical and Comparative Perspective*. New York: Basic Books, 1963.

Llewellyn, Karl N. "Law and the Social Sciences—Especially Sociology," *Harvard Law Review*, 62 (June 1949), 1,286–1,305.

Loevinger, Lee. "Recent Developments in Antitrust Enforcement," Antitrust Section, American Bar Association, *Proceedings* 18 (1961), 102–106.

Lombroso, Cesare, and William Ferrero. *The Female Offender*. New York: Appleton, 1895.

Lorenz, Konrad. *On Aggression*. New York: Harcourt, Brace & World, 1966.

Lou, Herbert H. *Juvenile Courts in the United States*. Chapel Hill: University of North Carolina Press, 1927.

Louria, Donald B. "Cool Talk About Hot Drugs," *The New York Times Magazine*, August 6, 1967, pp. 12–13ff.

Lowenthal, Max. *The Federal Bureau of Investigation.* New York: Sloane, 1950.

Lyle, John H. *The Dry and Lawless Years.* Englewood Cliffs, New Jersey: Prentice-Hall, 1960.

Lyman, J. L. "The Metropolitan Police Act of 1829," *Journal of Criminal Law,* 55 (March 1964), 141–154.

Lynd, Robert S., and Helen Lynd. *Middletown: A Study in Contemporary American Culture.* New York: Harcourt, Brace, 1929.

Maas, Peter. *The Valachi Papers.* New York: Putnam, 1968.

Madden, Edward. *The Structure of Scientific Thought.* Boston: Houghton Mifflin, 1960.

Malinowski, Bronislaw. *Crime and Custom in Savage Society.* New York: Harcourt, Brace, 1926.

Manchester, William. *The Death of a President.* New York: Harper & Row, 1967.

Mannheim, Hermann. *Comparative Criminology.* Boston: Houghton Mifflin, 1965.

———. *Criminal Justice and Social Reconstruction.* London: Routledge and Kegan Paul, 1946.

——— (ed.). *Pioneers in Criminology.* London: Stevens, 1960.

———. "The Criminal Law and Mentally Abnormal Offenders," *British Journal of Criminology,* 1 (January 1961), 203–220.

———. "Criminal Law and Penology," in Morris Ginsberg (ed.), *Law and Opinion in Twentieth Century England.* Berkeley: University of California Press, 1959, pp. 264–285.

Marcovitz, Eli, and Henry J. Myers. "The Marihuana Addict in the Army," *War Medicine,* 6 (December 1944), 382–391.

Margolis, Joseph. "Juvenile Delinquents: Latter-Day Knights," *American Scholar,* 29 (Spring 1960), 211–218.

Marrs, Wyatt. *The Man on Your Back.* Norman: University of Oklahoma Press, 1958.

Martienssen, Anthony. *Crime and the Police.* London: Secker & Warburg, 1951.

Martin, John B. (ed.). *My Life in Crime: The Autobiography of a Thief.* New York: Harper & Row, 1952.

Mason, Alpheus T. *Harlan Fiske Stone: Pillar of the Law.* New York: Viking, 1956.

Masotti, Louis H., and Jerome R. Corsi. *Shoot-Out in Cleveland: Black Militants and the Police, July 23, 1968.* Washington, D.C.: National Committee on Causes and Prevention of Violence, 1969.

Mattei, Kenneth D. "Use of Taxation to Control Organized Crime," *California Law Review,* 39 (June 1951), 225–234.

Matthews, Mitford M. *Dictionary of Americanisms on Historical Principles.* Chicago: University of Chicago Press, 1951.

Mattick, Hans W. "Form and Content of Recent Riots," *Midway,* 9 (Summer 1968), 3–32.

———, and Alexander B. Aikman. "The Cloacal Region of American Corrections," *The Annals,* 381 (January 1969), 109–118.

Maurer, David W. *The Big Con.* Indianapolis, Indiana: Bobbs-Merrill, 1940.

———. *Whiz Mob.* New Haven, Connecticut: College & University Press, 1955.

———. "The Argot of Forgery," *American Speech,* 16 (December 1941), 243–250.

Maxwell, Gavin. *God Protect Me From My Friends.* London: Longmans, 1956.

May, Max. "Jewish Criminal Law and Legal Procedure," *Journal of Criminal Law*, 31 (November–December 1940), 438–447.

McCaghy, Charles H. "Child Molesters: A Study of Their Careers as Deviants," in Marshall B. Clinard and Richard Quinney (eds.), *Criminal Behavior Systems: A Typology*. New York: Holt, Rinehart and Winston, 1967, pp. 75–88.

——, Irving L. Allen, and J. David Colfax. "Public Attitudes Toward City Police in Hartford," Paper, Society for the Study of Social Problems, San Francisco, August 1967.

McCall, George J. "Symbiosis: The Case of Hoodoo and the Numbers Racket," *Social Problems*, 10 (Spring 1963), 361–371.

McCarthy, Raymond G. (ed.). *Drinking and Intoxication*. New York: Free Press, 1959.

McClellan, John L. *Crime Without Punishment*. New York: Duell, 1962.

McClintock, F. H., and Evelyn Gibson. *Robbery in London*. London: Macmillan, 1961.

McCord, William, and Joan McCord. *Origins of Crime: A New Evaluation of the Cambridge–Somerville Study*. New York: Columbia Press, 1959.

McCorkle, Lloyd W., Albert Elias, and F. Lovell Bixby. *The Highfields Story: An Experimental Treatment Project for Youthful Offenders*. New York: Holt, Rinehart and Winston, 1958.

——, and Richard J. Korn. "Resocialization Within Walls," *The Annals*, 293 (May 1954), 88–98.

McKay, Henry D. "The Neighborhood and Child Conduct," *The Annals*, 261 (January 1949), 32–41.

McKelvey, Blake. *American Prisons*. Chicago: University of Chicago Press, 1936.

McKenzie, Donald. *Occupation: Thief*. Indianapolis, Indiana: Bobbs-Merrill, 1955.

McMillan, David R. "Work Furlough for the Jailed Prisoner," *Federal Probation*, 29 (March 1965), 33–34.

McNamara, John H. "Uncertainties in Police Work: The Relevance of Police Recruits' Backgrounds and Training," in David J. Bordua (ed.), *The Police: Six Sociological Essays*. New York: Wiley, 1967, pp. 163–282.

Mead, Margaret. *Coming of Age in Samoa*. New York: Morrow, 1928.

——. *Sex and Temperament in Three Primitive Societies*. New York: New American Library, 1950.

Medalie, Richard J., Leonard Zeitz, and Paul Alexander. "Custodial Police Interrogation in Our Nation's Capital: The Attempt to Implement Miranda," *Michigan Law Review*, 66 (May 1968), 1,347–1,422.

Meeker, Ben. "Probation is Case Work," *Federal Probation*, 12 (June 1948), 51–54.

Mehling, Harold. *The Scandalous Scamps*. New York: Henry Holt, 1959.

Meisel, Arthur. "The Code of Hammurabi: A Study of Babylonian Courts and Procedure," *Intramural Law Review*, 21 (May 1966), 191–223.

Mencken, Henry L. *The American Language: An Inquiry into the Development of English in the United States*. 4th ed. New York: Knopf, 1963.

Mendelsohn, B. "The Origin of the Doctrine of Victimology," *Excerpta Criminologica*, 3 (May–June 1963), 239–244.

Menninger, Karl. *Man Against Himself*. New York: Harcourt, Brace, 1938.

——, and Joseph Satten. "The Development of a Psychiatric Criminology," *Menninger Clinic Bulletin*, 25 (July 1961), 164–172.

Merton, Robert K. *Social Theory and Social Structure*. Rev. ed. New York: Free Press, 1957.

Merz, Charles. *The Dry Decade*. New York: Doubleday, 1930.

"Metropolitan Criminal Courts of First Instance," *Harvard Law Review,* 70 (December 1956), 320–349.

Meyer, Lee W. *Public Defenders.* New York: Institute of Judicial Administration, 1956.

Michael, Jerome, and Mortimer J. Adler. *Crime, Law and Social Science.* New York: Harcourt, Brace, 1933.

Miller, Arthur. *The Crucible.* New York: Viking, 1953.

Miller, Donald E., Alfred N. Himelson, and Gilbert Geis. "The East Los Angeles Halfway House for Felon Addicts," *International Journal of Addictions,* 2 (1967), 305–311.

Miller, Frank W., and Robert Dawson. "Non-Use of Preliminary Examination: A Study of Current Practices," *Wisconsin Law Review,* (March 1964), 252–277.

Miller, Norman C. *The Great Salad Oil Swindle.* New York: Coward-Mc-Cann, 1965.

Miller, Walter B. *City Gangs: An Experiment in Changing Gang Behavior.* Unpublished manuscript.

———. "The Corner Boy Gets Married," *Trans-action—Social Science & Modern Society,* 1 (November 1963), 10–12.

———. "Lower Class Culture as a Generating Milieu of Gang Delinquency," *Journal of Social Issues,* 14 (April 1958), 5–19.

———. "Violent Crime in City Gangs," *The Annals,* 364 (March 1966), 96–112.

Mills, C. Wright. *The Power Elite.* New York: Oxford University Press, 1956.

Mirsky, Jeannette. "The Dakota," in Margaret Mead (ed.), *Cooperation and Competition.* New York: McGraw-Hill, 1937, pp. 382–427.

Mohr, Johann W. "The Pedophilias: Their Clinical, Social and Legal Implications," *Canadian Psychiatric Association Journal,* 7 (October 1962), 255–260.

Molesworth, William. *The English Works of Thomas Hobbes of Malmesbury.* London: Scientia Aalen, 1962.

Monachesi, Elio. "Cesare Beccaria," in Hermann Mannheim (ed.), *Pioneers in Criminology.* London: Stevens, 1960, pp. 36–50.

Monroe, Jack J., and Robert Astin. "Stereotypes and the Drug Addict," *Journal of Clinical Psychology,* 14 (January 1958), 31–36.

Montagu, Ashley. "Chromosomes and Crime," *Psychology Today,* 2 (October 1968), 43–49.

Moore, Underhill, and Charles C. Callahan. "Law and Learning Theory: A Study in Social Control," *Yale Law Journal,* 53 (December 1943), 1–136.

Moreland, Donald. "John Augustus and His Successors," *Yearbook.* National Probation and Parole Association, 1941, pp. 1–22.

Morgan, Murray C. *Skid Road: An Informal Portrait of Seattle.* New York: Viking, 1951.

Morison, Samuel E. *The Oxford History of the American People.* New York: Oxford University Press, 1965.

Morris, Albert. *Criminology.* New York: Longmans, 1935.

———. *Homicide: An Approach to the Problem of Crime.* Boston: Boston University Press, 1955.

Morris, Lloyd R. *Postscript to Yesterday.* New York: Random House, 1947.

Morris, Norval. "Impediments to Penal Reform," *University of Chicago Law Review,* 33 (Summer 1960), 627–666.

Morris, Terence, and Louis Blom-Cooper. *A Calendar of Murder: Criminal Homicide in England Since 1957.* London: Joseph, 1964.

Mueller, Gerhard. "Criminal Law and Administration," *New York University Law Review,* 34 (January 1959), 82–116.

Mullen, James M. *Let Justice Be Done*. Philadelphia: Dorrance, 1952.

Murphy, Joseph P. "Training for and on the Job," *Yearbook,* National Probation and Parole Association, 1938, pp. 93–108.

Murray, Daniel E. "Ancient Laws on Adultery: A Synopsis," *Journal of Family Law,* 1 (Spring 1961), 89–104.

Murtagh, John M. "Arrests for Public Intoxication," *Fordham Law Review,* 35 (October 1967), 1–14.

Myers, Larry W. "Reasonable Mistake of Age: A Needed Defense to Statutory Rape," *Michigan Law Review,* 64 (November 1965), 105–135.

Mylonas, Anastassios, and Walter C. Reckless. "Prisoner Attitudes Toward Law and Legal Institutions," *Journal of Criminal Law,* 54 (December 1963), 479–484.

Nader, Ralph. *Unsafe At Any Speed*. New York: Grossman, 1965.

Nagel, Stuart S. "Testing the Effects of Excluding Illegally Seized Evidence," *Wisconsin Law Review,* (Spring 1965), 283–310.

Nahrendorf, Richard O. "Typologies of Crime and Delinquency; Classification or Methodology?", *Sociologia Internationalis* (Heft 1, 1967), 15–33.

Narcotic Clinics in the United States. Washington, D.C.: Government Printing Office, n.d.

National Advisory Commission on Civil Disorders, *Report*. New York: Dutton, 1968.

National Commission on Law Observance and Enforcement, *Report on Criminal Statistics*. Washington, D.C.: Government Printing Office, 1931.

Neigher, Alan. "The Gault Decision: Due Process and the Juvenile Courts," *Federal Probation,* 31 (December 1967), 8–18.

Nettler, Gwynn. "Cruelty, Dignity, and Determinism," *American Sociological Review,* 24 (June 1959), 375–384.

Neustatter, W. Lindesay. *Psychological Disorder and Crime*. London: Johnson, 1953.

Newcomb, Theodore. *Social Psychology*. New York: Dryden, 1950.

Newman, Charles L. "Trial By Jury: An Outmoded Relic?" *Journal of Criminal Law,* 46 (November–December 1955), 512–518.

Newman, Donald J. *Conviction: The Determination of Guilt or Innocence Without Trial*. Boston: Little, Brown, 1966.

——. "Pleading Guilty for Considerations: A Study of Bargain Justice," *Journal of Criminal Law,* 46 (March–April 1956), 780–790.

——. "Public Attitudes Toward a Form of White Collar Crime," *Social Problems,* 4 (January 1957), 228–232.

——. "White-Collar Crime," *Law and Contemporary Problems,* 23 (Autumn 1958), 735–753.

New York, Temporary Commission of Investigation. *An Investigation of the Loan-Shark Racket*. New York: The Commission, 1965.

New York [City], Citizens Committee on the Control of Crime in New York. *The Problem of Sex Offenses in New York City*. New York: The Committee, 1939.

Niebuhr, Reinhold. "Introduction," in Wilbur Schramm, *Responsibility in Mass Communication*. New York: Harper, 1957, pp. xi–xxiii.

Niederhoffer, Arthur. *Behind the Shield: The Police in Urban Society*. New York: Doubleday, 1967.

Noggle, Burl. *Teapot Dome: Oil and Politics in the 1920's*. Baton Rouge: Louisiana State University Press, 1962.

Noonan, John T., Jr. *The Scholastic Analysis of Usury*. Cambridge, Massachusetts: Harvard University Press, 1957.

Nye, Ivan. "Adolescent-Parent Adjustment: Socio-Economic Level as a Variable," *American Sociological Review,* 16 (June 1951), 341–349.

O'Brien, Eris M. *The Foundation of Australia, 1786–1800.* 2nd ed. Sydney, Australia: Angus & Robertson, 1950.

O'Donnell, Bernard. *Cavalcade of Justice.* New York: Macmillan, 1952.

O'Donnell, John A. "The Lexington Program for Narcotic Addicts," *Federal Probation,* 26 (March 1962), 55–60.

———. "Narcotic Addiction and Crime," *Social Problems,* 13 (Spring 1966), 374–385.

———, Karst J. Besteman, and Judith P. Jones. "Marital History of Narcotics Addicts," *International Journal of Addictions,* 2 (Spring 1967), 21–38.

Ohlin, Lloyd E. *Selection for Parole.* New York: Russell Sage, 1951.

Oldham, William. "The Common Thief," *Criminal Law Review,* (February 1964), 113–118.

Olmsted, Charlotte. *Heads I Win—Tails You Lose.* New York: Macmillan, 1962.

Orfield, Lester. *Criminal Procedure from Arrest to Appeal.* New York: New York University Press, 1947.

Oswald, Robert L. *Lee: A Portrait of Lee Harvey Oswald.* New York: Coward-McCann, 1967.

Oteri, Joseph S., and Harvey A. Silverglate. "In the Marketplace of Free Ideas: A Look at the Passage of the Marihuana Tax Act," in J. L. Simmons (ed.), *Marihuana: Myths and Realities.* North Hollywood, California: Brandon House, 1967, pp. 136–162.

Ottenberg, Miriam. *The Federal Investigators.* Englewood Cliffs, New Jersey: Prentice-Hall, 1962.

Overholser, Winfred. *Psychiatrist and the Law.* New York: Harcourt, Brace, 1953.

———. "Some Psychiatric Aspects of Criminal Responsibility," *State Government,* 34 (Spring 1961), 124–129.

Overstreet, Harry, and Bonaro Overstreet. *The FBI in Our Open Society.* New York: Norton, 1969.

Packard, Vance. *The Hidden Persuaders.* New York: McKay, 1957.

Packer, Herbert L., "The Crime Tariff," *American Scholar,* 33 (Autumn 1964), 551–557.

Paley, William. *The Works of William Paley.* London: Longmans, 1838.

Palmer, Stuart. *A Study of Murder.* New York: Crowell, 1960.

———. "Murder and Suicide in Forty Non-Literate Societies," *Journal of Criminal Law,* 56 (September 1965), 320–324.

Parker, William H. "Surveillance by Wiretap or Dictograph," *California Law Review,* 42 (December 1954), 727–737.

Parmelee, Maurice. *Criminology.* New York: Macmillan, 1918.

Parsons, Talcott. "A Sociologist Looks at the Legal Profession," in Parsons, *Essays in Sociological Theory.* Rev. ed. New York: Free Press, 1954, pp. 370–385.

Partington, Donald H. "The Incidence of the Death Penalty for Rape in Virginia," *Washington & Lee Law Review,* 22 (Spring 1965), 43–75.

Patrick, Clarence H. *Alcohol, Culture, and Society.* Durham: University of North Carolina Press, 1952.

Paulus, Ingeborg, and Robert Halliday. "Rehabilitating the Narcotic Addict," *Canadian Medical Association Journal,* 96 (March 18, 1967), 655–659.

Pechman, Joseph A. "Individual Income Tax Provisions of the Revenue Act of 1964," *Journal of Finance,* 20 (May 1965), 247–272.

The Penal Code of Sweden. Thorsten Sellin (tr.). Stockholm: Ministry of Justice, 1965.

Peterson, Richard A., David J. Pittman, and Patricia O'Neal. "Stabilities in Deviance: A Study of Assaultive and Non-Assaultive Offenders," *Journal of Criminal Law,* 53 (March 1962), 44–48.

Peterson, Virgil W. *Barbarians in Our Midst.* Boston: Little, Brown, 1952.

———. *Gambling—Should It Be Legalized?* Springfield, Illinois: Thomas, 1951.

Peterson, W. Jack, and Milton A. Maxwell. "The Skid Road 'Wino'," *Social Problems,* 5 (Spring 1958), 308–316.

Pettigrew, Thomas F., and Rosalind B. Spier. "The Ecological Structure of Negro Homicide," *American Journal of Sociology,* 67 (May 1962), 621–629.

Pfeiffer, John. *The Human Brain.* New York: Harper & Row, 1955.

Phillips, Harlan B. *Felix Frankfurter Reminisces.* New York: Reynal, 1960.

Phillipson, Coleman. *Three Criminal Law Reformers: Beccaria, Bentham, Romilly.* New York: Dutton, 1923.

Pickett, Robert. *House of Refuge: Origins of Juvenile Reform in New York State, 1815–1857.* Syracuse, New York: Syracuse University Press, 1969.

Pittman, David J. (ed.). *Alcoholism.* New York: Harper & Row, 1967.

———, and Wayne Gordon. *Revolving Door: A Study of the Chronic Police-Case Inebriate.* New York: Free Press, 1958.

———, and William Handy. "Patterns of Criminal Aggravated Assault," *Journal of Criminal Law,* 55 (December 1964), 462–470.

———, and Charles R. Snyder (eds.). *Society, Culture, and Drinking Patterns.* New York: Wiley, 1962.

Platt, Anthony. "Rise of the Child-Saving Movement: A Study in Social Policy and Correctional Reform," *The Annals,* 381 (January 1961), 21–38.

Ploscowe, Morris (ed.). *Organized Crime and Law Enforcement.* New York: Grosby, 1952–1953.

———. *Sex and the Law.* Englewood Cliffs, New Jersey: Prentice-Hall, 1951.

Pollak, Otto. *The Criminality of Women.* Philadelphia: University of Pennsylvania Press, 1950.

Pollock, Frederick. *A First Book of Jurisprudence for the Students of the Common Law.* 3rd ed. London: Macmillan, 1911.

———, and Frederic W. Maitland. *The History of the English Law Before the Time of Edward I.* 2nd ed. Cambridge, England: University Press, 1898.

Polsky, Ned. *Hustlers, Beats, Others.* Chicago: Aldine, 1967.

Popper, Samuel H. *Individualized Justice.* St. Paul, Minnesota: Bruce, 1956.

Porter, William Sydney [O. Henry]. *Complete Works.* New York: Doubleday, 1960.

Powers, Edwin, and Helen Witmer. *An Experiment in the Prevention of Delinquency.* New York: Columbia University Press, 1951.

President's Commission on Crime in the District of Columbia. *Report.* Washington, D.C.: Government Printing Office, 1966.

President's Commission on Law Enforcement and Administration of Justice. *The Challenge of Crime in a Free Society.* Washington, D.C.: Government Printing Office, 1967.

———. *Task Force Report: Crime and Its Impact—An Assessment.* Washington, D.C.: Government Printing Office, 1967.

———. *Task Force Report: Corrections.* Washington, D.C.: Government Printing Office, 1967.

———. *Task Force Report: The Courts.* Washington, D.C.: Government Printing Office, 1967.

————. *Task Force Report: Drunkenness.* Washington, D.C.: Government Printing Office, 1967.

————. *Task Force Report: Juvenile Delinquency and Youth Crime.* Washington, D.C.: Government Printing Office, 1967.

————. *Task Force Report: Narcotics and Drug Abuse.* Washington, D.C.: Government Printing Office, 1967.

————. *Task Force Report: Organized Crime.* Washington, D.C.: Government Printing Office, 1967.

————. *Task Force Report: The Police.* Washington, D.C.: Government Printing Office, 1967.

————. *Task Force Report: Science and Technology.* Washington, D.C.: Government Printing Office, 1967.

President's Commission on the Assassination of President Kennedy. *Report.* Washington, D.C.: Government Printing Office, 1964.

Price, W. H., and P. B. Whatmore. "Behavior Disorders and Pattern of Crime Among XYY Males Identified at a Maximum Security Hospital," *British Medical Journal,* (March 4, 1967), 533–536.

"Profile of a Bank Robber," *F.B.I. Law Enforcement Bulletin,* 34 (November 1965), 2–7ff.

Puttkammer, Ernst. *Administration of Criminal Law.* Chicago: University of Chicago Press, 1959.

Queen, Stuart A. *The Passing of the County Jail.* Menasha, Wisconsin: Banta, 1920.

Quinn, William F. "Narcotic Addiction: Medical and Legal Problems with Physicians," *California Medicine,* 94 (April 1961), 214–217.

Quinney, Richard. "Crime in Political Perspective," *American Behavioral Scientist,* 8 (December 1964), 19–22.

————. "Is Criminal Behaviour Deviant Behaviour?", *British Journal of Criminology,* 5 (April 1965), 132–142.

————. "Suicide, Homicide, and Economic Development," *Social Forces,* 43 (March 1965), 401–406.

Radcliffe-Brown, A. R. *The Andaman Islanders.* New York: Free Press, 1948.

Radzinowicz, Leon. *A History of English Criminal Law.* London: Macmillan, 1948–1953.

————. *Sex Offences.* London: Macmillan, 1957.

Rasmussen, Augusta. "Die Bedeutung Sexueller Attentate auf Kinder unter 14 Jahren für die Entwicklung von Geisteskrankheiten und Charakteranomalien," *Acta Neurologica et Psychiatrica,* 9 (1934), 351–434.

Ravkind, William M. "Justifiable Homicide in Texas," *Southwestern Law Journal,* 13 (Fall 1959), 508–524.

Rayback, Joseph G. *A History of American Labor.* New York: Macmillan, 1959.

Rechy, John. Book Review of *The Hustler!,* *The Nation,* March 8, 1965, pp. 254–255.

Reckless, Walter C. *The Crime Problem.* 4th ed. New York: Appleton-Century-Crofts, 1967.

————. "A New Theory of Delinquency and Crime," *Federal Probation,* 25 (December 1961), 42–46.

————. "A Non-Causal Explanation: Containment Theory," *Excerpta Criminologica,* 2 (March–April 1962), 131–134.

————, and Simon Dinitz. "Pioneering with Self-Concept as a Vulnerability Factor in Delinquency," *Journal of Criminal Law,* 58 (December 1967), 515–523.

Rees, John T., and Harley V. Usill (eds.). *They Stand Apart: A Critical Survey of the Problems of Homosexuality.* New York: Macmillan, 1955.

Reichstein, Kenneth J. "Ambulance Chasing: A Case Study of Deviation and Control Within the Legal Profession," *Social Problems,* 13 (Summer 1965), 6–17.

Reid, Ed. *The Shame of New York.* New York: Random House, 1953.

———, and Ovid Demaris. *Green Felt Jungle.* New York: Simon and Schuster, 1968.

Reid, John. "The Companion of the New Hampshire Doctrine of Criminal Insanity," *Vanderbilt Law Review,* 15 (June 1962), 721–767.

———. "Understanding the New Hampshire Doctrine of Criminal Insanity," *Yale Law Journal,* 69 (January 1960), 367–420.

Reiss, Albert J., Jr. "Police Brutality—Answers to Key Questions," *Trans-action—Social Science & Modern Society,* 5 (July–August 1968), 10–19.

———, and Donald J. Black. "Interrogation and the Criminal Process," *The Annals,* 374 (November 1967), 47–57.

Remmers, Hermann H., and D. H. Radler. *The American Teenager.* Indianapolis, Indiana: Bobbs-Merrill, 1957.

Remsberg, Charles, and Bonnie Remsberg. "The Aristocrats of Crime," *The New York Times Magazine,* December 27, 1964, pp. 9ff.

Revitch, Eugene, and Rosalie G. Weiss. "The Pedophiliac Offender," *Diseases of the Nervous System,* 73 (February 1962), 73–78.

Rheinstein, Max (ed.). *Max Weber on Law in Economy and Society.* Cambridge, Massachusetts: Harvard University Press, 1954.

Rhodes, Henry T. F. *The Craft of Forgery.* London: Murray, 1934.

Riccio, Vincent, and Bill Slocum. *All the Way Down: The Violent Underworld of Street Gangs.* New York: Simon and Schuster, 1962.

Rice, Craig (ed.). *Los Angeles Murders.* New York: Duell, 1947.

Rice, Robert. *The Business of Crime.* New York: Farrar, Straus, 1956.

Rickett, Allyn, and Adele Rickett. *Prisoners of Liberation.* New York: Cameron, 1957.

Rickles, Nathan K. *Exhibitionism.* Philadelphia: Lippincott, 1950.

Riesman, David. *Thorstein Veblen: A Critical Interpretation.* New York: Scribner, 1953.

———. "Law and Sociology: Notes on Recruitment, Training, and Colleagueship," *Stanford Law Review,* 9 (July 1957), 643–673.

Riis, Roger, and John Patric. *The Repairman Will Get You If You Don't Watch Out.* New York: Doubleday, 1942.

Rivera, Ramon J., and James F. Short, Jr. "Occupational Goals: A Comparative Analysis," in Malcolm W. Klein and Barbara G. Meyerhoff, *Juvenile Gangs.* Englewood Cliffs, New Jersey: Prentice-Hall, 1967, pp. 70–90.

Robbe-Grillet, Alain. *The Voyeur.* Richard Howard (tr.). New York: Grove, 1958.

Robin, Gerald D. "Patterns of Department Store Shoplifting," *Crime and Delinquency,* 9 (April 1963), 163–172.

Robins, Lee, and George E. Murphy. "Drug Use in a Normal Population of Young Negro Men," *American Journal of Public Health,* 57 (September 1967), 158–196.

Robinson, Louis N., and Rolf Nugent. *Regulation of the Small Loan Business.* New York: Russell Sage, 1935.

Robinson, W. S. "The Logical Structure of Analytic Induction," *American Sociological Review,* 16 (December 1951), 812–818.

Robison, Sophia M. *Can Delinquency Be Measured?* New York: Columbia University Press, 1936.

Robson, Lloyd L. *The Convict Settlers of Australia.* New York: Cambridge University Press, 1965.

Roebuck, Julian B., and Mervyn L. Cadwallader. "The Negro Armed Robber as a Criminal Type: The Construction and Application of a Typology," *Pacific Sociological Review,* 4 (Spring 1961), 21–26.

———, and Ronald C. Johnson. "The 'Short Con' Man," *Crime and Delinquency,* 10 (July 1964), 235–248.

Roeburt, John. *Al Capone.* New York: Pyramid, 1959.

Rogers, William P. "Plea for a Public Defender," *The New York Times Magazine,* April 21, 1957, pp. 26ff.

Rosenberg, Morris. *Society and the Adolescent Self-Image.* Princeton, New Jersey: Princeton University Press, 1965.

Rosenblum, Victor G. *Law as a Political Instrument.* New York: Doubleday, 1955.

Ross, Edward A. *Social Control: A Survey of the Foundations of Order.* New York: Macmillan, 1901.

———. "The Criminaloid," *Atlantic Monthly,* 99 (January 1907), 44–50.

Roueché, Berton. *The Neutral Spirit: A Portrait of Alcohol.* Boston: Little, Brown, 1960.

Rubin, Sol. *Crime and Juvenile Delinquency: A Rational Approach to Penal Problems.* Rev. ed. New York: Oceana, 1961.

———. "Allocation of Authority in the Sentencing–Correction Decision," *Texas Law Review,* 45 (February 1967), 455–469.

———. "Sentencing and Correctional Treatment Under the Law Institute's Model Penal Code," *American Bar Association Journal,* 46 (September 1960), 994–998.

Rubington, Earl. "The Chronic Drunkenness Offender," *The Annals,* 315 (January 1958), 65–72.

Rudwick, Elliott M. *Race Riot at East St. Louis, July 2, 1917.* Carbondale: Southern Illinois University Press, 1964.

Rumney, Jay, and Joseph P. Murphy. *Probation and Social Adjustment.* New Brunswick, New Jersey: Rutgers University Press, 1952.

Russell, Bertrand. *The Scientific Outlook.* New York: Norton, 1931.

Sackler, Howard. *The Great White Hope.* New York: Dial Press, 1968.

Salisbury, Harrison E. *The Shook-Up Generation.* New York: Harper & Row, 1958.

———. "'Lost Generation' Baffles Soviet: Nihilistic Youth Shuns Ideology," *The New York Times,* February 9, 1962.

Samuelson, Glenn W. "Why Was Capital Punishment Restored in Delaware?", *Journal of Criminal Law,* 60 (June 1969), 148–151.

San Mateo County [California], Juvenile Justice Commission. *Narcotics Inquiry Report.* November 16, 1967.

Sauter, Van Gordon, and Burleigh Hines. *Nightmare in Detroit.* Chicago: Regnery, 1968.

Sayre, Francis B. "Public Welfare Offenses," *Columbia Law Review,* 33 (January 1933), 55–88.

Schaefer, Walter V. "Federalism and State Criminal Procedure," *Harvard Law Review,* 70 (November 1956), 1–26.

Schafer, Stephen. *Restitution to Victims of Crime.* London: Stevens, 1960.

———. *The Victim and His Criminal: A Study in Functional Responsibility.* New York: Random House, 1968.

Schelling, Thomas C. "Economics and the Public Enterprise," *Public Interest,* 7 (Spring 1967), 61–78.

Schmidt, Wilbur J. "Wisconsin Jails and the Huber Law," *State Government,* 30 (November 1957), 243–245ff.

Schrag, Clarence. "The Correctional System: Problems and Prospects," *The Annals,* 381 (January 1969), 11–20.

Schuessler, Karl F. "The Deterrent Influence of the Death Penalty," *The Annals,* 284 (November 1952), 54–62.

——. Book Review of *Other People's Money. American Journal of Sociology,* 59 (May 1954), 604.

——. "Parole Prediction: Its History and Status," *Journal of Criminal Law,* 45 (November–December 1954), 425–431.

Schultz, Fritz. *History of Roman Legal Science.* Oxford, England: Clarendon Press, 1946.

——. *Principles of Roman Law.* Oxford, England: Clarendon Press, 1936.

Schultz, LeRoy G. "The Wife Assaulter," *Journal of Social Therapy,* 6 (2nd Quarter 1960), 103–112.

Schumach, Murray. "Crime Statistics: Are They Reliable?", *The New York Times,* December 22, 1968.

Schur, Edwin M. *Crimes Without Victims: Deviant Behavior and Public Policy.* Englewood Cliffs, New Jersey: Prentice-Hall, 1965.

——. "Sociological Analysis of Confidence Swindling," *Journal of Criminal Law,* 48 (September–October 1957), 296–304.

——. "Theory, Planning and Pathology," *Social Problems,* 6 (Winter 1958), 221–229.

Schwartz, Edward E. "Statistics of Juvenile Delinquency in the United States," *The Annals,* 261 (January 1949), 9–20.

"Science," *The Athenaeum,* No. 3280 (September 6, 1890), 325.

Scott, George R. *The History of Corporal Punishment.* London: Torchstream, 1938.

——. *The History of Torture Throughout the Ages.* London: Laurie, 1940.

Scott, Harold (ed.). *The Concise Encyclopedia of Crime and Criminals.* New York: Hawthorn, 1961.

Seagle, William. "Hammurabi: King of Babylon," in Seagle, *Men of Law: From Hammurabi to Holmes.* New York: Macmillan, 1947.

Seaton, George. *Isle of the Damned.* New York: Farrar, Straus, 1951.

Seavey, Warren A. "Principles of Torts," *Harvard Law Review,* 56 (September 1942), 72–98.

——, Page Keeton, and Robert E. Keeton. *Cases and Materials on the Law of Torts.* St. Paul, Minnesota: West, 1964.

Seligman, Siegried. *Der Böse Blick und Verwandtes.* Berlin: Barsdorf, 1910.

Sellin, Thorsten. *The Death Penalty.* Philadelphia: American Law Institute, 1959.

——. *Research Memorandum on Crime in the Depression.* New York: Social Science Research Council, 1937.

——. "The Death Penalty and Police Safety," in Canadian Joint Committee on Capital and Corporal Punishment, *Report.* Ottawa, Canada, 1955, pp. 718–728.

——. "The Negro Criminal: A Statistical Note," *The Annals,* 140 (November 1928), 52–64.

——. "The Significance of Records of Crime," *Law Quarterly Review,* 67 (October 1961), 489–504.

Sells, Helen F. *A Bibliography on Drug Dependence.* Fort Worth: Texas Christian University Press, 1967.

Selzer, Melvin L. "Alcoholism and the Law," *Michigan Law Review,* 56 (December 1957), 237–248.

Semmes, Raphael. *Crime and Punishment in Early Maryland.* Baltimore, Maryland: Johns Hopkins Press, 1936.

Severo, Richard. "Addicts and the State: Aim Unfulfilled," *The New York Times,* April 21, 1969.

Shannon, Lyle W. "The Spatial Distribution of Criminal Offenses by State," *Journal of Criminal Law,* 45 (September–October 1954), 264–273.

Shaplen, Robert. *Kreuger: Genius and Swindler.* New York: Knopf, 1960.

Shaw, A. G. L. *Convicts and the Colonies.* London: Faber, 1966.

Shaw, Clifford. *Brothers in Crime.* Chicago: University of Chicago Press, 1938.

———. *The Jack-Roller: A Delinquent Boy's Own Story.* Chicago: University of Chicago Press, 1930.

Sherwin, Robert V. *Sex and Statutory Law.* New York: Oceana, 1949.

———. "The Law and Sexual Relationships," *Journal of Social Issues,* 22 (April 1966), 109–122.

Shoenfeld, Dudley D. "The Sociological Study," in Mayor's Committee on Marihuana, New York City, *Report.* Lancaster, Pennsylvania: Cattell Press, 1944, pp. 1–25.

Shoham, Shlomo. "The Norm, the Act, and the Object of Crime as Bases for the Classification of Criminal Behavior," *International Journal of Social Psychiatry,* 11 (Autumn 1965), 272–279.

Shulman, Harry M. "The Measurement of Crime in the United States," *Journal of Criminal Law,* 57 (December 1966), 483–492.

Silberg, Moshe. "Law and Morals in Jewish Jurisprudence," *Indiana Law Journal,* 75 (December 1961), 306–331.

Silving, Helen. *Constituent Elements of Crime.* Springfield, Illinois: Thomas, 1967.

———. *Essays on Mental Incapacity.* Spingfield, Illinois: Thomas, 1967.

———. "Suicide and Law," in Edwin S. Schneidman and Norman L. Farberow, *Clues to Suicide.* New York: McGraw-Hill, 1957, pp. 79–95.

Simon, Carolyn. "The Case for Trial by Jury," *The New York Times Magazine,* July 15, 1956, pp. 12ff.

Simpson, Sidney P., and Ruth Field. "Law and the Social Sciences," *Virginia Law Review,* 32 (June 1946), 855–867.

Size, Mary. *Prisons I Have Known.* London: Allen & Unwin, 1957.

Sjostedt, Elsie M. *A Study of the Personality Variables Relating to Assaultive and Acquisitive Crimes.* Ph.D. dissertation, Purdue University, 1955.

Skolnick, Jerome H. *Justice Without Trial: Law Enforcement in a Democratic Society.* New York: Wiley, 1966.

———. *The Politics of Protest.* Washington: National Commission on the Causes and Prevention of Violence, 1969.

———. Book review of *Revolving Door, Yale Law Journal,* 68 (January, 1959), 625–632.

Smigel, Erwin O. "Public Attitudes Toward Stealing in Relation to the Size of the Victim Organization," *American Sociological Review,* 21 (June 1956), 320–327.

Smith, A. Delafield. *The Right to Life.* Chapel Hill: University of North Carolina Press, 1955.

Smith, Alson J. *Syndicate City.* Chicago: Regnery, 1954.

Smith, Bruce. *Police Systems in the United States.* 2nd rev. ed. New York: Harper & Row, 1960.

Smith, Dennis Mack. *Italy: A Modern History.* Ann Arbor: University of Michigan Press, 1959.

Smith, Ernest A. *American Youth Culture: Group Life in Teenage Society.* New York: Free Press, 1962.

Smith, Ralph L. *The Tarnished Badge.* New York: Crowell, 1965.

Smith, Richard A. "The Incredible Electric Conspiracy," *Fortune,* 63 (April 1961), 132–137, and 63 (May 1961), 161–164.

Smith, Robert E., John M. Rhoads, and Charles E. Llewellyn, Jr. "Exhibitionism," *North Carolina Medical Journal,* 22 (June 1961), 261–267.

Smith, Sandy. "The Crime Cartel," *Life,* 63 (September 1, 1967), 15–23ff.

———. "The Mob: Empire of Organized Crime," *Life,* 63 (September 8, 1967), 91ff.

Snyder, Charles R. *Alcohol and the Jews.* New York: Free Press, 1958.

Snyder, Orville C. *An Introduction to Criminal Justice.* Englewood Cliffs, New Jersey: Prentice-Hall, 1953.

Sobeloff, Simon E. "Insanity and the Criminal Law," *American Bar Association Journal,* 41 (September 1955), 793–796.

Society for the Reformation of Juvenile Delinquents in the City of New York, *1st Annual Report.* New York: Mahlon Day, 1825.

Söderman, Harry. *Policeman's Lot.* New York: Funk & Wagnall, 1956.

Solmes, Alwyn. *The English Policeman, 871–1935.* London: Allen & Unwin, 1935.

Solzhenitsyn, Aleksander I. *The Cancer Ward.* Rebecca Frank (tr.). New York: Dial Press, 1968.

"Some Aspects of the California Grand Jury System," *Stanford Law Review,* 8 (July 1956), 631–654.

Sondern, Frederick, Jr. *Brotherhood of Evil: The Mafia.* New York: Farrar, Straus, 1959.

Soviet Criminal Law and Procedure: The RSFSR Codes, Harold J. Berman and James W. Spindler (trs.). Cambridge, Massachusetts: Harvard University Press, 1966.

Sparling, J. Frederic. "Measuring Medical Care Quality: A Comparative Study," *Hospitals,* 36 (March 16, 1962), 62–67.

Spencer, John C. "White Collar Crime," in T. Grygier, Howard Jones, and Spencer (eds.), *Criminology in Transition.* London: Routledge and Kegan Paul, 1965, pp. 233–266.

Spergel, Irving. *Racketville, Slumtown, Haulburg: An Exploratory Study of Delinquent Subcultures.* Chicago: University of Chicago Press, 1964.

Spinoza, Benedictus de. "Theological-Political Treaties," [*Tractatus Theological-Politicus,* 1670], in *Chief Works.* R. H. M. Elwes (tr.). New York: Dover, 1951.

Stafford, Jean. *A Mother in History.* New York: Farrar, Straus 1966.

"State Sunday Blue Laws and the Religious Guarantees of the Federal Constitution," *Harvard Law Review,* 73 (February 1960), 729–746.

Stearns, Albert W. "Homicide in Massachusetts," *American Journal of Psychiatry,* 4 (July 1924), 725–749.

Steffens, Lincoln. *Autobiography.* New York: Harcourt, Brace, 1931.

Steinbeck, John. *Winter of Our Discontent.* New York: Viking, 1961.

Stephen, James Fitzjames. *A History of the Criminal Law of England.* London: Macmillan, 1883.

Stern, Philip M. *The Great Treasury Raid.* New York: Random House, 1964.

Sternberg, David. "Synanon House—A Consideration of Its Implications for American Correction," *Journal of Criminal Law,* 54 (December 1963), 447–455.

Sternitzsky, Julius L. *Forgery and Fictitious Checks.* Springfield, Illinois: Thomas, 1955.

Stock, R. W. "XYY and the Criminal," *The New York Times Magazine,* October 20, 1968, pp. 30–31ff.

Stonequist, Everett V. *The Marginal Man.* New York: September, 1937.

Straus, Jacqueline H., and Murray A. Straus. "Suicide, Homicide, and Social Structure in Ceylon," *American Journal of Sociology*, 48 (March 1953), 461–469.

Stryker, Lloyd P. *Art of Advocacy: A Plea for the Renaissance of the Trial Lawyer*. New York: Simon and Schuster, 1954.

"A Study of the Administration of Bail in New York City," *University of Pennsylvania Law Review*, 106 (March 1958), 693–730.

Sullivan, Harold W. *Trial by Newspaper*. Hyannis, Massachusetts: Patriot Press, 1961.

Sumner, William G. *Folkways*. Boston: Ginn, 1906.

Surface, William. *Inside Internal Revenue*. New York: Coward-McCann, 1967.

Sussman, Frederick B., and Frederic S. Baum. *Law of Juvenile Delinquency*. 3rd ed. New York: Oceana, 1968.

Sutherland, Edwin H. *White Collar Crime*. New York: Dryden, 1949.

———. (ed.). *The Professional Thief*. Chicago: University of Chicago Press, 1937.

———. "Crime and Business," *The Annals*, 217 (September 1941), 112–118.

———. "Is 'White Collar Crime' Crime?" *American Sociological Review*, 10 (April 1945), 132–139.

———. "The Sexual Psychopath Laws," *Journal of Criminal Law*, 40 (January–February 1950), 543–554.

———, and Donald R. Cressey. *Principles of Criminology*. 7th ed. Philadelphia: Lippincott, 1966.

Svalastoga, Kaare. "Homicide and Social Contact in Denmark," *American Journal of Sociology*, 62 (July 1956), 37–41.

Swados, Harvey (ed.). *Years of Conscience: The Muckrakers*. Cleveland: Meridan, 1962.

Sykes, Gresham. *Crime and Society*. 2nd ed. New York: Random House, 1967.

———. *The Society of Captives*. Princeton, New Jersey: Princeton University Press, 1958.

———. "Criminals and Non-Criminals Together: A Modest Proposal," *Prison Journal*, 48 (Autumn–Winter 1968), 4–16.

———. Review of *Criminology and Penology*, *American Sociological Review*, 25 (April 1960), 304.

———, and Sheldon Messinger. "The Inmate Social System," in *Theoretical Studies in Social Organization of the Prison*. New York: Social Science Research Council, 1960, pp. 5–48.

Szasz, Thomas S. *Law, Liberty, and Psychiatry: An Inquiry Into the Social Uses of Mental Health Practices*. New York: Macmillan, 1963.

Taber, Robert C. "The Value of Case Work to the Probationer," *Yearbook*, National Probation & Parole Association, 1940, pp. 167–179.

Taft, Donald R. "Influence of the General Culture on Crime," *Federal Probation*, 30 (September 1966), 16–23.

———, and Ralph W. England, Jr. *Criminology*. 4th ed. New York: Macmillan, 1964.

Taft, Philip. *Corruption and Racketeering in the Labor Movement*. Ithaca, New York: State School of Industrial & Labor Relations, 1958.

Taft, William H. *Popular Government*. New Haven, Connecticut: Yale University Press, 1913.

Tannenbaum, Frank. *Crime and the Community*. Boston: Ginn, 1938.

Tappan, Paul W. *Crime, Justice and Correction*. New York: McGraw-Hill, 1960.

_____. "The Sexual Psychopath—A Civic Social Responsibility," *Journal of Social Hygiene,* 35 (November 1949), 354–368.

_____. "Who is the Criminal?" *American Sociological Review,* 12 (February 1947), 96–103.

Tarde, Gabriel. *Penal Philosophy.* Rapalje Howell (tr.). Boston: Little, Brown, 1912.

Tawney, R. H. *The Acquisitive Society.* New York: Harcourt, Brace, 1920.

Taylor, G. Rattray. *Sex in History.* New York: Ballantine, 1954.

Teele, James E. "Suicidal Behavior, Assaultiveness, and Socialization Principles," *Social Forces,* 43 (May 1965), 510–518.

Teeters, Negley K. *The Cradle of the Penitentiary.* Philadelphia: Pennsylvania Prison Society, 1955.

Tennant, Peter F. D. (ed.). *The Scandinavian Book.* London: Hodge, 1951.

Tennyson, Alfred. "Godiva," in *The Complete Poetical Works.* W. J. Rolfe (ed.). Boston: Houghton Mifflin, 1898, pp. 95–96.

"Test Presentence Report and Summary of Ballot," *Federal Rules Decisions,* 27 (June 1961), 383–388.

Thigpen, Corbert H., and Hervey M. Cleckley. *The Three Faces of Eve.* New York: McGraw–Hill, 1957.

Thompson, George N. *The Psychopathic Delinquent and Criminal.* Springfield, Illinois: Thomas, 1953.

Thoreau, Henry David. *Life Without Principle.* [1863] Stanford, California: Stanford University Press, 1946.

Thrasher, Frederic M. *The Gang.* [1927] Rev. ed. Chicago: University of Chicago Press, 1963.

Tiedman, Christopher G. *A Treatise on the Limitations of Police Power in the United States.* St. Louis, Missouri: Thomas, 1886.

Timasheff, N. S. *An Introduction to the Sociology of Law.* Cambridge, Massachusetts: Harvard University Press, 1939.

Toch, Hans, and Richard Schulte. "Readiness to Perceive Violence as a Result of Police Training," *British Journal of Psychology,* 52 (November 1961), 389–393.

Tompkins, Dorothy C. *White Collar Crime—A Bibliography.* Berkeley: Institute of Government Studies, University of California, 1967.

_____. *Wire Tapping.* Berkeley: Bureau of Public Administration, University of California, 1955.

Tracy, Frederick. *Psychology of Adolescence.* New York: Macmillan, 1921.

Traver, Robert. *Anatomy of a Murder.* New York: St. Martin's, 1958.

Tulley, Andrew. *Treasury Agent.* New York: Simon and Schuster, 1958.

Tumin, Melvin M., and Robert Rotberg. "Leaders, the Led, and the Law: A Case Study in Social Change," *Public Opinion Quarterly,* 31 (Fall 1957), 355–370.

Turkus, Burton B., and Sid Feder. *Murder, Inc.* New York: Farrar, Straus, 1951.

Turner, J. W. C. (ed.). *Kenny's Outline of Criminal Law.* 17th ed. New York: Cambridge University Press, 1958.

Turner, Wallace. *Gambler's Money: The New Force in American Life.* Boston: Houghton Mifflin, 1965.

Tyler, Gus (ed.). *Organized Crime in America: A Book of Readings.* Ann Arbor: University of Michigan Press, 1962.

UNESCO. *Vagrant Children.* Paris, 1951.

United Nations. *Probation and Related Matters.* 1951.

United States Commission on Civil Rights. *Justice.* Washington, D.C.: Government Printing Office, 1961.

United States House of Representatives, Committee on Ways and Means. *Hearings on the Taxation of Marihuana.* 75th Congress, 1st Session, 1937.

United States Senate, Committee on Government Operations, Permanent Subcommittee on Investigations. *Organized Crime and Illicit Traffic in Narcotics.* 88th Congress, 1st Session, 1963, Parts 1 and 3.

———. Committee on the Judiciary, Subcommittee on Improvements in Judicial Machinery. *Free Press and Fair Trial.* 89th Congress, 1st Session, 1965, Parts 1 and 2.

———. Select Committee on Improper Activities in the Labor or Management Field. *1st Interim Report.* 85 Congress, 2nd Session, 1958.

———, Special Committee to Investigate Crime in Interstate Commerce. *3rd Interim Report.* 82nd Congress, 1st Session, 1951.

———, Subcommittee on Antitrust and Monopoly. *Administered Prices.* 87th Congress, 2nd Session, 1961, Parts 27 and 28.

———, Subcommittee on Constitutional Rights. *Wiretapping, Eavesdropping, and the Bill of Rights.* 85th Congress, 2nd Session, 1958.

———, Subcommittee to Investigate Juvenile Delinquency, Committee of the Judiciary. *Exploitation of Minors in Interstate Confidence Racket.* 84th Congress, 2nd Session, 1959.

Upham, Charles W. *Salem Witchcraft.* New York: Ungar, 1959.

Usher, Roland G. *The Pilgrims and Their History.* New York: Macmillan, 1930.

VanDen Haag, Ernest. "On Deterrence and the Death Penalty," *Journal of Criminal Law,* 60 (June 1969), 141–147.

Van Vechten, Courtland. "The Toleration Quotient as a Device for Defining Certain Social Concepts," *American Journal of Sociology,* 46 (July 1940), 35–42.

Veblen, Thorstein. *The Theory of the Leisure Class.* New York: Macmillan, 1912.

Verkko, Veli. *Homicides and Suicides in Finland.* Copenhagen: Gads, 1951.

Vold, George B. *Theoretical Criminology.* New York: Oxford University Press, 1958.

———. "Criminology at the Crossroads," *Journal of Criminal Law,* 42 (July–August 1951), 155–162.

Voltaire, François M. A. *L'Ingénu* [1767], in *Oeuvres completes.* Paris: Garnier, 1879, Vol. XXI.

Voss, Harwin L. "Differential Association and Containment Theory: A Theoretical Congruence," *Social Forces,* 47 (June 1969), 381–391.

Walker, Daniel. *Rights in Conflict.* New York: Bantam, 1968.

Wallace, Samuel E. *Skid Row as a Way of Life.* Totowa, New Jersey: Bedminster, 1965.

———, and José M. Canals. "Socio-Legal Aspects of a Study of Acts of Violence," *American University Law Review,* 11 (June 1962), 173–188.

Wallerstein, James S., and Clement J. Wyle. "Our Law-Abiding Law-Breakers," *Federal Probation,* 25 (March–April 1947), 107–112.

Walsh, Lawrence E. "Organized Crime," State Conference of Mayors, Los Angeles, July 15, 1959.

Walton, Clarence C., and Frederick W. Cleveland, Jr. *Corporations on Trial: The Electric Cases.* Belmont, California: Wadsworth, 1964.

Ward, Lester F. *Applied Sociology.* Boston: Ginn, 1906.

———. *The Psychic Factors of Civilization.* 2nd ed. Boston: Ginn, 1906.

———. *Pure Sociology.* New York: Macmillan, 1925.

Warner, Sam B. "Crimes Known to the Police—An Index of Crime?", *Harvard Law Review,* 45 (December 1931), 307–331.

Warner, William L., and Paul S. Lunt. *The Social Life of a Modern Community.* New Haven, Connecticut: Yale University Press, 1941.

Warren, Marguerite Q. "The Case for Differential Treatment of Delinquents," *The Annals,* 381(January 1969), 47–59.

——. "Recent Findings in the Community Treatment Project," in *Alternatives to Incarceration.* Sacramento, California: Board of Corrections, 1964.

Washburne, Chandler. *Primitive Drinking: A Study of the Uses and Functions of Alcohol in Preliterate Societies.* New Haven, Connecticut: College & University Press, 1961.

Wathen, Daniel E. "Criminal Responsibility: The Durham Rule in Maine," *Maine Law Review,* 15 (1963), 107–117.

Waybright, Roger J. "Florida's New Juvenile Court Act," *Miami Law Quarterly,* 6 (December 1951), 1–23.

Weber, Max. *The Protestant Ethic and the Spirit of Capitalism.* Talcott Parsons (tr.). London: Allen & Unwin, 1930.

——. *The Theory of Social and Economic Organization.* A. M. Henderson and Talcott Parsons (trs.). New York: Oxford University Press, 1947.

Wechsler, Herbert. "Sentencing, Correction, and the Model Penal Code," *University of Pennsylvania Law Review,* 109 (February 1961), 465–493.

Weihofen, Henry. *The Urge to Punish.* London: Gollancz, 1957.

Weinberg, Arthur, and Lila Weinberg. *The Muckrakers.* New York: Simon and Schuster, 1961.

Weinberg, S. Kirson. *Incest Behavior.* New York: Citadel, 1955.

Weiner, Saul, Grant Sutherland, Allen A. Bartholemew, and Bryan Hudson. "XYY Males in a Melbourne Prison," *Lancet,* (Jaunary 20, 1968) p. 150.

Wendell, Mitchell. "The Interstate Compact on Juveniles: Development and Operation," *Journal of Public Law,* 8 (Spring 1959), 524–536.

Wendt, Lloyd, and Herman Kogan. *Big Bill of Chicago.* Indianapolis, Indiana: Bobbs-Merrill, 1953.

——. *Lords of the Levee.* Indianapolis, Indiana: Bobbs-Merrill, 1943.

Wentworth, Harold, and Stuart B. Flexner. *Dictionary of American Slang.* New York: Crowell, 1960.

Werner, M. R. and John Starr. *Teapot Dome.* New York: Viking, 1959.

Wertham, Frederic. *A Sign for Cain: An Exploration of Human Violence.* New York: Macmillan, 1966.

——. *Seduction of the Innocent.* New York: Rinehart, 1954.

Wessel, Milton R. "Legalized Gambling: Dream and Realities," *The Nation,* 20 (January 18, 1965), 46–48.

West, D. J. *Murder Followed by Suicide.* Cambridge, Massachusetts: Harvard University Press, 1966.

Westin, Alan F. "Bookies and 'Bugs' in California: Judicial Control of Police Practices," in Westin (ed.), *The Uses of Power.* New York: Harcourt, Brace & World, 1962, pp. 117–171.

Wheeler, Stanton. "Criminal Statistics: A Reformulation of the Problem," *Journal of Criminal Law,* 58 (September 1967), 317–324.

——. "Sex Offenses: A Sociological Critique," in John H. Gagnon and William Simon (eds.). *Sexual Deviance.* New York: Harper & Row, 1967, pp. 77–102.

White House Conference on Narcotic and Drug Abuse. *Proceedings.* Washington, D.C.: Government Printing Office, 1962.

Whitehead, Don. *The FBI Story.* New York: Random House, 1956.

——. *Journey Into Crime.* New York: Random House, 1960.

Whitman, Howard. "Why Some Doctors Should Be in Jail," *Collier's*, 132 (October 30, 1953), 23–27.

Whittemore, L. H. *Cop! A Closeup of Violence and Tragedy.* New York: Holt, Rinehart and Winston, 1969.

Whyte, William F. *Street Corner Society.* Enlarged ed. Chicago: University of Chicago Press, 1955.

Wilde, Oscar. *De Profoundis.* New York: Putnam, 1905.

Wilkins, Leslie T. *Social Deviance: Social Policy, Action, Research.* Englewood Cliffs, New Jersey: Prentice-Hall, 1965.

Wilks, Judith A. "Ecological Correlates of Crime and Delinquency," in *Task Force Report: Crime and Its Impact—An Assessment.* Washington, D.C.: President's Commission on Law Enforcement and Administration of Justice, 1967, pp. 138–156.

Williams, Glanville. *Criminal Law—The General Part.* 2nd ed. London: Stevens, 1961.

———. *The Sanctity of Life and the Criminal Law.* New York: Knopf, 1957.

Williams, J. B. *Criminal Law Outline.* Rev. ed. Sacramento: California State Department of Education, 1954.

Williams, Robin M., Jr. *American Society: A Sociological Interpretation.* 3rd ed. New York: Knopf, 1970.

Williamson, Henry. *Hustler!* New York: Doubleday, 1965.

Will Your Business Be Next? New York: National Council on Crime and Delinquency, n.d.

Wilmer, Harry A. "The Role of the 'Rat' in Prison," *Federal Probation*, 29 (March 1965), 44–49.

Wilson, James Q. *Varieties of Police Behavior: The Management of Law and Order in Eight Communities.* Cambridge, Massachusetts: Harvard University Press, 1968.

Winchell, John W. "Intent in Criminal Law: The Legal Tower of Babel," *Catholic University Law Review*, 8 (January 1958), 31–42.

Wines, Frederick H. *Punishment and Reformation.* Rev. ed. New York: Crowell, 1923.

Winick, Charles. "Epidemiology of Drug Use," in Daniel M. Wilner and Gene G. Kassebaum (eds.). *Narcotics.* New York: McGraw-Hill, 1965, 3–18.

———. "Physician Narcotic Addicts," *Social Problems*, 9 (Fall 1961), 174–186.

———. "The Use of Drugs by Jazz Musicians," *Social Problems*, 3 (Winter 1959–1960), 240–253.

Wirth, Louis. *The Ghetto.* Chicago: University of Chicago Press, 1928.

Witmer, Helen L., and Ruth Kotinsky (eds.). *New Perspectives for Research in Juvenile Delinquency.* Children's Bureau 356. Washington, D.C.: Government Printing Office, 1956.

Wittels, David G. "What Can We Do About Sex Crimes?", *Saturday Evening Post*, 221 (December 11, 1948), 30–31ff.

Wolfenstein, Martha, and Nathan Leites. *Movies: A Psychological Study.* New York: Free Press, 1950.

Wolff, Hans J. *Roman Law: An Historical Interpretation.* Norman: University of Oklahoma Press, 1951.

Wolfgang, Marvin E. *Crime and Race: Conceptions and Misconceptions.* New York: Institution of Human Relations Press, American Jewish Committee, 1964.

———. *Patterns of Criminal Homicide.* Philadelphia: University of Pennsylvania Press, 1958.

———. "Uniform Crime Reports: A Critical Appraisal," *University of Pennsylvania Law Review*, 111 (April 1963), 708–738.

————, and Franco Ferracuti. *The Subculture of Violence: Towards An Integrated Theory in Criminology.* London: Tavistock, 1967.

Wood, Arthur L. *Crime and Aggression in Changing Ceylon.* Philadelphia: Transactions of the American Philosophical Society, 1961.

Wootton, Barbara. *Social Science and Social Pathology.* New York: Macmillan, 1959.

Wormuth, Francis D. *Origins of Modern Constitutionalism.* New York: Harper & Row, 1949.

Wright, Nathalia. "The Confidence Man of Melville and Cooper: An American Indictment," *American Quarterly,* 4 (Fall 1952), 266–268.

Wright, Richard. *Black Boy.* New York: Harper, 1954.

Wright, Thomas (ed.). *Queen Elizabeth and Her Times: A Series of Original Letters.* London: Colburn, 1838.

Wunniche, Brooke. "The 1951 Juvenile Court Law of Wyoming," *Wyoming Law Journal,* 8 (Spring 1954), 173–199.

Yablonsky, Lewis. *The Tunnel Back.* New York: Macmillan, 1965.

————. *The Violent Gang.* New York: Macmillan, 1962.

Yalom, Irwin D. "Aggression and Forbiddenness in Voyeurism," *Archives of General Psychiatry,* 3 (September 1960), 305–319.

Young, Pauline V. *The Pilgrims of Russian-Town.* Chicago: University of Chicago Press, 1932.

Young, Wayland. *The Montesi Scandal.* New York: Doubleday, 1958.

Zelitch, Judah. *Soviet Administration of Criminal Laws.* Philadelphia: University of Pennsylvania Press, 1931.

Zemans, Eugene, and Ruth S. Cavan. "Marital Relationships of Prisoners," *Journal of Criminal Law,* 49 (May–June 1958), 50–57.

Zola, Irving K. "Observations on Gambling in a Lower-Class Setting," *Social Problems,* 10 (Spring 1963), 353–361.

Zorbaugh, Harvey. *The Gold Coast and the Slum.* Chicago: University of Chicago Press, 1929.

Cases

American Motorcycle Assn. v. Davids, 158 North Western Reporter 2nd 72 (Michigan 1968).

Anderson v. United States, 237 Federal Reporter 2nd 118 (9th Circuit 1956).

Baltimore Radio Show v. State, U.S. Supreme Court Reports 912 (1950).

Boyse v. Rossborough, 6 House of Lords Cases 1 (1857).

Braunfield v. Brown, 366 U.S. Supreme Court Reports 599 (1961).

Commonwealth v. Fisher, 62 Atlantic Reporter 198 (Pennsylvania 1905).

Daniel M'Naghten's Case, 8 English Reports 718 (1843).

Driver v. Hinnant, 356 Federal Reporter 2nd 761 (4th Circuit 1966).

Durham v. United States, 214 Federal Reporter 2nd 862 (D.C. Circuit 1954).

Easter v. District of Columbia, 361 Federal Reporter 2nd 50 (D.C. Circuit 1966).

Escobedo v. Illinois, 378 U.S. Supreme Court Reports 478 (1964).

Estes v. Texas, 381 U.S. Supreme Court Reports 532 (1965).

Gault v. Arizona, 387 U.S. Supreme Court Reports 1 (1967).

Gideon v. Wainwright, 372 U.S. Supreme Court Reports 335 (1963).

Gregg Cartage & Storage Co. v. United States, 318 U.S. Supreme Court Reports 74 (1942).

Henselman v. People, 48 North Eastern Reporter 304 (Illinois 1897).

Irvin v. Dowd, 366 U.S. Supreme Court Reports 717 (1961).

Lambert v. California, 355 U.S. Supreme Court Reports 225 (1957).
Leonard v. Licker, 23 Ohio Circuit Court Reports (N.S.) 442 (1914).
Ex parte *Loving,* 77 South Western Reporter 508 (Missouri 1903).
Mallory v. United States, 354 U.S. Supreme Court Reports 449 (1957).
Mapp v. Ohio, 367 U.S. Supreme Court Reports 643 (1961).
Marchetti v. United States, 390 U.S. Supreme Court Reports 39 (1968).
McGowan v. Maryland, 366 U.S. Supreme Court Reports 420 (1961).
Mempa v. Rhay, 389 U.S. Supreme Court Reports 128 (1967).
Metoyer v. United States, 250 Federal Reporter 2nd 30 (D.C. Appelate 1957).
Miranda v. Arizona, 384 U.S. Supreme Court Reports 436 (1966).
Nardone v. United States, 302 U.S. Supreme Court Reports 379 (1937).
Olmstead v. United States, 277 U.S. Supreme Court Reports 438 (1928).
People v. Armstrong, 41 North Western Reporter 275 (Michigan 1889).
People v. Cahan, 282 Pacific Reporter 2nd 905 (California 1955).
People v. Hernandez, 393 Pacific Reporter 2nd 673 (California 1964).
People v. Horton, 308 New York Supplement 2nd 1 (1954).
Perkins v. North Carolina, 234 Federal Supplement 333 (Western District North Carolina 1964).
Powell v. Texas, 392 U.S. Supreme Court Reports 514 (1968).
Pugh v. Bowden, 54 Southern Reporter 499 (Florida 1907).
Robinson v. California, 370 U.S. Supreme Court Reports 660 (1962).
Rochin v. California, 342 U.S. Supreme Court Reports 165 (1952).
In re *Sharp,* 96 Pacific Reporter 563 (Idaho 1908).
State v. Adkins, 146 South Eastern Reporter 732 (West Virginia 1929).
State ex rel Colvin v. Lombardi, 241 Atlantic Reporter 2nd 625 (Rhode Island 1968).
State v. Pike, 48 New Hampshire Reports 399 (1870).
Sweeney v. United States, 353 Federal Reporter 2nd 10 (7th Circuit 1965).
Sweezy v. New Hampshire, 354 U.S. Supreme Court Reports 234 (1957).
Townley v. State, 355 Pacific Reporter 2nd 420 (Oklahoma 1960).
United States ex rel Berlandi v. Reimer, 113 Federal Reporter 2nd 492 (2nd Circuit 1940).
United States v. Buffalino, 285 Federal Reporter 2nd 408 (2nd Circuit 1960).
United States v. Currens, 290 Federal Reporter 2nd 751 (3rd Circuit 1961).
United States v. Freeman, 357 Federal Reporter 2nd 606 (2nd Circuit 1966).
United States v. McClung, 187 Federal Supplement 254 (Eastern District Louisiana 1960).
Weeks v. United States, 232 U.S. Supreme Court Reports 383 (1914).
Weigand v. Kentucky, 397 South Western Reporter 2nd 780 (1965).
West v. Campbell, Case No. 2814 (Criminal), Circuit Court, Carroll County, Maryland, May 1, 1969.
Wolf v. Colorado, 385 U.S. Supreme Court Reports 25 (1949).

Index

Abortion, 132, 133, 193, 223, 230, 324, 326
Abrahamsen, David, 5, 254
Acton, Lord, 81
Adler, Mortimer J., 23
Adultery, 245, 275, 325, 437
Advertising frauds, 299, 304, 307, 314–16, 319, 324
Air travel, 75
Airplane hijacking, 61
Alabama, 227, 327, 445
Alaska, 443
Albert, Ethel, 151, 154
Alcibiades, 59
Alcohol, 8, 11, 329–30; in aggravated assaults, 240; in check writing, 180, 280; in gang behavior, 374; in homicides, 231, 236; organized crime and, 207–8, 211; Prohibition and, 17, 72, 193; in property offenses, 283; sale of as criminal offense, 74; in sexual offenses, 248, 250, 251; violence and, 231, 284; see also Drunkenness
Alcohol and Tobacco Tax Division, 393
Allen, Francis A., 23, 317, 493–94
American Bankers Association, 179
American Bar Association, 214, 400
American Law Institute, 479–80, 492, 493
Amir, Menachem, 249–50
Anashkin, G. Z., 71
Anderson, C. L., 296
Anderson, Ronald A., 40–41
Andrews, T. Colemen, 312
Anglo-Saxon jurisprudence: blue-laws in, 62; ignorance of the law in, 46; police interrogation in, 415; punishment in, 436; on suicide, 64; see also England
Apfelberg, Benjamin, 265
Antitrust (monopoly) practices, 299, 307, 309–12, 393
Appalachin, New York, 211–12
Arapesh, 252
Arieff, Alex, 184
Aristotle, 64, 66, 307
Arkansas, 252

Arles, Council of, 64
Armed robbery, see Robbery, armed
Arnold, Thurman, 47
Arraignment, 413–15
Arrests, 125, 168, 413–14; age-levels and, 148–51, 155, 163; false, 182, 185, 291; in minority groups, 155–58, 227; sex composition in, 150–54; see also specific crime
Arson, 120, 223, 254, 293–97; arrests for, 148, 152, 157
Aschaffenburg, Gustav, 85, 297
Assault, 7, 10, 225, 279, 284; defined, 238–39; in gang behavior, 374; police and, 400; punishment for, 466
Assault, aggravated, 121, 128, 145, 239–40; age-levels and, 148, 240; defined, 122, 239; homicide and, 231, 239, 240; minority groups and, 155, 156, 240; sex and, 152; statistics on, 141, 143, 160; unreported, 115; weapons in, 240
Assault and battery, 120, 122, 238–41, 451; unnecessary surgery as, 308
Assault in burglary, 278
Astin, Robert, 340
Athelstand, King, 485
Atlantic City, New Jersey, 196
Audett, Blackie, 290–91
Augustus, Emperor, 15
Augustus, John, 485
Australia, 225, 226, 449, 464, 490
Austria, 333
Automobile arson, 294
Automobile theft, 102, 122, 161, 275, 394; arrests for, 125, 148, 152, 156; as embezzlement, 24, 25; as joyriding, 279; seasonal changes in, 145; statistics on, 141, 143, 160; unreported, 115
Aydelotte, Frank, 168

Babylonia, 57
Bail, 168, 413, 415–17; personal recognizance in, 416
Baker, Russell, 142

Baldwin, James, 386–87
Ball, Harry V., 240–41
Ball, John, 338
Baltimore, Maryland, 464
Bank robbery, 104, 105, 278, 288–91
Bankruptcy, planned, 208–9, 304
Barbara, Joseph, 211
Barbash, James, 176–77
Barnes, Harry Elmer, 73
Barnes, Marion, 22, 40
Barron, Milton, 184
Battery, see Assault and Battery
Beaney, William, 409–10
Beaumont, Gustave Auguste de, 55
Beccaria, Cesare, x, 84–87, 451
Beck, Dave, 207
Becker, Howard P., 303
Becker, Howard S., 345
Beggars, 169, 177–78
Bell, Daniel, 120, 143–44
Bender, Lauretta, 264
Benedict, Ruth, 266
Benefit of clergy, 485
Bennett, James, 394–95, 415
Bensing, Robert C., 229
Bentham, Jeremy, 85, 86, 451–52
Bernstein, Saul, 377–78
Bevington, Helen, 86
Bianchi, Hermannus, 19
Biderman, Albert, 112, 114, 123–24
Bigamy, 45, 401
Biggs, John, Jr., 479–80
Black, Donald J., 429
Black, Jack, 103
Blackmail, 267
Blacks, 8, 142, 154, 163; in arrest sta-
    tistics, 155–58, 360; in homicides, 156,
    227–30; homosexual activity of, 266;
    Kerner Commission on, 9–10; mari-
    juana and, 343–44; militancy among, 6;
    narcotics and, 338, 339; in organized
    crime, 198; personality patterns in,
    228–29; police and, 384, 386–88; in
    property offenses, 288; in rape offenses,
    252; shoplifting prosecutions of, 182
Blackstone, William, 40
Blau, Abram, 264
Bloch, Herbert, 125, 128, 192
Blum, Richard H., 329
Blumer, Herbert, 346
Blumrosen, Alfred, 33
Bok, Curtis, 193
Bonger, W. A., 85, 145
Bookmaking, 203, 215
Booth, John Wilkes, 236
Borchard, Edwin M., 407
Bordua, David, 283–84, 375
Boston, Massachusetts, 130, 230–31; po-
    lice in, 392
Bovet, Lucien, 88
Bowie, Carol, 184
Bowling, R. W., 257
Bradnox, Thomas, 60
Brancale, Ralph, 248, 269–70
Brandeis, Louis D., 35
Brennan, William J., Jr., 34
Bridgman, Percy, 82

Bromage, Kenneth G., 240–41
Brown, Claude, 316
Brown, John Mason, 421
Brown, William, 398
Bullock, Henry A., 229
Bureau of Internal Revenue, 195, 393
Bureau of Science Research, 115–16
Burgess, Ernest W., 318
Burglary, 44, 145; defined, 277–78; homi-
    cide during, 223, 237, 244; statistics
    on, 141, 143, 160; unreported, 115
Burglary, arrests for: age-levels and, 147,
    148, 163; in minority groups, 156; sex
    and, 151, 152
Busch, Francis, 3

Cadwallader, Mervyn L., 288
Cahn, Edmond, 64
Cairns, Huntington, 32, 322
Caldwell, Robert G., 317
California: civil commitment in, 482;
    crime rate in, 121; exclusionary rule
    in, 427; grand juries in, 419; on homo-
    sexuality, 267; on incest, 74; on juve-
    nile delinquency, 356; on preliminary
    hearings, 418; prisons in, 438, 466
California Youth Authority, 484
Calvin, John, 67–68
Cameron, Mary Owen, 183, 184
Camp, George M., 289–90
Campion, Father, 446
Camus, Albert, 448
Canada, 225, 226
Capital punishment, 437, 442–48, 451;
    abolition movement on, 443; dimuni-
    tion of use of, 444; in Soviet Union,
    69, 70, 442; suicide and, 65, 445
Caplovitz, David, 316
Capone, Al, 17, 138, 192, 195–97, 207–8,
    393
Cardozo, Benjamin, 38, 433
Carrarra, Francesco, 17
Carson, Edward, 422
Cason, Hulsey, 248
Cavan, Ruth S., 471–72
Caxton, William, 16
Cayton, Horace, 201
Ceylon, 145, 230
Chamberlin, Henry, 191
Charles I, 16
Chaucer, 367
Check writing, 178–81, 279, 280; see also
    Forgery
Chessman, Caryl, 254
Chicago, Illinois: organized crime in,
    194–96, 200, 201; police in, 383–85;
    robbery statistics in, 118–19; Town
    Hall crime patterns in, 7–8
Chile, 225, 226
China, 329
Chinese Americans, 156–57, 330
Christie, John, 448
Chromosome makeup, 48
Churchill, Allen, 6
Churchill, Sir Winston, 494
Civil commitment, 461, 481–83
Civil disorders, 9–10, 386, 388

Civil law, 317–18
Civil offenses, *see* Torts
Civil rights, 386, 393, 395, 437; of jail inmates, 464; in juvenile courts, 357–59
Clark, Ramsey, 155, 158
Clark, Tom C., 312
Cleckley, Hervey M., 483
Clemmer, Donald, 453–55
Cleveland, Ohio, 229–31
Clinard, Marshall, 161, 315, 319
Cloward, Richard A., 102, 374–75, 378
Cohen, Albert K., 247, 368, 372–74
Cohen, Sheldon, S., 312–13
Coke, Lord, 439
Cole, Robert, 330
Colosimo, Big Jim, 195
Commager, Henry, 432–33
Committee on Consumer Interest, 316
Commonwealth v. Fisher, 358
Communications, *see* Mass media
Community-treatment programs, 483–84
Comte, Auguste, 33–34
Confession rules, 409, 429
Confidence games, 102, 105, 171–78, 187, 305; attitude toward victims in, 104, 171, 177; history of, 169–70; in shoplifting false arrests, 185
Connecticut, 62
Conrad, John, 468, 470
Conscientious objectors, 38
Constantine, Emperor, 61–62
Consumer frauds, 307, 314–17
Containment theory, 99–101
Conwell, Chic, 174
Cooper, James Fenimore, 169
Coplon, Judith, 395
Corrections, 437–42, 460–61, 468–76, 481–93
Corrientes, Diego, 449
Cosa Nostra, La, 210, 212–14
Courts, 407–33; appellate, 426; bail in, 168, 413, 415–17; contempt powers of, 419; in criminal trials, 8, 42, 419–26; discretionary powers of, 86, 486; exclusionary rule in, 426–29; failure to convict in, 407–8, 432; fallibility of, 443; history of, 86, 424; integrity of, 408–9; lawyers and, 33, 422; on legal counsel, 414, 418, 422–23; medieval, 435; police and, 413–15, 426–32; probation granted by, 485–87; prosecuting attorneys in, 215, 408, 410–12, 417–22, 432; public defenders in, 422–24; social sciences and, 34; in tort law, 41; wiretapping evidence in, 430, 431; *see also* Judges
Courts, inferior (municipal), 409–13; arraignments in, 413–15; preliminary hearings in, 417–19
Courts, juries in, 408, 424–26; criminal responsibility and, 479–80; grand, 419; guilty pleas and, 412–13; history of, 59; petit (trial), 419
Courts, juvenile, 354–56, 460; constitutionality of, 357–59; establishment of, 357; female offenders in, 151
Cowell, John, 16

Cozzens, James Gould, 168
Creek Indians, 55
Cressey, Donald, 24, 25; on differential association, 92, 95, 97; on embezzlement, 292–93; on organized crime, 190, 213; on *Uniform Crime Reports*, 119; on white-collar crimes, 320–21
Crime, *xii*, 4; American attitudes toward, 73; as business enterprise, 5; capital, 415, 419; categorical risk of, 129; compulsive, 100; curiosity about, 3–5; as deserved, 75, 99; entities of, 43; environmental factors in, 90, 158, 163, 285, 286; epidemiology of, 97; in foreign countries, 140; functional aspects of, 23; investigations into, 7–12; known to the police, 124–26; law enforcement producing, 135, 389, 404–5; minority groups and, 154–59, 163; non-clergyable, 485; against the person, 125, 145, 159, 163, 225, 284–85; as political issue, *vii*, 7, 142, 386; polls on, 8; professional, 167–89, 279, 290; as psychological entity, 87, 90; public concern with, *vii*, 6–8, 25, 134–35, 142; reduction of, 80, 437; relativity of, 52–53, 73–77; reporting increasing, 132, 133; science and, *viii-xi*, 12, 16, 23, 26, 79, 493–94; as social deviance, *xi*, 18–21; social structure and, *xi*, 4, 6, 14, 21, 52–53; sociocultural matrix reflected in, 101–2; studies of, 83–84; techniques of, 94; typologies of, 101–7, 361; in U.S., 118, 130, 138, 144; unreported, 112, 114–19, 125, 126; *see also* Felonies; Misdemeanors; Torts; *and specific crimes*
Crimes, definitions of, 14–21, 23, 25, 26, 73, 318; behavioral, 101; increase of, 132; as a legal concept, 39–50, 87, 101, 279
Crime, organized, 190–216, 372; activities of, 190; bureaucratization of, 194, 196–197; control of, 214–16; cultural context of, 192–93, 197–98; growth of, 8; hierarchical arrangements of, 101, 190, 210; history of, 194–97; in labor unions, 206–7, 211; lawyers for, 216, 422; leaders of, 197–98, 202; in legitimate business, 190, 205–10; Mafia and/or La Cosa Nostra, 210–14; in narcotics, 190, 193, 211, 335–36; punishment of, 214–215, 449; silence of, 191; wiretapping against, 430, 431
Crime, against property, 125, 134, 140, 145, 155, 159, 163, 272–97; history of, 272–74; increase statistics on, 141, 143; typologies of, 278–85
Crime control, 13, 79, 134–35, 162; state programs for, 8
Crime measurement, 111–64; difficulties of, 111–13, 162; forecasts of future in, 130–34; indexes in, 126–28; nationwide statistics on, 118; in percentages, 112; population and, 121, 128–31; public attitudes reflected by, 125–26; reporting methods in, 119–26, 158, 162; sample

Crime measurement (*Continued*) composition in, 127–28; *see also Uniform Crime Reports*

Crime rate, 162–64, 467; age-levels and, 148–51, 155, 163; income and, 10, 132–133; as measure, 40; in minority groups, 155; 1967 compared to 1960 and 1966, 142–43; seasonal changes in, 144–46, 163, 239–40; sex and, 133–34, 150–54, 163; in U.S., 130–34, 162–63; urban-rural differentials in, 159–61, 163–64

Crimes Act (1790), 73

Criminal, the, 20, 50–52, 318

Criminal behavior, 389; affluence affecting, 133; age-group and, 127–28; behavior patterns in, 102–3; causes of, 480; chromosome makeup and, 48; containment theory in, 99–101; cultural crimogenisis in, 98–99; differential association on, 80, 92–98, 233, 299–300; encephalitis and, 253–54; environment affecting, 90, 91, 93, 106, 234–36, 240–41, 283, 304, 376, 480; ethical codes in, 40, 171, 185, 186; felonies as, 42–43; in ghetto, 154; group therapy affecting, 473, 474; investigations of, 31; law enforcement affecting, 134–35, 313, 388–89, 404–5, 407, 428; as learned, 92–93, 188, 253, 290, 300; toward legitimized social goals, 197–98, 206, 302; mental illness and, 476–81; misdemeanors as, 42–43; needs and values not explaining, 309; organization of society and, 77; punishment affecting, 134, 169, 314, 321, 389, 436–437, 439; racial variations in, 228; reinforcement of, 104; relativity of, 73–77; reporting systems on, 118; role-performance in, 101–2, 134, 151; sexual base of, 243; sociology of, 91–92; studies of, 83; techniques dealing with, 13; truncated behavior in, 101, 107; typologies of, 101–7; understanding of, 12, 79; *see also* Criminals

Criminal behavior, defined, 18, 24, 25, 26; civil commitment on, 481; as failure to act, 17; as social deviation, 20

Criminal behavior, professional, 167–89; force or weapons not used by, 167–68, 177; in-group reinforcement of, 172–173; insight of, 103; language distinctiveness in, 104–5, 173; rationalization system of, 171–72; self-concern of, 168; self-image of, 170–73, 188; techniques and skills of, 167–70, 290

Criminal capacity, 46–50

Criminal intent, 43–46; motive compared to, 46

Criminal justice: administration of, 24, 34, 52, 407–33; arraignment in, 413–15; controversial areas of, 409; defense attorneys in, 413, 414, 422–24, 432; for felonies, 413–26; guilty pleas in, 410–413, 423, habeas corpus in, 413; history of, 26, 424; mass media affecting, 418–420; material witnesses in, 415–16; for misdemeanors, 409–13; in preliminary

hearings, 417–18; prisoners' attitudes toward, 408; prosecuting attorneys in, 215, 408, 410–12, 417–22, 432; in Soviet Union, 70, 71; state witnesses in, 408, 417, 418; *see also* Courts; Judges

Criminal law, 21–23, 26; as agency of social control, 36; American roots of, 72–73; civil law compared to, 317–18; on criminal capacity, 46–47; criminal lawyers and, 422; criminal responsibility and, 476–81, 493–94; in defining crime, 40–41; history of, 56–60; jurisprudence in, 52; juvenile delinquency and, 354–56; norms of, 21; as reflecting the ethos of a society, 54; social sciences and, 34–35; social values reflected in, 60–61, 63; in Soviet Union, 69–71; technology affecting, 73, 75, 77; tort law compared to, 41–42, 301; white-collar crimes and, 301

Criminal responsibility, 476–82, 493–94

Criminalistics, 52

Criminals, 318; as criminaloid, 88, 302; hierarchical arrangements among, 105, 173, 176, 187; identification and in-group loyalty among, 105; life history of, 187–89; perceptions of, 103; physical characteristics of, 88–89; professional, *see* Criminal behavior, professional; psychological characteristics of, 90, 91, 95, 98; upperworld, 303; values and attitudes of, 103–4; *see also* Criminal behavior

Criminals, rehabilitation of, 52, 422, 424, 439–42, 454–57, 468–76, 494; administrators involved in, 11; for alcoholics, 327–28, 331–32, 487; civil commitment and, 481–83; community-treatment programs and, 483–84; Joint Commission on Correctional Manpower and Training on, 11; of narcotics addicts, 337–343, 481–82; parole and, 489–93; probation and, 484–87

Criminology, *xii*, 12–15, 79–107; areas of, 52–53; categorization in, 23–25; definitions of, 23, 39, 79; as deterministic, 49, 87; on organized crime, 190–92; particularism in, 89–91; research in, 80; science of, 79–84; social control studied by, 39; theories in, 80–82, 90–92, 101

Criminology, history of, x, 84–91; classical school, 85–87; positivist school, 87–90; social disorganization school of, 90

Cultural crimogenisis, 98–99

Curren Rule, 479–80

Dante, Alighieri, 67
Darrow, Clarence, 40
Davis, Clyde Brion, 199
Davis, David B., 443
Davis, Kingsley, 275, 351–52
Debo, Angie, 55
Defense attorneys, *see* Lawyers
De Fleur, Melvin, 97
Delaware, 436, 443, 466
Dentler, Robert, 281

Denver, Colorado, 464
Deodands, 435
Determinism, 49, 87, 480, 493, *see also* Free will
Detroit, Michigan, 386, 429, 463–64
Deviancy, *xi*, 18–21
Devlin, Patrick, 326, 384–85, 422
Dewey, Thomas E., 197, 205
Diana, Lewis, 488
Dickens, Charles, 402
Differential association, 80, 92–98, 233, 299–300
Dimock, Edward J., 423
Dioguardi, Johnny, 206
Disorderly conduct, 42, 149, 153, 157; drunkenness and, 327, 329
District of Columbia, 116
Doe, Charles, 85
Dole, Vincent, 341
Dollard, John, 92
Donnelly, Richard, 432
Dostoevsky, Fyodor, 51
Double jeopardy, 191
Douglas, William O., 46, 414, 420
Draft, 8, 138
Drake, St. Clair, 201
Drugs, *see* Narcotics
Drunkenness, 324–35, 401, 487; arrests for, 149, 153, 157, 329; causes of, 330; while driving, 149, 153, 157, 332–35, 411; police-case inebriate and, 330–32; *see also* Alcohol
Due-process protections, 482
Dunham, Warren, 256
Durant, Will, 38, 59
Durham v. United States, 478–79, 481
Durkheim, Émile, 4, 13, 85, 230
Dyer Act (National Motor Vehicle Theft Act, 1919), 394, 479

East, Norwood, 75
Eastman, Harold, 161
Economic crimes, 319
Ecuador, 226
Edelston, H., 181
Edwards, J. L. J., 43
Egypt, 74
Elliott, Mabel, 230
Ellis, Albert, 248, 269–70
Embezzlement, 122, 278, 279, 291–93, 307; arrests for, 148, 150, 153, 157; defined, 24, 25; laws changing on, 61; as middle class crime, 128; robbery as, 24; in Soviet Union, 442
Emerson, Thomas I., 306
Encephalitis, 253–55
England, 74; assaults in, 239; blackmail in, 267; burglary in, 277; on criminal responsibility, 477–78; deodands in, 435–36; drunken driving in, 334–35; early criminal law in, 56; felony-murder doctrine in, 223; gambling in, 203; grand juries in, 419; homicides in, 226, 231, 232, 237; homosexuality in, 268–69; jury trials in, 425–26, 432; police in, 391, 395, 402–4; prisons in, 465; prosecuting attorneys in, 422, 432;

punishment in, 56, 436, 442, 443, 445–446, 448–49, 449–50, 452, 464; robbery in, 286–87; statutory rape in, 256; on suicide, 64–66; theft in, 60, 276; wiretapping in, 429–30; *see also* Anglo-Saxon jurisprudence
Ennis, Phillip, 115
Epilepsy, arson and, 296–97
Erikson, Erik H., 6–7, 353
Escobedo v. Illinois, 428
Espionage, 393, 429, 442
Evans, Timothy, 448
Ex parte Loving, 358
Exclusionary rule, 426–29
Exhibitionism, 259–61, 263, 295

Fall, Albert, 304
Federal Bureau of Investigation (F.B.I.), 143, 162, 393–96; on bank robberies, 288–90; on rape, 249; urban-rural categories of, 159; *see also* Uniform Crime Reports
Federal Bureau of Narcotics, 337, 338
Federal Bureau of Prisons, 466, 467
Federal Communications Act (1934), 430
Federal Prisoner Rehabilitation Act (1965), 471
Federal Trade Commission (F.T.C.), 316
Feifer, George, 69–70
Felonies, 5, 42–43, 163; assaults as, 239; court trials of, 413–26; drunken driving as, 334; in felony-murder doctrine, 223, 446; juries or judges trying, 412; property offenses as, 277; punishment for, 42–43, 446, 466–67, 492; work release programs for, 470–71
Fences, 185
Ferdinand, Theodore, 130
Ferracuti, Franco, 231–33, 235
Ferri, Enrico, 85, 145
Field, Ruth, 32
Finland, 226, 231
Firearms, 8, *see also* Weapons
Fitch, J. H., 264
Floppers, 169
Folkways, 36–37
Forgery, 171, 178–81, 187; arrests for, 148, 150, 152, 157
Forman, Percy, 33
France, 54–55; homicide rate in, 226; police in, 391, 401–2; punishment in, 442, 450; on suicide, 64–65
France, Anatole, 46
Frank, Jerome, 425, 432
Frankel, Emil, 250
Frankfurter, Felix, 32, 395, 427
Fraud, 148, 150, 152, 157; *see also* White-collar crimes
Free will, 49, 50; in criminal capacity, 46; in criminal intent, 43; in criminal responsibility, 480, 481, 493; Pascal on, 47; in pioneer criminology, 86–87; in punishment, 441
French Guinea, 450
Freud, Sigmund, 266
Frontier tradition, 224, 225, 355–56
Functionalist views, 20

Gagnon, John H., 264–65
Galbraith, John Kenneth, 311
Gallo, Jon J., 268
Gallup polls: on crime and lawlessness (1968), 8; on police action in Chicago (1968), 384
Gambling, 190, 193, 198–200, 202, 211, 214, 429; in gang behavior, 375; legalized, 203–5; occupation tax stamp for, 215; police and, 387, 392, 396, 399, 400, 405, 428; poverty caused by, 203
Ganey, J. Cullen, 311
Gangs, see Juvenile delinquency, in groups
Gardner, George, 284
Garfinkel, Harold, 227
Garofalo, Raffaele, 85
Garrity, Donald L., 279–80
Gebhard, Paul H., 246–47, 249–52; on pedophilic criminals, 262–63; on voyeurism, 258, 259
Geis, Gilbert, 155
Genna brothers, 195, 196
Genovese, Vito, 212
Georgia, 327, 392
Germany, 65, 426, 464
Gibbens, T. C. N., 184
Gibbon, Edward, 3
Gibbons, Don C., 279–80
Gibbons, Thomas J., 120
Gibbs, Jack, 279
Gilbert, G. M., 256
Gillin, John, 250
Glueck, Sheldon, 34
Goffman, Erving, 174–75
Gogol, Nikolai, 55
Goldin, Hyman E., 58
Goldstein, Joseph, 400–1
Goldwater, Barry, 7
Goodman, Paul, 82–83
Gordon, Waxey, 393
Gordon, Wayne, 331–32
Gorer, Geoffrey, 203–4, 220, 403
Goring, Charles, 85, 90, 91
Great Britain, see England
Greece, 266, 333
Greek jurisprudence, 58–59
Gross, Hans, 85
Gross, Harry, 191
Grünhut, Max, 237
Guatemala, 226
Guilt, 73, 389, 483; about bank robbery, 290; correctional programs producing, 438; expiation of by money, 436; in guilty mind concept, 43–44; ignorance of the law and, 46; about juvenile delinquency, 7; pleas of, 410–13, 423; presumption of, 415, 432; prosecuting attorney and, 421; punishment before proving, 416; in sexual behavior, 262; in subculture of violence, 233
Guilty offenders, 407
Gusii, 252–53
Guttmacher, Mannfred: on exhibitionism, 260; on murder categories, 236; on rape, 250, 251; on voyeurism, 259

Habeas corpus, writ of, 413; denied in juvenile cases, 359

Hall, Jerome: on criminology, 23; on theft, 60–61, 276; on white-collar crimes, 317–18
Hallek, Seymour L., 246
Hammurabi, Code of, 56–58
Hand, Learned, 313
Handy, William, 239–40
Harris polls: on law and order (1968), 8; on prisons (1967), 468–69
Harrison Act (1914), 337
Hart, H. L. A., 326
Hartung, Frank E., 315
Haviland, John, 85
Hawaii, 443
Hawkins, E. R., 5
Hawley, Paul R., 308
Hawthorne, Nathaniel, 437
Hearn, Lafcadio, 275
Hecht, Ben, 5
Heckscher, August, 80
Heirens, William, 244, 304–5
Hemingway, Ernest, 248
Henry, Andrew F., 238
Henry, O., 170–72
Henry VII, 62
Hentig, Hans von, 88, 103–4
Herschell, Lord, 408
Hersey, John, 386
Hewart, Lord, 408
Hippies, 218, 220–21
Hippocrates, 296
Hobbes, Thomas, 21, 86
Hoffa, James R., 207
Holmes, Oliver Wendell: on criminal capacity, 46–47; on criminal intent, 44; on wiretapping, 430
Homer, 59
Homicide (murder), 10, 13, 42, 214, 221–38; alcohol in, 231, 236; arson and, 295; assaults and, 231, 239, 240; causes of, 233–35; city-size and, 229; correlates of, 226–29; court cases on, 408, 409; cross-national comparisons of, 225–26; as decreasing in U.S., 130, 225; defined, 222–24; as excusable, 224; felony-murder doctrine in, 223; as justifiable, 224, 451; mercy-killing as, 18; motives of, 235–37; Negroes in, 156, 227–30; patterns in, 229–33; punishment for, 234, 273, 436, 442–46, 466; in rural areas, 160, 161, 163–64, 229; seasonal changes in, 145, 163; sex in, 236, 237, 243, 244, 249; in Sicily, 211; statistics on, 141, 143, 160, 224–26; as subculture of violence, 232–33; suicide as, 64, 65, 236; suicide accomplices tried for, 65; suicide following, 232; suicide inversely proportional to, 237–38; traffic fatalities and, 333; unreported, 115; weapons in, 230–31; see also Manslaughter
Homicide, arrests for, 125, 231; age-levels and, 148; in minority groups, 155, 156, 227; sex and, 151, 152, 230
Homosexuality, 60, 193, 236, 245, 247, 253, 261, 265–69; causes of, 262, 265–66; consensual, 132; pedophilia and, 262–264, 268, 269; police and, 387

Honde, Yushi, 257
Hooker, Evelyn, 266
Hookers, 169
Hoover, J. Edgar, 393–96
Houston, Texas, 229
How to Win Lawsuits Before Juries, 421
Howe, Samuel, 490
Hoyles, J. Arthur, 439
Huber Law, 470
Hughes, Graham, 43–44
Hugo, Victor, 390, 437
Hull, Clark, 92
Hustling, 185–86, 374
Huxley, Aldous, *viii*

Iceland, 232
Icemen, 187
Idaho, 358–59, 418, 466
Iliad, 56
Illinois, 269, 327, 357, 445
Immigrants, 154
Imprisonment, *xi*, 437, 448, 451–57; alternatives to, 483–94; capital punishment compared to, 444, 446; history of, 451–53; rate of, 465–66; solitary, 452, 469; as successful, 456; as threat during probation, 488; variations in, 314; *see also* Prisons; Punishment
In re Sharp, 358–59
Incarceration, *see* Imprisonment; Punishment
Incest, 74, 262, 405
Income tax evasion, 299, 312–14, 405
India, 199, 415
Indians, American, 214, 272; arrest statistics for, 156–57
Infanticide, 38, 230, 232
Innocent, protection of, 407, 432, 433, 448
Insurance: arson and, 294; bank robberies and, 289–90; floppers and, 169; for professional criminal, 168; property offenses and, 297; against robbery, 124; as type of gambling, 199
Interest rates (usury), 66–69, 208; in Shylocking, 190, 208; on time payments, 317
Internal Revenue Service, 312–13
Iowa, 443
Ireland, 442
Irving, Washington, 16
Isbell, Harris, 342
Israel, 426
Italy, 55, 173, 368, 449

Jackson, Andrew, 10
Jackson, Robert, 480–81
Jails, 461–65, *see also* Prisons
James, Jesse, 138
Janosik, 449
Japan, 54, 226, 257, 465
Japanese-Americans, 214, 275; American arrest statistics for, 156–57
Jeffery, C. Ray, 56, 87, 480
Jesse, F. Tennyson, 235–36
Jewish jurisprudence, 58
Johnson, Guy B., 227

Johnson, Lyndom Baines, 7, 350–51; on wiretapping, 430–31
Johnson, Ronald, 177
Johnson, Samuel, 368
Joint Commission on Correctional Manpower and Training, 11
Judges, 407; education of, 33; in inferior courts, 409–13; public defenders and, 423; punishment options of, 436, 449, 461, 464, 491; sentencing by, 491–92; wiretap permission given by, 430
Juries, *see* Courts, juries in
Justices of the peace, 409
Juvenile Court Statistics, 360
Juvenile delinquency, 146–50, 163, 234, 350–78; adult standards threatened by, 353; age-range of, 355–56; in battery offenses, 240–41; behavioral systems in, 361–78; correctional facilities for, 11, 460; courts for, *see* Courts, juvenile; cross-cultural perspectives on, 368–71; definitions of, 15–16, 354; female, 134, 163, 355, 361; in groups (gangs), 374, 376, 367–78; history of, 139, 356–59, 367–68; increase in, 143, 146–47, 150, 360–61; public concern about, 6–7, 350–351, 353–54; quasi-professional property offenders in, 280; sample composition of, 127; in sexual offenses, 355; socially nonadaptive, 362–67; statistics on, 125–26, 148–51, 155, 359–61; as subculture, 362, 372–74, 376; theories on, 98; as typology, 361–62; value system in, 372–74

Kafka, Franz, 274
Kansas, 62
Kant, Fritz, 330
Karon, Bertram, 228–29
Karpman, Benjamin, 253, 267
Kassebaum, Gene, 474
Kaufman, Irving, 429
Kefauver Committee (Senate Committee to Investigate Organized Crime in Interstate Commerce), 194, 210, 214, 216
Kennedy, John F., 4, 10, 236, 293, 362
Kennedy, Robert F., 10, 236
Kentucky, 443
Kerner, Otto, 9
Kershaw, Alister, 235
Keynes, John Maynard, 312
Kidnaping, 120, 394–95
King, Martin Luther, Jr., 10, 33, 236
Kinsey, Alfred C., 256, 258; on homosexuality, 265, 266; on pedophiles, 263; on sodomy laws, 261–62
Kleptomania, 184
Kluckhohn, Clyde, 245
Kobrin, Solomon, 93
Korn, Richard, 408
Kossack, Nathaniel, 208–9
Kramer, John, 482
Kreuger, Ivar, 304–5
Krutch, Joseph Wood, 87
Kubla Khan, 329
Kupriyanov, Ivan, 370
Kvaraceus, William, 353–54

Labor unions, 206–7, 470
Lacassagne, Jean-Alexandre-Eugène, 75, 145
Larceny, 44, 145, 279; arrests for, 148, 150, 152, 156; of bicycles, 132–33; in crime reports, 120; defined, 122, 277; grand, 111, 277; petit, 277, 437; statistics on, 141, 143, 160; unreported, 115
Las Vegas, Nevada, 213
Laski, Harold, 72
Laswell, Harold, 54
LaVine, Robert, 253
Law and laws, xi, 8, 14, 451; attitudes toward, 13, 17, 31; American, 72–73; blue laws, 17, 61–63; crime defined and, 16–19, 21; as formal enactment, 37; ignorance of, 46; individual or society protected by, 324–26; on juveniles and adults, 354; police and, 384, 385, 387, 390, 399–401, 405; public opinion in, 26; on sexual offenses, 269; in social control, 36–39; social science and, 32–36; social values reflected in changes in, 60–61, 246; see also Criminal law
Law enforcement, 52, 134–35, 394, 432; as crime producing, 135, 389, 404–5; criminal behavior affected by, 134–35, 313, 388–89, 404–5, 407, 428; foreign, 401–4; officers of, see Police; of organized crime, 214–16; professionalization of personnel in, 133
Lawyers, 33, 35, 384; constitutional right to see, 428–29; court appointing, 414, 418, 422–23; criminal, 39, 422; on criminal responsibility, 477, 478; criminals' hostility toward, 408; as defense attorneys, 413, 414, 417–18, 422–24, 432; mens rea, 44; for organized crime, 216, 422; in probation hearings, 487; tactics of, 407, 421, 423–24
Lecky, William, 74, 139
Legal Aid Societies, 423
Leites, Nathan, 222
Lemert, Edwin M., 180–81
Leo, Pope (The Great), 67
Leopold, Nathan, 236
Lerner, Max, 72, 197
Lessing, Doris, 177
Levy, Sol, 254
Lewis, C. S., 439–40
Lewis, Nolan D. C., 254, 295–97
Lewis, Norman, 211
Lewis, Roy, 311
Lewis, Sinclair, 301
Lincoln, Abraham, 236
Lindesmith, Alfred E., 196, 198
Lindner, Robert, 236
Llewellyn, Karl N., 23
Loeb, Richard, 236
Lombroso, Cesare, x, xi, 85, 87–89, 296
London, England, 139, 167, 287, 402
Lorenz, Konrad, 220
Los Angeles, California, 9, 218; police in, 391, 392; public-defender system in, 423
Lotteries, 199–200
Louisiana, 252

LSD, 335, 347
Lynchings, 138
Lund, Robert and Helen, 103, 373

McCleery, Richard, 408
McClellan, John L., 206–7
McCord, William and Joan, 234
McCorkle, Lloyd, 408
MacCormick, Austin, 471
McKenzie, Donald, 187–88
Maconochie, Alexander, 85
Madden, Edward, 83
Mafia, 210–14
Maine, 227, 357, 443, 445
Maitland, Frederic W., 451
Malinowski, Bronislaw, 37
Mallory v. United States, 413–14
Manchester, William, 4
Manfield Society, 73
Mann Act (1910), 394
Mannheim, Hermann, 26, 85, 274, 320, 478
Manslaughter, 222–24; negligent, 120, 145, 146, 152, 156, 224; see also Homicide
Mapp v. Ohio, 427–28
Marijuana, 335, 343–48
Marijuana Tax Act (1937), 343, 344
Marrs, Wyatt, 19
Marshall, Thurgood, 328
Martin, John Bartlow, 188
Maryland, 467
Marx, Karl, 69, 341
Mass media, 3, 6, 93, 144, 219–20; homicide in, 221, 222; on parolees, 490; police shown on, 383, 392; trials covered by, 418–20
Massachusetts, 62, 278, 466, 485–86
Massachusetts Bay Colony, 58
Masturbation, 245
Mattick, Hans, 462, 464
Maudsley, Henry, 85
Mead, Margaret, 252
Melville, Herman, 169–70
Mencken, H. L., 200
Menninger, Karl, 4, 237
Mercy-killing, 18, 408
Merton, Robert K., 25, 303
Methadone, 341–42
Methadone Maintenance Program, 341
Methedrine, 346, 348
Mexican-Americans, 154–55, 158
Miami, Florida, 213
Michael, Jerome, 23
Michigan, 259, 324–25, 414, 443, 445
Mill, John Stuart, 12
Miller, Neal, 92
Miller, Walter B., 376–77
Mills, C. Wright, 309
Minnesota, 443, 445, 486
Minority groups: arrests in, 155–58, 227; in jails, 462; police and, 387–88, 398, 399
Miranda v. Arizona, 429
Misdemeanors, 42–43; assault and battery as, 239; criminal justice for, 409–413, 426; drunken driving as, 334;

Misdemeanors (*Continued*)
 property offenses as, 277; Sabbath-
 breaking as, 63; voyeurism as, 259
Mississippi, 62, 74
Missouri, 62, 358
Mitchell, John, 431
M'Naghten Rule, 477–79
Mobilization for Youth, 375
Model Penal Code, 269, 479–80, 493
Mönkemöller, Otto, 297
Monopoly (antitrust) practices, 299, 307,
 309–12, 393
Monroe, Jack J., 340
Monroe, Lawrence, 281
Monroe County State Penitentiary, 330–
 331
Montana, 418, 426
Montero, Pedro, 85
Moral aberrance, 18, 21
Moran, Bugs, 196
More, Sir Thomas, xi
Mores, 36–38
Morison, Samuel Eliot, 350
Morris, Albert, 222, 224–25, 231; on up-
 perworld criminals, 303
Mosaic Code, 56, 58
Motives, 46
Muckraking, 299, 301
Murder, *see* Homicide
Murder, Inc., 196
Murphy, George E., 345
Murphy, Joseph P., 489
Murtagh, John M., 327
Musica, Philip, 304
Mutilation, 436–37

Nader, Ralph, 301
Nagel, Stuart, 428
Nahrendorf, Richard O., 278
Napoleon III, 450
Narcotic addicts: rehabilitation for, 337–
 343, 481–82; methadone treatment for,
 341–42; preferring punishment, 440
Narcotics (drugs), 8, 11, 324, 335–45; arrests for, 149, 153, 157, 343; control of,
 337–39; in gang behavior, 374; among
 hippies, 221; opiate derivatives as, 325,
 335–38; organized crime in, 190, 193,
 211, 335–36; in patent medicines, 73,
 337; police and, 400–1; sale or possession of, 45; shoplifting to buy, 182–
 183; *see also* Marijuana
National Advisory Commission on Civil
 Disorders (Kerner Commission), 9–10;
 on police, 386
National Commission on Law Observance
 and Enforcement (Wickersham Commission), 118
National Commission on the Causes and
 Prevention of Violence, 10–11; on Chicago police, 385
National Council on Crime and Delinquency (NCCD), 463, 484–85
National Crime Information Center, 394
National Opinion Research Center
 (NORC), 115–17
National Safety Council, 333

Negroes, *see* Blacks
Nettler, Gwynne, 397
Nevada, 204, 418
New Hampshire, 200, 445, 466, 479
New Haven, Connecticut, 22
New Jersey, 463, 466, 473
New Jersey Maximum Security Prison, 455
New Mexico, 443
New York: blue laws in, 62–63; burglary
 in, 277–78; capital punishment in, 443,
 444; civil commitment in, 481–82; em-
 bezzling in, 291–92; felony-murder doc-
 trine in, 223; on homosexuality, 267;
 interest rates in, 68–69; prisons in, 452,
 467; public lotteries in, 200; on suicide,
 65
New York City, 138; bail in, 416–17;
 drunkenness in, 327, 332; gang be-
 havior in, 375–76; municipal courts in,
 410; organized crime in, 191, 201–2,
 213; police in, 388, 397; robbery in,
 118–19, 287; statutory rape in, 256
New Zealand, 226, 486
Newcomb, Theodore, 272
Newman, Donald J., 320, 412
Newport, Kentucky, 392
Newspapers, *see* Mass media
Nicaragua, 225, 226
Niebuhr, Reinhold, 83
Noonan, John, Jr., 66
Norris, Frank, 301
North Carolina, 227, 252, 470–71
North Dakota, 418, 443, 445
Norway, 226, 334
Nugent, Rolf, 68
Numbers (policy games), 193, 200–3, 214
Nye, Ivan, 352
Nyswander, Marie, 341

Occupational crimes, 319
O'Donnell, John A., 338, 340
Odyssey, 56
Office of Price Administration (O.P.A.),
 315
Ohio, 359, 427–28, 477
Ohlin, Lloyd E., 102, 142, 374–75, 378
Oklahoma, 74, 426
Oldham, William, 283
Olmstead v. United States, 430
Olney, Warren, 190
Omnibus Crime Control and Safe Streets
 Act (1968), 8, 133, 430
O'Neal, Patricia, 284–85
O'Neill, Eugene, 338
Oregon, 443, 463
Oswald, Lee Harvey, 4, 236, 362–67
Outlawry, 56, 436, 448–49
Ovid, 15

Packard, Vance, 184, 301
Palmer, Stuart, 235, 238
Panama, 226
Papuans, 272
Parasitism, 18–19, 21
Parchman, Mississippi, 471, 472
Parker, William, 204–5
Parmelee, Maurice, 18–19

Parole, 52, 416, 417, 447, 461, 484, 489-493; for alcoholics, 332; boards, 471, 491-93; in civil commitment, 482; defined, 490; records, 446; in Soviet Union, 71
Parsons, Talcott, 36
Pascal, Blaise, 47
Paulus, Ingeborg, 340
Pedophilia, 262-65, 268
Peel, Sir Robert, 402, 452-53
Penn, William, 442-43, 452
Pennsylvania, 358, 443, 466
Penology, 52
Peterson, Richard A., 284-85
Pettigrew, Thomas F., 227
Pfeffer, Arnold, 265
Philadelphia, Pennsylvania, 169, 452; crime records in, 120, 126, 182; homicide patterns in, 229-32; inferior courts in, 410
Philippines, 226
Pickpockets, 102-4, 172, 186, 445; slang about, 173, 187; techniques of, 168-69, 187
Pittman, David J., 239-40, 284-85, 331-32
Pius XII, Pope, 49
Plato, 64, 266, 451
Platt, Anthony, 356-57
Ploscowe, Morris, 260, 337
Poincaré, Henri, 82
Poland, 449
Police, 142, 383-405, on arraignment, 414; brutality of, 385, 397-99; civil rights and, 386, 426; class origin of, 386-88, 398; corruption of, 392, 396-97, 399; county sheriff and, 396; courts and, 413-15, 426-32; crime known to, 124-126; discretion of, 399-401, 405; dissatisfaction of, 388; exclusionary rule and, 426-29; federal, 392-93, 430; foreign, 401-4; in ghetto, 154, 386; interrogation by, 413-15, 427; justifiable homicide by, 224; law and, 384, 385, 387, 390, 399-401, 405; as lawbreakers, 396-97; local autonomy of, 215, 391, 402; methods of, 384-85, 389, 428, 437; national, 392-93, 401-2; numbers racket and, 201, 400; organization of, 391-97; President's Commission on, 133-35, 392, 397; professional criminals and, 172, 387; professionalization in, 133; reports to F.B.I. by, 119, 120, 359; role performance of, 383-86, 390-91; routine work of, 4; rural, 396; safety of, 445-46; social control and, 388-91, 403; training of, 8, 399; urban, 396-97; victims not reporting crimes to, 116-17, 239; victims of, 428; wiretapping and, 430-32; see also Federal Bureau of Investigation; Law enforcement
Politics, 54; assassinations and, 236; inferior courts and, 409, 410, 412; organized crime and, 195-96; police and, 392
Pollak, Otto, 182, 230
Pollock, Sir Frederick, 46, 451
Polsky, Ned, 173, 283-84

Powell, Leroy, 328
President's Commission on Law Enforcement and Administration of Justice, 7-8, 463; on bail, 417; on collaborative institutions, 474-75; on community-treatment programs, 484; on crime measurement, 131-34; on crime-related factors, 162; on embezzlement, 291; on foreign crime patterns, 140; on forgery loss, 179; on history of crime, 138; on hustling, 185; on juvenile delinquency, 354; on municipal courts, 410-11; on Negro arrest rates, 158; on organized crime, 213; on police, 133-35, 392, 397; on preliminary hearings, 417-18; on rape, 249; on reporting procedures to F.B.I., 120; on robbery, 285-86; on shoplifting, 182; on survey methodology, 117; on unreported crimes, 112, 114-15, 118-19; on white-collar crimes, 300, 305
Prisons, 52, 451-57, 465-76; community in, 453; conjugal visiting in, 471-73; group therapy in, 438, 473-74; history of, 452-53, 461; homosexuality in, 267, 472; informers in, 453-54; programs in, 458, 468-76; reform of, 457-58, 464, 469-76; security of, 455-56, 467; time served in, 467; in U.S., 462, 465-67; see also Imprisonment; Jails, Punishment
Probation, 52, 461, 484-89, 491-92; defined, 485
Professional criminals, see Criminal behavior, professional
Prohibition, 17, 72, 193
Property, defined, 275-76
Property laws, 64, 272-74
Property offenses, 272-97, see also Burglary; Crime, against property; Embezzlement; Larceny; Robbery
Prosecuting attorneys, 215, 408, 410-12, 417-22, 432
Prostitution, 60, 107, 149, 157, 253, 324, 325; female arrests for, 151, 153; narcotics and, 337; organized crime in, 190, 193; police and, 387, 396, 428; robbery and, 287; among shoplifters, 183; statutory rape and, 255
Public order offenses, 324-48; see also Drunkenness; Narcotics; Prostitution; Puerto Rico, 230
Puerto Ricans, in U.S., 154, 338, 375
Pugh v. Bowden, 358
Punishment, 435-57; attitudes toward, 54-55, 468; bail as, 415-16; banishment (outlawry) as, 56, 436, 448-49; corporal, 436; correctional techniques in, 437-442, 468-76, 481-93; criminal responsibility and, 476; as cruel and unusual, 482, 487; cultural crimogenisis produced by, 99; defined, 440; as deterrent to criminal behavior, 134, 169, 314, 321, 389, 436-37, 439, 444-46, 452, 453; for drunken driving, 334; for drunkenness, 328-30; for felonies and misdemeanors, 42-43, 446, 466-67, 492; for homicides, 234, 273, 442-46, 466;

Punishment *(Continued)*
judges' options on, 436, 449, 461, 464, 491; justice in, 439–40; justification for, 451; of juvenile delinquents, 358–359, 369; of mentally ill, 480; for narcotics offenses, 339; of organized criminals, 214–15, 449; pretrial detention as, 416; for property offenders, 273, 277; psychological barbarities in, 438; Roman Catholic Church on, 50; sentencing in, 491–92; for sexual offenses, 74, 252, 256, 259, 262, 267–69, 446–67; transportation as, 449–50, 452, 490; treatment and, 476, 481–83; for white-collar crimes, 99, 310–11, 314, 315, 319; *see also* Civil commitments; community-treatment programs; Imprisonment

Punishment, history of, 56–59, 272–73, 435–37; in classical school, 86–87; in positivist school, 87

Pure Food and Drug Act (1906), 73

Pyromaniacs, 295, 296

Queen, Stuart, 43
Quinn, William F., 342
Quinney, Richard, 97, 238, 319

Rackets, *see* Crime, organized; *and specific crime*
Radio, *see* Mass media
Radzinowicz, Leon, 81
Rape, 7, 42, 145, 223; categories of, 251–252; cultural perspectives on, 252–53; encephalitis and, 253–55; punishment for, 252, 446; unreported, 115, 249; women offenders in, 113
Rape, forcible, 10, 121, 130, 248–55; age-levels and, 148, 150, 248; defined, 248; minority groups and, 155, 156, 250, 252; in rural areas, 160, 161, 164; statistics on, 141, 143, 152, 155, 156, 160, 161
Rape, statutory, 193, 244, 255–57, 262, 411; in crime reports, 120; defined, 255; police discretion in, 401
Rasmussen, Augusta, 264
Ray, Isaac, 85
Ray, James Earl, 33, 236
Reader's Digest, 315
Rechy, John, 186
Recidivism, 80, 484; correctional programs and, 438, 474; among embezzlers, 292; among forgers, 181; in income tax evasion, 314; among juveniles, 240; rates of, 467; of sex offenders, 486; by training-school graduates, 461; in white-collar crime, 306, 321
Reckless, Walter G., 98; containment theory of, 99–101
Rees, John T., 267
Rehabilitation, *see* Criminals, rehabilitation of
Reiss, Albert J., Jr., 114, 397, 429
Reles, Abe, 191
Religion, 76; in addiction treatment, 341; blue laws and, 62–63; in criminal law, 60; on usury, 66–67

Research Institute of America, 206
Rhode Island, 324, 443, 466, 467
Rice, Robert, 50–51
Rickles, Nathan, 260
Riesman, David, 35, 83
Riots, 8–10, 12, 386, 388; by police, 385
Robbery, 285–91; aggravated, 10; armed, 7, 287–88; 446; of banks, 104, 105, 278, 288–91; defined, 122, 141, 277; as embezzlement, 24; homicide during, 223, 237; insurance against, 124; motive and intent in, 46; punishment for, 466; as receipt of stolen property, 23, 24; reports on, 7, 10; seasonal changes in, 145; statistics on, 118–19, 141–43, 160; technical artifice avoiding indictment for, 60–61; unreported, 115; *see also* Embezzlement; Theft
Robbery, arrests for, 125; age-levels and, 148, 150, 163; in minority groups, 155, 156; sex and, 152
Robin, Gerald, 183
Robin Hood, 449
Robins, Lee, 345
Robinson, Louis N., 68
Robinson, William, 292–93
Rochin v. California, 427
Roebuck, Julian, 177, 288
Roman Catholic Church, 49–50; on suicide, 64; on usury, 66–67
Roman jurisprudence, 15; history of, 59–60; personal justice in, 56; on suicide, 64; on thievery, 273
Romilly, Sir Samuel, 443
Ross, Edward A., 37–38, 302–3
Rothstein, Arnold, 191
Roueché, Berton, 330
Roxbury, Massachusetts, 376
Royal Society for the Prevention of Accidents, 334
Rubin, Sol, 22, 492
Ruby, Jack, 4
Rumney, Jay, 489
Russell, Bertrand, *viii*, 79, 245
Russia, *see* Soviet Union
Rutledge, Wiley, 423

St. Valentine's Day massacre, 196
Samoa, 258
San Francisco, California, 138
Satten, Joseph, 4
Schaefer, Walter, 52
Schelling, Thomas C., 25
Schrag, Clarence, 469
Schroeder, Oliver, Jr., 229
Schuessler, Karl, 293, 493
Schultz, Dutch, 197
Schumach, Murray, 144
Schur, Edwin, 177, 178, 192
Scotland, 38
Scott, George R., 436
Search and seizure, 405, 409, 426–28, 430
Seavey, Warren, 41
Secret Service, 393, 395
Sellin, Thorsten, 113, 182, 228, 446
Selzer, Melvin, 327

Senate Permanent Subcommittee on Investigations, 212
Senate Committee to Investigate Organized Crime in Interstate Commerce (Kefauver Committee), 194, 210, 214, 216
Senate Select Committee on Improper Activities in the Labor or Management Field, 206–7
Seneca, 64
Sentencing, 491–92
Sex, 8; in American society, 246–48, 253; arson and, 295; in gang behavior, 374; in homicide, 236, 237, 243, 244, 249; marijuana and, 346; normal and abnormal, 244–46; see also Homosexuality; Prostitution; Rape
Sex offenses, 13, 74, 106–7, 113, 243–70; categories of, 244; as disorderly conduct, 411; police and, 387, 397, 399; probation and, 486; punishment for, 74, 252, 256, 259, 262, 267–69, 466–67; society producing, 243, 246–48, 252–253
Sex roles, 151, 154; violence and, 220–21
Shakespeare, William, 16, 169, 368
Sherman Anti-Trust Act (1890), 393
Sherwin, Robert V., 246
Shoham, Shlomo, 21
Shoplifting, 102–3, 105, 170, 172, 182–85, 187, 443
Short, James F., Jr., 238, 375
Shulman, Harry, 124
Shylocking, 190, 208, see also Usury
Sicily, 210–11
Silberg, Moshe, 57–58
Silving, Helen, 41, 48–49; on suicide legislation, 65–66
Simon, Carolyn, 425
Simpson, Sidney, 32
Sinclair, Harry, 304
Sirhan, Sirhan, 236
Sjostedt, Elsie, 284
Skolnick, James H., 331, 385, 418
Slang (jargon), 104–5, 173, 187, see also specific crime
Smigel, Erwin O., 171
Smith, A. Delafield, 35
Smith, Betty, 260
Smith, Bruce, 396
Smith, Ernest A., 353
Social control, 13, 14, 26, 36–39, 52; in complex societies, 72; defined, 36; institutional, 36–37; legal, 36–39; police and, 388–91, 403; system of laws in, 36–39
Social dysfunction, 20, 21
Society, 63, 75–77, 433; contractual beginnings of, 85; crime defined and, 19–20; criminology on, 13; free, 431–32; institutions changing, 403; juvenile delinquency and, 352–53, 378; organization of, 77; parole for, 490; power structure of, 54; property offenses and, 272, 275; subculture and, 233; suicide and homicide produced by, 237–38; as victim, 324; see also Social control

Society, social values and, 76, 77, 373–74; criminal law reflecting, 60–61, 63; instrumental, 77
Society for the Reformation of Juvenile Delinquents, 16
Sociology, 302–3
Socrates, 59, 64
Sodomy, 245, 261–69
Solon, 59
Solzhenitsyn, Aleksander I., 456
Sondern, Frederick, Jr., 192
South Dakota, 314, 445
Soviet Union: criminal law in, 69; economic crimes in, 319, 320; juvenile delinquency in, 368–71; prison work programs in, 470; punishment in, 69, 70, 442, 450
Space exploration, 75
Spain, 225, 226, 442
Sparling, J. Frederick, 308
Spencer, Herbert, 88
Spencer, John C., 321
Spergal, Irving, 198, 375–76
Spier, Rosalind, 227
Spinoza, Baruch, 22
Steffens, Lincoln, 169, 301
Steinbeck, John, 31
Stephen, Sir James Fitzjames, 433
Stewart, Rosemary, 311
Stone, Harlan Fiske, 395
Straus, Murray and Jacqueline, 238
Student rebellion, 6, 8, 386
Sugar, Carl, 265
Suicide, 64–66, 237–38, 404, 445; drunkenness and, 327; exceeding speed limit as, 24; homicide followed by, 232; symbolic, 236
Sumner, William Graham, 37, 38, 389
Sutherland, Edwin H., 92–98, 101, 188, 299–300; on confidence games, 178; on homicide and rape, 249; an encephalitis, 254–55; on white-collar crimes, 301–7, 309, 317–21
Sutton, Al, 290
Swanis, 266
Sweden, 80, 472; homicide rate in, 226; suicide in, 65
Switzerland, 226
Sykes, Gresham, 438, 455–58, 475
Synanon, 341
Szasz, Thomas S., 483

Taber, Robert, 488
Taft, Donald R., 98–101
Taft, William Howard, 33
Tannenbaum, Frank, 94, 103
Tappan, Paul W., 22, 41, 216, 251; on white-collar crimes, 317
Tarbell, Ida, 301
Tarde, Gabriel, 85
Tawney, R. H., 273
Teele, James E., 237
Teen-Challenge, 341
Teeter, Negley, 73
Television, see Mass media
Tennessee, 314

Tennyson, Alfred Lord, 257–58
Tertullian, 15–16
Texas, 463
Theft: in gang behavior, 374–77; in high school students, 281; of jewelry, 187; law of, 274, 276–78; narcotics and, 337; petty, 42; punishment for, 437, 451, 464; social conditions and, 272, 275–76; types of, 279; vocabulary of, 173; working hours of, 284; *see also* Burglary; Larceny; Robbery; Shoplifting
Thigpen, Corbett H., 483
Thomas, W. I., 154
Thompson, George , 177–78
Thoreau, Henry David, 274
Thrasher, Frederic M., 371
Tiedman, Christopher, 68
Timasheff, Nicholas, 32
Tocqueville, Alexis de, 55
Tokyo, Japan, 275
Topinard, Paul, 15, 89
Torrio, Johnny, 195, 196, 393
Torts, 41–42, 301
Traffic fatalities, 224–25, 333
Traffic laws, 219; on drunken driving, 332–35; enforcement of, 13, 333, 388–389, 391
Traffic laws and speeding, 45; as attempted suicide, 24; sensual satisfaction in, 243
Transportation of criminals, 449–50, 452, 490
Treason, 393, 436, 442
Treasury Department, 393; on forgery, 179
Tres Marias, 471–72
Truancy, 354, 355, 366
Turkus, Burton, 196

Uniform Crime Reports, 119–24, 329, 394; on arrests of blacks, 155; on crime rates, 143; on juvenile delinquents, 150, 359; on volume of crime, 141–42
Uniform Vehicle Code, 334
United States Code (1968), 73
United States Supreme Court, 8; on arraignment, 413–14; on blue laws, 63; on civil commitment of alcoholics, 328, 332; on civil commitment of narcotics addicts, 338, 339; on corporations, 306; on ignorance of the law, 46; on juvenile courts, 357–58; on mass media trial coverage, 418–19; on probation, 487; on search and seizure, 427–30; on wiretapping, 430
United States v. Currens, 479–80
Ur-Nammu, 57
Usill, Harley V., 267
Usury (interest rates), 66–69, 208; in Shylocking, 190, 208; on time payments, 37
Utah, 418

Vagrancy, 42, 101, 149, 153, 157, 324, 325, 449
Valachi, Joseph, 210, 212–13
Vandalism, 149, 153, 157
Veblen, Thorsten, 83, 304
Vera Foundation, 388
Vera Institute of Justice, 332, 416–17

Verger, Jean-Louis, 235
Verkko, Veli, 231
Vermont, 443, 466, 467, 480
Victims, 324; of aggravated assaults, 240, 400; aid to, 10, 487; criminals' attitudes toward, 103–4, 106, 171, 177; of embezzlement, 291; field surveys of, 113–17; of forcible rape, 249–50; of homicides, 229–32, 249; of minority groups, 155, 158; of organized crime, 193, 208; of police, 428; of property offenders, 297; restitution to, 487; of robbery, 287–88
Violence, 72, 83, 143–44, 218–21, 284–85; alcohol and, 231, 284; consumer fraud causing, 316; crimes of, 7, 272, 466–67, 470, 486, 487; in gang behavior, 374; homicide as subculture of, 232–33; increase in, 142; in labor, 138; as learned, 220, 234; in minority groups, 155; in murders, 234–35; National Commission on, 10–11, 385; in organized crime, 190, 206; by police, 385, 397–99; predisposition towards, 48; in property offenses, 277, 285, 288–90; public attention on, 6; in racial disturbances, 138; in sex offenses, 251; sex roles and, 220–21
Virginia, 74, 227, 252, 314
Vocational Rehabilitation Administration, 11
Vold, George B., 192, 318
Voltaire, François, 3
Voting, by jail inmates, 464
Voyeurism (peeping), 257–59, 263

Walker, Edwin A., 365
Wall Street Journal, 68
Waller, Willard, 5
Walsh, Lawrence, 209
Ward, David, 474
Ward, Lester F., 34, 302
Warner, W. Lloyd, 373–74
Warner, Sam Bass, 119
Warren, Earl, 63, 490
Warren, Robert Penn, 82
Warren Commission, 362–67
Washington, 314
Watts, California, 9
Weant, Edward O., Jr., 60
Weapons, 8; in aggravated assault, 240; in armed robbery, 446; carrying concealed, 45–46, 113, 149, 153, 157, 404; in homicides, 230–31; probation and, 486; professional criminals and, 167–68, 177; in property offenses, 277, 278, 287–89
Weber, Max, 56, 199, 274
Weeks v. United States, 426–27
Weihofen, Henry, 465
Weil, Joseph (Yellow Kid), 171, 175
Welfare systems, 12; Kerner Commission on, 9–10
West v. Campbell, 60
West Virginia, 74, 443
Wheeler, Stanton, 244
White-collar crimes, 124, 170, 227, 279, 299–322; advertising fraud as, 299, 304, 307, 314–16, 319, 324; consumer frauds

White-collar crimes (*Continued*)
as, 307, 314–17; corporate, 305-6, 309-12, 319; defined, 299, 319–20; financial losses by, 305; history of, 301–5; income tax evasion as, 299, 312–14, 405; medical, 307–9; monopoly (antitrust) as, 299, 307, 309–12, 393; offenders in, 321, 387; punishment of, 99, 310–11, 314, 315, 319; as real crimes, 299, 301, 303, 317–18, 318–19; varieties of, 307; *see also* Embezzlement
Whitney, Richard, 304
Whyte, William F., 201, 371–72
Wickersham Commission, 118
Wilde, Oscar, 268
Wilkins, Leslie, 20
Williams, Robbin, Jr., 6, 374
Williamson, Henry, 186
Wilson, O. W., 414
Winchel, John, 45
Winick, Charles, 340, 344–45
Wiretapping, 8, 395, 409, 429–32
Wisconsin, 443, 445, 470
Witchcraft, 60, 448
Witnesses: defense attorneys and, 422; material, 415–16; prosecuting attorneys and, 422; right to subpoena, 418; state, 408, 417, 418
Wolf v. Colorado, 427, 428
Wolfenden Report, 269

Wolfenstein, Marta, 222
Wolfgang, Marvin E., 120–22, 229-33, 235
Women: in arrest statistics, 150–54; crime rate increasing of, 133–34, 163; in homicides, 230-32, 236, 249; in homosexual activity, 266; in jails and prisons, 462, 466; as juvenile delinquents,134, 163, 355, 361; narcotic addiction of, 337–40; as probation officers, 489; professional criminal's attitude toward, 170; in shoplifting, 183–84; suicide methods of, 65; theft scores of, 281; voyeurism by, 258–59
Wootton, Barbara, 478
World Health Organization: on suicide, 65; on traffic fatalities, 333
Wormuth, Francis D., 482–83
Wright, Richard, 387
Wright, Thomas, 169
Wyoming, 357, 466

Yolles, Stanley, 347
Youth culture, 352
Youth House, 363

Zelitch, Morris, 70
Zemans, Eugene, 471–72
Zola, Irving K., 198
Zuni Indians, 151

About the Authors

Herbert A. Bloch, the late Professor of Sociology and Anthropology at Brooklyn College, Dean of the Graduate School of the City University of New York, and Director of the Division of Graduate Studies at Brooklyn College, had a long and varied career in the field of social problems. A graduate of the City College of New York, he received his graduate degrees from Columbia University. He was long a member of the New York State Police and Public Safety Advisory Board, coordinated the Police Science Program at Brooklyn College, served as a consultant to various agencies—both public and private, state and federal—and conducted and administered staff in-service training programs at penal institutions and reformatories. A frequent contributor to scholarly as well as general journals, he also wrote several books, including *The Concept of Our Changing Loyalties, Disorganization: Personal and Social,* and co-authored, with Frank Flynn, *Delinquency: The Juvenile Offender in America Today.*

Gilbert Geis is Professor of Sociology at California State College, Los Angeles and (1969–70) Visiting Professor at the School of Criminal Justice, State University of New York at Albany. He received his B.A. from Colgate University, and Ph.D. from the University of Wisconsin. His career has included stints as a newspaperman, research director of the Oklahoma Crime Study Commission, and teacher at a federal reformatory. In 1964–65 he was a Fellow in Law and Sociology at Harvard Law School and he has also been a consultant to the President's Commission on Law Enforcement and Administration of Justice and the National Commission on the Causes and Prevention of Violence. He edited *White-Collar Criminal: The Offender in Business and the Professions,* co-authored, with William E. Bittle, *The Longest Way Home,* and has written extensively for professional journals.